The Letters
of
Thom Gunn

The Letters
of
Thom Gunn

Selected and Edited by

AUGUST KLEINZAHLER

MICHAEL NOTT

CLIVE WILMER

FARRAR, STRAUS AND GIROUX
NEW YORK

Farrar, Straus and Giroux
120 Broadway, New York 10271

Library of Congress Cataloging-in-Publication Data
Names: Gunn, Thom, author. | Nott, Michael, editor. | Kleinzahler, August,
    editor. | Wilmer, Clive, 1945– editor.
Title: The letters of Thom Gunn / selected and edited by Michael Nott, August
    Kleinzahler, Clive Wilmer.
Description: First American edition. | New York : Farrar, Straus and Giroux,
    2022. | Includes bibliographical references and index.
Identifiers: LCCN 2021059964 | ISBN 9780374605698 (hardcover)
Subjects: LCSH: Gunn, Thom—Correspondence. | Poets, English—
    20th century—Correspondence.
Classification: LCC PR6013.U65 Z48 2022 | DDC 821/.914—
    dc23/eng/20220213
LC record available at https://lccn.loc.gov/2021059964

www.fsgbooks.com
www.twitter.com/fsgbooks • www.facebook.com/fsgbooks

10 9 8 7 6 5 4 3 2 1

To Mike Kitay

CONTENTS

ACKNOWLEDGEMENTS

This book was made possible by Gunn's family, from Snodland to San Francisco, and it is to them we owe the greatest debt. In the preparation of this book, August, Clive and I have been helped by Thom's brother Ander; his niece Charlotte; his half-brothers Jamie and George; and his cousins Margot Corbett and Jenny Fremlin. Our deepest gratitude is due to Thom's lifelong partner, Mike Kitay, and to the friends who share his house, Bob Bair and Bill Schuessler. Their house on Cole Street, San Francisco – which they shared with Thom, too, for many decades – is the setting of many of the letters contained herein. I would like to extend my personal thanks to Ander, Charlotte, Jenny, Mike, Bill and Bob for their kindness and hospitality on numerous occasions in Penzance, Plymouth, Snodland and San Francisco.

Books like this are true collaborations. I was always aware of this, though the full collaborative weight was brought home to me when I started to sift through the thousands of emails that have been sent and received since this project began in earnest in spring 2017. August, Clive and I are deeply grateful to the many people who rifled through attics, back bedrooms and storage units in search of letters, and to those who answered queries or put us in touch with people who could. For their help in matters large and small we would like to thank John Ambrioso; William Arp; Don Bogen; Brian Bouldrey; Brandon Brown; Louis Bryan; Katherine Bucknell; Chris Burgess; Mike Caffee; Rick Carpenter; the late Douglas Chambers; Jessica Cole; Ben Coleman; Jack Collins; Roger Conover; Elizabeth Neece Conquest; Pablo Conrad; Jean Corston; Peter Daniels; Michael Davidson; Dick Davis; Randolph Delahanty; W. S. Di Piero; Edward Field; David Fitchew; Daisy Fried; Jack Fritscher; Nadia Fusini; David Galbraith; Maria Del Mar Galindo; Forrest Gander; Alisoun Gardner-Medwin; Thomas Geist; Timothy Gerken; Robert Glück; David Godine; Gordon Gould; Edward Guthmann; the late Donald Hall; Langdon Hammer; Hugh Haughton; Billy Hayes; Andrew Holleran; Michael Holmes; Richard Howard; Annie Ingrey; Panayotis Ioannidis; Patrick Dale Jackson; Glenn Jordan; Richard Kaye; Jim Kelly; Jago Lee; Cesar Love; Patricia McCarthy; Jane McPherson; Thomas Martin; Stefania Michelucci; Greg Miller; Jane Miller; Sam Miller; Joseph Mockus; A. F. Moritz; the late Richard Murphy; Christopher Nealon; Louis Keith Nelson; Richard Niland; John Niles; Raymond Oliver; Stephen Orgel; Margaret Owen; Craig Patterson;

Carl Phillips; Johnny Pomeroy; Neil Powell; Vincent Quinn; Belle Randall; Christopher Reid; Martin Rosen; Chuck Roth; Jerome Rothenberg; Lawrence Schimel; Michael Schmidt; Gordon Schneemann; Tony Scotland; Steve Silberman; Lee Smith; Timothy d'Arch Smith; Peter Spagnuolo; Gil Sutherland; Timothy Steele; Colin Still; Peter Swaab; Hal and Peter Tangen; Marcia Tanner; Anthony Thwaite; Clara Moriconi Timner; Claire Tomalin; Ben and Chris Townsend; Paul Trachtenberg; Jess Turner; Mark Turpin; Michael Vince; Dan Vining; Robert Wells; Edmund White; Hugo Williams; Dean Williamson; Anne Winters; Gregory Woods; and Stephen Yenser. Special thanks must go to Wendy Lesser and Joshua Weiner for stimulating conversations about all things Gunn, and for their assistance and kindness in supporting this book from the very beginning. Extra special thanks to Billy Lux for his friendship and humour from across the sea.

I transcribed the letters and am wholly responsible for any errors. My co-editors, August Kleinzahler and Clive Wilmer, have been unfailingly helpful, and I am grateful for their advice, openness and trust. We three met frequently during the course of the project to discuss Gunn's letters, to make our selections for this book and to work collaboratively on the annotations. It would have been impossible without them.

As Clive mentions in his recent edition of Gunn's *Selected Poems* (2017), this research would have been considerably more difficult had it not been for Gunn's bibliographers. Jack W. C. Hagstrom compiled and edited the two volumes of Gunn's bibliography: the first (London: Bertram Rota, 1979) with George Bixby, and the second (New Castle, DE: Oak Knoll Press, 2013) with Joshua S. Odell. I have spent many hours with these books and have fond memories of my visit with Jack, in New York, and Joshua (with Timothy Steele), in Santa Barbara, in autumn 2017. I am therefore particularly sad to report that both Jack and Joshua, who would have delighted in this book, died before it was finished. They will be much missed by Gunn enthusiasts, as well as by their families and friends.

Many librarians and archivists have helped with this research. We are particularly indebted to staff at the three main collections of Gunn material. They are James Eason, David Faulds and Dean Smith at the Bancroft Library, the University of California, Berkeley; Douglas McElrath at the Hornbake Library, University of Maryland; and Christina E. Barber and Margaret Dakin at the Robert Frost Library, Amherst College. The Bancroft Library holds the most extensive Gunn collection in the world, and we would like to extend special thanks to Dean Smith, who catalogued Gunn's papers back in 2007–8, for his personal interest in the collection. We also extend our thanks to Michelle Gait and Andrew MacGregor at the Special Collections Centre, the

Sir Duncan Rice Library, University of Aberdeen; Julie Swarstad Johnson at the University of Arizona Poetry Center; Colin McDowall at the Army Personnel Centre, Glasgow; Scot McKendrick, Head of Western Heritage Collections at the British Library; Robin Wheelwright Ness at Special Collections, the John Hay Library, Brown University; Alison Fraser and James Maynard at the Poetry Collection, University of Buffalo, New York; Caterina Fiorani at the archives of the Fondazione Camillo Caetani; Heather I. Briston at the Charles E. Young Library, University of California, Los Angeles; Sara Gunasekara at Special Collections, the Peter J. Shields Library, University of California, Davis; Heather Smedberg at Special Collections and Archives, the Geisel Library, University of California, San Diego; Yolanda Blue and Edward Fields at Special Research Collections, University of California, Santa Barbara; John Wells at the University Library, University of Cambridge; Julia Schmidt at the Churchill Archives Centre, Churchill College, University of Cambridge; Patricia McGuire and Peter Monteith at the Archive Centre, King's College, University of Cambridge; Kathryn McKee at the College Archives, St John's College, University of Cambridge; Emma Sheinbaum and Hekang Yang in the History Department at Columbia University; Benjamin Panciera at the Linda Lear Center for Special Collections and Archives, Connecticut College; Laura Schieb at the Rauner Special Collections Library, Dartmouth College; Valerie Stenner at the Morris Library, University of Delaware; Kathleen Shoemaker at the Stuart A. Rose Manuscript, Archives, and Rare Book Library, Emory University; Nigel Cochrane at the Albert Sloman Library, University of Essex; Robert Brown, archivist at Faber & Faber; Kelsi Evans and Ramon Silvestre at the Dr John P. De Cecco Archives and Special Collections, the GLBT Historical Society, San Francisco; Ellen Shea at the Arthur and Elizabeth Schlesinger Library on the History of Women in America, Harvard University; Caoimhe West at the Hull History Centre; Brian Moeller at the Huntington Library; Ruthann Miller at the Lilly Library, Indiana University; Laura Michelson at Special Collections & University Archives, University of Iowa; Elspeth Healey and Kathy Lafferty at the Kenneth Spencer Research Library, University of Kansas, Lawrence; Layla Hillsden at Special Collections & Galleries, Leeds University Library; Fran Baker at the John Rylands Library, University of Manchester; Cecily Marcus and Kathryn Hujda at Archives and Special Collections, Elmer L. Andersen Library, University of Minnesota; Christine Nelson, Drue Heinz Curator of Literary and Historical Manuscripts, Morgan Library & Museum, New York; Allison Chomet, Fales Library and Special Collections, New York University; Kate Edgar at the Oliver Sacks Foundation, New York; Angie Goodgame, Victoria Joynes and Samantha Sherbourne at Special Collections, Weston Library, Bodleian Libraries, University of Oxford; Sandra Bossert at the Department of Rare Books and Special Collections, Seeley G. Mudd Manuscript Library, Princeton University; Jo Anne Bilodeau at the City College of San Francisco; Jamie McIntosh at the National Library of Scotland, Edinburgh; Michael Oliveira and Loni Shibuyama at the ONE Archives, University of Southern California; Tim Edward Noakes at Special Collections & University Archives, Stanford University; Eric Colleary and Virginia Seymour at the Harry Ransom Center, University of Texas at Austin; Loryl MacDonald, John Shoesmith, Jennifer Toews and Danielle Van Wagner, Thomas Fisher Rare Book Library, University of Toronto; Amanda Vestal, Department of Special Collections and University Archives, the McFarlin Library, University of Tulsa; Kate Goldkamp and Joel Minor at the Olin Library, Washington University in St Louis; Jennifer Hadley at the Olin Memorial Library, Wesleyan University; Annie Pinder at the Parliamentary Archives, UK Parliament, Westminster; and Rebecca Aldi at the Beinecke Rare Book and Manuscript Library, Yale University.

Images included in the plates are reproduced by kind permission of the following: Ander Gunn; Charlotte Gunn; Christabel Holland; King's College Library, Cambridge; Mike Kitay; Sam Miller; Craig Patterson; Martin Rosen; Bill Schuessler; Marcia Tanner; Thomas Fisher Rare Book Library, University of Toronto; Deborah Treisman; Arthur Tress; Joe Watkinson; Clive Wilmer. Special thanks to Melissa Winters for her kind permission in allowing us to quote from an unpublished letter from Yvor Winters to Thom Gunn.

At Faber & Faber, we are grateful to Matthew Hollis and Lavinia Singer for their help and support. At Farrar, Straus & Giroux, we extend a firm handshake to Jonathan Galassi. We owe special thanks to our copy-editor, Donald Sommerville, proof-reader Hamish Ironside and indexer Margaret Christie for their care and attention.

The UK–US Fulbright Commission and the Irish Research Council provided support for travel and research.

David Godwin and Philippa Sitters have been warm and supportive agents. To them I extend especial thanks for helping steer this ship into a safe harbour.

On a personal note, I would like to thank Robert Crawford, Alex Davis, David Kinloch and Tom Normand, all patient and supportive mentors over the last few years. I am very grateful for conversations about Gunn with my former colleagues at the University of St Andrews and University College Cork. Likewise, poets Randall Mann and Andrew McMillan, fellows in the faith. And lastly a few friends, Hannah Britton, Tristan Carlyle, Caitlin Flynn, Katherine Furman, Elizabeth Hanna, Joanna Hofer-Robinson, Éadaoín Lynch, Anna Pilz, Sarah Sands Rice and Mamen Terol, who have all aided and abetted the slow passion to this deliberate progress.

M.N.

ILLUSTRATIONS

PAGE 1: TG with his mother, 1930 *(photographer unknown, image courtesy Ander Gunn)*; TG with his father and brother in the mid-1930s *(photographer unknown, image courtesy Charlotte Gunn)*; Ander Gunn and TG in the early 1940s *(photographer unknown, image courtesy Charlotte Gunn)*.

PAGE 2: TG at Cambridge, 1952 *(photographer unknown; image courtesy Mike Kitay)*; Mike Kitay at Stanford, June 1957 *(photographer unknown, image courtesy Glenn Jordan)*; Tony White in a production of *Coriolanus*, 1951 *(photographer Ramsay and Muspratt Photographers, image courtesy Sam Miller)*; TG and Karl Miller, San Antonio, Texas, July 1956 *(photographer Rory McEwen, image courtesy Christabel Holland)*.

PAGE 3: Tony Tanner, Tony White and TG, Cambridge, November 1964 *(photographer Marcia Tanner; image courtesy Marcia Tanner)*; Marcia and Tony Tanner at Stinson Beach, California, August 1967 *(photographer Thom Gunn, image courtesy Marcia Tanner)*; Don Doody in Palo Alto, July 1969 *(photographer Marcia Tanner, image courtesy Marcia Tanner)*.

PAGE 4: TG to Tony Tanner, 19 December 1966 *(image courtesy King's College Library, Cambridge)*; TG to Bill Schuessler, April 1974 *(image courtesy Bill Schuessler)*.

PAGE 5: TG and Ander Gunn with Ander's children William and Charlotte, June 1974 *(photographer Ander Gunn, image courtesy Charlotte Gunn)*; Mary Thomson, TG, Jenny Fremlin, Charlotte Gunn, Catherine Thomson and Barbara Godfrey, November 1979 *(photographer Ander Gunn, image courtesy Ander Gunn/Charlotte Gunn)*; Bob Bair, Mike Kitay, Bill Schuessler, and Jim Lay, *c.* 1978 *(photographer Thom Gunn, image courtesy: Mike Kitay)*; Don Doody, Bob Bair, Amy Kitay, Michael Belot, Bill Schuessler, TG, Mike Kitay and Martin Rosen, July 1985 *(photographer Jim Lay, image courtesy Martin Rosen)*.

PAGE 6: TG to Douglas Chambers, 27 May 1991 *(image courtesy Thomas Fisher Rare Book Library, University of Toronto)*; Billy Lux in New

York, mid-2000s *(photographer Arthur Tress, image courtesy Arthur Tress)*; Douglas Chambers at a book launch, Toronto, early 1990s *(photographer unknown, image courtesy Craig Patterson)*.

PAGE 7:   The wall collage in TG's workroom at Cole Street *(photographer Martin Rosen, image courtesy Martin Rosen)*; August Kleinzahler, with Patrick, *c.* 1990 *(photographer Deborah Treisman, image courtesy Deborah Treisman)*; 1214–16 Cole Street, San Francisco, June 2019 *(photographer Joe Watkinson, image courtesy Joe Watkinson and Charlotte Gunn)*; Clive Wilmer in Cambridge in the late 1990s *(photographer Carol Wright, image courtesy Clive Wilmer)*.

PAGE 8:   Mike Kitay and TG outside their house on Cole Street, late 1990s *(photographer Billy Lux, image courtesy Mike Kitay)*.

INTRODUCTION

Talk to anyone who knew Thom Gunn and one of the first things they'll tell you is that the man could laugh. 'His laughter, pumped by one of his heavy motorcycle boots thumping the floor, contained the raucous completeness of life,' writes W. S. Di Piero.[1] It is 'sudden, open, childishly joyful – as well as loud enough to triumph over the din at any restaurant in San Francisco,' writes Wendy Lesser.[2] 'He laughs a great deal, very loudly, with rumbustious pleasure. He enjoys any hint of the vulgar or the tasteless,' Clive Wilmer records.[3] 'Even when he was sober he had an enormous laugh, one that would often turn heads in public places,' remembers August Kleinzahler.[4] When not sober, Gunn was even more voluble. One time he swung by a party at Kleinzahler's apartment, plopped down on the sofa next to an unsuspecting young woman in a black velvet and gold Christmas dress, and boomed, 'I've been shooting speed for three days. I feel like I could fuck Hitler!'

Talk to anyone who knew Thom Gunn and one of the next things they'll tell you is that, no, he didn't talk about his mother. In fact, he didn't talk all that much about troubles of any kind. 'Whether it's his being English, or his mother's suicide . . .' Mike Kitay, his partner of five decades, told me, his voice trailing off. 'I always thought it was the mother's suicide, because he didn't want anything heavy. He couldn't handle anything heavy. He wanted it light.'[5] Lightness characterised much of their domestic life. 'Just before he swallowed a mouthful of food, he'd show it to you. YECH! The more grossed-out you were, the harder he'd laugh. Thom liked to shock. No, loved to shock. But that, of course, wasn't just at home.'[6] That great, chesty, boisterous laugh was one piece of armour, as was his desire for silliness and

---

1. W. S. Di Piero, 'A Symposium on Thom Gunn', *Threepenny Review* 102 (Summer 2005), 8.
2. Wendy Lesser, 'Thom Gunn's Sense of Movement', *Los Angeles Times* (14 August 1994), 18.
3. Clive Wilmer, 'Thom Gunn: The Art of Poetry LXXII', *Paris Review* 135 (Summer 1995), 145.
4. August Kleinzahler, 'Thom Gunn', in *Sallies, Romps, Portraits, and Send-Offs: Selected Prose, 2000–2016* (New York: Farrar, Straus & Giroux, 2017), 21.
5. Mike Kitay, interview with the author, 13 October 2018.
6. Mike Kitay, 'A Symposium on Thom Gunn', 13.

shock. After he retired from teaching in 1999, 'Thom kept saying how happy he was,' Kitay writes. 'He said it often; too often and too loudly. [. . .] He needed people to think he was happy. And mostly he appeared happy, even manic.'[7] But sometimes the mask slipped. 'Certainly in our conversations towards the end of his life,' Di Piero remembers, 'I don't want to make it sound as if he turned melancholy – that wasn't it – he was just a little quicker to bring up subjects that tended to deal with melancholy.'[8] Such reticence was typical Gunn: not a *cri de coeur*; barely worth mentioning. But his friends noticed.

Gunn detested the confessional. His work exhibits a certain anonymity out of kilter with much modern, post-war poetry on both sides of the Atlantic. 'This seems to upset many reviewers, American especially, of Gunn's poetry over the years,' Kleinzahler writes. 'They suggest that Gunn is a very cold chap, indeed, an emotional husk of a man. Presumably, they want to know why he isn't coughing up his guts all over the page as is the custom in contemporary American poetry.'[9] Gunn found his mother dead in December 1944: she had gassed herself, leaving her two teenage boys to find her. Some forty-seven years later Gunn wrote 'The Gas-poker', the only poem that deals directly with his mother's death. Though he was at last able to write the poem, its writing did not make him more open or encourage him to talk about his mother. As Kitay reflects, 'I think Clive says somewhere that, oh, now he can come out with it, finally. Yes, that's true in the poem. But I don't think it was true in any other way. He certainly didn't talk about it. He didn't talk about it before, he didn't talk about it afterwards. I'm not even sure I heard him say "suicide".'[10] The poem itself is no confessional outpouring: it is in third rather than first person; it makes use of allegory and suggestion in its image of the classical flute; its tone is as stark and distant as we might expect. As one friend suggests, 'He was clearly traumatized, for life, by his mother's suicide.'

Talk to anyone who has read Thom Gunn and one of the first things they'll mention is that his poems speak to them on a personal level. This is true of all poets who cut us to the quick, but with Gunn it seems all the more remarkable given the distance and reserve that we have come to associate with his work. Gunn kept a handful of fan letters. One of them begins: 'A letter of gratitude. And joy, the kind of joy one can feel, when having your inner emotions expressed verbally, that is the joy I have felt reading your poetry for over

7. Kitay, 'A Symposium on Thom Gunn', 13.
8. Di Piero, interview with the author, 10 October 2018.
9. Kleinzahler, 'The Plain Style and the City', *Threepenny Review* 60 (Winter 1995), 16.
10. Kitay, interview with the author, 13 October 2018.

ten years now. [. . .] One of my favourites from *Passages* is "Selves", such tenderness, I feel caressed by your language as I read it.'[11] Readers relate to Gunn because they can sense both hurt and the desire or need to hide it. Gunn may have buried his mother's suicide, and for a long time he also had to conceal his homosexuality. Publication of openly gay poems in the 1950s would have been illegal, and may well have brought his publisher to court; had that happened, Gunn certainly would not have made it to the United States. Instead he was forced to write poems such as 'The Allegory of the Wolf Boy', in which the boy leads one life by day, another by night. Today the poem has a clear queer reading, but in 1956 when it was written, Gunn had to appeal to a broader idea of doubleness – or 'sad duplicity' – so as not to arouse suspicion. As he wrote to his close friend Tony White midway through its composition, 'It is about queerness – or rather a certain type of queerness – but I think it is acceptable, because the allegory applies equally to any person who lives one life and fails to connect it to the life he really wants.'[12] This is typical of Gunn: to take a problem so deeply, personally affecting and to turn its focus outwards; just as he did, some thirty years after 'Wolf Boy', with his series of AIDS elegies.

'Wolf Boy' is one of Gunn's first major poems to deal with his obsession with doubles; an obsession that is difficult not to read biographically. Gunn was not just the leather-jacket-wearing, motorbike-riding tough that he is sometimes made out to be; nor the rambunctiously laughing, happy-go-lucky bon vivant that he often showed to the world. He once laughed about a profile piece in an American magazine: 'how can I complain,' he writes, when the interviewer 'falls so completely for the personality (I realize) that I project. (He never utters an unkind word, he has no troubles.) Very nice.'[13] Gunn's friend and fellow poet Jim Powell writes tellingly about this projected personality:

> Thom Gunn had no side (except when he chose to deploy it), leading many to mistake him for his garb (which was not front but surface), or for his stance, for his reserve. What he did have was depth, gulfs of it, 'intimate with [its] slaty cold.' Once I delighted him by quoting Herakleitos on the Delphic Oracle: *oute legei oute kruptei alla semainei* – who 'neither explains nor conceals but makes a sign.'[14]

11. Jørgen Frey to TG, 7 June 1988, Thom Gunn Papers, BANC MSS 2006/235, Bancroft Library, University of California, Berkeley. Hereafter Gunn MSS.
12. TG to Tony White, 21 April 1956, below.
13. TG, 'DIARY, vol 5: Sep 1986–Dec 2000', Gunn MSS.
14. Jim Powell, 'A Symposium on Thom Gunn', 9. The quotation 'intimate with its slaty cold' is from TG's poem 'The Antagonism' (*BC* 5–6).

In his correspondence, as in his poems, this depth is obvious. If letters are now a largely defunct genre, they had been for many people – and for Gunn especially – a chance to open up to those you most like, love and trust; a chance to speak plainly of what you think, feel and observe. Gunn's remarkable letters neither explain nor conceal – though they may err towards concealment – but signal his large, generous intelligence: both a literary and humane intelligence nurtured not only through books but through his range of experiences and friendships. As his readers, we are familiar with the values at the centre of his work: trust, openness, acceptance, innocence. As readers of his correspondence, we become aware of the value at the centre of his life. Friendship, Gunn remarks, 'must be the greatest value in my life. [. . .] I write about love, I write about friendship. Unlike Proust, I think that love and friendship are part of the same spectrum. Proust says that they are absolutely incompatible. I find that they are absolutely intertwined.'[15] If Gunn's poems at times feel like acts of friendship then his letters will strike a familiar note.

* * *

Thom Gunn was born in Gravesend, Kent, in 1929. He spent much of his childhood between Kent and Hampstead. His parents divorced when he was ten; he was fifteen at the time of his mother's suicide. In 1950, after two years of national service, he went up to Trinity College, Cambridge, to read English.

In Cambridge he came to terms with his homosexuality and fell in love with his lifelong partner, an American called Mike Kitay. Gunn wrote his first book, *Fighting Terms*, while at Cambridge and it was published in 1954. That year, Kitay returned to the USA and Gunn followed him, taking up a creative writing fellowship at Stanford University. In 1958, after a year teaching in San Antonio and another two working towards a PhD at Stanford, Gunn began teaching at the University of California, Berkeley. He gave up tenure in 1966, took some years away from the classroom, and returned in 1975 to teach one semester a year until his retirement in 1999.

Eight major collections followed *Fighting Terms*: *The Sense of Movement* (1957), *My Sad Captains* (1961), *Touch* (1967), *Moly* (1971), *Jack Straw's Castle* (1976), *The Passages of Joy* (1982), *The Man with Night Sweats* (1992) and *Boss Cupid* (2000). Gunn also published *Positives* (1966), a collection of poems alongside photographs by his brother Ander; editions of the work of Fulke Greville (1968), Ben Jonson (1974), Ezra Pound (2001) and Yvor Winters (2003); two volumes of prose, *The Occasions of Poetry* (1982) and *Shelf Life* (1993); and his *Collected Poems* (1993).

15. Wilmer, 'Thom Gunn: The Art of Poetry LXXII', 184–5.

Gunn and Kitay settled in San Francisco in 1961, where they took an apartment in North Beach. In the late sixties their relationship expanded to include other men. Gunn advocated promiscuity; Kitay was a serial monogamist. In 1969, Kitay's boyfriend Bill Schuessler joined their household – the 'family', they called it – and two years later they moved across town to Cole Street, in the Upper Haight. When Kitay and Schuessler split up, the family stayed together: both moved new partners into the house. 'Everything that we glimpsed,' Gunn wrote of his 'queer household', 'the trust, the brotherhood, the repossession of innocence, the nakedness of the spirit – is still a possibility and will continue to be so.'[16] Gunn died at his Cole Street home on 25 April 2004.

* * *

The person who had the most enduring influence on the life of Thom Gunn was his mother. Ann Charlotte Thomson was born in Snodland, Kent, in 1903. The fourth of seven sisters, she was known as Charlotte and was strong-willed, with a lively intelligence. After leaving school, she worked as a journalist for the *Kent Messenger* in nearby Maidstone where she met the charming and ambitious Herbert Gunn. They married in 1925 and had two children: Tom (William Guinneach, born 1929) and Ander (Dougal Alexander, born 1932). After a short time in Cheadle, on the outskirts of Manchester, where Bert was northern editor of the *Daily Express*, the family moved to Hampstead in 1938.

In the thirties and forties, Hampstead was the artistic and intellectual hub of London: artists and writers were drawn to the area because of its relatively low housing costs. British artists such as Barbara Hepworth, Henry Moore and Ben Nicholson were joined by those fleeing Nazi Europe, such as Naum Gabo, Walter Gropius and Piet Mondrian. The Gunns lived among this progressive, artistic, intellectual culture. Their house, 110 Frognal, was close to University College School and only a short walk from Hampstead Heath, which became the boys' playground.

By the time the Gunns moved to Hampstead, however, their marriage was breaking down. They were both having affairs: Bert with his fellow journalist, Hilde Marchant, and Charlotte with Ronald 'Joe' Hyde, who worked with Bert Gunn at the *Daily Express*. They had only been in Hampstead a few months before Bert moved out, leaving Charlotte and the two boys in the family home. Thus we find 'Tom', probably aged nine, writing across London to his father:

---

16. Gunn, 'My Life up to Now', in *The Occasions of Poetry*, ed. Clive Wilmer (London: Faber & Faber, 1982), 184.

Thank-you for the lovely toy theatre, we have played with it from early morn till sunset. [. . .] I go to a garden party to help "poor Spain" on Saturday.[17]

Charlotte, Ander remembers, 'read the Daily Worker, the Communist newspaper and hung red flags out whenever she could in order to shock the neighbourhood'.[18] This echoes a story Gunn told his friend Don Doody: 'She had certain social obligations as the wife of an important editor,' Doody recalled. 'And Thom said at one point she went to dinner and wore a brooch made of diamonds and rubies in the form of a hammer and sickle. She said, "I've got to do this, so I'll do it my way."'[19]

In the next letter, also from 110 Frognal, Thom writes to his Aunt Mary, one of Charlotte's sisters. The date is February 1945. He describes various events: a dispute with his father about the cost of university; the birth of his half-brother Jamie; the purchase of 'a lovely sports-coat of Harris Tweed and various other necessary articles of clothing'.[20] Then, at the top of the fourth page, he writes:

Margot cooks very well, and John is quite nice (of course Margot is) but I have a slight suspicion he doesn't approve of pacifism. We are very happy, though once I woke up in the morning feeling quite prepared to follow Mother to the grave![21]

Six weeks earlier, Thom (15) and Ander (12) had found their mother dead. She had taken her own life inhaling gas from a gas-poker, a tool used to ignite coal fires. She had blocked the door to the kitchen with a writing bureau and left a note pinned to the door instructing the boys to go next door to find Mrs Stoney, their charlady. When they could not find her, they found the back door from the garden into the kitchen was unlocked.

Thom's cousin Margot and her husband, John, both worked during the war at the codebreaking centre at Bletchley Park until John was transferred to another branch of the Foreign Office in London in January 1945. Looking for somewhere to live, Margot remembered, 'We were more or less commandeered by the aunts into moving into the house in Hampstead.' Margot, then twenty-two, had been married for less than a year and had no experience running a house. 'My husband had never even met the boys,' she

17. TG to Herbert Gunn, c. Early 1939, below.
18. See Edward Guthmann, 'A Poet's Life: Part One', San Francisco Chronicle (25 April 2005), C3.
19. Guthmann, 'A Poet's Life: Part One', C3.
20. TG to Mary Thomson, 10 February 1945, below.
21. Ibid.

recalled. 'Two teenage boys in a state of shock and grief. It was really weird entering the house so soon after Charlotte's death. The fridge was still full of her food.'[22]

In his notes to the *Selected Poems* (2017), Clive Wilmer reprints Gunn's diary entry for 29 December 1944, the day of his mother's death. It stands alone in a small notebook, and Gunn did not begin another diary until 1962. It is worth quoting here partly to compare his private voice at fifteen to the voice he uses in his letter to Aunt Mary, and partly to show his acute understanding, even as a teenager, of his mother's mental state in the moments before her death:

> But oh! mother, from the time when I left you at eleven on Thursday night until four in the morning, what did you do?
> She died quickly and peacefully, they said, but what agonies of mind must she have passed through during the night. I hate to think of her sadness. My poor, poor mother [. . .][23]

We do not hear a voice like this – as vulnerable and overwrought – in his correspondence, with the exception of letters to his life partner Mike Kitay during their difficulties in the early sixties. The voice we do hear, though, is typically more measured – not unlike Gunn's description of his mentor Yvor Winters's reading voice as 'a controlled resonance, suggesting large emotions barely held in reserve'.[24] This is not to suggest that Gunn's letters are not witty, light-hearted, exuberant and digressive: they are, but their reserve often asks the recipient to read between the lines. It is a voice not unlike that of 'The Gas-poker':

> Forty-eight years ago
> – Can it be forty-eight
> Since then? – they forced the door
> Which she had barricaded
> With a full bureau's weight
> Lest anyone find, as they did,
> What she had blocked it for.   (*BC* 10–11)

Written in 1991, the poem is a narrative account of two boys finding their mother's body. Gunn borrowed a trick from Hardy, writing the poem in the third person. 'Then it became easy,' Gunn said, 'because it was no longer

22. Margot Corbett, email to the author, 20 September 2018.
23. Gunn, *Selected Poems*, ed. Clive Wilmer (London: Faber & Faber, 2017), 271.
24. Gunn, 'On a Drying Hill: Yvor Winters', in *Shelf Life* (London: Faber & Faber, 1994), 198.

about myself. I don't like dramatizing myself.'[25] This remark becomes even more significant when we remember 'My Mother's Pride' – the poem that precedes 'The Gas-poker' in *Boss Cupid* – which begins, 'She dramatized herself / Without thought of the dangers.'

What are letters, though, if not a dramatization of oneself, events and experiences? Gunn understood that letter-writing is an act in which one's voice is modulated to the demands and expectations of the recipient. He says as much in his sequence 'Transients and Residents', about San Francisco friends Chuck Arnett, Jere Fransway and Don Doody. In its last poem, 'Interruption', Gunn italicises the line '*I like loud music, bars, and boisterous men*'. Just as we sense that the speaker is communicating something about himself, it is immediately undercut in the following lines: 'You may from this conclude I like the things / That help me if not lose then leave behind, / What else, the self.' As Joshua Weiner, a student of Gunn's and one of his most perceptive critics, has written, 'The gesture is not allowed to stand; the poet turns on it sceptically – the self he seeks to leave in order to discover new possibilities of being becomes a kind of cipher for assuming each identity he meets.'[26] Gunn continues:

> In the letters that I send
> I imitate unconsciously the style
> Of the recipients: mimicking each friend,
> I answer expectations, and meanwhile
> Can analyse, or drawl a page of wit,
> And range, depending on the friend addressed,
> From literary to barely literate.
> I manage my mere voice on postcards best.   (CP 379)

'People do have difficulty with my poetry,' Gunn told Kleinzahler and John Tranter, 'difficulties in locating the central voice or central personality. But I'm not aiming for central voice and I'm not aiming for central personality. I want to be an Elizabethan poet. I want to write with the same anonymity you get in the Elizabethans.'[27] Something similar happens in his letters. He uses mimicry and imitation to tailor a role for each recipient and thus fulfil their expectations. To 'manage' a voice implies both overseeing and handling

25. James Campbell and Gunn, *Thom Gunn in Conversation with James Campbell* (London: Between the Lines, 2000), 19.
26. Joshua Weiner, 'A Symposium on Thom Gunn', 10.
27. Kleinzahler and John Tranter, 'An Interview with Thom Gunn', *Scripsi* 5, no. 3 (1989), 175–6.

it, as though it were a kind of burden.[28] The verb brings to mind 'stage-manage', as though Gunn considered his voice to be a theatrical production in need of organisation and coordination. That he imitates 'unconsciously' further implies that his habit of mimicry is somehow innate, an inbuilt or reflex action; though the fact that Gunn can say this means the imitation cannot be entirely unconscious. Like the images of shields and armour we see throughout his poems, imitation is a form of protection. Inherent in writing letters is a kind of vulnerability which Gunn keeps in check through staging his voice.

The roots of this role-playing can be traced back to Cambridge, where Gunn developed his 'theory of pose': 'Everyone plays a part, whether he knows it or not, so he might as well deliberately design a part, or series of parts, for himself.'[29] A place rich in tension, Gunn suggested, could be found 'between the starting point – the bare undefined and undirected self, if such a self ever existed – and the chosen part'.[30] This theory was both literary in character (he refers to Donne, Yeats, Stendhal, Sartre) and born of personal experience: a feeling of unbounded energy, 'like the elimination of some enormous but undefined problem' he experienced on a walking trip through France in the summer of 1951.[31] It spurred him through his literary apprenticeship, during which he wrote a poem a week at Cambridge and started publishing in college magazines: 'viewing myself as an actor trying to play a part provided rich material for poetry'.[32]

Occasionally Gunn *was* an actor playing a part. One May Week, he played First and Second Servant in a production of *The Taming of the Shrew* held in Trinity Fellows' Garden. 'It was Cambridge at its sweetest,' Gunn wrote, 'Shakespeare, the moonlit summer night, the park-like private gardens of wealthy colleges, friends I hoped would be friends for life – different kinds of happiness rolled into one.'[33] Life and theatre merged to such a degree at Cambridge that the atmosphere must have been extraordinary for a young poet. From the toy theatre his father bought him as a child and roles in school productions of Shakespeare, to his actor friend Tony White (a model for his idea of pose) and Mike Kitay's acting and directing work, theatre was an abiding presence in Gunn's life.

28. Clive Wilmer discusses the importance of the word 'burden' in 'The Gas-poker'. See 'Poor Lovely statue!', *Times Literary Supplement* (23 June 2017), 17–18.
29. Gunn, 'Cambridge in the Fifties', in *The Occasions of Poetry*, 162.
30. Ibid.
31. Gunn, 'Cambridge in the Fifties', 159.
32. Gunn, 'Cambridge in the Fifties', 162.
33. Gunn, 'Cambridge in the Fifties', 164.

Names are significant in Gunn's correspondence for their ability to define roles and relationships. Using different names – for himself and for his correspondents – allowed Gunn to manage his voice, just as the use of characters and personas in his poems gave him enough distance from the reader to keep self-expression in check. Calling his aunts Mary and Catherine childhood names like Sam and Kay defines the relationship and the kind of letter he is going to write. Signing himself 'your sexy old friend, Osbert Sitwell' (to White) and 'your favourite uncle, Affluent Gunn' (to Kitay) serves to distract from whatever confidences or emotions have been expressed in the letter; or, rather, to assign them to one particular Gunn voice or character. Sometimes such monikers were not Gunn's coinages at all. One friend, Douglas Chambers, had 'a spelling-correcting typewriter: when he writes to me it corrects my name, which is obviously wrong, to Thor, thus "Dear Thor". There are few gods I feel less in common with.'[34] Chambers, among other names, was 'Duggle', 'Elegant creature', 'Wild boar' and 'Unwithered Dug'.

Gunn's mother often used variants of her name, and was at times known as Ann, Nan, Nancy and Charlotte, each denoting a small shift of character or circumstance. His cousin Margot remembers going to see the new-born at Gravesend, where the Gunns were living in 1929. 'It must have been that day when my aunt Nan said, "He looks just like a little Tom." So Tom he was from the very beginning, never William.'[35] In the earliest letters in this collection he signs himself Tom. It wasn't until Cambridge that he began signing himself 'Thom', having changed his name by deed poll from William Guinneach Gunn to Thomson William Gunn in 1950, exchanging the Gaelic version of his father's surname for his mother's maiden name.[36] Gunn called Cambridge 'an escape into my life. It was then that I started to spell my first name with an "h". It seemed to me to be nothing more than a delightful affectation when I came to Cambridge, but I can now see that this was an attempt to become a new person; it was my announcement that I was going to be somebody new.'[37] That Gunn escapes 'into' his life rather than 'from' it only re-emphasises the idea that playing parts offers numerous, positive opportunities for reinvention. If Cambridge – and 'Thom' – was one escape into life, his move to California in 1954 was another.

From that moment, letters became his primary means of communication with the old country, from his brother Ander and the Snodland aunts to his editor at the *London Magazine*, John Lehmann, and his best friends from

34. TG to Clive Wilmer, 20 February 1990, below.
35. Corbett, email to the author, 20 September 2018.
36. Wilmer, 'The self you choose', *Times Literary Supplement* (25 April 2008), 13–15.
37. Campbell and Gunn, *Conversation*, 21.

Cambridge, Karl Miller and Tony White. To each he uses a different voice, though all are identifiably Thom Gunn: to Ander the somewhat overbearing tones of an older brother; to his aunts the conspiratorial, mildly shocking voice of their 'naughty nephew' up to no good in far-flung cities; to Lehmann and Miller the urbane tones of a young poet growing in confidence and not entirely free of pretension; to White he was gushing, a little infatuated, and discussed as openly as he could his reading, his thinking, his writing and his new American life.

* * *

The only thing 'mere' about Gunn's voice is that we have heard so little of it beyond his poems and essays. In a couple of major interviews – with Clive Wilmer in the *Paris Review* (1995) and James Campbell for the BBC (2000) – Gunn's voice is modulated for public consumption, edited for print and broadcast. Since his death, two editions of *Selected Poems* have appeared, the first chosen and introduced by August Kleinzahler (2009), the second by Clive Wilmer (2017) with accompanying notes drawn from Gunn's archives at Berkeley and Maryland, and select correspondence. Gunn's *Letters*, however, goes one step further than these books in being the first to present Gunn's private words for public consideration. What is collected here is just a fragment of Gunn's correspondence – around a tenth of what we have uncovered – and a smaller fragment still of what remains to be unearthed in institutional archives and private collections. While putting this selection together it became clear that, in the words of Kleinzahler, 'Gunn's letters serve as one of the most indispensable epistolary chronicles of an era, especially in the U.S., of the Eisenhower fifties transforming into the revolutionary sixties and seventies, and then the revanchist, reactionary Reagan eighties and the AIDS epidemic, all seen through the lens of a gay, ex-pat English poet.'[38]

In the absence of a biography, it has been tempting to focus more on Gunn the man than Gunn the poet, but as well as offering what we hope is a compelling narrative, we also aim to offer a portrait of Gunn as a writer, looking more closely into what he called the 'continuities' of his life: 'between America and England, between free verse and metre, between vision and everyday consciousness'.[39] Literary interest, then, has guided our choice of letters, from Gunn's anxieties about his early poems to reflections on his body of work towards the end of his life. Such was his range of interests and sympathies he once joked, 'I am the only person in the world ever to have dedicated poems to both Winters and [Robert] Duncan.'[40] We can trace Gunn's

38. Kleinzahler, email to the author, 16 August 2019.
39. Gunn, 'My Life up to Now', 184.
40. Wilmer, 'Thom Gunn: The Art of Poetry LXXII', 171.

thinking from book to book: from an undergraduate interest in existentialism to the 'Gossip' poems of *Boss Cupid*, which bear traces of Frank O'Hara's *Lunch Poems*, all while maintaining what Wilmer calls 'a certain anonymity of tone' inherited from Elizabethan models like Thomas Campion.[41] Gunn's encounters with the American modernists offer considerable insight into his poetics. We glimpse Wallace Stevens, for example, on whom he began a doctoral thesis; William Carlos Williams, whose work he admired for its interest in things outside human emotion, and which was in part responsible for his more humane turn in the second half of *My Sad Captains*; and Pound, whose forty-seventh canto he called, in 1966, 'as good as anything in the last 50 years – only Hardy and Williams can equal it'.[42] Among the British, Basil Bunting emerges as a major figure. Gunn lectured on him at Cincinnati in 1981 ('the teachers in the English Dept meeting me in the hallways would politely ask "but who is Basil Bunting?"'[43]) and he began a monograph on Bunting in the mid-nineties. Other passions emerge. He confesses a youthful liking for Adrienne Rich, and in the mid-sixties he writes to Tony Tanner that 'My heroes are increasingly Pound, Williams, and Lowell. Maybe Stevens and Lawrence too. But not Yeats and Eliot.'[44]

Literature and literary figures are bound up unavoidably with literary gossip. From his bafflement at malicious reviews – 'Did I once kick Ian Hamilton's dog?' – to his dislike of how often poetry becomes subordinate to personality – 'I will never see the movie about Sylvia and Ted, the very thought of it turns my stomach' – Gunn is often candid and mischievous about his contemporaries.[45] 'I'm not really sure Heaney is that good,' he tells Chambers. 'I think he was invented by a committee of teachers with a sense of high fashion.'[46] He supposes John Ashbery never has 'any difficulty in placing his poems in an order: even passages within poems could be changed around'.[47] In a letter not published in this collection, he writes of Geoffrey Hill, 'But increasingly with his poetry I get a strange sense of archaic costuming. [. . .] Hill actually speaks of a lute as if he ran across people playing lutes all

41. Wilmer, introduction to Gunn, *Selected Poems*, xviii.
42. TG to Tony Tanner, 5 March 1966, below.
43. TG to Donald Davie, 19 November 1981, Donald Davie Papers, Gen MSS 439, Beinecke Library, Yale University.
44. TG to Tanner, 31 March 1966, below.
45. TG to Gareth Twose, 25 January 1992, below; TG to Clive Wilmer, *c.* November 2003, below.
46. TG to Douglas Chambers, 30 May 1984, below.
47. TG to Robert Pinsky, 1 June 1989, below.

the time, in the bus, outside the supermarket.'[48] Humour aside, the British have typically considered Gunn to be, not our man out there, but 'their man out there' in the words of Glyn Maxwell.[49] If the *Letters* makes one thing clear, it is that Gunn never lost his interest in British poetry: what was happening, who was good. This book situates Gunn among his British and American contemporaries for the first time, and offers unprecedented insights into his influences, his interests – fleeting and enduring – and his own sense of how his work measures up to past and present. In 1990, Gunn appeared in a casebook alongside Ted Hughes and R. S. Thomas.[50] Writing to its editor, A. E. Dyson, Gunn remarked, 'Like Keats, I always had a hankering to be admitted to the company of English poets, and the first third of your book, with its range of appreciative reactions, certainly makes me feel I am munching some sandwich at their picnic.'[51]

Readers wanting more biographical material will not be disappointed. Gunn's numerous passions are well represented, from loud music, bars and boisterous men to more domestic pursuits like cooking and gardening. He took particular pleasure in maintaining the yard at Cole Street. Less than a year after moving in he wrote to Tanner: 'I have sown or planted the following: radishes, onions, scallions, chives, parsley, lemon bergamot mint, hollyhocks, nasturtiums, lupins, alyssum, sweet williams, stock, phlox, pinks, sweet peas, snapdragons, tomatoes, basil, pansies, polyanthus. All the radishes have already been eaten – by snails, not by me.'[52] As for cooking, Kleinzahler writes, '[Thom] wasn't a greatly gifted cook (he was, after all, an Englishman, and an Englishman of a particular generation), but he was more than passable.'[53] Perhaps his cooking was best experienced in epistolary form. 'The secret of a perfect chicken is obvious, though it took me a while to learn it,' Gunn wrote to his two octogenarian aunts, Mary and Catherine, in the late 1990s. 'You baste with butter every ten minutes, so how can anybody fail when what you end up with is chicken meat soaked with butter?'[54] Their response does not survive.

48. TG to Belle Randall, 24 March 1983, Belle Randall Collection of Thom Gunn Letters, BANC MSS 2008/252, Bancroft Library, University of California, Berkeley.
49. Glyn Maxwell, 'How Late They Start to Shine', *Times Literary Supplement* (18 March 1994), 10.
50. A. E. Dyson, ed., *Three Contemporary Poets: Thom Gunn, Ted Hughes & R. S. Thomas* (Basingstoke: Macmillan, 1990).
51. TG to A. E. Dyson, 29 December 1990, below.
52. TG to Tanner, 19 March 1972, Tanner Papers, Archive Centre, King's College, Cambridge.
53. Kleinzahler, 'Thom Gunn', 12.
54. TG to Mary and Catherine Thomson, 22 June 1998, below.

As these pursuits imply, Gunn had a number of lives – his domestic, family life; his bar life; his writing life; his teaching life; his family back in England – and he was good at compartmentalising them. As a friend said recently in an interview, 'I think he had many people who he was friends with that never met each other at all.'[55] Occasionally his lives would intersect. After his reading at the Mermaid Theatre in 1974, Gunn hung out with Tanner (Berkeley), White and Holmstrom (Cambridge), Mary and Catherine (aunts), Jenny and Josie (cousins), Tom Arp (Stanford), and his editor at Faber & Faber, Charles Monteith, 'a bizarre bringing together of different sides of my life (lovely)'.[56] And those 'sides' do not even touch on his lives in the literary and leather scenes of San Francisco. Gunn's correspondence brings together all his friends and family, 'from literary to barely literate', and the voices in which he writes to them all.

In fact, we have two casts here: one a cast of recipients, the other a shadow cast. There is a whole host of people close to Gunn that have few if any letters included in this selection, from his childhood friend Ruth Townsend (née Pearce) and the woman who cared for him after his mother's death, Thérèse Megaw, to Gunn's difficult, itinerant friend Don Doody and his mentor and fellow poet Robert Duncan. The reasons are varied: the whereabouts of some collections are unknown; some are known to have been destroyed; other collections do exist but permission to read them has been refused. In Duncan's case, there are barely any letters or cards because he and Gunn lived so close to each other in San Francisco: they talked in person or over the phone. But from Gunn's mother to friends and lovers such as Allan Noseworthy and Charlie Hinkle, the people he writes *about* are just as important as those he writes *to*: both casts provide insight into his life and work.

Noseworthy's death was the prompt for 'Lament', the first of Gunn's AIDS elegies. He was the first of Gunn's close friends to die from the disease, and Gunn's letters to friends and family in the summer of 1984 reveal some of the details about Noseworthy's final days. We can see, too, some of the details that Gunn wove into 'Lament'. The next time he went to New York – where he used to stay with Noseworthy – he visited Noseworthy's friends and neighbours and went to his old apartment. All of Noseworthy's things were still there. 'I did notice that he had kept every letter, it looked like, that had ever been written to him,' Gunn wrote to his aunts, 'so I located an enormous bundle by myself and dropped them in a dustbin outside. As

55. Jack Collins, interview with the author, 20 June 2019.
56. TG, 'DIARY, vol 4: Jan 1974–Sept 1986', Gunn MSS.

a friend said who had to clear out Sylvia Plath's flat after her suicide: "The dead leave everything behind." Don't they just.'[57]

The elegies that make up the final section of Gunn's signature collection, *The Man with Night Sweats*, were written between 1984 and 1988, and in the letters we can trace the lives and deaths behind them. Christmas 1986 through autumn 1987 was an especially difficult time for Gunn. Jim Lay, Bill Schuessler's lover, died that Christmas. Schuessler nursed him through his last weeks, and Jim died at home at Cole Street. Schuessler, Gunn wrote to his brother, 'was dreadfully uncontrolled at first but has been getting very sensible: I took him to lunch on the revolving restaurant of the Hyatt Regency (on Embarcadero) on Boxing Day because he said he'd like to do "something grand." (I thought it was a very healthy thing for him to say).'[58] Then, from 8 August to 9 September 1987, Gunn lost four friends: Norm Rathweg, Lonnie Leard, Allen Day and Charlie Hinkle. Hinkle's death 'really did me in, or nearly. I thought I was doing pretty well with the others, being sensible, and going about my jobs as best I could, but that brought me as close as I have ever come to a breakdown.'[59] The final poem in the collection, 'A Blank' – in which the speaker sees, from a bus window, a man holding the hand of his adopted son – is based on a guy Gunn used to trick with, a 'sturdy-looking admirable young man' called Steve Rudser.[60] Gunn wrote to Rudser to ask his permission to publish the poem: 'Perhaps I am violating a confidence, perhaps I am making something public you do not want public. [. . .] If you want, I could change a detail or two where possible. Or if you want, I will simply not publish it.'[61] Rudser sent him a bunch of flowers. 'When I got [the poem], I was like, he did it! I won!' Rudser told me. 'It was like winning the lottery.'[62]

Another of Gunn's friends to succumb to AIDS was Larry Hoyt. They met in a bar in 1972, Hoyt dressed head to toe in leather. He was 'alarmingly young', Gunn (42) wrote to Tanner:

57. TG to Mary and Catherine Thomson, 14 December 1984, below.
58. TG to Ander Gunn, 30 December 1986, below.
59. TG to Clive Wilmer, 5 January 1988, private collection.
60. A 'trick' is a common term, especially among gay men, for a one-night stand. 'They'll say that [it] was an ex-lover,' Rudser remarked of the relationship portrayed in 'A Blank', 'and I wasn't an ex-lover. I was an ex-recreational partner. At that time, when no one could conceive of gay people getting married, your partner – your life partner – was your lover. Thom's lover was Mike Kitay. In ['A Blank'] the not terribly classy way of referring to it was a trick.' Steven Fritsch Rudser, interview with the author, 16 October 2018.
61. TG to Rudser, 9 April 1988, below.
62. Rudser, interview with the author, 16 October 2018.

21, certainly young enough to be my son. Very attractive and very bright. [...] Not that I (or he) am being monogamous – unimaginable, dahling – but we are seeing a lot of each other, which is a bit unusual for me. And I'm trying to do things for him I would have liked someone to do for me when I was his age.[63]

This speaks to Gunn's important role as a teacher and mentor, not only to the young men he met on Folsom Street, but also to emerging poets, including Jim Powell, Kleinzahler and Wilmer. It is interesting, in Hoyt's case, that Gunn cast his mentorship in filial terms. Some twenty years after he met Hoyt, Gunn echoed this sentiment in a letter he wrote to Dyson in which he discusses his ideal reader. Asked the question by Robert Duncan – whose ideal reader, Gunn reports, is 'a fat jolly woman rather like the best sort of aunt [...] who is faintly scandalized by his work and at the same time enjoys being scandalized by it' – Gunn speculates:

I realized it was my 20 year old self, or a simulacrum of him, full of dread about the future, and particularly of the future in store for the sexuality he has only just fully recognized, and that much of my poetry has been written as a kind of signal to him that 'it's really all right, you know.' So I think one of the impulses behind my writing has been to reassure – my past self, even my present self, and anybody else who needs the reassurance.[64]

He put it another way in a letter to Kitay: 'I need the Father-Figure.'[65]

Gunn had a difficult relationship with his own father. Gunn's ambivalence towards him is best expressed in the monologue 'From an Asian Tent' (1961): 'each year [I] look more like the man I least / Choose to resemble, bully, drunk, and beast'. After his parents divorced, Gunn's father was largely absent from his life. Only a handful of their letters survive, and Thom's tone is dutiful and distant. When Bert Gunn died in 1962, Thom told Robert Conquest, 'I was rather shocked that I couldn't feel anything at all. I'd half expected I might feel something in spite of the fact that I'd never had much to do with him and he was, finally, a ruthless and self-pitying man.'[66] As with Hoyt, there are traces of Gunn's parental impulses elsewhere. 'I never had any sexual feelings toward any of my students,' he told his brother in 1999, 'I felt too parental for that.'[67] Similarly, Gunn describes his relationship with male

63. TG to Tanner, 3 August 1972, below.
64. TG to Dyson, 8 September 1991, below.
65. TG to Kitay, c. March 1963, below.
66. TG to Conquest, c. March 1962, below.
67. TG to Ander Gunn, 27 May 1999, private collection.

prostitutes in Berlin as 'very platonic, almost fatherly on my part'.[68] Later in life, he was attracted to the homeless young gay men of San Francisco. At some level he must have felt abandoned and betrayed by his mother, and 'that feeling shows', Wilmer suggests, 'in the attraction he felt for boys who had been similarly abandoned; as somebody once said to me, he *mothered* those boys'.[69]

The next time Gunn's mother is mentioned in the correspondence is in the context of another death. In January 1976, Tony White, Gunn's close friend and confidant from Cambridge, died from a blood clot following a freak leg break while playing soccer at the age of forty-five. Writing to Tanner a week after he heard the news (communicated to him by letter), 'I must say I haven't felt a loss like that since my mother died. [. . .] [T]he world does seem enormously diminished, and I still can't altogether believe it.'[70] It is difficult to overstate White's importance to Gunn. Their friendship, after those first years at Cambridge, became one of correspondence punctuated by Gunn's visits to England – most notably the year spent in London in the mid-sixties, in a block (now demolished) on Talbot Road around the corner from White's own place. In the late 1950s, White was Gunn's primary confidant, and we can see in Gunn's side of the correspondence how their discussions shaped some of his most important early poems, such as 'Innocence' and 'Claus von Stauffenberg'. Gunn held White up as a 'model': 'He seemed to articulate in a bolder way than I ever could the kind of personal freedom that I had glimpsed on the road in France,' Gunn wrote in later life.[71]

In early 1960, Gunn wrote to White about his 'one real friend' at Berkeley, 'an ex-Cambridge Englishman (after our time) who is doing graduate work here. I think you would like him, but he is only about 24, and it is amazing what a difference that 6 years makes. I continually find myself almost in the position of a mentor (Jesus Christ) with him, and finally only a relationship between approximately equal people can be any good.'[72] This ex-Cambridge Englishman was Tony Tanner, who dedicated his first book, *The Reign of Wonder* (1965), to Gunn; that work, and Tanner's second book, *City of Words* (1971), helped make American literature a field of study in Britain. Tanner was appointed a fellow of King's College in 1960 but was a frequent visitor to the USA in the sixties and seventies, taking teaching and research positions at Emory, Northwestern and Stanford. Like White, Tanner proved an

68. TG to White, 18 November 1960, below.
69. Wilmer, introduction to Gunn, *Selected Poems*, xliv.
70. TG to Tanner, 27 January 1976, below.
71. Gunn, 'Cambridge in the Fifties', 163.
72. TG to White, 4 February 1960, below.

indispensable and stimulating companion for Gunn, and their letters contain some of the most vigorous discussions of art, literature and philosophy in this book. In late 1998, when Gunn returned to San Francisco from a reading tour, he found a letter from Wilmer informing him that Tanner would be dead within weeks from a combination of prostate, kidney and liver cancer. Gunn wrote to Tanner immediately. 'But you have always been a man of tremendous strength,' he wrote:

> I also must say that you have been without question one of the friends who has meant most to me in my life. I know it is difficult to keep up the full vitality of a friendship when separated by 6000 miles, but you have always been and will go on being a reference point and a reminder to me not only of affection but of the way to lead a life. Doesn't that sound pompous? But I mean it: I think of things you have said, jokes you have made, quotations, judgments, conclusions, funny stories, and they constantly recur to me as reference points as they do from Mike, my mother, Tony White and I am not sure anybody else in such profusion.[73]

Strength was another value Gunn prized. Of another friend, Chuck Arnett, Gunn remarked:

> We had nothing in common, but you don't need to have anything in common for a friendship. I am attracted to people who take charge, who decide what the party's going to be, who give the parties – not by Hitler-like leaders but by people who organize things. I think that's very sexy and very attractive. I admire people who are stronger than me, in fact, and although I may appear like a strong person, I appear to myself as a weak person so I'm always attracted by the strong.[74]

When Robert Prager, the interviewer, put to Gunn the suggestion that Arnett's life was a tragedy because he never made enough money from his art to support himself, Gunn replied: 'His life was not a tragedy. He was always having sex and doing drugs and having the time of his life.'[75]

He could easily have been talking about himself. Gunn's letters provide a kind of history of drug use and the gay scene in San Francisco. He was introduced to mescaline by Paul Bowles – 'a minor (and I think bad) American

73. TG to Tanner, 18 October 1998, below.
74. Robert Prager, 'Interview of Thom Gunn by Robert Prager on 25 July, 1996', Prager Papers, 1998–20, Gay, Lesbian, Bisexual, Transgender Historical Society Archives, San Francisco. Hereafter Prager MSS.
75. Prager, 'Interview of Thom Gunn', Prager MSS.

novelist' – in a San Francisco hotel room in 1958.[76] The drug Gunn is most associated with is LSD, and many of the poems in *Moly* are LSD-related. 'I learned from it, for example, a lot of information about myself that I had somehow blocked from my own view,' Gunn wrote.[77] Although he was experimenting with syllabics and free verse in the late 1960s, he thought metre was the proper form for poems about acid trips. 'The acid trip is unstructured, it opens you up to countless possibilities, you hanker after the infinite,' he rationalised. 'The only way I could give myself any control over the presentation of these experiences, and so could be true to them, was by trying to render the infinite through the finite, the unstructured through the structured.'[78] In 1970 he discovered MDA (methylenedioxyamphetamine) – 'I have on no other occasion had sex for SIX HOURS'[79] – a drug he would use for over twenty years. MDA is known as the 'love drug' for its enhancement of mood and empathy. Its hallucinogenic effects provide a different kind of high from the nowadays more common methylenedioxymethamphetamine (MDMA, ecstasy).

In his last years, Gunn took dangerous amounts of speed to fuel his nightlife. At his favourite bar, the Hole in the Wall Saloon, he fell in with a crowd of younger speedfreaks whom he would invite back to Cole Street for all-night drug and sex parties. One contemporary gay novelist described it as 'the whole San Francisco fantasy – handsome men with big dicks shooting speed'.[80] Drugs and promiscuity were large parts of Gunn's life, beginning with his move to San Francisco. During their difficulties in the early sixties, Gunn referred Kitay to the first 'Modes of Pleasure' poem. 'I realized all the bad possibilities of promiscuity when I wrote it in Spring 1959,' he chides.[81] In the poem, 'The Fallen Rake' sits at the bar, his looks gone. Nobody gives him a second glance and he is 'condemned / To the sharpest passion of them all.' It was not an end to which Gunn himself would surrender. 'All this speed at my age will probably kill me soon,' he wrote in 2000, referring to his young boyfriend John Ambrioso. 'But I cannot resist someone I find so disarmingly attractive.'[82]

Gunn had more of a problem with getting old than he had with death itself. There are moments in his letters that, in hindsight, are imbued with a

76. TG to White, 26 November 1958, below.
77. Gunn, 'My Life up to Now', 182.
78. Ibid.
79. TG to Tanner, 10 January 1971, below.
80. Anonymous, email to the author, 5 June 2019.
81. TG to Kitay, *c*. 14 April 1961, private collection.
82. TG to John Holmstrom, 21 May 2000, below.

sense that he knew what the last few years of his life would be like. 'I am 65 next year,' he wrote to Tanner, 'but by law they can't make you retire [. . .] and I will go on teaching till I go gaga – at least four more years! – as I can't deal with twelve months of unscheduled leisure.'[83] A few months after his sixty-fifth birthday he wrote a long letter to Chambers in which he meditates on death:

> I do think we – our generation on, that is – have had it unnaturally easy for most of our lives. ALWAYS people have experienced lots of death near at hand until the discovery of antibiotics in WWII – my parents had schoolfriends die, one of my mother's sisters died of TB while young, both my grandmothers died before I was born. [. . .] But it has taken AIDS to remind us of what every previous generation was familiar with, and to be aware that if we personally live to an advanced age, we shall be out there alone and in the cold. (So here's hoping I don't last more than another 10 years. I certainly don't want to outlast Mike. I may not mention him often in my letters, but I would find it very difficult surviving his death.)[84]

Gunn died nearly ten years later, in April 2004, from what the coroner termed 'acute polysubstance abuse'. Methamphetamine, heroin and alcohol were found in his system. 'In a sense he killed himself,' writes Wilmer, 'not in an act of willed suicide like his mother's, but by letting himself go, courting death. [. . .] It was a chosen death, but chosen by a man who had earlier chosen life.'[85]

It is true that Gunn does not often mention Kitay in his letters – to Chambers or anyone else – and certainly not at great length. The essential facts of their relationship are by now familiar. They met at Cambridge in December 1952, at a cast party for the Amateur Dramatic Club production of *Cyrano de Bergerac*. (Tony White played the lead, Kitay the meddler.) They quickly fell in love, and part of Gunn's purpose in applying for a graduate fellowship at Stanford was to follow Kitay back to the States. 'I read all the time about Mike Kitay, his lifelong lover who he followed to the United States,' Kitay told me, with typical self-deprecation. 'Really? I'm sure I played a part, but I think he wanted to come even before he knew me.'[86] And, after a fashion, they stayed together for more than five decades. In 1961 they moved to San Francisco and, with the help of a Guggenheim grant ten years later, bought the duplex apartment on Cole Street that they shared until Gunn's death.

83. TG to Tanner, 1 January 1994, below.
84. TG to Chambers, 26 September 1994, below.
85. Wilmer, introduction to Gunn, *Selected Poems*, xliv–xlv.
86. Kitay, interview with the author, 10 October 2018.

It is from the 1960s that most of their letters survive: from Kitay's bout of hepatitis in early 1961 and Gunn's recovery from the same illness in the summer of 1963, through to Gunn's year in London in 1964–5 and their reconciliation in San Francisco that autumn. It was a time of great trouble in their relationship. They were no longer sexual partners. They didn't know what their lives would look like if they stayed together, if they *could* stay together. During 1958–68, Kitay was back and forth between San Francisco and New York trying to carve out a career in show business. He directed plays, acted in musical revues, wrote for television. This period coincided with his and Gunn's worst troubles, and the strain of trying to figure out their relationship via letter took a heavy toll. For a while they separated. There were affairs. As Gunn told Tanner, 'Love by correspondence becomes a kind of obsession – fetishes are created, tone becomes all-important and at the same time elusive, momentary asides get worked up into big issues.'[87] Here we have only Gunn's side of the story, and he is by turns dismissive, condescending, exasperated and pleading. Mike 'wants our relationship exactly as it was eight years ago', he complained to Tanner, 'and he treats any change as a deterioration'.[88] Gunn wanted to be promiscuous; Kitay didn't. 'I don't know what I wanted,' Kitay said of that period:

> I didn't like being gay. The gay life, you know? Whereas Thom took to it like a duck to water. And the whole thing with sexual encounters. Thom was so active, and everything was fine and dandy. I liked being married. I liked the limitation, I guess. You know, we're there for each other. Which Thom was, in every other way. That's why I say [. . .] what did I want, for us to get back together as sexual partners? No. I didn't want it. Not consciously. That was over.[89]

In Gunn's final book, *Boss Cupid*, 'Rapallo' and 'In Trust' are addressed to Kitay. In the first, Gunn writes that if 'Coming to be resigned / To separate beds was not exactly / What we then had in mind, // Something of our first impetus, / Something of what we planned / Remains of what was given us / On the Rapallo sand.' In the second, 'Nothing is, or will ever be, / Mine, I suppose. No one can hold a heart, / But what we hold in trust / We do hold, even apart.' If Gunn's mother is one pillar of this collection, Mike Kitay is the other. With the exception of a handful of letters at the beginning, Gunn's life and work as we see them here are *with* Kitay. When Gunn returned to

87. TG to Tanner, 29 November 1960, below.
88. TG to Tanner, 15 August 1960, below.
89. Kitay, interview with the author, 13 October 2018.

San Francisco in autumn 1965, after a year spent in London, Kitay was living a few blocks along Filbert Street with another man – also called Tom – he thought he was in love with. Kitay went to see Gunn, who said 'Let's have no more of that nonsense.' Kitay recalls, 'It's not that [Tom] and I had an argument, there was nothing that happened other than I knew I didn't belong there. Somehow it was partly that I knew I couldn't . . . I wasn't ready to leave Thom Gunn.'[90]

M.N.

90. Kitay, interview with the author, 13 October 2018.

EDITING AND ANNOTATING THE LETTERS

Marginal insertions have been placed in text where Gunn clearly intended them to go, including instances where dashes or parentheses are required. He was fastidious about spelling, capitalisation, punctuation and grammar – all of which have been carefully preserved in the transcriptions and are presented without editorial comment. We have silently corrected minor spelling mistakes that we have judged inadvertent. Some misspellings are obviously intentional – 'pome' for poem, 'cuntry' for country – and these have been maintained. Gunn was an idiosyncratic speller of names (he never quite mastered Shiela/Sheila/Sheilah) and these, too, have been maintained unless the misspelling creates ambiguity, in which case a surname has been added in square brackets. This insertion has also been used to differentiate between people of the same first name where the context is unclear. Where Gunn clearly forgot an article or a preposition, we have added these in square brackets. We have tried to keep our use of square brackets to a minimum, knowing that a text full of editorial insertions is off-putting for most readers.

Gunn's other idiosyncrasy is his titling of novels, poems, films, paintings, plays and so on. He denotes these variously using single quotation marks, double quotation marks, underlining or nothing at all. No discernible pattern emerges across his correspondence and all original demarcations have therefore been maintained, with any obscure or ambiguous works clarified in footnotes. Where the full title of a work is mentioned in text, we have not seen fit to provide a footnote unless the work is obscure or has a special significance for Gunn. This is all to suggest that editorial apparatus has been kept to a minimum, and that the transcriptions of these letters are as faithful to Gunn's originals as possible.

The vast majority of Gunn's poems can be found in *Collected Poems* (*CP*) and his one subsequent collection, *Boss Cupid* (*BC*). For poems Gunn correctly names in the text, and which are collected in *CP* or *BC*, we have chosen not to gloss their publication history. Poems which Gunn mentions by working title, subject, theme or character but does not name are glossed with reference to *CP* or *BC*. We have glossed all poems from *Touch* which Gunn chose not to include under the heading 'Poems from the 1960s' in *CP*. All uncollected poems are glossed with details of their first (and usually only) publication in a journal, newspaper or anthology. For unpublished poems, we refer readers to the archive in which notes and drafts of the poem survive. Accompanying footnotes are provided for the purpose of bringing context to Gunn's life. Significant places, people and events are identified at their first mention. We have made extensive use of Gunn's diaries, scrapbooks, working notebooks and other writings to offer supporting biographical information. However, this book does not pretend to be a biography and factual notes have been kept as concise as possible. In most cases, footnotes refer to Gunn's experiences, his publication history, and wider cultural and political events where the letters demand additional clarification and explanation.

For undated letters, editorial dates have been assigned from postmarks and/or internal and external evidence, in most cases cross-referenced with other letters or Gunn's diaries. Dates supplied from postmarks and internal and external evidence are footnoted accordingly. On the rare occasion an exact date was impossible to determine, we offer an estimation, usually a span of months and occasionally the year. These are identified with a *circa* date. With the exception of love letters to Mike Kitay, Gunn was fastidious about dating his correspondence. The letters to Kitay in the early sixties have been the most troublesome to date, and their ordering here is as certain as we can determine. If a letter was started on one date and resumed later, both dates are clearly given in text, though we have taken the first date as the editorial date. Locations of the original manuscripts are also included in the introductory header for each letter. Where enclosures are mentioned in text, we have sought, where possible, to identify and footnote them.

One major regret concerns Gunn's use of postcards. Often he will allude to the visual image: we have done our best to describe and identify them while at the same time realising that most of the images – tattoos, advertisements for leather bars, homemade cards with pornographic pictures cut and pasted from magazines – are obscure and virtually impossible for the reader to track down. We realise that description is a poor substitute, but we hope that Gunn's visual humour – a big part of his correspondence – is not entirely lost.

In the interests of space, original layout and page breaks are not duplicated, though we have tried to reflect the layout of Gunn's sign-offs in the text. Addresses have been maintained in full. Where no address is given, we have sought to determine the most likely location through postmarks and internal evidence; inserted addresses are identified by square brackets. We would like to have included more letters in their entirety in order to recreate the shape and design of the originals, but the passages drawn from longer letters warrant inclusion for their literary and biographical merit. Where letters are abridged, omitted passages are marked with [. . .]. Although small,

Gunn's handwriting is mercifully legible and has saved innumerable hours of transcription. The character of his writing changed, becoming smaller and scrawnier as he aged. His undergraduate fountain pen made way for ballpoint. There are very few occasions where we have had to admit defeat as to knotted letters, words squashed into the margins of the page, or damage to the original documents. These are marked in the printed text with the probable reading and a question mark inside square brackets.

CHRONOLOGY

1903

3 April
: Birth of Herbert Smith Gunn (known as Bert), to Herbert Gunn, merchant seaman and marine engineer, and his wife Alice Eliza Smith, at 225 Old Road West, Gravesend, Kent.

28 September
: Birth of Ann Charlotte Thomson (known as Charlotte), the fourth child of Alexander Thomson, a farmer, and Daisy Collings, at 'Covey Hall', 27 Holborough Road, Snodland, Kent. Charlotte's siblings are Barbara (b.1898), Margaret (b.1900), Helen (b.1902), Christina (b.1905), Mary (b.1907) and Catherine (b.1909).

1921
: Charlotte Thomson begins work at the *Kent Messenger*, where she meets Herbert Gunn, a trainee reporter.

1925

12 September
: Herbert Gunn marries Charlotte Thomson in London.

1929

29 August
: William Guinneach Gunn (TG) born to Herbert and Charlotte Gunn; is quickly given the nickname 'Tom'; the family lives at 78 Old Road East, Gravesend.

1932

5 April
: Dougal Alexander Gunn, known as Ander, born in Gravesend.

1933
: The Gunns move to 44 De Vere Gardens, Kensington; Herbert Gunn is appointed news editor of the London *Evening Standard*.

1935
: The Gunns move to 36 St Mary's Avenue, Shortlands, in south-east London.

1936
: Herbert and Charlotte briefly separate; Charlotte takes the boys to live in Goudhurst, a village in Kent; Herbert and Charlotte later reconcile.

1937	The Gunns briefly move to St James's Street, Mayfair; then to 4 Daylesford Road, Cheadle, a suburb of Manchester, when Herbert is appointed northern editor of the *Daily Express*; as day boys, TG and Ander attend the Ryleys School in nearby Alderley Edge. Charlotte begins an affair with Herbert's friend and colleague at the *Daily Express*, Ronald 'Joe' Hyde.
1938 April	The Gunns return to London and move to 110 Frognal, Hampstead, when Herbert Gunn is promoted to assistant editor of the *Daily Express*; TG becomes close friends with Ruth Pearce, a neighbour; attends University College School (UCS), Hampstead.
5 November	Herbert and Charlotte separate.
1939	Herbert and Charlotte divorce.
5 June	Death of Alexander Thomson, TG's grandfather.
3 September	The United Kingdom declares war on Germany.
Autumn	TG and Ander return to the Ryleys School and board for a term; Charlotte begins living with Hyde at 110 Frognal.
December	TG and Ander return to Hampstead and UCS.
1940	
Spring	Charlotte marries Hyde.
July	TG's poem 'A Thousand Cheers for Authors' appears in the UCS magazine, *The Gower*.
September	Charlotte takes TG and Ander to stay with her sister Christina in Farnham, then to a hotel in Alton; they attend local schools for a term.
1941 January	TG attends the progressive Bedales School in Hampshire, where he boards; makes only day visits to London; writes 'The Flirt', a short story about adultery and divorce.
1942 April	Leaves Bedales; returns to UCS for last term of junior school.
Summer	Hyde leaves; Charlotte now living alone at 110 Frognal with TG and Ander; TG later calls this 'a golden period'.
Autumn	Attends senior school at UCS.

1943

December — Charlotte and Hyde reconcile; Hyde returns to 110 Frognal.

1944

29 January — Herbert Gunn marries Olive Melville Brown, a reporter on the *Daily Mail*.

Spring — Begins reading Hardy, Dickens and the Brontës.

27 December — Charlotte and Hyde separate again; Hyde leaves 110 Frognal.

29 December — Charlotte barricades the kitchen door then takes her own life using a gas-poker; TG and Ander discover her body the next morning.

1945

January–June — TG and Ander are looked after at 110 Frognal by their cousin Margot and her husband John Corbett.

Summer — Attains School Certificate; spends the summer with his aunts, Barbara in Allhallows, and Mary and Catherine in Snodland; 110 Frognal is sold.

Autumn — When school resumes, TG stays with his mother's friend Thérèse Megaw in Hampstead, during term, and with his aunts in Kent during holidays; Ander lives with Herbert and Olive in Chelsea.

1947

Summer — Attains the Higher School Certificate and leaves UCS.

Autumn — Lives in Snodland with Mary and Catherine until the start of his National Service.

1948

1 April — Begins his National Service in the Army with the Royal Hampshire Regiment at the Wessex Brigade depot in Wiltshire.

28 October — Transferred to the Royal Army Education Corps.

1949 — Teaches as an education sergeant at the Royal Electrical and Mechanical Engineers depot, Arborfield, Berkshire.

1950

23 January — Demobbed from military service.

January–June — Works in the translation office of the Paris Metro, a job organised by a friend of his father; begins writing a novel, later abandoned.

Summer	Hitchhikes around France with army friend Mark Myers; changes name from William Guinneach to Thomson William.
Autumn	Goes up to Trinity College, Cambridge, to read English.

1951

June	'Poem' (later renamed 'The Soldier') appears in *Cambridge Today*.
Summer	Hitchhikes through France with Myers, where he experiences 'the revelation [. . .] the elimination of some enormous but undefined problem'; reads all of Shakespeare.
Autumn	Writes a poem a week for the next two years; meets Karl Miller; attends F. R. Leavis's lectures.

1952

Spring	Meets Tony White, who becomes a close friend; White later introduces him to John Holmstrom.
21 June–2 Aug.	Picks fruit at Priory Farm Camp, near Wisbech; writes 'Carnal Knowledge'.
20 Aug.–8 Sept.	Hitchhikes through France and Italy; spends his twenty-third birthday in Siena.
Autumn	Becomes secretary of the Cambridge English Club; Miller is treasurer.
24 September	'The Secret Sharer' broadcast on *New Soundings* (BBC Radio).
5 or 7 December	Meets Mike Kitay, an American from Kearny, New Jersey, at a cast party for *Cyrano de Bergerac* at the ADC Theatre, Cambridge; Kitay is reading English at Cambridge on a Woodrow Wilson Fellowship.

1953

2 March	Invites Kitay to 'lunch, and wine' in his rooms at Trinity.
Spring	*Thom Gunn*, the sixteenth pamphlet in The Fantasy Poets series, published by Fantasy Press; writes 'Tamer & Hawk', about Kitay.
7–9 June	Visits Oxford; meets Donald Hall.
Summer	Graduates Trinity College, Cambridge.
Summer	Travels through Europe with Kitay, visiting Bruges, Heidelberg, Salzburg, Cologne, Frankfurt, Munich, Milan, Verona and Rapallo.

Autumn	Awarded Harper-Wood Studentship by St John's College, Cambridge, and plans to visit Rome for three months.
Autumn	'Lofty in the Palais de Dance' appears in the *Paris Review*.
14 November	'Tamer and Hawk' appears in the *New Statesman and Nation*.
December	Visits Rome, Padua, Milan and Venice with Kitay.
1954	
Jan.–Mar.	Lives in Rome at the Pensione Imhof, Via Modena.
15 March	Leaves Rome and returns to Cambridge; stays in the Central Hotel.
17 March	Awarded a creative writing fellowship at Stanford University.
1 July	*Fighting Terms* published by Fantasy Press, his first full collection.
Summer	Kitay graduates Trinity College, Cambridge; he returns to the USA to complete two years of service in the Air Force and is stationed at Lackland Air Force Base, San Antonio, Texas.
26 August	TG sails on the *Queen Elizabeth* to New York; stays with Kitay's parents in Kearny for three weeks; travels by train to San Francisco.
Late September	Meets his new supervisor, Yvor Winters; moves into a room at 334 Lincoln Avenue, Palo Alto.
October	Enrols in Winters's creative writing course and attends his other courses; begins reading Wallace Stevens and William Carlos Williams.
14 October	Meets W. H. Auden at Winters's house in Los Altos.
1955	
March–May	Writes 'On the Move'.
April	Accepts a teaching position at Trinity University, San Antonio.
June	Nine poems, including 'The Corridor' and 'Lines for a Book', appear in *Poetry*; is awarded the Levinson Prize by *Poetry*.
8 June	Meets Christopher Isherwood in Los Angeles.
9 June	Moves into an apartment with Kitay at 2638 West Craig, San Antonio.

13 June	Buys a second-hand 1950 Harley Davidson motorcycle; begins teaching at Trinity University.
December	'On the Move' appears in *Encounter*.

1956

16 January	Writes to Winters proposing a return to Stanford to begin a PhD on Wallace Stevens.
Spring	Writes 'The Allegory of the Wolf Boy'.
April	Awarded a scholarship and half-time teaching position by Stanford; Kitay awarded a Stanford scholarship to study drama; they plan to return to Palo Alto in the autumn.
26 May	Submits manuscript of *The Sense of Movement* to Faber & Faber.
28 June	Seven poems appear in the anthology of the Movement, *New Lines*, edited by Robert Conquest.
10 July	*The Sense of Movement* accepted by Faber & Faber.
August	Kitay leaves the Air Force; they holiday in New Orleans and New York; Kitay visits his parents in Kearny; TG stays in New York.
September	TG returns to Palo Alto, lives in his old room on Lincoln Avenue for the first quarter; begins teaching and graduate work at Stanford.
December	Kitay arrives in Palo Alto and enrols at Stanford; they move to a small apartment at 143 Alma Street.
26 December	Writes to Faber & Faber enclosing new poems for *The Sense of Movement*, including 'In Praise of Cities'.

1957

March	Gives a reading at UC Berkeley, at the invitation of Thomas Parkinson.
7 June	*The Sense of Movement* published by Faber & Faber.
3–8 July	Sails on the *Johan van Oldenbarnevelt* from New York to Southampton.
9 July–4 Sept.	Visits friends and family in London and Kent.
Summer	Kitay leaves Stanford and starts work as a director for the Comedia Repertory Company, based in Palo Alto.
5–10 Sept.	Sails on the *Queen Elizabeth* from Southampton to New York; returns to Palo Alto via Los Angeles, where he meets Kitay.
Autumn	Resolves to leave Stanford, having written almost nothing since finishing *The Sense of Movement*.

December	Josephine Miles offers him a one-year teaching position at UC Berkeley on the strength of *The Sense of Movement*; TG accepts.

1958

January	Begins writing 'Claus von Stauffenberg'.
18 May	Reads with Donald Davie at the Poetry Center, San Francisco.
June	Visits New York for a month; stays at William Sloane House, YMCA.
September	Moves to 3216 Telegraph Avenue, Oakland; Kitay stays in Palo Alto; TG begins teaching at UC Berkeley as a lecturer.
October	'Claus Von Stauffenberg' appears in *The Spectator*.
November	Has his first hallucinogenic experience when Paul Bowles gives him a mescaline capsule.
1 November	*Fighting Terms* published in the USA by Hawk's Well Press; TG extensively revised the poems for this edition.
December	Kitay leaves the Comedia Repertory Company and moves to New York.

1959

January	Kitay returns from New York and forms a new theatre group, Phoenix, with former members of Comedia.
March	Receives Somerset Maugham Award, given by the Society of Authors; plans to travel to Germany.
April	Becomes regular poetry critic for the *Yale Review*.
13 April	*The Sense of Movement* published by the University of Chicago Press.
Summer	Contract extended at UC Berkeley.
August	Spends two weeks in New York.
Autumn	Meets Tony Tanner, an English graduate student on a Harkness Fellowship at UC Berkeley.
December	Kitay moves to New York; Gunn plans to join him in the summer.

1960

May	TG meets Clint Cline; they live together in Oakland for six weeks.
July–August	Lives with Kitay in Liberty, New York, where Kitay performs with the Stanley Woolf Players, a local theatre group.

14–19 Sept.	Sails on the *Queen Mary* from New York to Southampton.
20–30 Sept.	Visits friends and family in London; meets Ted Hughes.
1 Oct.–30 Nov.	Spends a week in Hamburg before travelling to Berlin, where he stays until late November; writes 'Innocence'; submits the manuscript of *My Sad Captains* to Faber & Faber.
December	Spends a week in Copenhagen and returns to England for Christmas.

1961

January–June	TG and Kitay have a series of quarrels via letter; Kitay remains in New York for several months to recover from hepatitis.
9 January	Hughes introduces TG to Sylvia Plath, their only meeting.
13–18 January	Sails on the *Queen Elizabeth* from Southampton to New York.
February	Meets Oliver Sacks in San Francisco.
Late February	Moves into an apartment at 975 Filbert Street, San Francisco.
March	'Innocence' appears in the *London Magazine*.
Spring	Meets Donald Doody in Gordon's, a bar in San Francisco; meets Chuck Arnett, a dancer and artist; promoted to assistant professor at UC Berkeley.
Early July	Kitay returns to San Francisco and moves in with Gunn on Filbert Street; Kitay begins working as a director in nearby Redwood City.
1 September	*My Sad Captains* published by Faber & Faber.
19 September	*My Sad Captains* published by the University of Chicago Press.

1962

23 February	*Fighting Terms* published by Faber & Faber; in this edition, TG restored most of the 1954 text.
2 March	Herbert Gunn dies of cancer at his home in Wimbledon.
March	Kitay meets Tom Gee, a lawyer, and they begin an affair.
18 May	*Selected Poems of Thom Gunn and Ted Hughes* published by Faber & Faber.
Autumn	Kitay moves to New York to look for work as a director.

7 December	TG enters Mount Zion Hospital, San Francisco, with hepatitis; begins a diary, which he keeps for the rest of his life.

1963

7 January	Discharged from hospital.
January–May	Stays at Doody's apartment, 1045 Fell Street, to convalesce; begins work on 'Misanthropos'; starts reading Thomas Mann.
22 May	Returns to Filbert Street.
31 May	*Five American Poets*, co-edited with Ted Hughes, published by Faber & Faber.
8 June	Kitay returns from New York.
18 June–29 Aug.	Tours Mexico with Doody, and afterwards visits New Orleans, Chicago, Dallas, Amarillo and Salt Lake City.
September	Resumes teaching at UC Berkeley.

1964

March	Receives award from the National Institute of Arts & Letters.
18 June–5 July	Visits Doody in Chicago for four days, then to New York, alone; worries his relationship with Kitay is over.
6 July	Arrives in London, where he stays initially with Tony White.
31 August	Rents room at 80 Talbot Road, Notting Hill, close to White.
2 September	Meets T. S. Eliot at the Faber & Faber offices on Russell Square.
18 Sept.–16 Oct.	Kitay visits TG in London.
28 November	Gives a reading at King's College, Cambridge, at Tanner's invitation, and meets Clive Wilmer, one of Tanner's students.

1965

February	Begins work on an edition of Fulke Greville.
March	Begins work on *Positives*, a collaboration with his brother Ander.
8 March	'Misanthropos' broadcast on BBC Radio.
26 April	Begins essay on William Carlos Williams.
15 June	Submits manuscript of *Positives* to Faber & Faber.

15 June–13 July	Leaves London and spends three weeks in New York and Chicago before returning to San Francisco; stays with Kitay at Gee's apartment.
20 July	Moves back to 975 Filbert Street; Kitay stays at Gee's.
July	The essay 'William Carlos Williams' appears in *Encounter*.
August	'Misanthropos' appears in *Encounter*.
4–6 September	Attends Satyrs Motorcycle Club Labor Day run to Badger Flats in the Sierra National Forest.
12 October	Kitay leaves Gee and moves back to 975 Filbert Street.
9 December	Indicates to UC Berkeley that he wishes to resign his teaching position.

1966

7 June	Last day at UC Berkeley; though officially on unpaid leave, he does not intend to return.
12 June	Takes LSD for the first time.
20 August	Takes LSD with Kitay; Kitay's first trip.
13 September	Submits manuscript of *Touch* to Faber & Faber.
24 September	*Positives* published by Faber & Faber.
18 December	Meets Lonnie Leard in the Capri, North Beach.

1967

14 January	Attends Human Be-In at Golden Gate Park Polo Fields.
11 February	Sends letter of resignation to UC Berkeley.
27 Feb.–8 May	Travels to England: visits relatives in Cornwall and Kent; rents room at 24A Hedgegate Court, Notting Hill, for six weeks.
28 March	*Positives* published by the University of Chicago Press.
April	Writes six poems, his first since finishing *Touch*.
12 June	Kitay moves to New York; TG plans to join him within six months.
2 July	Meets Bill Schuessler in the Tool Box, a leather bar in San Francisco; Schuessler is visiting from Wisconsin for the Summer of Love.
31 July	Submits manuscript of *Selected Poems of Fulke Greville* to Faber & Faber.
28 September	*Touch* published by Faber & Faber.

1968

| 25 January | Death of Yvor Winters from throat cancer at his home in Palo Alto. |

l

30 January	*Touch* published by the University of Chicago Press.
3 Feb.–4 Mar.	Takes part in the California Poetry Reading Circuit.
14 March	Meets Elizabeth Bishop in San Francisco.
24 March	Doody begins bartending at the Stud; soon becomes manager.
12–19 April	Visits Kitay in New York.
18–19 May	Attends Northern California Folk-Rock Festival in San Jose; resumes taking acid, having given up after bad trips the previous summer.
31 July	Kitay quits his job in New York and returns to San Francisco.
11 September	Attends Society for Individual Rights poetry workshop run by Robert Duncan.
30 September	*Selected Poems of Fulke Greville*, edited by TG, published by Faber & Faber.
26 October	Attends Renaissance Pleasure Fair in San Rafael; takes acid and speed. The Fair provides the inspiration for his poem 'The Fair in the Woods'.
17 December	First Saturnalia party at the Stud.

1969

Jan.–Mar.	Teaches a quarter at California State College at Hayward (now California State University, East Bay).
22 March	Introduces Kitay to Schuessler, recently returned to San Francisco.
24 March	*Poems 1950–1966: A Selection* published by Faber & Faber.
Spring	Regularly takes acid and attends large concerts in Golden Gate Park.
April	Kitay and Schuessler begin an affair.
29 April	*Selected Poems of Fulke Greville* published by the University of Chicago Press.
June	Schuessler comes to live at 975 Filbert Street with TG and Kitay.
13 September	Has his twentieth acid trip at the Renaissance Pleasure Fair, San Rafael.
20 Oct.–7 Nov.	Gives eighteen readings in fifteen days on the Michigan Poetry Circuit.
6 December	Attends the Altamont Speedway Free Festival.
17 December	Second Saturnalia party at the Stud.

1970

January–May   Visiting Bain-Swiggett Lecturer in Poetry at Princeton
                 University; lives in New York, first in a hotel, then a loft
                 on Prince Street.

March–April   Writes several poems, including 'Tom-Dobbin' and
                 'Moly'.

27 April   Gives lecture 'Thomas Hardy and the Ballads' at
                 Princeton.

24 May   Submits manuscript of *Moly* to Faber & Faber.

16 June–18 Aug. Visits friends and family in Cambridge, London and Kent.

25–29 June   Takes part in the Poetry International Festival, London;
                 gives readings in London and Edinburgh.

September   Begins and abandons pornographic novel, 'San Francisco
                 Romance'.

4 December   Writes 'Hitching to Frisco', his first poem since April.

27 December   Takes MDA for the first time.

1971

Jan.–Mar.   Teaches a quarter at Stanford at Donald Davie's
                 invitation.

23 March   *Moly* published by Faber & Faber.

24 March   Awarded Guggenheim Fellowship.

3 April–4 May   Tony White visits San Francisco; they drop acid at a
                 ranch in Cobb.

May–July   Works as poetry editor for San Francisco counterculture
                 newspaper *The Organ*; publishes one poetry section
                 before the paper folds in July.

27 July   Purchases duplex apartment, 1214–16 Cole Street in the
                 Upper Haight, San Francisco.

13–15 August   First visit to the Geysers in Sonoma County, fifty miles
                 north of San Francisco, a popular gay and hippie
                 hangout.

1 September   Moves to 1216 Cole Street with Kitay and Schuessler;
                 various friends live in 1214, the upstairs apartment, for
                 the next decade.

1972

22 April   Meets Larry Hoyt at Ramrod, a leather bar in San
                 Francisco.

8 June   Submits manuscript of *Ben Jonson: Selected by Thom
                 Gunn* to Penguin.

1973

Jan.–Mar.	Teaches the winter quarter at UC Berkeley.
April	Gives readings as part of the Connecticut Poetry Circuit.
23 April	*Moly and My Sad Captains* published in the US, in a single volume, by Farrar, Straus & Giroux.
June	Has two poems included in *The Male Muse: A Gay Anthology*.

1974

3–15 April	Visits New York; meets Allan Noseworthy III, with whom a sexual relationship develops into a close friendship.
16 Apr.–19 June	Visits England; stays mainly in London but visits family in Kent and Cornwall.
10–14 June	Travels to Paris with Tony White.
20 June–3 July	Visits New York; marches in his first Gay Pride parade.
27 June	*Ben Jonson: Selected by Thom Gunn* published by Faber & Faber.
30 September	Money troubles; sells early notebooks to the University of Maryland.

1975

Jan.–Mar.	Begins teaching the winter quarter at UC Berkeley on a permanent part-time basis; this continues until his retirement in 1999.
April	Kitay and Schuessler split up; Schuessler stays at 1216 Cole Street, moving to the front room.
20 May	Gives a reading at Stanford where, in explanatory remarks about 'Jack Straw's Castle', he comes out as gay.
10 June	Meets Allen Day on Folsom Street; they become close friends.
19 June	Submits manuscript of *Jack Straw's Castle and Other Poems* to Faber & Faber.
27 Oct.–7 Nov.	Visits Canada; meets Douglas Chambers, a professor at Trinity College, University of Toronto, who becomes a close friend.

1976

9 January	Death of Tony White, from a blood clot following a broken leg.
9 February	Finishes article on 'Robert Duncan and Homosexuality'.
April	Writes memoir essay, 'Cambridge in the Fifties'.
20 September	*Jack Straw's Castle* published by Faber & Faber.

| 29 October | *Jack Straw's Castle and Other Poems* published by Farrar, Straus & Giroux. |

1977

| May | Kitay meets Bob Bair in the Stud and they begin a relationship. |
| 4–20 October | Visits New York, where he meets an architecture graduate student called Norm Rathweg. |

1978

3 Apr.–12 June	Teaches spring quarter at UC Davis, Sacramento.
May	Begins writing poems again after two and a half years, his longest period of writer's block.
July	Bair moves into Cole Street.
13 Sept.–9 Oct.	Visits England: stays with aunts Mary and Catherine in Snodland, Tanner in Cambridge, Ander in Leeds, and Thérèse Megaw in London.
27 November	Ex-city supervisor Dan White murders Harvey Milk and Mayor George Moscone; TG marches in candlelight parade to City Hall.

1979

21 May	White Night riots, a response to the lenient sentence given to Dan White for the Milk–Moscone assassination.
23 September	*Selected Poems: 1950–1975* published by Farrar, Straus & Giroux.
22 October	*Selected Poems: 1950–1975* published by Faber & Faber.
1–19 Nov.	Visits England and Wales, tours secondary schools giving readings; he does not visit England again until 1992.
12 December	Begins 'Talbot Road', a poem about his year in London (1964–5).
13 December	Diagnosed with Bell's palsy but recovers within a fortnight.

1980

18 January	Meets Wendy Lesser, founding editor of *Threepenny Review*.
28 January	Meets Robert Pinsky, his new colleague at UC Berkeley.
7 March	Receives WH Smith Literary Award for *Selected Poems: 1950–1975*.
30 June	Schuessler moves to the upstairs apartment in Cole Street with his partner Jim Lay.
2 August	Moves to a new workroom in the upstairs apartment.

8 October	Finishes 'Talbot Road', begun the previous December.

1981

7 April	Submits manuscript of *The Passages of Joy* to Faber & Faber.
22 Apr.–8 May	Visits Amherst College as the Robert Frost Library Fellow in Poetry; gives reading and delivers a lecture on early poems of Yvor Winters.
3 June	Finishes memoir/essay about Winters, 'On a Drying Hill'.
24 Sept.–3 Dec.	Visiting Elliston Poet at the University of Cincinnati; delivers public lectures on Basil Bunting and 'Misanthropos'.

1982

21 January	Finishes the essay 'What the Slowworm Said: Eliot, Pound, and Bunting'.
22 June	Meets August Kleinzahler.
28 June	*The Passages of Joy* published by Faber & Faber. *The Occasions of Poetry*, ed. Clive Wilmer, published by Faber & Faber.
18 August	*The Passages of Joy* published by Farrar, Straus & Giroux.
7 December	Resigns as consulting editor for *Threepenny Review* but continues to advise Lesser about poetry submissions on an informal basis.

1983

June	Finishes 'The Hug', a poem he began in 1980.
26 December	Meets Charlie Hinkle in Trax; they begin a sexual relationship that lasts until March, after which they remain close friends.

1984

February	Decides not to publish another poetry collection until 1992.
31 March	Begins writing 'The Differences', a poem about Hinkle.
8 May	Noseworthy, recently diagnosed with Kaposi's sarcoma, moves to San Francisco and stays at Cole Street.
4 June	Takes Noseworthy to hospital with pneumocystis pneumonia.
21 June	Death of Noseworthy.
18 July–9 Aug.	Writes 'Lament', about Noseworthy.

| 11–19 Nov. | Visits New York, stays with Rathweg and his partner Louis Keith Nelson; helps clear out Noseworthy's old apartment and throws away all the letters he wrote to Noseworthy from 1974 onwards. |

1985

13 January	Decides not to visit England in the summer; fears that Ronald Reagan's new anti-gay immigration policy means that he could not return to the USA.
12 May	Death of Josephine Miles; writes her obituary for *California Monthly*.
15 November	An expanded edition of *The Occasions of Poetry* published in the USA by North Point Press.
December	Writes six poems, including 'To Isherwood Dying'.

1986

4 January	Death of Isherwood.
8 March	Records programme about AIDS for BBC Radio.
13 September	Jim Lay reveals that he has AIDS.
5 December	Death of Larry Hoyt, from AIDS; writes 'Still Life', about Hoyt.
25 December	Death of Jim Lay, from AIDS.

1987

February	Kitay and Bair split up; Bair stays at Cole Street, in a separate room.
29 March	Learns that Hinkle has pneumocystis pneumonia.
4 June	Visits Hinkle; takes him to Speckmann's German restaurant; source of the poem 'The J Car'.
3 July	Finishes poem about Jim Lay, 'Words for Some Ash'.
8 August	Death of Norm Rathweg, from AIDS, in New York.
18 August	Deaths of Allen Day and Lonnie Leard, from AIDS.
9 September	Death of Charlie Hinkle, from AIDS.
October	Finishes 'The Missing', 'Her Pet' and 'To a Dead Graduate Student'; has written twenty poems in the last twelve months.

1988

3 February	Death of Robert Duncan, from kidney failure.
2 March	Death of Chuck Arnett, from AIDS.
1 April	Finishes 'A Blank', originally titled 'The Last Poem'.
15 June	Co-edits *Poems*, a posthumous collection of Hinkle's work, with William McPherson.

24 August	Finishes writing *The Man with Night Sweats* but does not plan to publish it until 1992.
21 December	Finishes elegy 'Duncan'.

1989

18 January	Schuessler diagnosed with AIDS-related complex (ARC).
30 June	Given security of employment at UC Berkeley; promoted from visiting lecturer to senior lecturer.
12 November	Bob Bair moves out of Cole Street; stays in San Francisco.
11 December	Death of Barbara Godfrey, née Thomson.

1990

8 January	Finishes 'An Operation', his first poem for a year.
17 February	Meets Robert Gallegos in a Folsom Street bar; later the subject of the poem 'American Boy'.
26 March	Sends manuscript of *The Man with Night Sweats* to Faber & Faber and Farrar, Straus & Giroux.
27 March	Receives Shelley Memorial Award from the Poetry Society of America.
May	Writes 'Saturday Night' and 'My Mother's Pride'.
June	Article on Isherwood, 'Getting it Right', appears in *Threepenny Review*.

1991

10–12 January	Visits New York to receive Lila Wallace–Reader's Digest Writers' Award.
11 June	Drafts 'The Gas-poker', about his mother's suicide.
12–17 Nov.	Visits Washington DC to make a recording for the Library of Congress; visits the National Gallery and the Phillips Collection.

1992

10 February	*The Man with Night Sweats* published by Faber & Faber.
16 April	*The Man with Night Sweats* published by Farrar, Straus & Giroux.
12 June	Submits manuscript of *Shelf Life* to Faber & Faber and the University of Michigan Press.
1–31 July	Visits London; stays with Thérèse Megaw in Hampstead; visits Tanner in Cambridge, Davie in Devon, and family in Cornwall and Kent.
7–9 July	Records interview with Clive Wilmer for the *Paris Review*.

27 July	Reads at the London Lighthouse, a centre and hospice for people with HIV and AIDS, in Ladbroke Grove.
26 August	Submits manuscript of *Collected Poems* to Faber & Faber and Farrar, Straus & Giroux.
30 September	Tests negative for HIV.
5–9 December	Visits London to receive the Forward Prize for the best collection of that year.

1993

15 June	Awarded a MacArthur 'Genius Grant' Fellowship.
19 June	Bob Bair returns to live at 1216 Cole Street.
5 September	*Collected Poems* published by Faber & Faber.
1–17 October	Visits Prague and Venice with Kitay; they fly back to San Francisco via Chicago to attend the MacArthur Fellowship ceremony.
19 November	*Shelf Life* published by the University of Michigan Press.
20–24 Nov.	Visits New York to receive the Lenore Marshall Prize.
7 December	Refuses the Queen's Gold Medal for Poetry.

1994

20 May	*Collected Poems* published by Farrar, Straus & Giroux.
4 July	*Shelf Life* published by Faber & Faber.
15 November	Tests negative for HIV.
30 Nov.–8 Dec.	Visits New York with Kitay.
6 December	Reads at the New School for the Academy of American Poets; meets Billy Lux.

1995

July	Agrees to write a monograph about Basil Bunting for William Cookson's Agenda Editions; abandons the book in 2000.
Summer	'The Art of Poetry' interview appears in the *Paris Review*.
6–22 September	Visits Madrid and Barcelona with Kitay.

1996

20 January	Meets Robert Prager in the Hole in the Wall Saloon.
April	Begins writing poems for the 'Gossip' sequence.

1997

21 February	Informs UC Berkeley of his decision to retire from teaching in 1999.
14–29 October	Visits Venice with Kitay.
11 December	Death of Clint Cline.

1998

12 January	Writes two 'Gossip' poems, his first since May 1997.
19–24 May	Visits New York to receive Award of Merit Medal from the American Academy of Arts and Letters.
July	Begins experiencing hallucinations as a result of amphetamine consumption.
13 August	Visits the AIDS Memorial Grove in Golden Gate Park, where he has an epigram carved in stone.
29 Sept.–15 Oct.	Visits New York and Washington DC to give readings.
14 October	Visits the National Gallery and drafts 'Painting by Vuillard', the last poem written for *Boss Cupid*.
5 December	Death of Tanner, in Cambridge.
17 December	Meets John Ambrioso at the Hole in the Wall.

1999

12–14 January	Records interview with James Campbell for BBC Radio; later published as *Thom Gunn in Conversation with James Campbell*.
20–28 March	Spends spring break with Ambrioso; they begin an affair.
30 March	Submits manuscript of *Boss Cupid* to Faber & Faber and Farrar, Straus & Giroux.
24 May	Retires from teaching at UC Berkeley.
Summer	'Front Door Man' appears in *Threepenny Review*, his final poem published in a journal or newspaper.
19 August	Works on introduction to Ezra Pound's *Selected Poems*.
4–5 October	Two-day celebration at UC Berkeley to mark his retirement.

2000

26 February	Refuses the Queen's Gold Medal for Poetry for a second time.
6 March	*Boss Cupid* published by Faber & Faber.
3 April	*Boss Cupid* published by Farrar, Straus & Giroux; *Ezra Pound: Poems*, edited by TG, published by Faber & Faber.
2–20 October	Visiting Hurst Professor at the University of Washington in St Louis.
14 October	Writes 'Lunch and then a Nap', one of his last, unpublished, poems.

2001

26 January   Taken to UCSF Hospital with suspected heart attack; later discharged.

11 May   Writes poem about Ambrioso, 'A Gratitude'.

28 November   Death of Mary Thomson.

2002

9–20 April   Visits New York, Amherst and Laramie, Wyoming, for readings.

30 December   Begins writing introduction for an edition of Yvor Winters's poems.

2003

19–29 March   Visits London to receive David Cohen Prize for Literature; TG is joint winner with Beryl Bainbridge.

13 June   Applies for domestic partnership with Kitay.

September   *Yvor Winters: Selected Poems*, edited by TG, is published by the Library of America.

Sept.–Dec.   Teaches at Stanford as the Mohr Visiting Poet.

2004

25 January   Death of Thérèse Megaw.

7 March   Meets Phil Monsky, who moves into TG's room at Cole Street.

19 April   Monsky moves out; TG reads to Robert Glück's class at San Francisco State University.

25 April   Thom Gunn dies from polysubstance abuse resulting in heart failure at his home on Cole Street, San Francisco, at the age of seventy-four.

2005

29 August   Memorial event in the Doe Library, UC Berkeley.

2007

4 May   *Thom Gunn: Poems*, edited by Kleinzahler, published by Faber & Faber; published by Farrar, Straus & Giroux as *Selected Poems* in 2009.

2012

19 September   Death of Catherine Thomson, TG's last surviving aunt.

2017   *Selected Poems*, edited by Wilmer, published by Faber & Faber; published by Farrar, Straus & Giroux as *New Selected Poems* in 2018.

ABBREVIATIONS

AL	autograph letter (unsigned)
ALS	autograph letter (signed)
TL	typed letter (unsigned)
TLS	typed letter signed
CT	(Ann) Charlotte Gunn, née Thomson
HG	Herbert Gunn
MK	Mike Kitay
TG	Thom Gunn
Aberdeen	Sir Duncan Rice Library, University of Aberdeen
Amherst	Robert Frost Library, Amherst College
Bancroft	Bancroft Library, University of California, Berkeley
Columbia	Butler Library, Columbia University
Emory	Stuart A. Rose Manuscripts, Archives, and Rare Book Library, Emory University
Essex	Albert Sloman Library, University of Essex
Faber	Faber Archive
Hornbake	Hornbake Library, University of Maryland
Huntington	Literary Manuscripts Collection, Huntington Library and Art Gallery
Kansas	Kenneth Spencer Research Library, University of Kansas
King's	Archive Centre, King's College, University of Cambridge
Leeds	Brotherton Library Special Collections, University of Leeds
London	Manuscripts and Archives, The British Library
Manchester	The John Rylands Library, University of Manchester
Morgan	Morgan Library and Museum, New York
New Hampshire	Milne Special Collections and Archives, University of New Hampshire
New York	Special Collections Center, New York University
Princeton	Princeton University Library Special Collections
Sacks Foundation	Oliver Sacks Foundation, New York

Stanford	Special Collections and University Archives, Stanford University
Texas	Harry Ransom Center, University of Texas at Austin
Toronto	Thomas Fisher Rare Book Library, University of Toronto
Tulsa	McFarlin Library, University of Tulsa
UCLA	Charles E. Young Research Library, University of California, Los Angeles
Yale	Beinecke Rare Book and Manuscript Library, Yale University
FT	*Fighting Terms*
SM	*The Sense of Movement*
MSC	*My Sad Captains*
T	*Touch*
M	*Moly*
JSC	*Jack Straw's Castle*
PJ	*The Passages of Joy*
MNS	*The Man with Night Sweats*
BC	*Boss Cupid*
OP	*The Occasions of Poetry*
SL	*Shelf Life*
CP	*Collected Poems*
SP	*Selected Poems*, ed. Clive Wilmer (2017)
JC	*Thom Gunn in Conversation with James Campbell* (London: Between the Lines, 2000)
JH	John Haffenden, *Viewpoints: Poets in Conversation* (London: Faber & Faber, 1981)
WS	W. S. Scobie, 'Gunn in America', *London Magazine* N.S. vol. 17, no. 6 (December 1977): 5–15
PR	Clive Wilmer, 'Thom Gunn: The Art of Poetry LXXII', *Paris Review* 135 (Summer 1995): 142–89

Bible references are to the Authorised (King James) Version. Shakespeare references are to *The Complete Works*, ed. Stanley Wells and Gary Taylor, 2nd edn (Oxford: Clarendon Press, 2005).

THE LETTERS

1939

TO *Herbert Gunn*[1]   ALS Ander Gunn

Early 1939[2]

[110 Frognal,
Hampstead,
London NW3][3]

Thursday

Dear Father,

Thank-you for the lovely toy theatre, we have played with it from early morn till sunset.

[. . .]

Miss Fuller a very kind and good-mannered misstress is leaving at the end of term. I gave 2s of my own money, towards her present (Ander said every single "persman" in the school likes her, quite true too,) Ander did too.[4]

I go to a garden party to help "poor Spain" on Saturday.

Ander wants a pistol you shoot little films out of, you get them from Selfridges if this is not too spoily. love

Tom

1. Herbert Gunn (1903–62), TG's father. See Glossary of Names.
2. Approximate date based on the separation of TG's parents in November 1938, and the reference to the Spanish Civil War: Franco declared victory on 1 April 1939 as the last significant Republican forces surrendered.
3. The letter is written on headed paper with the family's former address (4 Daylesford Road, Cheadle, Cheshire) crossed out in black ink. The Gunns moved to Hampstead in 1938.
4. Ander Gunn (1932–), TG's brother. See Glossary of Names.

1945

Saturday 10 February 1945

110 Frognal,
N.W.3

10 / 2 / 45

My dearest aunty Mary,

I'm so sorry I've not written for so long; thankyou for your sweet letter and the pound, which you ought not to have given us, as the clothes were free.

So glad you liked The Mummer's Wife,[2] have you read the [Tobias] Smollett books? Besides Vanity Fair, I've been reading dear Hazlitt and a lovely book, very scholarly but easy to read, that Hilde gave to mother,[3] about the French Revolution.

Father just came today. He said he might not be able to send me to a university because he wouldn't be able to afford it. I think this is nonsense, but he seems weak on the subject, and liable to have his mind changed quite easily. If he needs any argument, I could tell him that Hilde once promised to pay for me, but I don't think it will come to that.

The baby was born through a Cesarian operation – it is tiny and ordinary. It has been called (of all things) DAVID JAMIE ANDREW!!![4] [. . .] Father was terribly pressing and resentful and wounded when we couldn't come, so last week John said he thought we ought to go, so we did! and spent a dull 2 hours there. We saw a dreadful nurse, who told us "that the English always have been honest and always will be honest till the end of time" in a very firm voice. I thought it best not to answer this, but afterwards wished I had mentioned the Congress at Vienna and various other proofs of our hypocrisy!

We have managed to get 15/- each from father so far which is quite good, and I think he's going to be quite regular about pocket-money in future. He now has an account at John Barnes; and I bought a lovely sports-coat of Harris Tweed and various other necessary articles of clothing. The sports-coat cost £5 or something, which Margot said didn't seem bad. Father said it was shocking, but I think it's just his meanness. I'm going to the theater on the 24th with Holgate; so then I'll try and get tickets for Uncle Vanya.[5]

I'm sorry I've not tried before, which was very selfish and lazy, but I think it would have been very full up whatever. Would just any Saturday matinée do?

Margot cooks very well, and John is quite nice (of course Margot is) but I have a slight suspicion he doesn't approve of pacifism.[6] We are very happy, though once I woke up in the morning feeling quite prepared to follow Mother to the grave![7] Margot has been reading "Emma"; she has awful pains in her jaw, and catarrh, and so have I (the latter). Ander has a dreadful craving for a <u>dog</u>!! but I and Margot are very firm about refusing to let him have one, which father (sweet man) has counteracted, by saying to him that he has his complete permission to buy one. He says: Thankyou for the comic; and he has been clearing out the shed; and thankyou for the money. He's being quite sweet, and is not very bad-tempered.

I went to see Michael Wishart's show of paintings, which were rather disappointing, not being at all like his usual good style, and all being copies of Picasso and other people. Still, he's still nice.[8]

I would very much like to come down during the week's holiday, but am afraid neither of us will. Because I've got exams. (not School Certificate but "Mock Matric." which is a practice) during the week, and I don't think Ander wants to. I'm very sorry; but the term is very short, and we'll be able to come during the holidays. Give Jenny and Catherine my kisses and show Jenny the portrait of herself on the other side of this page.[9]

Your loving nephew

<u>Tom</u>

x x x x o o o

---

1. Mary Thomson (1907–2001), the fifth of TG's six aunts. See Glossary of Names.
2. George Moore, *A Mummer's Wife* (1885).
3. Hilde Marchant (1916–70), journalist, most notably for the *Daily Express*, and the author of *Women and Children Last: A Woman Reporter's Account of the Battle of Britain* (1941). Marchant and HG were lovers during 1938–41 while HG was an assistant editor of the *Express*; Marchant and CT remained friends.
4. David Jamie Andrew Gunn (1945–), HG's eldest son from his second marriage, to the *Daily Mail* reporter Olive Melville Brown (1912–90).
5. Michael Holgate, friend of TG's from University College School; Laurence Olivier starred in Chekhov's *Uncle Vanya* at the New Theatre, London (1944–5).
6. Margot Corbett, née Adams (1922–), TG's cousin, daughter of TG's Aunt Margaret (known as Peg); John is Margot's husband.
7. Ann Charlotte Gunn (1903–44), TG's mother. See Glossary of Names. She died by suicide in the early hours of 29 December 1944. See TG's diary entry on the day of his mother's death (*SP* 270–2).
8. Michael Wishart (1928–96), British painter and TG's friend from Bedales. Wishart reflected on their friendship in his memoir *High Diver* (1977), 'Mindless fellows . . .

mistook Thom's delicacy of form and thought for weakness, which developed his toughness.'
9. Jenny Fremlin, née Thomson (1941–), TG's cousin, daughter of Catherine Thomson. On the reverse TG has drawn a Picasso-style portrait of Jenny.

TO *Mary and Catherine Thomson*[1]   ALS Jenny Fremlin
Friday 11 May 1945

110 Frognal,
Hampstead,
N.W.3

11 / 5 / 45

Dear Aunts M & C,

Holgate had told me his Aunt had met someone at a wedding who had seen me on the milk-round; I was going to ask you about it – isn't it funny? Eric is Holgate's father.

I'm afraid your purse was never found – what a pity! – I suppose someone took a fancy to it and kept it. Also, I have been twice (on a Sat. morning, & afternoon) to the little shop in L. Square, but each time it was closed – God knows when they do their business!

Could Mary please send those [ration] coupons she is keeping for us; at last there is need of them.

Last Sunday I went to the Holgates for John's birthday party: There was a lovely cake, and on the top of it, between each candle, there was a little red flag (like those that are stuck in war-maps). The grandmother & aunt (Peggy) who came, are both very anti-Communist, and so were rather cross. All the same, they are rather nice.

I made two lovely red flags, dying two parts of a shirt all red, with my fingers looking as though they were dipped in blood! then, after they were dry, I ironed them out and painted hammers and sickels on them as you saw in Snodland. They were very nice, but not such a bright red as could be wished. I had to rush the last part rather, as Father had told me the war would be over on Monday, so I got up an hour early. Father made us come to him that evening to have a "celebration supper" at some grand place, but as VE day wasn't till Tuesday, we had a Florence-cooked supper. Father wanted us to come the next day as well, but we refused to.

The next day I went out with Holgate in the afternoon. We went to Piccadilly and then walked up with immense crowds to Buckingham Palace. It was just 3 o'clock, and we heard Churchill's speech (which we thought we were going to avoid) through loud speakers. After that, some people, who covered the whole of the Victoria Memorial, which graces (??) the front of the palace, shouted out "We want the King! We want the King! 1—2—3—4—G—E—O—R—GE—George! We want the King!" and so on. In the end, their graceless majesties appeared with their daughters dressed in khaki & blue, gave their regal cross between a wave & salute, & disappeared after a time. However stupid they are, it was fun seeing them; and it's nice to say I've seen the King & Queen on VE day, and the crowds were most impressive, as they were all over the rest of London. Great gangs of people marched up the Mall with flags and so on; people were drunk, and plump old men dressed in morning dress, and women dressed like dowager duchesses, fell drunk onto the road. A lot of people fainted, but as there were Red Cross and St. John men every few yards with flasks and bottles at their belts, they were always brought round quickly. Several girls were kissed by force, but they only laughed. I had a rattle (tiny in comparison with some people's, which sounded like pneumatic drills), and bought a paper hat (1/6,[2] everything was a horrible price; I should think the street-sellers made about 3 times as much on every article as it really was worth, but people didn't mind paying) – oh yes – a paper hat, and on it was written "SQUEEZE me tight," and a red, white & PURPLE (like Jenny's flag) rosette.

After Buckingham Palace, we walked down to Trafalgar Square, where we went up the steps of Nelson & looked down to Whitehall, which was so crowded, even more than where we'd been, that it didn't look as though you could move a step, if you were in the middle of it, but probably we looked like that, too. Then we heard, above our heads, the bells of St Martin-in-the-Fields, which were very sweet and clear (some bells had started at the end of Churchill's speech) and we went into the church itself and almost got caught for a service! From there we went to Leicester Square, and so you see we quite made the Victory Tour, and probably a much nicer one than the King & Queen are now making! It was really very exciting, I wouldn't have missed it for anything –

But the evening was even more exciting: there were one or two little bonfires on the Heath, and Mrs (Lady) Pearce gave Ander some fireworks from before the war, which were very successful. We went twice on the roundabout, whizzing around happily at ten o'clock at night, in the bright lights surrounded by dark. Then we went up and saw all the flood-lighting, and saw quite far off in a place covered with grass, with a few trees, and surrounded by an ugly little fence, an enormous bonfire. People were very destructively & madly pulling down the ugly little fence and putting it onto the bonfire, so all of us (the Holgates, Butterfields) set to work also with 10 other U.C.S. boys, some soldiers & other people, to help destructively & madly pull down the ugly little fence too! There were lovely green phosphorous fireworks and guns & rockets and searchlights and beautiful things that exploded in the air and came down in bright ashes like shining grain; and all the time everybody was pulling up the fence (there was about 200 yards of it, all round) and every time we brought some more along and chucked it onto the huge bonfire, people cheered. There was an enormous ring of people, and we all danced and sang around the fire till past one. I was so tired. But Ander didn't come home until about 2. But then, he'd not been all round London that afternoon. They went on dancing & singing round it till dawn. I went the next day to see the destruction but there was amazingly little, only all the fencing gone, and a black ring of ashes out of which dejected-looking keepers picked the metal and unburnable stuff. It was very merry.

We have chopped down the holly-tree, we are going to grow grass over the place where it was, and in the autumn plant a laburnum.

[. . .]

We are getting regular pocket-money at last. Father was very nice about it when I asked him, so we now get 10/- a fortnight each (though the Holgates get more than twice as much. Still, I suppose we don't really need more). Margot, of course, says she didn't have any when she was young. She also says it as though it was a great virtue. But of course, all reactionaries do. She is, as usual, despondant, sulky, and generally miserable. She talks, as a rule, to no-one, till John comes home, but the cat. I admit this kind of wimsicality is very amusing in Lewis Carrol, but when the Alice is 22 years old, and it goes on almost every day, it is not really so strikingly opposite to dull.

        Your nephew,
          Tom.

P.S. Sorry in pencil. Hope you can read it.

1. Catherine Thomson (1909–2012), TG's youngest aunt. See Glossary of Names.
2. In pre-decimal coinage, one shilling and sixpence, equivalent to 7.5 p.

1948

> No 22022206 Pte. Gunn T.[1]
> Royal Hamps: Reg.,
> Corunna I Platoon
> X Training Coy.,
> W. B. T. B.
> Kiwi Barracks,
> Bulford Camp,
> Wilts.
>
> 30 / 5 / 48

Dear Mary and Catherine,

I am writing this in the middle of a severe and lengthy attack of laziness, which began yesterday with the rain, and has not gone yet. I went to bed for most of the afternoon, reading, speaking (and sleeping), as did most of the other people in my barrack-room who stayed behind. Then we stayed up till about 12 in the reading-room listening to Verdi's opera Otello. I have only just got up this moment.

We have a new corporal sleeping in our room. Luckily it is a notable change for the better – our new corporal is less officious, and has even been reduced from the rank of sergeant for not being severe enough during parades.

Do you remember the very objectionable person I told you about, who only had a very limited vocabulary and that nothing but obscenities? One day we came back from the rifle-range and found a civilian policeman waiting for him. Apparently he had stolen the storeman's watch the previous weekend. He was taken away to the guard room, where we have seen him at intervals since then, and we have heard nothing of him.

This is a shockingly short letter, but I must get on with various little Tasks.

Love

Tom

1. TG was enlisted into the Royal Hampshire Regiment to begin his National Service on 1 April 1948; was transferred to the Royal Army Education Corps on 28 October 1948; served until 23 January 1950; and was released into the reserves on 13 February 1950. His military testimonial refers to him as 'a tower of strength, teaching both advanced Army classes and backward recruits. He has been kind, patient and most generous with his own time, running the unit library and television service.'

TO *Mary and Catherine Thomson*   ALS Jenny Fremlin
Wednesday 23 June 1948

> No 22022206, Pte Gunn T.,
> Royal Hamps. Regt.
> attached to the H. Q. Company,
> A.S.E. & Depot R.A.E.C,[1]
> Buchanan Castle,
> Drymen,
> near Glasgow.
> (Scotland, you know.)[2]
>
> 23 / 6 / 48

Dear Mary and Catherine,

I meant to write to you before, but it's rather a business settling in – and even now we're not in our proper barrack room (we are sleeping in a room called the Ball Room, dangerously near a passage where sergeant majors and officers of all kinds continually flit with gloomy groans).

We are still on fatigues (I was helping carry a piano half way across the camp this morning, but most of the time we mow grass or shovel coal), and are to be till our course starts in a week this Friday. We only wear denims for very dirty jobs – otherwise everyone wears battledress.

The whole place is very badly organized: there was no truck for us at Glasgow station till we had waited an hour or so and telephoned the camp; when we did arrive nothing seemed ready for us; there is very little food (though what there is is very good); and there are grotesque shortages – of electric light bulbs (only 5 among 30 of us), chairs (2), wash basins (2), lavatories (2), basin plugs (0), of door handles (every N.C.O.[3] carries a spare door handle about with him as an essential part of his equipment).

The R.A.E.C. officers are a different shape altogether from infantry officers; being short and round and often with glasses, whereas the infantry officers were languishing and wilting like lilies. – The most terrifying people here are easily the Sergeant Majors who are all aged guardsmen, <u>very</u> fierce, and at least 7 foot high.

Some people say they would prefer to be back at Bulford; but I don't mind it very much. For one reason, there is a library of reasonable dimensions; there is a slightly more civilized atmosphere, and there is the loveliest (and most salubrious) country. Loch Lomond is only ¾ of an hour's walk away, and there are many very large mountains which I hope to gather together enough energy to climb.

On Sunday I went, with two others, to Balloch, at one end of Loch Lomond, where we ate 3 ice creams, a tea, and a bag of chips, went out in rowing boats, and walked by the Loch. Every female we met read aloud our shoulder flashes to each other with great interest. Scottish women seem much more flirtatious than English! There are quite a number of ATS in the camp,[4] who join in everything we do – there will be two in each of our classes.

My postcards are very much admired. Luckily I have a windowsill over my present bed, on which I stand the box that frames them. – I am reading 'Kangaroo' still, but don't like it very much. Lawrence is so absurdly serious. I am getting some time to read French, and I am rereading Antony & Cleopatra in a very Glorious edition out of the library.

I went to the film of Nicolas Nickleby in hall in the camp on Tuesday.[5] I thought it rather a bad film, but I am not very fond of the book, which is anyway very unsuitable for filming. It was not improved by the facts that the projection was a little blurry and the loudspeaker only allowed you to hear about a third of the dialogue.

Sergeants are ten a penny here, but very <u>uppish</u>, as they were privates like us only a short while ago. Hope I shall be one too quite soon! A letter written all over the place, I am afraid. It is now tomorrow (the 24th)!

Love, Tom

[. . .]

1. ASE = Army School of Education; RAEC = Royal Army Educational Corps.
2. See 'Buchanan Castle, 1948', *London Magazine* N.S. 19, no. 9–10 (Dec 1979–Jan 1980), 45; uncollected. Its working titles include 'Soldier as Poet' and 'Poet as Soldier'.
3. NCO = non-commissioned officer.
4. ATS = Auxiliary Territorial Service, the women's branch of the British Army (1938–49).
5. *The Life and Adventures of Nicholas Nickleby*, dir. Alberto Cavalcanti (1947).

1951

Saturday 10 February 1951

L4 Whewell's Court
[Trinity College, Cambridge]

10th ? Feb '51

[. . .]
Dear Father,
[. . .]
I have been to some quite interesting meetings lately. Tom Driberg was
speaking in the Union, & [Vladimir Peniakoff] at a club I belong to.¹ Also
saw a most interesting 1932 film by Cocteau – A Poet's Blood. Superb – even
better than 'Orphée'.

I have come to a decision recently which is the result of at least a year's
thought. I have been consciously trying to find a solution since early last
summer – and have at last decided that my only proper course is to become
a conscientious objector. I dare say people will attribute to me the reasons
they always attribute to objectors: cowardice or dislike of army discipline.
Of course I did dislike the army, like most people; and I should probably be
terrified when it came to fighting, like most people; but I think you will do me
the credit of believing that these are quite irrelevant. I simply see no reason
why I should believe right what my reason and emotion tell me is wrong, and
I think one ought to act on one's beliefs (or beliefs have no value). It should
be unnecessary to say such a thing – but I have found large numbers of people
who believe in doing what is easiest, large numbers who believe in doing
what is most expedient, and large numbers who believe – if they believe
anything at all – 'ours not to reason why, ours but to do and die'. I would
like to emphasise, then, that (1) it is for moral reasons that I take this step
(though of course I would disagree – who wouldn't? – politically with a war
with against Russia), (2) I think it is usually only by individual action that
one man can bring about any good, (3) I do not believe a bad means can ever
bring about anything but a bad end, (4) this is not just an impetuous action
on the spur of the moment – I shall not change my mind, and I have been

thinking about it for a long time, (5) it is inconsistent with my already having done national service, but I feel no obligation to stand by something done at the age of 18, when I had not thought on the subject with any thoroughness. – I wrote out six pages of detailed reasons and arguments last week for you, but decided not to send them because they looked rather pompous and I thought you would understand even if I gave them at such short length as this. But I have worked out my ideas on the subject as well as I can, and am still working them out, so that I hope to be able to present them clearly to a tribunal. If I am to be called up on the Z reserve, it is a good opportunity to show I am willing to undergo a certain amount of discomfort for my opinions (i.e., if necessary, prison!!!) instead of the relative convenience of undergoing the 15-day summer romp.[2] I have got into contact with the Central Board of Conscientious Objectors in London, and (through them) with the representative in Cambridge, and have also written a registered letter to Army Records to tell them (as advised by the Central Board of C.O.s) and have persuaded a friend to do the same. I am thinking of joining the Peace Pledge Union, which is the best non-religious pacifist organisation. I hope you will excuse me for not having told you before I acted – but (apart from Ander) you are the first person outside Cambridge whom I have told about this. I thought it best to commit myself to save complications – that is, because I knew that whether people agreed or disagreed my reasons would still be the same. (I don't expect my aunts – except Barbara – to be in the least sympathy.) Whatever you think, don't worry about me: I shan't be going to Wormwood Scrubs – yet, anyway!!! I doubt if I shall have my tribunal till late summer, if then. I quite see the danger of being arrogant, conceited, and martyrish about it; but I hope it is not a real danger: I do not consider that I am doing any more than any individual person should do. I hope I have your sympathy if not your agreement.

Don't let this disturb the excellent editorship of an excellent magazine![3]

     Love,

         Thom

P.S. Sorry this is such a tomb-like sermon of a letter. Questions on points of doctrine invited.[4]

---

1. The Cambridge University Socialist Club, where TG 'read aloud from left-wing poetry of the thirties' (*OP* 158).
2. Class Z Reserve was a reserve contingent of the British Army. Following the Second World War, a Z Reserve of soldiers and officers who had served between 3 September 1939 and 31 December 1948 could be required to undertake refresher training or return to full-time service, if they were under forty-five years of age.

3. HG resigned the editorship of the *Evening Standard* in August 1950. He bought the magazine *Modern Housewife*, renamed it *You*, and installed his wife Olive as editor.
4. HG published an extract from this letter, and his reply, anonymously: see 'Father v. Son: Z Call-up Controversy', *You* (April 1951), 18–21. The exchange was kept anonymous 'in deference to the wishes of the father'.

TO *Alice Collings*[1]   ALS (postcard[2]) Jenny Fremlin
Saturday 21 July 1951[3]

[Blois, France][4]

Dear Great Aunt,
　Am being awfully <u>jolly</u>. Getting very good lifts – today went 100km in an army lorry – some soldiers on their way to fetch a broken down lorry.[5] They insisted that I shared lunch with them, & gave me <u>piles</u> of meat & wouldn't let me pay!! Am at present near Blois.
Love, Thom

1. Alice Collings (1862–1958), TG's great aunt. Collings lived much of her life with the Thomsons at Covey Hall and was responsible for home-schooling some of TG's aunts.
2. The postcard shows Chartres Cathedral.
3. Date supplied from postmark.
4. Location supplied from postmark and internal evidence.
5. During his first summer vacation from Cambridge, TG read the complete works of Shakespeare and hitch-hiked through France (*OP* 159). See 'South', *Times Literary Supplement* (12 June 1987), 633; uncollected.

1952

TO *John Coleman*[1]   ALS Coleman Family
Sunday 9 March 1952

Trinity [College, Cambridge]

March 9th I think

Beloved John,

I wish I had come to see you & Margaret[2] off when you left – Raef and I had
intended to shoot rockets from the platform.[3] John Farrowleigh understands
that you require robins, and I believe has sent a squadron of them to tour the
London parks.[4] We do so miss you both – where is a cult without its objects
of worship?

We all went to look at Roy Campbell the other day, speaking to the
Shirley Society (Cats Officers Mess Culture Club) about Leavis. He was a
scream: everybody went away determining to read his books and to go to
more of Leavis' lectures. Absolutely incoherent: looked like a cross between
Mr Gladstone and a sergeant major; spoke half the time of his experiences
fighting men and bulls, the other half of socialism and the Brit Council (with
which, curiously, he identified F.R.L.). Thought you might be interested.

I got so swinishly drunk at your farewell party that I never said goodbye.
We finished up some of the wine (that is, Karl[5] and I) at Raef's yesterday.
Karl bought innumerable garments from Raef – a dinner jacket & three pairs
of trousers – has also bought Pat Harrison's mackintosh. Well-dressed man,
Karl, quite staggeringly neat. Also sane, but not tediously so. [. . .]

I think I am editing the next Fortune Press anthology: at first I refused
on the grounds that I could not find more than about 30 poems – but they
were so humble, saying I could make it as short as I liked, and giving way
on everything.[6] They send letters typed on pink wrapping paper. Raef is
designing a dust cover, and I am going to try and improve on the typography
of the last one. – You simply must be in it – the very backbone. You seemed to
have objections, but I shan't do it at all if you won't let me print 4 or 5 or 6 of
your poems (truth!). Could I reprint the 2 sonnets, and Two, and either one
or both the poems in the summer number of the Review (1951)? (Rapunzel
and the other.) I have copies of them all. But really the whole thing is an awful

15

racket – 'Cambridge Poetry' that is: John Mander[7] is being so awkward at present, manufacturing a synthetic tradition, and has he says published an edition of his magazine entirely devoted to horrid Harold [Silver]. – The Fortune Press have a funny tone, certainly: in their last letter the following sentence occurred, completely isolated:

'Any suspicion of nepotism should be avoided, as this is so damaging.'

I shall take no notice, – only my friends can write well!

[. . .]

Raef has just told me it is not impossible you will come here for a day next week. Do hope so. Don't bother to answer this if feeling terribly depressed: everybody must be writing to you and it is vile having to write letters at the best of times (for you I mean, not for me).

       Love,

          Thom

1. John Coleman (1927–2001) read English at Downing College. His 'affectionately witty manner', TG wrote, 'struck me as the last word in sophistication' (*OP* 161).
2. Margaret Owen, née Baron (1932–) read law at Girton College and met TG through Coleman. She was also a member of the Amateur Dramatic Club (ADC), where she met MK.
3. Raef Payne, a friend of TG's at Cambridge; went on to be a schoolmaster at Eton.
4. Possibly John Farrelly, a friend of Karl Miller's at Downing College.
5. For Karl Miller, see next letter.
6. *Poetry from Cambridge, 1951–52*, ed. Gunn (1952).
7. John Mander (1932–78), writer and poet, studied at Trinity College. TG described Mander as 'an Etonian Marxist' and thought the poetry he wrote at Cambridge 'had a vigour somewhat lacking in mine' (*OP* 158). For Mander's 'magazine' see TG, '*Oasis*: an experiment in selling poetry', *The Bookseller* (15 March 1952), 782–5.

TO *Karl Miller*[1]   ALS Emory

Monday 14 July 1952[2]

                      till Aug 2: at Priory Farm Camp
                           West Walton
                             Wisbech
                             Cambs

                             July 14

Dear Karl,

After I last saw you I talked mainly about films, with Alan till midnight.[3] I hope you enjoyed the revue. Next day I left the sinful flat and hitched to where I am now. It is quite an agreeable place: we earn very little, but as Coleman said it is good to be in the open air all the time – a cure for introspection. I have been a proper extrovert since I came here. I have made 2 very good friends whom you would like very much – one a magnificent Jamaican who is going home next month, he is 30 and helps us by summing up our sexual difficulties in coherent terms; the other you shall meet next term – a Frenchman called Guy, very generous and very high spirited – one of those people who, in your own phrase, expend surplus energy to no particular purpose but very effectively. (To reassure you, both are as heterosexual as a Cradock.)

Trinity has given me a scholarship – I hope Downing has done the same by you. I feel desperately sorry for you, fortnighting with the t.a.[4] – (relax). I have written a poem which I enclose: it is founded on real life, as you shall see.[5] There is a chance that I shall have saved up enough to go to Italy in August after all; on the way I hope to drop in at Cambridge & see Romeo & Juliet.[6]

You told me to let you know if anything new turned up on "the sexual horizon". As soon as I got here I found myself surrounded by girls, so as they flirted with me I flirted with them which is so easy. Round about the 3rd evening I became involved with a girl called Ann – at first sight something very attractive about her. A kiss became prolonged and the situation became inescapable. I felt very vigorous during the first week or 2 and was prepared to experiment without stop, and while we still had confidence in each other and there was still exploration to be made everything was well. The main lights of the camp wr turned out at 11, and there were various beds laid about the recreation room so there was plenty of opportunity for exploration and experiment. She never, I am convinced, suspected for a minute that I loved men, and I was very nice to her. She said at the very beginning that as she was a Roman Catholic she would not have intercourse with me: however it was obvious I cd persuade her to in a few days.

But tho I was very interested until my curiosity was satisfied mere curiosity is soon satisfied, and I never for a minute imagined I felt any passion. To my credit, I never pretended to be more than casual. I carried off casualness with panache for a while; but I began to get bored, & there is also a feeling of <u>fear</u> of being committed to an attitude one does not sincerely feel so I had to make the necessary break, and I now see I was more unkind than I had meant to be. I knew that I cd have persuaded her to do anything I wanted – but I would not have been adequate to deal with her afterwards. And it did not seem worth the interest of the experiment if it were to be so joyless. Guy & Ozzie (the Jamaican) are at present trying to persuade me to make love to a dear little girl from Leeds whom they assure me has indicated I would not be disagreeable – you would think her very lovely, and she is – but I have learnt by the affair with Ann that one must not enter on such things if one cannot be happy in them and make the girl happy. It is a pity to be perverted. Meanwhile, living like an animal is beginning to pall somewhat – the first 3 weeks were all right but the next 3 are going to be a terrible bore. Ozzie is going at the end of this week & only Guy is staying on. Guy is continually happy, but has a lot of trouble with various girls & odd hours of depression when he comes to me, most unsuitably, for advice.

This (on being read) looks very conceited & "all very disorganised", but I thought you would like to know. Have read absolutely no complete book since the exams started some 6 or 7 weeks ago; somebody here lent me a book called 'Pleasures of New Writing' and I read a few of the stories I had not seen before – one by Lionel Trilling which was not so bad as the others; but the only one that gave me any real pleasure was one I had read before by Wm Sansom.[7] He magnifies until something is vivid. I hope you have found time to do some writing? Here is a poem I hope I have room for: (P.S. I sent up more poems to Lehmann for New Soundings,[8] & he said cd he keep The Secret Sharer & perhaps make use of it so long as it hadn't been printed before – even in a university magazine. I had to tell him it had, so expect it back. Disappointing.)

[. . .]

This [poem] is very derivative. Do write to me if you have time.

Thom.

P.P.S. You must not worry about what J. Coleman said of percentages of homosexuality in your character – no one who knew you could seriously think so. Besides, he was drunk and talking nonsense.

P.P.P.S. This is very cramped, but I only had 2 pp of notepaper. English Club: I met a cretin who is the next president of the Shirley & he says they have got Redgrove for next term so thr is no point in trying him.[9]

---

1. Karl Miller (1931–2014) read English at Downing College and was TG's first close friend at Cambridge. See Glossary of Names.
2. Date supplied from internal evidence.
3. Alan Bowness (1928–2021) read Modern Languages at Downing and later became a prominent art historian and Director of the Tate Gallery (1980–8).
4. TA = Territorial Army, the British Army's part-time reserve force, which traditionally used fortnight-long summer training camps.
5. The poem is 'Carnal Knowledge' (CP 15–16).
6. George 'Dadie' Rylands and John Barton directed Romeo & Juliet for the Marlowe Society at the Cambridge Arts Theatre, and at the Scala Theatre, London, on 11–13 August 1952. Tony White played Romeo.

7. *Pleasures of New Writing*, ed. Lehmann (1952). The Sansom story is 'On Stony Ground'.

8. John Lehmann (1907–87) edited the BBC radio programme *New Soundings*, on which TG's 'The Secret Sharer' was broadcast in September 1952. See Glossary of Names.

9. TG was president of the English Club, and Miller its secretary (1952–3). Their guest speakers for Michaelmas Term included Angus Wilson and Dylan Thomas.

TO *John Holmstrom*[1]   ALS (copy[2]) Bancroft

Monday 15 December 1952

27 Holboro Rd,
Snodland, Kent

15 Dec 52

Dear John,

You didn't date your letter, but I am sure it was at least 4 weeks ago. If I haven't answered before now, it's partly a feeling that I ought to allow myself at least a whole morning to answer your great blackboards of typing, for which (don't mistake me) I am grateful, but before which I feel the sort of awe one always has towards big things like cathedrals or your letter. Mine will be inadequate, I know, because I don't think I have the energy for more than five thousand words, and my critical faculty isn't as developed as yours.

I liked most of your comments on my poems very much, the more so because when you said something I knew already it was always something that nobody else but myself had noticed. In the main I agree with the order of merit you place them in – I myself think The Beach Head and A Mirror for Poets are the best – though I can't agree with your placing of Incident on a Journey,[3] which is a mere exercise which didn't engage me much in the writing and doesn't in the reading.

To clear up some things you asked (this reads like the Rejoinders to Rejoinders in 'Scrutiny'):[4]

1. 'Night-exposure in the hair' refers to were-wolves in the previous line. They are exposed to anyone who catches them unawares, they are wolves at night, and, being wolves, they are covered with hair instead of skin.

2. John a Gaunt verse. You can't exactly dash thro a person (except in the crudest sense) but you can dash thro a relationship, or an affair, bringing the emotional climaxes near together so exhaustingly that you bring it to a premature end.

19

3. I didn't realise dust in the universe was so complicated, but I expect you're right. It is just that if one believes in immortal souls, then they are as lasting and material as dust. Dust is immortal because it always <u>stays about</u>, in some form or another: Body becomes dust, dust only becomes another sort of dust. Soul hangs about and can't get annihilated any more than this immortal dust. (Explanation more confusing than thing explained?)

4. You're right about the Wystanishness of <u>A Mirror for Poets</u>: the whole poem is, I feel, what one calls unrealised.[5] It was written over a period of 3 months last year. Originally it had two other (horrid) verses, but I still don't think I've got it right. The reason why I like it is that even if it doesn't say all I meant, it says more than I usually succeed in saying.

5. Paphlagonian King. Character in Sidney's <u>Arcadia</u> (one of the subjects of the poem), who goes thro a lot of what King Lear goes thro. I thought when I wrote it that he was better known than he appears to be.

6. You're dead right about classical imagery – I realised when writing <u>The Wound</u> that it is altogether too easy, too stock-responsy and too hackneyed. But I used it partly <u>because</u> of that: so that I could depend on the reader's having a simple familiar picture before him, on which I could build anything original I had to say. However I don't seem to have succeeded in doing this, and had better lay off Foreign Mythologies in future.

7. For the rest, I'm glad you don't like <u>Two Ghosts</u>: I am rather worried that so many people <u>have</u> liked it.[6] It is I think the only poem I have ever written and revised and finished and everything in half an hour; and its subject is so trivial and unnecessary, without much reference to what humans feel. Sorry you didn't like <u>Lerici</u> more: I think the middle bit is the best and most stendhalian thing I've done.[7]

Then you make some general observations, of which I agree with only the flattering ones. <u>Of course</u> I don't mind your questioning whether I should write poetry at all. I often wonder myself. I really think it's impossible to decide until one knows exactly how one is to develop. And writing poetry, like writing individual poems, is often an affair of self-persuasion – by which I don't mean self-delusion. I think <u>your</u> vocation, if one must call it that, may be more pronounced.

There are extraordinary similarities between our verse. I don't know whether 3 years of Cambridge is to blame for this: I suspect so. The people we most resemble, in general, are Empson and Graves – tho distantly most of the time.[8] I am more like Empson, you like Graves. Now this is a bit frightening, in view of the minute efficiency of those two. I admire them both limitedly: both are damned efficient, but neither have, really, done anything <u>big</u> with their talent: only lovely exercises which they can repeat and repeat.

Perhaps you disagree. But I have found them at first helpful and encouraging influences, then more lately dangerously limiting . . .

You say, could I try writing more directly for a bit?

I feel I am as unreserved as I am competent to be in my poems: I only try to treat what I am sure I can deal with, and I think that my reserve is beginning to grow less – I had thought not gradually enough. You see, my chief fear is of writing again the awful sexy stuff – sentimentality and pornography of inexperience – that I wrote between 16 and 18.[9] I don't want to write of my emotions according to their intensity, but to the competence with which I can treat them. Of course it isn't as conscious as this, which is a rationalisation (but I hope a correct one): one explores in writing, naturally. And I want to explore as large a country as I can while I still have some of the flexibility of being young. To work within the limitations of one's own sexual emotions can come later when I have tried out as many different ways as possible of expressing them.

By this I don't mean <u>masks</u> (in the sense of disguises) for homosexual passion; but I want to be able to write of other things, so that I can work out relationships between them and myself – which I am still coleridgian enough to think is the best thing one can do in poetry. [. . .]

One's fear is that these hard times may never give one a subject and one will have to go on writing little exercises on set subjects that pretend to be inspirations.

       Love,

          Thom

1. John Holmstrom (1927–2013) studied at King's and was a childhood friend of Tony White, who introduced him to TG. Holmstrom was gay and someone in whom TG could confide his sexual feelings. See Glossary of Names.

2. Holmstrom transcribed this letter and sent it to the Bancroft Library, with the heading: 'December 1952, after an initial exchange of poetic oeuvre'. The original letter is held in a private collection.

3. This is a different poem to 'Incident on a Journey' in *FT*; see *Chance* 3 (April–June 1953), 70; uncollected.

4. *Scrutiny: A Quarterly Review* (1932–53) was founded by L. C. Knights and F. R. Leavis. One of the most important critical reviews of the twentieth century, it gained notoriety as the quintessential Leavisite publication.

5. '[Auden]'s someone I'm profoundly grateful to for giving me by his example the feeling that I could write about my experience,' TG remarked: 'That's what his example did for me: it made things seem easy, and the poetry I wrote then [. . .] was riddled with Audenesque mannerisms' (PR 149–50). See also TG to McClatchy, 24 September 1983, below.

6. 'Two Ghosts', *Oasis* 5 (February 1952), 8; uncollected.

7. TG was passionate about Stendhal, most notably *The Charterhouse of Parma* (1839). See TG to Wilmer, 23 August 1994, below.
8. Empson and Graves were important poets for the Movement generation for their emphasis on rational judgement, intellectual precision and interest in the metaphysical poets; for the Movement, see also TG to Conquest, 11 March 1955, below. TG reviewed Graves's *Poems 1953* (1953) in *Gadfly* 3, no. 3 (31 October 1953), 35–6, and Empson's *Collected Poems* (1955) in *London Magazine* 3, no. 2 (February 1956), 70–5; both uncollected. See also TG to White, 25 November 1955, below.
9. See 'My Suburban Muse' (*OP* 153–6).

TO *Karl Miller*   ALS Emory
Thursday 18 December 1952

                                                          27 Holborough Rd,
                                                          Snodland, KENT.

                                                          18 Dec 52

To be read at breakfast with an unflinching expression. –

Dear Karl,
    This will be another haste-written letter, as I am on the verge of going to my post office. (I have the mornings off, or have had, so far, because I am on evening duty.) [. . .]
    Happier times loom. I mean Paris.[1] Tho I have not yet had word from Margy, I have got another letter from John, who says that he can put us up (us = you, Tony,[2] & me) in the Poissonerie up to and including the night of the 2nd Jan. He also says he'll meet me when I arrive, on the evening of the 29th. So, rather than reverse this I'll leave England (Folkestone) on the morning of the 29th, and you follow what day you please. – Unless you find you can come that day, after all. I am looking forward ecstatically to seeing T again. One invariably finds it surprising (tho god knows, experience shd show it's the rule rather than otherwise) that the absence of a person presses them upon the memory & imagination quite disproportionately. Somehow, without anticipating it, I have found myself thinking about him for days on end. Perhaps there wd be a chance to sleep with him in Paris. Perhaps, but one mustn't set too much store on such a thing coming to pass. Anyway I know you'd never hinder me. And what a place for it to happen; Paris, the hot lips of Europe. But this is silly talk.
    [. . .]

Am reading Plato, who is <u>so</u> impossible. What is Justice, asked jesting Gunn?[3] With a sneer which is something more than a jest. I like the social history & the Symposium, but doubt if I'll be able to answer an exam question on those. Also <u>Women in Love</u> – and anything I've ever said against Lawrence is retracted. I'm a proper great-tradition boy now, aren't I, what with liking Conrad and tolerating James. <u>Roderick Hudson</u> was less satisfactory as a whole: at the end I found myself asking, as always with James 'What the hell is it <u>about</u>?' There is this quite wonderful writing <u>around</u> something – something which for all one knows might well be an hallucination.

[. . .]

Dearest love, my dear boy,

Thom

1. TG gives an account of this trip in 'Cambridge in the Fifties' (*OP* 165–6).
2. Tony White (1930–76) met TG in spring 1952. See Glossary of Names.
3. 'Pilate saith unto him, What is truth?' (John 18:38). 'What is truth? asked jesting Pilate, and would not stay for an answer' is the opening line of Francis Bacon's essay 'Of Truth' (1625).

1953

TO *Donald Hall*[1]   ALS New Hampshire
Wednesday 13 May 1953

Trinity College
Cambridge

13 May 53

Dear Don,

Thank you for your magnificent letter. Nice of you to ask me to submit to Paris Review.[2] Of course you can use what you like from the Fantasy.[3] I have several new poems – by when do you want them?

Have just been looking through all I have written in the last few months and am faintly depressed. I get the feeling that I started writing a few years ago with something like the proper Poetic vigour, & that everything since then has been weaker and phonier, tho more polished – all my writing an artificial inducement, a recapitulation, by reference to past work. I used to be afraid I would stop writing; now my fear is not that, but that I won't get any better. Kind of you to bind up the wounds that Toynbee inflicted,[4] but tho I don't think <u>that</u> criticism is particularly apt of any of the beginnings he quoted, I do think I and some of the others can be criticised for living on something other than the present feeling – i.e. other people's work or what I have written before. Why, for instance, there should be so many quotations from Shakespeare in that old drear Carnal Kn, I don't know. It looks as tho it's John Dover Wilson rather astonished at why he should be in that particular bed. I was not very pleased, either, that I alone of all the people in the book had informative notes appended giving one or two facts I didn't even know myself.

Your suggestion to give me introductions to people in Harvard (if I do go there) is most kind. I feel encouraged by what you say about the American Literary Scene. I had hoped it was like that. Or at least different from what it is in England, where as you say it's all a racket, and values are much more social than critical. Leavis, with all his limitations, does see that; which is why he's hated by the Mortimers and boudoir-kings of the Sunday papers.[5]

Also, I'd like to accept your offer of the loan of A.C.R's poems, which I want very much to read.[6] Have been trying, in fact, to get a copy. If you could send it some time, as you suggested, I'll return it when I see you and meanwhile care for it as if it contained my own Works . . . Saw one of hers, England and Always in a New Yorker just now.

No, I have never been a lion. Not too fond of animals. This is a chaotic letter. Begun one week ago, which I lost. I meant to write a longer one. Tripos is sort of near, and I keep on thinking how I must work. I know it's always fashionable in universities to say one doesn't do any work, but I just seem to go to films. Health to Kirby and a Poetry Fellowship to you.

Yours,

Thom

1. Donald Hall (1928–2018) received a BLitt from Oxford in 1953. See Glossary of Names.

2. Hall was the first poetry editor of the *Paris Review* (1953–61).

3. *The Fantasy Poets Number Sixteen: Thom Gunn* (1953). Its six poems are: 'Incident on a Journey', 'Wind in the Street', 'The Wound', 'The Beach Head', 'The Right Possessor' and 'A Village Edmund'.

4. Philip Toynbee reviewed *Springtime: An Anthology of Young Poets and Writers*, ed. Fraser and Fletcher (1953) in *The Observer* (May 3, 1953); quoting the opening line of 'Carnal Knowledge', Toynbee refers to its 'slick and empty facility'.

5. Raymond Mortimer (1895–1980), sometime literary editor of the *New Statesman* and book reviewer for the *Sunday Times*.

6. Adrienne Rich's *A Change of World* (1951) won the Yale Series of Younger Poets Competition.

TO *Mike Kitay*[1]   ALS Mike Kitay
Thursday 21 May 1953[2]

Heaven.

21st May

My darling,

You are working, so I cannot speak to you. I hope you're not cross that those people came in, or, if you are, only that they prevented you from working. Because I was thinking of you while they talked and didn't look at you, for loving you so much I'd have looked too tenderly. I love you, Mike Kitay, and not only because you're handsome and beautiful-voiced and graceful; I love you wholly, so much with all of myself, that I don't know what to do or say when there are other people by. And I <u>am</u> in love with your looks as well, because they're a part of you almost as much as what you say and think, but I'm so permanently in love with you all that I'll love them whatever they became. You are 22, my darling darling, and I love you because you are 22, and because you are as you are, and because you are here, and because you love me, & for 222 reasons none of which explains it. I just can't say why, but I know more certainly than ever before (and you must believe me), that this is for good; and I want there to be no Goodbye, and no parting, and never to share you, and love you and love you and love you.

T

P.S. This is only 1/22 of what I want to be able to say.

1. Mike Kitay (1931–) met TG at a cast party for the ADC's production of *Cyrano de Bergerac* in December 1952. See Glossary of Names.
2. Date supplied from internal evidence.

TO *Tony White*[1]   ALS Tulsa
c. June 1953[2]

Trinity [College, Cambridge]

Dear Tony,

Most sorry not to have said goodbye to you (right ventricle of my heart) at the party the other night. I was in the other room for about an hour, and when I came back, you and your coat were gone. All the sorrier – I do regret Something,[3] you see in that I'd been seeing so little of you this term. Which was mainly or completely my fault, but not thro my lack of love for you – and I hope you haven't thought so. I'm glad you knew about the Mike K etc, for besides the fact that one likes one's friends to know facts about oneself, it's some explanation for my having neglected you and Karl. I do hope to see you soon, in London or Cambridge or North Africa, – before the end of the year at least: apart from the fact that you are likeable, you are exemplary: 'our Sidney and our perfect man'[4] your actions are clean and direct. God knows that's rare enough. I myself am much weaker as the last term has borne out: being in love I wanted to give all my time to loving and simultaneously remain the same person as before – that is seeing my friends as much. They have to be reconciled in some way, but I didn't get very near to a reconciliation – it was like holding on to a pendulum rather than being the perfect Existentialist who stands at the works of the clock & swings the pendulum [. . .].

26

Hope you don't think this is all gush; but I meant to say something like this the other night & would have if I hadn't missed you. I know getting notes like this is a bit embarrassing, but imagine it's spoken and not written & it'll be acceptable, and anyway embarrassment is one of the feelings to be eliminated in our New Order. So I repeat, I wish I'd said goodbye to you, I hope to see you soon, and you continue to be my most admired man. Answer this when you feel like it.

Thom

[. . .]

1. Tony White (1930–76), actor and writer. See Glossary of Names.
2. Date written in by White.
3. The refrains of TG's 'Incident on a Journey' (*CP* 33–4) are variations of the phrase 'But I regret nothing'.
4. A line from Yeats's 'In Memory of Major Robert Gregory' (1918).

TO *Helena Mennie Shire*[1]   ALS Aberdeen
Wednesday 9 September 1953

as from London, but any answer, to: c/o Thomson
27 Holborough Road,
Snodland,
Kent.

9th Sept 53

Dear Mrs Shire,

It is very long since my paltry postcard sent from I can't remember where, but I only got back from the European tour about ten days ago, and for nine of those ten days I have been subjected to writing with a biro, which with me means a series of inkless but very deep pained marks. I went through Belgium, Germany, Austria, & a bit of North Italy, and count myself lucky to have been able to borrow tremendously from the American I was with, and see so many places.[2] I have come to a startling conclusion about Germans, which I may confide to you next month. I saw diverse operas – The Rosenkavelier in Cologne; Figaro and St Joan at the Stake (which I hated but superbly done) by the Munich State Opera; and Aida in a Roman amphitheatre at Verona – directed by the film man [G. W.] Pabst, it introduced the Nile on to the stage in tanks – Aida came up it in a boat – and for the triumphal march 2 elephants, 2 dromedaries, and best of all a sacred bull which casually left droppings in the middle of the stage: laughter of 20,000 drowned triumphal march.

[. . .]

I am at last on the brink of reading All the Eliz & Jac Drama besides Shakespeare. Really, so far I have only read Marlowe and Jonson and Ford – not even Tourneur.

Also on the brink of another broadcast – on the notorious 'First Reading'. I have 5 poems to be broadcast, I understand, among them the one you helped me with: 'A Mirror for Poets'. Slight disappointment was that if I'd come back 3 days earlier from Europe I should be reading them myself. But I am promised a better reader than the previous 2 times.[3]

Went to the New Statesman the other day to ask if they could trust me to review a book. Mr [Kingsley] Martin passed me on to Miss [Janet] Adam Smith, who was not over impressed but gave me a copy of a terrible book on Masefield.[4] I read JM – Everlasting Mercy etc. as a result, and he isn't quite so bad as I expected. (Have you any good lines on him?)

Love to all family,

Thom

1. Helena Mennie Shire (1912–91) was TG's main supervisor at Cambridge. See Glossary of Names.
2. The 'American' was Mike Kitay. TG's late poem 'Rapallo' (BC 96–7) is about this trip.
3. John Wain's radio programme First Reading replaced Lehmann's New Soundings. TG's poems 'For a Birthday', 'A Kind of Ethics', 'Matter and Spirit' and 'Cameleon' [sic] were broadcast on 24 September 1953. 'A Mirror for Poets' was broadcast on G. S. Fraser's programme New Poetry on 16 September 1953.
4. TG reviewed Muriel Spark, John Masefield (1953) in New Statesman and Nation (21 November 1953), 651.

1954

TO *Karl Miller*   ALS Emory

Saturday 9 January 1954

9 Jan 1954

c/o American Express,
38 Piazza di Spagna,
Rome

Dear Karl,

It's months ago that I got your long and affectionate and thoroughly nice letter, which warmed my heart muchly. Now that I've finally started this, I must make it a long one too, and tell you all about everything.

Since I received yours, I went with Mike to Venice. [. . .] Venice was perfect – almost too perfect to live in. Snow came, deep, and the Venetians stared at it appalled, not knowing quite what to do with it. Also went to the opera, Don Carlo; then to Milan, whr we stayed in a crazy boarding house, shit filthy and kept by four ghouls – all looking like Charles Adams characters. But all this is a long time ago.

Rome is the best place I've ever been in.[1] The right size, the right weather, the right proportions of good looking buildings to slums, the right complications. Also, the right attitude of the inhabitants. I mean as opposed to London or Cambridge or Paris. In London and half of Cambridge one tries like mad to conform; in Paris and the other half of Cambridge one tries like mad to nonconform. Here, nobody cares what you do, which is much healthier and less dull altogether. Tho perhaps the Northern frustrations may be necessary to make one a good writer, or is that all just crap. But one's certainly impressed by the ease with which they carry their maturity ('they' = the foreigner tourist's term for Italians). In England & Germany, certainly, there is either an ease without maturity, or else a so hardly struggled-for maturity that ease is impossible. The thing I lack terribly here is Mike. He's not being happy in Cambridge, I think, and perhaps I ought really to have stayed behind this term so as to be with him. He's more wonderful the longer I know him – but a lover's ravings will bore you. I hear vaguely that some misunderstanding took place between you and him the other day, with the help of that dreary old [Robert] Gottlieb. [. . .] I'm sorry, anyway, because it's a good deal my fault that you and Mike haven't been nearer.

I'm certainly pleased not to be in Cambridge. At present I think of it as the Valley of the Shadow of Death – everybody trying like crazy to be something or other that they'll never succeed in being, and all the sex gossip – talking about without doing, and everything and everything. It's only when I'm away from it that I begin to realise the hugeness of its negation to anything healthy, constant, or genuine. I know I sound as tho I'm overstating, but I'm not: it's fine for two years or even a bit more, but if one doesn't realise by the time one goes down that it's no more valuable than a piece of orange peel, one's deluded and damned. It's not the hurrying about and 'keeping busy' and parties I object to: those are rather pathetic, but it's the fact that you can't escape it while you're there, that you have to come across the Harry Porters and Malcolm Burgesses – people you would normally not dream of even knowing, so that you either have to put yourself completely outside all the attempted gaiety and smartness or be bored and resigned to it all or else become as phoney as the rest. And the kinds of phoneyness at Cambridge, in their subtle differences, the way they surprise you from behind, is legion. – Well, I'm getting boring, but I had to say it, because I've only realised it clearly since I've been abroad.

[. . .]

I've not been writing too much. I chug away at my long poem: I've done roughly half by now: but it's reached the stage whr it's almost a trial of strength I have too much pride to drop having brought it so far.[2] I think it does contain some very good bits, tho. Have written one or 2 absolutely worthless short poems. I hear I had a little cunty thing in Lehmann's new effort: David Gascoyne wrote me an incredible letter, asking me in Bloomsbury-type jargon if I had read Stefan George.[3] I wrote back very politely saying no, and that far from expressing 'intense spiritual topicality . . . the inner experience it commemorates, being the authentic characteristic spiritual experience (or "initiation", properly understood)' of my generation, (don't you love his language,) I thought it was just a lopsided and failed love poem. – I'm having two poems in the next Botteghe Oscure (also bad).[4] I so need the money. Just hope my book will set people right about me when it comes out – this month I believe.[5] I've written up to the Spectator, who are well disposed towards me, asking if they'd contemplate giving me reviewing to do.

I've met various people of varying interest. Meg Greenfield I see every now and again: I get on well with her, but consider her a trifle sexless. (I gave her, fictitiously, your love, because she speaks of you with such affection.) Not sexless, tho, a terribly rich and terribly thin young American woman who invites me to huge & luxurious suppers in her huge and luxurious apartment (with surely the most distinguished lavatory in Rome). At least, I don't understand her motives, doubt if she cd be attracted by me, but anyway I enjoy her suppers & wines. [. . .]

Also know the Princess Caetana who edits Botteghe Oscure.[6] She gives good meals as well. Lives in a palace (lawks) and is very old and distinguished and energetic and likeable. The rest of her family seem awfully dim to me. Went down to her castle in the country, once: near Anzio, and beneath a mountain on which the Cyclopes are supposed to have lived. Last time I went to see her I met a funny tubby piggy man coming away & as soon as I saw her she said 'You've just missed Cyril Connolly.'

The best person I've met is a German painter with the same name as yours.[7] He is, undoubtedly, one of the elect – he has the right pride and discrimination and sense of humour; and he does do things. I mean, not only fucking, or painting for that matter, but he acts rather than talks about [them]. And he's had an incredible life – too long to repeat here, but impressive, I'll tell you when I see you. He was in Berlin at the end of the war – aged ten, in the Hitler Youth, he was supposed to fight the Russians.

I've not been reading too deeply or widely. The book that most impressed me was Faulkner's 'Light in August'. Which completely brings me over to him, lock stock and – well, I'm no gun. Also read The Princess Casamassima – not much good. Am at present rereading Yeats' Autobiographies, which as you know I dote on. Have dabbled much among the standing pools of minor poetry that are to be found in the British Council library: Pound (I can't see what all the fuss is about with that man) [. . .]

[. . .] Awful about your friend who committed suicide. When Mike dies you'll have another homosexually suicided friend in the shape of me. You must be doing Plato now – isn't he, finally, awful? [. . .]

Looking thro your letter again, as I just did to answer your questions, I see once more what a very nice letter it is and I remember once more what a very patient and good friend you are to me. Forgive the lateness of it, and the crotchety tone (even in Rome there seem endless things to protest against, and I suppose one has one's troubles here, tho they're mostly troubles from England) and remember how fond I am of you. Are you going to Princeton next year? I'll perhaps be going to a Californian University (!) Any urgent message, as if thr wd be one, can be sent thro Mike, who writes often.[8] But write yourself, and soon, to your loving friend

Thom

1. TG spent ten weeks in Rome on the Harper-Wood Studentship for English Poetry and Literature, a travel grant he received from St John's College, Cambridge.

2. TG published two extracts from his abandoned long poem 'The Furies'. See 'The Furies', *Chequer* 2 (May 1953), 14–15; and 'Ralph's Dream', *London Magazine* 2, no. 1 (January 1955), 48–51; both uncollected.

3. 'Earthborn', *London Magazine* 1, no. 1 (February 1954), 64; uncollected. Gascoyne's letter can be found in TG's papers at the Bancroft Library.

4. 'Apocryphal' and 'Excursion', *Botteghe Oscure* 14 (1954), 173–5; uncollected.

5. After several delays, Fantasy Press published *Fighting Terms* in July 1954.

6. Marguerite Caetani, née Chapin (1880–1963), literary patron and cousin of T. S. Eliot. She founded *Botteghe Oscure* in 1948 and edited it until its demise in 1960.

7. Carl Timner (1933–2014) painted a portrait of TG that has been lost, though a reproduction can be found in one of TG's scrapbooks (Bancroft). TG's poem 'Before the Carnival' is subtitled 'A painting by Carl Timner' (*CP* 44–5). See also TG to Chambers, 2 July 1984, below.

8. These letters are lost.

TO *Donald Hall*   ALS New Hampshire

Tuesday 23 February 1954

you'd better reply to: St John's College,
Cambridge.
but written, still, from Rome!

23 Feb 54

Dear Don,

How can I thank you for all you've sent me, forms, advice, and lastly huge yellow letter with poems. The latter took some three weeks to reach me, as I suppose this one will. Forms, poems, prospectuses, samples, facts, etc etc, were all sent in to Stanford, and I hope it possible they may have the desired result at the beginning of June.[1] If not, well, another year in Rome, which isn't so bad either. I don't know if I'll ever be able to settle down in one place: one could characterise it as a romantic Wanderlust, but right thro my youth (what with having a journalist father, and then the war) I was continually on the move, and then thro choice I have been the last five years or so. Or perhaps it's a feature of our generation: displaced persons – Exile.

[. . .]

Thank you for all the advice about Wynters: I was tactful in my wording – as tactful as I could be.[2]

Congratulations on all your successes. My recent one was with that drip of a poem in Lehmann's new mag. Got mentioned in most reviews of the mag, Spectator said mine was the best thing in it 'but closely followed by Louis MacNeice and Elizabeth Jennings,' which I think grotesque criticism.[3] [. . .]

At last I've started working at a better rate. I enclose some of the results. Ralph's Dream is an extract from my long thing – not the best, not the worst – just a specimen.[4] Words in Action I feel is a bit empty – almost, if not quite, self caricature – I wrote it last autumn, may have sent it to you before.[5] The rest are written during the last few weeks, and may be changed a bit before I send them anywhere. Out of the dark may not be completely to your taste . . .[6] The four sonnet-length ones do not form a sequence – if only becos they are in different rhyme schemes, most of them I drafted in the open air and I cd never remember the rhyme schemes of those I'd already written. District in R. is straightforward, perhaps to dullness.[7] But After a dream, The Separation, and Off the Record, are I think fairly good work for me, tho not my best.[8] (But they're too recent for me to judge, I suppose.) – Sorry none are typewritten.

[. . .]

I'm now very hurried – if I don't end now I won't get my lunch. So goodbye for a while, love to yourself and Kirby – send me another batch when you can, and another lovely letter – to Cambridge. (I leave Rome March 15th, for Paris & London).

Thom

1. Hall was a creative writing fellow at Stanford University and helped Gunn apply for the same fellowship.
2. Yvor Winters (1900–68) ran the creative writing programme at Stanford. See Glossary of Names.
3. Anthony Hartley, 'Review of Reviews', *The Spectator* (22 January 1954), 24–6.
4. See TG to Miller, 9 January 1954, n. 2, above.
5. 'Words in Action', *The Spectator* (12 March 1954), 288; uncollected.
6. 'Out of the Dark' is unpublished; held among TG's letters to Hall (New Hampshire).
7. 'A District in Rome', *London Magazine* 2, no. 7 (July 1955), 14; uncollected.
8. 'After a Dream' is unpublished; held in the TG collection at the Hornbake Library, University of Maryland. 'Off the Record' is an early version of 'High Fidelity' (*CP* 76); a manuscript copy can be found among TG's letters to Hall (New Hampshire).

Wednesday 10 March 1954

Rome

March 10th 54

Dear Tony,

I just dropped my pen point downwards on the floor and even after reparations with scissors it doesn't write quite the same, so the writing of this is likely to be thick and eccentric.

I was very very glad to get your letter. It was really my turn to write to you and I don't know why I didn't – prolonged aggers on my part I suppose coupled with doubt as to what you must think of me, apart from travelling around.

[. . .] Paris & London both make furious efforts to <u>be</u> something; Rome does not try at all; it knows it's important, & it doesn't need to. – I won't start painting word pictures or anything, but there's a casualness, a nonchalance about the whole of it (at least at this time of year) that puts you completely at your ease. It's a pity I'm leaving at the end of this week (I stay the summer in Cambridge), because I've been feeling more & more confident, the weather's getting hot, and I've recently had such a burst of vigour in writing that I feel I could keep it up for months. But I've spent my money, and this is Mike's last summer in England. Next year I may be either returning here on the same scholarship (& I'd stay for 12 months then) or else going to America, yes America, on another scholarship.

I say I've been feeling 'more confident' which may seem funny, but I had a rather low time in various ways from the autumn till January. Mainly because of awful and unnecessary quarrels with Mike. And I reacted in the worst way when I was alone at first, by a sort of indiscriminate & unpleasant recklessness. I honestly don't know what's going to happen between me and him, tho. It sounds like a very trashy novel to say so, but I can't bear to contemplate living without him & at the same time I don't see how (even after technical – sociological, passport, family (his) – difficulties are got over) we can live together: we're so amazingly and disastrously different in just the wrong ways. If he was a girl it'd be so much easier! I'd marry him & it'd all be resolved. – I suppose what happens to me next year, whether I return to Rome or go to the States, which is out of my power, will decide. But it's all very muddling and painful. Tho he's made me more happy, & can still, than anybody else ever could. I hope you forgive all this, I really dislike the sort of person who writes letters like this. But partly one has to explain to somebody, and to you I want and ought to explain more than to anybody else; partly Karl has got so impossible that whatever I say to him is immediately passed on to somebody like Harry Porter or Malcolm Burgess (who are worms, after all); and partly that I have behaved so specially badly to you that you ought to know why. Mike doesn't really like any friend of mine, except perhaps Alan who's harmless, and every quarrel we've ever had has begun with friends or involved them in some way. The thought of quarrelling any more makes me puke. Added to that he was jealous of you. Well, I don't know how I <u>should</u> have behaved, but I know I have behaved in the wrong way both to Mike and to you. – It's a case where existentialist principles fail to help: a Goetz would fling Mike off, but I've never had any intention or desire of doing that.[1]

Still, I should stop this shit before I start wallowing in the famous Self Pity.[2] I can trust you not to speak about this letter to anybody, and I'd prefer it if you didn't even mention my writing if we meet in front of Mike. That's weak of me, but there's so little time left that I certainly have with him that there aren't enough hours for me to attempt once again to put my position before him and try to make it strong. Anyway, I simply must see you again, and we must talk & talk. In the summer, when Mike has gone home & before I follow him. And when I've decided something about myself.

I go on admiring the existentialist authors, even if I can't act completely in accordance with them – it's my weakness as much as theirs. I'm interested to hear you say you're starting to reread Dostoevsky. Because it's just recently after having reread 2 of his books that I suddenly & unexpectedly decided that he wasn't one of my men. Very good writer, yes, but except for bits & fragments he's one of the most poisonously persuasive of those who <u>talk about</u> rather than act. – I think my great find in books read over the last 6 months is Huckleberry Finn; and my great find among painters is Caravaggio, about whom I cd go on for pages.[3]

[. . .]

Well, I haven't yet read thro what I've been writing, but you say you'd like me to cheer you and what I've written must do just the reverse. But at least it might bring us nearer to each other again, and I do think of you, constantly and with admiration. I'm sorry you're in such a dull job, your talents deserve something very different. What happened to the offer of a rep job in January? I hope you're feeling a bit less depressed now. You'll get a break, if nobody else does – your deservings are so much greater than anybody's.

[. . .]

I shall be untraceable for a month now – but write in April to me 'c/o St Johns College' (<u>not</u> Trinity). Vale.[4] Think well of me, if you can.

– Thom

1. TG alludes to the relationship between Goetz and Catherine in Sartre's play *Le Diable et le Bon Dieu* (1951).
2. An allusion to F. R. Leavis. 'Anyone who took Leavis's lectures will remember the way he'd say "self-pit-teh" when talking about, let's say, some poem by Shelley,' TG later remarked: 'I think he thought self-pity was a limitation in moral fibre' (JC 23).
3. TG likely saw Caravaggio's *Conversion of Saint Paul* (1601) during this trip; it later became the subject of 'In Santa Maria del Popolo' (CP 93–4).
4. *Vale* = Farewell (Latin).

TO *Tony White*   ALS Tulsa
Friday 14 May 1954

Johns [College, Cambridge]

14 May 54

Dear Tony,

Seeing Rosa[1] this evening brought very sharply to my mind that I must answer your letter, and not prove myself a coward any longer by leaving it. I've been walking about for several hours, and meeting the proctors didn't help my meditations.

I did finally get that scholarship to America, and perhaps really from every point of view it's a good thing if I do try and settle down there.[2] It's not melodramatic to say I've ruined one life here – I mean I've behaved so to all my friends that I no longer have any contact with them: except with you, & if you can think well of me now you must be mad. This evening being alone, & feeling bad, I couldn't think of a single person I could go and see. And apart from everything else I've virtually stopped writing. So I suppose there's a chance that after 5 yrs or so in another country I cd get back that balance between outer and inner that makes for friends and poems. And fit Mike in with them, by starting with him as something they have to be built around. – I wouldn't have believed before how much that sort of balance I referred to so loosely above really matters. Not having it means one can do anything, however weak, once one stops being the stranger in the group and tries to become either one of the group or else a complete stranger. Witness Palinode and the other poem.[3] To say I tried to get Lehmann to withdraw them when it was too late is no excuse, any more than it would be to say I felt unwell when I wrote them. Hungry of course is sentimental & incompetent. As for Palinode, it's an unpleasant piece of sophistry, and I don't believe what it says, and didn't at the time. At least, I suppose I believed I believed it, if that's not sophistry too. No, I don't reject heroes: they're the only people there are, and you yourself have much of them in you. But there is at least this complication – how does the hero love? If one believes that passion is important, as I think you do, and that heroes are the only people worth while (I mean of course 'heroes' in a very big sense), the sort of Goetz–Catherine relationship won't do, except as something viewed so coldly that one can see it doesn't apply to oneself. How does the hero treat a relationship? Well, of course there's no cut-and-dried answer: I suppose it depends on a constant control which is continually adjusting & modifying without becoming inconsistent; but you must admit that Goetz is incapable of contact with others except to dominate so much that there's no real give-&-take contact left, that Coriolanus though not stupid is no success, that Heathcliff's love would be – well, different, if he were not conveniently isolated by moors; and etc. The question is, if you feel to the utmost for another person who is by no means the same as yourself and is no more inclined to be dominated than you are by him, how are you to get that fruitful balance without isolating yourself with him, or else first isolating and then building up around both?

Well, that's confused, and it may well be more sophistry even to put the questions in those words. I'd like to think that like Brando I'm a very sick boy, but I know I'm not.[4] It's just that I built up a centre to my life with some labour – everything fitted with it, or at least cd be adjusted to it; and behold, along comes another centre that is utterly different, and has a life of its own.

That's pretty pretentious, really, at least on the surface, but I can't very well put it in other words. It would be nice to feel like a Balzac hero, starting with everything just grand and ending with a long-led-up-to downfall, pretty extreme; but it's not so simple. From one point of view it's a downfall, from another it's chapter one again. How to make it merely chapter one of a new volume in the same book?

I owe you much congratulation for your successful storming of the Old Vic.[5] Shall we see you as Coriolanus? Antony? the Bastard (Faulconbridge and Edmund)? And perhaps in cinemascope as well, just to show how nice you look close to. But seriously, much congratulations, and I'm very glad for you. Where will you be in the second half of June and the first half of July? Not Elsinore or Edinburgh, I hope, but London, where I shall be. I long to talk with you. Honestly you're the only one who can help me, and the fact that you still care to keep in touch with me makes me more grateful than I can say.

I enclose a few poems I wrote in Rome. Neither so bad as last autumn's nor so good as those I wrote under your influence. I hope you'll see where the emphasis should be put in the Jesus poem.[6] I wrote others as well, but they're either unfinished or no good. (Don't bother to return them. Just criticise.)

Love, and I really mean love,

Thom

1. Rosa Egli who, though not a student at the university, was involved with the Cambridge theatrical world.
2. Winters wrote to TG on 17 March 1954 to inform him, unofficially, that he would be offered a creative writing fellowship at Stanford. 'I think there is little doubt of your literary gift,' Winters wrote, before continuing, 'Your weakness, as I see it, is in your conception of what a poem is, in some measure; and beyond that of difficulty in choosing a theme clearly enough so that each detail will really carry proper weight.' This letter can be found among TG's papers at the Bancroft Library.
3. 'Hungry' and 'Palinode', *London Magazine* 1, no. 4 (May 1954), 25–6; uncollected.
4. Brando quit *The Egyptian* (1954) citing mental strain; his therapist was reported as saying he was 'a very sick boy'.
5. White spent two years in the Old Vic theatre company (1954–6).
6. 'Jesus and his Mother' (*CP* 64–5).

TO *Mike Kitay*   ALS[1] Mike Kitay

c. Thursday 19 August 1954[2]

[School House,
Allhallows, nr Rochester

Kent]

[1]

If ever I meet my death as the result of a sudden accident or illness, I would like someone to send the enclosed to the name & address on its envelope. Please don't read the letter: it's of completely personal matters and couldn't interest anyone.

Thom Gunn

P.S. Also please send these 2 leather cases of correspondence to Mike Kitay, who will know what to do with them.[3]

[2]

Babe,

This is to be given you if I die. I'm writing it a week before I leave England, August 54; and I hope it'll never need to be given you, and we can open it and laugh at it together one day: and I hope that when we die, it'll be in each other's arms. But know this, my beloved; whenever I die, it'll be with thoughts of you – you who have taught me what it is like to live. I love you so passionately, so utterly, my darling, that I am sure my love will go on existing for ever, when I'm dead – long after that. And that's not ridiculous, it is as strong as that. I know that you love me as much as that, too.

Thank you, my darling baby, for having made me so terribly happy, thank you for having loved me so, and for having been so good to me. I needn't say any more.

And baby, try to get over this and get somebody good and strong – woman or man – to love you. Really-really I want you to do that. Only please always love me till the end (even if you love that other as well). Again, thank you, my love. I don't know how to say how I love you – it's always the same old trouble, the words aren't big enough. You are always all I can care for. Look after yourself, my precious.

Monk[4]

1. The envelope reads, 'To be opened in event of my death. T.G.'
2. Date supplied by internal evidence.
3. These letters are lost.
4. A reference to an oversized, maroon dressing gown TG had from his time in the army. The long, wide sleeves made it resemble a monk's robe.

TO *Helena Mennie Shire*   ALS Aberdeen
Monday 11 or Tuesday 12 October 1954

334 Lincoln Avenue,
PALO ALTO, California.

11 or 12 Oct 54

Dear Mrs Shire,

It's a long time since I wrote to you, and now I do it must be just when you're having to deal with difficult new pupils and look hard for virtues in them and get them through The Book of the Duchess. [. . .]

After a frustrating and worrying stay in London, where I got taken up by Uncle Lehmann in a big way and isn't he just horrid, and where I had conjunctivitis, I went down to my [aunt Barbara], where I spent another frustrating and worrying time, equally unproductive, and there I had an appalling sore throat which lasted about a month. Your wan young friend then went to America, and was tremendously impressed by New York. It really is one of the cities, you know, doesn't compare with Rome of course, but is as good as London or even Paris. It's very exciting and dirty and noisy, which I like in a city. I stayed with the Kitays – Mike being already in service – and looked up a few random addresses. Then I stayed in Chicago for two days with an ex-president of the ADC (the Saturninus of Titus A.). He refused to take me to the slaughter yards, which was all I really wanted to see, but otherwise showed me various dreary sights. Then a crippling journey to San Francisco which is only an hour away but I've hardly seen it yet, & here I was in Stanford.

Stanford is a refreshing change from Cambridge. The big rush to be in the sophisticated social swim replaced by a positively rustic casualness and directness, which I must say I rather like. It's supposed to be the best university in the West, and I can well believe it. I bathe every day, it's terribly sunny, all that one hears of California. I have bought some incredible clothes (e.g. a red jacket) partly because I like them partly to tone in.

It's also a place where I think I'll be able to write. I've done one or 2 things, but I've written so little in the last 6 months that it'll take me quite a while to get hard-workingly regular again. The trouble is, hell, I don't really know whether I want to be a poet. By 'being a poet' you are resoundingly different from other people, and tho that has its attractions as I'd be the first to admit, you train yourself into a state of mind which you think superior to that of other people. Well it may be superior, but it misses a lot of things the others have & take for granted. You train yourself to observing the main experiences of life, but this habit of observation becomes part of your life, and so is a substitute for the action it admires. I suppose, if I improve and work hard, I could become quite well known in about 25 years, but looking around the well known now, I'm not sure whether I want to be like them, at all, at all. Quite frankly, every writer but one whom I met thro the English Club, and every writer I've met since then, nauseates me. Leavis & D. Thomas (what a pair) are the only active, famous, literary people I can admire and I don't have the strength of the one or the completely reckless energy of the other.[1] I'm not sure that I could disregard the Nasties so much as they, tho I hate to admit it, as I always like to think I can disregard people I don't like. I can disregard them for a short time, but they make their mark in the end, and reacting wildly against them is as bad as being easy with them & associating with them. And they are the people who miss the common experiences so resoundingly.

Well, when I started this letter, I didn't intend it should have an awful inchoate mass of egotism inserted in the middle of it. But that isn't the whole of the trouble with my writing, tho it's the main one. I don't know what to write about any longer, I seem to have lost most of that inexplicable vigour I had when I was writing at Cambridge. Tho this certainly is the place to train myself. I'm working under a very good man called Yvor Winters, a sort of American Leavis, equal in well-founded opinionatedness and in toadies (except that he & they often think exactly the opposite to FRL) and just hating Leavis himself. However, he's very approachable, a very nice man, much more balanced and doesn't feel himself <u>quite</u> so persecuted, likes people to oppose him (& I do, like crazy), and he & his family have been very kind to me, always having me out for enormous steaks. And besides, he likes my verse, and his criticisms are never too milkily kind or sweepingly harsh. He adores Melville, Fulke Greville & Jonson, doesn't much like Yeats, and very much dislikes G. Manly Hopkins, D. H. Lawrence, & Eliot. So you see he & I have both common ground & uncommon ground, which certainly makes things interesting.

Do tell me what your ballad researches are bringing up. Also if the ADC has regained any of its vigour. Also if Karl has regained any vigour.

I told you I was thinking about St Martin as a subject, did I? Well, here is a ballad yes a <u>ballad</u> about him.[2] No, I'm not converted, tho the poems I've written about Abraham & Christ recently might make it look like it.[3] NB it doesn't bring in the name of God: the beggar in this poem tho certainly more than a natural phenomenon is a phenomenon outside the poem, as unexplained as ghosts are, and the important verse is (meant to be) the last bathetic one. In fact – yes, you've guessed it – St Martin is an early existentialist. It isn't a very good poem, but I think the best I've done this year, God knows I've chewed over it long enough.

Did you know WBY <u>read & enjoyed</u> DHL? I'd always wondered, hadn't you? I've just been reading Ellman's 'Yeats, the Man & the Masks' which I think (humbly) better than Mr Henn's book, though I disagree with one or two of his analyses of separate poems.[4]

Reading this letter over shows it to be full of non sequiturs and rather stupid. So please forgive that. At least I'm not falling into Self Pity. Barrenness, yes, but not self pity (at least in public). My early training precludes that. (Nobody <u>looks</u> at FRL without <u>some</u> part of them changing to stone. [. . .])

I hope all your family are well and happy, and my special love to you and also to Seth. Do write when you have time, but if you don't have time before the end of the year I'll quite understand.

Love again,

Thom

P.S. [. . .] – On Thursday I meet Auden, who is going to give a reading at Stanford. He is going to spend an evening at Winters', who has never met him but dislikes all but 2 of his poems. So it'll be an interesting evening, with perhaps a display of fireworks to end it. I expect to dislike him but be very interested. He's one of the few writers I've ever deeply wanted to meet, but from curiosity & admiration not personal sympathy. After all he's Part of One's Past, isn't he?

Please forgive all those awful things of mine that get published in The London Mag. I'm honestly beginning to think that all Lehmann touches withers into stone or candyfloss.

[. . .]

1. TG met Dylan Thomas in November 1952 when Thomas read at the Cambridge University English Club.
2. 'St Martin and the Beggar' (*CP* 66–8).
3. 'Apocryphal' retells the Abraham and Isaac sacrifice story; the poem about Christ is 'Jesus and his Mother'.
4. T. R. Henn, *The Lonely Tower: Studies in the Poetry of W. B. Yeats* (1950).

TO *Donald Hall*　　　　　　　　　　　　　ALS New Hampshire
Saturday 20 November 1954

334 Lincoln Ave,
Palo Alto.

20 Nov 54

Dear Don,

I've delayed writing so long because I wanted to enclose a lot of poems and revisions. But I'm so long in typing them out that I shan't have them ready for at least 10 days, so when they're ready I'll send them under another cover to you. You can keep all the copies I send, and also you can have any of them not published for the Paris Review. If you want them. (I'll mark the ones already published.)

[. . .]

I'm getting on just fine with Winters. He has liked one or two of my poems and I have big arguments with him in class every day. He's a nice person to argue with, leaves one with no feeling of rancour, but finally I have to give up – how can one say to a man of 60 as admirable as he is that I just think his whole attitude to life – or most of it, anyway – is wrong. But it's amazing, even if this is true, how much good I get from him. I do realise what harm he can do to me – I have a tendency to over abstraction (forbidden word) anyway, and he can't but encourage that in me, and I don't like it. But he cleans up my rhythms marvellously, and for the first time I've begun to understand something about it. This in itself wd have made it worth coming here, but also I've begun to write something like 4 hours a day. Some peculiar poems have resulted, as you'll see, I don't like them overmuch but am a bit astonished I should have written them. Hope they lead somewhere, anyway. I am full of hope.

On the other hand, Cal Thomas has turned out impossible.[1] I must have looked too hard for virtues in him in the first place. He induces ungovernable irritation in me every time I see him! (Jealousy? No, I don't think so.) Still, we don't have much to do with each other, so that's all right.

[. . .]

I know little of how my book goes in England except that the Spectator is always claiming me as one of its tiresome group of new metaphysicals.[2] Just because one's coherent, it doesn't mean one is metaphysical. And others in the group, nice tho they may be personally, I'd as little like to be associated with as with [James] Kirkup or [Paul] Dehn. I wrote to them offering them an article defending romanticism, but haven't heard from them yet.[3] I also wrote to [G. S.] Fraser asking what happens about his anthology – haven't heard from him, either, which is annoying because I've shelved 2 perfectly good poems for nine months because of him.[4] Lehmann wrote one of his smooth letters asking for poems – he's printing an extract from my long poem, called Ralph's Dream, in December, so he can wait a while. I feel a bit guilty about that Long Poem – I've written only a half of it, haven't looked at it since March, yet I go around importantly printing bits of it as tho it were finished. And I bet it doesn't get finished for at least another 2 years, too. I feel like Coleridge. Printing extracts, I mean.

[. . .]

Did I tell you I met Auden? At Winters'!! Both being terrifically genial to each other and being so careful not to tread on each other's toes that they practically kept in different rooms. Auden was in the district giving lectures. He was really a tremendous disappointment, both himself and his lectures. I could hardly believe this was the Wild One of the Thirties, who whatever his faults then at least had the virtue of a strident tone of denunciation. But now you'd never know: a flabby dilettante, gracious living, complacent and trite. I looked thro Nones more carefully after he had gone, and it was all confirmed. Have you read that Phi Beta Kappa poem – the long one – of his? I disagree with Winters' poem 'To a Young Writer' but, hell, if I have to choose between them, I'd go for Winters every time.

[. . .]

Anyway, I like my position here – far enough away from Winters and near enough to him to get what I want from him and to be liked by him.

[. . .]

This letter is sickeningly egotistical, I feel, tho I haven't read it thro yet. So please forgive. I may be going to Texas at Christmas to stay with a girlfriend (the Tamer & Hawk, etc subject).[5] Or else she may be coming here, not decided yet. Tell Adrienne C. Rich that I went wild with joy over her last New Yorker poem. My love to the family, and to yourself. Poems will follow.

Thom

P.S. You'll be astonished to hear W has recommended me to read W. C. Williams, Pound, and Marianne Moore. I worked diligently thro Williams, and quite liked about 4 poems out of 600; am at present on Pound, about whom I feel really enthusiastic for the first time; from what I've read of M. M. tho, I think I'll hate her. Typical woman writer.

Tell me if there's any American poet you particularly think I ought to read. I've read comparatively few – am going to work thro all Stevens in the near future, but apart from that, of the modern, I've only read Lowell, Shapiro and bits of Hart Crane. And Frost, I suppose. Is Jeffers really as bad as W says he is? – I have a sort of feeling I like him from what I've read.

When I leave Stanford, I'm going to set myself a Romantic reading list: to include Blake, Wuthering Heights, etc. As a corrective.

1. Calvin Thomas Jr. (1927–2016) received a creative writing fellowship at Stanford the same year as TG. An account of his time there, including Winters's letters to him and his father, was published in *Poetry* 194, no. 4 (July–August 2009), 383–9.
2. TG refers to Anthony Hartley's essay 'Poets of the Fifties', *The Spectator* (27 August 1954), in which TG is loosely connected with what Hartley calls 'neo-metaphysical writing'. For the connection between *The Spectator* and the Movement see TG to Conquest, 11 March 1955, below.
3. TG had reviewed the reissue of Frederick C. Gill's *The Romantic Movement and Methodism* (1954) in *The Spectator* (13 August 1954), 211.
4. 'Helen's Rape' and 'Light Sleeping', *Poetry Now*, ed. Fraser (1956), 80–5.
5. The 'girlfriend' is code for MK; see 'Tamer and Hawk' (*CP* 29).

TO *Karl Miller*   ALS Emory
Friday 26 November 1954

334 Lincoln Ave.
Palo Alto, Calif.

26 Nov 54

Dear Karl Miller Downing,
    [. . .] – It was rather exciting about New World Writing: Fraser asked for
some poems last March, so I gave him some old ones that were quite good –
but didn't know where they were to appear.[1] New World Writing is really
just a fashionable collection of shit, with about 2 good things in it per issue,
but it has a fantastic circulation. In previous issues they've had collections of
young american, young irish, young welsh, even young arabic poets. Now,
presumably, Young Eng. I can make a fairly safe guess that my companions
will be (1) E. Jennings (2) Wain (3) Amis (4) Davie,[2] and (5) Larkin. Only the
last of these is any good, and God, the more I read him the more good I think
him. He's fifteen times as good as me. (And, without boasting, I'm fifteen
times as good as the other four.)
    [. . .]
    California – what I've seen of it – is pretty terrific. Now I write, it suddenly
occurs to me that its 'American-ness', as one understands that at home,
hardly ever crosses my mind. It's about as different from the rest of America
(Europe-conscious New York, and the great ignorant spaces of the Middle
West between, and the impenetrable South) as the rest of America is from
Europe. It certainly has its own dignity, & most of the things one thinks
about it at home are either untrue or irrelevant. [. . .] San Francisco is a
fantastic place – a very lovely place too, it can hold its own against some of
the best European cities, and is incidentally the queerest city I've ever been in.
    [. . .]
    I've been working, laboriously, thro American Lit [. . .] and at last I have
to come over, a trifle reluctantly, to Wallace Stevens – reluctantly, because
there's a something in him that I dislike even more than that something I
dislike in Eliot. But he's a very fine writer, and there's no denying it. [. . .]
    Well I must stop now, but do write <u>soon</u>, Karl Miller Downing, and tell me
all the crap. And non-crap, specially that. Give my love to a selected few: Mrs
Shire and Neal [Ascherson] are the only people I can think of in Cambridge,
and the Boys in London.
                    Love,
                Thom

1. As well as appearing in *Poetry Now* (1956), 'Light Sleeping' was published – at Fraser's doing – in *New World Writing* 7 (April 1955), 115–16.
2. Donald Davie (1922–95), poet and critic. See Glossary of Names.

TO *Tony White*   ALS (aerogramme) Tulsa
Thursday 16 December 1954

334 Lincoln Avenue,
Palo Alto, California, U.S.A.

16 Dec 54

Dear Tony,

Here is your awful friend writing to say he's sorry he hasn't written again – and only writing a short letter to say it in. Before I go any farther I promise to write in the first week of January and (1) repay the money I owe you (2) send you a pair of real Californian (TIGHT!) levis (3) send you a batch of poems I've written, which at least are a bit better than in the last year, and I hope will get better. And happy Christmas.

[. . .] I've picked up some useful friends, and a wild and lovely (both of them) married couple.¹ And have been reading much, and writing quite a lot; as I haven't done for a long time. [. . .]

Tomorrow I start on a 2 ½ day journey down to Texas, where I stay over Christmas and New Year with Mike. Very excited, as this'll be the first time I've seen him since England. He's in service down there – a 2 Lt. in the air force. I also am going to have an interview at a college down there, to see if I can get a job for next year so I can live with Mike. Don't worry – even if I'll get it, I'll return to England after that. That'll be the big test – if it all works out all right, then I'll feel justified in dragging Mike over to Europe (as he'd like to be dragged). If it conceivably doesn't, then a year together will give us the chance of finding out, and I have no more business in America, which is just like England really – only a good deal more of surface energy, a little more deep-down energy, and more variation of landscape. I feel surprisingly unsentimental about Europe – even Rome and Paris, let alone Cambridge. You are about the only person in England I regret not being able to see – my family well out of the way. – I do regret the theatre, tho. Stanford dramatics are not overgood compared with Cambridge: they did The Alchemist recently, and it was pretty bad. And San Francisco has only had Midsummer Night's Dream, Old Vic, which I didn't bother to see (I dislike ballet) – and the opera season there is over. So I have sought out the whole canon of Brando pictures, and have now seen all but Streetcar. (<u>Don't</u> see Désirée, by the way. B makes a lovely Napoleon, but hasn't got a chance.)

[. . .]

I've been reading Melville (✓✓), Hawthorne (ugh), and the other Americans all term. But at present I'm starting the 'Chroniques Italiennes',[2] and for the train I have packed Mickey Spillane, La Nausée (which I've never read), another short book of Sartre's – L'Existentialism est une Humanisme or something, and a life of Napoleon.[3] So you see I'm still on the right lines as far as Thought goes. And at least <u>try</u> to be as far as Life goes. Tho you, Peter,[4] Karl etc don't agree I suppose with the latter.

[. . .]

Also, who's in your bed nowadays? I daren't hope it's a man. (You don't have to answer this question. In fact don't, unless you have a lot of time to spare, bother to answer this till you've got my next letter.) [. . .]

My love all round, but keep it mostly for yourself. [. . .] And embody the Values.[5]

     Love,

       Thom

1. Tony and Charlotte Herbold took TG to his first gay bar, the Black Cat, in San Francisco. They went in the company of a woman called Mary, TG's 'date'. The bar, TG told Robert Prager, 'was a great revelation to me. Gay bars were enjoyable! Though Mary kept on saying, "Those poor men. I feel so sorry for them." I wasn't feeling sorry for them. I could see that they were having fun. And I realized I could have fun there too, so I went back there the next night by myself.' A transcript of TG's interview with Prager can be found in the GLBT Historical Society archives in San Francisco.

2. Stendhal, *Chroniques Italiennes* (1855), TG would probably have read these nine short stories in the original French.

3. The 'life of Napoleon' TG mentions is likely Stendhal's *Vie de Napoléon* (1817–18) and *Mémoires sur Napoléon* (1836–7).

4. Peter Wood (1927–2016), theatre director, knew TG and White at Cambridge, where he studied English at Downing College.

5. The 'Values' are summarised in a card White sent TG in early 1954: 'All my best wishes for panache, logique, espagnolisme, l'imprévu, singularité and MAGNANIMITY in the New Year from one Étranger to another' (*OP* 163).

1955

Monday 24 January 1955

334 Lincoln Avenue,
Palo Alto, Calif.

24 Jan 55

Dear Tony,

I really must throw everything up and write to you, I was terribly pleased
to get your letter. You sound semi-depressed, but I'm glad you like the Old
Vic enough to stay on another year. So you are to play the tender-hearted
cousin: I'd be <u>very</u> interested to see you do it, I'm sure well. I must look out
for reviews of the production in the periodical room here. What do you play
in Henry IVs?¹ <u>One day</u> you'll get Hotspur – your tailor-made part, <u>one</u> of
your tailor-made parts that is.

Before I forget, here's a cheque for what I think I owe you. Also some
poems. I'm sincerely very sorry to have been so caddish in letting the cheque
go so long, specially considering I said I'd pay you back in September. Many
thanks for it, it was much appreciated. I enclose a revised 'Lines for a Book'
(which I think is a bit of an improvement on the other), and 'Jesus & his
Mother' with one line altered for the metre's sake. You see I'm forswearing
that phoney appearance of sincerity I had from being almost unscannable.
Also some others, mainly written last term: 'Before the Carnival' is dated
'Rome' because I wrote a draft of it there & it is in essentials as I wrote it
there – but I've done a good deal to it since then. (Have you read any Tristan
de Corbière? <u>He</u> used to date his poems from places he'd never been, like
Jerusalem and Cairo.) 'The Corridor', 'The Paraplegic', 'Julian the Apostate',
and perhaps 'Filling in Time', are attempts to deal with existentialist subjects.
'The Corridor' in fact comes direct from a quotation I found in a book on
Sartre by a Miss Murdock.² It's a sort of <u>sound</u> poem, but rather dull. Shows
Winters' influence more than any of the others. 'The Paraplegic' got inception
(or <u>conception</u>?) from seeing Brando's first ~~movie~~ film, The Men.³ I think it's
probably too long, at least <u>I</u> don't think so, but people tell me it is. 'Julian'
is a bit too complicated: Winters dislikes the punctuation image, but I want

to keep it, because the poem is about the concept of the irrational. (A sort of 'Caligula' writ small.[4]) My real regret with this is that I'd have liked to have dealt more adequately with Julian's character – a peach of a subject – my favourite Roman emperor. Ibsen wrote an absurd play about him – he was born pagan, got converted to Christianity, succeeded Constantine (Christianity being then the official religion), decided paganism was best after all, made <u>that</u> the official religion.[5] I <u>think</u> he got converted back to Christianity again, but I'm not sure; if he did, I've altered the story. 'Filling in Time', I'm not sure at all whether it comes off: Mike likes it, but no one else.[6] Oh yes, and 'St Martin & the Beggar' is also existentialist, my favourite saint, so practical you know. (I thought of putting 'knight of infinite resignation' below the title of 'The Paraplegic', but thought better of it.) 'Hi Fi', 'Puss in Boots', and 'During an Absence', are trivia, really.[7] I sort of get the feeling that <u>all</u> these poems are peripheral, somehow: they just miss the centre. I was thinking a short time back of getting together another book – I have enough material – but reading thro what I've written since 'Fighting Terms', none of it seems to have any continuity, enough to justify being collected yet. So I'll wait a while. Hope you saw my London Mag effort, 'Ralph's Dream' – quite unexpectedly, I was awfully pleased to see it in print. I wrote it 18 months ago and would alter a few lines now, but I was more pleased to have it published than I have been over anything for a long time.

Sorry about all this egotism but I thought I'd get it out of the way.

[. . .]

Really I don't know quite what I make of America. I say this on rereading your vigorous and enthusiastic questionings. What you say, tho you say it better than I would have, is rather what I hoped for before I came here. But somehow the independence from Europe is not so complete – here or in New York, that is, & these are the only 2 places worth worrying about. Educated Americans depend more on Europe, anyway. Because that's not quite true – I depend on Europe a good deal, & if I were to hear Europe had suddenly sunk into the sea I'd feel all that mattered had gone. That's why I have to come back to Europe: all I really value that has been achieved is there. The good thing about America is that comparatively little has been achieved: not that its inhabitants think so, & certainly one can't be a Pioneer any longer – but it's still all beautifully potential. Too potential tho, except for a stronger person than me: America won't get over being only potential till its power (Political) & wealth decrease, and it becomes as decadent as Europe. California & New York are the easiest places for a European to arrive into. Texas is a different matter. I stayed there with Mike for a fortnight over Christmas & New Year and it is hell's own place, honest. To find a provinciality equal to the Madame

Bovary brand one goes to Texas: nothing like it exists in Europe now, I'm sure. Completely oblivious of anything but its great dusty hot self – oil magnates, segregation of negroes, despising the rest of America let alone the rest of the world. (And by contrast, I think because masculinity is made so unattractive, it – San Antonio at any rate – contains more girley homosexuals than any other place I've ever been in. The lipsticky sort, I mean.) So next year is going to be an interesting experience: what Peter calls 'the pressures of life' will be operating from all angles. Good for me, tho, to live in an exasperating place for a year – could lead to absolute barrenness in writing (in which case I'm no good as a writer, & it might as well happen then as later), could merely be a period of treading water, but could conceivably stir up a great & fruitful reaction! Well, I suppose that's hoping for a bit much, and it'll be by no means hell (Il Paradiso, perhaps?) living with Mike, after all.

The job I hope to be getting there is not, I regret to say, film-extraing (Hollywood is about 3000 miles distant from there, silly!) but teaching elementary composition & perhaps a few of the Beauties of the English Poets to moronic freshmen in a small unheard of college in San Antonio. (I plan to get a motorcycle to cover the enormous distances involved.) This should be stimulating, & if I'm absolutely no good at it, it'll only be for a year. – Of course, the job & extension of any visa are both still a bit up in the air, & I may not get either.

Being with Mike again was terrific. It was funny to find how that warm sort of relationship had really been forgotten by me except as a concept in the mind. I mean I had confidence in it & knew what it was, but it hadn't been 'realised' in 6 months, & things can grow dangerously abstract even in 6 months. I find I tend to juggle with abstractions a bit too easily – juggle them into being something they may not be. So it was a good reminder to me (and him too, I think), and we were both happy. It's a hell of a place for him to be in & I'm glad I might be able to make things a bit better for him for his 2nd year in service. That sounds patronising, and I don't pretend it won't be making me happy too, but I am glad for that reason more than anybody would think.

[. . .]

Yes, I miss you too, & I don't just say that because you say the same thing. I can't help feeling that you were the cause, direct or indirect, of most of my best poetry, and by implication of my straightest thinking and strongest grasp on things. Not, exactly, that I'm thinking crooked now, but I have so much less thoughts. That's an awful admission to have to make, but I certainly seemed to have reached a stage – in the last 6 months? – in the last 18 months? – where the restlessness has become dangerously less. The

50

restlessness before didn't exactly conduce to happiness of course, it never does, and I suppose essentially it was just prolonged adolescence; but without it, or rather with less of it (becos I'll never be completely without it) there's so much less drive towards any kind of fruitful action. Well (philosophically) one goes on, & I just hope one goes somewhere. Or, as the famous line in The Wild One: 'You don't go to any special place, man, you just go.'[8] Indeed. How bathetic can your friend get, I'll be quoting R. L. Stevenson on the subject in a minute. Must stop myself before I do.

Saw 'L'auberge rouge' the other day, a film which was banned in England for being anti-clerical, & by God it is anti-clerical – magnificently so – next time you're in France you must see it, it's really terrifically funny.

I quite agree about Wain, Angus Wilson, and all the rest of the shit. One might add the Anglo-American Merwin (poet), and others. One book I read which you would like: 'Lucky Jim' by Kingsley Amis – a sort of minor bestseller in England, I believe. He is usually associated with Wain, but also, less often, with me. And I'm certainly flattered by the connection. He has some things wrong with him, but a good many things right that few other people have – i.e. the knowledge that you have to reject all the bumblers and phonies, however pitiful or impressive they may seem, and you're tied hand and foot unless you do something really savage & destructive against them. Also he has a splendid sense of humour. You must read it when you have time – and don't be put off by the fact that it has been liked by so many of the phonies and bumblers themselves.

Yes, I know what you mean – 'the odd carnal encounter' & just how unsatisfactory it really is, as one knows it will be beforehand but just hopes it might be Different, and then afterwards you are back just where you were before. I say this specially now because I've been trying to look around for some sort of relationship – either Body, or else Mind, if possible both – to fill in the year away from Mike; but it doesn't seem to work terribly satisfactorily – the nicest people I meet (either B, or M) always seem to be on their way thro here to Los Angeles or New York or somewhere, the intelligent ones are ugly and finally their intelligence is all taken up with the enthusiasm for woman writers or something, and the goodlooking ones are just so dumb it isn't true. What a Young Man's complaint that is! Old Werther Gunn.

[. . .]

I'm not doing too much work really. I'm learning Italian, catching up with French poets like Valéry & Corbière, rereading Baudelaire (who for all you may say, is one of the Great for me: all Romanticism & the criticism of Romanticism magnificently side by side) and a few odd plays of Shakespeare, go to the gym to work off excess energy, get drunk once every two weeks (can't afford to more often; anyway I'd probably only be sick), go into wonderful San Francisco at every opportunity where I think I have more friends than here. – It's beginning to get fine again, the squirrels go bouncing all over the roof outside my window, oh to fuck with all these natural details, I must be going soft inside or something. I'd send you those jeans, only don't know your size – measure your waist and tell me the size when you write, 32 inches, 33, 34?

God, I wish you were here so I could talk to you. How I know what you mean when you say you're surrounded by nice people who don't share most of your enthusiasms – it's just so with me.

I've got a wonderful typewriter by the way – 30 years old, but with all the French & Spanish accents on, and even an umlaut. Hell, I must be like dreary old Walt Whitman & start introducing foreign words into my poems; then I'll be able to use all the accents.

It's late in the night now and I must stop. My love to Kerri,[9] Peter & John H when you see them, everybody.

Much love to yourself, success, action (ACTION),

Thom

P.S. And happy birthday next month.

1. White played the 'tender-hearted cousin' Aumerle in *Richard II* and Edmund Mortimer and Mouldy in the two *Henry IV* plays at the Old Vic (1954–5).
2. 'The Corridor' (CP 85–6); see Iris Murdoch, *Sartre: Romantic Rationalist* (1953).
3. 'The Paraplegic Lying on his Back', *London Magazine* 2, no. 7 (July 1955), 13–14; uncollected. See also *The Men*, dir. Fred Zinnemann (1950).
4. Albert Camus, *Caligula* (1944).
5. Henrik Ibsen, *Emperor and Galilean* (1873).
6. 'Filling in Time' became 'High Fidelity' (CP 76).d; a typescript can be found among TG's letters to Hall (New Hampshire).
7. 'Hi Fi' became 'High Fidelity' (CP 76). 'Puss in Boots' was collected in *SM*, but dropped from *CP*.
8. 'On the Move' was first published with an epigraph from *The Wild One* – 'Man, you gotta Go' – in *Encounter* 5, no. 6 (December 1955), 50. This is a slight misquotation: the actual line reads, 'Oh man, we just gonna *go*.'
9. Edward Kerrigan Prescott (1931–2009), an actor White knew from the Old Vic.

Friday 11 March 1955

334 Lincoln Avenue,
Palo Alto, Calif.

March 11th 55

Dear Robert Conquest,
    Thank you for your letter. You asked me to answer it soon, and must have
been wondering whether I ever got it. It was about ten days on the bulletin
board before I saw it, and for additional delay I've been having big internal
questionings about whether I'm in the Movement or not.²
    What it really comes down to is that I don't think the Movement
is a movement in the same sense that, say, the Imagists, the Thirties, the
Apocalyptics, were movements. These shared intentions that I deplore, but
that were positive intentions. But the different writers you name share little
else beyond a desire to get rid of the phoniness that was preparing in the
Thirties and that made the Forties an all-time low in Eng Lit; I am not sure
that beyond this sanitary measure these writers (e.g. Wain and E. Jennings)
have much in common. They share a healthy destructive attitude but very
little else. Certainly I agree with the necessity for some sort of framework:
but surely this is only a return to the most obvious strength in poetry, the
derivations from which have all been pretty eccentric. A knowledge that it is
the strength doesn't make a school (otherwise Herbert and Baudelaire would
both be in it), it is the starting point for a school. I wonder whether the
movement is real enough yet to produce an anthology, and whether, after a
few years, when most of the writers have done more considerable work, we
shan't discover ourselves miles apart, each having been a separate movement?
    This must seem a surly way in which to answer your letter, but it doesn't
mean that I am not grateful for your asking me to contribute, or that I am
backing out:³ I suppose the remedy is to go ahead and do big things. And
I suppose a return to rational structure and comprehensible language do
provide some sort of link, even though I feel that my interests and attitude
will never have anything in common with those of Elizabeth Jennings and
Enright.
    I hope you'll forgive this tract. To be more practical: if you still want to,
after this, you can use any of the things in Fighting Terms that suit your
purpose (though I'd rather you didn't use Contemplative and Active, which
strikes me now as vague and dishonest).⁴ Perhaps you could let me know
what you want to use, as I have slightly revised some of them and I wish to

revise others before they are published again.[5] I also enclose some others: some of these are due to be published in magazines during the next month or two, others are at present being offered to magazines (I'll let you know particulars when I write again).

If you still want suggestions for other contributors, how about Geoffrey Hill and Donald Hall? I don't know whether you have already considered Geoffrey Hill (Elizabeth Jennings would know his address), but he strikes me as being a strong vigorous writer who lets no nonsense slip into his verse, possibly better than either the two poets you were unsure about including, and at least as closely connected with the rest as I am. He and Larkin are two of the few younger poets who keep the intellectual framework and at the same time take full advantage of the suggestive possibilities of language. – Don Hall is an American who was at Oxford for two years. The fact that he is American may disqualify him, of course, but otherwise he is just your man. You may have seen what he wrote before he left England and not have been over-impressed by it – but what he has done in the last eighteen months is very, very impressive, and I think he would be a credit to such a collection.

[. . .]

Yours sincerely,

Thom Gunn

1. Robert Conquest (1917–2015), historian and poet. Conquest edited the *New Lines* anthologies (1956, 1962). See Glossary of Names.

2. 'The Movement' was the name given to a number of loosely connected English poets in the mid-1950s whose work is generally thought to be a reaction against the neo-symbolist excesses of George Barker and Dylan Thomas in the 1940s. J. D. Scott, literary editor of *The Spectator* (1953–6), coined the name 'the Movement' in an anonymous article: 'In the Movement', *The Spectator* (1 October 1954), 399–400. Writers associated with the Movement include Philip Larkin, Kingsley Amis, Donald Davie, John Wain, Elizabeth Jennings and TG.

3. Conquest had asked TG to contribute to his anthology *New Lines* (1956).

4. 'Contemplative and Active' was published in the original *FT* but dropped thereafter, as was 'A Village Edmund'.

5. TG revised the *FT* poems for the Hawk's Well edition (1958), but came to think these revisions a bad mistake. For the Faber edition (1962) he mostly restored the text of the Fantasy edition, and included the original Fantasy versions in *CP*.

Thursday 9 June 1955

2638 W. Craig,
San Antonio,
Texas.

9 June 55

Dear Ander – Hope you don't mind being used as typewriter practice: I am getting command of several different machines at once (the right country to do it in, I guess). You will be astonished to know that I got my driver's license two days ago, for a car. No relation of mine will believe this, I'm sure. But the Greatest is the motorcycle. Not that I have actually got this yet, but I will on Monday. It is second hand: a 1950 Harley Davison (do you know anything about American makes, I believe this is the best), engine re-bored and the whole thing repainted so that it looks quite smart, at only $250, which, considering that new it would have been something like double the price, is pretty good. I'd have more qualms about getting it if I were to need it more than a year, because such a cheap job would probably begin causing trouble in the second or third year I had it; but I consider that it will be all right for the year I need it, and that I gain even if I find I can't get a dollar for it when I am finished with it – which is likely. I don't yet know [how] to ride it, but the dealer is going to teach me, and I hope to have learnt by this time next week: I don't have to get a new license.

I am glad to get your letter, which reached me just after I came here. I spent a few days in Hollywood (YMCA) on the way down: met Isherwood, who turned out to be one of the very few Men of Letters I have ever genuinely liked: he is a script writer for MGM, and took me round the studios, bringing me within a few feet of Lana Turner, and introducing me to a delightful and gorgeous twin of Pier Angeli, who has a part in a movie he has written and that was being filmed.[2] This was all terribly interesting. Then in the evening Isherwood took me to meet a certain Gerald Heard, who has started a new religion called Vedanta (so far as I can see it consists of the thrills of a pseudo-mystical experience without the inconvenience of being a Buddhist or Christian) to which Isherwood and Aldous Huxley subscribe – but I do not. Huxley lives there too, but I didn't meet him. I loathed Heard, tremendous meaningless eloquence; not enough people question him. Personally, I don't believe much in the value of the mystical experience: I dare say it is possible, but it is a state dangerously near to an induced madness (cf Huxley on mescalin[3]). I argued with Heard, anyway.

55

I start teaching here next week: the stuff I have to teach is infantile, also dull; the faculty at the university is stuffy, also dull. However I knew this when I applied for the job, and it is good to have a reasonably paid job at all, I suppose. I am sharing an apartment with Mike Kitay, who is a wonderful person to be sharing with. He is also lending me money for the first instalments of the cycle: and I learnt to drive on his car. I read Dick Tracy in the comics every day; it is so hot that we sleep without even a sheet on us, but I seem to be able to stand the heat; I may be going to either Mexico or New Orleans for a few days either during or at the end of the year, though this depends on money; San Antonio is a pretty drab and dull place, but Texans are tremendously boastful of anything to do with Texas.

[. . .] Glad you're working at the Serpers again: remember (this is going to be an elder-brotherly remark) do try and put a little money aside, in case you find it hard to get a job this winter. Well, you can count me in on the patricide: notoriety in both Time and the Daily Worker speaks for itself, and I got a letter from Father proudly recounting all his little tricks.[4] Barbara is going abroad for the first time in her life in August, to Scandinavia! You just be careful about that rough cider; if you get the acidosis still you ought seriously to see a doctor. You <u>must</u> see The Blackboard Jungle: it certainly has some bad points, but there is a marvellous character called West who just <u>sends</u> me, man, and is really a bit like you (this is meant as a compliment) – also it starts off with a tremendous tune, which you have probably heard by now, called Rockin around the Clock.

If you ever see Ruth & Peter, or Thérèse, tell them I'll write (I never have, in the whole year).[5] The above is my permanent address.

        Love & phlegmy kisses,
           Thom

1. Ander Gunn (1932–), TG's brother. See Glossary of Names.
2. TG wrote about this meeting in 'Christopher Isherwood: Getting Things Right' (*SL* 173–9). Pier Angeli's twin was Marisa Pavan, and the film Isherwood scripted was *Diane* (1955).
3. Huxley's psychedelic experience under the influence of mescaline is the subject of *The Doors of Perception* (1954).
4. The letter is lost.
5. TG's childhood neighbour Ruth Pearce (1927–2011) married the sociologist Peter Townsend in 1949. TG and Ruth maintained a lifelong correspondence; TG's letters to Ruth are held in a private collection. For Thérèse Megaw (1906–2004) see Glossary of Names.

TO *Yvor Winters*[1]   ALS Stanford
Thursday 16 June 1955

2638 W. Craig,
SAN ANTONIO,
TEXAS.

16 June 55

Dear Mr Winters,

This is only a note to give you my address, if you haven't yet sent those poems etc. It's hot here, but not unbearably so: to my surprise I am liking San Antonio a good deal more than I did at Christmas. I'm not yet due to start teaching so I spend my time swimming and, in quiet desperation, reading Thoreau.

Don't bother to answer this if you have already written – I'll write at more length later on. I have been looking at apartments till I think only in terms of apartments, which doesn't help me take Thoreau too seriously: I don't know about the Good Life in New England, but in Texas the Good Life needs an air cooler, a refrigerator, and a cold shower.

I know it's easy to get sentimental just after you've left a place, but really without sentimentality it was a terrific year. It was a very great pleasure, to say the least, knowing you; and even if it hadn't improved my poems (which it did) it would have done me good, personally, working under you; and I love California more than I am ever likely to love any other place besides Rome. I suppose you must be sick of departing pupils pouring themselves out all over you.

I'll write again. My love to Mrs Winters and Danny.[2]

Thom

1. Yvor Winters (1900–68), poet, critic and teacher. See Glossary of Names.
2. Janet Lewis (1899–1998), novelist and poet, wife of Yvor Winters. See Glossary of Names. Daniel Winters was their son.

c. August 1955¹

2638 West Craig,

San Antonio,

Texas.

Middle of August, some time

Dear Tony,

Don't apologise for not writing – I know how difficult it can be when you're working hard. I was <u>very</u> pleased to get your letter, and especially all the news of your coming over here. You say for 6 months, but don't tell when. Tell me what month, roughly, you'll be in San Francisco, and what month you'll be in New York – the two ends of your tour.² I shall probably be teaching part of next summer – but I want to spend a few weeks in SF, and see it and Winters again before I return to England. [. . .] I shall certainly regret leaving America – somehow it – or rather California – has become a sort of spiritual home, tho you very likely won't find it that for yourself – or perhaps you will, I don't know. It is partly that it exercises particular faculties that one was born with but for which the necessity of exercise isn't recognised in England. Or it may be that it's just that the men here attract me so much; I have an awful tendency to transform sexual attraction into a moral value. You'll see what I mean about the butchness when you go to San Francisco tho, a queer bar there is only half ponces, whereas the equivalent in England would probably be 98/100 ponces. Or perhaps I'm wrong, I've never been to one in England. – One thing you're wrong about, tho, the New York ~~theater~~ theatre (!): New York has only about half the theatres London does, and about half of <u>those</u> have musicals permanently. [. . .] Has [Karl Miller's] anthology come out yet?³ Please discount the immature ignoble things of mine included in it – Cameleon, Earthborn, Matter & Spirit will none of them be printed in any collection of mine: I think I am a little better able to distinguish between my good & my bad now than when I said he could use those. – Teaching is pretty much hell: I get on very well with my pupils, hate the other teachers, get full of immense restlessness and impatience, long to be back in San Francisco. The main trouble is that, with lessons, preparation of them, correcting essays, I have no time to even <u>think</u> about writing poems. I fully expect to write nothing all year: and the thought of starting from bottom again at the end of the year fills me with despair.

Mike & I have a nice garage apartment, and are sweetly domesticated. I don't know how it will turn out later: I am equally afraid of sticking to him merely from habit, and of leaving him on some crazy impulse that I'd regret. But this is everybody's trouble, I guess – homo or hetero.

[. . .]

I have a marvellous motorcycle, which has thrown me several times, but is positively sexually beautiful to look at. A 1950 Harley Davison, if that means anything to you. It is like bringing up a child, it constantly does things that surprise me. Actually, it is going to fall to pieces under me, but it is very good till that happens. By the way, did you like On the Move, because I think that is better than anything else I have ever done. Rather inappropriately, it is going to come out in Encounter, but I wanted people to see it, and I print too much in the London Mag as it is.

I am going to have a booklet (probably) published from Harvard this autumn. Will send you a copy. It'll be far better than Fighting Terms, will contain 6 or 8 from there and about 10 or 12 that I've written since then. I'm going to call it 'The Sense of Movement' – this does, it is true, sound a bit like a title of Henry James (The Sense of the Past), but it has two such good, and appropriate meanings, viz. the meaning of movement, and the actual <u>feeling</u> that you are moving – that I want to use it.

The temperature here is 100 or over every day, and one has to wear dark glasses outside all the time, so I envy you London with only 85. One of my pupils fainted with the heat a few days ago.

Lehmann has asked me to take David Hughes' place as asst. editor when I return. He says to tell no one, so don't repeat. I don't think I want to accept really, (a) because I'm not smooth enough, & don't want to <u>try</u> to be smooth enough, to people like those I met at his party, (b) because, tho I don't dislike him so much as most people do, I could easily dislike him as much or more. However, the great advantage would be that it wd be at least a regular job for a year or two, and it would give me plenty of leisure – which I'm going to need if I'm ever to do any writing. So I'm gonna stall till Christmas, and either accept or reject then.

Love, do write, and excuse this letter, which was written in three different places,

Thom

1. Date supplied by internal evidence.
2. In the end White did not take part in the Old Vic North American tour (1956–7).
3. *Poetry from Cambridge: 1952–4*, ed. Miller (1955).

TO *Tony White* ALS Tulsa

Friday 25 November 1955

2638 W. Craig,
San Antonio,
Texas, U.S.A.

25 Nov 55

Dear Tony,

Now its Thanksgiving, which is a public holiday, and Mike is home on leave, I have time to answer the longest letter I've ever had. Though not at the same length. You give me just the criticism I need, and as you'll see I've acted on some of it, tho not as much as you might wish, perhaps.

Teaching has become much easier, though I still don't intend to continue it after next summer. God knows what I <u>will</u> do on my return to England: I have no intention of a white collar job in an office, and you may find me doing what you did for a summer, working on street mending. [. . .] The Lehmann job has probably fallen through, not through L's fault, but because David Hughes suddenly left for a job with a publisher, and L has to take on someone else now – and he can't take him on just for 9 months. Just as well perhaps – takes away the temptation of a smooth job.

Yes, I was sorry about James Dean: I wish he'd lived to be cast in an uncrappy film.[1] East of Eden was bad enough, but his second one (Rebel without a Cause, which is probably too rough to be shown in England) contains about the worst dialogue and story I have ever seen in a film with any pretensions. Still, I enjoyed it – it's all about (good looking) young toughs in motorcycle boots. (There's a wonderful bit with chains.)

I have written what was meant to be a scathing review of Empson's collected poems for the London Mag, which is meant to set everybody against me except those who can't read: it's calculated to irritate both Empsonists and Thomas-worshippers. (Actually, Thomas is a <u>bit</u> better, but you won't find me admitting that in print while the present idolatry continues.) Lehmann may not print it as it is, though: I think he will dislike it as much as anybody.[2]

Much to my pleasure, I got a hundred dollar prize from Poetry Chicago for some poems I had printed in it last June.[3] Apart from the money, I am preening myself because the previous recipients include Stevens, Hart Crane, Edwin Arlington Robinson, D. Thomas. (I think D.T. are tremendously appropriate initials for Thomas, don't you?)

Now for the poems of mine you go through – which by this time will probably be filling you with enormous boredom. I really can't thank you enough for taking such trouble to criticise them so minutely. I've just finished a large scale revision of about 25 of my poems for my next book in England, and about half of them have been much changed.

First of all, about punctuation: I think poetry can afford to be slightly under-punctuated as compared to prose. Some poems, if punctuated exactly as prose, would look very over-punctuated. And I think there is definitely a slight pause at the end of every line, which can sometimes make a light punctuation mark unnecessary (so long as the meaning stays clear). However, I agree that I haven't punctuated enough, and I've inserted some in many of the places you mention and in some others.

Holmstrom wouldn't say I was writing too much if he knew (a) how little I wrote last year between January and September, and (b) that I have written nothing – not a damn thing except some revisions – since April this year until now. Not doing anything makes me morose, ungrateful, arrogant, difficult to live with, etc. (Whereas working hard makes me morose, ungrateful, arrogant, and difficult to live with.)

Do I really still have this damn 'witty detachment'. That is why the metaphysicalle boyes claim me as one of their own (Wain, Hartley, Ltd.), but I hope I had left all that behind with His Cynical (Mythical) Mistress, Cambridge, and Donne. Certainly I have detachment: I have to detach myself to write at all – which is, has been, and ever more will be, the trouble with my personal life. But I don't think wit occurs in, for example, On the Move, or The Inherited Estate, does it?

[. . .]

I have to agree with you about the attitude to Christianity. Personal justification: ['St Martin and the Beggar'] was to be one of a series of about 10 poems stealing saints etc from religion for Existentialism: Jesus & his mother was another of the series, and the only other one that got written was one called Apocryphal which got into Botteghe Oscure and will never be printed anywhere else. (It reads like Longfellow.) This series was to go under the name of Blasphemies, which I suppose was very childish of me. – The other justification is a bit more valid: I think the ballad form does dissociate me from having to believe in it all literally. However, this is a bit dishonest. I was trying to use Christ and miracles merely as something that happened in those days just as lightning or floods happen nowadays. – You go to the root of the matter when you question my attitude to Xianity: that's the real trouble with the poem. – Tho not with Jesus and his Mother, where there is no need to treat Jesus as being divine – just a Man with a Mission.

(Of course I'm not a Christian, by the way. I'd sooner be dead.)

[. . .]

I defend every stanza in On the Move. They are all necessary: e.g. thunder and dust in the first stanza are general, but are given particular reference in the second, where they are repeated. The birds in the last stanza are those in the first. ('Saints' come into it because, though they are considered as much above humans as birds are below, they are like them in that there is no gap for them between intention and action).

Also, stanza one, etc., are necessary because the poem is not only about the motorcyclists – it is also about 'one' (presumably me, or anyone) standing on the edge of a Californian highway and seeing them go past. The fourth stanza has all the meat of the poem in it, and if it generalises, that's tough. There's nothing wrong with generalisation in itself, so long as it is not vague. To generalise, one doesn't have to be either Augustan, or like Eliot (where every abstraction is a groan). – And they do go away into the distance: "they burst away" – to towns etc.

The Corridor I don't go crazy about myself. It is consistent and clever, and says what I wanted to say, but it doesn't say it in a way that too much interests me. It is Camus existentialism (La Peste) rather than Sartre. (Though I got the image of the watcher thro the keyhole finding himself watched by someone else, from a book about Sartre, a quotation in it from his big book.) The watcher is not an existentialist till the last stanza, but his situation is existentialist all through. Do you see the distinction I am trying to make?

The Inherited Estate is meant in two ways besides the literal one. (Oh, the levels, the levels.) It is dedicated to Mike: I don't know whether it was on your copy but it is now: 'To an American in Europe.' Coming to Europe he reaches not only Europe (one meaning of the estate) but also the estate of man. The last is the important meaning, though the other would do – it is supposed to apply to either or both. I have made a good many changes in the poem since I sent it to you, I think, because you quote as difficult a line that's no longer in it. I'll type out the new version when I have time (NB: it is now the end of Thanksgiving, and several days later), and it'll also be in Conquest's Macmillan anthology next Jan or Feb.[4]

[. . .]

My God this is a pretentious letter. I hope I don't sound irritable anywhere in it – I have the feeling I may. But I'm not at all; I'm just standing up for my rights, but I'd sooner have my rights taken away by you or Mike or Winters than anybody else there is. I'm terribly grateful for your criticism: it is fair, and relevant, and, above all, useful.

I've just read through all this. It's like a summary for a letter, not a letter. I'll write more tomorrow.

Shit, I have just heard that my booklet (The Sense of Movement) is not to come out after all, as the press that was to have done it is defunct.[5] In that case I shall speedily transfer the title to my next book in England – better than The Corridor, after all.

Karl sounds as though he's doing well in Oxford. [. . .] I only met Alvarez once: can't say I like what I have seen of his poetry. (He's at Harvard again, isn't he?)[6]

[. . .]

My motorcycle is acting up like crazy. Gears awful. My own fault for having got a 2nd-hand one. I know it's something of a pose (even more in the U.S. than in England), but what else can one do? One can to a certain extent be what one wants to be, and though doing this may start as a pose (and finish as one, if one's no good), there is a chance of its becoming the real thing.

Sorry if this letter is incoherent in parts: I should have typed it, but it would never have got written if I had.

Love (and also to J.H.)
Thom

1. Dean died in a car accident on 30 September 1955.
2. See TG to Holmstrom, 15 December 1952, n. 8, above.
3. TG won the Levinson Prize for Poetry in November 1955.
4. *New Lines*, ed. Conquest (1956).
5. TG originally planned to publish a pamphlet called 'The Sense of Movement' with Pegasus in the USA, combining new work and a selection of poems from *Fighting Terms*. Pegasus had published Donald Hall's pamphlet, *To the Loud Wind: and Other Poems* (1955), earlier in the year and Hall had suggested that they publish a pamphlet by TG. The publishing costs of Hall's pamphlet, however, bankrupted Pegasus and Hall wrote to TG to apologise. See Hall to TG, 17 November 1955, in TG's papers at the Bancroft Library.
6. Al Alvarez (1929–2019), writer and critic; poetry editor of *The Observer* (1956–66).

TO *Helena Mennie Shire* ALS Aberdeen
Tuesday 27 December 1955

> 2638 West Craig,
> San Antonio,
> Texas.
>
> 27 Dec 55

Dear Mrs Shire,

I think I owe you a letter from about ten months back – perhaps more. This is a compromise between a Christmas and New Years letter, as you'll see by the date. But though I'm so lazy, it doesn't mean I don't think of you often – thinking is easier than writing. – I got that job for which you sent me the letter of recommendation, and I'm teaching for the year at a small and rather bad college down here. I must say I like America – and saying that from Texas is saying a great deal, as it's hardly the best part. [. . .] I came here, bought a motorcycle, and started teaching. At first teaching was unspeakably horrible, nerve-racking, girls weeping when I gave them low marks, correction of essays, etc., but now I have come round to it much more: I seem to get on very well with my pupils, though I find my fellow teachers unbearable. One can get a certain warmth, which I suspect is not entirely vanity, from getting people to think about new things. My most enjoyable class is in 16th century Eng lit, for which I made a somewhat reserved use of C. S. Lewis' Hearty History. He is <u>wrong</u> about the "Drab" poets – admittedly a lot of them <u>were</u> drab, but many weren't, and he can't get away with that statement about the word drab's not being detrimental. It has connotations, Mr Lewis.[1] Have you ever read any of Fulke Greville's religious poems, by the way? His Sonnet C (Down in the depths of mine iniquity) is at least as good as Donne's Hymn to God the Father.

[. . .]

I have ideas for a book of essays, mainly on poetry, but I don't know when I shall get time to make a real start on it before next summer. I have written the basis for three of the essays already – two of them to be published as reviews in the London Magazine, one on Empson's poetry, and the other on Wallace Stevens'.[2] But these are much shorter – especially the Stevens review – than I want them to be finally. The themes of this book to be: (1) plain speech (as in the best Fulke Greville, Stevens etc.) rather than ambiguous speech (Empson, Dylan Thomas) (2) agnosticism as the great malady of the last 100–200 years, as opposed to Christianity and atheism – both of which can lead somewhere. Also, I sent a MS of poems to the Fantasy Press some

time ago, for a new book, to be called The Sense of Movement – also with these themes. I think they will accept it – if not, I'll be free of my contract and can send it to Macmillan's, whom I have reason to believe will accept it.
[. . .]

My motorcycle is wonderful. Did you see The Wild One, which was only shown at Cambridge?[3] Well, motorcycles are considered disreputable over here – only hoodlums ride them – and it is considered ODD for a teacher to ride one. This does much to help me feel at home at the university.

I would enclose some poems, but I can't remember what I sent you last time. Most of my best recent ones are to be in an anthology called New Lines to come out in England next March or April.

[. . .] How are you? – I hope your leg is not giving you trouble again (try a motorcycle) – and I hope work is at its most exciting and you have many potential firsts. The reason why America is difficult to judge is mainly because it is so big. What I mean is this: if there is an Abuse (i.e. a corrupt city administration, a naughty senator, racial discrimination) anywhere in a country the size of England or France, it can be stamped on at once by the central administration in London or Paris. But the administration here is so much more complicated, and it may be that Washington cannot stamp on it either directly or at all. This does not mean that the whole of America is guilty for the abuse, as the whole of England would be guilty for a similar abuse happening in, say, Newcastle or Nottingham. – I didn't understand this till I came over here.

You have never had so disjointed a letter. If you can't understand it, send it back and I will correct and rewrite. I am very influenced by the style of freshman themes. Do write a note, however short.

Much love to everybody,

Thom

---

1. C. S. Lewis, *English Literature in the Sixteenth Century* (1954). Lewis uses 'drab' to describe poets Winters calls 'plain' – Gascoigne, Googe and, in his later work, Greville – all of whom are contrasted with ornate poets like Sidney and Spenser. For TG's preference for Winters's essay 'The 16th Century Lyric in England', first published in *Poetry* in 1939, see TG to Chambers, 9 October 1984, below. Winters prized the 'plain' style and criticised Lewis's book in *The Function of Criticism: Problems and Exercises* (1962), 191–200.

2. TG reviewed Stevens's *Collected Poems* (1955) in *London Magazine* 3, no. 4 (April 1956), 81–4; uncollected.

3. Although *The Wild One* (1953) was banned by the British Board of Film Censors until 1968, some local councils overturned the BBFC's decision and screened the film. In Cambridge it was shown at the Rex Cinema.

1956

ALS Stanford
Monday 16 January 1956

2638 West Craig,
San Antonio, Texas.

16 Jan 56

Dear Mr Winters,

I have been meaning to write to you for the last month or so, and now that I do I seem to have chosen just the wrong time – the end of the semester, with a tower of term papers to demolish standing at my elbow. I enclose a poem I've been working on for quite a long time now: I thought I might as well send it to you so that you know what is being written about you nowadays.[1] I think it too much emphasises just the division (between 'rule and energy') that it is saying should be remedied. Also it is rather too reminiscent of Greville's 'At night, when colors all to black are cast'. I may change 'breed' in the last line to 'raise', which has an interesting double-meaning (perhaps too interesting). However, it is dedicated most respectfully and admiringly to you, and I hope you don't object to what it says. I am willing to alter any misrepresentations!

I see our friends are becoming successful: I was very glad that Cal's poem was in Poetry, and liked it far more than I had at first – most impressive.[2] Don Hall is being claimed as pretty well the Young Poet of the century: his book contains some poems I wish I could have written myself – I find some of his syllabic poems (e.g. Je suis une table) especially good.[3] I have been reading [J. V.] Cunningham's The Quest of the Opal recently: I must write to you about this later – I find it almost as troubling as I do interesting. Well, interesting is a mild word, but what I mean by troubling is what he says about choice ('All choice is error') which seems to me logically true but not true as it works out in life. However, it is the first thing that has given me new ideas in a long time. – I am also wondering about writing a libretto of The Scarlet Letter, an idea that seems more exciting the more I think of it – but I have to find a composer first.

Now to the practical purpose of this letter. First of all I must apologise for suggesting the following so late; I may be too late, in which case I have only myself to blame. I have at length decided that I ought to work for a PhD, not only because it would be good for me, but because it will be necessary if I want to teach in America, which is what I think I want to do. For a subject I want to take modern American poetry, more precisely Wallace Stevens. I may be wrong, but it strikes me that Stevens has been neglected as a PhD subject. I am wondering about one of the following angles: (1) the influence of French poets on him (this would be very difficult, and possibly not fruitful); (2) Stevens as agnostic – showing how his failure (and the failure of much 19th and 20th century thought) can be related to the agnostic attitude; (3) the poem as an "object" – i.e. presented without judgment – e.g. 13 Ways of Looking at a Blackbird and many worse poems – and why such an endeavour must fail. – The second of these ideas attracts me most: however, it may be too large, and the others may be too restricted.

Now you'll see what this is leading up to: I would like to return to Stanford next year and work under you, if you'll have me. I know I would work best under you, especially on the subject of Stevens; and as my engagement to the Texane is now <u>off</u> (your recent poetry fellows have bad luck) I'm free to go where I want.[4] I hope you will not be over-delicate in saying whether you would want me to work under you or not. The enclosed poem is not intended as a bribe.

[. . .]

I must apologise for asking so many things of you just at a time of year when other people must be asking the same things. Don't bother to answer my first letter or the first part of this. My regards to your wife: I have been reading her collected poems in order for the first time – before I had only read a few separately, and not the best ones. I think the last in the book are the finest (and the first one). Has she written any since the Collected Poems?[5]

       Yours,

          Thom.

P.S. Don't bother to return the poem.

---

1. 'To Yvor Winters, 1955' (CP 69–70).
2. Calvin Thomas, Jr., 'For a Girl Killed at Sea', *Poetry* 87, no. 1 (October 1955), 14.
3. Donald Hall, *Exiles and Marriages* (1955).
4. Winters's homophobia meant that TG hid his relationship with MK, referring instead – on this evidence – to a fiancée in Texas. 'He would have been *appalled* at the idea that I was queer,' TG said later (PR 159).
5. Janet Lewis, *Poems 1924–1944* (1950).

Saturday 21 April 1956

> 2638 West Craig,
> San Antonio,
> Texas, U.S.A.
>
> 21 April 56

Dear Tony –

What's this about your leaving the theater? I know what you'd say to me if I said I was going to stop writing, and I say the same to you about this. Of course I don't know the details – but anyway you are far too good an actor to be spared. There are going to be creeps around in any job, and there are probably worse than theatrical creeps in some jobs. So I hope your severance with the theater is not permanent. It would be a very great waste. See?

I was delighted to get your letter – and very excited by the news – and I'll be a better correspondent from now on. And from now on will be a good long time: it seems I'll be at least another year in the U.S. – I'm going back to California next year, with the somewhat fantastic intention of getting a PhD. This is a process of at least 4 years, and I don't know whether they will really renew my visa after 1957 – anyway it's quite likely I might come back for a while in the summer of 57. This is a big reversal from my previous attitude – that I'd get finished once and for all with universities. But teaching is about the only job I could do which would give me the leisure for writing (freelance I could never live on, I write badly when there is the pressure of time), and the university atmosphere in America – at least at Stanford – is not so sterile as that in Cambridge. However, as always, it's still a bit tentative and depends on visas and things. I suppose there's no chance now of your coming over here?

The programme sounds marvellous. I am terribly grateful to all three of you for taking so much trouble over your absent friend.[1] Is it true the BBC records all its programmes? If so, I might be able to have it played over to me when I get back, perhaps.

The choice of poems sounds fine – a good contrast and variation between them. However, I'd much rather you didn't use <u>Light Sleeping</u> (which, incidentally, has been broadcast before): an enormous amount of apparatus to say something very simple, and a good deal of it rather clumsily written. Instead you could use <u>The Corridor</u> or else this new one I enclose, <u>The Allegory of the Wolf Boy</u>. I have been working on this for about 3 months, and I'm still too much in the middle of it to be able to judge it coolly. It is about queerness – or rather a certain type of queerness – but I think it is acceptable, because the allegory applies equally to any person who lives one life and fails to connect it to the life he really wants. However, do what you choose about this and The Corridor.

Now, At the Back of the North Wind. Simpler than it appears. The title and a few bits and pieces are from a book by a Victorian, George Macdonald, that I read when I was 8, but this was only a starting point and not specially relevant. The boy in the poem is growing up: up to now he has only known sensory things, which are in a continual flux – a flux with positive implications: summer and winter, the smells, the water freezing, cold and warmth, the North Wind, the hay. But he is suddenly presented with something he does not understand – a negative power of annihilation. The change of wind is his realisation of the big negative force that involves not the death implicit in change but annihilation. The force cannot change because it is abstract and abstractions cannot change. The force is contained (somewhat arbitrarily I think now) in the East Wind – the sort of wind that goes through Cambridge all winter.

Next question: I am exactly TWENTY SIX. I also have intercourse with piglets.

[. . .]

I have been reading an incredible book that I understand has just been published in England – "Dylan Thomas in America" by a scoundrel called Brinnan.[2] It is extremely shocking from several points of view: both the subject and that it should have been published. I can understand how he wrote it – to get it off his chest – but not how he should have published it. It is very badly written, very self-contradictory, and Brinnan was quite obviously in love with Thomas. But very interesting. Read it, if you have time. – I think, about Thomas, that I perhaps overstressed his badness in my Empson review. He did after all write a handful (a small one) of poems better than Empson has ever written; but I think the comparison between their types of badness a just one. Kathleen Raine sent a very odd letter, in defence of Empson, to the London Mag.[3]

I have not written much this past year but even so have enough poems for another book of about the same length as Fighting Terms. The Fantasy Press is now defunct, so it is going the rounds of the big publishers, but it may be too short for their liking.

Write and tell me how the programme goes, when you have time; also about what you are doing or want to do; also about everybody. My much love to Sasha[4] and J.H. Did you see Troylus & Cressida?[5] Was it good? What do you think of the latest smart names, Beckett & Brecht? Has Sasha ever found the rich man who was going to finance her magazine?

Little Thom.

Mike sends his love.

1. 'Thom Gunn: A Selection from his Recent Poetry' was broadcast on the BBC Third Programme on 11 May 1956. Sasha Moorsom produced the programme; White and Holmstrom read the poems.
2. John Malcolm Brinnin, *Dylan Thomas in America* (1956).
3. Kathleen Raine, 'Letter to the Editor', *London Magazine* 3, no. 3 (March 1956), 66–7. TG replied in the April 1956 issue, 64–5.
4. Sasha Moorsom, later Sasha Young (1931–93), novelist and broadcaster, read English at Cambridge and acted opposite White in the ADC's *Cyrano de Bergerac*. Thom had a lot of affection for Sasha; see TG to Holmstrom, 20 January 1986, below.
5. White played Diomedes in Tyrone Guthrie's modern-dress production of *Troilus and Cressida* at the Old Vic (1956).

TO *Tony White*   ALS Tulsa

c. May 1956[1]

[2638 West Craig,
San Antonio,
Texas.]

Dear Tony,

I understand from the BBC that you used the Wolf Boy poem. Of which I'm glad, hope you liked it.

Well, now things of horrible urgency are happening in Texas, melodrama unfitting to two quiet lives – which is why I am writing to you. Mike is being "investigated" for homosexuality. So far as we can tell, it started in this way: some ponce in the airforce (whom we don't know) was being investigated for dismissal from the services, and, having seen us in some queer bars around here, gratuitously brought up Mike's name, adding some equally gratuitous untrue accusations. The danger involved in all this is that Mike may be courtmartialed, and may even find it difficult to have his passport renewed. They searched our apartment, but luckily we were one step ahead of them, having been tipped off, and had sent a lot of incriminating letters out of San Antonio. But they did find some letters from two friends of Mike's whom he had known when he was at college (Rutgers) here in about 1950. There were several letters from one friend (queer) called Joe, which showed very definitely that he, Joe, was queer. There was also one letter from the other friend (Jerry), who is not queer: this letter had overtones which could be interpreted in several ways, however, and Mike once forwarded it to me when I was at Stanford, writing at the top – "Baby, read this and return." (You will see why I am telling you all this, in a minute.) – Mike managed to explain Joe by saying that Joe was frankly queer and very extravagant in his expressions to everybody, hetero or homo. However, when they asked about M's inscription at the top of the letter from Jerry, he said that the "Baby" was his, Mike's, girlfriend. They asked him who she was, and he said she was English, that he had met her at Cambridge, but he didn't choose to give her name. They said that they would need to know her name because they "might need to contact her", but luckily did not press him for her name just then.

Now this may seem all hysterical, but it isn't, because Mike could get into awful trouble if they can prove that he is. (I don't know about myself; but it matters less, because I am not in service.) Mike has been holding his own against them wonderfully so far, but there is the difficulty of the girlfriend, which may be very important.

Would it be possible, if they contacted her, for Sasha to say to them that she had gone with Mike at Cambridge? I think it unlikely that they would speak to her (the American Airforce Intelligence in England, that is), but it is possible, and we have to be prepared. If she confirmed that she had been M's Girl Friend, they would undoubtedly be satisfied with that, and not try to corroborate from anybody else in England.

Anyway, could you go and see Sasha as soon as you can, and ask her if she could bear to do this. (I would write to her, but I only know her BBC address: perhaps you could show this letter to her.) I know it is awkward for her, but she can't lose anything by it, and this could become very important.

If they approach her, she would say:

(1) She had gone with Mike at Cambridge
(2) She had heard him mention Joe as a very nice, homosexual actor friend of his at Rutgers (whose homosexuality he "tolerated")
(3) He had once forwarded Jerry's letter to her as an interesting document, to show how ~~nearly people can sound homosexual without being homosexual;~~ INVOLVED + ODD THE SITUATION WAS; she read it, but remembers nothing about it except that she returned it to Mike
(4) Neither Mike nor I are homosexuals
(5) Refuse to say anything else at all.

If Sasha can play her part in this worldwide investigation into the morals of the young, we shall be very grateful. No, seriously, very grateful indeed.

It looks quite possible, if things go badly, that I may be back in England this year after all! But I don't think things will go badly. We will beat them.
[...]
Much love and much gratitude to you both, and also much regrets for disturbing you all round like this,

Thom

1. 'May 1956' was written on the letter by White, and this date has been corroborated through internal evidence.

TO *Charles Monteith*[1] ALS Faber

Saturday 26 May 1956

2638 WEST CRAIG,
SAN ANTONIO,
TEXAS, U.S.A.

26 May 56

Dear Sir,

I enclose the manuscript of a book of poems called The Sense of Movement. I hope you will be kind enough to consider it for publication. I enclose a cheque for five shillings, which ought to cover the cost of its return if you do not want to use it.

I am twenty-six years old, English, and teaching this year in the United States. I have published poems and articles in various English and American magazines; an anthology of undergraduate poetry, Poetry from Cambridge (Fortune Press, 1953); and a book of my own poetry, Fighting Terms (Fantasy Press, 1954). A short programme of my poems was recently broadcast over the B.B.C. Third Programme.[2]

Yours faithfully,
Thom Gunn

1. Charles Monteith (1921–95), publisher and editor. See Glossary of Names.
2. See TG to White, 21 April 1956, above.

TO *Charles Monteith*   ALS Faber
Tuesday 10 July 1956

2638 West Craig,
San Antonio,
Texas, U.S.A.

10 July 56

Dear Mr Monteith,

I have just received your letter and am very happy at the news that you want to publish my book. I shall be most proud to be published by Faber and Faber. Thank you very much for accepting it.

The terms you mention (10% of the published price) are fine, and it is perfectly all right about the date of publication.[1] I don't know how long it will be before you can send me the contract, but it would be simplest if you could send it to me at this address before the end of this month, as I shall be leaving Texas about August 3rd to travel for a couple of months. However, if necessary, I can send you a forwarding address.

Yours sincerely,
Thom Gunn

1. *SM* was published on 7 June 1957.

TO *Tony White*   ALS (aerogramme) Tulsa
Friday 20 July 1956

2638 West Craig,
San Antonio, Texas.
(do not write to Texas any more,
as I'm leaving this address.)

20 July 56

Dear Tony –

I thought I'd drop you a note to tell you we're leaving Texas in a couple of weeks. The investigation is as yet unresolved, but Mike went to see the Director of Personnel, a sympathetic colonel, the other day, who said he would try and force them to bring it to a conclusion by the time M is due out (which is in about 10 days). So it seems probable everything will go well, from lack of evidence. Thank you and Sasha both very much. It was good knowing we could count on you even though we didn't make you actually do anything for us. If Mike does get out on time we're going for a big tour of the country in his car (I sold my motorcycle today; just as well, perhaps) New Orleans to New York; then three weeks in NY, while he stays with his parents; then New York to California.

The two most sensational pieces of news are (1) About 3 weeks ago we came home about 12 one night, and found Karl, Jane, Rory, and Rory's brother Alek sitting on the lawn.[1] It was really enormously nice seeing them again. Mike and Karl got on well for the first time ever, which made me very happy. I hadn't been too sure what a good idea it was for Karl and Jane to marry, but they seemed happy together – and anyway, what goddamned business is it of mine who marries who. Still, you'll be seeing them all very soon, and they'll be able to give you eyewitness accounts of what San Antonio is like and tell you more than I can get in this letter. (2) I've got a book of poems accepted by Faber (& Faber), which they'll be bringing out early next year. It contains all the poems that were on your programme, and about 20 others. A very gentlemanly, third-personish compliment from TSE was included in their letter of acceptance: 'Mr Eliot sends you his personal congratulations on the poems, and wants me to tell you he enjoyed reading them.' I must be slipping.

Karl mentioned that you may be joining the police force. With evident disapproval. But I must say it does not seem a bad choice. Opportunity for much action, and certain great layers of panache possible, I'd think. I still think it an awful pity for you to give up acting, but perhaps it hurts more than it's worth for me to say just that. It may be that I am being far more unfaithful to myself by teaching. I still find it enough effort, for there to be no danger of its milky easing-down, but I do wonder about how I'll find it after a few years. Oh well, I can always change my job. At present it keeps me greatly on my toes. America is not the honey-baited trap (hamburger-baited?) Peter Wood said it would be: it's more difficult getting poems published here, and there is much energy evident. The real problem is one of being married. I don't say being married in a camp way, because after all living with Mike is equivalent in most ways to actually being married. We are really pretty happy together, and we both intend it to be for good. But doing this – living with someone, or marrying – is the most crippling choice. Here above all the choice – living alone or else living with someone – involves, either way, such a huge renunciation of different things. Living alone gives one, on the one hand, an absolute freedom, an enormous independence, the power to change oneself constantly, there is nothing to hold one back, and on the other hand the feeling that one is missing what is one of the chief values – the power to completely know, almost to be, someone else. Living with someone just reverses it. There is this fixity. I am terrified to think that already if I were suddenly left on my own for a few months I would be completely unable to use that restlessness I value. Well, I don't actually <u>think</u> this – but it is a possibility, and I'm determined to find some way of preventing its being a possibility. The thing to aim at is for both Mike and me to be completely individual and still have the other thing as well. Poor Tony, I'm always speaking about this and it must bore you.

I hope to write more in the coming year than I have in the last year. Only 3 poems! Too little. So long as I am able to write I suppose I don't have too much to worry about. What is behind my writing is the same thing as is behind the independence business.

If you buy the Times Educational Supplement for August 3rd you will find a profile of me in it. I suspect it will be pretty bad, as they appear to have got all the information in it from my father, who knows less about me than most people.[2]

Have you seen Alexander the Great? It really is the panachiest ever except for some rather weak things near the end where they have him more or less losing his mind. But I've seen it twice, and intend to see it several more times: I hope you agree with me – there are some tremendous things in it. What do you think of Burton, by the way? You will know a lot about him from having worked with him. I have been much impressed by him since I saw his Hamlet, and his Coriolanus struck me as being just what I should wish it.[3]

I stopped teaching a week ago, and am trying to catch up with some reading – and I have a lot to catch up with. First I am rereading Le Diable et le Bon Dieu, which I like as much as I ever did – though its resemblances to Shaw never struck me so much before. – Is this Colin Wilson any good? He sounds partly good, partly a bit phoney, but I judge entirely by reviews. He emphasises the <u>will</u> – which is the important thing, after all, and which is what distinguishes the existentialist from the Romantic. That would be the fine thing, for a man to be entirely will, with no emotions left. It leads to death, but a fine death. – I look forward to reading Camus' new book,[4] which I ought to be able to get in New York.

[. . .]

Much love. Do write. Tell me everything. Long live the Values.

Love,

Thom

Will send you my Californian address when I get there in September.

1. Jane Miller (née Collet; 1932–), teacher and writer; Rory McEwen (1932–82), artist and musician.

2. 'Four Young Poets – IV: Thom Gunn', *Times Educational Supplement* (3 August 1956), 995. 'He is a tough thinker writing for intellectual toughs like himself,' writes the anonymous author. 'His rough-hewn lines display a dynamic energy, unmatched by his contemporaries; violence abounds, blood flows freely, and strong men – for whom he betrays a Nietzschian admiration – stalk through his pages.'
3. Richard Burton played the leading roles in *Coriolanus* and *Hamlet* at the Old Vic (1953–4) and starred in *Alexander the Great*, dir. Robert Rossen (1956). In the 1956 production of *Othello* at the Old Vic, White played Cassio: Burton and John Neville played Othello and Iago on alternate nights.
4. Albert Camus, *La Chute* (1956).

TO *John Lehmann*[1]   ALS (aerogramme) Texas
Monday 3 September 1956

New England, care of Donald Hall,
right now – will send an address
when I reach California at the end of the month

[39 Paul Revere Road,
Lexington, Mass., U.S.A.]

3 Sept 56

Dear John –
    Thank you very much for the cheque. I had already paid the contributors different proportions of it (according to how much got printed by each) in anticipation before I left San Antonio. So that's finished.[2] I'll send you the official receipt in a few days.
    [. . .]
    I met one young poet in NY whom I liked very much, personally and poetically. Remembering that you always urge new promising people to send up to the London Magazine, I have done so (urged him). Name is Ralph Pomeroy.[3] You may not like his work, of course, but there were some poems that I thought made it. Curiously like Hart Crane in the way he can mix extremes of good & bad writing, sometimes in the same poem. So you'll probably be getting some things from him, within the next few weeks – I believe Isherwood knows him – or knew him a few years ago – slightly, anyway.
    [. . .]
    I start off to the West Coast shortly, so don't answer this. I suspect Mike & I have managed our time so badly that we shan't be able to visit L.A. &

Isherwood, but we're sure to go down there some time before the end of the year. I want Mike & him to meet very much – made for each other! (Well . . .)
[. . .]
I am getting old, I was 27 last week. – By the way, next time I write anything for you I am going to send you a new contributor's note for myself. (E.g. Is 27, has been twice arrested, likes motorcycles and Elvis Presley, etc.) Has Elvis Presley hit England yet? He used to be a hustler in New Orleans: I have this from his fellow hustlers.

      Love,

          Thom

P.S. The Halls send their affection and regards.

1. John Lehmann (1907–87), poet and editor. See Glossary of Names.
2. TG edited the supplement 'Young American Poets 1956' for *London Magazine* 3, no. 8 (August 1956), 21–35. Its contributors were Philip Booth, Edgar Bowers, Donald Hall, Joseph Langland, James Merrill, Robert Pack, Adrienne Rich, Louis Simpson and James Wright.
3. Ralph Pomeroy (1926–99), poet and friend of TG.

TO *Tony White*   ALS (aerogramme) Tulsa
Friday 12 October 1956

                  Stanford University,
               STANFORD, Calif, U.S.A.

                        12 Oct 56

Dear Tony –
    It's high time I answered your letter of two months ago – for which many thanks. The boring travelling and everything is now more or less died away, and at last I have a bit of time. – Yes, the witch hunt seems to have died: no more has been heard of it. I understand that it is quite exceptional to beat the investigation in this way.[1] I met an airman who had been under investigation TWELVE months for taking the Daily Worker, & then only just managed an honorable discharge. – We had an enjoyable and highly eventful trip. The first day we smashed the car at a small place called Opelousas, Louisiana. We were arrested for careless driving, and were told we had to pay a bail of $100. However the sheriff was amiably corrupt (his French was also pretty corrupt), and $13 for himself disposed of it. So we drove the wreckage to New Orleans, where we had to stay a week waiting for it to be repaired. The second day we were there, we were arrested again, this time completely unjustified, for

Vagrancy by loitering. We were not even loitering. The two most ignorant cops I have ever seen, they thought we were hoodlums. However, it was fairly interesting: we were stood up against the wall (this was in Bourbon Street at 1 a.m.) and frisked, put into the paddy waggon, booked in at the police station (where Mike managed to dispose of a highly incriminating document I had had in my wallet), and would have had to spend a night in the cells if I hadn't luckily happened to have had the unused bail from the previous day to use as bail for this. Naturally, the judge next day dismissed the case. We made much protests, and I seriously thought of suing the cops if this wouldn't have taken so much time and money. – In New Orleans I met many male whores (merely met, that is) who claimed that Elvis Presley had been one of them in his poorer days. When the car was repaired we rocketed to New York, where Mike went to stay with his parents, while I stayed in New York. Everything happened there: I had my pocket picked, I made various interesting but inconclusive experiments with the more extreme evidences of perversion, I saw Jayne Mansfield (Marilyn Monroe's rival) from a few yards' distance, I met a few semi-celebrities – or would-be ones – who wrote. Then I spent a week in New England (where you wrote me) – this was dull: I met about 600 New England poets, all looking alike, all married, all sitting in their large flat gardens sucking their pipes, with their children & dogs, and complimenting each other on each other's work. But I had a very good recording done of me reading,[2] & heard a marvelous record of Pound reading the Bloody Sestina to the accompaniment of drums. This was marked Not to be played, because it was so fascist. You would have loved it.[3]

Then I came back to New York, and Mike's mother had got ill at the thought of him going off again so soon – psychosomatically, I'm sure, but the results were so genuine that he had to stay. So I flew across (this is terrific – have you ever flown), and Mike is not coming across till Christmas. Strangely enough, I don't find teaching here too uninteresting; apart from work, I keep much alone, have started writing again – I hope to have a few poems to send you in a month or two's time.

[. . .]

I saw a few plays and things in New York, the most interesting being Cat on a Hot Tin Roof, which strikes me as the best play by Williams. The incredible thing about him is that he is pretentious as hell, but the pretentiousness (usually) gets buried under the fineness of the main part. I should be more explicit, but haven't room to be.

[. . .]

Lehmann has asked me to be on the "Advisory Editorial Board" of the LM. This involves no pay, and I think it's just because he wants to have one of the younger generation displayed on his side rather than against him, as most of them are. However, I'm on no side, being for me rather than for the Thirties or the Fifties, and I've said yes mainly because I now have a good opportunity to push people I think are good. I made about 6 suggestions to him for making the LM better (doubt if he'll do anything about them). Can you think of anybody good – whom you either know personally or don't know – whom I can try to push? Has Holmstrom, for instance, written any poems recently? Have you got anything suitable? Could you write some vigorous article pulling down a few idols?

I must stop now. Hope you can decipher this. You must check me if being Faber makes me get respectable – I rely on you to do that. My love to Sasha, J.H., P.W., Karl, Jane.

Thom

1. The investigation into MK was later brought to trial and he was given a discharge under honourable conditions.
2. This refers to a reading TG gave at Harvard on 5 September.
3. Pound recorded 'Sestina: Altaforte' – nicknamed the 'Bloody Sestina' – for the Harvard Vocarium in May 1939.

TO *Robert Conquest*   ALS (aerogramme) Elizabeth Neece Conquest
Sunday 14–Thursday 18 October 1956

> Department of English,
> Stanford University,
> STANFORD,
> California.
>
> 14 Oct 56

Dear Bob,

Many thanks for your letter, which I am exactly two months late in answering. There have just been so many events that I haven't had time. – I saw the Spender review, and am still trying to make out what he means by Cambridge seduced by Oxford.¹ He doesn't seriously think that I have slept with Elizabeth [Jennings], does he? – My profile, incidentally, is mainly lies, except where it quotes from my answers to the questionnaire sent me, or paraphrases them.² I am not, unfortunately, an expert swimmer. I can barely splash once, breast-stroke, across a pool. Oh well, it is publicity. (This to be said in an airy tone.)
   [. . .]

I can't remember what made me break off, but here I am still without a decent pen and some awful kind of New Statesman ink (joke). I saw the review of New Lines in the London Mag – very peculiar – who is John Press, anyway?[3] [. . .]

The only thing that has happened to me here, apart from the sudden feeling that I am getting very old (or perhaps this is only a lasting hangover from drinking continuously in New York, which is a city I have fallen for in a big way incidentally) is that I have started writing furiously, many hours a day – in a way I haven't done for about 18 months. It is funny how I have bursts like this, almost as if I need to gestate at elephant-length before I can write anything. I have many ideas, am trying new forms, have several things in process – though God knows when they'll be finished. One is in terza rima – something I never dared before in case it turned out Empsonic. One is in syllabics. One is a canzone (i.e. same rhyme scheme as some of early Pound, c. 1908) about flagellation.[4] Though I was just reading Wallace Stevens' The Snow Man again, and then read what I'd written, and honest it makes me despair. Beside it I seem like dead wood. Do you know that poem? I'm beginning to think it has even more than Sunday Morning: it has all a poem can have. A single word like the just transforms the poem in the last line.

[. . .]

About Socialism: [. . .] I am a socialist, but such a vague and lazy one that I don't have much right to call myself one. I most feel one when I read mewling letters by Nancy Mitford or Evelyn Waugh or when I come in contact with the Pitt Club at Cambridge or with the Daily Telegraph or with the gracious livers – I must reread Sartre. I learnt a lot from him but perhaps I've got beyond him now. I think he is accurate in his definition of the situation, but slightly inadequate when it comes to metaphysicking. (There is one highly 'suspect' part of one of his nonfiction works where he says that one's decisions are finally based on instinct: something hardly true of his own heroes – Goetz, for instance.) I think he is most convincing in his plays, where the statements are less gnomic and the ideas are shown in action. Huis Clos and Les Mouches only give the situation with not much remedy, though they are both good plays; but Le Diable et le Bon Dieu and Morts sans Sépulture, two very successful plays, show the people doing things, and finding ways out. In spite of Iris Murdock's book about him, I think it's by the plays that he stands or falls.[5] (Christ what clichés.)

[. . .]

Much beneficence,
Thom

1. For Spender's review of *New Lines*, see 'New and Healthy', *New Statesman and Nation* (7 July 1956), 20–1.
2. See TG to White, 20 July 1956, n. 2, above.
3. Press reviewed *New Lines* in *London Magazine* 3, no. 10 (October 1956), 71–7.
4. TG refers to 'The Annihilation of Nothing' (terza rima), 'Vox Humana' (syllabics) and an early version of 'The Beaters' called 'Canzon: The Flagellants' (canzone). 'Vox Humana' and 'The Beaters' were included in *SM*, and a much-revised version of 'The Annihilation of Nothing' was included in *MSC*. TG later dropped 'The Beaters' from *CP*.
5. Sartre was an important influence on TG's early poems about existentialist heroes. 'I was very influenced by Sartre,' TG remarked, 'and in particular a short book called *Existentialism and Humanism*, and I certainly kept close to that text the year or two I was writing *The Sense of Movement*' (JH 36). For Murdoch's book about Sartre, see TG to White, 24 January 1955, n. 2, above.

TO *Tony White*   ALS Tulsa
Wednesday 12 December 1956

Dept. of English,
Stanford University,
Stanford,
Calif., U.S.A.

12 Dec 56

Dear Tony,

It was terrific hearing from you, and I should have answered earlier. But today I experience perhaps the only advantage of academic life – the Hols. [. . .] I get the feeling that writing becomes more and more difficult once one has got over thirty, and one's ideas and enthusiasms have begun to form a definite pattern, so one must try and make some sort of start before then. [. . .] For myself, every now and again I have a tremendous idea for a play – I work it out act by act, scene by scene – it seems an obvious success – then I start writing the first scene and I'm faced once more by the inescapable fact that I can't write dialogue. And somehow a verse play is even more impossible – unless it's to be one of those fey things that Yeats or Wallace Stevens wrote, and I have no wish to do those: I simply don't know what sort of verse, if any, can go on a modern stage.

[. . .]

Funny but the same thing has been happening to me – reading, I mean. I'd hardly read anything outside poetry for eighteen months. The library here is enormous, and gets a lot of books from England. Thanks for telling me about the Giuliano book.[1] It "strengthened" me (Arnold-wise, as poetry is supposed to do). He is the real Stendhalian – one that I would hardly have believed possible nowadays. And the book was mostly very well-written, though it fell to pieces at the end, and some of his similes are somewhat pretentious. I want to write a longish poem in two parts, which would be called 'In Our Time' if Hemingway hadn't already used it: the first part about Giuliano, the second about a Californian bandit who was shot in 1951 robbing supermarkets dressed up as the Man from Mars.[2] It's a perfect contrast: the outlaw who is still a part of his society beside the outlaw who is produced by his society but does not understand it; violence with an end beside violence with no end but immediate gratification; abstract (in the best sense) beside the particular; symbol (the belt buckle) beside fetish (the uniform of the Man from Mars, with a helmet topped by antennae and skull & crossbones). One day I may write this!

I also read Antony West's last book, which struck me as something of a disappointment: it was worth reading, certainly, but why does he have to apply his very perceptive mind to such conventional novelish material?[3] My big find is William Golding, who strikes me as the best English novelist since the war, 'Lord of the Flies' and 'The Inheritors', both tremendous, though I don't share some of the implied beliefs. But he has an enormously fresh outlook, is tremendously skillful, and he writes about the doubleness of violence – the way that the energy-side and the sinister side are mixed up and inextricable. Read him if you haven't already.

I have been having long self-questionings about just what I'm doing here and why I'm doing it. I'm half-teacher & half-student – the teaching I like unexpectedly much: it keeps me on my toes and is interesting in itself, and I never know whether a lesson is going to be a good one or not (it has also had the side-product of making me much quicker of speech); but the student-work just kills me – it completely bores me and it is completely useless – I know I could do it well if I tried, but I simply feel that I've got past the age when I <u>want</u> to try at it – I feel an enormous resistance against reading books that I don't feel like reading. I'll stick with it for the rest of the year, because I'm under contract for the teaching part, but next summer will be the occasion for a big Choice: continuing to teach or becoming a postman. The only advantage teaching has, as I said, (and it is an enormous one, as I see the more I look at it) is the huge vacations. But I don't know whether even these are worth it. I don't think I'll grow into a fuddy-duddy, but being surrounded by fuddy-duddies for the rest of my life won't do much good for my health.

I'll be back in England about June 27th – 30th. Will leave probably about the beginning of September. That means I'll be there all July and August. You must be in England part of that time. Can you be?

I enclose some poems. The Vox Humana one is fairly good for me, I think. It is in syllabics (i.e. same number of syllables to a line, but varying stress-pattern).

It's absurd we can't see more of each other. You are almost the only person I've ever really got ideas from, and I hardly ever write to you. You must come and live over here. One day I'll write you my best poem, if I'm still writing. (I must say, I constantly think that every poem is going to be my last one. The effort is like putting up a large apartment-house, which at any moment during the construction may fall down. This sounds pretty pretentious, but I sometimes feel like that.)

Mike comes over (for good) in a couple of weeks. I'm soon moving to a new apartment. He and I gradually civilize each other, but sometimes I get the feeling we're neither of us fit for the company of others even yet. Very unstable young men.

Poetry in England – to borrow Holmstrom's figure – is constipated, isn't it? I got 3 anthologies recently, that were filled with light verse, incompetent verse, pompous verse, and vague verse. The fact that one's forced to say Philip Larkin is the best poet of our generation is quite shaking: he's a nice quiet poet, but of no particular importance after all. Mander, if he had gone on writing, would have been able to knock them all back into their college blazers – or librarian's cushions.

– Have you read Valéry's poem L'ebauche d'un serpent? It has everything.

    Love,
        write soon,
          Thom

1. Gavin Maxwell, God Protect Me from My Friends: The Story of Salvatore Giuliano (1956). Giuliano (1922–50) was a notorious Sicilian bandit.
2. Forest Ray Colson (1925–51), dubbed the 'Man from Mars', was a bandit who staged five successful hold-ups of supermarkets in San Gabriel, California, dressed in tight-fitting black clothes, motorcycle boots, a leather American football helmet, goggles, gas mask and hood. He was shot and killed on 12 October 1951.
3. West, Heritage (1955).

1957

Monday 29 July 1957

as from: 32 Somerset Road,
London SW19
England

29 July 57

Dear Don –

Got your letter with poems on Saturday, and your other note today. Glad you got the book – I've had nine reviews so far – only two against, one in Isis, one in the Listener – the rest damn nice: the nicest, because liking it in spite of big and intelligent reservations, from Alvarez; one enormously comic one from Betjeman, who obviously doesn't like it but is damn fair; one vague and blurby and meaningless but highly appreciative from Muir, one detailed and badly written and jolly d. from TLS; one from Conquest who rather charmingly suggests that I am probably Yeats' successor.[1] I have also, somewhat unexpectedly, been making money hand over prick from the poems on the radio, a reading I did for the British Council (which for some reason is far better than the Harvard reading), and a lot of reviews I have done. When I went to get a copy in Bowes & Bowes (Cambridge) for the reading, the man there said: "Ah yes, I remember Thom Gunn. He's got in with the right boys in London." However, I get, as I got after <u>Fighting Terms</u>, the awful final feeling that a phase is over, that I've got to go on to a new set of subjects or at least a new way of looking at them, that I can't risk self-repetition. You know what I mean because from your letter that's what you've been going through as well. And somehow the book itself, now it's complete, is terribly <u>another thing</u> from me, separate, and when I am praised or attacked it is as though the attack and praise was for another person. Poor old Gunn, he's such a sensitive young poet.

I went to 2 literary parties – one given by Lehmann, one by the Spectator. At Lehmann's I met Elizabeth J, Wain (whom I unexpectedly found I like terrifically), David Gascoyne (no reaction), George Barker's first wife, George Barker's second wife, George Barker, Roy Fuller (good, nice, honest man),

David Hughes, and people whose names I forget. George Barker was damned sweet to me, which made me feel rather bad, because I was just about to write a very unfavorable review of his Collected P for the Spectator. Afterwards I toyed with the idea of returning the book or writing a dishonest review, but finally wrote as I'd originally intended to and the review will come out this week: after all, what I say is true and he's a grown man so ought to be able to stand it.[2]

England really is a bit too much: I mean I kept saying before I left in June that I was going to hate this summer but I was secretly expecting it would be rather marvelous, Matey, returning in triumph to the ways of my youth. However it's terribly neurotic making: the first week was really nightmarish – London so damned familiar but so damned constricting – my friends all grown old-looking – I just slept a lot and went to an American movie every day (always my 2 escapes). It is a bit better now, but I'm still just biding my time, waiting for when I go, and only just able to bear it. I find it difficult to know why I feel this complicated dislike of England, which is absolutely unreasoned. I think it may be that I never became at all a satisfactory person till I was pretty old, and associate the unsatisfactory side of myself with here. Certainly I feel a sort of inscapish and entirely motivated depression just by seeing certain streets, buildings, landscapes – a feeling of "Oh God, have I got to go through that again", though I'm fucked if I know what "that" may be.[3] However, I am still far from being a case for the psychiatrist.

[. . .] There have been various delays in the application for the visa so I have only just sent it in today – I am praying I shall make it by Sept 5th for the ticket I've got on the Queen Elizabeth – if I don't I may have to wait an extra 2 months or so over here. I have definitely decided, if they let me, to become a Citizen of your Country – quite as much to dissociate myself from England as to associate myself with America.[4] So I shall become an American Poet and rival of you, Louis Simpson, and Merrill.

I met Simpson, by the way, in New York, the afternoon before I sailed, and liked him enormously. I sent him a copy of my book, to Rome, and strongly suspect it'll never reach him. Still, a gesture. Quel panache, Gunn.

[. . .]

The Byrnies is about (or supposed to be about) the beginning of Thought: where symbols become concepts – the process being: perception of object > perception of associations > symbol of those associations > concept. I want to write one parallel about the opposite process, where object becomes fetish. This will be equally difficult, I think.

This is a most inadequate letter. I have decided the way to make money is to do reviews: wrecks one's prose style, perhaps one's judgment too, but

85

means you don't have to work too hard. When I have time (and balance) I want to write a sort of ABC of Reading for 16–18 year olds: it's needed, God knows, but I don't know whether it wd be possible to frame it as a text book.

I have written nothing, never can when I'm on the move so constantly, and don't expect to till I've been back in the States for at least a month.

        Write.

        Love,

            Thom.

1. John Betjeman, 'Round the Poets' Gallery', *Daily Telegraph* (7 June 1957), 12; anonymous, 'Wrenching Values', *Times Literary Supplement* (14 June 1957), 360; Robert Conquest, 'A New Major Poet?', *The Spectator* (14 June 1957), 786–7; A. Alvarez, 'Signs of Poetic Life', *The Observer* (16 June 1957), 19; anonymous review in *The Listener* (4 July 1957), 25; Peter Ferguson, 'New Poems', *Isis* (13 July 1957), 29, 31; Edwin Muir, 'Time and Place', *New Statesman and Nation* (13 July 1957), 59–60.
2. TG reviewed George Barker, *Collected Poems 1930–1955* (1957), in *The Spectator* (2 August 1957), 167; uncollected.
3. A reference to Gerald Manley Hopkins's idea of 'inscape': the unique essence of something that differentiates it from everything else.
4. TG never did become a US citizen.

TO *Tony White*   ALS (aerogramme) Tulsa
Monday 25 November 1957

English Dept,
Stanford U.; S.; C.; USA.

25 Nov 57

Dear Tony –

It was good as always to hear from you, especially in answer to what I remember as being a terribly inadequate letter of mine. I hope my next will contain a few poems: I am writing, though am also being more dissatisfied than usual with what I do. I feel I could write a poem for the gods right now if only I could find the right vehicle, i.e. "fable." This is partly the trouble – feeling like writing so seldom coincides with finding the best subject, which is why one seldom writes at one's best. I have several "intellectual" subjects in mind – Odysseus with the dead; acting; jazz; a few epigrams on French writers – but these do not engage me wholly.[1] What I <u>really</u> want, I suppose, is to write about handsome hoodlums, but (a) that wd probably end up as a self-indulgence, and (b) there is nothing much I have to say about them.

It would be nice to write a poem about Nazis, but I don't know what angle to take on them – I mean, just reading about them and never having known them, it'd be literary fantasy (but then perhaps Odysseus is as well). I'd adore some rich, wonderful, aged, disinterested man to give me $3000 a year for 3 years, so I could travel all over everywhere and get in all the new impressions before it's too late for them. I have a romantic superstition that I'll be finished by 30.

I saw 2 more reviews of me, one of which depressed me, one delighted. The first was by Hough, in Encounter, and though I know he's really wrong, it chastens me a good deal, for some reason.[2] If one gets too old to see these things (as he is) then why live? The other was an old one by Dannie Abse, and the phrase I delighted in was "he has a barely concealed viciousness."[3] Highly ambiguous.

Have been reading much. Trevor Roper, which was a weakly written book (Last Days of It), full of historical clichés,[4] but which whetted my appetite for more, so please send me a list of books (bibliography for The Decline of Generals). (I lost the one title you did give me.) A few novels, not worth mentioning. David Gascoyne, who appears to me outrageously bad, nothing to say, no way to say it. Roy Fuller, who was clean and honest in a bad time, but hardly anything more: his pessimism is so simplified and all embracing that it is not very interesting. Auden's The Orators, which I'd never read – it is like a queer scrapbook, strange and quite powerful in a Cocteau-ish way. Also his Age of Anxiety, which is full of good things, but so goddamn weak in its message. Though really, when I try to think of poets who say anything both valid (for me) and (Christ this pen) well-put, I can count them on the fingers of one hand: Baudelaire, bits of Hart Crane, many bits of Shakespeare, and I can't really think of anybody else who doesn't merely express beautifully things I could never agree with (e.g. Donne, Wallace Stevens, Keats, Rimbaud).

Trouble with pen broke about 10 trains of thought.

When I last saw Johnnie he was trying to contact you, he said – this was just before you were leaving for Ireland. Your adventures there (i.e. Holy Ireland) sound great – I wish I'd come: I mean a brother of Rommel's tank commander and then an American movie star – in a way the two sum up all the kinds of people it is desirable to know.

Mike's Chalk Garden is to start this Friday: next he does Huis Clos, and says he has a very good cast for it.[5] John Chapple (now a Captain) visits us for 3 days in January, on his way from Singapore.[6] Donald Davie was surprisingly nice: too exclusively literary in interests to be that good, but good in his narrow way. He gave me a Swedish anthology, in which 3 of my poems were translated.[7] I am also, I believe, to be translated into Czech[8] (with inserted communist concepts?)

God, it would be so good to go out pub crawling with you tonight – hundreds of black and tans and intelligent conversation. Mike excepted, the people in the immediate vicinity have nothing – all Ph.D. mentalities. If I had the money I'd go into the city (S.F.), only an hour away, every night, but I don't. There at least there are a few possible people who are people, and in a town there is always a chance of running into somebody interesting. – I'm still swaying this way and that about whether to teach or not: the fact that you hinted perhaps I ought to go through with it has something to do with my still wondering. It's great to think I might make some money steadily in about 4 years time, and I'm not one to sneer at steady money, adoring all forms of cash as I do, but it's a hell of a time to wait, having to work my heart out at a thesis, being bored with the people and the work, living in a subtopian wen, and with far less time for writing than I need. On the other hand, the ghastly thoughts of only 2 weeks holiday a year, and having to worry about money even more than I do now, etc. As I say, some financier with regrets about culture should supply me with money.

Write soon, Tone, Man.

Yours in Loot,

Th.

1. The Odysseus poem became 'The Book of the Dead' (*CP* 104–5); there is no identifiable poem about 'acting' in TG's notebooks from this period; the jazz poem became the unpublished 'Trio', held in the TG collection at the Hornbake Library, University of Maryland; and the epigrams became 'Readings in French' (*CP* 98).

2. Graham Hough, 'Landmarks and Turbulence', *Encounter* 9, no. 5 (November 1957), 83–4, 86–7.

3. Abse, 'New Poetry', *Time and Tide* 38, no. 32 (August 1957), 1000.

4. Hugh Trevor-Roper, *The Last Days of Hitler* (1947). TG possibly makes a casual reference to E. Nesbit's *Five Children and It* (1902).

5. MK was a director for the Comedia Repertory Company, a theatre group founded by Peter Kump (1937–95), a noted chef and cooking teacher.

6. Sir John Lyon Chapple (1931–), British Army officer and friend of TG and MK from Trinity College, Cambridge. Chapple went on to become Chief of the General Staff of the British Army (1988–92) and Governor of Gibraltar (1993–5).

7. *Åtta Engelska Poeter*, ed. Petter Bergman and Göran Printz-Påhlson (1957). The anthology includes translations of TG's 'For a Birthday' (by Printz-Påhlson) and 'Lerici' and 'The Corridor' (by Bergman).

8. Jiří Konůpek (1919–68) translated TG's poems 'On the Move', 'The Nature of an Action', 'St Martin and the Beggar', 'Human Condition' and 'The Corridor' in the Czech journal *Světová literatura* 4 (1958), 107–11.

Wednesday 4 December 1957

English Dept.,
Stanford University,
Stanford, Calif.

4 Dec 57

Dear John,

Here is a real letter, for a change, instead of a niggling note. I'm delighted you are taking the poems. For The Byrnies how about adding the following:

"Gloss: byrnie – a shirt or coat of chainmail
nicker – water-monster"

I hate notes, but you are right: before I read Beowulf I wouldn't have known what they meant. I also enclose a slightly revised From the Highest Camp (high camp?) – only a full stop added and a couple of words changed in 11th and 12th lines, but I think the alteration makes it a shade less didactic.

Actually, I'm not too satisfied (as you probably gather) with the work I've been doing in this last year. These poems, for instance, are I think well-executed, and even say something worth saying, but there is a certain primness about them that distresses me. What I want to do, what I try to do, is to come somewhere between the rational-statement poem of, say W. Stevens, or E.A. Robinson, or Hardy, and the near-sexual energy of Crane or Thomas. The energy plus the rationality. I find I come temperamentally between the two, as well. But I find constantly that I slip off to one side or the other – becoming either prim or repulsive. It's something worth trying for, I think, but hard and unsatisfactory to get there – as all poetry is, I suppose; if one is ever lucky enough to get IT, the unique combination which is one's own, as I may have (once or twice at the most), one can't stay there – the poem is finished, it is outside of oneself, one has to be on one's way, and it is only a landmark which looks as separate from oneself as somebody else's poem. One of my problems is how to get the important sexual business into poetry, I mean one can't write of motorcycles and hoodlums etc all the time, and there are other problems in dealing with the actual mechanics of sex. It isn't that I don't dare, but that I don't have the technique yet, I think.

Oh well, I now have 4 clear weeks with no travelling, no teaching, nothing involved. Perhaps I can hammer out something this time.

(The man who did most nearly to what I want to do was Baudelaire of course. There is a certain amount of 19th century junk in him, but even that he manages often to turn to good effect.)

[. . .]

About reviewing. I am really terribly sorry about the delay in that last one.[1] Yes, I do want to do more reviewing for you, but I find books of criticism awfully difficult to do. Most of them are so uninteresting that I take years reading them and making up my mind about them. What I really want to do is poetry (I suppose everybody does). I know you have a very good regular reviewer for that, [John Holloway], but if something ever turns up that he doesn't want to deal with for any reason (like the Empson and Stevens which I did last year) I'd be delighted to do it, and would do it quickly.

There's a chance I may leave here next year as I may be offered a year's teaching at Berkeley, 40 miles from here. Great advantages that I'd be earning a decent salary which wd be princely beside what I get here, it is a good university (as good as this one), would give me a little extra free time, and best of all is only a few miles across the bay from San Francisco. You would adore SF by the way (or have you been there?) – if you like Rome better than anywhere else in Europe then you'd like San Francisco better than anywhere else in America.

Love,

Thom

1. TG reviewed John Bayley, *The Romantic Survival: A Study in Poetic Evolution* (1957) in *London Magazine* 4, no. 9 (September 1957), 76–9.

TO *Tony White*   ALS Tulsa
Sunday 15 December 1957

Stanford

15 Dec 57

Dear Tone:

I'll type out some poems to enclose with this tomorrow – I'm not sure what, but I'd like your comments on whatever I send – or rather your diagnosis. What I've been doing lately strikes me as insufferably <u>prim</u>: but I don't quite know why, or how to get out of the state. <u>The Book of the Dead</u>, for example, has something lacking – I approve of what it says, and though it might have been said better with a more modern myth, I think it does it all right. But it lacks, somehow, verbal – and emotional – electricity. So inspire me, matey.

I read the Camus interview in the Observer the other day and found it quite exciting, I'm getting an aunt to send me a copy.[1] I like the remark about honor, etc. And I get the feeling that a lot of it makes clear several things that have been fuzzy in my mind, so I look forward to studying it. (Have you read L'Exil et La Royaume, by the way? No copy of it has yet come my way.) I suddenly realized something – by way of a single word – the other night: the direction in which I ought to go, as far as writing is concerned. The word being Conduct (the Stance is part of this!). Something Alvarez said in his review of me has been hanging in my mind for the last 6 months, viz. that my first bk dealt with doubt, and my second with choice.[2] So I have asked myself what about what comes after? Of course, conduct is an easily spoken word – and hard to deal with: if one looks on it as a concept succeeding the concept of choice, it is so particular (it comes out of a general situation, but is something particular in itself) that I don't know whether I'll ever be able to do anything adequate on it. And of course, also the concept is a somewhat artificial one, being that conduct is determined by the type of choice.

I'm finding it difficult as hell to write just now – I need chiefly to get away alone to get a lot of things clear with myself, but there's no prospect of that in years, I should think, what with lack of money, and other things. So I'll try to make out as it is. Best of all, I suppose, would be frequent conversations with you, which I miss all the more acutely as they are still so fresh in my mind and I can see how vividly you help me make things clear and also push me forward to other things. One thing: I'll have to leave Stanford in the summer – suburban surroundings, a lot of work for too little money, boredom, and – mainly – the fact I've been here so long, these are too much for me. Two possibilities for the summer and after – either a job, any job, in San Francisco, or else teaching full time on a good salary at Berkeley (whr Barton was, and is still remembered!)[3] Apparently they are "interested" in me there, and have made one very tentative approach, to which I responded with enthusiasm. It is almost a part of San Francisco – or rather it is a separate town divided from SF only by a huge bay and a long bridge, and thus is as much part of it as Strood is of Rochester, if you're familiar with Kent. – My longing to live in a city again gets greater and greater all the time: partly because it is a place of choice, and the possibilities of choice are perpetually renewed (this is getting close to jargon) – whereas in the country one is confined very much in an already performed choice, out of which there's no getting. I go up on a spree every now and again – last night was one – but knowing I'm there only for the day makes me set too much store by it, I try to cram in too much, I exaggerate the pace. I love this part of California, though: and I'm sure you'd agree with me. There is just enough "tradition" (Spanish, Chinese, pioneer) for it to have depth, and little enough for it not to be oppressive. And it is a violent and surprising town too, in some ways. If only I cd get hold of it in a poem: but every time I try to, the effect is of a Whitmanian catalogue – every detail is so impressive that I can't bear to leave it out.

[. . .]

I've been reading Hart Crane's Letters, a fascinating book.[4] I also find it rather frightening – seeing such resemblances between himself and me – and I don't mean just queerness, either. Queerness is not a disease, but the way society looks on it is liable to cause reactions in one that are, at least, destructive. The lack of rest can become an inability to stay in one place, to keep up one pursuit, to think about one subject. There's nothing wrong with the first, but the other two caused Crane to practically stop writing after the age of 30 – the last 2 yrs of his life – which, I take it, was the main reason he killed himself.

This is a highly egotistical letter, so I'd better stop before there's any more of it. Has [Peter] Wood got married yet? What are you doing now (still vile French farces)? Have you seen The Kidders, which sounds interesting? I am reading Rimbaud, thoroughly for the first time. [. . .]

Write as soon as you get a chance.

        Love,

            Thom

> My love, regards, remembrances
> (where suitable) to Wood, Karl,
> J.H., your parents, Sasha.
>   Irene was on television (much
> praised too) the other day, but I
> didn't hear about it till afterward.[5]

Gloss on the poems:
> The Book of the Dead is the title of the particular book in the
> Odyssey whr all this happens. The last thing Tiresias says is – 'you
> will leave Ithaca and finally land alone in a strange country and walk
> until you come to a man in a field with a winnowing fan, and you
> will say, "Friend, lend me your winnowing-fan," and work beside
> him.'
> The epigrams are not to be taken too seriously.[6]

1. Jean Bloch-Michel, 'Camus: The Lie and the Quarter-Truth', *The Observer* (17 November 1957), 16. TG pasted the article into his scrapbook.
2. 'The tenseness of his early poems was that of a man actually in doubt; in his latest volume he is, instead, continually writing about choice,' Alvarez wrote. 'His troubles

seem to be relatively at a distance, so his work is cooler, less involved.' See 'Signs of Poetic Life', *The Observer* (16 June 1957), 19. TG pasted the review into his scrapbook.

3. John Barton (1928–2018) knew TG and White at Cambridge, where he directed plays for the ADC and the Marlowe Society. He directed more than fifty productions for the Royal Shakespeare Company, with whom he was affiliated for more than five decades.

4. *The Letters of Hart Crane, 1916–1932*, ed. Weber (1952).

5. Irene Worth (1916–2002), an American actor known for her work on the London stage, likely met White at the Old Vic. Opposite White, she starred in the Marlowe Society's recording of *Troilus and Cressida* (1961); in the same series, she played Volumnia in *Coriolanus* (1960), with White in the title role.

6. 'Readings in French' (*CP* 98).

1958

TO *Tony White*   ALS Tulsa
c. January 1958[1]

[Apt. 4, 143 Alma,
Palo Alto, Calif.]

Dear Tony –

I'd just sent my last letter when yours arrived – most welcome, as always, and many thanks for the book-list especially. I have so far only had time to read the Fitzgibbon, which is excellent, having just the virtues so painfully absent in Trevor Roper: i.e. his generalizations emerge from the narration rather than being moralizing paragraphs thrust into it.[2] It is often very well written – the last few paragraphs of the book, especially, have a terrific restrained rightness. Claus von Stauffenberg is now one of my heroes, too. I have started a poem about him which may or may not turn out. – It is the perfect subject, too, for a modern tragedy – the great noble figure (no Willy Loman[3]), magnanimous, the courage, the plot, even perhaps hubris – having favored the unknown of Nazism in the first place as being preferable to the known evils of Communism & the W. Republic. Though perhaps the tragedy has been already written: I haven't read the original play, but I saw the film of The Devil's General twice last week, and it is great. Also [Curd] Jurgens is great. Hope to see it a third time before it leaves this area: God knows when I'll get another chance.

30 Jan

[. . .]

Did I tell you I'm going to one of Barton's alma matrae, Berkeley, next year? Hard work, but money. Perhaps I'll be able to save enough to really go out on a limb the following year.

No I haven't written a poem on loot, though I'm going to some day. Meanwhile here are some recent attempts. I feel very dissatisfied at everything I've done since I returned from England – somehow the attitude behind the poems is wrong. In Sta. Maria del Popolo is the best I've done in some time, I think, I hope. But I can't make up my mind whether the 2 middle stanzas help or confuse the shape of it. I send you a short & a long version – the only difference is that one has extra stanzas. (The painting, incidentally, is a terrific one.[4] Reproduced if you're unfamiliar with it, in the 3rd vol of Skira's Italian Painting. Not possible to buy, but can be looked at furtively in book shops.) Is it dishonest or obscure to write about paintings, I wonder? You implied reservations about it when I showed you Before the Carnival. I think perhaps it's all right if one does not make merely an allusion, but explains what the painting looks like (& means). Black Jackets is supposed to be a brother-piece to The Byrnies, which I showed you, & which is I think to be in the February London Maggers. The Byrnies showed objects taking on meaning, this shows – or tries to show – objects losing meaning. The last 2 lines come from a newspaper description of a body. – The other poem is balladiquesque. Slight, I think.

Hough's review in Encounter was slimy. Can't remember why – oh yes, he said I had a fine "technique" but I shouldn't try to state anything because in this century we cannot have any clear concepts (philosophy was I think the word) – presumably because the Great Chain of Being got broken some time since the Elizabethans and one may only describe images now – he holds Ted Hughes up for me to imitate.[5] Actually he puts it a good deal more persuasively than this, but I no longer feel sensitive about it. I mean there isn't time to worry that much. You should just see what the Glasgow Gazette & Bristol Courier wrote about me – let alone Isis!

Am reading Le Cid again, to my great happiness. Plan to read Cinna next, which I remember as being even better.[6]

There is nobody, but nobody, round here, who completely understands the values. Well, there is one who comes close, but he is married, which takes a good deal of freedom from his ideas. Continually the reservations. I suppose I ought to be, embody, the values, so that I don't make demands on you to keep jogging me. I do need the jogging, though.

                    Yours,
                Thom
[. . .]

1. Date written in by White.
2. Constantine FitzGibbon's *The Shirt of Nessus* (1956) is the main source of TG's poems 'Claus von Stauffenberg' (*CP* 111) and 'Innocence' (*CP* 100).
3. Loman is the common-man protagonist of Arthur Miller's *Death of a Salesman* (1949).
4. Caravaggio, *The Conversion of St Paul* (1601), painted for the Cerasi Chapel of the church of Santa Maria del Popolo, Rome.
5. For Hughes, see TG to him, 24 April 1980, below.

6. Pierre Corneille (1606–84), French tragedian. The figure of the Corneillean hero was an important influence on TG's early poems. *SM* begins with an epigraph from *Cinna*: 'Je le suis, je veux l'être' ('I am that, I choose to be that').

TO *Thomas Parkinson*[1]   ALS (aerogramme) Texas
Sunday 6 April 1958

Stanford

6 April 58

Dear Tom Parkinson,

[. . .]

I never knew you were going to live in Hampstead. I lived there between the ages of 8 and 18, went to school there, played on the Heath – it's nice to think of you there. I hope you went tobogganing – by all accounts you've picked the worst winter since 1947, and <u>that</u> was memorable. Here, we just have floods, but they are pretty bad too.

I'm enormously pleased to be teaching at Berkeley next year. Have just been reading Watt's book, which is <u>brilliant</u>.[2] Yes, I've met Davie twice, and like him very much indeed, we are to do a reading together in the city next month for Mrs Legs Diamant.[3]

Have you come across the Daily Sketch yet? (the world's most unscrupulous newspaper) My father is the editor of it.

My love to your wife and daughter (if she remembers me).

Yours,

Thom

1. Thomas F. Parkinson (1920–92), professor of English at UC Berkeley and an authority on W. B. Yeats. Parkinson was instrumental in TG's appointment at Berkeley.
2. Ian Watt, *The Rise of the Novel: Studies in Defoe, Richardson and Fielding* (1957). Watt taught at Berkeley (1952–62).
3. TG and Donald Davie read together at the San Francisco State University Poetry Center on 18 May 1958. Ruth Witt-Diamant (1899–1989), professor at San Francisco State University, founded the SFSU Poetry Center in 1954 and was its director until 1961.

TO *Tony White*   ALS Tulsa
Tuesday 8 April 1958

English Dept.,
Stanford University,
Stanford, Calif., U.S.A.

8 April 58

Dear Tony –
  [. . .]
I was enormously pleased about Karl.[1] He has sent me a pamphlet to
review, which I shall do.[2] Though need for money has made me accept 2 other
reviews as well, and this dull grub-street occupation takes all my time, so I
have no time for writing poems. I wrote a poem on Claus Von Stauffenberg,
which I sent to Ld. Altrincham (did I tell you he asked me for a short poem for
a poetic number of his magazine), but it was too long – or too bad – and he
sent it back.[3] When I got it back, I was glad, seeing how bad it was – and
will rewrite it one of these days: at least it has a lovely last stanza. Will send
it to you when it's worth sending. – I agree with what you say about Von
Stauffenberg's religion. At the same time it is very difficult for people like you
and me to understand the justification religion can have for somebody who's
been brought up in it: it can be – especially Catholicism – a source of values,
even though I find it hard to see the necessity for a mystical justification of
them. I am really very proud of being born when I was – I'm convinced that
our generation was the first that could grow up <u>unselfconsciously</u> atheist:
for the others the rejection of God was something so terribly deliberate.
(Bradlaugh-ish).
  The Nazis are a great subject for a whole set of poems. And yet, though the
subject fascinates me, I'm not sure how far I understand them. Complete lack
of any contact (except for 3 weeks) with Germany. – Was glancing through a
book about Camus by a man called Thody (you may have read it), where there
is a very interesting part describing the Lettres à un ami allemande, which I
haven't read.[4] There, C. is writing, apparently, to a Nazi, showing how both
their attitudes start from similar assumptions. – Sometimes it seems to me
that Nazism, and its spread, are related to the sort of contagious attraction
of various sadists I have known. I mean for their practices, not their physical
attraction. It is almost as though the Nazi occupation of Europe was like
some huge sadist beating party, to which more and more people kept on being
invited, until it got completely out of control. But this would only explain
the <u>followers</u>: it doesn't explain the leaders, people like Hitler and Himmler.

Can one put down the leaders (most of them) as fools? I doubt it. At the same time, can one attribute to them the intellectual daring of completely surrealist or nihilist motives, of a complete negation of humane values? Not this, either. And if they are not (1) either compulsively or fashionably sadistic, (2) mere greedy fools, or (3) existentialists more daring than have ever existed before, then what are they? One's forced back on the possibility of the image of people who are sentimentally patriotic, and just happen to have greater technical resources and less scruples than their like ever before.

I feel the last paragraph was a bit confusing. Of course, there were probably different motives for most of them, but what I can't make out was the principal and most common motive. Besides Nazism, Soviet Communism is almost banally easy to understand.

You put enormously well – and much better than I had said it – what I meant about 'conduct'. You're right about the Existentialistic impasse: I think it is Camus' triumph that he realized so early that it is an impasse.

Delighted you like The Feel of Hands. Your interpretation of it is exactly right. (You say "impersonal, almost like engines" – I once used the word 'engines' in this sense, in a poem I never finished. Incredible.) And your other comments were most helpful. The only other poem of those I sent you which I like is the Paul one. I really think it gains from dropping the middle 2 stanzas: while they elucidate explicitly they confuse a reader by making the poem top-heavy – they make the proportions wrong, so one wouldn't understand the emphasis.[5] Though I feel regrets at dropping them, because I like the writing – which is as you say Merlin-esque.[6] I don't know whether I made the last stanza of the poem clear: what I'm trying to say is – there are two gestures possible in Life: (1) holding your praying hands clenched over your eyes (involving all the suggestions of cutting off perceptions, of holding oneself in, of the defensive posture), and (2) Paul's attitude in the picture. At the same time I didn't want to be cheap at the expense of the old women in the church: after a certain age you cannot physically make the large gestures – especially if you are poor, ill, etc etc.

[. . .]

I am to have an American edition of Fighting Terms, and have been revising it as honestly and thoroughly as I can. Of course, about ½ the poems should be thrown out, but I've only dropped 2. Will send you a copy when it comes out. Sorry this letter is so short and so slovenly.

Much love,
Thom

1. Miller became literary editor of *The Spectator* in 1958.

2. TG reviewed Geoffrey Moore's *Poetry To-day* (1958) in *The Spectator* (23 May 1958), 661.
3. Lord Altrincham [John Grigg] (1924–2001) edited the *National and English Review* (1954–60).
4. Philip Thody, *Albert Camus: A Study of His Work* (1957).
5. The 'Paul' poem is 'In Santa Maria del Popolo' (*CP* 93–4). An earlier version of the poem had six stanzas.
6. See 'Merlin in the Cave: He Speculates without a Book' (*CP* 81–4).

TO *Robert Conquest*   ALS (aerogramme) Elizabeth Neece Conquest
Monday 26 May 1958

[Stanford]

26 May 58

Dear Bob –

I owe you at least 2 letters, and many thanks for Anode or Two,[1] which I am very happy to have, as it contains some of your best poems. 'Guided Missiles Exp. Range' has grown on me; for some reason I didn't take much notice of it in your book,[2] God knows why, because it's a fine poem – strong and tight and really big. The phrase "loveless haste", for instance, has a rightness that is at the same time exact description and enormously suggestive – though in a controlled manner. (Similarly the word "rigour" in the line before it.) This is surely one of the main differences between the Boys and the sensible writers: that the boys cultivate phrases with infinite suggestiveness (and consequently little or none), while the others control suggestions – however many there may be – to the relevant ones. I first learnt this in reading Donne at Cambridge.

Glad you liked the Moore review.[3] When I said I found his book frightening, I wasn't making a gesture: I do find it frightening – and no less so because I happen to be one of the chaps he likes. And one of the awful things about his book is the fact that he is so sheerly unintelligent. I mean, even John Lehmann would have done a far better job. Yes, I was being a bit gratuitous about the photographs: but hope no one took those remarks too seriously. I do find pictures of poets enormously funny, though, including those of myself. I would have said 'Gunn trying hard to look like a hoodlum in repose' – only one can't draw attention to oneself that much.

[. . .] Have written very little lately – i.e. nothing. Have been reading Rimbaud, who really was extraordinarily good. The trouble is, it looks so easy when he does it, so everybody gets tempted to do the same – but anybody who wants to write poetry in which there is a systematic disordering of the senses must dare to systematically disorder his senses in life (let alone have talent). Rimbaud dared to – Hilary Corke, Christopher Logue, Ginsberg don't, though the last one may pretend to. Poetry is after all a kind of action (just as thought is), and only a deranged man can write great deranged poetry like Rimbaud's, just as only somebody who has learnt life-saving can perform the action of saving someone from drowning. This may seem suspiciously romantic, but I don't think it is: Baudelaire and Donne and Valéry wrote poetry that is consistent with their lives. But one doesn't have to know anything about their lives to see this. Of course, I don't want to write deranged poetry – even great deranged poetry. For Logue, etc., I suppose it is just a way of not being James Kirkup, whom I suppose he has the sense to despise.

Very funny about Ginsberg and Corso. (Also about the George Barker incident.) Actually, they don't trouble me any more than Dame Edith [Sitwell] does, – what troubles me is that they should be taken seriously. [. . .] The thing about free verse, surely, is that only about 8 or 10 people have written good free verse in English – most of them, for some reason, Americans. It's a valid and difficult form, though in an odd way very restrictive as to tone – but it is not incantatory prose. Stevens' The Snow Man has a very subtle (but discernible) rhythm; Howl (apart from being nonsense) is a mere catalogue, as bad as bad Whitman (who is always bad, anyway). I must say England has gone to the dogs – first Suez, now falling for Ginsberg.

Nice of you to say I'm better than Osborne. I found his play quite impressive, though.[4] I haven't seen any of the magazines you speak of, Epoch, etc – or else I've forgotten them. The quarterlies over here I find on the whole great tombstones of boredom – articles like The Symbolic Use of the Color Mauve in Faulkner's Late Novels, safe academic verse, stories very deliberately in stream of consciousness Technique. I saw the Sewanee review of you, however, and was very pleased about it.

One reason I delayed answering your last was that I wanted to mention St Martin's Press to the chaps at Faber, but the only two I've corresponded with are somewhere in New England now, and I can't get at them. I'm extremely pleased that S. M's P is doing Larkin, indifferent about Wain. I just give up Wain (a) because he's not as good as he tells everybody, and (b) because, as Ian Watt said to me, how can one man sincerely hold all those attitudes at the same time?

I must get the Kinsella.[5] Davie, also, told me how good it was. [. . .]

Thanks again for the book.

Yours,

Thom

[. . .]

1. Conquest's *Anode or Two: Some Poems* (1957) was a limited edition roneograph of science fiction poems produced for the 15th World Science Fiction Convention held in London in September 1957. TG's copy can be found at the Bancroft Library.
2. Conquest, *Poems* (1955).
3. See TG to White, 8 April 1958. n. 2, above.
4. John Osborne, *Look Back in Anger* (1956).
5. Thomas Kinsella, *Another September* (1958).

TO *Tony White*   ALS Tulsa
Thursday 17 July 1958

> Till Sept 1: Apartment 4,
> 143 ALMA St.,
> PALO ALTO,
> California, U.S.A.

> After that: c/o English Dept.,
> University of California,
> BERKELEY,
> California, U.S.A.

> 17 July 58

Dear Tony –

I owe you a letter, and also one that is of a decent length. I enclose a couple of poems, and since I've just typed out these copies and what I want to say about them is still fresh in my mind, I'll start with them. Neither of them satisfies me. The Von Stauffenberg poem is still in the state in which Altrincham refused it. I want to keep it in some form, not only because of the subject, but because in some parts of it I have come near to what I wanted to do. I wanted to write a poem statue-like without being frigid (like a Cornelian hero).[1] Something composed and powerful. The first stanza troubles me: I was trying in it to get the atmosphere at the beginning of the Devils General movie – winter, deprivation, as a symbol of fear. Should I perhaps substitute with exposition of Von S. – and if so, what? The one or 2 people I have shown the poem to have never heard of him and say they want to know more of the background to indicate that the attempt on Hitler was not merely that of one wolf on another. At the same time (a) I surely show that he is different from Hitler (and the Nazis) in the poem, and what more can I do here than assert and hope my assertion will be believed, and (b) just <u>what</u> background would it be a good idea to introduce here? So do you think I should cut the first stanza, rewrite along the same lines as it stands, or rewrite in a completely different way?

Do you think any other stanzas could be cut out? Should I get rid of the rather 30's-ish imperative at the end of stanza 5? What do you think of the last stanza? Would "<u>snow</u>" in the last stanza be meaningless if there were no first stanza?

The other poem I merely send because I happened to write it about 6 weeks ago. I think I may scrap it altogether. Too damn literary, too abstract, too damn many antecedents. And I'm not sure it says anything at all clearly.[2]

I'm in a state with writing in which I can't work on a <u>line</u> without getting restless, in which I find it impossible to write down anything that has any connection with life. There is a shocking smell of paper, if you see what I mean. I somehow get the feeling that it may be 2 or 3 years before I get into the swing again: I feel strangely impotent (you remember J.H.'s "My muse was constipate"?) and perhaps the best thing would be to finish off Von Stauffenberg and the Odysseus poem[3] and anything else around, and stop writing until I find something really jogging my elbow.

I was delighted to hear about the reception of John's play.[4] (Lehmann wrote me about how he liked it, not knowing that I know John.) Surely Eve's husband must have an <u>extremely</u> delicate stomach? (I enclose reviews. Thank you.) Peter W is a cunt to have acted like that.

Look, if you are able, at a review Frank Kermode wrote of me in the last issue of "Listen" (it can be got at Better Books in Charing X Rd).[5] The most marvellous review anybody has ever received of anything, and from a man I admire. The disturbing thing about being called a potentially "great" poet is that it gives one a hell of a lot to live up to, and for an impotent-constipate like me it is sort of frustrating. Makes me feel I ought to die quick in case I let him down, you know.

I came back last week from a month in New York, which was wonderful, and revelatory as it always is. I learn more about people and myself in NY than anywhere else. There was one guy you would have liked, or at least found very interesting – a huge blond motorcyclist (also on holiday) from Milwaukee, of German descent (very obviously), who turned out to be a masochist. I saw various plays, the only one I really went crazy for was West Side Story, a musical about gang warfare in New York that was based fairly intelligently on Romeo & Juliet, and was very moving at times. The score was enormously, beautifully slushy, just like Puccini. Also saw The Music Man, one of the most nauseating, homey, comfy musicals I have seen since The King & I. Also a play by a man called [Edwin Justus] Mayer – Children of Darkness, based in a rather remote and indirect way on Jonathan Wild the Great. The play was too epigrammatic and Shavianesque for my liking, but the direction was awfully good, quite a famous man called Quintero did it. Also saw The Visit, which I believe is going to London – with the Lunts, and my old friends [Peter] Woodthorpe and [Eric] Porter. (Needless to say, I did not go back to greet said old friends after the performance.) Woodthorpe was billed just below the Lunts, and was really rather bad, Porter was fine, though, I also, to my surprise, found myself liking Lynn Fontanne a good deal. A little like a slim Edith Evans in some ways, but terribly impressive for the part. Unfortunately I met Woodthorpe anyway, by mistake.

I move thirty miles north in a couple of weeks, by which time I shall be 29. In a way I'm sorry I took the job at Berkeley – but I need the money too badly. I'm 7/8 decided to give up universities altogether next summer. Certainly nothing will persuade me to finish up my PhD. It has become an endurance test in which I am not interested and for which I am underpaid. I got offered a job in a tough-queer bar in New York, which I would have taken if I hadn't already signed this damn contract.

Congratulations on your garage job. After this, I return to my yearly plea for you to return to acting. It's my business not only as a friend but because I'm part of the public you would benefit by acting for them. The explanations you gave me for quitting are still not adequate (tough talk, this). I mean, say you had to work with all the ponces in London if you acted and with your ten best friends if you stay in the garage, you should still act. My giving up teaching would not be a parallel to your giving up acting – my giving up writing would be. I'm not pretending you're an Olivier (yet, anyway), but your talent is far too big to be just stopped suddenly. And your talent is also so much a part of your character that the feeling of waste you'll get in a few years' time (if you don't go back to the theatre) is going to be far greater than the irritations of the nasty theatre background. In a way, I think quitting could be looked on as an oblique form of cowardice, in that you didn't want to wait long enough to fail – fail either from your own fault or not. But it's a risk (failing) one should invite. Stauffenberg invited it: he would have been nothing if he hadn't. One is living only when one has put oneself in a position where it is possible to fail, and the larger the possibility of failure the greater one is.

I feel that you haven't really finally made up your mind against acting and I hope you'll think about it again and discuss it with somebody intelligent like Irene or J.H.

Don't take this wrong, anyway.

Expect you're in Ireland right now. Hope you are having a good time.
        Yours,
                Thom

1. For Corneillean heroes see TG to White, *c*. January 1958, n. 5, above.
2. Possibly the unpublished 'Trucker' (Hornbake), a poem about conduct which TG rewrote substantially as 'A Trucker' (*CP* 126).
3. 'The Book of the Dead' (CP 104–5).
4. Roger Gellert [John Holmstrom], *Quaint Honour* (1958).
5. Frank Kermode, 'The Problem of Pleasure', *Listen* 2, no. 4 (Spring 1958), 14–19.

TO *Randolph Stow*[1]   ALS (aerogramme) Daniel Brown
Wednesday 8 October 1958

                                                [Apt. 2,
                                        3216 Telegraph Avenue,
                                                OAKLAND]
                                            California, U.S.A

                                                8 October 58

Dear Randolph Stow,
    I have been so long in answering your letter that you must have thought I was not going to answer it.[2] It took about 6 weeks to reach me, as it happened, and found me in the middle of moving from one part of California to another.
    I was very happy to get it, anyway. It is a great feeling when you see that you have, after all, made a complete communication to someone else who is not already a friend, even if he is a continent or so away. This sounds slushy, of course, but you must know for yourself that it is true.
    I am particularly pleased that you should like 'On the Move' and 'Market at Turk' (this last is liked by very few people apart from myself). Yes, you are right about "the generation": one mustn't speak about it – look what's happened recently with Angry Young Men and the Beat Generation – but nevertheless it's there: a particular and unprecedented kind of exuberant godlesslessness, a kind of despair that is not only liveable in but lived in. You are dead right about Sartre, who was, I guess, my main "influence" for 4 or 5 years, though I'd make a reservation here and there about him now. The rest of the influence (with these poems anyway) is from having had a motorcycle for a while myself and from having friends who ride them. The mere riding of one is, in a strange way, a sort of controlled irresponsibility.

I like the names bodgies and leatheries, that you mentioned. I met an Australian the other day who told me that "bodgies" is equivalent to "hoods" over here, but he couldn't tell me anything about leatheries. Are these specifically bike-boys, or just anybody in leather jacket and boots?

There is another (another!) poem that I wrote to do with this in this month's issue of Poetry (Chicago). Black Jackets is the name. If you can't get at the magazine and are interested I could send you a copy. I think it may be the last I will write on this particular subject – it is already getting repetitive.

I have only read one of your poems, as your book[3] is not available over here – and that was in some book club periodical or something rather a long time ago, so I can only say that I remember it as being very direct and impressive. It strikes me I could probably send for a copy of your book to England. I share your enthusiasm for Ted Hughes, though he can sometimes do appalling things: at his best he has a fine explicit vigor – a vigor that is almost absent from English and American poetry right now.

Thank you again for your letter, which gave me great pleasure. I hope that you'll forgive me for taking so long to answer it, and also that I'll hear from you again.

     Sincerely,
       Thom Gunn

1. Randolph Stow (1935–2010), Australian novelist and poet.
2. Stow's letter is lost.
3. Stow, *Act One: Poems* (1957).

TO *Tony White*　　　　　　　　　　　　　　　ALS Tulsa
Wednesday 26 November 1958[1]

Apt 2,
3216 Telegraph Avenue,
Oakland,
California, U.S.A.

November 26

Dear Wolfe,[2]

The trouble with sending your friends such long and interesting letters is that your friends will have to wait, sometimes for months, before they have time to follow your own high standard. But really that was about the best letter I've ever had sent to me. This won't come up to its standard, but I imagine will be written in several sessions, as I've got a lot to say.

Many thanks for that <u>great</u> Motorcyclista (I haven't checked this spelling with it) emblem. A fine piece of loot, that. I haven't stuck it on anywhere because I never wear my motorcycle cap except when I am writing poetry drunk (my equivalent to Balzac's cowl), and I don't know how I could get it on my leather jacket. So I keep it loose and fondle it often. What is so endearing about it is that the silver motorcycle looks almost like a flower. I wear my German belt, by the way, constantly. It is admired, envied, and despised – but more admired and envied than despised.

I think it must have been about 2 months ago I last wrote to you. I'm living in Oakland now, anyway, which is a few miles from Berkeley, where I work. Thus I avoid the highly-charged self-conscious atmosphere of Berkeley itself (e.g. coffee shops full of boys in grotesquely thick sweaters and girls in black stockings, all dropping names like Kierkegaard, etc – though Zen Buddhism is the selling thing right now). Oakland itself is a port and shabby transit town: beautifully free of any characteristics except shabbiness and impermanence. Gertrude Stein and Isadora Duncan once lived here, but you certainly wouldn't know it. It reminds me of Chatham, but without the occasionally pretty houses you find in Chatham.

I see Mike at weekends, and occasionally he surprises me by climbing in through the window on week-nights. He is finishing up at Palo Alto right now, is coming to stay with me for about 10 days, and then goes to New York – either for a couple of months, for a year or two, or for ever. Depending on whether he manages to impress anybody that he is a good director. He <u>is</u> a good director, actually – I think you'd agree if you had seen his last few productions – but New York is probably an even more difficult place than London to prove this. If he can't stick it, he'll come back here; if things go well with him, I'll join him there. Our plans, you see, are as hazy as ever.

Don't apologize about the Von Stauffenberg poem – if you and Karl thought it ready to be published then I was happy for it to be published. That was one of the reasons for sending it to you: to see if you thought it finished. I'm interested what you say about the 2nd stanza (i.e. it could be unclear who 'They' are). The only way to find out whether I ought to alter it is to take a poll of friends. I've recently got down to regular writing in a way I haven't in over a year. Many irons in the fire, some of which will probably never get even warm. The only two in anything like an interesting stage I enclose. Warning: these are in an extremely unfinished state, especially the poem to you.[3] More unfinished than any I have shown to you before, probably. I'd like any comments you may have on them: <u>Loot</u> is in sapphics, a form I am not sure I like at all, now I've started on it. I have made big variations on the sapphic form because English must be kept up,[4] but at present it has so many anapaests that it is very jumpy and sing-song. So I shall cut down on them as much as I can. I have come to dislike the anapaestic line (or even the line with several anapaests in it): there is so little you can do with it – the stresses are too heavy and the un-stresses too light, so it becomes inflexible and like Tom Moore.[5] Slips by you altogether. – I hope I have not seemed too supercilious about your powers of pig hunting. (How do you think of Megalopolis for the title of my next book, 6 years ahead?)

The other poem is about San Francisco.[6] Both poems are really rather "minor", I'm afraid. I increasingly feel that perhaps my good time is over, and I am destined to be an Edwin Muir for the rest of my life. I'm not sure that it matters if I am, really: there's plenty of things to be done, places to be travelled.

Talking of travel, I've applied for the S. Maugham Award. Doubt if I'll get it, but if I do, I plan to spend a few months in Germany. I need quite badly to be reminded of my Northernness – I agree with you about this very much, what you say of Ireland and Sicily. It would be nicer to go to Italy again, where everything is so easy and beautiful; but I need a savage, ice-hard winter by which to remind myself that my ancestors lived in caves and not out of doors. The ideal in writing would be the logic of the Romance languages combined with the knowledge of the desperate need for emotional discipline that one gets from living in a cave. Figuratively, if you see what I mean.

The University of Chicago Press (a good publisher, though it does very little poetry) is bringing out The S. of Movement in the spring. I am very happy about this. Meanwhile, my revised Fighting Terms has been in transit from Spain, where it was printed, to New York, where it is to be published, for over three months. I suspect that the ship it was on has gone to the bottom of the sea. It was supposed to come out around the end of August.

I have been reading very randomly. Bolitho disappointed me a bit.[7] He has too much the Lytton Strachey manner – though I certainly prefer him to LS – refusing to take most of his people seriously. Tarn is better on Alexander and Voltaire on Charles XII.[8] It was an interesting book, but too damn frivolous. (I suspect you agree with me.) I am at present reading Voltaire's book. Suggested project: I wonder if the Penguin Classics wd be interested in a translation of it? – I've also read Nigel Dennis' Boys and Girls Come Out to Play, which I strongly recommend to you; and William Cooper's Disquiet and Peace, which is a terribly interesting book, though Cooper doesn't exactly have my own interests.

I will try to remember to enclose Kermode's review in this. (Please return.) Will enclose my only American review, which don't bother to return.[9] S.F.

Morse was the friend of Wallace Stevens, and has edited his posthumous works. – Kermode's review of Stevens struck me as irrelevant to much of S's best work, and rather hurriedly written. I agree, Stevens is a damn difficult writer. I took two years getting underneath the surface of it all, and even now find most of his work trivial or repetitious or plain incomprehensible. He published too much. But about a third of his poems are the best things written in this century. Forgive the portentous tone. I wrote a review of his collected poems for the London Maggers in 1956, which I think was quite good, though I underestimated his later work. The best poems to make a start on him with are: The Snow Man, Sunday Morning, Lions in Sweden. And one has to keep in mind that he has three characteristics that I, and probably you, find intensely unsympathetic: (1) he started as an Imagist, and, though he was from the start much more than somebody like H.D, he never completely lost sight of Imagism; (2) he is an agnostic – this means he is unable to accept the Christian discipline or the atheist discipline, but is a complete relativist; (3) he believes in a sort of mystical Coleridgean Imagination – a concept both in him and Coleridge I find pretty wishful thinking – and vague wishful thinking at that. (Sunday Morning is a fine exposition of his agnosticism – a very early poem; Notes Toward a Supreme Fiction of the Imagination – it is an impressive but confusing poem, written quite late.) In spite of all this, though, he is next to Yeats in my pantheon (and God knows, there is even more that is phoney and boring about Yeats: I find 'the wild wicked old man' about the most silly character in all modern literature).

Now to the big subject, art and conduct. I knew, at any rate, that you hadn't completely made up your mind about the theater: I might have thought so if it hadn't been for one or two regrets you hinted at last year. I grant all that you say (though you were a good deal more than you will admit). But the answer to give you is this – you seem to regard yourself as only capable of one style of acting: the heroic, the Shakespearean-Cornelian, what you call the flashy soloist. I agree that this kind has all the dangers you speak of, but it is not the only kind. So far as I know, you never tried another kind, and actually didn't have much opportunity to in the Vic. And there is another kind – at least one other (I'm never too sure how seriously one can take Brecht's kind). Right now the Method seems to be having a [illegible] vogue in England which sounds as superficial as the vogue of Angry Young Men. But that the vogue is superficial means nothing. (What I know about it is somewhat second hand, mainly from reading snippets of Mike's books and discussing it with Mike.) There is also a certain amount of jargon attached to it, which is boring, but also irrelevant. It strikes me that this kind of acting, acting from within, is exactly the opposite to the kind you gave up, to the make-believe world. Used intelligently, it is a discipline and an education: it involves an understanding of a part, and to understand a part one needs to interpret life – i.e. judge it, experience it. Also, it is a terribly flexible discipline in that it does not really restrict one to a single temperament of acting, as the heroic does: it varies with the part, with the actor, and with what the actor has in him to bring into play upon the part. The fact that it is popularly identified with Stanley Kowalski means nothing – this is again fashion: the answer to this objection would be merely to point out the astonishing variety of what Brando himself has achieved – there are no points of connection, really, between his Kowalski, his Waterfront character, and his German officer. It is a terribly flexible method if one is intelligent about it.[10] And to suggest this is for you is not to assume that you would be continually blessed with parts from intelligent dramatists, Ibsen, Sartre, and so on: when you are confronted with a part in [Terence] Rattigan (or worse) you have to treat it as a part that must be built up from the start again, as the author would have written it if he had had his eye on the way people live. – You may have considered it before, and said 'Not for me', but surely, such is its flexibility, it is for any actor (unlike the heroic style), being a discipline and a means of understanding rather than a style.

[. . .]

God, I wish I could work on you in person. I'm sure I could make you see what I mean then. And you will have to make your mind up permanently one way or the other, fairly soon, because, as a practical consideration (however irrelevant it actually is) your youth and looks will help you get jobs. Not that I'm suggesting you will wither away January 23rd, but you see what I mean.

Sorry to have mentioned Von S. in my attack. Unfair and rhetorical.

Then you turn my arguments round against myself. About the doctorate, I have no need to worry. Most people need a doctorate over here in order to get a job teaching in a university: a tiny handful, if they can teach all right, manage without because they have published novels or poetry. I am, or can be, one in the second group. It has already been made clear to me, unofficially, that if all goes well I could stay on at Berkeley indefinitely, and even get on the 'scale' for promotion within a few years, just as if I had a Ph.D. And Berkeley comes close to Harvard, Yale, and Princeton as a university. – I am not sure, however, if I left here next semester, (a) how ready they would be to have me back later on, or (b) how easy it would be to get a teaching job in another university. – But I am only 29! What I mean is, do I want to stay here, in the same job, in the same area, all my life? Do I really want to start the crawl up the same scale I shall end on? (As it is, I am earning fairly comfortably – or would be, if I didn't owe the dentist $500 and friends $500.) What I am concerned with is living in a way so that I get often enough woken up, so that I remain restless, and am able to continue writing. Teaching itself has no direct effect on my poetry – nor does being a tramp. As a teacher or a tramp I start and stop writing poetry for fairly irrelevant reasons. But one reason that makes me write – i.e. that stirs me up inside as well as outside – is being in a new place, and new circumstances. If I stayed at Berkeley for the rest of my life, or even for the next 5 years, I am fairly certain that my output would be reduced to three pieces of Horatian verse a year – or, since I have a conscience, perhaps to nothing.

As for the PhD, it is now unthinkable I should go back to it: it is mental slavery of a sort that, if I had another year of it, my mind might suddenly die! So you see my problem. Being in the proper condition to write is such a precarious thing, anyway, that I feel whatever I do will be the wrong thing. I completely agree with you, by the way, about the emotional exhaustion involved in job-hunting.

[. . .]

Oh yes, I forgot to tell you. A couple of weeks ago I met Paul Bowles, a minor (and I think bad) American novelist. He looks like a ponce but doesn't act like one. And he gave me a mescalin pill (the results of which are similar to haschisch). And I went through <u>all</u> of the effects: uplift, giggles, supernatural confidence <u>plus</u> the uplifted feeling, mighty perceptions, calm and adoration at the "rightness" of everything ("rightness" is the only word), then colors – rockets exploding in green, much green, much blue, then shapes – ugh – fat and with turbans on (must come from De Quincy, though I've never read him), then cramps in my legs, and the most appalling sense of isolation imaginable – the only person in the world – like being the first man on another planet. I'd take one again if I had the chance, though: it was fascinating.

I am still about 15 ½ pages short of you, but even so write again when you have time. My love to the Irish maid and the Dadie. Come over here quickly. America needs you.

Yours,

Thom

1. Date supplied through internal evidence.
2. A reference to the Irish republican and rebel Wolfe Tone (1763–98), whose memoirs White was reading at the time.
3. TG later summarised the idea of poetry as a kind of loot in his short essay 'Writing a Poem', first published in 1973. Writing a poem, he notes, 'is a reaching out into the unexplained areas of the mind, in which the air is too thickly primitive or too fine for us to live continually. From that reaching I bring back loot, and don't always know

what that loot is, except that I hope it is of value as an understanding or as a talisman, or more likely as a combination of the two, of both rational power and irrational' (*OP* 152). The loot symbol preoccupied TG for a long time and led to two distinct attempts at poeticising it, only one of which was published: 'Loot' (*CP* 127–8).

The 'poem to you' TG mentions here is his earlier, unpublished, version. It was directly about White and attempted to deal with the key issue of *MSC*: conduct. TG worked on this poem for two years before abandoning it: see TG to Tanner (11 November 1960), and TG to White (18 November 1960), both below. TG and White shared 'the values' (see TG to White, 16 December 1954, above) and TG later dedicated 'Innocence' (*CP* 100) – a poem about the dark potential in the values, negative conduct – to White.

4. 'English must be kept up' is a quotation from Keats's letter to John Hamilton Reynolds (21 September 1819) where he discusses Milton as a bad influence.

5. Thomas Moore (1770–1852), Irish lyric poet.

6. This refers to an early draft of 'A Map of the City' (*CP* 103).

7. William Bolitho, *Twelve Against the Gods: The Story of Adventure* (1957).

8. W. W. Tarn, *Alexander the Great* (1948); Voltaire, *Histoire de Charles XII* (1731).

9. Samuel French Morse, 'A transatlantic view', *Poetry* 92, no. 5 (August 1958), 318–29.

10. Stanley Kowalski is the male lead in Tennessee Williams's *A Streetcar Named Desire*. In the 1951 film, dir. Elia Kazan, the part was played by Marlon Brando. TG is discussing Stanislavski and Method acting as interpreted by Lee Strasberg at the Actors Studio in New York, of which Brando and James Dean were alumni. The other Brando films mentioned are *On the Waterfront* (1954), dir. Elia Kazan, and *The Young Lions* (1958), dir. Edward Dmytryk.

1959

Wednesday 25–Friday 27 February 1959[1]

Apt 2,
3216 Telegraph,
Oakland,
Calif.

25 Feb

Dear Tony,

[. . .] – Mike is having big problems right now: he headed a rebellion in the group against the stupid producer, who was inefficient, had managed to lose $7000, and was a cynical-sentimental piece of shit (also in love with Mike: many embarrassing letters), but finally stupid producer's capitalist father <u>bought</u> the group for his son, so the rebels all resigned. Meanwhile Mike has returned from New York at the invitation of the rebels (when they thought they were being successful), thinking he was Castro, but he was Napoleon at Waterloo. So he and the other rebels are hoping to form another group. It may not work: if it doesn't, he'll somehow have to fish up enough money to go back to N.Y. or else try with one of the groups in San Francisco. – This is to summarize the whole harrowing story.[2]

I am being harrowed, slightly anyway, by having to teach at 8 o'clock every morning (barbarous American custom), but otherwise, to my surprise, am liking teaching far more. I mean the circumstances that go with it rather than the thing itself. I am left to myself and get quite a bit of leisure now that I'm settled in. So now it's 50–50 whether I'll stay next year. Rather than make a Sartrean choice I'll let it depend on whether I get the Somerset Maugham Award I applied for – small but enough excuse to dive off to Mexico or Germany. So perhaps, ha ha, we'll end by taking each other's advice – you acting, me teaching. That was a nervous laugh, not a hearty one.

Stephen Wet Spender is here, I have met him. He acted very nervously, as if I'd offered to knock him down, when I met him. I flattered myself that this was because of my reputation as a Tough, and because of my Restoration-like lampoons on him but noticed afterwards that this was his manner with everybody.[3] Like a caricature of the vague poet: actually a sham – he knows very well what he is about.

Did I tell you I'm having a record made of me reading, to come out in England in a couple of months?[4] The cover is to be made of black horsehide, with studs and rivets.

I received the exciting news the other day that I'd been "exposed" to syphilis. The Public Health Department told me, and didn't appear at all interested in the fact that their informant was a man (I can't remember who he can be, but he's quite a gentleman to have let me know (through them)): if they were, they'd probably get people concealing venereal diseases, which would be bad for public health. Anyway, they are frenziedly efficient, and gave me a blood test, of which the result came through today. Alas, I am completely healthy. I say "alas" because it really would put me one up on Peter Wood, wouldn't it? Still, I have two more blood tests to come, but it is really very unlikely I have it.

[. . .]

I suppose I haven't written to you since before Christmas. Had a fine vacation, painting the town my own colour. Have also become an occupant of the local Skid Row (ref. enclosed poem, which is all accurate in details), and got in good with the local down-and-outs.[5] If I was Balzac, I'd make use of them by writing novels about them. Poets are more scrupulous.

If you don't come over here, I must come over there to see you. I need an infusion of strength and Values. Actually I need it very often. It's not (I think) that I'm becoming soft so much as muddled, or purposeless (which is probably equally bad). I also get madly depressed about my own lack of talent. I may be better than anybody else in England but Larkin and Ted Hughes, but that isn't particularly good. I want to be better than Rimbaud + Baudelaire + Donne and unfortunately do not look likely to be. Too mousy, alas. There's little likelihood I'll come to Europe this year (unless I get that Maugham thing) as I've spent all my money paying vast dentist bills and paying back money I owe Mike, which he needs now he's workless. But perhaps 1960. Jesus, I'll be 30 then.

[. . .]

The enclosed poems: Map of the City is a revision. The "malady" is perversion of course – in heterosexual parlance – but in terms of the poem it is "love of chance." Loot I haven't yet revised to my satisfaction: you're right about the Auden-like facility of it – I don't know what I can do about it. All-Night Burlesque I like, but the one or two people I've shown it to do not.[6] An Inhabitant will probably never get into print, but I'll try, anyway. Modes of Pleasure is fearfully abstract, but intended to be, really: about the aging, lonely ponces you see in bars, Rastignacs at the age of 50, with <u>nothing</u> to support them – as all their actions have been valueless.[7] The Improvisation I don't know about: I suspect it could be improved a good deal, but don't know how.[8] Perhaps it's not worth improving. (I haven't sent this last after all – I'll work some more on it.) (The word <u>turk</u> in An Inhabitant is prison-argot for those men – in prison – who rape other men at knife point. I got this, I am sorry to say, from books, not from people.)

27 Feb

I must say I can imagine few things more interesting than sharing a flat with a Nazi Youth, even a former one (I hope former Nazi Youths don't turn, like former Communist Youths, into Present Middle-Aged Liberals). – Yes, San Francisco is certainly as good as the pictures of it. Some of the best pictures I have seen of it occurred in a crappy film called In Time of Love and War.[9] [. . .] I will redo Loot – or try to. I know what you mean about the worlds of idea and action, their irreconcilability. But I have no comfort for you – it is bad to compromise, it is bad to fail, it is bad not to attempt their reconciliation. At least one mustn't give up. The most one can hope for is a few short periods when they appear to be reconciled, and also for a bit of knowledge learned about them as one goes along. I must say this moral counsel makes me almost weep as I say it, it is so touchingly written.

Excuse this awful letter. Yours are a real source of strength to me. And your criticisms of my poems are (as they have always been) more to the point, and more helpful than anyone else's.

My love to the lobsters.

Yours,

Tiger

1. Date supplied through internal evidence.
2. MK and several others split from Peter Kump's Comedia Repertory Company and formed another group, Phoenix.
3. TG's 'Lines for a Book' (CP 56) alludes to two Spender poems – 'My Parents' and 'The Truly Great' – which begin (respectively) 'My parents kept me from children who were rough' and 'I think continually of those who were truly great'.
4. *Listen: Thom Gunn Reading 'On the Move'* [and other poems] (Hessle, Yorkshire: Marvell Press, 1962). TG recorded the poems in Oakland on 20 January 1959.
5. 'An Inhabitant', London Magazine 7, no. 5 (May 1960), 14–15; uncollected.
6. 'All-Night Burlesque', The Observer (26 April 1959), 22; uncollected.

7. TG refers to the first of two poems called 'Modes of Pleasure'(*CP* 101), first published as 'Pleasure' in *The Observer* (29 November 1959). See also 'Rastignac at 45' (*CP* 122–3); from Balzac's *La Comédie Humaine*, Rastignac is a Gunnian sexual adventurer.

8. 'The Improvisation' was a working title for TG's unpublished poem 'Trio'; see TG to White, 25 November 1957, above.

9. *In Love and War*, dir. Philip Dunne (1958).

1960

TO *Tony White*   ALS Tulsa
Thursday 4 February 1960

Apt. 2,
3216 Telegraph Avenue,
OAKLAND,
Calif., U.S.A.

4 Feb 60

Dear Tony –

It's at least a year since I last wrote to you, and you've sent me three letters meanwhile. Every time I thought of writing to you I've put it off till I could spend several days on it and send you a gargantuan letter, but obviously this is only a secret excuse for being lazy, and if I don't answer you now I won't till I see you next.

I just turned up the start of a letter to you dated Dec 8, and it reads like Henry James in his last years. I hope all of my letters aren't like that after two months. I often think about you – in fact, I often find myself telling people about you, how admirable a person you are. You had more to do with making me the kind of person I am than anybody else I've known – something you probably realize as well as I do. I mean, you helped me establish the Values: and the Values are still the values, with very little modification (or at least with no more modification than the difference between Sartre and Camus), and they are still something to try to live by however much I may fail. This, anyway, by way of answer to your absurd remark that you hope your letter didn't turn up like an embarrassing face out of the past. More like a face in the present and future, and one that is always in my mind. (This is not meant to be so mushy as it may sound.)

Your last letter was full of despair, but hell it's a sign of something when one can still feel despair. I sometimes wonder whether I haven't got to the stage where I can't feel anything any longer. You have had a good life, in that there's nothing phoney about it, you try to tell the truth, you try to live what you believe. I have never known anybody else like that. I don't know what to wish for you, any more than I know what to wish for myself. That you may become the novelist I am sure you can be, perhaps. What saves you is the very lack of rest, the very power to feel despair, that makes life hell for you.

I've not been such hot shakes myself. Wrote virtually nothing all last year, didn't travel anywhere outside the States last summer, still teach and am in the same place. It was a relief when I started writing again about six weeks ago – I am <u>making</u> myself work at it, be articulate even when I don't want to be, get something down on paper rather than nothing. The results are not that good, the poems are not exciting, but if I stop writing – and I would, I think, if I had another silence comparable to the last one – I would lose a considerable justification for everything and would go very soft. I enclose a few things which I suppose are probably finished.

[. . .]

I'm going to be in England for about a week at the beginning of September and a week in the middle of December (between which times I'll be, perhaps, probably, unless I change my mind, in Berlin). I want to see as much of you as possible both times. And maybe I'll be able to persuade you to come to California – "new styles of architecture, a change of heart."[1] Mike is in New York, trying to see what can be done for a young director. Nothing, so far, but I wrote to Irene Worth (who is there) about him, and maybe she can help. In the summer I'll be going there, and will get some sort of job to last me out till the end of August (all that I've saved will have to go for the Atlantic crossing). Then in Sept I'll bring Mike across – probably – and he'll come to Berlin as well – this will be all on Maugham money.[2] Many thanks, by the way, for your advice about revue material: he finally got a revue together (much of it pirated) and it was so successful that he (and the others in it) were able to live on the proceeds of doing it on a stage in an arty bar.[3] Toward the end of it he directed Dillon, a play neither he nor I liked very much – but he directed it very well.[4]

I seem to remember that we were writing to each other about me in the role of teacher. Frankly I am being cowardly (in the main) about this: I enjoy it more than almost anything else I can see myself doing, it gives me time to write poetry when I'm able to write poetry, and it does nobody any harm unless they are willing to let it. One can be as independent and vigorous as a teacher as in almost any other job, and more so than in most. At the same time, I know that for my own good I need a change of scene, even if it's only a few hundred miles away – to, say, Los Angeles – and that 3 months in Berlin would count merely as a vacation: I'd still be coming back here (that's why I want to impress you – in the sense of press-ganging you – you'd count as a change of scene all by yourself). My great terror of slowing down – you can't start rapid motion again once it's lost – and maybe outside pressure can keep me from it. Or maybe not. – So I have my familiar problems, you see, and you must be very bored with them.

On the Cultural Front (as they used to say in the war): I read Macaulay's history last spring, which is an immensely great book, especially the first two thirds or so – a fantastic intelligence and powers of discrimination.[5] Read it (or have you already?). Camus' death breaks me up, as Gerard Phillippe's did in a somewhat minor fashion: as you say, he was not to be spared.[6] I read La Peste again this summer, and it struck me even more than before as the great book of the century: I can't think of a single other work of prose – nor a Collected Poems by anyone, for that matter – which is as important, as well done, says so much. I mean since Stendhal. La Chute struck me as mysterious – ambiguous to say the least, but there's no reason why this should have pointed to a decline. It was a vigorous kind of mystery, at least. – I also read Alan Bullock's Life of Hitler, which I'm sure you have read, Claus. – Saw no plays of much interest in New York: Sweet Bird of Youth had a great first act, and some good bits in the third, and an immensely good and subtle and convincing performance by Paul Newman, whom I'd always assumed was a glamor boy and nothing else ("a rugby tough and glamor boy," I seem to remember something like that in a Profile in Varsity).[7] The Triumph of the Will (Riefenstahl movie about the Nuremberg Rally) has been running in San Francisco for the last 9 months or so: tremendously impressive – the audiences all come out at least ½-Nazis. It is so easy to see it as "history", though. In a way, it makes me feel very old (I am 30, by the way, as you will be in some 19(?) days). – I'm sure you saw Look Back in Anger (movie) and it struck me as better than the play, and probably the best film ever to come out of England. Burton gives an English Brando performance, doesn't he? – And I also saw He Who Must Die (French title was not supplied), French film about Greeks, which I found terribly moving, for which I am scorned by all the smart people. It's a pity it's Christian, true, but I think it's more socialist-revolutionary than Christian.

I get pretty lonely up here now that Mike has gone. I only have one real friend – an ex-Cambridge Englishman (after our time) who is doing graduate work here.[8] I think you would like him, but he is only about 24, and it is amazing what a difference that 6 years makes. I continually find myself almost in the position of a mentor (Jesus Christ) with him, and finally only a relationship between approximately equal people can be any good. Apart from him, I have virtually nothing to do with the people at the university. I drink a lot, I sleep around rather indiscriminately – that's about it. (Not that I drink that much: I'm not in any danger of becoming an alcoholic. So don't worry.)

Last weekend – or rather for about 4 days, as it was between semesters in this strange American system where they end a semester 2 weeks after Christmas – I went down to Los Angeles, where I met a lot of interesting people. The last day and evening I spent at Isherwood's. God, he is a nice and unphoney and happy person. He infects all the people around him with his clean kind of honesty: when I was there, anyway, I met Gavin Lambert, who was once editor of Sight & Sound and has written a pleasant book called The Slide Area, and William Inge, a wreck – the American Terrance Rattigan, and a rather attractive stunt man.

I'm sure I've missed out a lot of things I wanted to tell you, but if I'd waited to remember them all I'd never have written the letter. Happy Birthday – our thirties are all before us. My love to Holmstrom and Karl and Jane (I wrote Karl a note two weeks ago).

Yours,

Thom

1. The last line of Auden's 'Petition'.
2. TG won the Somerset Maugham Award in 1959 but did not use the funds – for travel to foreign countries – until autumn 1960 when he travelled to Denmark and Germany.
3. MK wrote parts of and performed in *Six Appeal*, a musical revue directed by Glenn Jordan, at the Pagliacci Playhouse in Redwood City.
4. Anthony Creighton and John Osborne, *Epitaph for George Dillon* (1957).
5. Thomas Babington Macaulay, *The History of England from the Accession of James the Second* (1848).
6. Camus died in a car accident on 4 January 1960; Gérard Philipe (1922–59), a charismatic French actor, had died of cancer on 25 November 1959.
7. TG wrote a profile of White in the Cambridge student newspaper *Varsity*. '[White] has been called in turn "the Cambridge glamour-boy" and "a rugger-tough P.T. instructor",' TG wrote: 'Like Coriolanus, his favourite hero, he refuses to be "false to his nature". And it is a supremely confident and active nature. One suspects that his real ideal is some swaggering unscrupulous Sabatini hero – and it is normally difficult to retain whole-heartedly such an innocent ideal at the age of 22.' See 'Tony White', *Varsity* 17, no. 5 (November 8, 1952), 4; uncollected.
8. Tony Tanner, whom TG met at a dinner given by F. W. Bateson. See next letter and TG to Wilmer, 9 January 1999, below.

TO *Tony Tanner*[1]   ALS (aerogramme) King's
Wednesday 20 July 1960

62 CHESTNUT St.,
LIBERTY,
New York, U.S.A.

20 July 60
(anniversary of
Von Stauffenberg's bomb!)

Dear Tone, Mate,

As I'm sure you know, you were universally missed at Berkeley. I got your card, and assume that the sharks of the Atlantic didn't get you on the way home. I'm wondering how you're feeling – a mixture of exasperation and delight, I suppose. Anyway, I've talked about you with so many people you know, and described you to so many you don't know, that the least I can do is drop you a note every now and again.

A couple of weeks after you left I met a guy from Michigan, of real hillbilly stock, now an Xray technician, who had just moved to California.[2] He moved in with me for the 5 or 6 weeks before I left for the east, and is now living in my old apartment. We developed quite an affection, of a sort I really thought I'd got too old for, and I was only sorry you and he couldn't have known each other: you both have the same kind of warmth.

Meanwhile I've come here, to be with Mike for the summer, Mike being in a crappy company that does a crappy show in neighboring hotels.[3] Actually I don't see Mike for more than an hour a day, and that is late at night, with other people present, when he is tired. So I feel less close to him than when we were writing to each other with 3000 miles between us. Lack of any kind of success in the theater is doing disturbing things to him: he's vague and irrational and irresolute, and I don't even know whether I can get him to come to Berlin with me. I could bully him into coming there and then returning to California with me in January, but that wouldn't be much good so long as he still entertains the delusion that there's a Chance waiting for him somewhere in Manhattan. (There isn't.) So I'm pretty irresolute myself.

Apart from seeing Mike, I find Liberty a huge bore. No sex, no friends, no good bars, not enough money, not enough books to read, not enough talent to write poems. So I work on reviews, eat, shit, go for cuntry walks. I have caught poison ivy in my hands – I hope this letter is not infected: if it is, your having it will be quite a novelty in Greater London, won't it, Elvis? I am reviewing Auden's latest book, which is very sad, being his worst ever, not bad so much as dull, and Lawrence Durrell's Collected, which is a ghastly pretentious mess.[4] More voices, as we say in Yale. I saw Psycho, a movie, which you really ought to see, partly because Tony Perkins is very good in it, but mainly because it's the most frightening horror movie I've ever seen. Also the most sick. Incredibly sick.

[. . .]

I sail on the 14th of Sept, which is a little later than I'd planned. I hope you'll still be around in London between the 20th & 30th of that month? Even if you're in Cambridge by then, I'll be seeing you, anyway, because I'll spend a day there. – I expect I'll be at this address for at least the next month, but don't answer if you don't have time.

There is a new Sinatra song, one of his best, called River, Stay Away From My Door, and a new Ella Fitzgerald recording of Too Darned Hot. And there is an incredibly good Dinah Washington called This Bitter Earth, which you must hear because it sounds like the best Billie Holliday.

Incidentally I heard a terrible B.H. record the other day, which I assume must date from her decline. Oh yes, and in New York I saw Gypsy, and it was lousy – acting, directing, script – the only good thing being the score (Stephen Sondheim and Jules Stone) which I knew already and prefer on the record. My one theatrical experience.

[. . .]

Before I left California I saw 2 (heterosexual) pornographic movies. The first I'd ever seen. Sort of nice. Also went to a champagne party, where the champagne never gave out (and I was there for 5 hours). Though, it may sound pretentious but I don't enjoy champagne that much.

It'll be good seeing you again.

Much love, Claus,

Thom

1. Paul Antony 'Tony' Tanner (1935–98), literary critic and key figure in the study of American literature. See Glossary of Names

2. Clint Cline (1925–97) and TG remained friends until Cline's death.

3. The Stanley Woolf Players performed *Father of the Bride*, based on the novel by Edward Streeter (1949).

4. TG reviewed several collections including Auden's *Homage to Clio* (1960) and Durrell's *Collected Poems* (1960) in 'Manner and Mannerism', *Yale Review* 50, no. 1 (September 1960), 125–35; uncollected.

TO *Tony Tanner*   ALS King's
Monday 15 August 1960

62 Chestnut St.
Liberty, NY

(do not answer, as I'll be
gone from this address soon)

15 Aug 60

Dear Tony,

If I've delayed answering your letter it's because I've been collecting myself together in an attempt to emulate. But, oh well, I won't be able to emulate it, so what the hell.

It was a wonderful letter, the kind I can never write. – You must know by now whether you've got the thing at Kings. I enormously hope so, even if you don't. Nothing happens here, really: but I'm writing quantities of new poems, of which I'll enclose a few, and in a few weeks will be out of here on the merry ocean. Am at present reviewing Ted Hughes (I <u>did</u> get 2 copies, so I'll bring you one when I come over).[1] Even started writing a Stendhalian kind of autobiography, but decided that it's necessary to be more self-absorbed than I am to write that, so stopped around my eighteenth year (not so good when I admit that it didn't <u>start</u> till my fourteenth). Or maybe I compliment myself too much, and was merely lazy. The thing was prompted by a feeling of general unsatisfactoriness, in turn caused by being too much alone for the last 5 weeks – I only see Mike for an hour or so each day, and apart from that there are only farmers in the bars to talk to. The farmers are all right when not talking about fishing or baseball, neither of which I know anything about. And you know, Cecil, one does wonder what one <u>is</u>, doesn't one? What one, as it were, <u>amounts</u> to?

To hell with that kind of attitude too. I made a resolution several years ago never again to allow myself to get in a situation of being completely alone, unless I was doing something, and here I find – being forced to break it by the special circumstances of Mike's being here – how dead right I was.

I am not feeling the anticipation I might on going back to England, for two reasons – I feel I've already had the worst of it, and I'm only there for nine or ten days in any case. Your description of being back was great: at last it put into words what I felt in 1957. Back in it, and not only back in it, but <u>knowing</u> it through and through. So do your damnedest to get Marcia over.[2] I mean be unscrupulous. Because, remember – for her it will be as fascinating as it is for a European to come to America. Sometimes, in fact, I wonder whether it isn't simply that: Americans coming back after London or Paris would find over here the same accumulated shit that they had forgotten even smelt. You're right when you connect it with being back in your adolescence: everything relates to one's adolescence, nothing relates to one's experience abroad – and that experience is impossible to communicate even to one's best friends unless they have had it themselves: telling them anecdotes of one's American life in the hope of getting them to see its total richness turns out to be completely frustrating – they have no way of understanding.

[. . .]

My business with Mike is awful too in a different and somewhat quieter way. Briefly, he wants our relationship exactly as it was eight years ago: he finds me changed (well, I don't play with teddy bears any longer), and he treats any change as a deterioration. Well, he knows I love him, and I know it too, so he'll just have to get used to it, I suppose. A somewhat brutal remark, but what happens when Tristan and Isolde (or Roland & Oliver, for that matter) marry? The old intensity of passion becomes something out of place, and should give way to something equally good but different. Or maybe I'm wrong, and am really just a eunuch too, of a sort. Such a suspicion does cross my mind. But what hurts me is to see him hurt yet to know that I'd only be phoney if I were to act as if we'd just met.

This all takes place at late hours, when we're both tired, so maybe it's misleading.

This letter is full of shit, I realize. I just read through what I've written. I expect a short story or two from you, Mate, before the end of the year, by the way.

You ask me what I think of Marcia, which is difficult considering I only ever saw her in your company. She struck me, & I may be wrong, as marvellously extroverted. Excuse the word, and I mean it as laudatory: I mean it to imply a giving-ness, & a delight in appearance and sensation that is finally more important than in finding what goes on underneath. Because a person like her is able to judge from the appearance and sensation what goes on underneath when it is important and is never going to be taken in by phonies. Maybe this is meaningless and maybe also wrong. I think she is wonderful, as you know. For some reason I judge her partly by Clint, the Michigan boy I told you about (who will be there when I get back). He has a kind of generosity of the spirit that I've almost never come across before, an insistence that I should enjoy everything as much as he enjoys it, and having himself an unequalled capacity for enjoyment. I meant it when I said I wished you & he could have met: you would have liked each other incredibly. Well, when you come back. – Here I am, in love with two people, and classically unable to see a way of resolving the classic situation. Not that it should be unresolvable. So maybe I will do something extraordinary and resolve it. Fucking hopeful, that.

This had better come to an end, anyway. I enclose a few poems.[3] One, I suspect, is unprintable, but I'll try to get it printed just the same. Editor, think of the <u>challenge</u>. [. . .]

Much love,

Thom.

1. TG reviewed Hughes's *Lupercal* (1960) and other collections in 'Certain Traditions', *Poetry* 97, no. 4 (January 1961), 260–70.
2. Marcia Albright, later Tanner (1940–) was an English major at UC Berkeley when she met Tony Tanner. See 'Marcia Tanner' in Glossary of Names.
3. The enclosed poems are no longer with the letter.

TO *John Lehmann*   ALS Princeton
c. November 1960[1]

c/o American Express,
Berlin-Dahlem,
Clay Allee

Saturday

Dear John,

The night before I got your card I had a dream about a whole new book of poems by you! So you've been in my unconscious as well as conscious mind.

I'm enjoying Berlin, as I said, though my impressions are too disordered to say much about it. It's not as I expected, though I'm not sure what I expected, really: the Berlin of Mr Norris and Sally Bowles with a lot of rubble, maybe. It's hard to imagine Isherwood's Berlin as having ever been here – or having been here as recently as 30 years ago – and the rubble has all been cleared away in the West.[2] Though I met one man straight out of Isherwood's, or maybe Dr Magnus Hirschveldt's, Berlin:[3] he took me to his apartment and started showing me the most awful pictures of hangings, mutilations, etc. I fled the apartment, and found I didn't know where I was, lost and drunk. (I love Bäranfang, by the way – do you know it? a honey liqueur that is or was the Russian national drink.)

I've met a lot of nice people, though I find queer bars outside America very epicene, very girly. I think it must be only in America you get bars exclusively for the butch (as opposed to money-butch). However there are a lot of attractive Germans outside the bars – I don't mean directly outside I mean all over the place.

Since I don't drink and sightsee all the time I've been doing a lot of reading: partly catching up on some good English novels, Nigel Dennis, Alan Sillitoe. Also a strange one called <u>Thin Ice</u> by Compton Mackenzie. This I found very depressing and I didn't like its constant implication (also, I seem to remember, in Proust) that there is something basically effeminate about being queer. But it wasn't too bad a book. I'm now reading Sartre's latest play, which strikes me as something of a recovery.[4]

I was going to send you or Alan Ross[5] some of my new poems, but I sent the batch first to Stephen [Spender], since it's about 5 years since I had anything in Encounter. And he took them all, 7 poems.[6] (Rape!) Still, it'll be nice having so many out together.

Incidentally, it sounds as though a hell of a lot of new anthologies of recent verse are being prepared. I've been asked permission for poems by Elizabeth Jennings, [Thomas] Blackburn, Alvarez, and Hall. From the sound of it, all the anthologies will be covering the same ground. Macneice once wrote a wise review for you in which he complained about the unnecessariness of so many anthologies.

Talking of E.J. – her reviews get worse and worse. I realize that she is too good-natured to make any unkind criticisms, but it's still possible to write good-natured reviews that tell you something about the books discussed (Louise Bogan's early reviews, in her book, are fine examples). But Elizabeth's are useless – that recent one in the London M. said <u>nothing</u>. (This is of course said without malice toward her. One couldn't feel malice toward her.)

I hope to take in Copenhagen for a week or so before I return to England, never having been there. It's a place I've always wanted to go to.

Very happy Ralph P is in love. Wish he wouldn't be so conscious of his age: I was worried at 29 about being 30, but as soon as I <u>was</u> 30 I was delighted and look forward now to my forties with much eagerness.

Charles Monteith wants me to give him a manuscript by February. I keep wondering whether the book I've got here is any good: I have very deliberately tried to learn a new tone from Marianne Moore, William Carlos Williams, and even Wallace Stevens, and I'm not too sure that I haven't turned into a [Charles] Tomlinson (temporarily) i.e. an excellent mimic of the Americans of the '20s. Well, when I send in the manuscript I'll say this to Eliot and see what he thinks.

I'll be around the first 2 weeks of Jan, as there's no quick crossing to be got before the 13th – so I will certainly see you for longer than that half-hour in September.

Love,

Thom

1. Date supplied through internal evidence.
2. Christopher Isherwood's novels *Mr Norris Changes Trains* (1935) and *Goodbye to Berlin* (1939) are collected in a single volume as *The Berlin Stories* (1945).
3. Magnus Hirschfeld (1868–1935), physician, sexologist and prominent gay-rights advocate who practised in Berlin-Charlottenburg during the Weimar Republic.
4. Jean-Paul Sartre, *Les séquestrés d'Altona* (1959).
5. Alan Ross (1922–2001) succeeded Lehmann as editor of *The London Magazine* in 1961, renamed it *London Magazine*, and edited it until his death.
6. 'Das Liebesleben', 'Flying Above California', 'Hotblood on Friday', 'Lights Among Redwood', 'Loot', 'Rastignac at 45' and 'Telegraph Avenue', *Encounter* 16, no. 3 (March 1961), 3–5.

TO *Tony Tanner*   ALS King's

Friday 11 November 1960[1]

c/o American Express,
Berlin-Dahlem,
Clay Allee,
Germany.

11 Nov

Dear Tony,

It was fine to hear from you and you really do write awfully good letters. As you may well guess, I'm enjoying Berlin. As always, for the first two weeks I was disgruntled and bewildered ('what is there here besides a lot of pastel-colored workers' flats and a few heavy Empire relics? it's cold and I don't understand the language,' etc.) but after that I suddenly find myself in the place, and knowing it, and loving it the more I know it. I really do get terrifically sentimental about places – big towns, that is: first with London when I was 14 or 15, then I have had big affairs with Paris, Rome, San F., and New York. Even a flirtation with L. A. One's first problem here is to connect Berlin with the past: I was continually trying to see SA men in the streets, and the ghosts of political rallies, but the effort was absurd – with the almost total demolishing of the city, it has made a complete break. One can find relics of the past, but they're very few. You feel so much that a new generation

126

has taken possession. What does strike me is that of the 4 Berlins (empire, Weimar Republic, Nazi, and post-war jungle) this – the 5th – has most in common with the 2nd. I've been rereading "Goodbye to Berlin" and detail after detail strikes me as a marvellously accurate description of the feeling here now. There is the same kind of recklessness, nonchalant hedonism, unscrupulousness – but totally without the feeling of immanent catastrophe in the early 30s. You do not feel the nearness of Communists, in fact you have to keep reminding yourself of East Berlin: West Berliners go into East Berlin as little as possible – they say they go there only for the theater, and some are reluctant to go even for that – and obviously they try to keep the whole problem out of mind as far as possible. – On top of all this I find myself rich for the first time in my life: a very peculiar feeling, not bothering how much you spend. I understand at last why the rich cannot understand poverty, since I suddenly find myself in the same position: someone says they can't afford another drink or they don't have a bed for the night (whether it's true or not), and you think – 'how absurd, what's 7 marks?' and give it to them, a piece of paper. Money really is paper when you have all you want. A pity I can't take it back to England, because of the nature of the award, but I've been sending some of it to Mike and Clint, both of whom need it. (And I don't even feel generous, as I would if it were dollars).

I have made marvellous progress with the language, simply from having it spoken to me continually. I only had one year of German at school, so had to use that as a basis. (Almost no one, by the way, speaks more than a few words of English.) Have made a lot of friends, from All Walks of Life. People are madly interested by the fact that I live in America. My identity bracelet charms everybody out of their senses. I have been on the backs of more motorcycles & drunk more cognac (prost, gulp, prost, gulp, etc) than ever before in my life.

[. . .]

I am more delighted than I can say that you & Tony W got on so well. Since you are probably my two best friends, I kept on telling myself this couldn't happen, it'd be too good. Well, about Karl: I didn't "take offense" at him when I last saw him, but I felt irritated that he was exactly the same – the mannerisms of his Cambridge self had hardened into habit, and the very fact that he was the same meant that his potentialities were not the same. There always used to be a potential bigness about him, but now – as far as I cd see – he seems pretty self-satisfied and totally lacking the power of self-criticism. During a five-minute bicker between him & John Coleman about whether he should have tipped a waiter or not, I felt a strange weary indifference to them both (Coleman, whom you don't know, is equally disastrously unchanged) as if I had been hearing them have the same quarrel every day for the last 6 years I'd been away.

Tony W, by contrast, is a much bigger person than when he was at Cambridge (he was big enough there) – he has looked outward, at the tangible world, without constantly wanting to make it refer to himself, but with a sense that it existed in its own right and that something could be learnt from it. This is roughly what I'm trying to say in the poem to him I enclose.[2] (Maybe I'm getting unclear!) Consequently he has become a quieter person, but with a rich and warm kind of quietness.

[. . .]

It's cold as shit here, or rather a witch's tit. If you ever see any attractive posters of any sort, snatch them for me: I told Mike I'd try to bring him posters from Germany & England, for purposes of decorating rooms (he is perversely fond of large sheets of paper with lettering on), and I haven't had much luck yet here. I have made up an epigram: 'Carolyn Kizer is the Madame Verdurin of Seattle.' (Thank you.) I have got some German motorcycle boots.

     Love,

          Thom

P.S. God am I delighted about Kennedy. – Have you seen John Betjeman's Life-Poem. My favorite lines are the ones where he explains that since he couldn't aim with a gun he knew he <u>must</u> be a poet.

1. Date supplied through internal evidence.
2. This refers to an unpublished poem called 'Loot': see TG to White, 26 November 1958, above.

TO *Tony White*   ALS Tulsa
Friday 18 November 1960

c/o American Express,
<u>Berlin-Dahlem,</u>
Clay Allee,
Germany

18 Nov 60

Dear Tony –

If my writing is a thought unsteady, that is because I have a hangover. A cheerful one, luckily, but it leaves me with a feeling of extreme fragility. I was drinking cognac last night with a young truck driver & a friend of his, and the Berlin capacity for cognac seems unlimited, but mine isn't.

I'm doing very well for meeting people of interest, as you may gather from my nonchalant name-dropping in the last paragraph. I spent Wednesday (a religious holiday) with a family I've got to know: the mother is 80, has lived in Berlin all her life, and is good to pump. Then the son and daughter in the afternoon took me to see where Hitler's bunker was, etc. I've met a dull American who ought to be nice from the way he lives – on odd jobs for the last 3 years, with practically no money – but isn't; however he's extremely useful for giving me tips about East Berlin: most West Berliners refuse to accompany me over there and won't say a good word for it. I've met a guy who worked under Stauffenberg during the war, but refuses to talk about him (I've been told by someone else this is because he, this man, was in the Hitlerjugend, and is scared to talk about the past at all in case this gets known by the wrong sort of person). I've met various extremely young male prostitutes who are overwhelmed by the fact that I live in der oo ess eh and insist on attaching themselves to me for hours at a time (I need hardly say this is very platonic, almost fatherly on my part). And also this man who drives a truck for a sausage company, and by night a motorcycle for himself, and is really fine.

[. . .]

So I'm enjoying myself. At the end of the month I go to Copenhagen, and maybe from there for a few days in Stockholm, though this depends on how easy it is to get a ship back from Sweden to England. I'm coming back for Christmas, and don't sail back to America till Jan 13, so hope to see a lot of you.

[. . .] I tried turning that poem about you into syllabics, but it obstinately remained in bumpy anapaests, whatever I did.[1] It's odd how I can never write a decent poem to you. It's also odd, come to think of it, how I don't seem to be able to write personal poems any more. Atrophy of the emotions? Thank god, that's what I've been waiting for. – I'm trying to get a Nazi belt for this friend of mine in Calif., but can't find any nowadays. Where did you get yours and mine in England?

[. . .]

If you feel like writing, the above is my address this month – & from Dec 1 till about 22, c/o American Express, Kopenhagen (Køpanhavn?), Denmark.

Hilarity! Gusto!

From your sexy old friend

Osbert Sitwell

Did I tell you my favourite dedication by the way?

"To Ella and Barry Fitzgerald"

(some funny book published in the USA).

1. See TG to White, 26 November 1958, and TG to Tanner, 11 November 1960), both above.

TO *Tony Tanner*   A L S King's

Tuesday 29 November 1960[1]

Berlin

(from tomorrow on, address:

c/o American Express,

Copenhagen,

Denmark)

Tuesday

Dear Tony

Got your fine letter this morning, when I was feeling a little melancholy at the thought of leaving Berlin tomorrow. I imagine I will find Denmark, by contrast, a little soft. Berlin is so finely resistant that what one gets from it one feels one has really <u>won</u>, really wrestled out of it. It's still too near for me to speak about, but I would seriously like to be able to spend a couple of years here sometime – there is so much I don't yet know about it. Anyway your letter restored the backbone to me.

I have quite thoroughly explored E. Berlin which is in most ways a good deal more exciting than the West. W. Berlin is flourishing and capitalist, covered with new rather Scandinavian-looking apartment houses in attractive pastel colors, expensive shops, all the ruins nicely patched up where possible, the cops politely in the background like English cops, the girls with beehive hairstyles, the boys with Italian shoes. East Berlin is totally different but unlike most people I don't find it depressing, just interesting. All the ruins are still very much ruins – many of them are being dynamited, either because they are irreparable or because they are Imperialist or Fascist in association. The huge famous equestrian statue of Frederick the Great which stood on Unter den Linden was carted away by the Russians (tho apparently it wasn't badly damaged) because F the G was a Fascist. Almost all the interesting buildings are in the East, as the center of the town was formerly there, built with French money exacted after the Franco-Prussian war. And you really see what it's like to be in a Communist state: everybody in working clothes (tho blue jeans are frowned upon), hearty exhorting posters, and everywhere more cops than you've ever seen before – though they all look about 16 years old. And then a marvellous theater, to judge from what I've seen. I saw Aida at the Opera – I hate the thing, but the scenery was fantastic. And Brecht's Mother Courage at the Berliner Ensembler, which was without doubt the best production I have ever seen of anything. Luckily I knew the play, so I could follow it fairly well, and I have never seen anything like it. A good production of Brecht is almost enough to make one a communist, just as Chartres Cathedral is almost enough to make one a Catholic.

To my surprise, I delight in the language. It has a lovely slopping casualness and flexibility when it's informal that I never guessed at. I have big resolutions of studying it so hard when I get back to Berkeley that I will be able to read Brecht and to speak it as well as I can French. At present I am learning the Thousand Most Frequent German Words.

I can't say how sorry I am about Marcia. These are weak words, but she is silly to act up like this, and perhaps cowardly. That's the trouble of letters – the only kind of love-relationship that can be successfully conducted through them must be utterly unreal, the rhetoric of Heloise & Abelard; with us ordinary people who don't find a sexual kick in rhetoric, love by correspondence becomes a kind of obsession – fetishes are created, tone becomes all-important and at the same time elusive, momentary asides get worked up into big issues. Maybe at least – this is all I can say – she didn't mean what she wrote quite so definitely as you think.

Your remarks about the poems are, as ever, very helpful. Surprised you both liked 'The Inhabitants' – I had given it up as a bad job, but will take another look at it.[2] [. . .] 'Sinatra' and 'Out of Breath' are dead losses.[3] 'Blackie' I persist in liking, though it is minute in scale and nobody likes it at all.[4] I am overjoyed that you like 'Innocence', and forgive me if I say a few things about it and ask for your further advice, because there are real problems with it I can't work out by myself and I think it could become one of my best poems. (Karl sent me a telegram asking for a poem, so I impetuously sent him this & Blackie. Good good.) And in it I'm trying to deal with a problem I've never before fully faced in a poem, the problem of the consequences of energy (which I admire) without moral sanction.

No, I am not trying to sell the SS man as something fine in his own way. But I am trying to show how like he is to most people, or rather how easy it would be for most people to (in the right circumstances) be in the SS. Think back on the army – you were slightly brutalised there, even if only for a time – weren't you? And I think there is ultimately rather little difference, in war, between the attitude a soldier has toward killing (which is never clean, a neat hole thro the forehead) and that he has toward atrocity. – By attributing innocence to this man I am not exonerating him or the SS, but I am attacking innocence.

In the first 3 stanzas I am deliberately keeping myself from judging <u>against</u> the boy (except in the line about 'hardening to an instrument' which is more against the SS than him), because I am trusting the last 2 stanzas to do the work for me. Surely these 2 stanzas show that the 'courage, endurance, loyalty, and skill' are virtues meaning nothing without the virtue of wisdom (vide. Plato passim), and that innocence is <u>not</u>, as popularly supposed, a virtue, but a mere vacancy, into which anything can be put, including horrors.

I am now going to go through the poem at boring length, line by line. Forgive the pedagogical approach, but I need your advice. (There are a few slight revisions.)

> 1.   Culture of guilt and guilt's inheritance
>   Adopted him as neither heir nor pupil:
>   He grew up in a slum, and by that chance
>   Self-pity was as foreign as a scruple.

First, is this stanza really necessary? I'd like to drop it, if the poem still has meaning without it. If it should stay, is it necessary to know he grew up in a slum? (I think you'll say no.) You say I'm throwing out pity with the self-pity. No, I'm not, but <u>he</u> is. I don't like self-pity but I do like pity, but I see no need to comment here, since surely the end of the poem makes the point at sufficient length, tho by implication. What I'm implying here is what strikes me as an unfortunate fact: that the despicable Christian tradition does help one feel humanity, and that one cannot feel pity without having felt self-pity. Or am I totally wrong?

> 2.   The Corps trained virtues that were plain to see
>   – Courage, endurance, loyalty, and skill –
>   To a morale firm as morality,
>   Hardening him to an instrument, until

The 2nd line here: these <u>are</u> virtues, and they are present in any efficient military organization, and I have read nothing which gives me cause to doubt their presence in the SS. And they are just the virtues such a boy (from the slums?) would recognize as such. Doesn't the following line sufficiently imply that they do not add up to Virtue: they amount to 'a morale <u>firm as</u> morality', but do <u>not</u> amount to morality, Stupid. And the last line qualifies them still more.

> 3. (until) He embodied thankfully, within the year
>   Compact beneath the swarthy uniform
>   A total innocence, child-like and clear,
>   No doubt could penetrate, no act could harm.

Yes I agree <u>joyfully</u> was a bit much. Is <u>thankfully</u> any better? I have altered <u>noble</u> (in line 2) to <u>swarthy</u>, because it helps the reader to realize he's in the SS, which I don't now name as such, in the poem. The last 2 lines of this stanza are supposed to describe innocence in a way that is accurate and at the same time would be approved by the great romantics, Blake & Emerson, whose ideas at least partly led to Nazism. Again, I am trusting in what follows to give a moral context.

> 4.   When he stood by the Russian partisan
>   Being burned alive, he therefore could behold
>   The ribs wear gently thro the darkening skin,
>   And sicken only at the Northern cold,
>
> 5.   Could watch the fat burn with a violet flame,
>   And feel disgusted only at the smell,
>   And see how all pain finishes the same
>   As melting quietly by his boots it fell.

This stands about the same as before, I think, except for one line. Is there enough punctuation? (Would commas at the end of the third, fifth, and seventh lines help or not?) Do 'behold', 'watch', and 'see' strike you as merely elegant variation or a brief record of his progress in insensitivity? I have trouble with the penultimate line: does it say enough to you?

Forgive the demands I'm making on you. Write back if you have time.

Love,

Thom

---

1. Date supplied through internal evidence.
2. 'The Inhabitants' is an early version of 'Kurfürstendamm': see TG to Tanner, 31 July 1961, below. Not to be confused with 'An Inhabitant': see TG to White, 25 February 1959, above.
3. 'Sinatra' is unpublished (Hornbake). 'Out of Breath', *Encounter* 18, no. 1 (January 1962), 96; uncollected.
4. 'Blackie, the Electric Rembrandt' (*CP* 118).

1961

TO *Mary and Catherine Thomson*   ALS Jenny Fremlin
Saturday 14 January 1961[1]

Cunard Line
R.M.S. "Queen Elizabeth"

14 Jan 61

Dear Sam and Kay[2] –

Well I got an immense red case, which expands to even more immense and is as light as a coathanger. Thank you very much for all that money – it was most kind of you.

[. . .]

I didn't have time to see Father again, so I suppose he'll be getting a bit hurt, maybe justifiably. Ander told me I ought to at least phone him, but I forgot till I was at Southampton so sent him a telegram. I know he likes telegrams. Everybody, including Ander, tells me his job is pretty insecure, as the S. Dispatch is expected to be the next paper to fold.[3] I have no idea whether he has any money saved or not. I get the feeling, anyway, that he might have difficulty in finding a new job, as apparently his drinking at work has become serious enough for quite a lot of people to know about it. He's a sad man now.

(I hope you can read my writing: it's the ship swaying that makes it uneven.)

The day before I left I heard from Faber, that they had accepted my new book. Also it's quite probable that the anthology I'll be doing with Ted Hughes will be accepted.[4]

[. . .]

Spent a day at Cambridge. It was cold and damp and awful, so I was saved from being sentimental about it!

Love, (and to Jenny & Douglas!)
Thom

1. TG posted this letter at sea. The postmark reads 'Southampton, paquebot' and is dated 25 January 1961.
2. Sam and Kay are TG's childhood names for his aunts Mary and Catherine.

3. In June 1961 the *Sunday Dispatch* merged with the *Sunday Express* and HG resigned as editor.

4. *Five American Poets*, ed. Gunn and Hughes (1963).

TO *Mike Kitay*   AL Mike Kitay

c. February 1961[1]

[Apt. 2,
3216 Telegraph Avenue,
OAKLAND,
Calif., U.S.A.]

Monday

[. . .]

You'll notice I'm keeping rather far away from important subjects, baby. I feel mentally, emotionally, even physically exhausted – something even people at school, & Ralph Pomeroy too, have noticed. I felt one day, after the last phone call, that I was out of the worst. But I'm not really. And my hopes for the future are more a matter of the will than out of any conviction. Your letter tomorrow will I expect be about what I must do, and not mention anything you are prepared to do for me. I will keep off the subjects, anyway, my darling, till I have your questions for answering, which I hope will be tomorrow. You must know what I've been going through and I don't need to tell you about it. I love you very, very dearly, my darling, and will do anything you ask that I am able to. We can lead rich lives together if we allow each other to, my beloved. Oh baby, please settle for me. I'll never be your ideal, but you'll never find your ideal on earth.

Have seen various people you know, in Jack's.[2] Architect, California's finest boy, has a creepy ugly lover, and looks a wreck. Greensleeves, maybe California's 2nd finest, looks as good as ever. There is a queer, colossally big London Jew called Wolf, a medical student, and friend of Jonathan Miller, who says my poetry changed his life – it caused him to get a bike and wear leather, and he tears around like a whirlwind – and came out here to be a doctor, here because I live here.[3] And he really means it, too. Funny how I've influenced so many people either thro knowing them or thro my poetry. This sounds mock modest, but it isn't: I hardly feel, nowadays, like anybody who could ever have affected a person in the world. – Anyway, knowing my poetry alone had this effect somewhat offsets a review I've had in the Sewanee that is the most violent, & it seems to me the most unjustified, I've ever had or am likely to have.[4] I mean ONE reader who understands what I mean

so thoroughly that he acts on it, is enough to counterbalance such a review (Quote: "The S. of M. is one of the dullest books I have ever read. I have nightmares thinking of the energy and the good intentions that went into it.")
[. . .]

[. . .]

All right, I'll plunge into the most controversial part. The Nature of Love. You say "To love is to submit . . . To love is to cease being one's own man . . . To love is to be less than yourself in order, finally, to be more than yourself." You also say love is to conquer. God knows love isn't such an abstract thing that it is always the same, and with the same effects. I believe that the love of the operatic heroes and heroines is a real enough thing – sincere and absolute – that is; but their embrace is a kind of glorified death wish, in which the validity of any other kind of action is denied, and we feel it is fitting, and very satisfactory, that they should always end in the tomb. For them, love is a retreat from the world, and essentially tragic, and since they can't kill the world & at the same time refuse to have any thing to do with it, Radamès & Aida & Tristan & Isolde & Romeo & Juliet, the lot, end up in the tomb – in a permanent embrace all right. – On the other hand, I used to believe in a love that conquered without submission; in a love where, since we were both men, there should be no submission; and, yes, in spite of the New Testament tone of paradox, in which you were all of yourself and more of yourself. How else, I thought, could it be worth it? Otherwise, the first half of one's life would be a lie, and the second half (love) would be a kind of religious conversion that had nothing to do with the first half. – Admittedly the terms are a trifle abstract here, but I know you don't accept the operatic love, and I now know you don't accept the second kind (what I believed could be). And, baby, you are your own man: you have never not been, and I believe I wouldn't love you if you weren't. I will go along with your kind of love in any case, babe, but I want to know what relation it bears to each of these kinds. And you may think you've made it clear to me, but you haven't, baby, made it clear what it is, except in negative terms. [. . .]

Yes, I know what I've left out. I've left out the fact that our love has been very special, is very special, that no two pairs of people love in the same way, that though love may be absolute at times, no two absolutes resemble each other. But it seems we have to define it here, and reach a definition in general terms (your idea more than mine). I have sometimes wanted the death-wish love, and so have you; I have more consciously wanted the other definition, and I should think you have too. I think love is a kind of unevenness – in that is varies between the two, but I need to know, baby, exactly to which side it most tends. There is a terrible danger – and I mean to me, just as much as to you – in unconsciously modelling one's love on het. love. But one can't, our love has to make its own, homosexual terms, which CANNOT be the same as between a girl and a man. Babe – I'm not clinging to unattachedness, to uncommittedness – but I am, or want to be, a man just as much as you are. I wanted us to be individuals "our own men," and each other's men.

    [. . .]

Thursday

[. . .]

    I know that these words and many others in this letter are scarcely calculated to win you back to me, my lost darling. I want to win you back more than anything else in the world – more than anything else I have ever wanted – but I respect you, my beloved, and will not be phoney about my means of trying to get you back. You will still find me difficult, but I will try harder than with anything ever before to be what you want me to be, in fact to act as though I have been wrong. It is important for us to live together again. Tell me whether to come to you or wait for you to come here soon. I can't go on like this much longer. Please, my darling Mike.

1. Date supplied through internal evidence.
2. Jack's on the Waterfront (1952–63) was a leather-friendly bar in the Embarcadero, San Francisco.
3. Oliver Wolf Sacks (1933–2015), neurologist and author. See Glossary of Names.
4. James Dickey, 'The Suspect in Poetry or Everyman as Detective', *Sewanee Review* 68, no. 4 (October–December 1960), 660–74.

TO *Mike Kitay* AL Mike Kitay
Monday 20 March 1961[1]

[975 Filbert Street,
San Francisco,
California,
USA.]

Montag

Hello, my Jewish Colleen, this is your Rock 'n' Roll Transvestite, e.g. Geraldine or Gerald Johnson. Today's my good day, because I got a long and delirious letter from the Boy. My beloved husky man. I love you.

    Hundreds of questions, but I'll try to answer them all. I'm head over heels with joy that you will be here mid-May at the latest. But I'm glad you are determined not to strain yourself, or over-exert that is. Better for you not to be here till June than have a relapse.[2] Oh! . . . I'm suddenly less happy. I'd been assuming today was not March 20 but April 20. [. . .]

I love you. Well babe, about my saying "for a few years on Filbert Street." I mean it in every way you suggest. I meant it, first, if we simply decide to change apartments. But I am not so committed to Berkeley as you think: I certainly don't have what they call <u>tenure</u>, and I could find probably as good a job in NY, given one year to do it in. And I wouldn't mind. I will say that SF is the one city I really don't mind the prospect of living in for ever, but would have great pleasure in spending 5 or 10 years in NY. What I expect at the best is this: that you will get directing to do, after a while, in SF and that this will lead within a few years to NY. But I'm prepared to move whenever you say, doll. But in view of everything I think it would be pointless for us to go to NY within say the next 2 years (tho I'm open to persuasion). As for what happens if one of yr parents dies: yes of course the other shd live with us (if he or she could stand me). However, I think that would entail some kind of acknowledgment of our queerness. [. . .]

No I'm not writing. The reason being almost certainly the restless depression I've felt this year. I have a strong desire to write openly queer poems, not for publication – or else for publication under a pseudonym. Subject: the sailor on leave, innocently unscrupulous, his debauches not showing in his appearance. Subject: "Driving to Florida" – Mother & the truckers.[3] Subject: orgy. Subject: the successful queer marriage. Subject: trade. At the same time I haven't been able to find a good style; I don't want them to be pornography, but I want them to have sex in them. Maybe these subjects are really for essays & not poems.

[. . .] Yes, I did make it with Wolf, & it was indefensible, since I find him extremely unatt. Well, not extremely, and some people go mad crazy about him, but I like something (a) more beautiful and (b) more subtle. But for the first time in my life I did what I consider so wrong, i.e. slept with someone because he was so devoted, which I find immoral, really, the one form of sexual immorality. But he literally came to California because of me, and bought a bike which he still rides all the time because of me. And I still feel a rather owing responsibility, since he wants me far too much (though it's not love, by my definition, it's obsession) – I mean I feel like Pygmalion with Galatea, or like Yeats wondering 'did certain lines of mine / Send these men to get killed by the English' (mad misquotation, that).[4] But I haven't slept with anybody worth talking about. There is an officer in the navy I made (he doesn't know I know his job) who wants to stay with me for a convenience over weekends, & pay rent, until you come, & I'm not sure how to refuse him. [. . .] Met a leather trucker last night, and if that sounds exciting, let me assure you he wasn't. (So I didn't take him home!) – Strangely enough, I must have looked att for the first time of the year on a Sat night (well I did look about 5 yrs younger, with that fantastic burn), because no less than 3 gorgeous guys cruised me in turn, each of which would be normally the best thing in 6 months, and I was so ultradepressed (in spite of my chipper note that day, to you) that I went to bed alone.

Actually that night I felt strangely, & rather strongly, of each of these guys: I don't want him on any terms but one – I would like for Mike & me to take him home and fuck him in turn.

[. . .]

I love you always, my butchie. Remember to make that trucker when you're better & before you leave NY, heh heh. Don't worry about leaving NY, either, babe. I love it too, and if you want I could start looking for a job there this fall, to take up summer 1962. This would be no sacrifice on my part: SF & NY are both lovely places. Don't start jacking off until you're pretty strong, now, baby, however sexy you get to feel. I love you and love you, and look forward only to your getting here.

1. Date supplied through internal evidence.
2. MK contracted hepatitis in late February. He stayed in New York to recuperate, thus delaying his return to San Francisco.
3. 'Driving to Florida', *The Observer* (31 March 1963), 27; uncollected. See TG to MK, *c.* 27 February 1963, below.
4. 'Did that play of mine send out / Certain men the English shot?', in Yeats, 'The Man and the Echo' (1938).

TO *Charles Monteith*   ALS Faber
Wednesday 5 July 1961

975 Filbert St.,
San Francisco,
California,
USA.

5 July 1961

Dear Charles,

Many thanks for your letter. Of course I like your first idea very much, of appearing in a volume with Ted and Larkin: I'd be most flattered by the company I'll be keeping.[1]

Your second question, about a book on Berlin, is more difficult to answer straight off. I'd like to think about it for a week or two. It strikes me that a straight travel-book is hardly called for: there's plenty of that in books and newspapers already. On the other hand what might be possible is something as far from the conventional travel-book as <u>Letters from Iceland,</u> though I wouldn't imitate that.² So I'll think about it for a while and let you know.³

     Best,

         Thom

1. Thom Gunn and Ted Hughes, *Selected Poems* (1962). Larkin's publisher, the Marvell Press, vetoed his inclusion.
2. Auden and MacNeice, *Letters from Iceland* (1937).
3. TG wrote to Monteith on 25 July 1961 to turn down the proposal, remarking that '[I] should have kept thorough notes or a diary [. . .] As it is, what I'd be able to write at this distance would be too vague and scrappy' (Faber Archive).

TO *Tony Tanner*

ALS King's

Monday 31 July 1961

975 Filbert St.,
San Francisco

31 July 61

Dear Tony –

You will be shrieking with annoyance justifiably that I haven't yet sent the books and tie. I hope I haven't badly inconvenienced you. To tell the truth, one or two of them are surprisingly difficult to get and I may have to send them in different editions, but I will make a final search in Berkeley tomorrow. And I'll send you the books on Wednesday, so they'll reach your home about mid-August. I'm practically certain I won't be able to find James' notebooks. They are not even obtainable in hard-covers. But I'll look for them second-hand. If I can't get them, tell me some other book(s) I can let you have. – The Fitzgerald books turned up months ago, as I probably told you. Thank you, they are marvellous.

I haven't gone anywhere this summer, and I guess I won't till next June, in fact, which is rather a bore. But I'll make up for it then by a real junketing round the whole country, and maybe touch Canada. (Any chance that you'll be finished enough to come over by then?) San Francisco, however, is a fine place to live in: I patrol the streets like a poète maudit, but feel neither maudit nor especially poetic. I keep nicely far away from Berkeley, and thus have no news for you of friends. Sean (Shawn?) had disappeared from the record shop when I got back in January, and Fred doesn't know where. Fred seems vigorous and happy working for the radio. Meisenbach was sensationally proclaimed innocent a few months ago, to the anger of Senator Walter and frustration of the cops.[1] [. . .]

And now for the, as it were, real me. I got sort of emotionally tangled up, or maybe desensitized, by the awful, continuously awful situation with Mike for the first 6 months of the year. One can only take so much and then Nature steps in. It's like your having to sleep when you are physically exhausted. Or like fire-sprinklers starting to operate when a room reaches a certain temperature. Not that the situation of M's and my correspondence was his fault more than mine. It had reached a stage of complication where guilt, though continually speculated about, had become irrelevant because impossible to determine. So anyway he became well enough after his hepatitis to come out here at the start of this month, and we'll see what happens. The situation is in some ways as hellish as before, in other ways better. At least the letter-shit is done with. At the same time I think it's becoming evident to me that we can't live together without a continual emotional storm, something I can't take. & yet I feel blackmailed by circumstances: he needs me more than I need him, and also I can't just kick him out, having failed largely in the theater (tho not thro his own fault), without friends here, without anything, even good health. Well, all this is probably as incoherent as I feel. I had a while of quite intense writing in April and May, but since then haven't written a line, or even thought of doing so. The Observer is printing 4 poems, maybe all together, which you'll see quite soon.[2] I'd particularly like to know what you think of "The Goddess," the only one that is totally new this year. "Kurfürstendamm" is one of the four, in a new version, but I'm beginning to regret their having it: it's so goddamn gentle and stylish. I'll write out a poem at the end of this letter that Alvarez said he wanted to have printed, but the editor wouldn't let him. I think it funny, in a repulsive sort of way.

Have read recently Martin Esslin's book on Brecht, which I recommend, and Norman Mailer's Advertisements for Myself and plays by Edward Albee. You ought to read these two last as part of the inexhaustible source material for your thesis. Mailer is 1/3 boring, 1/3 wildly self-pitying and irritating, 1/3 brilliant and brave. The self-pity and the bravery are intimately connected, and so is his wrongness and rightness. Albee strikes me as far far better than Genet, Ionesco, Beckett, & even Osborne. This is a relief, I mean since they and their reputations get on my nerves, whereas he is the one OK name in drama that I can like. Though it's difficult with him, as with Williams (T I mean, not W.C.), to tell how much of his talent is in brilliant talk and how much extends to ideas. Also read a neat novel called A Separate Peace, which you <u>might</u> like & I'm sending you.

[. . .] Saw Winters a couple of months ago, which was very pleasant, in spite of the fact that he told me <u>all</u> my recent poems (including "Innocence") were journalistic and melodramatic and I ought to give up poetry for a few years and concentrate on criticism.[3] He is also too old to be told he is wrong. There are two rules he doesn't recognize (1) that once you have started you must write as much as you can, and only stop (temporarily) when you have no ideas and the paper seems to have a nauseating stench that you can't stand, and (2) that you usually need to write 6 bad poems before you can write 1 good one.

My brother has a son, so I am an uncle.

Show this letter to Tony W. I got a nice postcard from him in Wien, and will write to him as soon as I think it likely he is back. I owe him a letter from months back. – Look after yourself, and don't marry till you're sure you want it for life. Says your grandfather. Here's the poem:

A Crab

A crab labors across my thigh.
Oh. The first time I got crabs, I

experienced positively
Swiftian self-revulsion: me

– unclean! But now I think instead
'I must get some A200,'

and feel (picking it up, watching
its tiny beige legs, a live thing

that wriggles in all directions)
neither disgust nor indifference,

but a fondness, as for a pet.
I'm glad it's nothing worse, and yet

it slipped and swung from one of us
to the other, unfelt because

the skin was alive with so much
else. It was a part of our touch.[4]

My next book comes out in paperback here in September, and in England (hard-backed) around the same time. Don't buy a copy – I'll send you & White copies.

Alles gute

– Thom

1. Robert Meisenbach, an English major at UC Berkeley, was arrested during a student protest against the House Un-American Activities Committee hearings in San Francisco in May 1960. He was charged with felony assault and later found not guilty.
2. 'From an Asian Tent', 'The Goddess', 'Knowledge' and 'Kurfürstendamm', *The Observer* (24 September 1961), 28.
3. Winters's letter (26 June 1961) can be found in TG's papers at the Bancroft Library.
4. 'A Crab', *London Magazine* N.S. 1, no. 11 (February 1962), 40; uncollected.

TO *Mary and Catherine Thomson*

ALS (aerogramme) Jenny Fremlin

Wednesday 30 August 1961¹

975 Filbert St.,
San Francisco,
Calif., USA.

30 August

Dear Aunts –

Thank you for your letter. The day after, I heard from Bar, enclosing the photographs taken at Christmas. There was one lovely one of the five sisters. I'm sorry about Godfrey being ill.

I was thinking today, it's strange how none of you look or act as if you are in your fifties and sixties, but then I realized I took my standards of age from Alice [Collings], and she must have been born old.

Yes, I've seen pictures of William Gunn. Father hadn't yet bothered to go and see him when A. & Margaret wrote, which was about a month after his birth. And I suppose Herbert has plenty of time now he's not working. – Unfortunately, he and Olive will be in San Francisco next month – I hope briefly, but know no details: he sent me a telegram on my birthday saying "hope to see you in mid-September."

My new book comes out in England on Friday, here two weeks later. I am on my guard for bad reviews! Will send you a copy of the American edition, as that might make a change, in spite of the fact that it has been given what is probably the ugliest cover any book has ever had, and one that looks more appropriate to The Scarlet Pimpernel or The Tale of 2 Cities than anything else. You will see.

San Francisco is marvellous. No, silly, it's <u>New York</u> where it gets so hot they have to sit on fire escapes. Though there's a little rain here in the summer, there are big sea-fogs, and the average temperature, the year round, is in the fifties and sixties. But a very pretty place to live, really: houses mostly painted white, many hills, views of the sea and bridges and things, most pretty. Why it has the highest rates in the country of alcoholism and suicides no one seems able to understand. You'd think Chicago would.

Didn't go away this summer, but will travel round the country all next summer, I think. – Got promoted at the university, so will have slightly more advanced courses to teach this year. – Karl Miller is now literary ed. for the New Statesman (he was for Spectator), Tony White has just published a translation of a French novel over here & in England.[2]

Yes, the posters travelled very well, and are now all over the walls. And the new suitcase is strong and handsome.

    Much love to you all,
      Thom
[. . .]

1. Date supplied through postmark.
2. Claude Faux, *The Young Dogs*, trans. White (1961).

TO *Herbert Gunn*   ALS Ander Gunn
Saturday 30 September 1961

            975 Filbert St,
            San Francisco,
              Calif.,
               USA.

             30 Sept 61

Dear Father –

Got your cable yesterday, and apart from being disappointed not to see you was rather worried. I figured it was probably not your heart, since the doctor would have told you to stay put in NY rather than return to England, but that's not much comfort. Do write me a note, or get Olive to, as soon as you feel like it. You must feel pretty exasperated to cut off your American trip like this. I hope you had a good time, anyway, for the few days you were in New York. And also that your journey back was comfortable. Make sure you do what the doctor says – i.e. rest up when he tells you to – and take things as easy as you can. Maybe in a year or two you'll have a chance to come over for a bit longer, and make it to this nice city then. In any case I'll be back during the summer of '63, for which I've started saving already – maybe I'll be returning to Europe for good then, though I'm not sure yet.

Anyway, Father, take good care of yourself and get well.

All my love,

Thom

TO *Tony Tanner*   ALS King's
Saturday 7 October 1961

975 Filbert,
San Francisco,
Calif., USA.

7 Oct 1961

Dear Tony –

I have the copy of [*Time and Tide*], postcards from everywhere, and a long letter to thank you for. God how I envy you being in Berlin – I guess it was just about a year ago today that I got there. Tell me, is it still possible to get into the East? Did you go there?

I can't thank you enough for the review.[1] It was the first to come out, and by far the most intelligent thing (& also the most flattering) ever written on me. You see it was quoted in advertisements? – The book is out over here, I believe, but it's not visible anywhere. Maybe it's just a myth. However, Fighting Terms comes out from Faber next spring in a slightly de-revised version, and also a paperback selection of me and Ted Hughes (also from Faber).

I suppose you're back in Cambridge now, for either the Lent or Michaelmas Term, I always forget which. That swinging supervisor, T.T. of Kings, he always conducts supervisions in his leather jacket against a background of Miles Davis.

Yes, you're right about everybody's life after 25 being a mess. I mean in your early twenties you do seem to be grasping something, some kind of coherence, but after that you've either got it and it's meaningless or else it wasn't coherence at all, just another kind of incoherence. I'm not sure at this point whether to moan for a while or appear stoical. Well, I'll moan. Mainly about my own sense of inadequacy. I mean really my choice is between a comfortable domesticity, in which I am bored to the point of not writing a line (I haven't since June), but which certainly has its virtues, and on the other hand a kind of endurance in a vacuum, given a local meaningfulness (but no more than local) by affairs and poems. I guess I really want the latter, but at the moment I'm too much of a goddamn coward to really plump for it, since it means losing the other. And, well, finally also, I'm afraid of what I'd be doing to Mike – that's the hell of it, and that's why it isn't even a clean choice of the sort I've described. Jesus only knows what he'll do if I leave him – Jesus knows what he'd become. He's a fine and good person, but he has come to depend on me, on my being there, in a way that terrifies me. I don't feel up to such a need, and at the same time I feel guilty in that it's my fault that it's there, and I encouraged its growth in the first place. So I sit on, from day to day wondering, about myself, about him, and growing more and more incapable of any real action which would do myself good, or him good, or us good. [. . .]

I see from your letter that you were uneasy about my reactions to your review. Well, you needn't be. I don't deserve such praise, and maybe you find a greater coherence in the whole of my work than is really, alas, there, but it's sound and careful and well-written. (Like your other things for Time and Tide.) You are right to take Vox Humana as being central – nobody else has realized that – and also in tracing the cross-references of "risk." I feel marvelously proud that what I hoped was there really is, apparently, there in the poems. – In taking the exiled king and gardener as key-figures in the first book, you are in a way giving them an importance and the book a unity that was not consciously intended, but in doing this you are critically justified – I mean in discovering themes that are there, then naming the themes in terms of the book. I mean, for example, that Sh. was probably not aware of the distinctions between kinds and uses of imagery in Macbeth and Othello, yet a critic is right to point them out and to name them. I'm not sure I've made myself clear but you see roughly what I mean.

I've been listening to Mahagonny repeatedly on records. I agree about The Inheritors: it's very great and very original in every detail. I've been rereading Conrad's anarchist books with great satisfaction: they contain all that's important in thought that was to follow for the next fifty years.[2] Even Sartre's "nausée" is there (in a passage of the Secret Agent). And I reread Felix Krull, which was even better than before.

Nothing to tell you about school: I only work Monday, Wed, and Fri, and stay behind in the city for the rest of the week. So I see few people, and am largely out of the way, which delights me. As I've said before, I doubt if I'll feel like continuing there beyond a couple of years. – How good about all these offers of jobs that you've had. It would be nice, wouldn't it, to get one from London Univ., so that one could live there? In London itself, I mean. I too became an uncle a few months ago. My father lost his job on the Sunday Dispatch and came to this country on holiday, he was coming here but got no farther than NY where he caught some virus and turned back. I feel, heartlessly, somewhat relieved. That incredible man, incidentally, never took the trouble to cross London to take a look at his first grandson, who is now three or four months old. – My best to Helena Shire and anyone you see. And cover Tony White with kisses from me. (That would be an amusing scene!)

Love,

Thom

[. . .]

1. Tony Tanner, 'An Armour of Concepts', *Time and Tide* 42, no. 35 (31 August 1961), 140–1.
2. *The Secret Agent: A Simple Tale* (1907), and *Under Western Eyes* (1911). TG may also mean the stories 'The Informer' (1908) and 'An Anarchist' (1911).

TO *Christopher Isherwood*[1]   ALS Huntington
Monday 11 December 1961

975 Filbert,
San Francisco.

11 Dec 61

Dear Christopher,
    Very good to hear from you, and thank you for your remarks about the book.[2] Fred Mintz called the day after your letter arrived, and we're very happy you told him to look us up. I've spent two evenings drinking with him, and find him very bright and sweet-natured and attractive.[3]
    I don't know whether I told you at the time, but London was something of a surprise. People seemed much more relaxed and happy than I'd ever found them before. But, as you say, it's good to be back here. It's great about Don's success in London and also in New York.[4] Send him my congratulations: if the show is still on in March I'll be able to go to it, since I'll be in NY for a week then.
    There's no need to worry about teaching creative writing. The least one can teach them is the elementary rules, and though the majority of them don't go on writing once the course is over they at least <u>read</u> with more enthusiasm and perception. And for the one or two (out of thirty) who do have some talent, you can do a lot – they get a lot of practice at a time when practice is necessary, and a lot of reactions at a time when it's difficult to get useful reactions. Not that I teach it well: my classes in this tend to be very hit and miss.

It's wonderful having Mike back in California. After we've been apart for any length of time, we always have a difficult time for a few months, as I guess many people do, but those months are over now. He works his ass off directing a revue on the Peninsula, which starts at the end of this month, but he seems reasonably recovered.[5] I only wish he could drink (not that I tempt him).

It's very good living in San Francisco, though I do occasionally feel a bit like Lord Rochester. There are a lot of interesting people, and I like living in a city which looks so attractive all the time.

Did I tell you how I liked the London Mag interview (especially that remark about Sound and Fury: I've never been able to finish it either).[6] And it's exciting to think of reading a new novel by you next month.[7] Your prose is the best written since 1900: it is the only one which has the virtues of both formal and colloquial styles, and which can be now unobtrusive and now capable of splendid rhetorical effects and still the same kind of prose. If I make myself clear. I said in a short thing I wrote recently that I would like one day to write poetry with the same type of power as your prose: and the more I think about that, the more I hope it.[8]

I have become an uncle, by the way, and get sentimental over photographs of my nephew.

Much love from us both,

Thom

1. Christopher Isherwood (1904–85), British-American novelist and playwright.
2. Isherwood wrote to Gunn (28 November 1961) praising 'My Sad Captains' and calling him one of the most important poets in England. This letter can be found in TG's papers at the Bancroft Library.
3. Fred Mintz, a San Francisco doctor who was a friend of Isherwood.
4. Don Bachardy (1934–), Isherwood's long-term partner.
5. *The Son of Six Appeal* opened on 12 January 1962 at the Tunn in Redwood City.
6. Stanley Poss, 'A Conversation [with Isherwood] on Tape', *London Magazine* N.S. 1, no. 3 (June 1961), 41–58.
7. Isherwood, *Down There on a Visit* (1962).
8. 'I feel uneasy about the split in my work between the two kinds of poems I write, the metrically intense and the syllabically casual,' TG reflected. 'Each excludes too much of the other. The poem I want to write, in fact, is one in which the qualities of each could exist: it would be a kind of equivalent in poetry to the best of Isherwood – for example, the passage about the liner in *The World in the Evening* or the first two pages to the second 'Berlin Diary' in *Goodbye to Berlin*, where the particularity of the things described does not diminish the intensity of their implications and where the language is plain, unornamented, and eloquent.' See TG's response to a questionnaire on diction in *London Magazine* N.S. 1, no. 11 (February 1962), 40.

1962

ALS (aerogramme) James Gunn

975 Filbert St.,
San Francisco,
California, USA.

12 March 62

Dear Olive,

I was in the East on a lecture tour when your telegram arrived, and they didn't know where to forward it, so I only got it yesterday on my return. I know how inadequate it sounds with a loss like this, but you do have my deepest sympathy and if there is any way in which I can make things easier for you in this difficult time, please have no hesitation in asking me. I am glad that Father's illness was not longer, and that his death was peaceful.[2] I am glad also that you and he made each other so clearly happy and have two such fine boys as Jamie and Georgie, who must be great comfort to you. I realize that there is nothing to be said that can make you any less unhappy, and so I will not try. The death empties your life of its center, and the pain and emptiness are as vivid and real each morning you wake up as they were at the start. Do believe in my very great sympathy.

Love,

Thom

P.S. Do not feel that you have to answer this letter soon – or at all, if you don't feel like it. I am sure your life is difficult enough without having to answer letters.

1. Olive Melville Brown, later Olive Gunn (1912–90), journalist, second wife of HG.
2. HG died of lung cancer on 2 March 1962.

c. March 1962[1]

975 Filbert St.,
San Francisco,
Calif., USA

Thursday

Dear Bob –

Good to get your letter. Karl is silly. New Lines no 2 could be very good. I don't know who to recommend to you, being a bit out of contact. Hugo Williams certainly seems the best new one in years, I agree. I don't remember the name [Edwin] Brock. Wish you liked Hughes: he still has his extravagances, but there's something that's solidly good poetry beneath it all. And it's not his fault he's liked by Alvarez and Edith Sitwell any more than it's mine that I'm liked by Alvarez and Cyril Connolly.

I warn you, though: I have written only two decent poems since the book. [. . .] One, The Goddess, was in the Observer last summer. The other is the crab poem, about which you are dead right, by the way: it is a deliberately sentimental poem, but I'm not sure that the deliberately sentimental is any more excusable than the undeliberately.

My father died recently, and I was rather shocked that I couldn't feel anything at all. I'd half expected I might feel something in spite of the fact that I'd never had much to do with him and he was, finally, a ruthless and self-pitying man.

[. . .]

This is a rather hurried letter. Forgive shortness.

     Best,

       Thom

1. Date supplied through internal evidence.

975 Filbert St.,
San Francisco,
Calif.

31 May 62

Dear Bob –

Sorry about my misreading in the review. Didn't see AA's – did he on the whole like the book? Not, I suppose, since he didn't put you in the anthology.[1]

All right [. . .] your woolly-haired friend wants to change the subject to that of your anthology. The question of Ted Hughes is what brings up the problem. The problem is this: there are too many anthologies of new poetry that come out in any case, and how do you justify New New Lines? And in your justification, how is it possible to omit Ted Hughes?[2]

I don't mean this as aggressively as it maybe looks, but I think it is a problem. The old New Lines did clearly establish what had been only intermittently clear – that there were 8 poets who shared (if nothing else) a belief in the rational structure of poetry.[3] And it was a very good anthology.

But this battle has been more or less won, and even if it's more "less" than "more", exactly the same point doesn't need making again. What should this anthology establish? I think it would be unwise and over-limiting for it to be an anti-Alvarez anthology. Alvarez emphasizes topicality, which is bad, I agree, but he emphasizes a fairly controlled energy, which is good – and though his idea of reconciling DHL and TSE is on the surface ridiculous (like Davie's of reconciling Pound and Winters), I can see what he means, and appreciate it, in the same way as I saw what Davie meant.

Now, when you come down to it, isn't Hughes a better poet than Elizabeth Jennings, Wain, Holloway, or even Enright? I'd say he's better at his average than they are at their best. (I'd also say he's better at his best than I am at my best.)

Forgive my usual cribbing. However, I do think these are important questions. And to put it personally, I don't want there to be a suggestion of ganging up on Alvarez, very simply because his gang contains Hughes (though knowing Hughes, I'm sure completely unwillingly).

      Best,

        Thom

1. *The New Poetry*, ed. Alvarez (1962).

2. *New Lines II*, ed. Conquest (1963). Hughes was included. Conquest wrote in a late essay that 'there was some surprise that Ted Hughes was in it. [. . .] But Thom finally said that at least I must admit he was as good as John Wain, who was being included again this time (saved by some echoes of Theodore Roethke). That did the trick.' See Conquest, '*New Lines*, Movements, and Modernisms', in *The Movement Reconsidered: Essays on Larkin, Amis, Gunn, Davie and Their Contemporaries*, ed. Leader (2009), 307–16.

3. There were nine poets in *New Lines* (1956), Amis, Conquest, Davie, Enright, TG, Holloway, Jennings, Larkin and Wain.

TO *Oliver Sacks*[1]   ALS (postcard[2]) Sacks Foundation
Wednesday 26 December 1962

26 Dec 62

Dear Wolf – I could not read your address on your card. The reason you didn't find me at home is that I am in Mount Zion, as a patient – with – yes – hepatitis.[3] I am on cortisone, after 2 weeks of jaundice & getting worse, & maybe show a bit of improvement. What a laugh, anyway! I am full of optimism. Much best to Mel & look after yourself.

Love,   Thom

1. Oliver Wolf Sacks (1933–2015), neurologist and author. See Glossary of Names.
2. The postcard is a photograph of Mount Zion Hospital and Medical Center, San Francisco.
3. TG entered hospital with hepatitis on 7 December 1962 and was discharged on 7 January 1963. In hospital he began a diary which he maintained, almost daily, until his death in April 2004. The diaries can be found in TG's papers at the Bancroft Library.

1963

TO *Tony White* ALS Tulsa
Thursday 7 February 1963

as from:[1] 975 Filbert St.,
San Francisco,
Calif.,
USA

7 Feb 63

Dear Tony –

I will now start remedying my total lack of communication. I have had an illness called hepatitis, a laughable complaint that kept me in bed eight weeks. I am just about better, but still occasionally pretty weak. I was a month in hospital, and for the last month have been staying with Don Doody, a bartender friend I hope you will someday meet, a very fine man who understands Camus much better than I do.[2] So I have been reading in big quantities, Dostoevsky, Tolstoy, and Camus. Tony T has also been marvelous. It has been interesting, in a way, standing back from things for a while. I think I see myself a bit more clearly. (Ha ha, I am going to join the Catholic Church.)

I've also done, or started, a lot of writing, though reading it through last night it all looks pretty damp.

I'm sorry to be on-&-off like this, but it now seems a bit unlikely I'll make England this year. I might be strong enough around May, but I'd prefer, I think, to come over next year, spend a full 6 months, and not have to be careful. By careful I mean this: not only can you not drink for a year after this thing, but you are inclined to have bouts of weakness. I'm not sure that I can visualize myself in the clutch of such bouts of weakness, but then that's probably just lack of imagination. – So what happens next year? You come over in the spring, and I'll come back to Europe with you in the summer? In any case I want to see you <u>soon</u>. Apart from other reasons, I have to use you as a tuning-fork, for the broken down piano of my ethical organization. Such language.

Meanwhile, without you, I have to test myself in rather childishly obvious ways; for example, I was reassured to get a letter (out of the blue) of hurt egoism from Stephen Spender, saying he was upset by the fact I had let that old poem of mine that referred to him be printed in an anthology, and ending his letter "so I must refuse to have any further personal relations with you" (any _further_!).[3] I feel rather pleased, in that, of all the young men of the early 1950's – Davie, Wain, etc. –, I'm the only one this happens to.

[. . .]

What are you doing (a) for pleasure (b) for your own good (c) for money? I hope they all coincide. I am thinking of writing a prose book – more in class (b) than the others – in which I set the world right about poetry. It will take 5 years to write, by which time somebody quicker than me may have already accomplished this.

There is a good play on with the rather silly title 'Who's Afraid of Virginia Woolf?' by Edward Albee, who strikes me as probably the best man around over here since T. Williams decided that any male whore was Jesus Christ.

I am worried about Tanner's love life. He isn't getting enough of it. Sex, I mean, not love. Wish I knew some lithe girls to introduce him to. I think he had such a good time when he was last in America that living in Berkeley this time is something of a come-down to his expectations. Berkeley is just an ordinary suburban-university town after all, a bit like Reading without the factories. – I'm trying to persuade him to live in San Francisco, but he seems undecided. Mike has been on a directing job in the East for the last few months, so Tony has had the use of his car, which makes things slightly better.

[. . .]

Write to me about your ethical organization and any funny jokes you have heard. Don't get hepatitis. It is unmanly to lie in a bed and be waited on. [. . .]

Look after yourself,

Thom

1. After leaving hospital, TG stayed with his friend Don Doody for four months at 1045 Fell Street, San Francisco.
2. Don Doody (1931–2006) met TG in Gordon's, a bar and restaurant in North Beach, in 1961. See Glossary of Names.
3. A copy of this letter can be found in the Jack W. C. Hagstrom (AC 1955) Thom Gunn Bibliography Papers at Amherst College.

c. Monday 18–Wednesday 20 February 1963[1]

1045 Fell

[San Francisco]

Monday

Hello Babe –

Started writing last night, a junky letter, but tore it up today. It was lovely to hear your pretty voice on the phone. Tom called today, and sounded as though he'd had a good time.[2] [. . .]

As I say, I am a good deal stronger now. I get tired toward the end of the day, but there is not much reason why I shouldn't go home soon. I'll be seeing Cerf tomorrow, & if he OKs it probably go back to F. Street next week. I have a vague superstitious feeling that I must look after myself all on my own to regain my manhood. Or maybe gain it.

[. . .]

Wed.

Something broke me off here. On Tuesday I saw the dr & he "discharged" me, as from a gunn. That is, as he said, I can do anything I like. Except drink or use paint & cleaning fluid. I see him again in 6 weeks. In spite of this, and in spite of good Mr. Sun, who shines hard every day, I have been quite depressed the last three days. Various reasons, many reasons – but when I name them they don't quite seem to explain the depression. On top of which I had to cheer up Don yesterday, since he was extraordinarily depressed. I guess it is good for me, every time I am miserable I get outdone in unhappiness. Ted Hughes left his wife Sylvia and she committed suicide. I feel very sorry for him, poor bastard. I don't know, I feel depressed in all the conventional ways and for all the conventional reasons: I am a moderately egotistical, moderately generous, moderately strong, moderately intelligent man, like everybody else. I try to stop from blaming anyone else for my failures, but my failures nevertheless loom large. And the trouble is, even if they had been less of failures, they would still be failures. Since I am only moderately anything. The fact that they exist makes the degree of them irrelevant. Well, so I try not to feel sorry for myself, and try to accept my failures. My latest pastime is to try to check every recognizable urge of vanity by reminding myself of what I am really, underneath the vanity.

I have written to cancel my tickets to Europe. I will stay at Filbert Street for the next 3 months and write poetry and start another book and prepare next year's courses. I'm sure I could go to Europe for the summer only, but don't want to. I had planned to go for 6 months and so will do that in the summer & fall of '64. Don is driving down to Mexico in June, and then back here via New Orleans & Canada, & wants me to come with him. Maybe I will. – Shielah's castle in Mexico has crumbled into gold-dust, I suppose.[3]

I love you very much baby, and want very much to see you soon. I don't think I have ever caused you very much happiness, when I think about it. I am very glad you have been working at directing, my darling, and Tom says impressing some people.

I get the feeling that you will say of this letter that it's like what you wrote when recovering from hep. Except maybe you are in some rather important ways a good deal stronger than me, and the strength of your endurance – endurance of illness & failure and me – for the last few years will now start to pay off, and will go on paying off for a long time. – While I become daily more aware of my weaknesses – of vanity and dishonesty and cowardice – and the awareness is starting to turn me into a figure of stone.

At least I will make sure it is stone and not foam rubber, though I'd prefer flesh every time.

I mean, I look across at the oven, and think how clean it would be simply to put my head in it, except for all the inconvenience later on to other people. It would save so many people, over the next 40 years, from being misled by me, or betrayed, or even – less dramatically – simply bored by me. Don't get alarmed, I'm not going to put my head in it: I'd always want one last cigarette or walk by the sea. In fact I'm one of the very few people I've ever known well who has not seriously tried to kill himself.

[. . .]

I love you always.
I wouldn't send this letter only I'm tired of tearing up letters that would depress you, so remember Polyanna W. Gunn always bounces out of it.

x x x x x x x x

1. Date supplied through internal evidence.
2. Thomas H. Gee (1931–), MK's on and off boyfriend from March 1962 until October 1965.
3. Sheilah Dorcy (1936–) met MK through the Comedia Repertory Company and later produced several of his plays and revues.

TO *Mike Kitay*   AL Mike Kitay

c. Wednesday 27 February 1963[1]

[1045 Fell St,
San Francisco]

Wed

Hello Baby –

It was lovely to hear your pretty voice with the snow storms of Boston in the background. Your last letter, which I got on Monday, was lovely too, if hurried. I'm sorry you read that letter – tho it was my fault for sending it – not because I didn't mean it, but because it wasn't enough of the truth. I mean I found it was possible to look a good deal farther into myself. Wasn't it true, really, that beneath my appearance and self-delusion of being charitable and long-suffering during your affair with Tom, I was actually (if only by omission) encouraging it, so that, the more guilty I could make you, the more innocent I could appear myself? Probably. In fact, for a day or so of distaste with myself, I could see that much of my life and much of my life with you, has involved this pattern of setting-up guilt so as to be able to assure myself of my own innocence. – Well, it must seem positively insulting for me to admit this at such a late date, when it scarcely matters, really, who was most guilty. This is why I didn't want you to read that letter, since in its priggish consciousness of self-restraint it was pretending a good deal more innocence than I can pretend. I can't apologize with the excuse of unhappiness, since tho I was unhappy you were a good deal more so since your capacity for unhappiness is a good deal greater than mine, I think; and I can't sneer at Tom, since it was up to you to get happiness where you could (though you should have left me) and it was your business whom to choose. And actually a good laugh against me that Tom should be someone so unlike me.

The strange thing is that since I came to Fell Street I have felt this curious coolness in my attitudes. It is something to do with the pleasure of regaining strength (which I am, steadily) combined with the residue of that distance that illness gives you to your life. By coolness, I mean an awareness of at least more clear-sightedness than I had had before. Thus, that day or two of distaste for myself that I spoke of ultimately involved a kind of pleasure (and I do not mean masochistic pleasure) that I could finally, for the first time in several years, make a large perception about what I am rather than what I want to be. (I have often been perceptive about what I want to be, cf. most of my poetry. It is not difficult like the other, though.)

I have a strange, largely superstitious feeling about Filbert Street. That once I'm there I'll fall into a kind of hepatitis depression – all the depression I have <u>not</u> felt ever since I left hospital – and that my perception about myself will become self-pity and so unworkable. Well, right now I have a good reason for not going back. After I next see the doctor, or the week after, i.e. at the end of the month, I will probably be a man and face it. That is, I will be a man when I am strong enough to move all the furniture around so as to make the place unrecognizable from the place I left on Dec 7.

I am up and down in health a bit still, but that I expected. I mean it's more or less alternate days of energy and lack of it. But I am making most of my meals now, often get Don's & my food at Safeway, went to an awful movie with Don (Sundays & Cybele – Tony T gave it one star, Don half a star, and I minus a star), and apart from going to bed about an hour before Don & Bryan, am up as long as they.[2] – Clint Eastwood goes on my list: he is good enough to get hepatitis with Judy Garland and Jim and George and me.

I am still reading a long life of Tolstoy, and also Kafka's short stories (which I find enchanting), and am rereading Camus. I have started a lot of poems, and finished six. The best I sent you, Breakfast, which I hope you liked, as I think it is one of the best I've ever done.[3] I enclose two others, one of which you have seen in about 10 other forms. It's funny how egotistical my poetry is: I mean Breakfast is not about Peter at all, but myself as I see myself in his situation;[4] Driving to Florida is not about Don Magner, but becomes me as the masculine principle being smothered by the feminine principle, in my imagination;[5] Tending Bar is more <u>actually</u> about Don D., I guess, or rather it becomes abstractified a bit to one of the definitions (or "notes toward a definition") of strength.[6]

[. . .]

Well, Babe, I'm sorry I haven't written in so long. [. . .] If you are short of money, tell me, and I will send you forthwith. I'm rolling in it, and since I live on hamburgers and don't drink I keep saving more and more. I love you, my sweetheart.

1. Date supplied through internal evidence.
2. Bryan Condon (1930–2013), Doody's flatmate at 1045 Fell.
3. 'Breakfast' (*T* 24).
4. Peter Tangen (1928–2008), painter and friend of TG and MK.
5. See TG to MK, 20 March 1961, above. Donald Magner (1934–2016) looked after MK when he contracted hepatitis while in New York in 1961.
6. 'Tending Bar', *Critical Quarterly* 6, no. 1 (Spring 1964), 33–4; uncollected.

TO *Mike Kitay*
c. March 1963[1]

[1045 Fell St,
San Francisco]

Tuesday

Hello B –

Two letters from you today. Both depressed, both depressing. [. . .]

Babe, my darling, you ask for answers, but you know all the answers as well as I do, my beloved. You need Tristan, and I need the Father-Figure. I am not being sarcastic about you any more than I am about me, just using shorthand. And I am not Tristan. And you are not the Ideal Father. If you want marriage that badly and marriage only, am I much good to you? We haven't had sex in a year in fact – but virtually longer than that, so we cannot pretend that we still have the same relationship. (Yes, I know, you said that first.) And yet I do need your presence, my darling – you are still, as I said last week, a part of me that I could never, never get rid of.

[. . .]

I don't know what I'd say in answer to this letter if I was you, Sweetheart. I love you and care for you very much, remember that please. I feel very much as though I'm sending this letter through a vacuum. And there is a vacuum in our relationship: or, to put it another way, it's a fiercely clung-to abstraction, very real but without many recent reference points – you have been away the last six months, before that was six months of Tom, before that a period of constant quarrels. This is why I spoke some months ago about Phase VI. I don't at all want a repetition of what we've had together in the last two years, because what we had together then was laughable – we'd have had more if we were separate. So if we live together we have to make a new start, and a different one, and a modest one. Modest in that we live together because of our need for each other, and recognize that, and want to make each other stronger, not trying to deliberately weaken each other.

I think I am being honest in this letter but maybe I just look evasive. The choice seems to be yours whether to come back, but it is really both of ours whether to live together. Well, Babe, I am trying to help that choice be made with the smallest risk of mistake when I try to define how we should live together – the smallness of our expectations must be a guard against the risk of repeating the last 2 years. I am not blaming you more than myself for Tom, but the fact that he was your husband meant that I wasn't your husband. I haven't seen you since you broke up with him, but you can't expect me to be a Patient Griselda waiting for you to be finished. This is what I mean by smallness of expectations. We are the most important people in each other's lives, but though that is a lot, it is all, isn't it really?

I love you, my darling.

x x x x x x x x x x x x x

1. Date estimated through internal evidence.

TO *Mike Kitay*

AL Mike Kitay

Thursday 11 April 1963[1]

Write to Fell St until
I tell you not to.

Thurs

Get Laid for Easter.

Hello, Fair Crittur –

Well, the days are full of blithe activity. I told you about going to Joan Sutherland. Yesterday we went to Barbra Streisand at the Hungry Eye, a very lovely singer with a fine manner, whom you have probably heard of. The bartender from the Tool Box, Chuck, we went with, said it was one of her best nights.[2] He has been to see her 4 times. On the way went to City Lights, trying to get the Observer I'm in.[3] They didn't have it, but the man told me my paperback of Sad Captains is sold out over here, 5000 copies! They had sent to the publisher for more but there were no more. I find this very surprising in view of the fact that it has scarcely had more than 3 favorable reviews in the US, & those made it sound uninteresting. So I have not the faintest idea who the 5000 buyers are. [. . .]

An answer: I saw Tom in the Tool Box 2 or 3 weeks ago, in the Rendezvous on Sunday. – Maybe the Mexican trip & tour of the country is not completely off. I will try to talk Don into it. I suspect he has the money left but it would wipe him clean.

[. . .]

And then there is your nice and intelligent long letter. One thing I cannot do is ask you to risk your career, the possibility of jobs, etc. I mean I don't ask you, & it's sort of a separate question also, isn't it. – I don't want to talk about Tom so let this be the last time. You say I don't understand, but I do, really. I knew you wanted to make it work with him, but that he was such a booby that it was impossible (which introduced a convenient safeguard so

160

that it cd be prolonged). I also know you were trying to get a reaction from me, and it was partly (entirely!) my awareness of this that made me think to hell with you both, I'll feel nothing & show nothing. & I also know that you were trying to give College Boy Ideal a chance, except that Tom was not C.B.I. – ~~his difference from me was not between types, but~~ he was as different from C.B.I. as I was. You may not believe this, but one of my main feelings was depression that your judgment could be so unutterably lousy. However, that isn't my business. In any case, I do think this was your sort of attempt – an abortive attempt – at a 2nd marriage. It was so at the start. However, it wasn't at all a thoroughgoing attempt (1) because, however you felt about him, you knew he wasn't worth it, and (2) because your eye was on me, how I wd react, at the time.

Later: I love you poppet. Found your sex-filled letter today at Filbert (I'd had to go back to pick up a parcel from the post office). I really don't know what to say to you by way of advice. Speaking unselfishly, I would say if you want to get married as fully as you do, you should stay in NY. You do not like promiscuity, and one of 2 things wd happen here – you wd be promiscuous, which would depress you; or you would find the guy you want, in which case you would move out. Well, you know all this, my darling. I get the feeling I spend my life in telling you things you already know. – I have the feeling, at times, that I don't have very much time left, and that I should make the most of it in trying harder to become the person I want to be.

Take no notice of the last 2 lousy paragraphs. Still haven't had sex in I don't know when. 4½ months. I was saying to Don yesterday, I wish I could see somebody I found pretty enough to regret not being able to get, even. The pretties have all run away somewhere.

My diet is very strange. I eat hamburger almost every day of the week. And yoghurt from a sense of duty. And lots of fruit. And I eat breakfast at 12 or 1, a big meal, usually with Don, at 5 or 6, and a Snack at about 11. – You will be interested to know I am having much the same trouble as you with not taking sleeping pills. I sleep all right normally, but after a night out find it difficult. Oddly curious, that. Now I will take the dog for a walk, since she is making noises likes she wants to piss somewhere.

x x x x

1. Date supplied through internal evidence.
2. Chuck Arnett (1928–88), American dancer and artist. See Glossary of Names. The Tool Box opened at Fourth Street and Harrison in 1961 and was the first leather bar in the South of Market neighbourhood. Arnett painted a large mural of leathermen in the Tool Box: see 'Homosexuality in America', *Life* (26 June 1964), 66–73.
3. 'Driving to Florida'; see TG to MK, *c.* 27 February 1963, above.

Monday 6 May 1963[1]

Monday

Dear Wynken Nodd,

I felt like going on a drunk after your call last night, but the doctor says no, so I went to see The Birdman of Alcatraz and afterwards drank orange juice & 7up. It was in a way very lovely talking to you baby, though.

This is supposed to be the letter in which the level-headed Gunn gives Crazy Mike some good advice. By my troth, Gaffer Gunn, 'tis a fine head of hair ye have there. – Mend thy ways, Crazy Mike, and thou too shalt grow hair unto thy waist. (Mike's hair starts growing rapidly. They waltz until they trip over Mike's hair.)

– Just got a note from you.

I repeat that it isn't my choice to make, baby, at all, at all. Obviously I'm going to say – again – come out here, and at once. Your depressions and unhappiness get out of control in the East, they do not here. The ironical thing is that you can get work in the East, and not here. But there's no point in being near work you don't feel like doing & can't do. I think it is a very great loss to you and – really really – to the stage if you give it up, but it's like a boxer getting too old or something: if you're physically incapable it's ridiculous to hang around wishing you're physically capable. [. . .]

I said on the phone that I must also think of myself, and you obviously thought this unforgivably selfish in the circumstances. But what I mean is this – I must live a life that enables me to keep writing, since this is really all I am left with, for all its self-distrust and doubt. Now, I was writing until you came from NY in 1961 and I started writing this year: I honestly don't think it worried you that I didn't – couldn't – write a line during the era of the great quarrels and the era of Tom Gee, the whole time you were here. This wasn't selfishness on your part, I think, it just didn't strike you. But it contributed to my unhappiness, which in turn made it more difficult for me to write again. Writing was once easy for me: it is when you start, I guess, but now it is very lengthy and difficult, so if I do not arrange my life according to it I simply do not have a chance. – It was certainly not your <u>presence</u> that stopped me in 1961 and 1962, but it was all that went on that made me too depressed to do anything but drink. I never knew in what mood you'd be when I came in (I too need a species of security, I guess). I'm not complaining about the past, baby, that would be silly, but only saying yet again that things must be different. I hope I never have two years again like those, and wouldn't willingly enter them again, now I'm out of them, under any circumstances. If

I didn't know it was a virus, I'd say that hepatitis was a logical culmination of them – the liver (the center of the body) turning against the rest of the body in revulsion at a life it doesn't want to lead.

This last paragraph I mean merely for what it says, not to keep you away, my darling. I love you very much and I want your good: I am incredibly worried about you, as you must know. I wasn't angry (as you thought) at your long letter, but very very upset by it and unhappy. And couldn't answer it.

So go on a bus to the Palisades. And walk there all afternoon. And don't start thinking till you've been there an hour or two, so that you can get a bit tranquil. And then decide to come back to California & be a teacher. (Gunn's home therapy, outlined above.) And come out damn quickly – you've been deciding to decide for eight months now and that's long enough. If you'd come out before there would be more time before I go to Mexico. – I love you, you lovely man (and obviously everybody else considers you lovely, you've been doing so much screwing). I must get up (I'm still in bed). There is a cat on my feet and another cat in the bed under my knees, so getting up may be difficult. Look after your precious self, my beloved, and decide what is right for you. x x x x x x x x x

1. Date supplied through internal evidence.

TO *Mike Kitay*   AL Mike Kitay
Tuesday 28 May 1963[1]

Filbert
Tuesday

Hello Hebrew,
   [. . .]
Let me define what I mean by selling out, a phrase I did not mean to apply to you even indirectly. It is when somebody has worked all his life toward achieving a personal freedom of activity, and then adopts a life in which this freedom will be inhibited, eventually diminished, and finally made away with. [. . .] For you to become a teacher I would look on as rather the reverse of selling out, babe: you have theoretically all the freedom in the world right now, but in fact it is unrealized by activity.

Well it is about one, and sunless, and I have that somewhat limbo feeling between sleep & waking you must know so well. Ugh. – I still haven't seen yr last letter but one, since Don forgot to bring it. – We are getting 2 kittens from his Siamese cat at the end of the summer. I know the mother well, &

she is the essence of intelligence, and Don tells me the father is very butch.
[. . .]

The only time I was in love with Don was the last 2 weeks I was in bed, & then I knew what it was, having heard of patients falling for doctors or analysts. I mean I knew that in a position where I had resigned myself to temporary dependence, then the person I'm dependent on becomes a kind of father figure, doing everything for me, etc. So I knew it for what it was & didn't take it seriously.

In answer, in part, to another part of your letter: you always credit me with lack of feeling because I often don't show feeling. I'm sure my feeling threshold is also much higher than yours, but also I don't particularly want to show it. Maybe it's having read too many boys' stories when I was little, or something, but I admire the understatement of feeling more than anything. In that feelings are tricky, and are always available, and everybody has too many of them; whereas the mind is a control, and is never as strong as it ought to be, and most people have almost none of it. Like in Handel and Vivaldi and Caravaggio and Racine, if you see what I mean: the feelings in them are <u>contained</u> within a clean and strong framework. It is not that feelings are less important than the mind, but that they have a tendency to anarchy and the mind doesn't, and if they are allowed full power – with me, anyway – one is Hitler (and one's always <u>potentially</u> Hitler), while if the mind is allowed as much power as it can take, it can never take very much power anyway. – This is not what I <u>am</u>, but what I say to myself. It's a lousy sketch of the human psychology, certainly. – But you say you would be crippled by the loss of both Tony & Don. I [would] feel very bad at losing them, but I refuse to allow myself to be crippled again. I was crippled for about 5 years in my teens, and I was crippled in 1961 and 1962, but I hope I am strong enough (& lucky enough) to be able to prevent it again.

Well, maybe this is very objectionable to you, my darling. It is not meant to be so. I do love you very much. But my love for you must be framed by a concept of myself otherwise it is mere surgings, meaningless, and bound to sink like a flood into a marsh, see. My sweetheart, I do look forward to seeing you again.

x x x x x x x x x x x x x x x x

> There is a poem, obviously in answer to On the Move, by Alan Stephens (a friend) in the latest Poetry, entitled My Friend the Motorcyclist.[2] It is a very lovely poem, & I'm flattered as all hell that he wrote it.

1. Date supplied through internal evidence.

2. Stephens's 'My Friend the Motorcyclist' imitates the syllabic form and rhyme scheme of TG's poems 'Considering the Snail' and 'My Sad Captains'.

TO *Tony Tanner*   ALS King's

Saturday 31 August 1963[1]

975 Filbert

31 Aug

Dear Tony –

Two days ago we came back to San Francisco, which is – at Filbert, anyway – the veritable Pussy-Land that Mexican cabdrivers were always offering to drive us to. Don recovered himself after we left Chicago, and was profuse in apologies to me – yes, Don apologizes. He did say, actually, driving back from the airport where we deposited you, "I do hope Tony knew how pleased I was to see him." After that, I spent a few days away from that awful family and came back to find the mother had fallen and broken her hip and spine. However, when we left she was mending. Then we drove to West Texas, New Mexico and Colorado, which was as good as any part of our trip. Around Amarillo is "Hud" country – beautifully understated and flat and lovely. And Denver struck me as one of the prettiest towns I had seen, and also a real town, if you get me. So, except for Chicago, it was a hugely successful summer.

And now I am 34, and there are poems to finish, and poses to adopt before I sleep.[2] Mike is on the whole returning to good health, being as there is nothing organic wrong with him. Last night we went to Vesuvio's, and both us old tabbies had some beer.

I said I would write you about Victorian poetry, but actually all the books dealing with it are at school.[3] Tennyson is the best of the mid-Victorians, and the book I recommended was by Harold Nicholson.[4] He certainly pointed out some good poems by T that I'd have missed otherwise, particularly a latish one, Horatian, entitled "To the Rev (XY)" or some such name, and having as third line "And only hear the magpie's chatter."[5] (This is a peculiar reference, I admit.) Auden published a selected Tennyson, which has a long introduction, I think.[6] – Browning's most exciting poem is "Childe Roland to the Dark Tower Came," which you probably know. The first few stanzas seem to be influenced by Donne! Elizabeth BB was devitalizing him, so he took his leave of her for a couple of days, and wrote this poem in some inner room, refusing to see her. – For the ultimate effect of Browning's style, see the first version of Pound's first canto, as published in Poetry (Chicago) around 1915 or so.[7] In it Pound describes both B's style and what he himself was aiming at. – [Thomas Lovell] Beddoes is the other interesting poet: one stunner is the song by the unborn creature in, I think, "Death's Jest Book." All the songs in that play are worth reading. [George] Darley is a dead loss, and [Thomas] Hood even more so. – Lionel Johnson may be worth looking up, the poem Yeats quotes in his autobiography, "Dark Angel," is quite good. And probably you could bring in Hopkins and at least half of Hardy and Bridges as Victorians. God Speed to you, young man. Childe Tanner to the Dark Tower came. – I would indeed be very delighted to share the dedication with [Marcia].[8] [. . .]

I have been reading things like H.G. Wells, but mainly playing with the cats since I came back. Damn it, I wish I could keep travelling for ever. I wouldn't write anything, but I'd have a great time. Thank you for the picture of Tony Tanner, Tony Curtis, it almost made me throw up. The third Tony (White) seriously thinks of coming here in January. Encourage him. See you next summer,

     Love,

        Thom

1. Date supplied through internal evidence.
2. See Robert Frost's 'Stopping by Woods on a Snowy Evening' (1923), 'But I have promises to keep, / And miles to go before I sleep.'
3. Tanner was writing a series of lectures on Victorian poetry.
4. Nicolson, Tennyson: Aspects of His Life, Character, and Poetry (1923).
5. 'To the Rev. F. D. Maurice' (1854); the line is 'And only hear the magpie gossip'.
6. A Selection from the Poems of Alfred, Lord Tennyson, ed. Auden (1944).
7. Ezra Pound, 'Three Cantos: I', Poetry 10, no. 3 (June 1917), 113–21.
8. Tanner, The Reign of Wonder: Naivety and Reality in American Literature (1965).

Monday 23 December 1963

975 Filbert,
San Francisco,
Calif.

23 Dec 63

Dear Tanner –

Many thanks for your two very helpful letters. I delayed answering them because I wanted to act on them and show the results, but put off and put off. I will enclose it, I hope finished, also the Dying Lady, a bit revised, and two new ones. I have got quite far with the long poem, which is called "For the Survivor"¹ it will be probably in fifteen parts, that is unless I decide to cut some of them out. I have most of it in a very rough draft, but a decent showable draft won't be ready till at least the summer, and that done I could finish it in England. It is a new feeling for me, who have written such short things always, of being committed to a big structure, with the misgivings that maybe not only matters could go wrong with the structure of the separate parts but with the way the whole is put together. This must be a familiar feeling for you, though. Well, I cross my fingers and hope about it, anyway.

[. . .]

I am feeling that ungratefulness at San Francisco that I feel every year during the two months of winter. I.E. I think, as every year, of moving to England. While being certain that next year will cure me of that. I must say, though, that I look forward enormously to being in England for a while, seeing you and White & my brother, and living in London.

I have seen Jules & Jim again, and like it as much on the third time as the first. And the Loneliness of the L-D Runner, which struck me as funny in parts but rather poor, really. And 8½, which is like Ezra Pound, "procedure by random association" – good harem scene, but a big bore in What It Has To Say, and it <u>has</u> to, doesn't it? And Tom Jones, which I could happily see several more times. It is maybe derivative in techniques, but it's really so enjoyable I couldn't worry.

I also read The Transposed Heads & The Tales of the Law & The Black Swan – the two last I agree with you are two of the best things Tommy Mann ever wrote. They sum up so much that is good in him, the ambiguities that are so carefully under control and are not confusions, the delicacy of moral concern, the concern over disease as health and health as disease. Also I dragged thro The Beloved Returns, which I understand is pretty sparkling in the original if you know the whole of Goethe well in German. I am now reading Joseph and his Brothers, and after that (next December?) will read Buddenbrooks. As you see, with The Survivor and Tommy Mann, I have my life pretty well mapped out till the end of next year.

I read all Thomas Hardy's poems and am now working my way through Pound, for this new course next semester. I must say, there isn't really much <u>there</u> in Pound, is there? I am sending you Alan Stephens' new book, but it won't get to you for at least a month, as I had to order it.[2] I think it's the best new book of poems since – since (fill in name you want) _____. It is really splendid, twice as good as his first book, a book that makes me envious as no one else's does, because he has both more vigor than me and more delicacy, and he also thinks better. Of course, no one over here will even know about it, and he probably won't get famous for 40 years. Meanwhile Jon Silkin is a widely-appreciated Young Poet.[3]

Tell me, when you have time, if you prefer The Bitch of Dead Buckram in this version.[4] You somewhat misread The Dying Lady, which was my fault – she does the nibbling – I hope it's clear now.[5] Corpus Christi is probably rather too much worked upon,[6] it has too <u>much</u> going on in it, like Berlin in Ruins and that Godawful Doctor poem.[7] There's bit of Hans Castorp in it (in his blankets outside the sanatorium, and one of Mann's favorite words in that book, 'soldierly') and a bit of Odysseus (!!!) but they are not particularly noticeable & don't help it much.[8] Tending Bar I mean as a kind of substitute for the other poem of that name rather than as an addition to it.[9] I hope it's better, anyway. The second & 3rd stanzas are still a bit rough. ('To count the breakage' you may or may not know is a term (Eng. as well as Am.?) for counting the number of bottles of liquor consumed in a bar in a given night.)

A. Alvarez is coming here in January. Somebody wrote me that he "is now in the international literary set, now off to a weekend at Mary [McCarthy]'s near Paris, now to a party given by Hannah Arendt in New York." I find this hugely funny. I get on quite well with him, actually, since I am politic and sly when it comes to somebody who has got me a profitable option with the Observer. Can't say I like his theories of poetry any more than Conquest's or Davie's, with both of whom I am also politic and sly, mainly because what they say often seems rather plausible and because I'm not always sure what my own theory of poetry is.

[. . .]

Looking back through this letter it seems like a list of movies, books and poems. Other things continue, however, like time, mutability, and the age-old problems that have nonplussed mankind in their various and sundry manifestations.

I couldn't go on with that paragraph. Actually I had intended to make a wise comment or two on my psychical-passional state, but I am so many faceted [. . .] that I find it difficult to sum myself up other than by the term, possibly derogatory, more likely laudworthy, of "many-faceted thing"!

Here I will go from you,

         a sincere shake of the hand

         and a cordial offering of the emotional clasp

              from

                   A Many Faceted Thing

1. An early title for 'Misanthropos' (*CP* 133–51).
2. Stephens, *Between Matter and Principle* (1963).
3. Jon Silkin (1930–97), poet, academic and founding editor of the magazine *Stand*.
4. 'The Girl of Live Marble', *The Observer* (19 April 1964), 28; collected in *T*, but cut from *CP*.
5. 'The Dying Lady', *The Observer* (9 February 1964), 26; uncollected.
6. 'The Vigil of Corpus Christi' (*CP* 170–1).
7. 'The Doctor's Own Body', *The Observer* (15 December 1963), 25; uncollected.
8. Castorp is the protagonist of Mann's *The Magic Mountain*.
9. 'Tending Bar', *Critical Quarterly* 6, no. 1 (Spring 1964), 33–4; uncollected.

1964

TO *Donald Hall*   ALS New Hampshire
Tuesday 25 February 1964

975 Filbert,
San Francisco,
Calif.

25 Feb 64

Dear Don –

Good to hear from you, even though I haven't yet answered your last. Yes, you did send me a manuscript of your book,[1] and I did actually write a long long letter about them over Christmas, which I ended by throwing away. It wasn't that bad, it just didn't say explicitly or clearly enough what I wanted to say. The trouble is that now when I have the slightest reservation about your work, I feel I ought to write a book supplying background argument establishing what I think imagery should do, what I think about surrealism, etc. etc., before I can get down to the particular points.

Actually I do, in a lazy kind of way, think of writing a prose book. But then I've been thinking of doing that for about 5 years now.

Hepatitis was really good for me! Or maybe it was a summer in Mexico and the South West. I have been writing steadily for the last year, and at last (I think) I am beginning to get some good results. There have been a lot of crappy things of course, and some of them have had to be published before I could see how bad they are, but I'm beginning to see more clearly what I can be doing now. I have been working on a kind of long poem for the last 9 months, in which I have a peculiar faith. I hope to finish it around the end of the year – don't have time till I've been in England a couple of months.

[. . .]

They seem to be getting very upset over syllabics in England. Every time I open the TLS let alone other mags., there seems to be a manifesto for or against. I don't know why, seeing free verse has been around so long. Though from the bit of [George] Macbeth that I see quoted, they are so bad that maybe I do see why. Somebody said Macbeth "invented" syllabics.[2] Really! As I see the lineage, it's like this

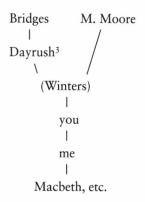

Bridges   M. Moore
|
Dayrush[3]
\
(Winters)
|
you
|
me
|
Macbeth, etc.

    Though the only bit I'm sure of is that I learnt how to use syllabics from studying your poems. [. . .]
        Love,

           Thom

1. Hall, *A Roof of Tiger Lilies* (1964).
2. TG challenged this suggestion: see *Times Literary Supplement* (12 March 1964), 215.
3. Elizabeth Daryush (1897–1977), poet. 'I have been ridiculed for praising her by various people who have never read her,' wrote Winters, 'among them Mr. Thom Gunn, who has never learned to spell her name.' See Winters, *Forms of Discovery* (1967), 347–8, and TG's 'On a Drying Hill: Yvor Winters' (*SL* 197–212).

TO *Charles Monteith*   ALS (aerogramme) Faber
Thursday 28 May 1964

                    975 Filbert St.,
                    San Francisco,
                    California,
                    U.S.A.

                    28 May 64

Dear Charles –
    This is just to tell you that I'm leaving this address in three weeks time. I'll be staying a few weeks in New York next month, and will phone you soon after I reach London.[1] Meanwhile if you need to forward any mail or anything (not that I expect any) you can send it to my brother.
    [. . .]

I wonder if you have ever considered being the English publisher of Gary Snyder [. . .] He has what they call "a growing reputation" in England as well as here. He was rather mistakenly associated in people's minds with the Beats at first, but actually he is a careful craftsman, and his work is very unGinsbergian: he was influenced at first, clearly, by Pound, but in the best way and by the best of Pound (e.g. E.P.'s Cantos 2 & 4!). His first two books "Riprap" and "Myths and Texts" – which I find really splendid – were both brought out by little publishers here, but clearly his next book will be published by one of the larger houses. It strikes me that his first two, anyway, could well be brought out in England as one volume.[2] – I scarcely know him, by the way, so this suggestion is completely altruistic, i.e. he doesn't know I am making it to you. – You can get a small idea of what his work is like from the selection in Donald Hall's Penguin anthology,[3] but I think his best work is in his second book, not represented there. If you are unable to get it in London – and the only place would be somewhere like Better Books – I could bring you a copy when I see you. – In any case, he is worth your consideration, and I am sure F&F would not be losers by publishing him.

I look forward to seeing you in a couple of months.

I intend to be in London the best part of a year. It sounds very much changed, from all I hear.

> Best,
>
> Thom

1. In 1964 TG received a National Institute of Arts and Letters Grant that allowed him to spend a sabbatical year in London.
2. *Riprap* and *Myths and Texts* were collected in *A Range of Poems* (1966); see TG, 'The Early Snyder' (*OP* 36–46).
3. *Contemporary American Poetry*, ed. Hall (1962).

TO *Mike Kitay*   AL Mike Kitay
Wednesday 11 November 1964[1]

80 Talbot Rd
W2

Wed (i.e. Nov 11)

Dear Babe –

A letter from you yesterday, and then a letter from you today! That's what we Anglicans call God's Plenty. I should really be typing out me article,[2] but

I feel more like writing to the Queen of Kearny, especially after such a bad start to the day as all my gas going out, so I had to limp out into the cold and collect sixpences.

I have disposed well of the problems you speak about in the first letter. I simply see a select few people, and say no to everybody else. In fact the No's in my letters get more and more uncompromising, in one I wrote yesterday I said "let us put lunch off till the spring." A rather ridiculous sentence, if everybody did that they'd be hungry. I have Supper on Mondays with White, and we discuss a Book, like Aristotle (no shit, back on the old self-improvement kick). I must say the years have made him very gentle and considerate. In the middle of the weeks I go to see the Teddington Gunns.[3] At the end of the weeks Tanner & Marcia turn up. You ask how are they? Christ knows. I'm beginning to think that on the whole they slightly get on each other's nerves. Anyways, I have stopped speculating on them. [. . .]

Noel Coward on Camelot: "It's Parsifal with all the jokes taken out."

Tony Tanner dreamed that he had invited both the Beatles and the Rolling Stones to High Table at King's. Really that man's sleeping life is of a piece with his waking life.

[. . .]

Spent Guy Fawkes' night at Ruth's, making sure her children didn't explode themselves with fireworks & also making sure the bonfire didn't get out of hand. It really took me back to my childhood.

[. . .]

Babe, don't worry about worrying me. If you feel like being unhappy in a letter to me, I am happy at least that you are writing it to me rather than holding it in and having no one to say it to. So don't worry about that, at least, my precious. And you are precious to me, baby. [. . .] If Peter [Tangen] couldn't put you up [in New York], could Glenn?[4] If neither could put you up, try to find out if you would be able to cash traveller's checks signed by me. You would then have enough to live on for a couple of months. Please do not scruple to accept these, my darling. I am not trying to buy your affection or sell my own blame or do anything but simply provide you with some money when you need it, as you have often done with me and as I have no doubt you will do with me in the future. I can send you $300. [. . .]

No, I need nothing. If & when I do, I'll ask you to send it. Please do not send me anything for Christmas, as I know you are poor.

Do send a note to Peter Wood, saying I told you to. [. . .] He is immensely curious to see you, after having heard about you over a period of some 12 years, and I'm sure if he does have time he will. He is nice, really, and I think you would like him – as much as I do, anyway.

Interesting that you are to be arrested. Mike the Jail Bird, "The Ballad of Kearny Jail!" a smash-hit musical by an old lag, Mike "Tickets" Kitay.

Yes, I see why you are depressed about Kinmont [Hoitsma].[5] It shows how insensitive I am, I think, that if I'd simply <u>heard</u> about him I'd have had no particular reaction, and that it took actually seeing him there and talking to him for me to be depressed by him. Actually, it's him rather than his situation that is so depressing. Well, maybe he needs to be kept, maybe he even finds Cecil Beaton attractive.

I love the joke about "you piss all over my date, etc."

I don't think you'd <u>really</u> like to go to a party. They are mostly enough to make you an old misanthropos and go live on a hill at the end of the world.

I miss you and love you, my darling. Give my best to Glenn and Peter. And <u>keep well</u>. And take plenty of vitamins and no sleeping pills.

              x x x x x x x x x

1. Date supplied through internal evidence.
2. 'Poets in Control', *Twentieth Century* 173, no. 1024 (Winter 1964-5), 102-6; uncollected.
3. Ander and his family lived in Teddington, south-west London. See 'Last Days at Teddington' (*CP* 237).
4. Glenn Jordan (1936-), television director and producer, met TG and MK in Palo Alto in 1958.
5. Cecil Beaton's last boyfriend (from the early 1960s until CB's death); Olympic fencer.

TO *Mike Kitay*   AL Mike Kitay
Thursday 17 December 1964[1]

                                                  80 Talbot Rd.,
                                                    London W.2

                                                      Thursday

Mike Lovely,

No letter from you yet this week, which I suppose is the Christmas mail, but I hope you continue in your triumphant restoration of wit to TV and are earning more money and have got some contract, my sweetheart. & also have started writing a <u>play</u>. [. . .]

This letter is being written rather late really, the reason being that on Monday the BBC said they wanted to see a draft of ['For the Survivor']. So I spent that day, Tues, & Wed, in not only typing but getting it presentable. & when I read it through yesterday before sending it, Jesus what a pompous boring thing it seemed. Oh Gunny, are you simply tedious in your middle age? I'm afraid so.

Otherwise it has been a week moderately fully of discomforts, rising to an artistic climax during one hour on Sunday morning during which I broke a plate, found the water-heater wouldn't produce hot water, and lost a filling weighing at least an ounce from one of me teeth. Who said God doesn't play favorites?

Anyway, I had all my lunches and dinners, which was awful enough. Lehmann came, gave me his disconcerting peck on the face (I <u>wish</u> he wouldn't, but it seems hard to insult a man in his fifties), talked about cocks, talked about minor poets, gave me another dry peck, and left. He did it is true bring with him this gorgeous butch dog with a great curly face who kept on leaping about, then disappearing for a moment to return bringing a tube of Tackle[2] proudly back to us. Doris, I thought I'd die.

Then my <u>big</u> social event was on Saturday. Well I had all the lights lowered, the candles lit, the doileys laid out and the place-cards, and the under-stairs maid was briefed on all to do, and – they arrived. Actually it was very nice – two Tonies and a Marcia, and I cooked surprisingly well.

And I saw The Outlaw – Jane Russell's first film. She is absolutely gorgeously comically dumb. And beautiful, I'd never realized how genuinely sexy she had once been. Terribly funny in a kind of wonderful dated way, the whole film – huge sustained bursts of Wagnerian themes every time she is even <u>about</u> to kiss the hero, who was rather sexy, called Jack Buetel.

[. . .]

I am going down to Kent for Christmas for a few days – a bit reluctantly, but it will probably turn out nice seeing all those relatives. I mean they're all nice people. It's just that Christmas would come quite often enough if it were once every three years. – Also it will be healthy not to drink, I have got a bit liverish these last few days (more than 2 years after, god what a systematic illness old hep is).

I ran amok in the toy-shops getting things for my nephews and niece. Now I keep playing with their toys, which I haven't taken to them yet. There is one you would love, it is a great green frog that hops under the bed, I keep feeling it is really Fletcher.[3]

[. . .]

My precious, I do hope you are well – and successful still. Success is very good for your health, I am sure, and in any case it's only justice to you. You are wonderful to have written all those sketches. I would love to read them, if you are able to send me copies, if you have copies. Put them in a big envelope and send them surface mail.

Title for the long poem? I once mentioned this before:
"In the City of Kites and Crows" (Coriolanus)[4]
The trouble is, it doesn't really fit the content of the poem in detail. – I <u>have</u> taken out a good deal of the foliage and flowers you didn't like. Probably some more should go. I feel that probably at least half the poem should be cut, but what half, which halves, oh dear.

Sorry about this letter. I have the feeling I'm always apologizing for my letters, and rightly apologizing. Hope you have gone to a merry party or two, my precious. I love you, my sweetheart, and in the New Year they are planning to make you Pope. (It's part of the Catholic plans for recognition of the Jews.) Keep yourself warm and well, my handsome baby.

    x x x x x x x x x x

1. Date supplied through internal evidence.
2. An acne treatment.
3. Fletcher was one of TG and MK's cats.
4. *Coriolanus* (4. 3. 53); a possible title for 'Misanthropos'.

1965

TO *Charles Monteith*   ALS Faber

Monday 25 January 1965

80 Talbot Rd.,
London W.2

25 Jan 65

Dear Charles –

Well, I have finally finished the Long Poem, so I can think of other things. It is to be done on the BBC some time or other.[1]

Thank you very much for the two books. I have thought of two poets for a "Choice." One is Hardy; the trouble with him is (a) I should think most of his work is still bound by copyright, and (b) selections from him already exist, though not very good ones. So I imagine he is out of the question. The other you may consider more promising – Fulke Greville. Greville is very little known, and what there is by him in anthologies is not his typical or best work. The Oxford edition of his poetry has been out of print a long time.[2] And he is a terribly good poet. I would be delighted to do a book of him, if I have your approval.

Incidentally, I wonder if you would be able to recommend a second-hand bookseller who might be able to get me a copy of the Oxford Greville. I have been out of England so long that I don't know much about this kind of thing. Not that there is much hope of my getting a copy (I have tried before). I can easily work from library copies.

Best,

Thom

1. 'Misanthropos' was broadcast on the BBC Third Programme on 8 March 1965.
2. *Poems and Dramas of Fulke Greville, First Lord Brooke*, 2 vols, ed. Geoffrey Bullough (1939).

ALS British Library

80 Talbot Rd.,
London W.2

9 Feb 65

Dear Al,

Thank you for a very fine evening last week. You are a far better cook than I will ever be.

I enclose a new poem or rather new series of poems, probably also too long for the Observer.² Hope you like it (or bits of it) even if you can't use it. Sling it back if you can't use it, anyway.

You may well be right about those parts of Misanthropos that you don't like, though I'm too close to it all still to be able to judge. Just the same, I don't think it's fair to Winters to refer to him in describing them. He can't be blamed for the kind of style I'm writing in the couplet and blank verse poems – I'd started on the metrical-epigrammatic before I'd ever heard of him. The 'Elegy on the Dust' has Marvell and Herbert behind it, not Winters. I have written one poem (in my second book) which is a deliberate evocation of YW's style, the poem called To Yvor Winters, 1955, and I think if you compare that one with any of the metrical poems in Misanthropos you'll see a big difference.

I say this rather by way of a footnote to our discussion than an attempt to start it again.

Best, and thank you for reading all the crap I send you –

Thom

1. Al Alvarez (1929–2019), writer, critic and poetry editor of *The Observer* (1956–66). Alvarez had played an important part in establishing TG's reputation through book reviews in *The Observer* and in his anthology *The New Poetry* (1962), to which TG was a key contributor. It might be argued that his turn against such poems as 'Misanthropos' initiated the decline in TG's reputation.
2. 'Confessions of the Life Artist' (CP 159–63) was first published in the *New Statesman*.

80 Talbot Rd.,
London W.2

25 Feb 65

Dear John –

Many thanks for your comments. I think you misunderstand my motives in ['Misanthropos'] – I don't <u>want</u> the absence of humans. What I wanted was (1) to see how someone (myself?) would act in the absence of humans without hope of ever seeing any again, and (2) to isolate him in the poem, for this purpose. I had thought I have quite a good old upbeat and rush of optimism at the end of the poem (you are, oddly, at one with Alvarez in disliking the last part)! As for the other absences – of plants and animals – those I suppose are deliberate, though there are plenty of references to them, in that I cut out one or two poems that were positively webs of foliage. The trouble with plants is that you can like them, but they can't like you back, it's a real one-way relationship. – Glad you like the 'Memoirs of the World' section. It is very nice of you to have read the whole thing through and to have told me what you think of it. Yes of course you may keep the copy. As I say, I'm sorry it is a carbon.

You say you wish I "didn't pull my poetry-making self so far away from my life-enjoying self." This certainly gives me qualms. One of my troubles (one of my writer's troubles, I suppose) is in not being able to get down on paper the whole of what I find valuable or true about what I experience. (This is perhaps especially difficult for a poet, as opposed to a novelist?) I have a great delight in the trivial and casual – things one may see on the street – that are somehow lovely because they are part of the whole absurd and pointless and wonderful expression of energy ("life-energy," that is). But I have not yet found a good framework for these – the mere recording of them would not be very impressive.

At the same time, I don't think I am being at all dishonest in the attitudes behind my poetry. Not that you say I am dishonest but you imply that they are different from the attitudes I act on as a "life-enjoying" person. My enjoyment, in both important and trivial things, is very great because I'm as aware as any Elizabethan of the mutability/ephemerality of the things I enjoy. And I don't even have God to believe in, as the Elizabethans did. If I write bleakly, it's because life <u>is</u> pretty bleak, and I don't see any way of denying it. What I'm particularly concerned with are the ways in which one can operate fully and at one's best <u>at the same time</u> as perceiving the total bleakness. (This is why I see Camus as, not the greatest, but the central writer of the last twenty or thirty years.) I hope one day I'll be able to do it better, and get more in, than what I do now. God knows I don't see myself as having achieved anything so far.

You didn't expect a pompous letter like this in answer, did you? Don't bother to answer it – I'm just trying to elucidate a bit, not start an argument.
Love,
Thom
[. . .]

TO *Clive Wilmer*[1]   ALS Clive Wilmer
Thursday 25 February 1965

80 Talbot Road,
London W.2

25 Feb 65

Dear Clive –

I have kept these poems of Sylvia Plath's for months. Thank you very much for sending them: I have read them through a good deal.[2]

I am still not quite sure what they add up to. Each poem is a series of exclamations and images loosely connected by the theme stated in the title, but the connection is often very loose. Only about two of the poems (e.g. "The Rival", and "Kindness") have any construction worth talking about. The result is that together they make a kind of rambling hysterical monologue, which is fine for people who believe in art as Organic but less satisfactory for those who demand more. Nevertheless there are some incredibly beautiful passages, where an image suddenly emerges from the crowd of other images and <u>takes over</u> for a few lines. The garden in "Edge" is an obvious example, but almost every poem has a passage like this, long or short, where the image becomes an enormous and compelling actuality, and where the movement is an exact and urgent transmitter of the emotion. The trouble is with the emotion, itself, really, it is largely one of hysteria, and it is amazing that her hysteria has produced poetry as good as this. I think there's a tremendous danger in the fact that we <u>know</u> she committed suicide. If they were anonymous poems I wonder how we'd take them.

Don't mistake me. I did enjoy them, and they have tremendous passages, but I don't think they are great poetry as Alvarez does.

The book of her collected posthumous poems is finally to come out, in the next month or so.[3] I am afraid we are due for one of those boring literary wars over it, the kind that the journalist-poets haven't indulged in since the death of Dylan Thomas. Myself, I don't feel inclined to take sides.

Thank you again.

Best,

Thom

1. Clive Wilmer (1945–), poet, critic, and lecturer. See Glossary of Names.
2. Wilmer sent TG a clipping of Plath's poems 'Edge', 'The Fearful', 'Kindness' and 'Contusion', from *The Observer* (17 February 1963), and 'The Last Poems of Sylvia Plath', *The Review* 9 (October 1963), 3–19, which includes 'Daddy', 'Lady Lazarus' and 'Ariel'.
3. *Ariel* (1965).

TO *Belle Randall*[1]   ALS Bancroft
Thursday 18–Saturday 20 March 1965[2]

80 Talbot Rd.,
London W.2

18 March 64[3]

Dear Belle,

I am filled with rather large feelings of guilt. I mean, to be a month or two late in answering a letter is understandable, but as long as this! I did write a long beginning to a letter last autumn, about how I met TS Eliot, but I seem to have lost it. London is for you, really. One day you will come here and decide it is a mixture of the best in New York and the best in San Francisco. I suddenly realized, when I was here, that this had always been my great ambition, to live in London. All my childhood was spent in a nice kind of suburb, which was not the same kind of thing at all. I am living in a rather fine district, about as racially mixed as could be imagined – West Indians, Poles, Irish mainly, but also Greeks and Spanish and English. I like this very much, as you may imagine: it makes for a kind of general good humor and amusement by people at each other's ways. (Though it was here that they had the anti-Negro riots a few years ago.[4] But you see very few signs of anti-Negro feeling here now.)

I have been working like a prince. I mean, at least hard, I don't know if well. Often when I have gone away to write I suddenly find that I'm able to do nothing, but I had enough started and shaped out this time for me to have a foundation. I finished the long poem, which I'm sending you by surface mail (won't reach you for a month). It still needs a bit of rewriting in places, I think. I also wrote a weird series of tiny poems, in syllabics, called The Life Artist. [. . .]

I found out why people say you cannot write if you live in London. If you accept every invitation to lunch you find there is very little of the day left, by the time you get back in the afternoon, what with having had some rich publisher's or editor's wine, you feel past writing. So I decided early on to go out to lunch only once a month.

I met Mr Eliot a few months before he died. He was already rather weak and would start long sentences and get lost in the middle of them. He was an immensely big man, did you know? Very wide, very tall, very large head. He had a signed photograph of Groucho Marx on the wall.

There is a street here – in the East End by the docks, that you would like. On one side is the Thames, with ships docked. On the other side there are Victorian cottages, but just behind them, rising above them, there are more ships, in canals and artificial docks. So you have ships and water on both sides of you, and it is like a road through a river.

I had an "interview" in the Observer the other day. It was shocking – untrue. I say this in case you read it. I would hate you to think I actually said what I'm given as saying.[5]

Do you like Robert Lowell's new book?[6] "The Flaw" I think is one of the most beautiful poems he has written, and I like a lot of others in it. – I also read John Berryman's book, "77 Dream Songs," and found it quite funny, but where it was not funny I couldn't make head nor tail of it. – And have you ever read "The Old Wives' Tale" by Arnold Bennett? You would like it very much. It is like a Victorian novel without any of the faults of a Victorian novel, and beautifully felt, without even any sentimentality in the feeling.
[. . .]

20 March

I saw Olivier (twice) playing Othello. He plays the part like a West Indian, with a West Indian intonation, walking on the balls of his feet, and his first entrance was sniffing a huge red flower. Beautifully done – it made the part really alive for me for the first time: I've always found it rather dead since I saw it played by Jack Hawkins like a British officer unaccountably in black-face (with trouble in the married quarters). And Olivier's interpretation also made wonderful sense of certain transitions (or lack of transitions) in the early tempting-scenes with Iago. It was the best performance of anything I have ever seen, I think, except possibly Helene Wiegel as Mother Courage.
[. . .]

I should be leaving here toward the end of June, but may well not reach California before September.

Love,

Thom

P.S. My best to your mother and John.

1. Belle Randall (1940–), poet and TG's former student. See Glossary of Names.
2. Date supplied through internal evidence.
3. TG misdated this letter.
4. A reference to race riots that took place in Notting Hill in 1958.
5. Kenneth Martin, 'Love me, love my poem', *The Observer* (7 March 1965), 23. TG is quoted as saying, 'My mother committed suicide. I'm told my father was a tyrant in the office. There were other things I wouldn't mention in an interview. I had an eventful childhood.' TG annotated the interview in his scrapbook: 'These 4 sentences were not connected, and occurred in different contexts. The first 2, also, were supposedly spoken off the record.'
6. Lowell, *For the Union Dead* (1964).

TO *Charles Monteith*

ALS Faber

Thursday 26 August 1965

975 Filbert St.,
San Francisco,
Calif.

26 Aug 65

Dear Charles,

Thank you for the letter. I'm glad Ander brought in the book, and very glad you liked it. Now I'll wait and see what your colleagues think of it![1]

By the way, a friend of ours jokingly referred to it as "the Gunn Brothers' Guide to Humans": if you were to accept it, maybe such a title would help it to sell better???

You will notice that I've been rather evasive about the Misanthropos book of poems. I did promise I'd send it to you this summer, and then didn't. I have about enough poems for it, really, but I'm not sure that a lot of them are that strong. I know about half, or maybe three-quarters of the book, is strong enough – but not the rest. So my hope is to substitute better poems for the weak ones, during the next few months.[2] (As for Misanthropos itself, I think it falls off a bit toward the end, but I don't think there's anything else I can do to strengthen it!)

I promise (pledge myself, swear, etc) by Chaucer, Shakespeare, etc., to send you this book by next summer at the latest. Or may I turn into the new Austin Dobson!

[. . .]

> Best,
>
> Thom

1. *Positives* (1966).
2. TG came to think of *Touch* (1967) as a flawed collection: he omitted it from *CP* and included its best poems in a section called 'Poems from the 1960s'.

TO *Tony Tanner*

ALS King's

Saturday 28 August 1965

> 975 Filbert,
> San Francisco,
> Calif.
>
> 28 Aug 65

Dear Tony –

My much congratulations to you and Marcia. Usually when a friend marries, one just has to smile bravely at the friend's choice and be as agreeable as possible before the effect of his choice starts to turn him into somebody different, but when two friends marry that is the cause for genuine happiness. And I am awfully happy for you both. Mike sends wellnigh equivalent congratulations. May you both live for ever and have a hundred pretty children!

I'm finally getting down to a bit of work, though I still find a lecture course on the whole of English poetry rather too much to contemplate without a slight feeling of sickness. – The riot business on campus was really incredible, I find as I read and hear more about it. Do you know that one day a few hundred students declared a Free University in the Admin Building, and graduates started giving lectures on "God and the Theorem", etc.[1] There is likely to be a lot more trouble this year – too many students are expecting and half-hoping for it. Myself, I am turning into a crusty old Tory, I meet so many professional liberals that I find myself defending Johnson in Viet Nam to them. No Englishman who has not been here will believe it, but I haven't met anybody in weeks who will agree with me that there is anything wrong with Communism. Joan Baez, you have had more influence than you think.

Heard from Monteith yesterday. He is quite enthusiastic about the book Ander and I did together and has practically accepted it – but wants to get an estimate of the costs of production before he <u>does</u> accept it. It looks like in the bag, though, Monteith's big bag.

[. . .]

My phone must have belonged to two whores. Strange men call at 3 in the morning and say "Is that Judy?" When I say no (in my high-pitched voice) they then ask for Diana. Judy must have been the good one, Diana the one you fall back on.

Mike's show continues being marvelously successful.[2] He has a chance of doing a play, off Broadway of course, in New York next year, if he can find a good play. I thought of Charles Wood's <u>Cockade</u> (it is too late for [John] Arden, who has already been discovered, in a big way, by NY), since it is 2/3 good, and very modishly "cruel" and queer. And it seems unknown over here. [. . .]

I have decided that what Milly Theale <u>has</u> must be syphilis. Otherwise people would mention what it was. It <u>is</u> a funny book (I have still not finished it), I do like it when Milly observes the American tourists in the National Gallery. One of the pleasures of getting older is that I can find more and more funny. Sir Luke Strett did puzzle me for a while, the way he's able to diagnose things on the basis of three minutes conversation, I was rather afraid that he was God, in fact; but then I realized with great relief that I'd come across him before, quite often, in science fiction. There is always a doctor there who sits a patient in a chair full of sensitive electrical impulses which do the diagnosis for the doctor. And of course Sir Luke Strett must have such a chair.[3]

I am writing a few poems. I cannot feel great confidence about them, but maybe they will turn out better than I think. At least I'm keeping my hand in. Will send them to you in a month or two if I haven't torn them up. They are all metrical, you'll be interested to know.

I am reading Jonson's poetry, all through, for the first time. Very extraordinary – like in the song called Big John that [Doody] is so fond of, he was a big, big man.

It is strange, now that Mike and I do not live together, I find it much easier to talk to him frankly about himself, myself, and us, in a way that he always (rightly) complained I didn't for the last two years.

[. . .]

Do you want Gary Snyder's new book "Six extracts from <u>Mountains and Rivers Without End</u>"? – a slight falling-off, I don't think he ought to write a long poem. Saw him the other day, he is such a nice man (and I know Marcia would find him handsome, even I do slightly) – he has just received a $10,000 award from somewhere, and is off to live in Japan again.

Much love, more congratulations, eternal happiness,
Thom

1. The Free Speech Movement (1964–5) demanded that the UC Berkeley administration lift the ban on campus political activities. TG missed most of the protests while in London.
2. MK directed *Funny Side Up*, a musical revue, at the Sir Francis Drake Hotel in San Francisco.
3. Milly Theale is the American heiress, and Strett her doctor, in Henry James's *The Wings of the Dove* (1902). Tanner was an authority on James – his favourite novelist – and his enthusiasm was infectious; he encouraged TG to read more of him.

TO *Tony Tanner*   ALS King's

Friday 24 December 1965

975 Filbert St.,
San Francisco,
Calif.

24 Dec 65

Dear Tony,

I have all these pals called Tony, see? And I'm never sure which is which. You I believe are the song-and-dance man,[1] and I note that I owe you a letter, but I can't remember how I know you. On the other hand you may be the translator, or the organ-grinder. (Stop grinding that organ.) – This dreadful archness is to cover up my shame for not having written. I keep getting these lovely things from you: today the John Lennon book,[2] another time long witty letters, another time a signed Stones programme. (I worked out Marcia's, yours and TW's handwriting for those signatures. Shiela's and Sean's I could only guess at.)

The best thing I had from you you didn't even send, and that was your essay on Pope.[3] It is seriously one of your very best, perhaps even better than your Under Western Eyes essay. I was due to give a lecture on Pope the next day, so I scrapped my own beginning, borrowed the mag from the faculty library where I had just read it, and read the first section aloud to my students, of course acknowledging you. After the lecture, three graduate students came up to me separately to check the reference, saying it was the best thing they had ever heard on Pope. One day you must collect your essays into a book, so that they are properly available. [. . .]

It is Christmas hols now, as you can see from the date. Not only have I had no time to write letters, I have had no time to write poetry. Haven't even read much: last book I read was The Awkward Age, which you put me on to, and which I expect I told you I find the funniest novel I have ever read. Laugh! I thought I'd piss my pants. I have read other things, to support me in my dreadfully ambitious course – my fault that it was so ambitious – on the whole of English poetry from Chaucer to Hardy. I found that Leavis in Revaluation is very useful, though less so toward the end of the book (impossible on Wordsworth, though I didn't find anyone good on Wordsworth). I also found that Winters is dead right about the Elizabethans: Gascoigne is a fine poet and Ben Jonson (whom I read thoroughly for the first time) is one of the most exciting poets in English (a lecture course on his poetry would be a rewarding albeit demanding experience for you!). – The term has been impossible, though: ridiculous committee work, etc, etc. So I told [James D.] Hart that I was leaving in the summer. 'Weally, Thom, I'm stunned,' he riposted. Eventually we agreed that he could give me another year of leave, without pay of course, and I could then make up my mind about leaving. But I don't see myself changing my mind, so in any case you'll be seeing me toward the end of next year. – San Francisco meanwhile has never seemed so exciting, but maybe this is partly because I know I shall be leaving it. It'll be nice to have a memory of it as the ideal city. I'm just not sure I really should live always in the ideal city.

I got your Saul Bellow book, but have only glanced through it.[4] I must read at least Herzog before I read your book. Meanwhile I've lent it to Doody. DD is in splendid shape, seeming oddly enough rather continuously happy nowadays. I have been encouraging him to write a pornographic novel, do not know whether he is. He & Bryan & their two roommates gave a fine party last Sunday. I started drinking at 6, around 12 we all went to a bar, at 2 DD and I went off to another party that started up, at 3 I passed out for the first time in my life since I was 20! Mike's show is still on: it has had 180 performances or something. [. . .]

I like the Byrds very much. The recent Beatles LP is as good as or perhaps better than anything they sang before.[5] I have seen Help 3 times.

I have sent various things which should soon start arriving. A couple of pamphlets of poetry, later E.A. Robinson (I wish you luck, there are forty pages of good poetry in twelve hundred!), and recently WCW's essays (I wish you even more luck).

My Fulke Greville book is due at the publishers next week. It will not reach them then, however. In fact it will reach them about a year late so far as I can see. No TIME.

I hear great reports of conjugal happiness, it sounds as though St Edward's passage is, as it were, warming frosty Cambridge. And it must be frosty. I hear another kind of report about the weather. Remember you felt a little guilty at not being in England for the winter of 1962? Now is your chance to atone for the feeling. I suggest a naked snow bath in the drifts over King's Parade.

[. . .]

The Viet Nam thing is fantastic. Maybe I was wrong in what I wrote of it several letters ago, though I must say I do not see the rights of the situation very clearly – certainly as it was in the middle of the year and earlier.[6] But right now it seems clear that it will be a war lasting several more years and one of increasing nastiness. You cannot believe how depressing it is to see San Francisco so full of teen-age servicemen. Johnson is marvelous with home affairs – more of a socialist than anyone since Roosevelt – but is totally out of his depth in foreign. He seems to be leaving it all to the generals. It is still a highly unpopular war here, as you can tell from even such unlikely places as film reviews in the Chronicle, but a few more months of Our Boys getting killed and it will be quite popular, I imagine.

x x x x x for Marcia

x x x x for yourself (one less to show I'm no queer)

and a happy new year, and look after the old organ: remember, if it drops off, you won't get another. <u>Wishing</u> won't get you one, that's certain.

       Much love,

           Thom

Mike sends enormous love to you both.

1. The 'song-and-dance man' refers to the actor, director, and choreographer Tony Tanner (1932–2020) who made his name as a revue performer on the London stage.
2. Lennon, *A Spaniard in the Works* (1965).
3. Tanner, 'Reason and the Grotesque: Pope's *Dunciad*', *Critical Quarterly* 7, no. 2 (June 1965), 145–61.
4. Tanner, *Saul Bellow* (1965).
5. *Rubber Soul* was released on 3 December 1965.
6. See TG to Tanner, 28 August 1965, above.

1966

c. Thursday 18 February 1966[1]

975 Filbert St.,
San Francisco,
Calif., USA

Thurs, some time in Feb

Dear Don,

[. . .]

I guess I will be going back to England. I have already told them here that I'm leaving at the end of the semester. Why I am leaving Mike I really don't know – maybe I won't. Decisions are easier to make when you're absent from someone than when you're around the actual warm vulnerable human being. So maybe I'll stay on here, for all I know.

[. . .] I have been doing, for me, wild things. I wrote a whole book of short poems, all in free verse, between Feb and May of last year. They are based on pictures by my brother, photographs, and I was using the opportunity to frankly experiment. I won't enclose any with this, but send you the book when it comes out in September or so. There are 38 poems, and they range from captions merely arranged as verse to poems I think come off, and come off as free verse. There are about three of the former, ten of the latter, and the remainder somewhere in between. Virtually nobody has seen them besides the publisher: I felt, for once, I must do what I could without advice.

I did so much writing last year, and grew a cubit, which is why I must stop teaching a year or two, so as to fill out to justify that cubit. What I mean is what I did may be poor, but I think I learned a few things. I wrote two series of poems besides the one I've just mentioned: a long didactic thing called Misanthropos [. . .] which so far as I can tell only Stephen Spender likes. It is an attempt to bring syllabics and meter closer together by including them in the same poem. I don't think I did bring them closer together, though I have a curious affection for the big clumsy thing that resulted. I also wrote a series of short things in free verse (actually unrhymed syllabics) called The Confessions of the Life Artist, which I'll send you if you haven't seen it. So far as I can tell, only Alvarez liked <u>that</u> one. The trouble is, I know why S.S. & A.A. liked these two poems – solely for the different types of subject matter. S.S. liked the one because it seemed humane and vaguely philosophical. A.A. liked the other because it was a frank confession of someone very unpleasant indeed.

You'll see from what I enclose that I still have a hankering to hold on to what seems the greater toughness of poetry written in meter at the same time as I'm trying to explore the tenderer measures of the present in free verse. (I think I'm through with syllabics: in fact I know I am, the thought of writing a poem in syllabics makes me sick. The form has served its purpose with me, I suppose.) The great problem, for me and I think for all of us, is to find a line that can contain the virtues of both. Lowell has I think done it, but in quite an idiosyncratic way, and one needs something serviceable, all-purpose, which will suit, if they use it, Gary Snyder and Edgar Bowers[2] and you and me. It may well be impossible, but the search is necessary. For those who wrote in the Old English alliterative line, the idea of the iambic line must have seemed impossible. It seems to me (1) the great virtue of the iambic line is that it deals beautifully with the past – it is marvellous for summing up, but apply it to the present (outside of Shakespeare, who is prepared to break it up & mix it with prose) and it is a shade too histrionic to be the unarranged exploration that one engages in in the present (it ends as a Browning monologue in fact, full of theatrical exclamations); (2) the great virtue of the non-iambic line is simply that unarranged exploration, perceptions crowding in, used, deserted for other perceptions – but try and deal with the past in such verse, and the verse loses all life, since it has to be spontaneous or it is nothing. One wants to get a line that can accommodate the experience of the present plus, if necessary, the implied understanding of the present. Obviously the latter is always <u>partly</u> there, but it is almost never so strong or so important or convincing as the <u>experience</u> in free verse. – I seem to have got myself into an Ars Poetica of the sort our friend [Anthony] Hecht a bit unfortunately did a month or two ago. I didn't mean to do this. Oh well, I was just trying to show you what I'm trying for.

[. . .]

Berkeley and San Francisco are nice and very wild places these days. I find my students are much more awake, much brighter than they used to be. A cliché of rebellion is better for young people to follow than a cliché of acceptance, apparently. They are so alert, and I find myself learning a lot from them. But last semester I was working so hard at school (e.g. committees, MA and PhD orals, tenure meetings, let alone preparing a new course as I went along – you know it all, I'm sure) that I didn't write a line from September till Christmas. [. . .]

Edgar Bowers came up. He is a nice person. The only poet I've met since I returned, but I'd forgotten what a nice sense of humor he has and how friendly and intelligent he is.

I've been reading Davie's book on Pound.[3] I must write him a fan-letter. A book of criticism that not only helps one's reading but could help one's writing.

Come across any good new poets lately? I mean besides George Macbeth and Anthony Thwaite, of course. I can't say I've read anybody who has struck me as very exciting, but I might well have missed people now I've given up reviewing. And, boy, am I glad I did give that up. Half my judgments were 100% wrong. Now I can just <u>wait</u> until my mind quietly changes.

There is a bar in San Francisco where they have Go-Go Boys. About thirty other places have Go Go <u>Girls</u> (i.e. topless dancers), but only this one has boys dancing topless. They are very bad, but it is very funny.

How is your Whitman selection? I got bogged down in my Greville book. I won't finish it for years. It <u>is</u> worth doing (I think) but it involves so much scholarship, and I'm not used to that kind of thing, Yvor. I'm having to modernise the text, which is harder than it sounds, and also provide notes. Expect to see it out in 1980.

[. . .]

      Love

          Thom

1. Date supplied through internal evidence.
2. Edgar Bowers (1924–2000) was a poet greatly admired by TG. See TG to Bowers, c. Summer 1967, below.
3. Davie, *Ezra Pound: Poet as Sculptor* (1965).

TO *Tony Tanner*   ALS King's
Saturday 5 March 1966[1]

975 Filbert

March 5

Dear Tanner – child of the celebrated 'Jack' Tanner of Man & Superman and the celebrated 'Ma' Tanner of Look Back in Anger – progeny of the theater –

There is no date on your letter but I know I got it a long time ago, and I knew it was high time for writing when Henry Smash[2] told me of new events in your life, like you will be lecturing at Northwestern this summer and have been promoted to Lecturer (I thought you were one already, or was that Jr.

Lecturer?). Congratulations on the latter – and as for the former, all of us, Henry, Bryan, etc, <u>all</u> of us, hope you can make it to San Francisco. Maybe we could even put you both up here – with Whitey here (if he <u>is</u> here by then) that would be a happy drunken household. (I assume Marcia would be coming over with you – or would that be too expensive?)

School is much better this semester. I taught worse than ever before last semester, but this semester I'm teaching better than ever before. Partly because in several ways I have an easier schedule, partly because two of the 3 courses I have taught before, partly because spring is always better than fall when I spend half the time lamenting about goldengrove unleaving and other such useless nostalgia.[3] > Result is that I get more time for drinking > Result is I am happy > Result is I write poetry again.

I enclose a few jottings – some started before last September, as you'll recognize. I am thinking of calling my next book, which is ready to send off in the summer, OUT LINE. The word outline occurs in far too many poems in the book & this will be a crude way of disarming the reader. Also it could mean a line going <u>outward</u>, see, like the kind of line I'm trying to write now. My preoccupation is in trying to get a form that combines the virtues of the iambic line (which deals with the past) and the virtues of the free verse line (which deals with the present). The thing may of course be unobtainable!!! <u>Snowfall</u> you will remember in a 9 stanza version: I hope you find this version a bit better.[4] <u>Fillmore Auditorium</u> is where I actually went a few weeks ago – and danced in my crude fashion (as taught by friends at Cambridge).[5] In it I am trying to use the Williams-Olson-Westcoast three-part line. (Though I hate Olson, who has the most inflated reputation of our time.) I am being influenced by my students, I think. I'll be very interested in your reaction to this poem, since Mike is the only person I've shown it to. Of the short poems, I don't know if any come off. The Old Man in the Brit you'll recognize: it was in Positives, but Ander didn't find the photograph up to standard so the poem had to come out too.[6] The Sierras poem I like, but maybe that is because the experience it is based on was so good, like Birkin among the primroses.[7] I have about 5 other poems, being written, I'll finish by & by & send you soon I hope. Give these to Whitey when you see him, could you?

I am really, after teaching him for the 2nd time, converted to Pound. Most of the second canto and the whole of the 47th are as good as anything in the last 50 years – only Hardy and Williams can equal it. Eliot, Winters, Lowell etc, come slightly lower – they do not experience so directly. On the other hand they do try to understand their experience – which I suppose as a human being one <u>ought</u> to do – but the attempt to understand removes some of the vividness of the experience. Have you read Pound's essay on James, by the way? (It's in EP's selected essays. Is rather wrong in some ways, but in others astonishingly right for 1919.)[8] Davie's book on Pound is first-class, as good I think as Dekker's.[9]

I seem to be getting extraordinarily pompous, don't I? Oh well, that's what happens when you're my age, you see.

[. . .]

I am writing an article on Gary Snyder for Agenda (English mag.), an introduction of Snyder to the English.[10] (Actually they've caught on very well by themselves, it strikes me.) His collected poems are to be published in England – to contain a new book, I think, The Back Country, not yet out over here. – The English are funny. Till about 1955, they pretended American poetry didn't exist, or if it did exist it was like Australian poetry and unimportant. By 1966 not only good American poetry but all American poetry is devoured. Not only good young people like Snyder & Creeley but Olson, the deadness of whose poetry it would be difficult to equal.

[. . .]

A FABLE The English poets lived in a large pond and were very happy in the 1940s and 1950s.[11] They hopped about, being frogs, and admired each other's green sleek skins or despised each other's distasteful sleek skins. The King was a huge Log named G.S. Fraser, which sat in the middle of the pond inert but appreciative of everything the frogs did. They hopped about on it daringly but only caused it to sink a little deeper. At length they got tired & besought the gods for a new King. So the gods sent the Log to Leicester University and gave the frogs not one new King but about 20. The names of these kings were Edward Lucie-Smith, A. Alvarez, Anthony Thwaite, etc., and they were terrifying. They had long, sharp beaks which they used for maiming, and sometimes even devouring the frogs. The frogs wisely hid in the weed. The storks were left with nothing to do but attack each other, and started to jab at each other with their strong pointed beaks. They are still at it to this day. Some of the frogs got tired of watching the fights, but not daring to come out of the weed started to write a little poetry out of sheer boredom.

Doody went to Chicago and then New Orleans. He will be back here in April.

[. . .]

Must stop. Forgive this ponderous letter.

Love to Marcia

(Have you got her pregnant yet?)

— give Whitey a push Westward when you see him

— come here in the summer
Love to yourself,
Thom

1. Date supplied through internal evidence.
2. Henry Nash Smith (1906–86), with whom Tanner worked while at UC Berkeley.
3. A reference to Gerard Manley Hopkins's 'Spring and Fall' (1880).
4. 'Snowfall' (*T* 50).
5. 'Fillmore Auditorium', *Occident* 1 (Spring–Summer 1967), 60–1; uncollected.
6. 'The Old Man in the Britannia', *Poetry* 109, no. 2 (November 1966), 70; uncollected.
7. 'The Sierras' is unpublished. A draft of the poem was published in the *D. H. Lawrence Review* 43, no. 1–2 (2018), 167. Birkin is a character in Lawrence's *Women in Love* (1920).
8. *The Literary Essays of Ezra Pound*, ed. T. S. Eliot (1954), 295–338.
9. Donald Davie, *Ezra Pound: Poet as Sculptor* (1965); George Dekker, *Sailing After Knowledge: The Cantos of Ezra Pound* (1963).
10. TG's review, 'Interpenetrating Things', is reprinted with its companion piece, 'Waking with Wonder', as 'The Early Snyder' (*OP* 36–46).
11. A parody of Aesop's fable 'The Frogs Who Demanded a King'.

TO *Tony White*   ALS Tulsa
Saturday 26 March 1966

975 Filbert St.,
San Francisco,
Calif., USA

26 March 66

Dear Tone –
    As usual I've been too long in answering you. I won't repeat the usual nagging message at length: just hope you'll be here soon. I hear from Tanner you are still around the district, helping out at the Brit (by which I take it that Arch has been made manager and has already taken it over). [. . .] I do know somebody who will be opening up a bar in a few months, and undoubtedly you could get a job bartending there, but equally undoubtedly it will be a queer bar: I imagine being a bartender in a queer bar would be unpleasant enough for somebody queer, but for somebody straight it would be a 100% bore. A nicer possibility would be for you to be Mike's and my kept boy, which we would be more than delighted to do.
    I am sure I shall be here till at least the autumn (1) because I am lazy, and San Francisco is such an agreeable place to be, and (2) because I am in

a writing streak, which I'm pretty sure will continue after the end of term. I am not being quite so hard-pressed at school right now, and am doing wild experiments. I sent some poems to Tanner, which I hope he has passed on to you by now. I have a lot of others in various stages but none ready to send you yet, though I had hoped I would.

It is very good knowing I have so much to work on. Simply for the work, not for the possibility of success. I think during the past year I have for the first time reached a real indifference to being a career poet. I honestly have no intentions of being a Great Poet. (Two kinds of people only, become great poets: Dante & Shakespeare and Chaucer, who have such big minds and talents that they have it all there; the other class is the class of first-class bores, Spenser, Shelley, and Yeats, who decide to be great poets, act like great poets, take big subjects, and work very very hard in embodying large notions in very pompous poetry. (Yes, Yeats.)) I am also very indifferent to the literary critic or reviewer's opinion of my career: 'Gunn is developing again, he is in his fourth period now.' I certainly tried for indifference to such things before but I think I have it only now. Now I am more interested in writing poems, i.e. making efficient and maybe moving communications, to you and Tanner and people like you, and who knows there may be several thousands of people who as suitable recipients are like you and Tanner. Maybe I am not being clear, or more likely maybe I am sounding priggish, but anyway I have reached – for the time – a sweet simple silence in my own mind on the subject of my reputation, and I hope I can repress vanity enough to keep it that way.

Perhaps I told you, Don is off travelling, but he ought to be back in the next three weeks. Bryan brought Mike and me a cat, which was very lovable: unfortunately it ran away after 3 days and has not returned since. We left the back door open and a dish of cat food in the hallway to tempt it back. This ruse has tempted four other cats in at various times – you wake to find a strange cat purring on your chest, but it's the wrong cat and the wrong face as some song says.

Nowhere Man is the first Beatles song ever that I do not particularly like. It strikes me as an imitation of the Kinks' Well Respected Man, which was much better.

Sex is almost too easy in this city. I find myself continually going to marvelous orgies where I meet unbelievably sexy people. If I were to tell my English queen friends about them they would think I was bullshitting or hallucinating. One has it made, as it were.

[. . .]

The writing of this is so illegible because I am writing this on the roof on a sunny but very windy day.

Con molto troppo,

A kiss for Shielah,[1]

Warm busses for the Cambridge folks (to whom tell them I will write very soon),

> Love,
>> Thom

---

1. White's then-girlfriend, the actor Sheila Ballantine (1928–).

TO *Tony Tanner*   ALS King's
Thursday 31 March 1966

975 Filbert St.,
S.F., Calif.

31 March 66

Old Thing –

[. . .] You will be very amused to know that I have (again) written a letter to the TLS. It is meant to be a funny letter. It contains an expression from Batman, the TV show here, so may be considered obscure rather than funny by the few Englishmen who see it.[1]

Life is gorgeously gorgeous. For example: next week is Easter holiday, the sun is hot over me as I write this on the roof and I am making my yearly retreat from 50 year old Mappa-Mundi to 36 year old level-pampas, I get on well with Mike, we have somehow acquired two inoffensive Siamese cats, I am doing vast amounts of writing, the pressure of work is much less this semester, Don will soon be back, I spent last night getting drunk with a handsome blonde architect I had just met. Things are fitting together well. If this is the country of the young ('Fish! In one another's arms,' etc), I can postpone Byzantium for quite a bit yet.[2] Not that by Byzantium I mean England. I must make up my mind about when to return to England. I'll decide in June (in January I said I'd decide in March).

Talking of Yeats I found an interesting connection of all his poetry. Too long to explain here – also it's probably a commonplace. I'm always discovering marvelous facts that have been known for 500 years. I do find him an irritating poet, I must say. There are some early things and things from the middle I find great, and The Tower is the best book. But after the Tower – childish obscurity, that fucking vatic tone, sexual hysteria, insensitive

196

meter (often), etc. I do like Lapis Lazuli, though, with all that bit about the best people being gay. No, I seriously like it. BUT take Under Ben Bulben. Take it! Take it away! Note the section beginning 'Send war in our time, O Lord'. Note it! Is it excusable? It is not excusable! Sentimental fascism (all Yeats', not implied by 'Mitchel's cry', which refers to a specific war for a specific purpose) from someone who mostly kept out of the fighting all his life. The Mask of the timid intellectual is Hitler. – I've been teaching, him as you gather. Interesting course. Eliot is, actually, finally a bit dull most of the time. My heroes are increasingly Pound, Williams, and Lowell. Maybe Stevens and Lawrence too. But not Yeats and Eliot. Maybe this is merely a fashionable reaction to the fashions of a few years ago, but what bugs me so especially about WBY and TSE is their inhumanity, i.e. lack of humaneness, their contempt for ordinary nice rather silly harmless people.

I had thought I'd have some more poetry to send you, but though I have about 10 poems begun I don't have anything quite finished. I am writing a poem in iambic lines of different lengths with irregular rhymes (& some lines have no rhymes) i.e. like Lycidas etc.[3] Maybe this is the answer! Certainly it's possible to get a great variety of effects, ranging from the strictures of a 4-foot couplet to something almost as loose as free verse, without seeming inconsistent. Strangely enough, I've never tried this form before. – Many thanks for your very useful comments on the poems I sent you. You seem to think you wrote a poor letter. On the contrary: there are some things in it so good I shall have to steal them for the essay I shall someday write comparing metrical & free verse.

I knew you'd like Snowfall (I don't myself now), but I think I like Fillmore Auditorium better than you do. I think I finally do understand the 3-part line – with the help of my students, really. The middle part of the poem is very like EP's second canto – not a direct resemblance, but a general one. The last part is sentimental, yes – and it is very like the ending of Blackie the Electric Rembrandt, which is also sentimental. I guess I tend to get sentimental about pretty boys. You are helpful about the other poems. I shall drop the Sierras and the Painter.[4] I'd be surprised you liked No Speech from the Scaffold if several other people didn't like it too. It's a bit too Gunny for my liking. Funnily enough, it comes from notes made in about 1958 – first I tried it in meter and it didn't work – about 1961 or so I tried it in syllabics & it didn't work – now it emerges in free verse!

[. . .]

I am pleased that I stop teaching in nine weeks time. Actually I am stopping mostly because I am an indolent bastard, but indolence does help with the poetry sometimes. Why, look at Keats.

[. . .]

Alas, neither you nor Mike like <u>Outline</u> for a title. <u>Out Line</u>, actually, but I guess that makes it no better. I'll have to think of another. Mike gave me my last title i.e. the title for the <u>poem</u> of My Sad Captains too. Think of a good title to do with walls, boundaries, outlines, etc, please. There is a marvelous sentence from your friend Morgan Le Fay Forster,[5] about memory (I quote without book) 'that dull glow of which intelligence is the bright advancing edge' (Aspects of the Novel). Beautiful, but hardly title-material. <u>Dull Glow</u>, a book of poems. No. <u>Bright Advancing Edge</u>. No. <u>That Dull</u> might do, though. How about (as titles for a book) <u>Memoirs of the World</u> or <u>Elegy on the Dust?</u>

[. . .]

Much love,

Thom

1. See *Times Literary Supplement* (14 April 1966), 327.
2. TG garbles the opening of Yeats's 'Sailing to Byzantium' (1927).
3. 'The Produce District' (*T* 55–6). 'Back to Life' (*CP* 175–6) – a revision of 'Kurfürstendamm' – is written in a similar form.
4. 'Painter Carrying Paintings' was abandoned.
5. E. M. Forster, like Tanner a fellow of King's, Cambridge, was known to his friends as Morgan.

TO *Tony Tanner*

ALS King's

Friday 10 June 1966[1]

975 Filbert Street,
San Francisco,
Calif.

Friday

Tansy Precious –

Or rather, since you started your last letter to me 'Cher', I should address <u>you</u> as 'Sonny.' I have a whole wardrobe now of flowered bellbottom pants: all because you encouraged me.

[. . .] I will not be back in England till the start of next year (and, besides, I'm too lazy), and right now I am pausing – work stopped three days ago – to look around me,[2] find <u>where I am spiritually</u> and <u>metaphysically</u>, and to sample a few of the manifold pleasures that I am assured life has. Really though, I feel a touch bewildered, and I am splitting the time between cleaning the apartment (which needs it, as Mike is working days now) and reading 'The Tragic Muse'. I will not, pretty certainly, be returning to work at Berkeley, much as I like that place, and I will, pretty certainly, return to England, but not all at once. (Brighton in 1969?)

I will do a little typing, & enclose a poem or 2. I hope you like them. The Produce District is to be in Poetry (Chicago) some time or other. It is rather new for me, I think, and consequently I find it very hard to judge. I have shown it to two other people, and they pretty well completely disagreed with each other. Pierce Street is rather old for me, and I <u>think</u> it's all right, but it's scarcely a departure, though I do like the pretty effects of the rhymes. (Borrowed from Pound! Who got it from Cavalcanti!!) This poem was to be the start of a sequence of 5, which I sent Whitey. However, of the five, I've cut out the last 2, am reworking the second, and enclose the third (to be judged as a separate poem) 'Chuck's Painting', which I'm very bewildered about.[3] Again, there was disagreement on this.

I heard from Whitey shortly after you told me he was not coming. As you thought, sad but not surprising. I would be truly delighted if I thought Shiela <u>were</u> the reason. One doesn't want one's friends to stay single, and one certainly wants them to get affianced to such groovy creatures as Romney[4] and Shiela. But I hardly dare hope that.

I would like your definition of sentimentality in my poetry. Excessive, unwarranted and/or unsupported feeling?

[. . .]

I am taking LSD for the first time on Sunday. I am about the last of my friends here to take it, but I didn't think it would mix with those three damn lectures a week. Don has taken it twice. See what I mean about him being different? I remember a big argument he had with you when he said he wouldn't even smoke grass.

You are dead right, <u>naturally</u>, in what you say about WBY and EP, and maybe what I go on to say is personal. Maybe it isn't, though. With say Canto 2 or 47 or the other splendid bits of Pound, I completely forget all the bullshit about Usura not to speak of the remarks about Musso, Hitler, the Jews, buggery ('James I, that old bugger', true, of course). With say 'Sailing to Byzantium' or 'The Tower', on the other hand, I do <u>not</u> forget the Yeatsian bullshit – on the contrary it is constantly infringing on and threatening the enormous virtues of such poems. What is the difference? Is it solely that I am newer to Pound and have had time to get tired of Yeats? (Rhetorical question.) I don't think so. There is (as Davie points out) ultimately something of an impersonality about Pound: he is not a <u>person</u> even like Keats or Ben Jonson let alone like Yeats. And Yeats' poetry is almost strictly poetry of personality: there are exceptions, but this is largely true, though I forget if his use of the world personality agrees with the common use. The personality is greatly complicated by the anti-mask business, but actually the search for (and assertion of) the anti-mask in the paraphrasable content of the poem only serves to emphasize the actual 'real' personality of Willie himself in the unparaphrasable parts (notably verse movement). And the personality I find by and large very obnoxious. And when personality becomes such an important part of the <u>content</u> of a man's poetry, I am unable not to judge it. Rereading this, maybe I've left out the last step. All the longing-for-violence business, 'send war in our time,' wicked old men and 70-year-old rapery is very much a part of that humorless personality, a personality finally almost incapable of an ounce of humility before anything except Yeats himself. (I may not have convinced you but at least I've justified myself.)

I am able to be much less clear about Eliot's stuff. I just find it at best rather inhumane and at worst (rather a lot of the time) a bit boring. Maybe one is wrong to make 'humaneness' a requirement, but I certainly find it difficult to have much liking for a writer who doesn't possess it. Eliot is as much of an egotist as Milton, and I find it pretty well impossible to read much of Milton any more (though I would never admit this when looking for a job). Of course modern poets, Williams & DHL are very humane, so is Stevens (though not at first glance maybe), so (very much) is Lowell, and so (ultimately) is the Pound of the Pisan Cantos <u>and</u> earlier. Samuel Johnson is a humane writer, and maybe a better example than any of these – because ultimately he (1) doesn't set up his own world as the only world there is, and (2) he realizes there may be certain situations into which one must collapse into pure feeling (e.g. the famous remark about the end of Lear).

I like 'The Waist Line.'

Went to the retirement party given for Winters, at Stanford, last Sunday. He didn't seem as entirely displeased to see me as I had expected.

[. . .]

R. Lowell came out here in May. I hadn't met him in years. He is a sweet, polite, rather sloppy person. I like him very much, I think.

Resolutions: 20 pushups a day (from general principles, not necessity); limit self to one pack of cigarettes a day (little point to getting cancer, really); hold self up straight (erection looks nice). [. . .]

Happy Hols.

Give Romney an intimate kiss from me. [. . .] Mike sends hot love to both. Give Whitey a kiss on his privates, from all in San Francisco.

And fervent, engulfing, unmanageable love from me to you, Rock

    x x x x

[. . .]

1. Date supplied through internal evidence.
2. A probable allusion to the line 'And waits and looks around him' in E. A. Robinson's
'Eros Turannos' (1916), one of TG's favourite poems. TG later borrowed the line in
'7 a.m. in the bar' (*BC* 67).
3. 'Chuck's Painting' is an early title for 'Bravery' (*T* 16–17).
4. TG's nickname for Marcia Tanner. He was familiar with Romney Marsh from a
childhood spent partly in Kent.

TO *Tony Tanner*   ALS King's

Friday 12 August 1966¹

975 Filbert
San Francisco
Calif.

Friday

Old Thing –

It is so foggy today that the air is full of droplets. Good for the flowrets,
no doubt, but not sunbathing weather. And me Muse feels pretty costive. So I
bethink myself, and ponder: why not write an arch riposte to Tanner? Maybe
I will cut out the archery though.

I have seldom received a more delightful, Old Thing, or <u>long</u> letter than I
got from you a few days ago. Packed was it with wisdom based on goodly
love. I cannot hope to equal it. [. . .]

So far, this is tearable up material.

I have heard that Ted Hughes is living on Murphy's island and assume
that is where TW is, so obviously the center of things has shifted.² Imagining
Ted Hughes and Tony White meeting without other people present is almost
impossible, it is like Batman and Superman meeting. – Incidentally, some
months ago I received a record which had ¼ Ted Hughes reading, ¼ Sylvia
Plath, ¼ Peter Porter, and ¼ me, which was why I was sent it.³ Yesterday
I finally conquered my well-known and occasionally violent repugnance to
hearing myself read, and listened to the record, and it is wildly interesting.
For the first time I am pleased to possess a poetry record. I am standard-dull,
Sylvia Plath is very interesting but quite bad (she overstresses some of her
ironies so they sound like review-sketch sarcasms), and Ted Hughes is the

best reader I have ever heard. He is incredible. The best reading is of a poem called WODWO (have you any idea what that means, by the way?): he has for the start a fine resonant voice and I'd say a good deal of dramatic skill, but his honesty keeps him from milking the resonance or being too dramatic.
[. . .]

I went down to Palo Alto to dinner with the Davies last week. I agree, he is a lovely man. His wife is odd. Obviously, they have an enviable marriage, and equally so she is basically all right, but there is something rather strident about her – as if to say, Look I've read all these books you and Donald are talking about. I imagine she'd be rather better once she got used to one. He said, drunk, some rather interesting things about writing in America: in America things (one's subjects) are isolated, in England they are crowded together and often not clearly distinguished. This is a geographical fact, but it affects writing, and I think is relevant to what you said about American writing, of which more later. – He heavily advised me to read Ed Dorn, whom I am reading right now. I am puzzled by his high valuation. There is something very attractive there all right and a spasmodic rhetorical power (particularly in the short poems, e.g. the first in 'Geography'), but – at this stage of reading – it strikes me as very spasmodic and there is an awful lot that is long-winded (and discursive in the wrong way) and (worse) rhythmically very insensitive. What do you think of Dorn?

Also, I am puzzled by Davie's thinking Wm. Stafford the best youngish American poet after Lowell. He strikes me as very limited and rather folksy. – I suppose, finally, I'm old-fashioned in my demands: what I like about Snyder is rather closely connected with what I like about Keats. Creeley strikes me as the best of the Black Mountaineers – i.e. better than Duncan, better than Dorn, far far better than Granddaddy Olson: Creeley knows about rhythms – almost all of his poems are rhythmically very exciting; and he is economical – and shortness makes for intensity.
[. . .]

I find what you say about American writers all living in different worlds suggestive and exciting. Very true, and it explains a lot. Of course, they have their schools, but so many of them. Meanwhile, just to take a few examples, Bly (midWest), Stafford (NorthWest), Snyder (SF and Japan), Wilbur (East) – have nothing to do with each other. On the other hand, Davie, Hughes, and myself, different as we are in interests, share a hell of a lot of techniques. Maybe it is to do with all having been to Cambridge and consequently having had to study the Metaphysical poets intensively. There's a lot of Donne-derived conceits even in recent Hughes, I noticed from this record, and it's there in Davie, and of course most nakedly in myself. Of the books you mention, I read some early short stories by James Purdy (Dream Palace something) and considered them like, but worse than, Tennessee Williams' short stories which till then had been the worst I had ever read. Was The Sot-Weed Factor by John Barth? I read about 50 pages, and stopped there because it was so incompetent. City of Night I read about a third of & then skipped through the rest because I knew the originals of I think all of the bars he mentions. (I must know him by sight!). It is a promising subject, and somebody with a gift for observation could do something marvelous, like Colonel Jack or Moll Flanders, but Rechy is hung up on (a) himself and (b) symbols. I thought it was incredibly bad: self-pity of a sort one seldom comes across nowadays, egotism, dull dull. Whenever he had a chance to describe something accurately that would be outside most people's experience & thus interesting, he instead described his own reactions to it. – You see, I'm not the person to ask about recent fiction![4]

I'll enclose 1½ new poems. 'Touch' I hope comes off. I think it may be the best free verse I have written since two of the poems in Positives. On the other hand maybe it is too cliché, too fashionably bare. I'm in a real fix, style-wise: I think you are right that I do best with meter. The Byrnies has certain qualities that are all my own and a good deal of intensity. But I'm no longer able to write like that. You liked 'Snowfall', but it's pretty tame stuff compared with the best or the second-best in my last 2 books. I am interested and excited by the kind of thing I'm doing in 'Touch' or the old woman poem for Positives.[5] But I am aware that when I use free verse it is slack, compared to The Byrnies, and – comparatively – derivative. So I am as it were between two worlds, but I've been waiting some time for the next one to be born, and I don't think it has been yet.[6] – I have been doing a bit of revision on old poems for the next book, and as a book it is going to be very curious. My other books have had a certain unity, both in preoccupation and style: this one won't, which I think explains why I am having so much trouble in finding a title for it. – The other "poem" is The Color Machine with a second part added. I am certainly not prepared to defend the prose poem in English, and I'm sure I'll never write another. The most I'd be prepared to say is that maybe some of the rhythms have a curiousness to them.

And I accuse John Rechy of self-pity!

I am growing tomatoes outside the back door. It all started with a rotten tomato which seeded some months ago. A few days ago the first embryonic tomato appeared [. . .]. Triumph and the miracle of life.

[. . .] Thank you for the article on The Ambassadors.[7] I think you are very right in it. [. . .] It isn't an article of the same kind of brilliance as your Pope one, though, being more a detailing of what is there than an evaluation,

I suppose. Also, why don't I like The Ambassadors, a perfect book, nearly as much as The Wings of a Dove, a pretty imperfect one? I can't say that the subject of the latter brings in more of life, — I'm not sure it does, really – but it certainly evokes more interested responses from me, particularly Kate and Densher. And part of what makes Kate and Densher so exciting and human is that we don't know everything about them, whereas we know almost too thoroughly much about Strether. Oh I don't know, this is arguable, and incoherent on my part.

[. . .]

Ha, ha. You are down to 160 pounds. I am up to 162 pounds. Suddenly about 2 months ago, all my 29 inch waist pants became too small for me. Naturally, I thought they had shrunk. But happening naked in someone's bathroom on a weighing machine, I weighed myself out of curiosity and found I have joined the rest of the human race. Well, at least I'm normal now, it was a bit uncanny before.

Don made an abrupt disappearance to Hawaii 2 weeks ago. i.e. he told no one he was going. He must have been too happy here? I don't know, he is very complicated. I suddenly realized yesterday, thinking about him, that I expect he will one day commit suicide. Which I don't, need I say, mean as a joke.

Bryan is probably going to move to North Beach. We see him often. He & Mike send their most tremendous love to you both. Mike is writing for a TV station.

Little Mr Cat and little Miss Tomato send their weeny, furry kisses.

With a respectful embrace to you both, and a clean wink,

   I am

    Thom

The Stones do get better than ever, don't they?

1. Date supplied through internal evidence.
2. Richard Murphy (1927–2018), poet and friend of Hughes and White. For a time, Murphy and White were neighbours in Cleggan, a fishing village on the Galway coast.
3. *The Poet Speaks 5: Ted Hughes, Peter Porter, Thom Gunn, Sylvia Plath* (1965).
4. Tanner was researching his second full-length book, *City of Words: American Fiction 1950–1970* (1971). It was originally to have dealt with poetry as well as fiction.
5. 'The Old Woman' (*CP* 167).
6. An allusion to Matthew Arnold's 'Stanzas from the Grand Chartreuse' (1855).
7. Tanner, 'The Watcher from the Balcony: Henry James's *The Ambassadors*', *Critical Quarterly* 8, no. 1 (Spring 1966), 35–52.

TO *Tony Tanner*   ALS King's
Tuesday 13 September 1966

                                                   975 Filbert,
                                                San Francisco,
                                                         Calif.

                                                   13 Sept 66

My Lord
    (though I understand your <u>original</u> name was Frank Ifield)¹
Have received many splendid goodies from you – viz. a long letter, a dirty
postcard, a color supplement, books. In the middle of all this, I think I have
drunk more in the last 10 days than ever before in my life, starting in the
mountains two weekends ago and ending up on Grant Avenue on Sunday.
Monday I had only one beer. Tuesday, today, I'm getting back to the great
good place, I mean the stance of sobriety, and I will today shuffle together
my papers, which I shall coolly appraise, and start on an essay about Robt
Lowell.
    Also I'll send Touch to the publishers. Yes it will contain the pamphlet. But
it will not contain about 15 shitty poems written in the last few years. I have
come to dislike the Life Artist series a good deal, but I included it, though I
shortened it from 12 to 10 sections. On the other hand I think I do like most
of Misanthropos. It weakens toward the end, becoming a rather didactic
structure only (a bit like Camus' short stories), but I think I am pleased with
what goes before. Not that anyone else is. Apart from you, Whitey, and Ma
Doody, not a soul has breathed a comment on it except Stephen Spender. If I
press anybody, he will say 'Well, it's rather <u>difficult</u>' !!! But the new book is a
curiously mixed collection. – Thank you for your comments. I am dropping
The Color Machine.² Delighted with your liking (the poem) Touch. (It is to
<u>Mike</u>, idiot.) It has a good deal to do with reading, and trying to like, Edward
Dorn, I think. I was very amused by your dialogue (about 'hard with self' etc)
and won't do that kind of thing again. I agree with your distrust of organic
imagery and am aware that in Back to Life I am endorsing a XIXth century
cliché (we are leaves on a branch), but I endorse it only <u>so far</u>: i.e. I am trying
to find out how far it is true and how far not true. Paraphrase "OK, we are
like leaves on a branch, we have some kind of instinctual connection, some
kind of deep sympathy, but at the same time this isn't much good to us except
at certain happy moments. It is of as much importance to see ourselves as
separate as it is to see ourselves as connected. And the final tests are always
going to be of us as separate beings." This is my <u>intention</u>, of course, which

may not be (as Frank Ifield Leavis would put it) realized. I do find all your comments very valuable, by the way, maybe when you are older you may write criticism.

Maybe I told you these two graffiti:

(1)   <u>To the Inverts of the 21st Century</u>
Children of a future age
Reading this indignant page,
Know that in a former time
Love, sweet love, was thought a crime.

(2)   Please flush the toilet, these Hungarians will eat anything

Mike and I took LSD together a few weeks ago. It was the biggest trip I had taken (500mg., apparently). Hallucinating solid for about 3 hours. – Do you know by the way that of all the times – it must be about 50 – I have smoked grass I have NEVER got really high on it?

We – all of us – have found a bar that suits all of us, me, Mike, Don, Bryan, and it would you two as well. We conceal it from Tom Gee and such like. It is the only really bisexual bar I have ever known and is very wild and delightful, as well as being close – on Grant Avenue.[3] Bryan & Don (who is back) now live very close – right by Safeway if you remember where that is, in a gorgeous wooden triangular house (with a sun deck, of course). So I see a lot of both. The whole district is now full of teenagers who look & dress just like English teenagers, if you can imagine that.

Yes, Revolver is incredible. My 3 favorites, & I guess yours, are Eleanor Rigby, the one Paul sings with the horn in the middle ('She wakes up / She makes up / She takes her time . . .'), and the last one sung by John ('Turn off your mind, relax, & float down stream') which seems to be an invitation into the heart of darkness. The first two almost make me weep, they are so good. And the lyrics have become so good too (lyrics after all, were not always the best part of their songs). Query: is the Yellow Submarine the same thing as 'the little yellow pill' in Mothers Little Helper? (Panathol or something.)

Which brings us to Lady Jane. I am not going to read your introduction till I have reread Mansfield Park, & am now in the middle of it.[4] What makes you think I don't like Jane Austen? She's a good, hard, tough disciplined lady with the best style in the world, and I always think of her as similar to the early Hemingway in her structure and the way she makes economy part of her subject.

As I say I spent a weekend camping in the Sierras again with some motorcycle friends. The air is so thin up there it is heady. You have a gorgeous feeling of strangeness and the vividness of things, like Kirilov looking at a leaf,[5] or like a small amount of acid, simply from the air. It is like a trip, really, in that it is a marvelous side-road, it has nothing directly to do with anything, I no more intend to live in a forest on top of a mountain than I intend to live on a trip: it is something beautiful, non-verbal, and practically meaningless. And I love to court such things, knowing I could never be happy as a Thoreau or an acid-head.

Your comments on Heaney are exactly right. It is a good book, and with luck (a great deal of luck) he will get better: he is direct and honest and almost always interesting.[6] Slightly limited in his subject matter maybe, but so much better than R.S. Thomas whom I find an honest bore. You are right about the overgreat search for 'hard' images, but they are often very successful. He doesn't know the first thing about meter yet, though: there should be a compulsory 2 day course in meter taught by all English departments in the Freshman year. I didn't know much about it till I met Winters.

Went down to see Winters the other day and spent a very good afternoon with him, drinking bourbon and discussing poetry. I hadn't really talked to him in years. He is a lovely man. His critical ideas have hardened dreadfully in the last 10 years, though. He very sweetly gave me first editions of his first 2 books – the first a pamphlet of 1921 – which he said had turned up in an attic.[7]

[. . .]

My love to you and to your good wife

('good wife' does conjure up a nice homely little creature in a white apron – Marcia is a gorgeous creature not a good wife, so:)

My love to you and your gorgeous creature

T.

---

1. For TG and Tanner, Frank Ifield (1937–) typified the vacuous mediocrity of British pop music in the period before the Beatles and Rolling Stones emerged.
2. Although TG did indeed drop the poem from *T*, he later included it in *M*.
3. The Capri (1964–72) was a bohemian gay bar in North Beach.
4. See Tanner's introduction to *Mansfield Park* (Harmondsworth: Penguin, 1966), 7–36.
5. Kirilov is a character in Dostoyevsky's *Demons* (1873); Camus discusses him in *The Myth of Sisyphus* (1942).
6. Seamus Heaney, *Death of a Naturalist* (1966).
7. Winters, *The Immobile Wind* (1921) and *The Bare Hills* (1927).

TO *Tony Tanner*   ALS King's

Thursday 27 October 1966

975 Filbert St.,
San Francisco,
Calif., U.S.A.

27 Oct 66

Dear Tony,

I went to New York for 3 weeks, and I was very happy to find your letter
when I came back. Mike is off now for a week, visiting his parents, and he
took that copy of Mansfield Park with him, so I cannot be as explicit as I
want. It was nice reading it again: it really is extraordinary how by the end
of Vol 1 you think you can never like Fanny Price and how by the middle of
Vol 2 all her interests have become yours. Partly this is sheer skill – with
Jane Austen so much in command of her material, the reader is prepared to
sympathize where she indicates he should sympathize – but I do find your
remarks about her being 'a Christian heroine' and comparable to Milly Theale
very apropos and helpful. I think you explain how her negatives become in
context positives. And god knows we don't have to take her on trust, as we
do Milly. I have only one reservation about yr introduction, and it's here
I wish I had the copy of the book. You speak at times as if Jane Austen
had far more explicit intentions about putting Fanny in a certain tradition
than I think she really had. Or she may have had them, but we can't know
she did. The Shakespearean critics are far worse about this kind of thing,
of course (e.g. 'Shakespeare <u>meant</u> The Winters Tale to follow the course
of certain vegetation ceremonies not fully described till Fraser'), but I don't
think one can be too careful about the way one records one's perceptions
about a writer's intentions.

I got a note from Winters which depressed me enormously, partly because
he was going out of his way to say nicely what he had to say. He finds
all my recent poems, with the possible exception of Snowfall, 'genteel' and
'approaching polite journalism.'[1] I think by this he means they lack intensity.
The trouble is, I think he may well be right.

One nice thing has happened recently, anyway. You know how I've said
that I have never got high on grass? Well last night I went round to see a
friend who turned out not to be in but his friends were busily smoking and
I really did turn on, for the first time. Considering I have been in a state of
largely unmotivated but deepening depression of the last few weeks, this sure
was a welcome turn to Dame Fortune's wheel. The high was unsensational,

enormously pleasant, and surprisingly lengthy, i.e. it went on for about 1½ to 2 hours after the last joint I smoked. So at last I know what it's all about!

On the other hand I've begun to change my ideas about LSD. At least for me. Doody turns on with it about twice a week now, and it certainly seems good for him in that he is very relaxed and chummy in the times between. The apostles of it (not him) say Trust your body. But unfortunately I think my body must be rather untrustworthy. Much incipient paranoias, etc. I'll take it a few more times, anyway, just to see.

New York was very beautiful and autumnal. I saw Albee's new play, A Delicate Balance. The first two acts are largely unnecessary, but the last act was beautiful and moving. He does write so well – even in those first 2 acts. – I saw the movie of Virginia Woolf a few weeks ago, & then reread the play. I really think it is better than anything by Williams or Osborne, let alone Miller or Pinter.

[. . .]

I got a long letter from Whitey in Ireland, the longest and funniest and nicest he has ever written. Apparently he is now Richard Murphy's <u>nurse</u>. A new and interesting job for him. Did you ever meet Murphy? An egotistical prick, I thought.

I get an uneasy feeling, as in the last 2 sentences, that I repeat myself from letter to letter, and can imagine a chain of overlapping letters with familiar little refrains.

Oh yes, I like 'I'm only sleeping' (it was on the previous record to Revolver over here), though you are the only person I've known even mention it. And the latest Stones single has a fine cover with the Stones in drag, which you may have seen, or may be similar to the short you saw about them: they are mostly in women's army uniforms, with Mick Jagger as a negro nurse.[2] Obviously I'll have to get Ander to take a series of pictures of me in crinolines or tutus. I must keep up.

It's nice to read your descriptions of the trials of teaching. Is it Horace who wrote some poem about standing on the shore watching a ship go down & feeling so good because he's not in it?[3] I feel like that at the moment, though I do not mean to imply you are in anything but a most buoyant and gallant craft. A man of gallant craft, that Tanner. (Horace <u>who</u>?)

I did start work on an essay on Robt Lowell, but I'm not sure now that I'll write it. I find I like so little of him before this last book, apart from about 6 poems. Lord Weary's Castle is mostly very, very bad [. . .]. And The Mills of the Kavanaughs is a good deal worse.

I read Pericles again a few days ago. Not bad really. I think probably Shakespeare <u>did</u> write those first 2 deplorable acts, after all. I'd like to see it done, I think it would stage quite effectively. Christ, do I sound patronizing.

I wish I was able to spend a day or two talking with you. You'd restore a certain balance to me I seem to be rather lacking right now, poor discouraged kid that I am.

Apologizing for this shitty letter,
> and cordially shaking your hand,
>> with love to your wife Marshall
>> (Jesus, am I confused about the sexes)
>>> Th.

1. 'Your dissipated adventure in syllabics (or something) has weakened the whole texture of your perceptions,' Winters wrote (20 October 1966): 'Your rhythms, when I can find them, are uninteresting; the diction is genteel but unimportant. I cannot remember the poems; they blur into each other and into nothing. [. . .] You simply approach polite journalism.' The letter can be found in TG's papers at the Bancroft Library.
2. 'Have You Seen Your Mother, Baby, Standing in the Shadow?' was released on 23 September 1966. TG refers to a photograph on the American picture sleeve.
3. TG is thinking of Horace's Ode 1.14, 'O navis, referent'.

TO *Yvor Winters*

ALS Stanford

Friday 16 December 1966

975 Filbert,
San Francisco,
Calif.

16 Dec 66

Dear Arthur,[1]

It must be a month since I received the copy of your book, and longer since I received your note, but I wanted to read the book through carefully before I wrote.[2] The book is very impressive, much more than I had assumed it would be. I'm sorry if that sounds patronizing – I don't mean it to be so. I agree that the best poems are those I had already read in your Collected Poems, though I would have included more than you did (particularly more from The Bare Hills), but it makes a difference reading them in their original context. One understands more from seeing their original companions. I take back what I said about your free verse being like Williams' – that remark resulted from a faulty impression and lack of study. Most of the free verse in your book reminds me of nobody else, and though there are echoes of Williams and others in the language and images (of Stevens' poem about the lines between the stars in 'The Cold'?), they are very few for a young man. One of the things I find most interesting about the book – and one that sheds some light on later poems – is the general feeling of hallucination. By this I don't mean you took drugs: one can cultivate such a feeling without them. There is an intensity of detail in most of the poems, as if the detail had a hidden significance. I also find a frequent sense of the slowing down of time, of abnormal concentration on a sensory detail during that slowing, and of the transformation of that detail into something else, accompanied by a feeling of intense wonder allied to terror. Sometimes, when this enters the structure of a poem, the poem as a whole gets very obscure – there are a few I don't yet grasp, one of them is Digue Dondaine, Digue Dondon, which may be about madness but may equally not be, for all I can tell. – Anyway, this hallucinatory power isn't abandoned in your later poems, the knowledge of it is retained and used, as for example in the use of the word 'swarmed' in 'Sir Gawaine', which Tate admired so much (and it is admirable).

[. . .]

As for your comments on my poems, you are probably right.[3] I will be sending you a picture book I did with my brother. Most of the writing in it is intended as captions rather than poems, but there are about five I would claim as poems. The last one in the book I think is the best poem I have written in free verse. The others are of little importance. I have decided to give up free verse (I gave up syllabics two years ago), since I don't seem to be doing very well with it, and am going back to meter. But I expect the period of retraining in meter to take some time!

I'm in the middle of writing notes for the selection of Greville's poems that I told you about. Bullough established an admirable text, but he did not clear up all difficulties.[4] The job is difficult but interesting. When I've finished this, I have to write a long introduction on Greville, in which I will endeavour not to plagiarize from your lectures. (By the way, I think Greville's long poem about Monarchy is one of the worst long poems in the language![5]) So I won't be starting on the essay I intend to write on your poetry for quite a long time.

Thank you again for the book, and even more for the two early editions that you gave me. They give me much pleasure, and many of the poems are very beautiful. I don't always agree with Alan Swallow, but he is completely right on his jacket cover in saying that the book shows you as one of the great experimental writers.

My best to Janet and you,
Thom

1. Winters's full name was Arthur Yvor Winters, although he published his work as Yvor Winters.

2. *The Early Poems of Yvor Winters, 1920–1928* (1966).

3. See TG to Tanner, 27 October 1966, n. 1, above.

4. See TG to Monteith, 25 January 1965, above.

5. Greville's *A Treatise of Monarchy* (1670) can be found in *The Remains: Being Poems of Monarchy and Religion*, ed. Wilkes (1965).

1967

TO *Thomas Parkinson*   ALS Texas
Saturday 11 February 1967[1]

975 Filbert,
San Francisco

Saturday

Dear Tom –

My decision, as you probably guessed, is to resign from the department. Very good things are happening to me, which I hope will show up eventually in my writing, and I really think it will be better for me to take off from teaching for a few years. I wrote to Jim Hart today.

I am going away next week, but ought to be back in June, at the same address (above) as always. I hope to go on seeing you!

     Best,

        Thom

1. Date supplied through internal evidence.

TO *Mike Kitay*   ALS Mike Kitay
Thursday 27 April–Wednesday 3 May 1967[1]

[24A Hedgegate Court,
Powis Terrace,
London W.11]

Thurs

Hello Babe –

It is sunny and it is nice, as Gertrude Stein would have said, with such admirable simplicity. Went last night to Love for Love, directed by Wood.[2] [. . .] Really ideal: I suddenly realize this must be the first thing I've seen directed by PW since Cambridge. It was not wigs and satins but dirty-looking hair and Hogarth, which is apparently more accurate anyway. And everything, the pace and all, was beautiful: there must be a tendency – a temptation I mean, with Congreve, to treat it as Oscar Wilde, very fast and flashy with one's epigrammatic Noël Wilde voice on.³ But the lines are quite funny enough without that. It was very measured and not at all fast, but always interesting. It is also the first time (& this includes Shakespeare plays too) that I have ever enjoyed an irrelevant song introduced into the action (i.e. as in "Restoration Piece"). And Olivier was marvelously poncy; and Miles Malleson (whom I saw doing the same part in 1945 when it was last done) very funny; and the best of all, maybe, was someone called Robert Lang, who we saw as Roderigo in Othello. I always say a production at the National restores me faith in the theatre.

I have been thinking that when I get back to SF it might be more profitable than getting a part-time job (at first, anyway) to write a book of general interest which would get me $800-1000. I am thinking of a book about San Francisco, part guide, part history, and reliable as such, but also to be enjoyable for people who have never been there and so full of anecdotes and atmospheric impressionism.⁴

[. . .]

Fri

[. . .]

Went to Stratford yesterday for the first time in my life. Had a cheerful ride in Holmstrom's car, with Karl & Holmstrom and Tony W, and got home at 3 this morning. Saw Coriolanus, directed by [John] Barton.⁵ It was SHOCKINGLY bad. The lead was played by Ian Richardson: I doubt if he is queer, but he looked like a little bleached-blond hairburner, and Barton's every reading of the play was wrong. It was absolutely amazing. Apparently he is very influenced by the Brecht production a few years ago. Coriolanus comes over as totally unsympathetic, unglamorous, uncomplicated, pompous, and nelly as all hell. Naturally the play was a colossal bore, as a result. Bore except for one thing, the Aufidius (Coriolanus' rival), who appeared all too seldom, played by a young American called Edward Cicciarelli, who has played at Lincoln Center apparently: have you heard of him or seen him? He is just about the most gorgeous thing on earth, and moves like a sexy tiger or something. Of course, his blonde wig suited him and he was probably well-made up, but since he was only wearing an armoured jockstrap much of the evening one saw a lot of fine body apart from an incredible flashing smile. My dear, I've never seen anybody LIKE him on the stage!

As you can see, I've been too busy to even think. I enclose a copy of a poem I doubt if you'll like.⁶ I think it's something of a departure, but not in a direction that interests me much: probably the most formal poem (in tone, anyway) I've ever written. I find it a tremendous problem nowadays not to repeat myself: I'm always starting poems and then finding they are terribly close to poems I wrote a long time ago – I mean in what they say. Ted Hughes has a new book out, and it makes me almost melt with envy, it is so good – but how can one feel envy for something so solid and beautiful.[7] He is so good he will not live.

Oh yes, I saw Barton. Difficult, having disliked his production so. He still looks quite Jesus-y, but has put on a little weight, and anyway was very tired.

Wed May 3

[. . .]

You will not be surprised to hear that my life is Hectic. Saturday I went to the East End, to see my sexy friends, tho not for sex. Very interesting & very nice. The mother of one of them turned up while I was there, something of a monster, I am trying to write a poem about her which will reveal her memorable character. Incidentally, one of these guys was telling me that the rent for a room, goodish, in the East End, is about 15/- a week, and for a small flat that could hold two 30/- a week. 30/- being $4.20. My god, even Greece couldn't be <u>that</u> much cheaper. But of course different weather (we even had a little <u>snow</u> yesterday.)

Positives has sold out here, but will not reprint. I heard this today from Monteith. So hold on to your copy. It will become a Scarce Book!

I spent most of Sunday drinking & eating with my friends Mick & Peter.[8] In the evening we saw a telly-film called East Side West Side. A real jewel – it had James Mason and Ava [Gardner] and Barbara [Stanwyck] in it. Barbara got very passionate at a few points. Every line of dialogue was very classic, having appeared in several other movies before.

Monday was a most peculiar day. Last week I had suddenly realized that the Australian novelist, Randolph Stow, whom I met 2 yrs back in SF, lived in London & I had promised to go and see him. He asked me to lunch. He is rather nice, very bright, very unattractive, and (I had assumed) straight. He pumped Scotch into me and himself all afternoon. Toward the end of the afternoon he kissed me. Oh dear. Luckily it was about time I left. My assumption of course had been wrong. Then I had dinner with Lehmann, Scotch & wine, & some little probably hustler friend of his came along & we 3 went out to a pub where I drank a lot of beer and next morning I was overhung by God the Father himself.

Well anyways, yesterday to Snodland where several aunts. My aunt Mary has another small 'lump' on her breast, which is to be taken off this week. She has been convinced it is not serious, but it could be. They are all very brave and practical about their lumps, but it makes me very sad. Apparently my aunt Peg who died of her lungs recently had started to get cancer of the breast just before she died.

My poem about skindivers is much better than the enclosed, but is not quite finished yet, but I think (hope) you will like it.[9] My poetry is rather unpopulated right now, I mean not enough people in it.

[. . .]

Roger must be about due to have his balls fixed.[10] We must do this in June and no later. We'll have his nose looked at at the same time.

[. . .]

Well, baby, I adore you. This is written in haste, as must be apparent. My Twiggy, may I sign myself:

Branchy

(James Branch Cabell)

All my love to you, you pretty and holy man.

x x x x x x x x

1. Date supplied through internal evidence.
2. Peter Wood directed Congreve's *Love for Love* for the National Theatre at the Old Vic.
3. An allusion to Noël Coward (1899–1973).
4. TG abandoned this project.
5. John Barton directed *Coriolanus* for the Royal Shakespeare Company.
6. Probably 'Sunlight' (*CP* 223–4).
7. Hughes, *Wodwo* (1967).
8. Mick Belsten and Peter Flannery were Gay Liberation Front activists.
9. 'From the Wave' (*CP* 198–9). TG wrote to Michael Vince (25 January 2000), 'The poem was about a rather chilly January walk along a dull beach in San Francisco with some friends. We were suddenly astonished by the appearance of a bunch of surfers. A few days later, and I was in England on a visit, so most of it was written by my aunts' stove in England.'
10. Roger is one of TG and MK's cats.

TO *Edgar Bowers*[1]   ALS UCLA

c. Summer 1967[2]

975 Filbert,
San Francisco,
Calif 94133

Friday

Dear Edgar,

How lovely to read a poem like 'Living Together'.[3] You really do it, time after time, and it is worth it, waiting between the poems, for something like this. This is simply a fan letter, which you certainly should not answer, to say how happy your poem has made me. And very happy.

Best,

Thom

1. Edgar Bowers (1924–2000) was a poet greatly admired by TG. A former student of Winters's, he first met TG in 1959, probably on Winters's recommendation. TG was one of the judges who awarded Bowers the prestigious Bollingen Prize in 1989. His *Collected Poems* appeared in 1997.
2. Date supplied through internal evidence.
3. 'Living Together' was published in *Denver Quarterly* (Spring 1967) and became the title of Bowers's third book (1973).

TO *Tony White*   ALS Tulsa

Tuesday 15 August 1967

975 Filbert St.,
San Francisco,
Calif., U.S.A.

15 August 67

Dear Flower Child –

All this time and I haven't written you a word. So I felt characteristically guilty at receiving your long letter.

I arrived in New York at 5a.m of a gorgeous summer day, knowing I couldn't check into the YMCA before 1p.m. So I went to the Zoo and then rowed around the lake of Central Park and then slept a little in some grass, and this was a delightful start. New York City itself seemed for the next ten days merely an appendage to Central Park, existing by courtesy of the cheetahs etc. – Then to Montreal, where Don Doody and the guy he's staying with put me up in a veritable palace – or rather a house that had been a merchant's some few hundred years back. The Expo was fine, I saw almost every movie there – all very multiple-senses and light-show – but Montreal itself charmed the hell out of me, no wonder de Gaulle wants it back. I want it too. They speak a French which would interest you very much – it is not like French with an American accent as in Louisiana, but very run together with many consonants slurred out of existence: thus though the educated speak with quite a French accent the uneducated pronounce the name of their town Mon'réal. And the town constantly reminds me of North France, England, and the United States all at the same time.

(Why has my writing got so microscopic? Marcia and Dr Freud would have something to say about that.)

Then to Chicago for a week, which was pleasant, especially since the Tanners were near, and I saw them a couple of times. – One thing I do notice on returning to the U.S. this time which I have never noticed before: a very bad feeling of tension, of suppressed violence, etc. It was certainly there in NY and Chicago. It was certainly absent in Montreal. It is present in San Francisco, but less than in other places. Tanner says it is less because of the provincial nature of San Francisco – he may be right. – Meanwhile the political outlook is as frightening here as it must seem from England: everything seems to get worse with every morning's newspaper, and I wouldn't be surprised if there was some kind of quasi-military quasi-dictatorship in this country within a few years, unless the Vietnam war is put an end to, which does not seem likely. Left and Right have got so extreme that they can no longer discuss things with each other. And then there are the Black extremists – whether they are left or right who can tell.

Coming back to San Francisco was as lovely as always, just the same. Mike has taken a job in New York for a while. He had always wanted this kind of thing – cocktail parties and Show Business – until he actually got the offer. Then he said: 'I've decided I don't really want that kind of thing after all. I like being lazy in the sun in San Francisco and wearing old clothes and being unambitious.' But it seemed a good idea for him to get it out of his system and I said if he decided he did like New York by about November then I'd follow him there around that time. Luckily this seems unlikely and it looks like he'll be returning here for good.[1] – Now the Tanners have left (two days ago) I have no Major Friends left in the city – they, Mike, Don and Bryan all being away. Obviously I shall have to make some new major friends. Though you could save me that trouble by coming here yourself. That room is waiting for you.

It was really fantastic having Lord Tanner and Lady ('my good wife') Romney Marsh here. Such high jinx. Such drinking orgies. Such eating orgies. They are the only people I know who serve crab and caviar as <u>snacks</u> before a meal. We turned on <u>and</u> got drunk at the same time. Actually I am spending this week recovering from them physically: TT and I would put away ¾ gallon of wine together most evenings. [. . .]

As for me, I've kept myself fairly busy since I got back. I finished the Introduction to Fulke Greville, thank god, and sent in the whole book to Faber's. I wrote that article for Karl, and was very flattered that he put it on the first page of his first issue.[2] [. . .] Then I've written several poems, of which I've "discarded" a few. They lie in the dirty clothes basket waiting for God's laundry – no one else could make them work. But I enclose two so far undiscarded. One a bit too Donnean, maybe, the other more than a bit Lawrentian.[3] Actually the second, 'Three', I like because of the things I am trying to say in it. Of course, I may not succeed. I'm firmly back with meter now, and am getting poems refused right and left by the mags. I hope it's because they are unfashionable rather than because they are bad. (I <u>know</u> they are unfashionable.)

Get Tanner to tell you about (A) the Park and (B) the Avalon Ballroom.

I had my ear pierced. I now wear things through it. I am so fearfully butch.

Have you heard a group (local in origin but nationally known) called Country Joe and the Fish? They are very good. TT calls the use of the organ 'astral' which is a great word for it.

I have been rereading Daniel Deronda, and had forgot how good it is. The Zionist parts <u>are</u> dull, but they are a very small part of it and harm it much less than the bad parts of War and Peace harm that book. And as a whole I think the book does almost come up to War and Peace. Almost. I'm rereading Middlemarch now, but so far don't like it nearly as much.
[. . .]

Yes, the new Beatles single. 'It's easy.' Some of their songs, this one, and Strawberry Fields, make me feel so <u>happy</u> every time I hear them.

I thought the first Listener – all I've seen – was so good that I took out a subscription to it.
[. . .]

Incredible about Joe Orton being hammered to death by his lover, isn't it?
[. . .]

I am,
              warmly,
                        your humble servant,
                                  well-wisher,
                                            ethical coadjutor,
                                                      companion-in-virtue
                                                                and a public humility of demeanour,
                                                      Your Humble Servant

1. MK was a story editor at Channel 13, the New York PBS television station (1967–8).
2. 'The New Music', *The Listener* (3 August 1967), 129–30; uncollected.
3. For the 'Donnean' poem see next letter; the Lawrentian poem is 'Three' (*CP* 195–6).

TO *Tony Tanner*   ALS King's

Saturday 28 October 1967[1]

975 Filbert,
San Francisco,
Calif.

Saturday

My Lord,

An idle hour or two and, of course, I am thinking of the delicious Tanners –
I have no other good reason for writing. How those Tanners fill the air around
me, aromatic yet bodiless presences – one actually reaches out for them,
thinking them there, but one 'cries to dream again', for it is insubstantial air
that one so poignantly punches.[2]

I also enclose a poem or two, or <u>will</u> enclose them, because I have a line
or two to clean up in one of them first. 'The Sand Man' is based on a real
man, of course: maybe you remember him.[3] He was a labor leader, beaten
up by some thugs in the '30's, and so got a brain injury, and after that was
on the beach at Aquatic Park almost every day of every year. I started the
poem about 6 weeks ago, did a few drafts of it, then the next day thought
I'd go down to Aquatic Park to see whether I could notice any details of
hallucinatory vividness about him. He was not there – he had died in his bed
the night before. Lawks, it was enough to make you feel that art is Satanic or
poetry the kiss of death, or something Thomas Mannish. – The other poem
enclosed is shamelessly sentimental, my last poem relating to sunlight, I hope.
You will notice it's related to Aubades, and Romeo & Juliet, & Donne, & so
on, where the mistress' eyes and the sun are confused; this doesn't <u>redeem</u> it,

of course – it's at best pretty but maybe is impossible.[4] I'd like to know what you think. (I do like the rhythms of the third stanza, though.) But I'd like to know much more whether you think the Sand Man comes off, since that matters much more to me. I really do think it's about time I stopped writing about sunlight – beaches – nakedness, though, as I find myself getting a bit tiresome on the subject.

Doody turns up here for three weeks soon, of which I am glad, as I get a bit lonely both living on my own and having no really exceptional friends here. Though I'm not complaining: life is very pleasant of course. We have our local elections on Nov 7th, and we're all wondering whether Proposition P will pass (the one for the immediate withdrawal of troops from Vietnam). I've been told my name will appear in the paper soon as one of its 'independent sponsors'. Of course you've read & heard all about the 'End the Draft Week' here and in Washington and elsewhere. All very ugly. – Obviously the next president will get in on a promise of ending the war, I pray it will be Rockefeller, I mean I pray he will stand.

I don't think I mentioned in my last that I read Creeley's new book.[5] It is terrible. I now realise that the kind of interest 'For Love' had for me was based entirely on untypical poems, where he was doing things he wasn't prepared to follow up. I think he is, not a fake, but as bad as a fake, and it is terrible that he is such a big influence. A poet who is uninterested in language (and he is, he simply won't admit its validity – his poems are like algebra in some ways) lacks the ONE indispensable prerequisite for writing poetry.

By contrast, Robert Bly's new book is very pleasing and full of attractive vivid images.[6] Ultimately I think he's pretty frivolous, and he is easy to parody. A good parody would be a poem entitled 'Passing By Oakland Induction Center, I think of the Police Barbarity of Last Week', and the poem would be full of agreeable surrealistic imagery of say feathers falling on a man in a coal-mine, without a reference to Oakland, the demonstrators, the police, the war, etc. But after Creeley I felt grateful for any kind of skill.

Winters' book of crit came out, at least I got an advance copy tremblingly signed and it is about to come out.[7] It confirms my best hopes and worst fears. The tone of much of it is terrible – dogmatic, arrogant, defiant, and almost always unnecessarily so. And he puts down too many people who don't need to be put down that hard. And there is a deplorable last chapter in which he discusses most of his students (I am a good poet but not a great poet, he says. Actually he writes a very perceptive bit about my poetry, and I make no complaints). It is true this chapter was written in the few days before he went into hospital for his last operation, but it's the idea of it that is worse than the execution. – I have told him all these criticisms, incidentally. – And all this is a great pity, because the argument of the book is a noble argument, and it goes right to the core of what is important about poetry – it discusses that central question of how discourse and image should be related, the question Kermode went into in part of 'Romantic Image'[8] and Clive Wilmer touched on in his Granta article.[9] And many of the discussions of poets and analyses of particular poems are brilliant, it would be difficult to imagine how they could be better done. But that nasty embattled tone keeps intruding, so it is ultimately a very mixed book even though I think a great many teachers and poets are going to find it extraordinarily useful.

What a literary letter this is.

[. . .]

I hope you are (1) Now heavily bearded.

(2) Even now writing to Stanford to accept their job.

Proposition Q: We need Tanners in the Bay Area. Yes X   No ☐

So here's cheers, kid, to all you hold valuable, to the God of your choice, and to your cuddly wife the Marsh-woman (or Lady of the Fens)

E. Lucie Smith, most repulsive man in England

to Marsh X   to you X

to your unborn children (x x x x x x x x x x x)

1. Date supplied through internal evidence.

2. *The Tempest* (3.28.140–1).

3. 'The Sand Man' (*CP* 193).

4. 'The Discovery of San Francisco' is unpublished (Bancroft).

5. Robert Creeley, *A Sight* (1967).

6. Bly, *The Light Around the Body* (1967).

7. Winters, *Forms of Discovery: Critical and Historical Essays on the Forms of the Short Poem in English* (1967).

8. TG reviewed Frank Kermode's *Romantic Image* (1957) in *London Magazine* 5, no. 2 (February 1958), 62–5; uncollected.

9. 'Clive Wilmer on Thom Gunn', *Granta* (22 April 1967), 20–1.

TO *Tony Tanner*   ALS King's

Sunday 3 December 1967

975 Filbert,
San Francisco,
Calif. USA

3 Dec 67

Hello, Dear,

Well it's raining hard & I started drinking this (Sunday) afternoon, but then I had a meal & sobered up, and as I came back in the rain just now I thought to myself "How very nice it would be of me if I conferred some kind of missive on the good Tansy." My life is full of such generous impulses nowadays.

Speaking of generous, or rather not speaking of it, I had a visit paid me the other day by a person called Watson, a "Johnian" as he called himself, as unpleasant a piece of work as I've come across in many a year.[1] He had a bad word for everyone, and seems to live in a very closed world, closed anyway to all except Old Johnians and a few courtesy-Johnians. What was all the worse was that he seemed quite intelligent, it wouldn't have mattered so much if he weren't. Extremely conceited, too, I suspect. Well, I suppose it takes a Colonial to be so repulsively English these days, god knows the English themselves aren't.

Ian Watt phoned me this morning, and though you were not the subject of the phone call (he wanted to know how big my cock is, actually), I brought you into it. I gather, and this was put so diplomatically by the author of "The Rise of the Novel" that I dare not say more than "gather", that they think, down there at Stanford, you are turning them down. If you are not aware that you are giving them this impression, but instead think you are playing for time, think again. They get this impression all the more because word has reached them (I am quite certain through the nasty Watson, since he said much the same to me) that you are "very anti-American" these days. I̲ know you were just speaking about politics, and told Ian so, but they do not.

John Berryman has just published a huge book of the poems he never printed in the early 1940's. It is called "Berryman's Sonnets." (Like "Shakespeare's Sonnets", see?)

Thank you for telling me to go to "Bonnie & Clyde", I liked it very much.

Thanksgiving was heaven. I had Don staying with me, and also a splendid man from Los Angeles whom I'd met a few weeks before, a rather sexy University professor, of all the outlandish occupations.[2] And then Don's

223

ex-lover and Cecil Beaton's ex-lover, who are lovers for the moment, came over, and we had lots of dexamyl and beer and turkey and apricot wine and grass. Waves of sheer love pulsed around and one by one we collapsed on the floor in sheer wiped-outness. It was all terribly happy, and one did feel that one was giving veritable thanks for something or other, though maybe it was only for being part of the warp and woof of life itself. (A homosexual dog, by the way, could colloquially be called a warped woof.)

Many thanks for your useful remarks about the poems. Something is wrong with The Sand Man, and you are a lot of help in identifying it, but it's something I obviously must put aside for a few months as it all puzzles me a good deal. It started out such a big poem, and then it shrank & shrank. [. . .]

There are some very splendid songs around. Of course the Eggman song (which is about a crisis of identity?),[3] and its lovely flipside, the best of Hello Songs. And the Stones 'We Love You.' And have you come across the Bee Gees' "Every Christian Lion-Hearted Man" and the Small Faces' "Itchykoo Park" (some fabulous electric orgasmic sounds).

[. . .]

Ian Hamilton has a way of hitting nails on the head (and driving them right out of sight). I expect he's right about me. Though I had no intention of writing a Victorian novel in Misanthropos, I didn't intend the central character to have any "character" – he was <u>universal</u>, see, Ian? I ought to have called him "Man", I guess.[4]

[. . .]

I've been reading R.P. Blackmur's poetry. A book called <u>From Jordan's Delight</u> published in 1937. Find it in the Univ Library & read it. It is really awfully good.

Oh yes, I did try methedrine, that dangerous substance that I've been telling people not to take. Only once. It was very exhilarating, but I'd better not take it again.

I wore my byrnie for Thanksgiving. I force myself to wear it once a month, so as to wear it out.[5]

I was sorry Proposition P (the peace proposition) lost in the election here. I was asked to be one of its "independent sponsors" and said yes. I thought I would be in the list of famous writers, along with Isherwood and people, but actually I was in the list of local homosexuals (in an advt in the local San Francisco "homophile" magazine).[6] I was rather pleased by that!

Isherwood came to see me the other day. Very nice to talk with him after all these years. One interesting thing. He was saying how attractive Auden used to be, & "For years we used to screw like weasels," he added off-handedly. Somehow it was so obvious I never thought of <u>that</u>. – Also, the talentless John Rechy has a new "novel" coming out, which contains unkind caricatures of Isherwood, his lover Gavin Lambert, and his ex-lover.[7] Of the latter, confidences are revealed, and a sad time is foreseen for Gavin L. Well, that's the end of this piece of paper, I think.

Love to both, x x x x x x x The Walrus

1. George Watson (1927–2013) taught English at Cambridge and was a Johnian: a fellow of St John's College.
2. TG met John Zeigel (1934–2021), a former love interest of Isherwood, in Febe's, a leather bar on Folsom Street, in October 1967. A year later, Isherwood wrote to Don Bachardy: 'Zeigelita is also going up to San Francisco for a whirl with Thom. I guess Mike doesn't mind this any more.' See *The Animals: Love Letters Between Christopher Isherwood and Don Bachardy*, ed. Bucknell (2014), 354.
3. The Beatles, 'I am the Walrus' (1967).
4. Ian Hamilton, 'Dead Ends and Soft Centres', *The Observer* (12 November 1967), 28.
5. TG bought a byrnie – a chainmail shirt – in June 1967. That summer, Tony and Marcia met him at one of the free concerts in Golden Gate Park. 'We came across Thom lying down on the ground, wearing a chainmail vest,' Marcia recalls, 'and nothing else on underneath it. It was boiling hot. There was his hairy chest and then hot metal burning into his skin, his flesh. He was trying to look very nonchalant but he was obviously being crucified. It was horrible. But he wouldn't take it off because it would've spoiled the whole look of the thing.' See 'The Byrnies' (*CP* 106–7).
6. See 'Vote Yes on P', *Vector* 3, no. 12 (November 1967), 11. *Vector* ('a voice for the homophile community') was the official publication of the Society for Individual Rights.
7. Rechy, *Numbers* (1967).

1968

TO *Tony White*   ALS Tulsa
Saturday 27 January 1968¹

975 Filbert St.,
San Francisco,
Calif., U.S.A.

Saturday

Dear Whitey,

It was splendid to get your letter. You do write good letters nowadays. I wish I could do as well. Anyway, I thought I ought to answer it now since I shall be away all of Feb on the Poetry Circuit. The word circuit always reminds me of Methodist ministers, but I shall try to be as unMethodist as possible. – I will let you know how I feel about readings after next month. Meanwhile I do think your idea of a three-ring English circus, a Hughes–Murphy–Gunn dance team on bareback horses, very good indeed. As you say, it would get you over here, and we could make lots of money. [. . .]

Here is a poem you haven't seen. I sent an earlier version to Tanner in the Fall and he made some useful criticisms, which I acted on, so this is quite changed from the one he saw.²

[. . .]

My friend (and mentor) Yvor Winters died yesterday. I am very sorry he had such a painful time of it the last few years, with cancer of the mouth. He meant quite a lot to me, even though I've seen him only once a year for the last nine years. And a very loveable man, in his dogged and awkward and sometimes outrageous way.

And Marshall McLuhan has a haemorrage of the brain and Gerald Heard is largely paralysed. A nasty irony there: McLuhan despises the mind, and Gerald Heard had all those Homer Lane theories of illness being repression (as in 'Miss Gee').³

I have given one of my readings already. It went quite well. I think, actually, it was the best I have given, and that I have improved a bit in the last few years. I hope it was a good augury for the next eighteen or so, anyway!

Did I say how much I liked the new Stones LP? I have come to like it even more than the new Beatles.[4] Brilliant, though I still can't make out a lot of the words in the songs. And you ought to look out for Country Joe & the Fish, who I believe are touring England. Tanner has their first LP, but they have come out with a second even better. They are a local group, part of what the trade papers call the San Francisco Sound.

There is a lovely bit in Harold Nicolson's diaries.[5] He, with John Strachey, Joad, and others, was originally in Mosley's 'New Party' before they realized what he was turning it into. In 1931, Nicolson writes 'We have a meeting of the Party. (Mosley says) that we need no longer to hesitate to create our trained and disciplined force. We discuss their uniforms. I suggest grey flannel trousers and shirts.'

I have had nothing but colds and flu, laid end to end, since about October. More than any other winter. The weather is perfectly mild and I am really very fit, so I can't help concluding that it's all because smoking joints is such a social thing, mouth to mouth. 'I get colds with the help of my friends.'[6]

My friends miraculously keep out of reach of the law, though so many others keep getting arrested and though several of my friends are really getting pretty big time in dealing in grass and acid. But I suppose it's because they have the sense not to deal in it continually: one guy I know made $18,000 in selling acid a short while ago, but it was all out of his house in under a week, and he will live on the money for a few years and not bother to deal again till the money runs out. It is all very interesting, very capitalistic – like home industries, the whole week there were guys in the kitchen putting the white powder into capsules (and licking their fingers and getting loaded), the phone went continually, people kept dropping by to pick up their 'lots'. The first dealer sells them in large lots (of about 500 capsules) to people who then sell them in smaller lots of 100 to people who sell them in tens or fives to the actual consumers. All this is not because of capitalist ideals but because it is dangerous to be found with many in one's possession and so people want to get rid of them quickly. And the customers are a real trip – hair down below their shoulders, colossal earrings etc.

[. . .]

X X X X

Th.

---

1. Date supplied through internal evidence.
2. 'The Sand Man' (CP 193). See also TG to Tanner, 28 October 1967, above.
3. See Auden's 'Miss Gee' (1938).
4. The Rolling Stones, *Their Satanic Majesties Request* (1967); the Beatles, *Magical Mystery Tour* (1967).

5. Nicolson, *Diaries and Letters 1930–1939* (1966).
6. The Beatles, 'With a Little Help from My Friends' (1967).

TO *Janet Lewis*[1]

ALS Stanford

Tuesday 30 January 1968[2]

975 Filbert,
San Francisco,
Calif.

Tuesday

Dear Janet,

Ken Fields[3] phoned Friday morning to say that Arthur was dead. I am sure that you know I feel the greatest sympathy for you. You expected his death, but it must be a terrible loss just the same.

It is very difficult to believe that I shall never see him again, but he will go on influencing the minds of those of us who worked under him, for the rest of our lives. That is such a stiff and formal statement to make, I know, but it is true. And it is even harder to speak about the love we felt for him, a love the extent of which he was too modest to realize.

Please don't answer this letter. I feel for you very much.

Thom

1. Janet Lewis (1899–1998), novelist and poet. See Glossary of Names.
2. Date from postmark.
3. Kenneth Fields (1939–), poet and academic; former student of Winters's.

TO *Tony and Marcia Tanner*

ALS King's

Thursday 15 February 1968

Los Angeles

15 Feb 68

Hello Tanners,

I meant to send you a picture postcard, but not being able to get at shops all the time from my hill I thought I'd send you a short letter instead. For all I know there may be a letter from you waiting for me at home, but I won't find it till I get back there on March 1st.

I am having a splendid hedonistic time here. My host (John Zeigel, a teacher at Cal Tech, whom I have mentioned before) is a prince of generosity, and has a bosky garden on a hill ~~over~~ (Mount Washington, in Highland Park) overlooking almost all of L.A., which provides an enormous light show every night. I am giving regular poetry readings with great vigor, and to my surprise I have become so lacking in nervousness that I am reading pretty well – certainly better than ever before. They are a bit trying, of course, as all work is, and can seriously interfere with drinking schedules. The night before my reading at UCLA I got as drunk as I ever have in my life – there was actually an hour of consciousness of which next day I remembered nothing at all. I woke up the next day surrounded by naked bodies and uniquely hungover. While I gave my reading I kept wondering whether any poet had ever thrown up on the stage during a poetry reading. Luckily I got through it all right. Anyway, days here start with bloody Marys.

We went to Jimi Hendryx, at the Shrine, which is quite a place. Also there was an English group, the Soft Machine (the drummer and vocalist was naked), and a SF group (I think), the Blue Cheer – both very good.

Did I say that Winters died. With maybe a vulgar showmanship (but I didn't intend it that way), I finished my reading at Stanford with my (old) poem to him and then My Sad Captains. Wes Trimpi wept.[1] I felt like Charles Dickens.

I have been having 2 types of dream lately and only two – they are all very vivid. Type one is of dead people, type two is sexual dreams. Among type one was a <u>very</u> strange dream where I found my mother dead. I thought, callously, 'Oh no, not <u>again</u>. I think I'll let somebody else find her body this time.' Which I did! Also in this dream I got on very well with my father. I think my analyst, if I had one, would be rather pleased with this dream.

I have been seeing a marvellous American Indian with the real name of Sky Highchief. Probably for literary and cinematic reasons, I find American Indians very sexy. However, there aren't many, are there?

Did I thank you for your Henry James? Thank you very much indeed. I feel guilty about having asked for it, all the more because I dislike the book so much now I read it! But I do like your introduction, which is much more sensible and has a much better sense of proportion than old Hank shows about Nat.[2]

Well, Folks, I'll be closing off now. By the way –

[. . .]

– Stay safe.

How is Whitey? I got a resilient letter from him, saying how depressed he had been and describing the shit he had been through – but the resilience might be bravery, only.

X X X
X X X
X X X
X X

1. Wesley Trimpi (1928–2014) and Helen Pinkerton Trimpi (1927–2017), poets and academics, were close friends and colleagues of Winters at Stanford.
2. See Tanner's introduction to Henry James, *Hawthorne* (1967), 1–21.

TO *Tony Tanner*   ALS King's

Tuesday 21 May 1968

975 Filbert,
San Francisco,
Calif.

21 May 68

Dear Tance,

I got your little portrait by Francis Bacon, and very depressed indeed you did look at not hearing from me for so long. The truth is, what with my richly-travelled life – 5 weeks in S. Calif., other trips within Calif., visits to N.Y., Boston, Vancouver, Denver and San Jose – I have made lots of money to live on this year but haven't written a letter or a poem, to speak of, in lots of time. I only have 2 more readings to do – both in L.A., one tomorrow & one next month – and then will call it quits for the year, whatever quits may be. I have begun to get a distinct impression of motels and hotels: if there is no picture (in oils or ceramics) of a bullfighter on the wall of your bedroom, then you are in either a very expensive or a very cheap hotel indeed.

Ted & I are to do a replacement for (John Hayward's) Faber Book of Verse.[1] Nothing less. It will take us years and years. But it should be fun, rather like taking the Tripos again, but in poetry only. Two long-term requests, then: (1) if you ever run across a good poem or poet you think it likely we might miss, do tell me (though we plan to be exhaustive, I'm even going to read William Diaper, whoever he is); (2) and also could you tell me when you come across good collections of popular (anonymous mostly) poetry, i.e. broadsides, songs, etc. I am haunted by the idea that there might be something as good as Tom o' Bedlam knocking about (not that I believe that to be popular poetry, it is very sophisticated and literary, & I suspect it's by somebody who was very famous, though I can't guess who).

No of course I wouldn't pass on anything you say, to Ian Watt (though I would do the reverse, i.e. pass on what <u>he</u> said, to <u>you</u>). You must be right about him (Davie), judging from his funny outbursts of irritation in the Listener. – By the way, you'd better come to Stanford, I add selfishly, because I'm not likely to be back in England for years and years. I'm too lazy to make more money than I need for living on, so I don't see myself saving enough to go back, for a long time. – My object is to form a Snyder-type Tribe here, with you & Marsh, Whitey, and about ten people from here. (<u>Of course</u> you don't want to go to Essex, why ever should you?!)

My drug-life is starting to get interesting again. (I hardly count grass as a drug any longer!) Last weekend I went with about twelve nice people (among them Don) to a pop festival, 2 days long, in a fairgrounds near San Jose.[2] Some interesting groups – I am starting to like the Electric Flag, Big Brother was splendid as usual, Country Joe & the Fish were greatly inferior to their records, and the Doors gave the most fantastic performance I've ever seen from a group. And some interesting things happened. There is a new drug, a capsule, called a 'hog', as of last week, when a lot were distributed at a dance sponsored by Hells Angels (who ride Harley Davidsons, known as hogs). So a man & woman turned up at the fairgrounds and, Kesey fashion, gave away 4000 capsules.[3] They gave them away to promising looking people, one of them Jerry, Don's splendid friend (well mine too, but Don is in love with him).[4] So I took one, having already had laid on me a cap of psilocybin, a marvellous mushroom thing you probably took some ten years ago. And I had an afternoon that was – well – memorable. A steady euphoria for hour after hour. Of course, 3999 other people were somewhat high also. I would sit with some of my friends in the shade for a while; then at times I would stand in the sun with one or two of them & have a prolonged wordless euphoric understanding with them. We would start sentences and there would be no need to finish them, the sympathy was so great. Well, <u>you</u> know. Toward the end of the afternoon 3 cops came up to Jerry, his identification was in his car, and we all knew he had all sorts of illicit pills & things in his car. But they had thought he was the one who had made the hogs, he convinced them he wasn't, so he wasn't busted, & bounced back to us ten minutes later. But even this didn't bring me down, the euphoria continued, and while he was away I remember feeling a bit sorry that I couldn't feel worse about him. Anyway, one result of this is that I know I am now ready to take acid again. You remember I had scared myself out of it; now I feel good & confident that I can handle it as at the start.

Did I tell you I am going to teach a quarter next year at the Calif. State College at Hayward, fairly near Berkeley?

You ask me how the war affects me. Acutely depressing and confusing, it drives a lot of ordinary people to nasty extremes. I suppose I am selfish, if I really cared I would demonstrate. Though I must say it's beginning to look as if the center cannot hold, anywhere.[5] Were the results of Enoch Powell's speech as ugly as they sounded from over here?[6]

I read a nice book called Growing Up Absurd by Paul Goodman. You have probably read it. It struck me as very reasonable. Even rather conservative, if anything. Very good, though.

I know what you and Whitey & Ted mean about territory, but I don't think it applies much to me. Partly because I'm less influenced by the roots business than any of you (certainly less than Ted), and partly because if I have any roots, I seem to have put down as many here – or almost as many – as in England, I am at my best – in my writing, anyway – when I am trying to reconcile opposites, E.g. Apollonian – Dionysian, impulse & self-discipline, etc. (Maybe this is why I write bad free verse – if you understand me.) (Much of my content is very impulsive stuff (basically the kind of thing in 'A Map of the City', in My Sad Captains), but usually it only becomes something more when the metrical form examines it.) & one of the most important of these living-between-opposites is being an Englishman in San Francisco. Incidentally, I discovered, during my readings, that Misanthropos is all this kind of thing, first in its main structure – he is the only person in the world, he is not the only person in the world; and also in its detail, poem contradicts previous poem, particularly the section VII, [VIII], IX, X, XI, XII. I think I learned that from Baudelaire. – It's worth a thought, by the way, that two of the greatest influences on me are Donne & Baudelaire, both of whom were set books for the Tripos when I was at Cambridge. Thank god they were good set books. But they were very good for me.

I'm enclosing a recent poem by the Snyder (from Poetry mag) which I think is one of the nicest sex poems I have read.[7]

Lots of other lovely things have happened. I spent a splendid week in NY, with M, where I gave my best reading of my life. Mike comes back in a few weeks & turns on every day now. I must introduce him, heh heh, to psilocybin.

Tenderest love to both you babies, biggest hugs & wet kisses,

x x x x x x x Thom

---

1. TG and Hughes never completed this anthology. Material relating to the project can be found in Hughes's papers at the British Library and Emory University.

2. The Northern California Folk-Rock Festival (18–19 May 1968).

3. Ken Kesey (1935–2001), novelist and subject of Tom Wolfe's book about psychedelic drugs, *The Electric Kool-Aid Acid Test* (1968). Kesey organized Acid Tests: parties at which he and his friends, the Merry Pranksters, served LSD-laced Kool-Aid to the public.

4. Jere Fransway (1928–96) is the dedicatee of 'The Fair in the Woods' (*CP* 209–10) and the subject of 'Falstaff' (*CP* 374–5). See Glossary of Names.

5. See Yeats's 'The Second Coming' (1920).

6. Powell's attack on mass immigration became known as the 'Rivers of Blood' speech because of its reference to 'the Tiber foaming with much blood' from Virgil's *Aeneid*.

7. 'Song of the Taste' (1968).

TO *Tony Tanner*   ALS King's

Monday 30 September 1968

San Francisco

30 Sept 68

Dear Tanner,

We all miss you, and the deluge of postcards you have sent us only brings the tear to the collective eye. Maybe next year you can return and bring Marsh with you on a visit to Fascist America.

Mike and I are getting on splendidly, more so than for years. Quarrels such as we used to have are almost unimaginable. Look, we have come through.[1] And he really seems pretty sustainedly happy. He has been going through a Tanner reading list, by the way, 'V'[2] and [Bernard] Malamud and etcetera. Yesterday we dropped Christmas trees, if you recollect those energetic little capsules, and had a rare old drunk evening. As often, I think mine is still working. – Something funny and unexpected is that Don has started telling me he <u>likes</u> Mike. He likes him because he is in general more relaxed, is liked by various of Don's friends, turns on, and enjoys the Stud.[3] So I said to Don, all right, <u>show</u> him you like him. Which he is doing, to Mike's pleasure and surprise. Well, we shall see. But if they continue getting on together it could certainly make an old lady's life easier.

Don has succeeded magnificently with the Stud. There are now more murals, there is dancing and affability, and it is probably the most packed bar in town. He is moving into those rooms above (where we went your first night, remember) with Chuck Arnett and a few other nice people. Apparently there are 16 rooms up there!

I sent your books after a rather unpardonable delay, and they should have reached you by now. I read the Terry Southern and was very impressed by some stories I wouldn't have expected from him (especially the one about the razor fight).[4] I find him an enormously sympathetic writer – did you read Flash & Filigree? yes, you must have – except I wish, in my probably pedantic way, that he would distinguish between 'like' and 'as'.

I'm reading Constantine Fitzgibbon's Life of Dylan Thomas. It is very good, with a kind of ideal attitude for a biographer – affectionate but critical. Did you know that except for 20 poems, all his published poems were contained in embryonic form in notebooks written before he was twenty years old? I find his life quite reassuring, being something of a non-writer myself this year. I don't think I can delude myself that there are external reasons for my having written so little – I just don't feel the proper enthusiasm + obsessional-interest-in-subject when I sit down to write nowadays. I have a few things I tinker with, but I don't want to go farther with them till I have that right feeling that I recognize when it is there. Oh well, it will come again, but less and less as I get older. I suspect I have at most two more books in me. I wonder why so many poets dry up, and so few novelists, dramatists, etc? I think it might be to do with the shortness of the form, you use up subjects so quickly. If I were a novelist I might have written a whole novel about motorcyclists and another about Julian the Apostate, but a few poems use up those subjects completely, all I have to say about them, and any more about them (not that I want to write more about them) would just be repetitious. Edwin Muir said something wise about all this, I remember, though I don't know where.

Strangely enough, Robert Duncan has taken me up lately, coming to see me and asking me to dinner.[5] I say strangely because we have known each other slightly for ten years and also because he clearly has read at most two or three poems by me. He is a nice man, rather egotistical, and a great talker. By great I mean he talks a lot and any time spent with him tends to be occupied with his monologues. I have met splendid monologists, Aldous Huxley being one and Chet Helms, who runs the Avalon Ballroom, being another, and Robert Duncan is not one of those. – He is fantastically learned, especially in funny areas like the occult. His lover, Jess Collins, is a painter, and very modest (he needs to be) and sweet-natured.

I must be a masochist, otherwise I would stop reading the papers. Since the Chicago convention I have come round to believing that "the revolution" will take place.[6] And the revolutionaries will lose, of course, and we'll end with an Ian Smith or a Vorster. And it will be time for me to return to England.[7]

I have had very vivid and odd dreams all this week. Two nights ago I dreamt I had rheumatic fever and fell in love with a male nurse (who was also a hippy). Last night I was one of the first group of people to land on the moon. What will tonight bring?

The reviews of Touch over here have been consistently shitty. Doesn't matter, really. There is only a handful of reviewers who know much about poetry, after all. The rest are all trying madly to be now people. (Touch just came out in paperback, a pink book.)

Have you seen a movie called The Producers? Most of it is really up to the best Marx Bros standard. You must both see it.

I see from Life Mag that I was in Hamburg the same time as the Beatles. If only I had strayed into their beer cellar. – Isn't Hey Jude one of their all-time best.

Maybe I'll have another try at writing an autobiography.[8] Mike bought me a rocking chair for my 39th birthday, and that's what an old man should do in his decline – write his life from a rocker. Not that I feel 39. 20 years old is more like it.

On which note I shall stop. Excuse the eccentricities of this letter, and put them down to that pill I took yestere'en.

X X to you

X X to Marsh

and throw a bit of cucumber skin in front of Geo. Watson, Gent., next time he ponces along Trinity Street when he greets you Tone[9]

1. An allusion to D. H. Lawrence's poetry collection Look! We Have Come Through! (1917).

2. Thomas Pynchon, V (1963).

3. Doody managed the Stud, a gay bar at 1535 Folsom Street. Initially a leather bar, Doody transformed it into a druggy, hippy 'head' bar that was one of the most popular in San Francisco.

4. Southern, Red-Dirt Marijuana and Other Tastes (1967).

5. Robert Duncan (1919–88) became a major influence on TG's writing. See Glossary of Names.

6. The 1968 Democratic National Convention was held in Chicago against the backdrop of ongoing protests against the Vietnam War and civil unrest following the assassination of Martin Luther King Jr. It was marred by the violent repression of peaceful protest.

7. For TG, Ian Smith, Prime Minister of Rhodesia (1964–79), and John Vorster, Prime Minister of South Africa (1966–78), represented the survival of fascism in the post-fascist, post-war era.

8. TG made a great many false starts at writing an autobiography. He did draft several chapters, copies of which can be found among his papers at the Bancroft Library. The four autobiographical essays he published are collected in OP (151–88).

9. See TG to Tanner, 3 December 1967, above.

TO *Donald Davie*[1]
TLS Essex

Wednesday 27 November 1968

975 FILBERT,
San Francisco,
Calif.

27 Nov 68

Dear Donald,

This is just a note to say thank you for your review, in which I thought you were very generous to me and to Greville.[2] And I liked your reservation, really. No, I can't claim that the 'plain style' is any longer <u>central</u> to the poetic tradition, but I would like more people to recognize it as one of the valid styles. You do recognise it as such. I am getting so tired of people – whether Winters or Robert Duncan, Conquest or Alvarez – who claim that there is ONE tradition and all the rest is virtually trash. There are, for us nowadays, anyway, a lot of valid traditions. I have to admit this, since I find myself able to admire such diverse people, have to leave myself open to the possibility that, say, Ginsberg might one day learn to write well.[3]

Anyway, thank you for the review again. It really warmed me. I'm looking forward to seeing you up this end of California. If it weren't for North California, I doubt if I'd want to live in this country.

Best,

Thom

1. Donald Davie (1922–95), poet and critic. See Glossary of Names.
2. Davie, 'Forgotten Poet', *The Listener* (24 October 1968), 540–1.
3. See TG to Hall, 26 March 1969, postscript, below.

TO *Tony Tanner*
AL King's

Wednesday 25 December 1968[1]

[975 Filbert,
San Francisco,
Calif., USA]

Christmas Day

Sir:

What better day to start a letter to you than Christmas Day? It certainly is being a wild Christmas, none of your drab suburban get-togethers this year.

The Stud closed for a night to give its 150 closest friends a party in the bar. The place was decorated with polythene so as to look like a kind of Venusian Fingal's Cave, with flexible stalactites, etc.[2] And everybody, including Mike and me, said it was the best party they'd ever been to. One thing that helped was that everyone was offered acid, and so about 70 of us were on a reasonably heavy trip. So after the party some of us went upstairs. As one guy said, 'I had one look at the road outside and I knew I wasn't ready for it yet.' Mike (who was wearing leather bellbottoms – no shit) was still hallucinating mildly 12 hours after. – And Jerry Franzway gave a smaller but as splendid party last night. [. . .] [We] ate a lot of wonderful food and went through a lot of grass. Jerry found an old bag full of the classical acid, Blue Cheer (after which the rock group got its name – every different lot of acid has its name, what we took at the Stud was called Cheap Thrills) and distributed it to those who wanted it. I didn't this time. I had decided on a good old place to reach with grass and hash, reached it, and stayed there about six hours with the help of the boosting joint every now and then. [. . .] I discovered someone in a corner having a bad trip so elected myself Nurse [Edith] Cavell. I have got very good at this, but it bores me out of my mind. However if I'm stoned it's not too bad. – So as you can see, it's all happening at San Francisco. You should both have been here, Sir and Ma'am. – I must say I find it difficult to believe I shall be teaching again in eight days time. I've decided to blow my students' minds with outrageous costumes, i.e. frilled shirts, bell bottom pants etc. That'll give them something to think about in Hayward.

[. . .]

I have now read The Armies of the Night. Yes, you are right when you say Mailer is the best prose writer around. At least maybe you do not say it, but he says it. It could be he is the best writer around. (Which he also says.) His personality is unpleasant, but one just has to stick with it.

Enclosed a few poems I jotted down over the holidays. (Untrue, of course: I started one twelve years ago and one eighteen months ago.) Questions: does the meter of line 2 of 'Words' strike you as difficult? Did you read it with the right stresses when you first read the poem? The first foot is supposed to be an anapaest, but I get the feeling one can't start a line with an anapaest after a line with a feminine ending? Or maybe it works? (I sound like [Robert] Bridges, but us impulsive Hell's Angels of poetry are really deeply dedicated to our craft, Raymond.[3]) What do you think of the punctuation of 'Justin'? Specifically of lines 2 and 3 should they be enclosed in dashes? & I want the last line to be both a noun phrase and an adjectival phrase, Mr. Empson, so is it best to end the preceding line with a comma? – The long poem you may well consider unforgivable.[4] First he writes poems about drugs, and now it's dreams and astrology. Who does he think he is, Willie Yeats? The title comes from the Bible, God setting the sun & moon in the sky 'for signs, and for seasons' (a good title for my next book). The moon was in Scorpio when I was born, I am told, and I am further told that that means sexual perversion. Ooh. I don't feel the reference is obscure nowadays, because so many people know this kind of thing; & what's more I think more & more people will know it, until in about 20 years time astrological assumptions are going to be as much behind people's thought as Freudian assumptions are behind them now – both non-sciences but full of useful metaphors.

Quite an egotistical letter, this. Throw it away. [. . .]

P.S. Is the structure of 'For Signs', clear? Part 1 is me awake in moonlight, Part 2 is dreaming, Part 3 is an essay on the moon (the high style, fine writing, etc. i.e. genteel bombast, at which I am so good).

1. Date supplied through internal evidence.
2. Chuck Arnett decorated the Stud for the annual Saturnalia party, which coincided with Doody's birthday (17 December).
3. Probably Raymond Williams, who was a colleague of Tanner's at Cambridge.
4. 'For Signs' (CP 188–9).

1969

975 Filbert,
San Francisco,
Calif.

Monday

Hello young Tanner,

An overcast afternoon and it seems right, being indoors, to write to you. No great news. January was not too happy a month, but February seems much nicer. Mike has gone to New York for ten days, and it is good, every now and again, to live alone for a short spell.

[. . .]

I'm halfway through the term [at Hayward]. I wish the students were better i.e. knew how to write. Stanford and Berkeley spoiled me.

I had a truly big experience the other day. There has been a new batch of acid made by a friend (the same friend who has made most of what circulates in our group): it was very strong – the strongest Don or Chuck Arnett had ever had, and Chuck has dropped it as many times as anybody in the world. Of the nine people who had dropped it, five threw up and went into a deep sleep for a couple of hours. All nine, as Don said, had one thing in common – they all came face to face with essentials about themselves. One – a rather nasty boy with a lot of dope experience – left for San Diego the next day and has never been seen since. So when Don suggested I drop it too, my first impulse was that I wasn't up to it. But I thought about it 2 days, and felt it was a challenge, and also knew I wouldn't have such a chance often in my life, so on Saturday afternoon I went round to the household and dropped. Well, I didn't throw up or pass out, but that two hours at the center of the six or so I was on it were about the most interesting in my life. After the first hour, which consisted of fairly familiar but continually stronger light-hallucinations and distortions, suddenly – click – I was in a new place, where hallucination was so strong that it was completely part of reality. It was completely incredible, life was a complete <u>flowing</u> so that nothing had a permanent identity, least of all myself, and in fact I didn't even know what time I was living in. (Don had dropped too but certainly kept his sense of humor. At one stage I said to him, 'What age am I in?' and he said 'nearing middle-age, dear.') Meanwhile Don became a lot of different people to me, at one stage my father, for example. At another stage we went on the roof and I had a conversation with God. It may seem strange for somebody brought up completely without religion to do such a thing, but by God I meant, and Don knew I meant, It, the source of the universe, etc. I can tell you, I put some pretty challenging propositions to God, and he gave me no answer. Of course I didn't see him, because it was not a human-shaped god I was speaking with. But I could see anybody who was relevant – as I say, including my father – except for Mike, interestingly enough. And there was a time when I felt quite a need for Mike to be there. I had various moments quite close to panic but Don was really splendid with me, in that he didn't <u>comfort</u> me when I asked panicky questions (& that would have been <u>my</u> impulse) but answered them honestly with difficult answers, which made me work out the problem on its own terms rather than dismiss it. E.g. at one time I said 'Well, if I don't have identity and I don't have love, what is there?' And he said 'honor.' Though I didn't understand what he meant till some hours later, when he said that by honoring oneself one can honor other people. And then, click, the peak was over, and I went into the kitchen and we all sat round the table with some beer and the rest of it was an ordinary nice acid trip, though the skin on their faces shone like snow for another few hours.[2]

All this is no doubt rather boring. People who go on about their trips <u>are</u> very boring. But this was a trip different <u>in kind</u> from any other, and I still feel beautifully clean-brained from it. I was in the Stud for a while later in the evening, and I noticed something I've noticed before when I'm coming down from a trip: one seems to other people the most beautiful one has ever been. Partly, I think, because one has such an air of self-sufficiency, partly because one's pupils are still enlarged and look full of wonder. – I feel rather proud to have been there and survived: I doubt even Ken Kesey has dropped acid any stronger. It's as if I've been to a place I never even hoped to get to. And it is good for me. I'm not one of those people who get all religious in trying to get everyone to drop acid, because I can't spot those who are potential schizophrenics, but anybody who wants to should, I think. Mike has dropped four times now, and it has been pretty good for him in opening him up. One thing it does (& grass too, to a much less degree) is to present as possible still the choices one had thought were settled long ago. Which is why confirmed homosexuals can become bisexual (for a time, anyway). Not that I see that as likely to happen to me.

End of acid-letter.

Two Listeners came today. Something is very depressing about England. I suppose something is just depressing about the U.S.A., but San Francisco, as you know, is not in the U.S.A.

Haven't had time to do much writing. In any case, I am now confronted by subjects so big I must do a lot of thinking before I write about them. I'm not even sure they can be written about.

Haven't heard from T.W. or from the Gunns.

>   Love,
>
>   Thom

1. Date supplied through internal evidence.
2. TG wrote about this acid trip in 'At the Centre' (*CP* 220–1).

TO *Donald Hall*   ALS New Hampshire
Wednesday 26 March 1969

> 975 Filbert,
> San Francisco,
> Calif. 94133
>
> 26 March 69

Dear Don,

[. . .]

I've begun to realize that I like giving readings – mainly an ego thing I'm sure, as since I've got better at them I enjoy that feeling of manipulating the audience.

You remember how I used to say I didn't like other poets. Well, I suppose that was never really very true, as I can think of plenty I liked when I said it, but I suppose that dreadful London thing – Lehmann-people, and the hangovers from the Soho group of the '40s, and the camp followers – was enough to make me scared of the scene. And of course there are still plenty of horrific people around. But the people living here are full of charm. I see quite a bit of Robert Duncan and Elizabeth Bishop (who lives on the other side of this hill). Elizabeth turned Duncan on to grass last year – for the first time in his life! Isn't that wild? I plan to turn him on to acid soon. When I drop acid I see people as angels, but he sees angels anyway, so Blake only knows what he'll see then. Elizabeth is a person of a certain superficial formality – in a very nice way – beneath which is really a great openness to experience. So picture this: at a wild 12-poet benefit reading for the strikers at San Francisco State a few weeks ago, Michael McClure and his literary hells angel friend Free Wheelin' Frank pass me a joint that smells more of hashish than grass and I pass it on to Miss Bishop, who doesn't blink, but calmly takes an enormous puff on it. – Ferlinghetti has always been polite with me, but really rather disapproves of me. Gary Snyder, whom I've met only twice, is back in San Francisco, and it would be nice to see something of him. I really think he has more going than anyone else our age. – By all this I don't mean I have abandoned old loyalties! Though it's true I have never felt farther from poor Winters, who had a wretched and embittered death, and whose passion for poetry became so often such a perverted kind of love. But I still like and admire Edgar Bowers – who is so loosened up now that whenever I see him he does nothing but smile and smile (though he talks too, of course). I have got to know Charles Gullans this last year: I cannot stand his poetry but what I like about him as a man is that he recognizes and dislikes his own primness and makes valiant and not always successful efforts to defeat it. – So I'm plenty social with poets nowadays.

I know what you mean about not really <u>minding</u> if I dislike your poems. You reach a stage when you know surely enough what you want to do, and the ways in which you are aiming at it, that the opinions of even those you respect are not very important if they don't understand your direction. This is why I haven't minded my last book having had on the whole rather shitty reviews. It's a rather poor book, actually, but reviewers disliked it for the wrong reasons – I can't be bothered any longer with <u>their</u> assumptions about what poetry should be – and it was important for me to write the poems in the book as part of my direction toward something else. There's an All's Well that End's Well on the path to every King Lear.

As a matter of fact I've abandoned syllabics for ever, and I've been writing very single-mindedly in meter for two years now. I don't care what can be said against meter – I can see it as the form in which I can do the most there is for me in poetry. I'm trying to get into it a good deal of what I learned from free verse, <u>plus</u>. I'm trying to get all of myself into it! (Wow.)

More specifically I see myself as always having been up to one thing, and I want to carry it even farther. That is, I take, mostly, pure romantic experience-for-its-own-sake and then try to give it meaning by rendering it through the human inventions of metrical and stanzaic form. My difference from most of the good people around is that I'm not primarily interested in capturing the thing-in-itself or the experience-in-itself and in producing it on its own terms, I am interested in <u>why</u> it seems important. My difference from YW or from awful less consistent rationalists like Roy Fuller is that I do see experience as a good and that I approach it as far as I can without pre-assuming what its meaning will be.

I think maybe I'm getting obscure, if not pompous. My trouble this morning is that I had only 4 hours sleep last night and I was given a nice yellow dexamyl, so I am verbose without being what you might call keenly intelligent.

I wish you would come out here. Life is such fun here. I just taught a quarter at the State College at Hayward – but that was the first time I had taught in three years. And I have been quite euphoric much of those last three years!

[. . .]

Don't bother to answer this. You must be busy right now. Be in good health.

      Love,

           X X X Thom.

P.S. Did you see Ginsberg's latest book?[1] At last he has written some good poetry. I mean 'Visitation Wales' mainly, but there are a couple of others I like where he seems to be turning outward to really look at and experience the things he previously generalized about.

1. *Planet News* (1968).

TO *Tony Tanner*   ALS King's
Saturday 19 April 1969

                    975 Filbert
                San Francisco
                Calif 94133

           19 or so of April 69

Hello!

It may be your last letter I have here to answer, or again it may be not. It is very interesting anyway. I certainly should have answered it before, but experiences have been following each other so hot and heavy lately that I have barely had time to think about them after, let alone write about them. First, anyway, some surprising plans. I teach next spring at Princeton, where they have some sort of endowed professorship for poets – two days work a week and ten thousand dollars. And just a seminar + creative writing, and a lecture or two. Then the rest of the week in New York City. (I must pick your brains about seminars this summer – I have never given one, and surely they don't need to be so deadly dull as they were at Stanford when I did graduate work.) Well, anyway, I hope I surprise them at Princeton.

This will provide enough money for Mike and me to visit Sydney for 6 months, later next year. Our head friends will have already done a little Australian mind-expanding there, and will probably already have a chemical factory and a few acres of ground under cultivation by then. – If you have had time to read that seminal work, Tom Wolfe's book about Ken Kesey,[1] then you will understand more clearly what seems to be in our minds. Right now, there are about 6–8 of us who plan on going.

I am reading Wm James, as you suggested, and it is a beautiful book.[2] I haven't yet come across the word vastation, but I did find the lectures on Conversion very applicable to what happens to most people on their first acid trip. Marginal values leap into the center and take over from what were often selfish habits, etc. The world is full of light. And so on. The acid experience is mostly religious in effect, I have come to realize (I don't think I thought so a couple of years ago), but religious in a much more subtle way than you'd guess from reading [Timothy] Leary. – Marcia's remark about my poems is much to the point. Maybe it's really just that I swing along with every fashion, Sartre one year, acid the next. Right now I am not at all sure where I am going, but it is certainly an interesting exploration. With drugs you get glimpses, but only glimpses, of other ways of knowing, and of forces beyond you, but I don't think any person or system has ever been able to name those ways of knowing or those forces. I have had a curious fancy more than once on acid that just at the edge of my vision there are a few giant pillars or maybe figures.[3] I do not want to see those figures very clearly, because if I do they may turn into the doctor and the mid-wife delivering me into a new life, to which this life is only a preface. And I'm certainly not ready to leave this life yet, it is far too enjoyable.

Anyway, your Romantic Poet friend encloses a nice printed copy of an old poem and a new one.[4] Well, you know what the new one is about. Pretty ambitious. (I thought at one time of calling it 'Poem About Everything'.)[5] Don has seen it and has not yet made any comment, which may mean he doesn't think much of it. Mike likes the last stanza. I like the line 'The blue line bleeds and on the gold one draws,' which has a kind of lush Tennyson–Swinburne–Pound thing going. I'll be interested to know what you think of it, anyway!

I continue seeing Robert Duncan every now and again. I now find him completely delightful. He talks far too much, and has at times a kind of fetching silliness that reminds me of Stephen Spender. But he is a very good poet, he has some really good ideas at bottom (some of them, anyway), he can be very witty, and his silliness is not like Spender's a cover for dishonesty or cowardliness. – Snyder is back in San Francisco, with a gorgeous Japanese wife and an equally gorgeous baby. I had lunch with all of them (I mean Duncan too) the other day. Snyder continues to blow my mind – I taught 'The Back Country' at Hayward in March and it really is completely solid: probably he's even better than Ted, though maybe that's because I find his attitudes more sympathetic than Ted's (which at times, after all, get a bit close to melodrama).

[. . .]

A lovely movie, the best I have seen in years: 'Monterey Pop'. You would like it for the music anyway, but it is much more than the music.

Last Sunday, Mike and a friend called Bill and I went to GG Park, where there was lots of music and pretty people and pretty trees etc.[6] With us we took a friend of Bill's from Milwaukee, a young painter called Jim.[7] We all dropped acid (no, I didn't, I dropped something much milder called THC, as I was feeling rather hungover). About 4 hours later it became apparent that Jim was freaking out, and was getting more and more panicky. So we drove back to Bill's place. Jim refused to leave the car. I phoned DD to see if he had any thorazine (which is the stuff to bring people off trips), but he had none and said 'Lay him down on a bed, lay lots of love on him, and make sure you don't communicate any of your own panic to him.' Meanwhile two cops in a car had cruised along the street twice looking rather curiously at our group, so I decided it was time for Mike & me to leave any drugs we had on us in a little doorway (later we retrieved them intact). Finally we got Jim out of the car & upstairs, and then I did almost 6 hours of relief work. Afterwards I felt really proud of myself: I knew just what to say and do, having had at least one bad trip myself, DD had helped me in confirming what to do, and I think I learned something from going through it all. I also think Jim learned something about himself. First time, anyway, I have successfully cast myself as father figure. (Later I learned that it was only Jim's 2nd trip, the first also having been bad.)

By contrast, on Tuesday, somebody reserved a private beach called Kirby's Cove, right by Golden Gate Bridge on the Marin side, facing the city and the ocean. We dropped when we were coming down the long road to the cove, overlooking the sand, an abandoned fort, the woods behind – lots of flowers and trees and sea. As pretty a place as I've ever seen, and I knew it would be the best trip ever, as it was. There were about 40 people there, some girls, at least one married couple, and everyone dropped and everyone went naked until it got too cold. Then we made an enormous fire in the woods and left about 9 in the evening. I can't describe how beautiful it all was. A kind of barely controlled euphoria – no, that makes it sound almost hysterical, and it certainly wasn't close to that – there was much more of a feeling of discovery + a feeling of adequacy and delight in the things discovered.[8]

I hope you will be here by June 9. Any chance? Don has planned a vast party at the Avalon Ballroom. All his friends, and all their friends – hopefully as many straight people as queer. There will be tickets, and when you are let in you will be encouraged to eat your ticket (heh heh). There will be bands, including the Grateful Dead. Again, there are parallels in the Wolfe book on Kesey. Once I said to Don, 'you know I identify most with Sandy in that book' (Sandy is a little unstable) 'who do you identify with?' He said, of me, 'well that speaks volumes' (as it does), and then 'of course I identify with Kesey.' (Which also speaks volumes.)

Yes, I like Brautigan's writing too. It reminds me very much of word-play and verbal fantasy that people sometimes share when they are stoned on grass. And I think that may be part of the reason why he is such a bestseller among young people. And of course it is all very nice and very relaxed. I have seen him around North Beach for a long time, and met him once [. . .], but I don't think he recognizes me now. I enjoyed your description of the Meistersinger, which I have never seen. I think you & Marsh were rather surprised a couple of years ago when I was trying to explain how moved I had been by the Walkyrie – it was really just the same thing you are speaking about in your letter 'music seems the natural medium of expression.' I think I said at the time that it seemed as if words and music had come from the same source – though I'm not sure what I meant by that, as I don't follow German well enough to understand it when it is sung.

[. . .]

I don't think your American informant is correct in saying that the news media are suppressing news of the student & black uprisings. We read detailed depressing accounts of them in the morning papers and could see just as much of them on TV. Also a good many of the reporters for newspapers & commentators on TV are fairly left-wing in inclination (tho I'd never admit that to a Bircher[9]), and I don't think they'd stand for it.

X X X X X X

1. Wolfe, *The Electric Kool-Aid Acid Test* (1968).
2. William James, *The Varieties of Religious Experience: A Study in Human Nature* (1902).
3. See 'Being Born' (*CP* 218–19).
4. The 'old poem' is 'The Fair in the Woods' (*CP* 209–10).
5. The 'new one' is 'At the Centre'; see TG to Tanner, 10 February 1969, n. 2, above.

6. Bill Schuessler (1946–) later moved in with TG and MK. See Glossary of Names.
7. Unidentified.
8. TG wrote about this trip in 'Grasses' (CP 216).
9. The John Birch Society, a right-wing, anti-communist organization founded in 1958, prominent in American politics in the 1960s and early 1970s.

TO *Donald Hall*   ALS New Hampshire
Wednesday 9 July 1969

975 Filbert,
San Francisco,
Calif. 94133

9 July 69

Dear Don –
[. . .] I hope, anyway, I thanked you for your comments on the poems I sent. They are always useful, the things you say about my poetry. What I mean is that some of your criticisms make me realize just why and how something should be changed, and even when I don't accept what you say it (at least) tells me something about what I have done, and also helps me in my attitudes in what I have still to do. – All this may seem very obvious, but I know very few people who are any help – very few, you can count them on the fingers of a mutilated hand. Three, maybe. Then there are about five or ten people (to whom I am very grateful) whose reactions are interesting without being helpful in a practical sense.

We are really aiming for totally different things nowadays. But that's all right – we can like each other's poetries, and see each other's aims as being valuable. You have this power of sympathetic criticism as much as anyone I know, and maybe the most important product of your critical side was the Penguin Anth. of Contemp. Am. Poetry.[1] By saying this I am not putting down your written criticism, it's just that the anthology is about the only important one to have come out since we were freshmen. You don't miss anybody of importance who was available at that time, and the book was a brilliant introduction for the English to a body of verse they couldn't at that time even guess at. And all the other English & American anthologies are pale beside it.

[. . .]

I have ambitious projects of a pamphlet mixing poetry and prose. A kind of acid pamphlet. I first dropped acid three years ago, but it was only toward the end of last year I started to see ways in which I could use it in poetry. I may

247

be wrong about them, but I have to try them. The trouble is, I have promised the pamphlet for the end of August, and I don't really know whether I'll have it ready by then.[2]

My chief danger nowadays seems to be sentimentality. Not gush, but the placing of a high value on such things as wonder, acceptance, etc., without completely producing in the poem the wonder-ful side of the things to be accepted.

[. . .]

I am really pretty happy nowadays. If I could have foreseen the life I live when I was leaving Cambridge, it would have struck me as an improbable dream. Which also makes me realize how easily it could all come to an end!

I wonder why there is no good poetry out of England. In 1963 or so I would say it was because they didn't know the young Americans, but now they are imitating Creeley, Snyder, everybody, to tedium, and without even trying to translate into English terms. Meanwhile there is Ted Hughes and Larkin. Larkin is fine in his way – and it's a perfectly good way – but I keep having to remind myself that he is in years more contemporary with myself than with Thomas Hardy. Ted is splendid – a real loner, and will get better and better, but he's the only really exciting person in England and he's hardly a new poet. Apart from him there is Seamus Heaney and people – Heaney is not very good really, with his careful stumblings, but he is brilliant compared with the absolute boringness of Lucie-Smith and the BBC crowd, or of the Agenda people (who recognize the good Americans, but can't do anything themselves). And I suppose there are the Beatles – but the words of the Beatles are not poetry of the order of Dylan, after all.

I don't know why this is. I sense a rather widespread irritability in England nowadays – not just in literature but in everything, an irritability and sense of futility. Maybe that's what is behind the lack of good poetry. Very different, after all, from the feeling here: it's a cliché I'm sure to say that Americans are hopeful and violent, but it's true enough in the context I [am] speaking of, and hopeful violence is a much better incentive to poetry than irritable futility. It means one can imagine influencing an audience to action (surely that is what links such really different people as Bly and Snyder).

Are there many good poets in New York under 45? I can't read [Ted] Berrigan, and the others I have read fade from my mind some minutes after being read. Well, I suppose Denise L[evertov] lives in New York, and now you will surprise me by telling me that Robert Bly has a secret farmhouse in Manhattan.

Excuse this boring letter. But write to me sometime and send me some poems.

[. . .]

Love,

Thom

1. *Contemporary American Poetry*, ed. Hall (1962).
2. TG likely means his poetry pamphlet *Sunlight* (1969).

TO *Tony Tanner*   ALS King's

Saturday 20 September 1969

975 Filbert,
San Francisco,
Calif 94133
USA

20 Sept 69

Dear Tony,

   Glad to get your witty card and letter. Witty card was received the day of a special expedition to the Renaissance Fair, was shown round home, and then taken down to Don Doody. Then Don ushered us and about 50 others onto a hired bus, and gave us little brown acid-tablets on the bus, and we were all well and truly into it by the time we got to the fair. He had decided to try something a little heavier on us all, this time, and I actually hallucinated quite a bit for an hour (which I quite seldom do), people were dropping like flies, and it was a very fine afternoon, we all agreed. On the way back, crossing G. Gate Bridge, we saw the sun setting. From some freaky combination of mist and reflection, it was taking on the most extraordinary shapes. If I'd been alone I'd have believed I was hallucinating, but it was real. We all watched with great pleasure, and at the last change we broke into appreciative applause. The sun had really outdone itself!

   Well, how lovely it was to have you both here. We profit from you, too, I hope you know that. You set our unsteady minds working for the next year. But we enjoy you even more. I hope you liked your glimpses into the garden of the gods, and hope you will return there at times.[1]

   I like Gaudier-Br.'s interpretation of Sestina: Altaforte.[2] His mishearing adds a peculiar beauty and ambiguity to various of the lines (viz.):

Damn it all! all this our South stinks piss.

· · · · ·

In hot summer have I great rejoicing
When the tempests kill the earth's foul piss.

· · · · · ·

249

> Better one hour's stour than a year's piss
> > (hear! hear!)
> . . . .
> The man who fears war and squats opposing
> My words for stour, hath no blood of crimson
> But is fit only to rot in womanish piss.
>
> . . . . .
> May God damn for ever all who cry "Piss!"
>
> . . . .
> Hell blot black for always the thought "Piss!"

You really have to go back to Swift before you find anybody similarly opposed to the bodily functions.

Actually I can understand Gaudier-Br.'s mishearing. I once heard a recording of EP reading this poem (in the Harvard Poetry Room – no one was supposed to hear it till after Pound's death) and he sounded like an old Irish fisherman.[3] (Not Richard Murphy, either.)

In three weeks I go to NY, and then I do my performance around Michigan. Then back here from Nov. to January.

I creep through my lecture on Hardy at a less than snail's pace.[4] One great thing about writing weekly essays as an undergraduate was that it kept one in practice for writing prose. I now find this kind of thing as difficult as writing 30pp. of poetry, and much less fun, and much less to show for it. – He is an absolutely splendid poet, though. Even at his worst (and it is bad), I cannot feel irritated. – I am reading Tess for the first time since I was 15, and it really is pretty good, isn't it? Interesting how similar it is to the poetry – Pound says of Hardy that he is 'immersed in his subject matter', and I interpret this to mean that though he may moralize he is never rhetorical.[5]

Which brings me to Tennyson. Thank you very much for finding the source of those lines. But what a pity they should be an epic-simile. The characteristics of the epic simile seem to be as follows: (a) it should be so long that you forget the context (b) it should be irrelevant to the context anyway (c) it should be much better written than the context. (By context I mean thing it's compared to (tenor? vehicle?).) This applies to Milton too. Tennyson's slow-arching wave is completely real and there. The trouble is it doesn't describe the way a man can fall from a horse, and the Red Knight's fall itself is so unvivid that you forget all about it, and just think of the wave.[6] I suppose that's part of the result of Milton's curse on Eng lit.

Maybe you disagree. I've started reading the Idylls of the King, anyway, after being checked ever so slightly by the dedication (where pronouns referring to Albert are capitalized – He and Him, as for God). My objections to Tennyson remain much the same. He is pleasing, readable, and melodious – more important, he has a fantastic eye for detail, which we must all envy – but there is a fatal tendency to rhetoric.

There is a passage in the Idylls of the King that I told you (2 years ago) I learned by heart when I was a mere stripling. My silly edition doesn't have line numbers but it is in The Passing of Arthur – the 9th and 10th verse paragraphs from the end. ('But, as he walk'd . . . since the making of the world.') (It also comes in the 'Morte D'Arthur' published in 1842.) I can understand why I liked it so much when I was 14, it is rhetoric rather of the sort (though it's more sophisticated) that you find in Kyd and Marlowe. Very artful, Tennyson knows exactly how to get his effects.

> He heard the deep behind him, and a cry
> Before. His own thought drove him like a goad.

Clever, that line end making a pause between 'cry' and 'before'. And the speed of the remainder of that second line, driving the reader forward too. Then the next five lines

> Dry clash'd his harness in the icy caves
> And barren chasms, and all to left and right
> The bare black cliff clang'd round him, as he based
> His feet on juts of slippery crag that rang
> Sharp-smitten with the dint of armed heels –

Yes, the same kind of thing. Here all the noise is indicated by the hardness of consonants, the hard 'c's, and so on. Which is replaced by the next two lines (which we know so well), all full of liquid 'e's:

> And on a sudden, lo! the level lake,
> And the long glories of the winter moon.[7]

Enormously impressive, and there have been few poets who could do it so well. But it is all writing, if you see what I mean, it doesn't take me into any experience I can imagine as like anything one goes through. I am not making the mistake of pretending good writing is ever without artifice – that's what writing is, artifice – but this is nothing else but. I find it stagey, and the excitement is in the words rather than in any experience they create for me. I can understand why Hopkins (consciously) and Hardy (I think only half-consciously) reacted so much against this kind of thing – deliberately roughening their poetry. Another sort of artifice, of course, but an artifice that recalls the feel of our own experiences, which has its roughnesses.

This is probably all old stuff to you. What I like about Tennyson I still like greatly, of course, and it certainly includes that 'slow arching wave' and a lot else. But I suspect you 'place' Tennyson a good deal higher than I do, and I wonder why. I'm not playing the FRL—YW game of hierarchies, I hope, but one does have – however roughly – poets one considers essential, poets one considers very good, and poets (in the third rank) one considers valuable for the comparatively few things they do well. In this last rank I'd put Beddoes and Tennyson (and Wilfred Owen and Dryden, if you'd like to know!!).

Oh well, I'm in bed today with a cold, and my pen runneth over.

I was a bit snappish that last day we were all together. I'm sorry. Rather tired, I think.

'Long, long, long' – yes or no?[8]

We all send love.

X X X X X X X X
Thom

P.S. Better <u>anything</u> than a year's piss.

1. See 'The Garden of the Gods' (*CP* 213–14).
2. See Pound, 'Sestina: Altaforte' (1909). Pound and the French sculptor Henri Gaudier-Brzeska (1891–1915) were close friends.
3. See TG to White, 12 October 1956, above.
4. TG's lecture, delivered at Princeton in April 1970, became 'Hardy and the Ballads' (*OP* 77–105).
5. TG perhaps means Pound's admiring remark about Hardy's poetry: 'Now *there* is clarity. There *is* the harvest of having written 20 novels first.' See *The Selected Letters of Ezra Pound, 1907–1941*, ed. Paige (1950), 294, and chapters 51 and 52 of Pound's *Guide to Kulchur* (1938).
6. Tennyson, 'The Last Tournament' (1872), ll. 458–68, from *Idylls of the King* (1859–85).
7. Tennyson, 'The Passing of Arthur' (1842), ll. 352–60, from *Idylls*.
8. The Beatles, 'Long, Long, Long' (1968).

TO *Tony Tanner* ALS King's

Tuesday 25 November 1969[1]

975 Filbert,
San Francisco,
Calif 94133
USA

I dreamt last night that I was at a vast indoor meeting being addressed by Hitler. He may have been Spiro Agnew too, but it got me plenty paranoid, I can tell you. During the course of his speech he referred to the 'truly disgraceful

Moratorium of last Saturday.' Surrounded by Nazis and Birchers as I was, I heroically shouted out and raised my hand in a clenched revolutionary salute. To my surprise I was joined by half the audience.

I woke.

Does this mean that San Francisco is an improbable dream?

(No.)

Dear Tanners,

That was the little bit that comes before the movie titles and credits. It will be taken up later.

We've had elections since I last wrote, and to everybody's surprise [John] Lindsay got in in New York. And I'm especially pleased by that, since I'll be living in NY for several months.

And I gave 15 readings in 18 days through Michigan and Ohio. I think it was the period of most concentrated strain I have spent since let's say the first few weeks of basic training in the army. I only relaxed and enjoyed myself in one place, which was Kalamazoo (as in 'I met a girl in . . .'). For some reason, there all the students I met were like bright San Franciscans, and all the faculty I met were like bright San Franciscans. For the rest – well, it varied. Two questions I got one time were 'Mr Gunn, what are your goals?' and 'How do you relate to the scientific?' A whole new bunch of people every day – very nice even when dull, as they usually were. A whole new <u>place</u> to adjust to, a whole new <u>head</u> to shit in (toilet, I mean; that phrase looks like Céline). A couple of memorable mornings, on my own, in hotel rooms, of real neurosis: what am I <u>doing</u> here? can I <u>make</u> it? the bell-boys are <u>snickering</u> at me. – However, I'm proud to say, the neurosis never emerged publicly. I was very nice to all the people whose names I'd just forgotten, and I read well: I mean (without immodesty) I think I developed a very finished performance (and it was a performance, down to the bits between the poems: something spontaneous from one reading would get incorporated in the next reading, etc.) and I never went below a certain level.

It was interesting, though. One thing was that I was introduced to several new Americas. And this is the thing about it over here, isn't it? An intensely political person will say to me every now and again: Why do you choose to live in America when you can live in England? Well, quite apart from personal reasons, I'd say that whereas there are several Englands (Philip Larkin's England, Agatha Christie's England, the Beatles' England, Tony Tanner's England and a few others) there are <u>hundreds</u> of Americas, and I haven't got to the end of them yet.

And the other thing (related) was to see how successfully I could carry around Michigan a San Francisco in the head. True, it was only for a few weeks, and I had my bad interludes, but in essentials I was able to do it under difficult conditions, so I think I could, if necessary, do it for much longer under easier conditions. (This maybe has to do with why I think one should try dropping acid in England. "One"!!!)

I was very glad to get back, and a week after my return went to see Crosby, Stills, Nash and Young at Winterland with Mike, Bill, and a dazzling guy from NY whom I'd met the previous night. We dropped, and it was wonderful. (Have you heard C, S, & N's "Suite: Judy Blue Eyes"? (Young was added after they'd made it.) A single. Get hold of it. A fantastic sound. Beautiful. Best thing since The Band.)

An interesting thing about reading aloud is one gets to see what one has done in a poem, and gets to judge it more easily. And this does not depend on audience response. One or two poems of this year I really think successful, – but on the other hand I gave up reading 'The Naked Peace Marcher' (tho it was much liked) from sheer embarrassment at such sickening self-indulgence.[2] You were right, and so was Belle Randall, and it's out as out can be.

Sometimes a Great Notion. [. . .] I find this book pretty unusual: it is a naturalistic novel, for one thing, and I think it is directly in the line of Frank Norris, Dreiser, and co – though much more interesting, never dull in fact. For another, it is a heroic novel. How unusual in the 60's! (And what an awful movie it will make.) – I am fantastically impressed by it, (maybe I said all this before) it takes unbelievable risks all the time, and if with half of them it falls flat on its face, with the other half it succeeds out of all likelihood. Hank and Viv come off, after all. I don't know how, but they are there. (Lee does not, and it's a great pity.) But it's a wonderful book.

My favourite phrase in the book is: 'No man is an island, honey.' I still keep laughing over that.

[. . .]

Davie has a book of poems out in England called Essex Poems. There is at least one I like, called Sylvae. I always love the thought of England covered in thick forest, and full of foxes and wolves and Herne the Hunter. Some of the other poems seen pretty directionless, though. I hear he is telling his creative writing class at Stanford that their prime object in writing must be to declare themselves American. (That's his hang-up, not theirs!)

Acid worked just classically with you. I am very happy. What you say about trees (soft explosions etc) and air. Yes. That is exactly what it does (can do). Maybe I don't any longer believe acid can change the hearts of the whole human race, but it can do it to ¾ of them. Not that you ever needed a change of heart. But even for you it has enlarged the field of goggling.

We have a bet going over 'Long, Long, Long.' In face of your continued obstinate silence, I am assuming that I have won the bet, and expect $10 of English foods – veal & ham pie, sausage rolls, Yorkshire pudding – to be airmailed to me immediately.

[. . .]

I came back and bought a fringed jacket with a vengeance. White leather, and fringes to my knees.

[. . .]

Have you seen TW in Lear yet? My first reaction was total amazement. My second is delight. What a break-through for him to acknowledge that acting is something he still wants to do.[3]

[. . .]

Mike's happy. Bill's happy. Someone I wrote to describing our house now, with Bill living here, wrote back: 'it sounds like a French art movie.' I was amused. At the same time I find it strange that anybody should find our set-up strange. Everybody's set-up is a bit different from everybody else's, after all. The only strange thing about our house is Mona.[4] No idea how a Hitlermädchen like that ever got so fully accepted by such lovers as we are.

I visited Princeton when I was in the East. It certainly will be a very easy job. When I returned from my afternoon with them I felt very uneasy, and finally localized the cause. I had been using my Englishness on them and they liked it too much. Too easy. And of course (I could have foretold it) Princeton loves an Englishman. I'll change that in February.

Not that I'm American, but I'm not (really) English either. The one thing I share with Sylvia Plath is that we are both Midatlantic poets. And I'm a Midatlantic person too. At least I believe so. Even if I were to go back and live in England for the rest of my life (God Forbid) I'd stay Midatlantic – or, let's say, half-San Franciscan half-English. What does Marsh feel like? It's a feeling, a sense of loyalties or lack of them, a sense of belonging and not-belonging. I find London exotic and I find San Francisco exotic.

Dear me. What am I talking about?

Well, here's the end of a page. It would be nice to talk to you several hours, but that will come next summer.

                    X X X X X X
                        Love,
                            Guntrip

1. Date supplied by postmark.
2. 'The Naked Peace Marcher', *Journal for the Protection of All Beings* 3 (1969), 29; uncollected.

3. White played Edmund in Jonathan Miller's *King Lear* at the Nottingham Playhouse (1969) and the Old Vic (1970).
4. Mona was one of TG and MK's cats.

TO *Elizabeth Kray*[1]   ALS Academy of American Poets
Friday 12 December 1969

975 FILBERT ST.,
San Francisco,
Calif. 94133

12 Dec 69

Dear Betty Kray,

I am sorry to have been so long in answering your letter, in which you ask me for a list of books. I have not listed fiction, as my own reading of contemporary fiction is too random for me to be much help. And my list of poetry is a short one, as I think it will be more useful this way. It would be tempting to list all the twentieth century poets I myself like, but it strikes me that a poet like Wallace Stevens would be difficult to teach well to teenagers, so I have stuck with books about which I am certain.

I think the first aim of someone teaching poetry in a high school should be to continuously demonstrate that poetry is of many sorts and is all around us; that a rhymed political slogan is poetry of a kind, for example, and that the lyric of a song by the Beatles, the Rolling Stones, or Bob Dylan may be poetry of a very high order; that inevitably most people have commerce with poetry in some part of their lives. The book that first demonstrated this to me was

1) THE POET'S TONGUE, edited by W.H. AUDEN and JOHN GARRETT. It is thirty years old, and I believe is not published over here, but it is in print in England, and is a book I think any high school teacher should get hold of. It is an anthology of all kinds of poetry, from all times, and successfully demonstrates the range and possibilities of poetry.

The teacher should also have copies of

2) THE BOB DYLAN SONG BOOK, and

3) THE BEATLES SONG BOOK (to be published this month). 'Sir Patrick Spens' is a poem not immediately available to most teenagers.[2] But many of them already know and like the Beatles' 'Eleanor Rigby', which is a ballad right in the same tradition.

I think the following could also be successfully taught:

256

4) WILFRED OWEN: Collected Poems

5) D.H. LAWRENCE: Selected Poems (ed. Rexroth), (Compass Books) and even

6) EZRA POUND: Selected Poems (New Directions).

The Pound would be less easy to teach than the other two, but there are plenty of poems in it ('The Ballad of the Goodly Fere,' the Cathay poems) that could be much enjoyed by teenage students.

Of really contemporary poets, I would include the following:

7) GARY SNYDER: The Back Country (New Directions) and any of his other books the teacher could get hold of.

8) ALLEN GINSBERG: Howl and Other Poems (City Lights)
                and   Planet News.

These are two poets who can most successfully speak to teenagers (and to a good many others of us). True, there are references to sex and drugs, and I don't know what school policies may be about these. I think poems about sex and drugs are particularly good for teenagers to read, and if these two poets have to be bowdlerized out of the suggested program then I doubt if the program can be much good.

9) SYLVIA PLATH: Ariel

10) TED HUGHES: Lupercal
         or   Selected Poems.

I would hesitate to suggest Robert Bly or James Wright. They are fine poets but I think people under eighteen would have a good deal of difficulty with them.

As I say, sorry to have been so long. Don't bother to answer this. I am sure you have plenty on your hands.

         Love,

               Thom Gunn

1. Elizabeth Kray (1916–87) was the first executive director of the Academy of American Poets.
2. 'Sir Patrick Spens' is a Scottish ballad about a disaster at sea.

1970

TO *Tony Tanner*   ALS King's

Monday 19 January 1970

Department of English,
Princeton University,
PRINCETON,
N.J. 08540

19 Jan 70

Hello.

Oh. The letter of yours I brought with me from San Francisco is one I've already answered. You sent me one since then. It is still in San Francisco. I'll answer it in August, after I return from England, where I will be seeing you.

I thought I'd give you the above address, even though I'll only be down there 2 days a week, – as I suppose I might move from this hotel.[1] It's nice and relaxed and full of groovy people, but it really is incredibly dirty, even by my unfastidious standards. I may stay from sheer lethargy and from liking to be in the middle of Greenwich Village. Meanwhile all my powers of choice are numbed by the cold. I'd forgotten cold like this <u>existed</u>. I crouch by radiators. The leather pants I got from dandyishness are a severely practical defense.

I hope Marsh's fainting stopped, and was nothing serious. My mother used to faint every year or so. I always felt a little envious of the fainters, and used to try to imagine what it was like. Horrible, I should think.

I have been experiencing the usual sense of displacement that I get for a week or so after I displace myself. Seeing a movie called 'Putney Swope' raised my spirits a bit. I wonder whether it will ever get to England. It is marvellously funny (some people hate it, but you'd like it). It is about a black man who gets elected to head of an advertising agency by mistake, and then starts making very unusual commercials. My favorite commercial shows a black man, quite average looking, surrounded by his average-looking family, eating a breakfast cereal. A voice addresses him and he looks at the camera. 'Mr (So and So),' it says, 'do you realize that (Something) Breakfast Cereal contains 19 milligrams of niacin, 45 units of ergosterol,

145 ESP units of XYZ, etc, etc.' The camera pans in on him and he says with true astonishment 'No shit!' – A lovely moment, even if I do ruin it.

I have also been reading Borges, at last. Which brought my spirits right down again. Though he is pretty good. One might also say succinct. And also terribly funny. I like the story about the French symbolist poet whose life-work was to write three chapters identical to three of Don Quixote. I like him best when he is frankly the mad librarian, less when he resembles Poe and Kafka.

As you may guess, we were all at Altamont, with some 200,000 to 300,000 others. I guess you have read all about it in the papers. We were about half-way back, and saw no trouble (which was right on the edge of the stage), though we were <u>aware</u> of troubles from hearing them over the mike. Like when Marty Balin of the Airplane got knocked cold by a Hell's Angel. I see Keith Richards has said there wouldn't have been the same trouble if everybody there had been English. Which is bullshit – the violence was caused by Hell's Angels, which the Stones were crazy enough to have hired to guard the stage. There is a good deal of feeling against the Stones locally – for good reason, really. But they did perform <u>beautifully</u>. Very good account of the whole disaster in the mid-December <u>Rolling Stone</u>, which I must say I think is about the best-written paper out.[2]

[. . . Doody's] new sailing date for Australia is August 29! He provided two beautiful mass trips in the Stud, numbers being kept down and the doors closed. One was a Christmas party, the Saturnalia like that of 1968, where the whole place inside was transformed into a kind of Beerbohm Tree Forest of Arden, lots of branches from George's ranch (where you tripped), pools, glades, three real birds, stage turf on the ground.[3] We all dropped, of course – as we all did on New Year's Eve in the Stud, when – though there were no props – I had one of the most Bacchanalian evenings of my life. Gorgeous. No content, but lots of euphoria.

We were a bit worried about him in early December when he had a real Doody-type freakout, managing within about a week to quarrel with almost everybody he lived with. It looked rather serious for a bit, but now they are all friends again, if a touch wary of him. The general trouble seemed to be this: Jere and he and some others have got together to open up a shop (a very nice one) at Jere's new place. Lots of work was needed – carpentry, etc. Naturally everybody from Folsom Street, being old friends of Jere's, did a lot of the work, Don originally encouraging them. But Don apparently got jealous, that they were acting as if they were more a part of Jere's commune than of his own. Everybody was surprised, in that they had not realized they belonged to Don. – But that's all blown over, anyway.

[. . .]

Since you brought up John Ashbery and since I passed a vague judgment on him in my last letter I thought I would take him up again. I quickly put him down. Totally incomprehensible. And you don't even feel like wanting to know what he means.

[. . .]

When I was at Cambridge I saw John Barton's production of Edward II. Toby Robertson played Edward II – Tony White played Gaveston. And it's just possible that the word butch originated with that performance.

I took enormous pleasure reading Sense and Sensibility again. Even more than I did in rereading Mansfield Park (I couldn't say why, because M.P. is a much better book). And then I read your introduction and found it fascinating, and very good, and completely correct.[4] It's a funny thing when one is writing about a good writer – one can't go wrong if one emphasizes their most unlikely qualities – the melancholia of Jane Austen, the classical austerity of Stendhal, the baroque melodramas in T.S. Eliot. Not that I'm suggesting you are being gimmicky – it's all there if the writer is any good, he contains his opposites, and they need emphasizing. – No poems to send, and none likely for a while. – Have you heard Jefferson Airplane's 'We Can Be Together' (first song on their last LP). Too much.

The central heating is sending me to sleep, so I must out into the cold, of which I may die. What an awful letter!

                    X X X X X X X X X X X
                    Duke Gunn

1. Hotel Albert, 23 East 10th Street, New York City.
2. 'The Rolling Stones Disaster at Altamont: Let It Bleed', Rolling Stone 50 (21 January 1970).
3. Herbert Beerbohm Tree's production of As You Like It (1907–8) recreated the Forest of Arden using real grass, foliage, and rabbits.
4. See Tanner's introduction to Sense and Sensibility (Harmondsworth: Penguin, 1969), 7–34.

Friday 13 February 1970

c/o Department of English,
Princeton University,
PRINCETON,
NJ 08540
USA

13 Feb '70

My dears,

I'll write this now but probably not send it for a few days as it looks as though I am getting close to finishing some poems and I want to enclose them.

New York is – well, not San Francisco, nor London either. But it's not Inverness, let's say.

It is fucking <u>cold</u>. I mean, there have been days this past month when I have been colder out of doors than ever in my life (i.e. even colder than in Cambridge). Also, the evening after I wrote you, someone broke into my room (I was not there) and took money, all my grass, my typewriter, and that fringed jacket I told you about. Curiously enough, I didn't care that much: I felt I had nothing much left to lose. They missed a few things like passport and acid, which I am keeping at Princeton.

Peter Tangen (the painter) has been enormously kind.[1] Constantly has me to delectable dinners and has found me a gorgeous loft for three months from mid March to mid June. It will be a delight living there – I'll be subleasing it from a lady art critic who is going to Spain for a while.

Princeton is pretty odd. Have you ever been there? The students are very bright and good, but the English faculty all resemble Charles Monteith – gracious, distant, proper, and very lacking in warmth. They are awful, really, I'd take Monteith any day, but they are so aware that they teach at an institution that can have no rival in this world. And their conversation lacks life. (I think they are probably all bibliographers.) And not one of them has asked me to their house (oh yes, one did for a momentary drink) – not that I <u>want</u> to go to their houses particularly, but I wonder why they don't ask me. – However, they tell me they are very pleased with me, and that I am taking my job much more seriously than previous poets they had had there!

Not that I'm unhappy, just rather bored. For the first (and I hope only) time in my life I seem to be using sex as something interesting to engage in because I can't think of anything better. I mean, one can read only so many hours a day. – But it'll be better when it's warmer and I can go for walks in the park. – Haven't found anybody I want to drop acid with yet.

I went to see the guy who published Sunlight, and he is also a book collector and seller and so on.[2] 'I have one thing that might amuse you,' he said, and showed me a first edition of Fighting Terms. On the fly page on the left was a book plate 'From the library of John Masefield, O.M., Poet Laureate', and on the right in a funny handwriting rather like that of my late great aunt was written, almost like two lines of free verse:

> clever ugly indecent intellectual
> last poem good example

That's me, all right! Well, at least the old boy kept up. I bet few people of his generation ever possessed a copy of the first edition of my first book!

Apparently Ted is to come out with a whole book of Crow poems this autumn. Should be wild. Everybody, including me, says with each book 'where can he go from here?' and then he pushes on into a new bare territory. Have you read his Senecan Oedipus? It's not out here yet.

I haven't been reading the papers in some while, but I hear that Death has been taking quite a toll lately. Olson, Bertrand Russell, and Louise Bogan. Wonder what they will find to discuss while waiting for the Pearly Gates to open?

These poems enclosed are all a bit odd, and maybe none of them comes off. The one about the grass is my first French Symbolist poem. At least I think that's what it is.[3]

Oh yes. There is an interview with Robert Graves in the Paris Review.[4] In dipping into it I came across the following. The interviewers asked him why his World War I poems didn't have the bitterness or savage anti-war feeling of Sassoon's and Owen's. And he answered: 'Well, you see, both Owen and Sassoon were homosexuals. They just couldn't stand seeing the fields covered with the dead bodies of mangled young men. Now, just imagine what it would be like for you and me if we had seen them covered with the bodies of women.'

A mind-blower, that. Reminds me of Alvarez patronizing me sexually: he was speaking about his troubles with some girl, and then said: 'Well I don't know why I'm bothering you with all this,' as if to say a homosexual couldn't possibly be expected to understand a heterosexual's romantic problems.

I read Janet Lewis' one modern novel, with the rather awful title Against a Darkening Sky. It is her worst book, but even her worst is pretty fantastic. Her reproduction and analysis of people's unverbalized feelings is always incredible. She's about the only person writing in English who ever makes me think of Tolstoy – not in scope, but in her understanding of how beautiful (and interesting) the ordinary person can be. If you don't believe me, read the first 100 pp of The Invasion, if you ever get time – or even The Trial of Soren Quist. (She really must have had a lot to take, living with Winters.) I really think she is one of the best writers living. This is no reproachful hint that you ought to have put her in your book – she's not really a post-war novelist, and she's not really very American (though she's not very European either, except in some of her subject-matter).

I'm reading The Last Chronicle of Barset right now, first time since I was 16, and frankly as escape literature. It's not that bad, actually. He is a <u>little</u> gooey with some of the young girls (but nothing like as bad as Charles or Wm Makepeace), but he has a splendid sense of humor, and some of the dialogue is really tremendous. Now I think of it, though, he lacks just that Tolstoy power over the ordinary that Janet has: most of his characters are terribly ordinary, and you feel a lot of easy sympathy or unsympathy for them, but you never feel their real devastating beauty as you do in Tolstoy.

Well, I must wash my hair, and restore it to all its real devastating beauty.
       X X X X X X X X X X X X
       Th

1. See TG to MK, *c.* 27 February 1963, above.
2. George Bixby, publisher of Albondocani Press, later compiled *Thom Gunn: A Bibliography, 1940–78* (1979) with Jack Hagstrom.
3. TG enclosed 'To Natty Bumppo' (*CP* 212), 'Phaedra in the Farm House' (*CP* 191–2), and 'The Inside-Outside Game' (*CP* 180). The 'French Symbolist poem' is 'Grasses' (*CP* 216); see TG to Tanner, 19 April 1969, n. 7, above.
4. 'Robert Graves: The Art of Poetry XI', *Paris Review* 47 (Summer 1969), 119–45.

TO *Tony and Marcia Tanner*   ALS King's
Thursday 2 April 1970

c/o LIPPARD,
138 Prince St.,
NY,
NY 10012

2 April 70

Dear Tanners,
I'm not sure whether I'd moved into the above address when I last wrote, but I'm here now, anyway, very happy with it. It is I should guess 90 feet by

about 20, and at times I feel a bit like those characters in Les Enfants Terribles camping (bivouacking) in the ball room. But I like that. And at last I have somewhere to stay in and read when it's raining and snowing. (It snowed heavily on Easter Sunday.) There is a rat, I haven't seen him yet though I've heard him, but I am prepared to meet him halfway if he'll do the same.

I enclose a funny little series (or as the New York poets say, 'suite') of poems.[1] To adopt John Masefield's admirably succinct method of literary criticism, I would sum them up as cerebral, restless, experimental, odd. (You see I'm kinder on me than he is.) I think the first three are the best. I think in the first poem I have succeeded in writing echt Projectiv Verse.[2] (Probably my last attempt.) The order is not very important – there is a rationale behind it, but it is loose, and poems could be added or taken away. I also enclose a nice Florentine anonymous half-horse, which is my idea of Dobbin to a T. Or Tom's idea of Dobbin to a Th? (Forgive me. I am reading Ulysses.)

At Princeton they do try hard to be English – visitors for the year are, or have been, Elizabeth Bowen, Nathaniel Tarn, Lawrence Durrell, Frank Kermode, & me. The first was writer-in-residence last semester. Nathaniel Tarn, I met when he was a boyfriend of a girl I knew some 17 years ago. His name was then Michael Mendelsohn, a name I infinitely prefer. He seems a passable but not very interesting poet. I don't know him very well yet, but I suspect he is rather egotistical and am almost sure he has no sense of humor. Durrell was here only for 2 days, & I deliberately missed him. Kermode was here to give a series of lectures (the Gauss Seminar, in which [Erich] Auerbach's Mimesis was originally given). I went to his last one – it was neither good nor bad, it seemed to be making an obvious point but was not disagreeable to listen to since it consisted largely of plots of novels I hadn't read. One thing endeared him to me, though. He finished the lecture and was on his way out when someone introduced me to him. 'Pleased-to-meet-you,' he said, and rushed away. Later he came up to me, at the party afterwards, and said 'I'm sorry I had to leave you so quickly, but I have terrible diahorrea.'

I've been catching up on reading to prepare me for your book.[3] Viz. Portnoy's Complaint & An American Dream. You are right about both, of course. The first reads as a whole no better than the 70 page extract of it I read a couple of years ago. It is terribly funny, of course, and I kept laughing aloud (I loved it when the Vassar girl consents to suck his cock and then holds it in her mouth 'like a thermometer.' I've known people like that). But for all the clever structuring, the structure is meaningless. And the last line of the novel is plain cheap. So it remains a collection of very good jokes. The Mailer book is something else again – the usual dream-hero, of course, but such lovely writing. I remember your remarks (in your lecture) about the parapet, and they are good and true! (The ending is a Huck Finn ending, though, isn't it?) I'm now reading The Deer Park, in which I notice there is reference to a handsome character called Tony Tanner. But I do wish Mailer could have a hero who was small, terrible at fucking, with an undersized cock, timid, and completely untrained at boxing. It sure would make a change.

[. . .]

I'll fly to England on June 16th, I think. I would love to stay with you for a week, but you must honestly tell me if this would fuck up plans or even slightly disturb your and Marcia's work and/or sex-life. When would you like me to come, if you want me to come? I'll be free the whole time except for some grandiose readings I'll be giving in London, with lots of other poets, on June 25, 26, & 27, & also one on the 28th in Edinburgh.[4] I'll be doing a whole reading to myself at the Mermaid later on, too, I don't know the date. But I really have no plans for the 2 months I'll be in England. I guess staying on a few days in Edinburgh could be fun, & I'll have a couple of weeks in Kent, but I'll probably spend most of the rest of the time at my brother's in Teddington (rather far out) if their house is big enough. (He drives a mini-cab now, by the way.)

[. . .]

Oh – you must see Bunuel's The Milky Way. Not as good as The Exterminating Angel (few movies are), but <u>very</u> funny. It has, in particular, the funniest Virgin Mary, really <u>sickly</u>, – I broke up every time she appeared.

Love

X X X X X X

Thom

I look forward to reading your book. If you have a carbon of the ms, could I read it when I stay with you.

(I remember when I was 17, I thought 'ms' was the most exciting word in the language. It was so professional. I thought not about 'manuscripts', but about 'mss.')

1. 'Tom-Dobbin' (CP 200–2).
2. A reference to Charles Olson's essay 'Projective Verse' (1950).
3. City of Words (1971). See TG to Tanner, 12 August 1966, above.
4. TG took part in the Poetry International Festival in London and Edinburgh.

TO *Charles Monteith*   TLS Faber

Friday 10 April 1970

c/o Lippard,
138 Prince Street,
New York, N.Y. 10012

10 April 70

Dear Charles,

[. . .]

I am doing a fair amount of writing. It looks as if I shall have a new book of poems to submit to you this summer, say mid-August.

Meanwhile, here is a suggestion you might think about. About three years ago, a book came out here, The Earlier Poems of Yvor Winters, 1920–28. These are largely poems Winters omitted from his Collected Poems, a book which has appeared in England. I was a friend of Winters, as I suppose you know, and was influenced a fair amount by his later work, but my admiration for this book has nothing to do with friendship, and the book itself has remarkably little to do with his later work. These early poems are almost all in free verse, fully in the experimental movement of the 1920s, very exciting, full of wild hallucinatory imagery, etc., and not showing any clear derivations apart from that of Rimbaud, maybe. I would like to be able to push this a little, since it hasn't been noticed much, and I am sure that it will take its place soon among the important bodies of poetry brought out in the 1920s – as important, I think, as what William Carlos Williams was doing, and almost as important as what Wallace Stevens was doing.

So I wonder if F & F would be interested in publishing this with an introduction by me? It is published over here by Alan Swallow with a rather putting-off introduction by Winters which could be omitted from the English edition. (I think I could get the permission of Winters' widow to omit it, if that were necessary.) Routledge and Kegan Paul presumably have an option on the book (they published the Collected Poems in England, didn't they?), but it certainly looks as if they aren't interested in picking it up.[1]

I think once people were to notice the book they'd really be excited by it. Maybe F&F will not be interested, or maybe the business with Routledge and KP is too complicated to unravel, but it would be a worthwhile thing to do, and I suspect that over a number of years you would find it going into several editions.

Best,

Thom

1. Winters's *Collected Poems* (1952) was a severely pruned selection of his poems. It was a major concession on his part to permit the publication in 1966 of *The Early Poems of Yvor Winters*, which brings together the poems from several early experimental collections. Most of these had been excluded from *Collected Poems* and exemplify a style, form and manner he had rejected more than thirty years before. Faber did not agree to publish *The Early Poems* in the UK.

TO *Tony and Marcia Tanner*   ALS King's
Wednesday 22 April–Saturday 2 May 1970

c/o Lippard,
138 Prince St.,
NY, NY 10012

22 April 70

Dear Tanners,

The sun woke me (at Princeton today) at 6 this morning, so I've been up several hours, and thought I'd start a letter to you. Mike has been here for 3 weeks, dividing his time between me & his parents, and that has been of a goodness. Also the weather is tip-top, as you English say, and I'm always very weather-influenced.

I saw The Damned (prob. called Götterdämmerung in England), and it is the heaviest thing you can imagine. (I mean heavy <u>slow</u> not heavy good.) Even tho by Visconti. Avoid 2 ½ hrs of boredom. – I have been reading Jane Kramer's 'Allen Ginsberg in America', which some have called similar to Wolfe's Kesey. It is not. It's worth reading (or hearing on TV), but the style is coy & <u>New Yorkerish</u>, and one constantly feels her on the edge of actual misrepresentation. She finds him so quaint! And she is so taken with the fact that his father and stepmother eat bagels and lax that she makes a regular Jewish-comedy scene of it. As she has earlier made a regular hippie-comedy scene on Haight Street earlier. She's full of whimsey. – Also I read Barbary Shore, which I think I understood better when I remembered 1950 was the time of Calder Willingham & Truman Capote. I continue with Ulysses, and am reading The Two Noble Kinsmen. And I found The Deer Park <u>totally</u> splendid. The scene between Teppis & his two sisters is a kind of comedy I didn't even know Mailer had in him. I think I agree with Mailer that this is his best book.

And I taught a good 3-hour class on Charles Olson (with the help of my students), which astonished me. Nothing like teaching a poet for getting to understand him. I still don't like him too much, though. (Maybe the last page of 'In Cold Hell, In Thicket' is OK – but E.P.-derived).

End of book notes. Start of ego notes. I have cut that funny sonnet (part IV) out of 'Tom-Dobbin', & sent the rest off with the enclosed 'Moly' to the London Mag. I liked the first 2 lines of the sonnet, which are the most grotesque I've ever written, but the rest was somehow too rhetorical. As if the 'meaning' had been decided on before-hand, and the writing was simply a presentation with no exploration involved. I hope you like 'Moly'. Do you remember what moly is? It is the flower Hermes gave to Odysseus so that O. wd not be subject to Circe's spells. The poem, my poem that is, is spoken by one of the freaked out sailors. The phrase 'human title' is stolen from Shakespeare (2 Noble K.). (The other enclosed poem I don't know about. Maybe it's not worth printing.) The word moly is in dictionaries, so doesn't need a note.

Now – big question, which I have also asked Whitey. Shall I call my next book (which is almost finished) MOLY? For: it is a nice word (holy-moly, says Marcia), and it also covers a good deal of the contents of the book – I see Moly as the antidote to the piggishness in man (some might see it as the thorazine to be used for an acid freak-out, but let it be, that ambiguity). Against: doesn't it sound rather too much like a Ted Hughes title? – Alternative title: SUNSHINE. For: it covers the sunlight imagery that is supposed to grow during the book, and it is also coming, more and more, to be a synonym for acid (having been originally just one batch of acid, San Francisco, April 1969) – in London too, I gather. Against: too trendy in its second meaning. Another alternative would be something like The Metamorphoses (but a Roman chap used that one), because I've recently realized almost all the poems in the book are about changes in people, but all the associated words (transformations, alterations (!), changes) make lousy titles. How about Inscape Epiphanies by Exfoliating Personae, I wonder?

(That was a joke. I have such a poor sense of humor that you do not always realize when I am not serious. So I am bound to tell you my last sentence was not serious.)

Did I tell you my favorite of all graffiti: (in a queer bar) 'We are the people our parents warned us against.' I've since found that this is also a title to a recent book. It's a sentence that burgeons in the mind as the months pass.

Ted H. sent me his Seneca's Oedipus, with a fascinating letter on the performance. I think it is a play that must have worked marvellously in performance but doesn't read well – like a libretto without the music. I suspect he's aware of that.

I tried to get Faber to bring out YW's Early Poems, with an introduction by me. They wouldn't. Now I'll try Routledge, maybe have a better chance. The poems are marvey-poo. If you don't believe me, read 'Josés Country' (also in Collected Poems). That last three lines: he <u>must</u> have been taking peyote (or maybe intensive study of Rimbaud could have done it; or maybe both together).

A nice note from Whitey, suggesting maybe I could use his flat for some of the time I'm in England. He is selling it, and moving along the road. If you see him, I wonder if you could make a point of saying how proper it would be for me to pay him rent (if it is available for me), as I am sure he will make a struggle over that question. The point is, he needs the money, I am sure, and I would have to pay somebody some rent in any case.

I am finally to give my Hardy lecture next week (my first public lecture ever). Then 2 weeks later a poetry reading. Maybe I'll read them the one about Tom watching Dobbin fuck.

2 May

Somehow I never sent all that. I've been typing out my new book. It is not long – only 26 poems if one counts 'Tom-Dobbin' as one poem. I am including that, and 'Moly', and the enclosed 'Nice Thing.'[1] But <u>not</u> the enclosed 'Diagrams,' which doesn't really make it I think. I won't send it to Faber for a month or so, but I want to see what it all looks like together. The poems all seem to 'cohere', at least, I mean they join together rather nicely at the ends.

The reviews will be really something. I mean, it's almost as if I am <u>inviting</u> them to discuss acid and homosexuality rather than the quality of the poems.

'Nice Thing' is a poem I started last year and got finished recently. I imagine Marcia will find it more enjoyable than you will. I shall also be quite surprised if Faber consent to print it. I can just picture poor Uncle Charles trying to write the letter in which he tells me that though <u>he</u> thinks it's all right <u>the others</u> don't want to print it. Well, we'll see. Maybe I do him an injustice.

Will be seeing you next month, I hope. I think Whitey may meet me. I've hinted that he might, anyway.

X X X X X X

Thom

P.S. I gave my lecture. Big success!

1. 'Nice Thing', *Massachusetts Review* 23, no. 1 (Spring 1982), 132; uncollected.

Friday 1 May 1970

c/o Lippard
138 Prince St.,
NY, NY 10012

1 May 70

Dear Donald,

Thank you very much for your prompt answer. I too am going to England for a couple of months this summer, and I think the first rule to adopt for the sake of one's equanimity is to avoid reading all weeklies and Sunday papers (and supplements too, of course) – except the Listener. Even the TLS rouses me only to amazement at England's provinciality – probably because Ian Hamilton is the big power there.

Of course, the orthodoxy of admiring Hughes-Plath-Lowell-and-Berryman at the expense of all else will be replaced in a few years, maybe by an orthodoxy of admiring Olson-Creeley-and-Duncan at the expense of all else. They are <u>all</u> pretty good poets: what is annoying is that the first lot of critics can't see any good in, say, Duncan, and that (I am afraid) the second lot won't be able to appreciate the large virtues of Hughes.

I know that when you are speaking about your 'baffled and contemptuous fury' on returning to England, you are speaking about something bigger than all this, but I think 'all this' is pretty typical of England now – how the English, for example, either ape America for the wrong things or else ape a small and hardly characteristic kind of Americanness. (Alvarez being the perfect example, of course.)

[. . .]

OK, here is a new poem.[1] I wonder if it needs a note. Actually, the word 'moly' is found in all dictionaries (at least I don't spell it molü![2]), but then I wonder how many people bother to use dictionaries. I do hate footnotes to poems, though.

[. . .]

Love,

Thom

1. 'Moly' (*CP* 186–7).
2. Pound spells it 'molü' in 'Canto XLVII'; see *The Cantos of Ezra Pound* (New Directions, 1948).

Sunday 24 May 1970

till June 16: c/o LIPPARD,
138 PRINCE St.,
NY,
NY 10012, USA

24 May 70

Dear Charles,

Here's the new book, if you want it. It has a rather Hughesian title (Moly, Wodwo, Lupercal . . .) but it is the best I can think of, and I don't think the rest of the book is very like Ted (wish it was!).

[. . .]

If you do want to publish the book, you might suggest to the designer of the dust-jacket that yellow is a very nice color – that is, there is so much sunshine in the poems (more and more, the later you get in the book) that it would be rather appropriate to have sunshiney colors on the cover.[1]

[. . .]

　　　Best,
　　　　　Thom

1.　The first edition hardback of *Moly* was given a bright yellow cover.

1971

TO *Tony Tanner*   ALS King's

Sunday 10 January 1971[1]

> 975 FILBERT,
> San Francisco,
> Calif. 94133
>
> 10 Jan 70[2]

Dear Tony,

We got your splendid Christmas card, which is certainly one to be kept. I don't think we sent any, we were not in the sending vein last year.[3] But <u>this</u> year – this will be a marvellous year, whether a sending one or not. I had a lovely dream that you and Marsh and Whitey and <u>all</u> of us were having a lot of fun in some strange place in San Francisco.

I think you might even find America's tensions a little bit lessened. They were so great at the time of the election, when Nixon and Agnew were exacerbating them, that they couldn't but go down after. Difficult of course to judge such feelings, people have a great tendency nowadays to judge their personal vibrations as public ones. – I greatly miss the concerts in the park, for instance, where one got an incredible and beautiful sense of community and of 'peace through conversion', but simply because they've been banned it doesn't mean that that community has vanished.

Wow, what do you think of John Lennon's new record?[4] I hate the whole idea of confessional poetry – it is the ultimate in egoism (egotism?) – and I think very few confessional poems, outside Baudelaire, in a few lines, and 'Skunk Hour' come off, but I find the new album great. Must be the music. The music at the beginning of 'God' for instance is mindblowing, and to the dryest words <u>ever</u> to be found in a pop song. – Have you seen the interview of him (first half) in the Rolling Stone?[5] Interesting but awful, really. I wonder if the impulse to be nakedly honest is not in itself and unavoidably also an impulse to self-dramatize? I am bored by people's egos. I find my own boring enough, and wish it were less. (Now follows a paragraph of ego.)

I dropped acid for Christmas day and hallucinated, quite uncomfortably, for well over two hours. However, the trip as a whole was rewarding, as it always is, even if I was something of a burden to Mike and Bill and another guy with us. I discovered something quite interesting: that I have been (not unconsciously) idealizing the situation when I was a child after Father left home – I must have found the household of my mother and Ander and me very comfortable, so comfortable in fact that I have succeeded in reconstructing it now – Mike as my mother, Bill as my younger brother. [. . .] – The only thing that disturbs me about such knowledge is the question that, if Mike is really secretly my mother and Bill my brother, then what importance are they as themselves to me, as opposed to simply being symbolic embodiments of needs? Well, there's much to be said in answer that is reassuring, but it continues to disturb me that the submerged part of myself is still that far lost in the primeval jungles and swamps. I've always liked to see myself as such a free-willer.

A few days later I took a very interesting capsule called MDA with another guy.[6] A mild psychedelic, and a very wild aphrodisiac. I have on no other occasion had sex for SIX HOURS! I had heard about MDA for a couple of years (one or two of the people at Sharon Tate's were on it when they were murdered), but I've come across very few other people who've had it. Right now I'm trying to get hold of some for Mike and Bill and also for Don, who were all rather "intrigued" by my account of it. Like total sensuality, man.

I enclose a few odd little experiments in the field of verse composition.[7] Dunno what you'll think of them. Dunno what I think of them, though I do like the Country [and] Western song. Encolpius is the main character (his name means Crotch) in the Satyricon.

Bill made Marcia's cheesecake and it was fantastic. I had already had it, when made by Marcia, so I knew it would be.

I still am without American publisher for Moly, which is annoying. I hope it comes out this year, over here.[8]

[. . .]

I've taught for a week at Stanford. A very nice easy job, I must say, and Stanford is an easy place to be. Though Donald Davie is a hard person to follow. I always think myself to be a fairly good teacher, but I can tell an awful lot from seeing a teacher informally with his students, and seeing Donald with his like seeing you with yours makes me pretty modest. He is a lovely man, and it is nice to be meeting him more often than I did. He is also quite puzzled by me, I always suspect, and I'm never quite sure of the source of puzzlement.

Well my dears, get safe through that English winter, and get here safe for your Californian spring.

Love

X X X X

Thom

1. Date supplied through internal evidence.
2. TG misdated this letter.
3. Allusion to *Richard III*, 4.2.119: 'I am not in the giving vein today'.
4. *John Lennon/Plastic Ono Band* (1970).
5. 'John Lennon, Part One: The Working Class Hero', *Rolling Stone* 74 (21 January 1971).
6. Not to be confused with MDMA, MDA became popular in the 1960s as a 'love drug' for its enhancement of mood and empathy.
7. TG enclosed 'Encolpius', *Antaeus* 3 (Autumn 1971), 107; uncollected; and 'Sparrow', 'Hitching into Frisco' and 'Baby Song' (*CP* 247–8).
8. TG's original US publisher, the University of Chicago Press (UCP), rejected *Moly* on account of the only modest success of *Touch*. Farrar, Straus & Giroux (FSG) wanted to publish *Moly* and a standoff over rights ensued with UCP, with Faber attempting to mediate. *Moly* did not appear in the USA until 1973 when it was published by FSG in a joint edition with *MSC*, which UCP had allowed to go out of print.

TO *Donald Davie*   ALS Yale
Sunday 21 March 1971

975 Filbert,
San Francisco,
Calif 94133

21 March 71

Dear Donald,
    Enclosed Vining's poetry.[1] I agree that he is very good, certainly he would count as one of the very best of the 40 or so mss I read. His main influences seem to be Whitman and Rod![2] But both used individually, and very nicely. I particularly like the way he is exploring possibilities of the structure of the poem as a whole. Of those I remember from the mss I read, only [William] Decker seemed to be doing this with the same curiosity and success. – As you say, he isn't quite as good as Rod – but that would be expecting too much. Sometimes the direction of his surrealism seems a bit unsure, and he doesn't use it all in the confident way Rod does – Rod ventures out on what seems a gratuitous flight of fantasy, and then you find everything in it is made relevant. I liked the first two of Vining's best – it would be interesting to know how recent they are.

274

Thank you very much for your version of 'Last Days at Teddington', in which you loosened the meter up a bit. I know you meant this merely as an indication of what <u>could</u> be done, but I have to read it also as a possible poem in itself, and frankly I find this version of the poem very sloppy. I don't think one can do such a thing at so late a stage of composition – one can make minor changes of rhythm, one can make such large changes as adding a stanza or deleting half the poem, or one can throw the whole poem out, but I think it is too late to change the entire rhythmic intention, which has to be decided on very early. You'll know what I mean if you think of trying to change a fairly completed free verse poem into a metrical poem, or vice versa. (One of the few criticisms I ever had of your book on Pound is of that part where you rewrite a free verse passage – Perigord? – as metrical verse.[3] Your rewrite is bad metrical verse, full of fill-words that help meter rather than meaning, because the meaning had already been completed. The passage had to be thought of as metrical at an early stage, when the metrical needs could still be answered by words that are a part of the meaning, not an addition to it. – Of course I still think very highly of the EP book as a whole.) – When I spoke of starting a poem in meter, the other day, and going back to do it in free verse, I meant I'd gone back to the <u>first notes</u> for that poem and developed them differently, not that I'd gone on to make, say, version 7 of the metrical poem into free verse. So I think, if one's going to do the Teddington poem in loosened meter, one has to make that decision very early – the rhythmical character of the poem is not something that can be changed like a piece of clothing, and can't simply add an unevenness to every other line.

Please don't take that last paragraph for ingratitude. I'm very grateful for your rewrite as a general criticism, and you certainly helped me very practically in one line, which I've rewritten. But it certainly seems too late to change the rhythmical movement of the poem as a whole, and it has to stay 'tight' if it is to stay at all.

I do have doubts about the possibilities of loosened meter. It comes off in special cases, with special people: I can think of two – Pound moving from Anglo Saxon meter to the free verse of Canto II; and Stevens constantly and miraculously. There must be other people who have done it well, but very few. In general it ends as verse that is not quite meter and not quite accentual. It seems to indicate a rhythmical indecisiveness – whether in late Yeats, or Robert Lowell, or Allen Tate. At its worst (e.g. Lowell's <u>Sunday Morning</u>) it's as if Alexander Pope were to decide he didn't look modern enough, and muddied up some perfectly good couplets. Hard meter can make for a variety of intensities, loose meter usually only for clumsiness (A clumsiness sometimes associated with histrionics – the connection may be fortuitous, though). Of course I'm not just speaking of free verse or of accentual verse, both of which have their own rhythmical decisiveness.

Didn't mean to run on so much. The problem is interesting, though, because it comes up so often nowadays.

The problem certainly does not come up in Cochrane (and Lady Cochrane), which alternates good free verse and good metrical, and a lot of the poem's power comes from the cleanness of the contrast.[4] Marvell is not so invisible as you seem to think, but the more visible he is the clearer the effect, and that's all to the good. I particularly like the metrical half or so of the poem. At the same time the poem does have a problem, one that for me it shares with a lot of your work. A few weeks ago you did broach the subject of learning in poetry, but something happened and I don't think we got down to discussing it. My own attitude – as you might guess from all I've written in the last 10 years or so – is that I don't want to make any but the smallest demands on the reader, as far as background information is concerned. There may be some 'learning' behind the poem, but I try to absorb it into the poem and leave it as something that either the reader might guess at as a source or else as something that is my own secret, not very relevant to the effect of the finished poem as a whole. I'd be the first to admit that my attitude amounts to a prejudice, and that it has plenty of exceptions. E.g. of course Pound: he is so good one is prepared to do a lot of work in reference books to find his meaning more clearly. But what I like so much about many of your poems – including your quite old 'To a Brother in the Mystery' – is that anybody can grasp what is going on with a minimum of special, or historical information. – It's a difficult matter to argue about, of course, to draw lines between special and ordinary information. But in further studying your poem I will get most rewards, I expect, from thinking about such lines as 'sailed / Past impetus that failed' or such phrases as 'the scathed Andean pass', rather than from looking up some book to find out who 'O'Higgins' was. It is a lovely poem, though, and I like the relation – or opposition – set up between public and private life.

This is a far longer letter than I intended.

I guess Doreen is back by now. Love to both,

 X X X

 Thom

1. Davie was responsible for selecting the poetry fellows (known as Stegner Fellows) on the Creative Writing Program at Stanford. Dan Vining, a screenwriter and journalist, was a Stegner Fellow (1971–2).
2. Rod Taylor (1950–), poet, screenwriter, director, and musician. Taylor was a Stegner Fellow (1969–70) and TG reviewed his debut collection, *Florida East Coast*

Champion (1972), see 'New Lineaments' (*OP* 135–7). TG's poem 'Night Taxi' (*CP* 386–8) is subtitled 'for Rod Taylor / wherever he is' and is indebted to Taylor's poem 'San Francisco Connection'.

3. Davie rewrote 'Provincia Deserta', not 'Near Perigord'; see *Ezra Pound: Poet as Sculptor* (1965), 60–3.

4. For Davie's 'Lady Cochrane' see *Collected Poems*, ed. Powell (2002), 249–52.

TO *Tony Tanner*   ALS King's
Thursday 3 June 1971

975 Filbert,
San Francisco,
Calif. 94133,
USA

3 June 71

Dear Tony,

Well, that was a sudden and sad parting. I saw Henry Smash last week and you have no cause for self-reproach about your teaching at Berkeley, so cut that out Tanner! Whitey writes that you are in a nursing home in Cambridge, and maybe that's just as well: Ve haf vays to make you rest. So, Babe, I hope by now all those taut strings in your head are a little loosened and you can soon start enjoying your lovely self as much as you ought.[1]

You will hardly believe this, but we are about to buy the FIRST house we looked at. It is on Cole Street, which crosses Haight – but is about ten blocks from Haight, and in a very cool neighborhood, mostly longhairs. Big bright rooms, a studio for Bill, and a small back yard with sun on it all the day. So when you next come to see us that's where you'll be coming. We won't move in there till early August as we have a wall to pull down, a window to put in, and several doors to install where there are now some ornate Moorish arches. We're all going to be sorry at leaving North Beach, but North Beach is going through rather bad changes and the Haight is going through some pretty good ones – and though we won't have the Bay right beside us we'll have the whole of Golden Gate Park just around the corner, and getting to know all the different parts of that will be nice.

I know how disturbed you were when you left, and probably we all contributed to that, tho certainly in different ways, but – you dear old thing – to disturb you is the last thing I could want. I am often wrong about everything, as you know. But I hope you know I love you.

And love to Marsh,

X X X

Thom

P.S. Tolkein is very restful reading. Like being back in your childhood yet very impressive, I think. He's the ultimate Romantic poet.

I've just about got my first lot of people's poems for Organ.² Wonder how it'll look.

1. Tanner suffered from bipolarity and had a breakdown in May. He was forced to leave California at short notice and return to Cambridge to recuperate. At the same time, he and Don Doody had a major quarrel from which their friendship never truly recovered.

2. For its final issue, TG edited the poetry page of countercultural newspaper *The Organ* and included work by Belle Randall, Rod Taylor, David Ignatow, Gary Snyder and Donald Moyer. See *The Organ* (July 1971), 21.

TO *Tony Tanner*   ALS King's

Monday 16 August 1971¹

SF

16th Aug

Dear teetee – that's a name out of A.A. Milne now, isn't it?

Quite a quick answer to yours, mainly to tell you how happy I am that you are on the mend. A good instinct that took you back to Cambridge – and it is <u>very</u> healthy that you are learning how to enjoy being lazy. It's fun enough to spend a whole lifetime over, isn't it? I certainly take note of the fact that you're not completely out of the pit yet, but the important thing is that you know you're on the way up. And I liked what you said about being aware of possibilities again. That's it, isn't it – I really think that's what marks the difference between despair and happiness.

I've been going through quite a little house-thing myself, and am consequently much better able to understand how your moving triggered off such a depression. To start with, I am <u>consciously</u> aware that I prefer the house and neighborhood that we're moving to. With a few natural regrets for North Beach, but not excessive ones. But the work on the house drives me into frequent downers, and my dear you wouldn't believe the dreams I've been having. Lurid and easy-to-interpret. Obviously moving after 11 years in one place (I think longer than I've ever lived in one house in my life) does very curious things to the stability of some hidden little man inside of me. Though

278

Bill's dream has been the best, it was (1) that the three of us were moving to a house just four blocks from his parents' home in Milwaukee, (2) our real estate agent was giving an exam that all three of us had to pass before we could live in the house, (3) he forgot to study for the exam, so before it was due to start he went for a walk to get his ideas straight, and (4) lost his way and was unable to find where the exam was being given. So we are all freshly understanding of how you felt a few months ago.

You are right about the unforeseen expenses. I will say no more. However, it should be very nice once we move in and feel stable again – the first will take place Sept 1, the second maybe in December.

[. . .]

In the middle of all this, I had a splendid interlude this last weekend, which relaxed me no end. A friend took me from Friday eve till Sunday eve to the Geysers, near Geyserville, about 100 miles north of here.[2] I must say, California is endlessly, lushly beautiful, and there was some country round there that outdid even the best I'd seen. There are some ancient bath houses there, each pool with different temperatures of water – wet, drippy, green light, etc. Everybody who goes there is much reminded of the baths at the start of Fellini's Satyricon. I first arrived there late at night, completely stoned on grass, and it was a weird and nice way to see it first – (they stay open all night). The day time attendant came around with a joint, and bent down by the baths where people were standing, and inserted it in the mouths of everybody in turn – so we wouldn't get it wet with our hands. Then my friend & I took our sleeping bags to a hill, and the stars were as bright as in the desert, especially Mars, which is apparently very close to earth right now, and was brighter than any star I've ever seen. My air mattress immediately deflated, but I slept pretty well anyway. In the morning I found myself in the middle of this fabulous landscape, a hissing geyser I'd heard all night at the top of the hill, and a cliff a few yards away above a pretty river. And the weekend was a total nudity trip – most people were pretty long-haired and young, but everybody young and old, male and female, lived naked most of the time they were there, except when going up to the (truly lousy) café – on the property – for food. In the mornings, most people climbed up the stream (not a hot stream, but still warm enough, the temperature of the air being in the 90s), over rocks for about half an hour, to get to a series of deep pools just below a waterfall. This was Thomas Bewick in California – really.[3] The banks had got so high by this point that it was a ravine, the sides all covered with marvellous mosses. There were rocks where you could sunbathe and talk. And the wonderful thing about all this is the naturalness of being naked. Probably about a third of the guys there were gay, and the rest were mostly heterosexual couples. A few rather aggressive-looking ex-Marines who kept their shorts on. But even with them everything was fine, because they were smoking just as much grass as they drank beer, and there was a lot of good feeling! And it's easy to be nice in beautiful surroundings. Then in the afternoon there was a bit of psychedelia back near the baths. And in the evening much soaking in baths, with quite a bit of both heterosexual and homosexual orgy. Again, this seemed very natural – just like the world ought to be. About two in the morning, the bar by the café closed, and a lot of old men in cowboy hats came down with beer cans in their hands to have a look at all the titties. They didn't seem to get any (titty, that is), but everybody was very nice to them, and they shared their beer with us, and anyway they looked a little too drunk to be able to do much. Well, this is no doubt a rather gushy account, but it really all was a slice of the Garden of Eden, the redneck being quite ready to lie down with the longhair.[4] On Sunday afternoon we climbed up to look at one of the geysers – a hot climb, and it was even hotter at the top. Quite near the top there were little hollows beside the path, gushing out steam and with various very brilliant mineral deposits around them. I didn't like [it] all that much – it made me feel the insecurity of what we're living on, I mean what's to prevent a scalding geyser from suddenly appearing in the already small back garden at Cole Street? And for quite a distance around the geyser, most of the top of the hill in fact, it's a real moon-landscape – rubble and grey stone. – Otherwise, an idyllic weekend. What a strange time and place I live in. (I mean, apparently a year ago people couldn't go nude in this place till after 11p.m.) Maybe this is what Clive would call hippie sentimentality, but the beautiful naïve impulses that started up about 6 years ago are much too powerful to be obliterated by the shit that has been piled upon them, and that they have sometimes directly caused themselves.

I was very grateful indeed for Clive's review.[5] I will write him a note in September. He is most sharp – nobody else has noticed the sun–moon opposition that the book moves between. I only hope I deserve the things he says of me.

Glad about Robert Coover. The Babysitter, which I read at your place, is one of the funniest things I've ever read.[6]

Isn't the Oz trial shocking and depressing?[7] There is a point where American fascism and English conservatism (as documented in TW's Alfie Hinds book) come to exactly the same thing.[8] Maybe public opinion can shame the judges, as it did in the Cambridge case last year. Neville's speech to the judge makes a lot of good sense to me. But the judgement and the sentences are monstrous.

I'm reading H.G. Wells' short stories again. I often come back to them. They are very good stories – and people in the 1920s were very silly to sneer at him!!!!

These last two lines are the most I can manage by way of lit crit these days. I look forward to your book. I'm so happy you are getting better, and now it's Marsh's turn to look after herself.

Much love to both   X X X X Thom

1. Date supplied through internal evidence.
2. See 'The Geysers' (*CP* 239–46).
3. See 'Thomas Bewick' (*CP* 258–9).
4. See Isaiah 11:6.
5. 'Clive Wilmer on New Poetry', *The Spectator* (29 May 1971), 742–4. In his review of *Moly*, Wilmer concludes that the only 'significant flaw' in the book is 'a kind of hippie sentimentalism that creeps into a couple of the poems'.
6. See 'The Babysitter', in Coover's *Pricksongs & Descants: Fictions* (1969).
7. The 'School Kids Issue' of the countercultural magazine *Oz* – in which teenagers were given complete editorial freedom – was the subject of a lengthy obscenity trial in 1971. *Oz*'s three editors – Jim Anderson, Felix Dennis and Richard Neville – were found guilty under the Obscene Publications Act, though the verdict was overturned at appeal.
8. White ghosted Alfred George Hinds's memoir *Contempt of Court* (1966).

TO *Tony Tanner*   ALS King's

Monday 27 September 1971

1216 Cole,

SF, Calif 94117

27 Sept 71

Hello young fellow,

It is 11p.m. and Mike and Bill are in the next room planning where they will put various signs,[1] I am on my bed just having finished your book and 2 beers, and our three other housemates are busy upstairs – Don is scraping paint off his mantelpiece, having become hugely domestic. A cosy scene indeed, we are six, plus 3 cats and 2 dogs, and the whole house becomes beautifully bigger & full of possibilities every day (though a fellow's dreams – <u>always</u> about moving – do seem to continue at night with a certain persistence). We are kind of getting to the end of all our work, now doing only 2 hours painting a day. Don has two very nice roommates – I don't think you know them, but you might, they are both old friends: Al Hilliard, who was earlier this year black bartender at the Dead End (where TW went a lot with us) and Paul Faola, a good cook and occasional bartender. Three or four times a week someone cooks for the whole house and guests – I have cooked for 12 several times already – and indeed (the back stairs are so short) it is like having 5 roommates. So things are working out very well: it is really, I realize, the way of living I've wanted for the last 6 years or so. I guess I am something of a bully, in my quiet way: first I manipulate things so that Bill comes to live with us, and then I manipulate things so that Don does too – and it happens with just the two others I'd hoped for (Al & Paul).

I got your book about a week ago, and let me tell you – since you apparently don't know it – it is very good indeed.[2] In about 6 years time you will read it through & realize this. What I like especially is that it is a book about ideas, and just those ideas I most want to see explored by such a mind as yours. And the writing is, almost throughout, sensitive and vigorous, seeming at times to be narrating a plot but suddenly the reader finds himself already submerged in, surrounded by ideas, that he already understands because he thought he was following a plot-line.

When you described the book to us, and described your critics' reactions, it certainly did sound pretty bland. No evaluation of the books, and Barth it seemed put on the same level as Mailer! But I'd forgotten how your favorite sentence from Sartre was that bit about perception necessarily involving evaluation. In fact it is extremely clear how you evaluate every novel you write about – you do not press the point, you do not make a hierarchy (and your last 2 pages are particularly well put) – but if I cared, I bet I could make a hierarchy, a regular pyramid with an apex of the novels you most admire and a base of the novels you least admire (John Barth). And the pyramid would be derived from your book alone, not from your conversation. So there is quite enough evaluation in the book, and just of the right sort.

It is a beautiful book, keeping me constantly interested, constantly instructed. Of the people I hadn't read, I now want to read most The Bell Jar and Malamud. And possibly The Recognitions, & even John Updike (one quote from him, about the seagull, is really lovely well-observed stuff).

[. . .]

And the way you have of bringing all your experience and reading to bear on a point so relevantly, it's wonderful mate.

(And it's all so nicely produced, with a particularly nice dust-jacket I've liked every time I pick up the book.)

My serious advice to you, for my further education, is that the subject of your next book and emotional breakdown should be Melville – or at any rate Moby Dick. Maybe you have this in mind – you give a few little hints and half promises about it. Moby Dick is, after all, one of the best books ever written, and you are one of the best writers and thinkers alive, and probably this is your destiny anyway so you might as well submit to it.

Signed,

The Three Fates

I'm going to NY for 2 weeks in December, I have 3 readings there which will cover it, and it'll be nice to go. New York is the ultimate city, after all, and I like to dip into its entropy before returning to the West Coast to wash off all that entropy in the Pacific flow.

One terrifying thing happened in moving. We were taking the (very heavy) refrigerator up the front stairs on a dolly, but without having tied it on, as we should have. Jim (the guy Don loves, who was a saint in helping us) was guiding it up the stairs, and Mike and I were lifting beneath. About fifteen steps up, the refrigerator suddenly jumped off, somehow slipped by me, and pursued Mike down the stairs. Mike must have been very quick, as it was about 6 inches behind him all the way down. He made it, of course, and it was OK, but one thing that was so interesting was that in disaster the mind is so quick – I mean <u>my</u> mind – even while I couldn't act fast enough to do anything about it, in a few seconds I could imagine it first crushing his ribs, then when it took a kind of spin crushing his whole body, then seeing him bedridden for the rest of his life, then seeing him dead. All in something like 4 seconds. – We all had to sit at the bottom of the stairs for a cigarette before we started taking it up again. I was too chicken to go up with it that time (we had about 7 helpers) but Mike lifted it in just the same position. The refrigerator works very well still.

A kiss to your fractured foot.

A hope that you enjoy teaching a lot this term.

A fart to George Watson, the one person since Oswald Le Winter to whom I took an irrational dislike. (Another fart to Graham Hough, while I'm farting.)

An embrace to Romney and you, full of nectar.

& my best wishes to your Lares & Penates.[3]

I have written several poems, weird & funny. I am going to add a few & Olwyn is going to publish them on expensive paper & of course you'll have a copy.[4] But you won't see them till then, nor will anyone. Maybe I feel defensive about them, but anyway I want it to be a surprise for everyone.

X X X X X U No Hoo

P.S. By the way, have you read Little Dorrit? This was the one Dickens novel I'd never read. It is one of the very best + one of the four best (with Our Mutual Friend, Bleak House, & Great Expectations). So much that is good – and a marvellous dyke woman who has one confessional chapter that is like

Dostoevsky (Miss Wade, a nice name). I'm now rereading Dombey & Son – a nice enough book, but not of the same caliber.

[. . .]

1. MK decorated the house with his collection of vintage metal advertising signs.
2. Tanner, *City of Words: American Fiction 1950–1970* (1971).
3. The benevolent spirits and gods of the household in Roman religion.
4. *Mandrakes* (Rainbow Press, 1974), with illustrations by Leonard Baskin. Olwyn Hughes (1928–2016), literary agent and publisher, sister of Ted Hughes.

TO *Tony Tanner*   ALS King's
Friday 31 December 1971

1216 Cole St.,
San Francisco,
Calif 94117

31 Dec 71

Dear Tanner,

Even this is not a real letter, but more like a business note. I went to NY state for about 3 weeks. Did a reading at Rochester – a really nice place, right in the North, on some lake, – they have snow 5 months of the year and know how to treat visitors (beer and friendliness). Colgate was less good. For one thing, it is a highly elegant, much-pillared college on a hill by a village – a far too pretty place to do much work in. Also, they are <u>dreadfully</u> aware of how exclusive and special and much-pillared they are (tho I had barely heard of them, and had somehow the impression that Colgate was a State College in an industrial city). Then, to make matters worse, the really awful Richard Murphy was my host. I should add that it was he who fixed up both readings for me and also that he was very hospitable to me. But his conversation is so self-centred it is difficult to take for any length of time (e.g. 5 minutes). Also, half an hour before the reading, he informed me that Auden has a great distaste for me (something I'd been suspecting for some years). And a quarter of an hour before the reading, that the head of the department thinks my poetry is nowhere. Neither fact troubled me greatly, but they were curious facts to tell a fellow just before his reading, I thought.

[. . .]

Still not really writing, but I'm doing a little desultory work on a selection of B. Jonson's poetry I promised to do for Penguins.[1] He's an awfully good poet I must say. I think my Introduction will be unique among <u>all</u> essays and introductions to Ben Jonson in that it will be the only one to make no comparisons with Shakespeare. Contrasts I should say.

[. . .]

Well, this seems to have developed into a letter after all. – Murphy told me of some extremely dramatic goings on involving Alvarez, Ted, the Observer, and the TLS.[2] Sounds like Alvarez has got his comeuppance. He's an egotistical fool, really. Must look it all up in a library, when I next work for a university.

Plenty has been going on upstairs, though we are very tranquil downstairs. (We have a democracy, DD has an autocracy.) But where Doody lives, there will always be drama. First one roommate left, then the other. Then Jere Franzway (one of DD's ex-crushes, a fine man) had his shop get busted (for dealing), and so he moved in with his really vast entourage – usually 15–25 people. Which was more than Doody could take. But it's turning out nicely: at the beginning of the year he is going to share with Jim Dondson (another of DD's ex-crushes, a person so generous, open, and tactful that it is difficult to find any flaw in him, as Mike & I were agreeing the other day) and with a boy called Grady (DD's present crush) and Grady's girl-friend Renée. The last two are around 19 years old and pretty nice, it seems. We all suspect (except Don) that Renée will not stay very long, but who knows. If there is more drama in store it will probably be very minor – drawing room comedy rather than black comedy.

All the grass around is of such high caliber nowadays that even I turn on every day. The word for it in 1970 was 'heavy', in 1971 'mellow', wonder what it will be in 1972. ('Twee', maybe.)

I mentioned to someone in NY, a sculptor, about how many NY towns are called by Greek names, Ithaca, Syracuse, Utica, etc. Then for a few minutes we made a list of Greek names for towns not only in NY but elsewhere. So I said, 'Interesting, in the 18th century (American) people thought of themselves as Romans, in the 19th they thought of themselves as Greeks, I wonder what they think of themselves as today?' He gave a glance at my hair tied up behind and at my leather pants, and said 'Indians, of course.' Very interesting, and completely true. Sentimental nostalgia for the primitive. It would be rather interesting for someone to do an essay on the historical nostalgias of different ages. Except that it would probably turn out that most ages thought the Romans were the cat's whiskers. (Actually they were a repellent bunch of fascists.)

I met Mark[3] and David Hockney at the Stud. They wanted to go on to a bunch of new bars they had heard about. I said, 'Oh those bars are awful, they're very plastic.' David Hockney said, 'But we like plastic.'

Which I thought was a very funny remark.
Well my dears, have a good new year,
          with lots of spritely fun
                    & love from Mike & Bill & Don
          X X X X X X X Thom X X X X
P.S. I am going to see a hypnotist in the New Year, in an attempt to give up smoking. It seems a silly way to die. Certainly I want to live to be eighty.

1. *Ben Jonson* (1974); TG's introduction is collected in *OP* (106–17).
2. In November 1971 *The Observer* published the first of a two-part series called 'Sylvia Plath: The Road to Suicide', which became the preface of Alvarez's *The Savage God* (1971). An exchange of letters ensued in the *TLS* in which Hughes contended that Alvarez had 'misremembered' facts and had appropriated Hughes's own notion that Plath had 'gambled' with her suicide.
3. Mark Lancaster (1938–), artist and set designer, was artist in residence at King's College, Cambridge, 1968–70, and would have known Tanner.

1972

TO *Tony Tanner*   ALS King's
Thursday 3 August 1972

> 1216 Cole Street,
> San Francisco,
> Calif. 94117
>
> 3 August 72

Dear Tanner,

[. . .] I got your postcards from Cambridge and Japan – a little disappointed you didn't parachute down here while the plane was returning over Cole Street, but then there are probably other routes between England and Japan. I never could get used to the Copernican idea that I was not the center of the universe.

It is really being a pretty good year. If some trying things have happened, my spirits seem to cope with them OK, and the good things have far outnumbered the bad ones anyway. Olwyn Hughes usually writes beforehand to tell me when things are likely to be particularly loathesome for somebody with her and my sun sign (something about Neptune opposing our trine) – one time she was dramatically right, another time just as dramatically wrong. I have really started to like her a lot. I finally sent her my ten new poems, which she's going to bring out this fall – or when Leonard Baskin has finished the illustrations. It will be called <u>Mandrakes,</u> and I hope he has fun with that image. You can count on a copy from me, by the way; it will be far too expensive for anybody but eccentric millionaire book collectors and some of the wealthier American libraries.

I did a couple of days at the Univ of Arizona near Phoenix, or maybe I told you, & almost freaked out. I was surrounded by ignorant and boring pedants. I didn't even like many of the students. So I took too much speed and got twice as irritable. What an awful place. – On the other hand I went later to give a reading at Southern Methodist University in Dallas, and hugely enjoyed myself. A matter of mood, really, since that university wasn't much better than the other and Dallas itself (which I hadn't seen since the time when Don and I planned Kennedy's assassination) is falling to pieces.[1]

287

Don Doody by the way is now manager of a huge hotel–bar–sauna baths.[2] He is very excited as it is an open-ended project he can do anything with. Considering that a Turkish baths in New York now has a women's night, when there is a stage show, etc., almost anything is possible.

There was a sensational raid by the narcs on his apartment upstairs a few months ago, by the way. I saw it starting, by chance, from the street. Got him out of jail next day, anyway, and the case is still going on, but I don't think there is too much danger. He doesn't deal any longer, anyway. Come to think of it, I know very few people who do any dealing nowadays.

Went down to Stanford to give a reading again last week (my third in 18 months, they are gluttons for punishment). After the reading this black girl was getting very little-girlish and flirtatious, and finally she said 'I told Rod Taylor I wanted to meet you, but he said I try to seduce everybody I meet and I couldn't with you because you are homosexual.' I said: 'He's right about me; is he right about you?' Which disposed of that problem. (Rod Taylor is that marvellous poet I mentioned.)

I teach at Berkeley next winter for a quarter. I wonder if that will be my last teaching job for a while. I am to be represented in an anthology of poetry by homosexuals The Male Muse (!), whenever that comes out. I don't think much of the idea of such an anthology, but it seemed to me it would be cowardly to refuse permission to be in it.[3]

You will probably see the Davies by and by, since Donald is teaching at Tours for the next year. Marcia must not be surprised if Doreen deifies her, as I passed on the gazpacho recipe to Doreen and she finds it very successful. (Incidentally, ask Marsh if she has tried the chicken tarragon recipe in Julia Child. She probably has, but if she hasn't tell her it's fabulous – and it's also pretty simple and quick.)

I have all sorts of herbs in the garden. It is amazing how much better some are when fresh – especially thyme and basil. – I just counted 35 green tomatoes, and we've had lots of lettuce, radishes, scallions, and snow peas from the garden. And some of the flowers go on and on. If you want to know two that grow from seed easily and are in flower all summer, try PHLOX and PINKS. Beautiful. Sensuous. Far out. Pinks are the basic Shakespearean flower from which carnations and sweet williams derive. The color is named after the flower. Probably the flower was Indo European, along with honey and mother and all those other basic Indo European properties they filled their lives with. But this, of course, is pure speculation, he concluded with a leer.

No, I have not read Joyce Carol Oates either. But I did meet her a few years ago, and she is imprinted on my memory (even etched on it) as by far the thinnest woman I have ever set eyes on. A taller and thinner version of Ariel Parkinson. – But I have read Walker Percy's third book, Love in the Ruins. Very funny, but I wouldn't bother to recommend it. And boy is he a right winger (though I'm sure he wouldn't admit to being one). A better book, if you haven't read it, in fact enchantingly funny, is Hunter S. Thompson's Fear and Loathing in Las Vegas, which I read when it was serialised in the Rolling Stone, and which you'll love. – Oh yes, I reread The Awkward Age. I'm beginning to think that it is not only the best novel by James, but one of the best novels ever written. It makes so many beautiful points I find increasingly apposite. Especially how Mr Longdon has to accept in Nanda all of what she is rather than trying to reform her. The whole book is incredible isn't it? The bitch scene at Tishy Grendon's is so funny that when I got to the end of that section I had to go back & read it all over again.

I've recently been seeing a lot of a boy (named Larry) alarmingly young – 21, certainly young enough to be my son.[4] (Come to think of it, maybe I see him as Nanda?) Very attractive and very bright. And very sweet-natured: everybody I introduce him to likes him. – Not that I (or he) am being monogamous – unimaginable, dahling – but we are seeing a lot of each other, which is a bit unusual for me. And I'm trying to do things for him I would have liked someone to do for me when I was his age.

I have been several times to the Geysers, and bathed in those splendid streams, cold as well as hot.[5] I started an elaborate series of poems to the Geysers, modelled more or less on Ben Jonson's To Penshurst, which ended with me being torn to pieces in the hot baths, like Orpheus, but it hasn't got very far, since my head has got out of the habit of couplets and Mannerist exaggerations. But I modelled it on To Penshurst because the place embodies moral virtues for me in the same way P. did for BJ.

I've been doing a lot of nice acid this year, you'll be surprised to hear, & what is more doing a lot of it on my own. It has been very weak and easily-manageable stuff (as I've often said, with acid a difference in quantity is a difference in kind), and I particularly like doing it on my own around gay bars on a Saturday night. At the end of the trip you feel as though you have an epic behind you, the evening has been so crammed with incident and heroic action. Last Saturday I met a dude who had, it turned out, dropped at the same time as I had and we met while we were peaking. So we finished the trip together.

    [. . .]

        All love,

              X X X X X

                  Thom

1. Clay Shaw (1917–74), a New Orleans businessman, was acquitted of involvement in the assassination of President Kennedy, the only person ever prosecuted in connection with the murder. Doody, a friend of Shaw's, was interviewed by New Orleans District Attorney Jim Garrison in March 1967 regarding the assassination. TG and Doody spent two nights in Dallas in August 1963 at the tail end of their summer road trip through the US and Mexico. TG met Shaw several times in Doody's company.
2. Doody briefly managed the Barracks, a bathhouse off Folsom Street that is the subject of TG's poem 'Saturday Night' (*BC* 45–6).
3. *The Male Muse: A Gay Anthology*, ed. Ian Young (1973); TG's poems were 'The Feel of Hands' (*CP* 120) and 'Blackie, the Electric Rembrandt' (*CP* 118).
4. Larry Hoyt (1951–86). See Glossary of Names.
5. See TG to Tanner, 16 August 1971, above.

TO *Donald Davie*   ALS Hornbake
Tuesday 14 November 1972

1216 Cole Street,
San Francisco,
Calif. 94117

14 Nov 72

Dear Donald,
    Many thanks for sending me your article from the TLS.[1] I hope what you say is true: it certainly is nice to have such things said. You take the moly-poems as I would want them to be taken – more as examples than as teaching – and you get the point of why I wrote the book as I did, in a way that very few others got it.
    [. . .]
    The NY Times Book Review asked me to review your two books, so I did, without realizing I was going to disagree with so much of your prose book. But I hope the enclosed review you will find more 'amiable' than 'stringent' (two words you have used of reviews).[2] I have lots of serious disagreements with the prose book, but I was allowed only 1000 or was it 1200 words and I thought it better to spend more space on your poetry, because poetry is more important than criticism, and of course a <u>Collected</u> poems is equivalent to several shorter books.[3] The collection gave me very great pleasure, as I hope is apparent. You must be getting bored by me (and everyone else) liking To a Brother in the Mystery so much; but it <u>is</u> one of the best two or three poems you have written, and it has to be discussed in any critique of your whole work because it is thematically so central. It was good to come to old favorites again. 'Time Passing, Beloved' especially seems something

of a miracle still. On the whole I don't like <u>Brides of Reason</u> very much – the two poems that stand out from it, for me, are also the least typical, Woodpigeons at Raheny and Evening on the Boyne. <u>A Winter Talent</u> is a solid book, though. And both <u>Events and Wisdoms</u> and <u>Essex Poems</u> have gained a lot since I first read them. They are relaxed and personal without being loose or egotistical.

[. . .]

As for <u>Thomas Hardy and British Poetry</u>, my disagreements are many and go deep. Well, you didn't expect to write a <u>popular</u> book did you?

One thing that interests me, however, is that I am probably in many ways the Lefty you are against, and it is certainly good for me to have my cliché views of the Right broken down. I mean, this book reveals you to be far more conservative than I'd guessed; yet you are as humane, generous, and unselfish a person as I know, and I should think tolerant as well about most matters of importance, and these are all qualities I've been in the habit of thinking conservatives lack.

[. . .]

My biggest disagreement with you is about 'the nature of poetry.' I put it in quotes to apologize for the pomposity of the phrase, and it's pompous because it's too big a subject to cover in a letter. But I'm troubled in particular by two matters: (1) you seem to think that poetry <u>docet</u>, that it <u>teaches</u>, in a straightforward moralistic way. Or rather, I don't believe you think anything that simple, but if all I knew about you was this book I would. (2) Similarly, you say you are 'unable to follow' E.P. and others into mythological experience, again doing an awful lot of unnecessary and misleading simplification. I'm not sure that understanding of poetry is well served by too often posing the alternatives of belief or disbelief in a poet's claims. Claims to supernatural experience ("turning into a tree") and conscious fictions (Hardy's ghosts) are much less clearly demarcated than you suppose in this book. On the whole, we believe fictions as if they were true, while we read them, and the way in which we apply such belief to our own lives is as complicated and mysterious a matter as the way we apply the moral lessons of 'King Lear' to our own lives. But which of these do we 'believe': (a) Moses claiming he has communicated with God, (b) Blake claiming he sees cherubim, (c) the elfin pinnace in The Prelude, (d) your own dream-adventures at night?

I must stop here, I'm getting pompous and didactic, and really this is a matter for conversation rather than letters. I am certainly not trying to start an argument with you, but rather trying to play fair with what troubled me about your book, which I hope you'll interpret as the act of a friend.

I would like to have a long talk with you about this next year, though.

Love to Doreen and Patrick. I envy you all that nice French food. I recently made a repulsive garlic soup, not a recipe I would pass on!

     Love,

        Thom

1. Davie, 'The rhetoric of emotion', *Times Literary Supplement* (29 September 1972), 141–3.
2. For TG's review, see *New York Times Book Review* (7 January 1973), 5, 26; uncollected.
3. Davie, *Collected Poems 1950–1970* (1972).

TO *Tony White*   ALS Tulsa
Tuesday 5 December 1972

1216 Cole Street,
San Francisco,
Calif. 94117

5 Dec 72

Dear Tony,

My god I delay. I see your last letter was sent on Stauffenburgtag, as you say, and here it is the day before the anniversary of being ill in 1962, hepatitistag (and I just realized today is the day I met Mike, Cyrano party in 1952 – what anniversaries and saints' days accumulate as a man gets older). It's been a really good year in most ways. Of course that barrel of slime Nixon got in, but if it had been up to Massachusetts and San Francisco McGovern would now be president. Also there was a referendum (in Calif.) on marijuana, which lost 2 to 1 (not bad really), but which won overwhelmingly in San Francisco. Not that that makes any difference to the law!

And the other thing that's been bad has been so many people I know getting busted over drugs. A year ago if I'd wanted to buy anything I'd have known 10 people at least I could get it from at once, now it's hard sometimes to find one. [. . .] [Don] has <u>not</u> had a good year, having quarrelled with pretty well every friend he has except us. This has been difficult at times because we have not quarrelled with any of them. However I did have one tremendous long argument with him which may have been what caused him to make up with Jere Franzway, who is now living upstairs and is a moderating influence on DD. Actually, however pissed off I get at DD, I never wish he was living elsewhere. He's a person I really love for all his wrong-headedness. (Of course it could be all the rest of us who are wrong-headed.)

But in all other ways it has been a splendid year. The house is all one would want it to be. I've been writing moderately. Oh yes, and I have an American publisher again – Farrar Straus & Giroux (Scottish German & French), about as good as one can get. They are to bring out Moly & My Sad Captains in the spring, and of course I'm very happy about that.

[. . .]

Hope your eye is well by now, and that you are back to football. That must have been very painful and worrying, I should think. I've never had anything wrong with my eye.

Tanner says he has had an offer to do something at the Stanford Research Institute in 1974. I hope you will join me in trying to persuade him to accept it. Taunt him with being afraid of meeting Don. Hit him in the stomach if he tries to answer you back. Don't leave until you have a signed promise that he will come here.

And you know there is a room here for you. I plan to have its window prettily framed with nodding foxgloves. You just wouldn't believe the gardening I'm into. I'm even growing primroses from seed (I've never heard of anybody doing that) – not to mention bergamot, chervil, coriander (or alexolanus?), etc., he continued airily.

Haven't read an awful lot of anything lately. Got Ted's Selected Poems, and it is extraordinary.[1] I read it, and realized of course he's by far the best person writing nowadays – for all the bombast, the romanticism, etc., he is making interactions between language & experience that no one else (in English that is) is even capable of. Right now I'm reading some only just published poems by H.D., Hermetic Definition, written in the last couple of years of her life. Very interesting, very different from anyone else and from her early work – I don't even know whether I like them or not.

All send love

    X X X X X

      Thom

1. Hughes, Selected Poems, 1957–67 (1972).

1973

TO *Tony Tanner*   ALS King's
Monday 9 April 1973

1216 Cole St.,
San Francisco,
Calif. 94117
USA

9 April 73

Dear Giggles,

A long time since I got your letter, but it's been a busy (though very nice) year. But I'd better write now, as I'm going to leave for a series of 10 readings in Connecticut. Underpaid, but it'll mean a couple of weeks in the Big Apple afterwards, which is always fun. [. . .] And, since Easter falls in the middle of the readings, I can spend an Irish Easter in Boston.

I taught my quarter at Berkeley, and I must say I still like it – and its students – so much better than anywhere else [I've] taught. I'd been afraid I'd sentimentalized them after the years away. But they really are more representative of people outside the university, and also more worldly, more diversified. I found Stanford students a somewhat homogeneous bunch, and Princeton even more so. (Of course more of my classes were over 4–8 people.)

I got a new kitten on 21st December. If you want to know her name, remember Donne's poem written on that day, being the shortest day.[1] She is a tortoiseshell, at first she looked a bit like a hyena, but as she has got bigger the colors have spaced out very prettily. Our third cat – but the guy who wanted me to take her was so attractive I could not see my way to refusing him.

There is a most extraordinary series that has been on TV, called An American Family. When I saw the first instalment, I called it rivetingly boring, but it's got more interesting with every week. It is about a family – quite rich – in Sta. Barbara, and is all documentary – a cameraman came round every day and practically lived with them for about a year. The parents get divorced, the eldest son turns out to be gay, and there are two other sons & two other daughters. But what is so fascinating, of course, is that it is true, and from having found them all rather distasteful you start sympathising and seeing yourself in them. Really the most interesting and boring show I've seen on the Set.

[. . .]

Jolly letters from Tony the White fairly often. It would be nice if he and you were to come over at the same time. Though I suppose I ought to come over to England some time next year. Not that I want to, except to see you people and Ander & a few relatives. Looks like Mike and Bill will be coming over to England and France at the end of this summer. I choose to stay in my garden, getting drunk. (I've got some raspberries going in the garden (they should bear in 1974). Snow peas, beans, lettuce very rewarding.)

Yes I liked 100 Years of Solitude, though I found the ending a bit of a cop out. No, I've never read any Gorki. I've been reading Ovid's Metamorphoses (in English, of course) (one-upmanship!) an interestingly disorganised book;[2] and a really disgustingly funny pornographic book by Apollinaire called The Debauched Hospodar (one girl can only get excited when she has both hands in the wounds of dying people – luckily the hero meets her when she is working as a nurse during the Russian-Japanese war). Oh yes, and a fine book Jim Hart lent me called Americans and the American Dream, by Kevin STARR (O.U.P.), just out, beautifully informative about California. I love the idea of San Franciscans going out to the country to picnic on Potrero Hill. Of course, the best stories are about Mrs [Jane] Stanford. "An intense and somewhat spiritualistic religiosity grew with the years" causing great embarrassment to the President of Stanford (the Senator was dead) when she tried to have some of her more unusual religious ideas taught to all the students. "Encountering personal opposition, Mrs Stanford had the habit of stepping to one side, cocking her head to the ceiling, and asking, 'God, did you hear that?'"

I'm thinking of using this myself. How could one ever lose an argument?

I've been writing a few little personal essays for here and there. I think I am finally beginning to see a way to writing a book about my life. So many interesting things have happened to me that I would like to put them down on paper, but I have a dislike of all that confessional stuff people write. So I have been searching I guess for a tone, as a way of dealing with experience. Though don't expect to see any of it for years. I haven't written a word of it yet, and at the rate I write it wouldn't be finished for years.

Also some poems. Don't know where I'm going as usual, but it is mostly coming out in pamphlets, and I prefer to send you them to see what reaction you have to the directions I am or may be going in.

[. . .]

Have you read Henryson's tale of the Uponlondis Mous and the Burges Mous (town & country mouse)? I guess I read it as an undergraduate, but I'd forgotten it: it really is very funny, funnier than Chaucer, I think.

[. . .]

By the way, we had <u>double</u> the usual rainfall last winter and lots of frost. Very weird.

I've been reading Edmund Waller. None of it comes up to Go Lovely Rose, but there are some interesting oddities. Still, of all of us who are better than him, who can write anything like Go Lovely Rose.

          Love to Romney and your slim self X X X X X Thom

[. . .]

P.S. I'm feeling exhilarated because I turned down a $10,000 job to teach one term at the University of Michigan. I could have done with the money, but I'd have killed myself if I'd had to spend 15 weeks there.

1. Donne, 'A Nocturnal upon St Lucy's Day' (*c.* 1627).
2. TG read Mary M. Innes's translation, *The Metamorphoses of Ovid* (1955).

TO *Tony White*   ALS Tulsa

Friday 13 April 1973

          1216 Cole Street,
          San Francisco,
          CA 94117

          13 April 73

Hello, Young Sir,

[. . .]

Sad about Mr Kroll's block.[1] Almost simultaneously, my grandfather's farm, what buildings are left of it – barns, granaries, stables – in Snodland are being bulldozed, presumably for a housing estate. (The farm <u>house</u>, where two of my aunts live, is still O.K.) I was much more upset to hear that than I was to hear, by the same post, that my cousin Jenny had split up with her husband, though I like them both. Jenny is now living on Talbot Road, which she fell for when she visited me once. [. . .]

[. . .]

I think I'll probably come over some time in 1974. Less for England than for you, Ander, Tanner, and aunts!

          Love,

            Thom

1. 'Mr Kroll's block', where TG lived on Talbot Road, London W2 (1964–5), was demolished in the mid-1970s.

TO *Tony White*   ALS Tulsa
Thursday 13 September 1973

1216 Cole Street,
San Francisco,
CA 94117

13 Sept 73

Dear Tony,
   [. . .]
   I really don't know when I last wrote. I did a reading tour of Connecticut in the spring. Very small-time: 10 readings at a hundred each; but I really enjoyed it – it was efficiently set up, I enjoyed a lot of the people I met (that's ambiguous, I mean I liked them), and it is a pretty state. Easter came in the middle, so I went to Boston for three days and had a fine time there too. I'd never realized it would be so beautiful there. I met a nice young Texan who showed me round (just heard from him yesterday that he had been mugged, knifed, zipzap, and came near to death, in Brooklyn). Then to New York, which I've never enjoyed so much. It was beautiful spring weather, for a start, and NY doesn't always have a spring. Then some of the people I met introduced me to cocaine (one of the people was a singer for a group called Looking Glass), and that is a fine fine drug, far too expensive to make a habit of, but I've had it about 10 times now, and by the tenth time your body has learned whole new categories of excitement which it didn't know of even by the fifth time. Then I met my American publisher, the Giroux in Farrar, Straus, and Giroux, who gave me an excellent Armenian lunch with yoghurt soup (better than it sounds). And went to the Cloisters, a museum of medieval loot brought back by Rockefellers, and liked tapestries for the first time. And had a good 3 weeks.
   A strange figure was to be seen sometimes on Christopher Street: a man dressed in a kind of fairy frock, with a wand, and a knapsack where wings would be. He would appear and swoop up and down the street on roller skates, stopping by attractive motorists at times. This could be very unfunny, but it really worked, he did it so well. His name I think was Arena Rena. Though I feel sorry for a friend of mine who had never seen him, and one evening after taking a little acid started walking along the street, enjoying the

mild evening, and suddenly this gauzy thing swooped out of nowhere. And he thought it was a <u>real</u> fairy for a while.

By the way, did you ever do that acid you called a microdot? Have you done any since you came back? – I have done quite a lot, but always in small measures – i.e. about a third of what we did those two times. "Acid is a drug where a difference in amount is a difference in <u>kind of trip</u>" – Gunn.

Of course, maybe I wrote all this to you in my last letter.

Positives just came out in paperback, so I read it through for the first time since it came out, probably, and it took me back marvellously to 1964–5. That was a marvellous year. Maybe before I'm fifty I'll come back to England for at least six months. Next year, though, for a couple of months only.

I have written quite a bit, I suppose, but it all lacks that concentrated sense of direction of the Moly poems. Anyway I have hardly shown any of it to anybody, through a curious blending of arrogance and humility. But much of it will come out in 3 pamphlets – or short books anyway – that I think will all be published about the same time, one when it was promised for, one a year later than I expected, and one a year earlier.[1] I'll make sure you get them all – one, from Olwyn's press, with illustrations by Baskin, and another with illustrations by Bill.

[. . .]

You know the Oliver Sacks who is now so big as a writer in England (and deservedly)? I have known him for years. He apparently came out to do his internship in San Francisco because he liked my poetry (!), and I tried to help him learn to write. He was a very difficult person in those days, with a large ego and small sympathies, and though he wrote huge amounts it was – well, <u>deluded</u>, or I might say <u>obsessive</u>. It has been very interesting to see him whenever I'm in New York and watch him maturing into somebody with such large sympathies and somebody indeed so much more balanced and wise than myself. If you haven't read his book <u>Awakenings</u> you really should.

Oh, also, if you haven't seen a movie called <u>McCabe and Mrs Miller</u>, it is wonderful. The <u>Ulysses</u> of movies, in that you approach meaning in it purely through experience. & gorgeous visually too.

Ted has been buying cattle. Will his next book be called Cow?

Have you <u>met</u> his wife yet?

I've been reading <u>Dante</u>, darling! I found a good way of doing it with only minimal Italian. First I read a canto in Laurence Binyon's fantastic translations[2] then I go through it in the Temple edition of Dante Darling – which has Italian opposite literal prose English.[3] It is quite a revelation – almost of the order of Shakespeare, above that of Racine – indeed? – yes! He is comprehensive and inclusive like Shakespeare, you are amazed one mind can hold so much, and at the same time incredibly clean in style, on the whole very undecorated. "The author has an unusual imagination, and his book is an excellent buy" – Book World.

Yes, the Watergate hearings took over my whole evenings (they had complete replays on one of the stations).[4] A lot of people in such despair that the Country could get in such a state, but surely we all know it was in a bad way before that: the hearings made me incredibly optimistic in that all those gangsters could be exposed so completely.

Your letter was lovely. Yes I owe the Tanners a letter – and Ander too. The place is full of kittens. There were five born & I drowned two (very difficult even for a nazi like me), and now there are 3 growing & growing & nobody seems to want them.

> Love,
> Thom

1. TG refers to *Mandrakes* (1974), *Songbook* (1973) and *To the Air* (1974).
2. Laurence Binyon (1869–1943), poet, scholar, and curator of Oriental art at the British Museum, translated the *Divine Comedy* into English terza rima. *Inferno* appeared in 1933, *Purgatory* in 1938 and *Paradise* in 1943. Pound, who was friendly with Binyon, recommended his *Inferno* in the essay 'Hell' (1934).
3. The Temple Classics Dante was a multi-volume pocket edition of Dante's works published by J. M. Dent in the first few years of the twentieth century and frequently reprinted thereafter. The Italian text is accompanied by an elegant English crib, which can help a reader with almost no Italian to follow the original. Both Eliot and Pound first read Dante in this edition.
4. The Senate Watergate hearings were broadcast on live television from 17 May to 7 August 1973.

TO *Oliver Sacks*   ALS Sacks Foundation
Tuesday 2 October 1973

> 1216 Cole Street,
> San Francisco,
> CA 94117
>
> 2 Oct 73

Dear Oliver,

It is so long since I received your letter, and read, enjoyed, and admired your book (and related article) that I'm not sure where you are now. Well, I'll decide later where to send this. – Awakenings is, anyway, extraordinary. I remember when, some time in the late sixties, you described the kind of book you wanted to write, simultaneously a good scientific book and worth reading as a well-written book, and you have certainly done it here. I admired the Migraine book terrifically,[1] as you know, but there were a few parts difficult of access to someone like me (not most of it, just a few parts), and one can't say that of Awakenings.

I have also been thinking of the Great Diary you used to show me. I found you so talented, but so deficient in one quality – just the most important quality – call it humanity, or sympathy, or something like that. And, frankly, I despaired of your ever becoming a good writer, because I didn't see how one could be taught such a quality. The kind of deficiency I'm talking about showed up most extremely in the Doctor Kindly episode, but all over the place as well. It made for an insularity, a smallness of capacity, even when you were confronted with the whole of America as your subject (when travelling): the ego didn't change much when it moved to the other side of the country, and your deficiency of sympathy made for a limitation to your observation.

What I didn't know was that the growth of sympathies is something frequently delayed till one's thirties. What was deficient in those writings is now the supreme organizer of Awakenings, and wonderfully so. It is literally the organizer of your style, too, and is what enables it to be so inclusive, so receptive, and so varied.

I wonder if you know what happened. Simply working with the patients over so long, or the opening-up helped by acid, or really falling in love with someone (as opposed to being infatuated)? Or all three. Or most likely, your mind would have matured in that way whatever your circumstances.

Anyway, congratulations on a book that I think will be read for a long time and by a large audience. It is something to be very proud of.

I certainly do remember your discourse on Pain. That will be a fine book too.

One small cavil: I wouldn't have minded a bibliography. Not for pedantic reasons, but it can be helpful to know the date when a book was published, for example. & I don't think it makes a work unwieldy.

You would have been amused and have appreciated a certain irony if you could have witnessed me one evening a few months ago, holding forth on your book, positively inspired by some cocaine I'd snorted, giving a brilliantly organized and detailed account of it to a whole table full of people. Irony because of the inclusion of the Freud passage at the end of your book.

I just heard about Auden's death yesterday. It must be particularly saddening to you as a personal friend of his, but it makes a tremendous gap for all of us. Probably he was, apart from Shakespeare, the poet who most

deeply influenced me, who made it seem most possible for me to write myself.
I don't believe he liked me very much, or so I'm told, but that doesn't matter
any more than if I were to find that Keats didn't like me.

   [. . .]

        Love,

               Thom

1. Sacks, *Migraine: The Evolution of a Common Disorder* (1970).

1974

TO *Tony White*   ALS Tulsa
Wednesday 27 February 1974

> 1216 Cole St.,
> San Francisco,
> Calif. 94117,
> USA
>
> 27 Feb 74

Dear Tony,

I needn't feel quite as guilty as usual, because I hope I'll be seeing you in a month or two. Things sound awful in England, though people (e.g. Sheila) keep writing "it isn't so bad as it sounds." But I'll float in, with my American dollars, and judge all <u>that</u> for myself. Not that I have that many dollars now – we eat meat only about four times a week now, and I've taken up washing & ironing my shirts. Ironing isn't nearly so bad as it used to be when shirts didn't open all the way down the front – and as for vegetarian cooking, I've found out that real Indian cooking is far out. By real, I mean so real that you don't use curry powder but some of its ingredients!

I can't tell you what a good time you gave Mike and Bill. They sent you a letter that went surface mail, so you may not have got it yet. Enclosed was a small pamphlet Bill and I did together, my part of it quite trivial. I'll make sure that you get a copy of the Baskin book (which I don't have yet) and another rather nice thing that came out here, thus completing your Gunn Poetry Kit for the Winter of 74. Thank you for your kind words about the Statue of Liberty.[1] I was afraid it might be obscure. So I've finally written a political poem! I have one or two other things you won't have seen, but will bring them with me.

I have invented a new form. Really. It is based on iambic lines that rhyme, but it can be broken up anywhere as much or as little as one wants. Difficult to explain, but you'll see what I mean in a longish poem I write. The advantage is, that one can move from free verse effects to metrical effects in the same poem without breaking up the form and seeming sloppy.[2]

You may know Dylan toured the country. We were lucky enough to get to one of the two concerts he did in the area. It was quite simply the best concert I'd ever been to. One beautiful thing is that he could sing the "protest songs" of ten years ago and didn't need to change a thing, they seemed just as apt now. The times they are a changing, <u>still</u>. And boy, what a beautiful poet he is.

> e.g.   His clothes are dirty but his hands are clean,
> And you're the best thing that he's ever seen.   (Lay Lady Lay)

or –

> The beggar who is rapping on your door
> Is standing in the clothes that you once wore.
> (Goodbye Baby Blue[3])

I did a little trip down to Los Angeles, c/o the BBC, who made a 10 minute movie of me reading on Malibu Beach against a slightly improbable background of handsome teenage surfers.[4] I stayed in the hotel where the Lawrences had stayed in the 1920s! Spent a few hours with Isherwood, for the first time in years. He must be seventy but he has never lost his youth. Unlike Auden who could never remember what it was like, I suspect, after about 1940.

Also spent a few days at Oklahoma University, which was interesting. No one can say poets don't get a chance to travel!

San Francisco continues absolutely outrageous. Imagine a huge old doss-home converted into a "bath house", and you go in there especially on a Saturday night and there are at least 300 men in towels, all so laid back on drugs they can hardly stagger. And on holiday weekends, they are served "mescalin punch".[5] I mean the Satyricon isn't in the running. One would call it all decadent if it wasn't that people did it all with such a hearty enjoyment. (Hearty = healthy, apparently?)

I'll be doing another Mermaid [Theatre] reading, and also one at the Cambridge English Club. The latter partly because when I was President of it I always used to wonder if one day <u>I</u> would be coming back to give a poetry reading. Dreams of Glory fulfilled!

I haven't got my ticket yet, but I think I'll fly to England on April 17, and return to America on June 20. Of course there will be Snodland, Sittingbourne, & the Anders. I certainly <u>would</u> be glad of a place to stay in London, as you say, though it would probably be for only half the time I'm in England. But really I can't squeeze you out of your own places. It's not like you staying here, we had plenty of rooms at Filbert Street and we have even more on Cole Street. What I would be happy to do would be to sleep in a sleeping bag on your floor for the first week, and not interfere with you when you are working during the day.

What I'd love to do would be to go to Paris for a few days at the end of my stay. I'll be doing the Mermaid reading on June 9th, & they were so repentant at not having paid me for reading before that they are paying me £50 this time. So I was wondering if you'd be interested in/able to do a little French jaunt with me, if I could pay the fare and share some of the expenses. (Think of it as rent paid for use of your floor.) Do think about it anyway. Can you believe it is 20 years since I was last in Paris?

All Love, my Lord,

and love from Mike, Bill, & Don

Thom

I'm sure you know how tremendously I look forward to seeing you.

1. 'Iron Landscapes (and the Statue of Liberty)' (*CP* 231–2).
2. See 'The Bath House' (*CP* 242–6), the final part of 'The Geysers'.
3. Correctly titled 'It's All Over Now, Baby Blue'.
4. This 'movie' was broadcast as part of *2nd House* on BBC Two in January 1975.
5. A reference to the Barracks bathhouse.

TO *Tony White*   ALS *Tulsa*
Wednesday 17 July 1974

1216 Cole St.,
San Francisco,
Calif. 94117,
USA

17 July 74

Dear Tony,

I am sitting in the garden in my jacket. It is the one overcast day of the last 2 weeks, but the cockroach exterminator is here, squirting the whole house, & I hate the smell of his squirt. The garden, however, is splendid, jubilant, towering & overgrown, with tunnels for cats and even tunnels for humans. I really like big flowers, it seems, and there are lots of hollyhocks & delphiniums besides more medium-sized things that are all in flower too.

Well, I won't thank you again for all your kindness & generosity. It was endless, and made my three months. I love your room. Do I rightly picture you in it at the moment, he suggested coyly, or are you already on the way to Ireland?

As I told you, I did get a perm, in which I take much rather conceited pleasure, tossing my greying curls at the whole world. I thought I would arrive in San Francisco a leader of fashion, but 2 days after I got back there was a whole page devoted to men's perms in the women's section of the newspaper, so I find I'm Old Hat again.

[. . .]

I had an incredible time in New York. I spent a lot of time with a young guy who works as a bouncer[1] – the second night I was there, he took me to an immense party in a warehouse, dancing upstairs and an orgy downstairs in what seemed like a combination of crypt & catacombs – i.e. a huge cellary area with lots of strange little annexes and sidetrips, dripping ceilings, enclosures, passages, etc. I was on acid, so it seemed even more exotic.

[. . .]

I'm writing a bit – or at any rate playing around with the notes I took in England, dunno with what result. I suggested to Charles that I do a Selected Beddoes[2] – do you know him, I've always rather liked him. [. . .]

Love

X X X X   Thom

P.S. That was a great time in Paris, wasn't it?

---

1. Allan Noseworthy III (1950–84). See Glossary of Names.
2. TG did not make a selection of Thomas Lovell Beddoes. His letter to Monteith (8 July 1974) can be found in the Faber Archive.

TO *Tony and Marcia Tanner*   ALS (aerogramme) King's

Tuesday 30 July 1974

1216 Cole St.,
San Francisco,
Calif. 94117,
USA

30 July 74

Dear Tanners,

I've been meaning to write before, and suppose it's not too long till you actually get to California – about a month or so, perhaps? It'll be nice having you here for a good long time instead of having to see each other for such brief spells that one feels it has to be an occasion and one relaxes less easily. That

305

was a bit true of me, anyway, just about the whole time I was in England: it would have been better if I'd stayed longer and drawn things out more.

It was good in the pub after the reading, wasn't it? – Charles Monteith meeting my aunts (no that was in the greenroom) meeting Tanner & White meeting a rather dim American I knew at Stanford – astonishing juxtapositions. This Is Your Life. Whitey & I had a magnificent time in Paris, drinking constantly, eating fabulously, enjoying the chestnut trees, going to an extraordinary park I'd never even heard of called Buttes-Chaumont, meeting his aunt & uncle. I even finally started to like the Tour Eiffel when I saw it surrounded by fog one day.

Then we returned & Tony went North to work & there was the Monteith party, where a prodigious amount of wine was consumed, & Monteith took eight of us to a very expensive meal afterwards. At the party I was even nice to E. Lucie-Smith.

Then the next day I got a perm, so I now look like someone who has put his finger in a light-socket.

Then I went to New York for two weeks, where I really burned the candle at the middle as well as both ends. I almost fell in love, and New York in the spring was at its best. Rockefeller has given them the most savage drug laws in the whole country, but you can still get just about any drug you want as easily as a couple of years ago. I dropped some acid for the Gay Rights March, which I went on more because it seemed to me cowardice if I didn't than from real enthusiasm. But it had good explicit political purposes – the Gay Rights bill still hasn't been passed in NY – and I must say I did feel rather proud of the variety and sweetnaturedness of the people in the march. I'd never done much walking on acid before, and it was all the way from the West Village to Sheep Meadows in Central Park. Round about 30th Street I wondered would I ever make it, but the general enthusiasm carried me along. I believe there were 40,000 on the march.

Then came back here and have had a most delightful month. The garden is immense, towering and overgrown and beautiful, things are flowering I don't even remember planting. I'm working on several poems. Mike & Bill are working so hard I'm doing most of the cooking. Bill's childhood friend who lives in Paris is staying here for a couple of weeks, & I must say he is a total sweetheart. I have developed the habit of drinking sweet vermouth before dinner, which with wine during dinner & beer after doesn't help the reducing program any. (What reducing program?)

[. . .]

The impeachment thing is great fun, and I'm especially pleased that that shit [John] Connally turns out to be a bribe taker. The law & order people all turn out to be hypocrites. Incredible. I at least thought they were sincere.

Don I haven't seen yet. He is off in New Orleans on a death watch, as he calls it, nursing Clay Shaw till he dies of the big C.[1] (John Wayne called it that: 'How I licked the big C.')

Went to a fabulous Eric Clapton concert here.

I've given up all attempts at autobiography. I'm far too unsure of what I am to be able to write its history.

Some men have been installing new gas mains in front of the house for some weeks, some of the work even took place in the garage. Why is it that all of them are good-humored, friendly, & courteous, whereas hardly any of the numerous bureaucrats I have to deal with can even bother to be polite? That's not a sentimental observation, I give my word.

How did Marcia do in the exam? Not that, I assure you, I will think one whit worse of her if she didn't pass. I think I must rewrite Jack Straw's Castle.[2] My cat Lucie is pregnant again: La Vendée looms for some of those kittens.

Love

X X X X X X X X X X X   Th.

1. For Shaw, see TG to Tanner, 3 August 1972, n. 1, above.
2. For a note on the different versions of 'Jack Straw's Castle', see *SP* (242–5).

TO *Tony Tanner*   TLS King's

Tuesday 29 October 1974

1216 Cole Street,
San Francisco,
CA 94117

29 Oct 74

Dear Tony,

You asked me for a list, and I am sincerely sitting down to write one, even though I have three beers under my belt. Oh well, if this letter looks ridiculous tomorrow, I can always write another.

I have to admit, though, that I find it too difficult to give you an interesting list that is not unfair or at least biased. And my bias seems, rather obviously, to be toward the West and toward people I know.

So let me first list a few poets that others would list and I wouldn't: Galway Kinnell, James Wright, Denise Levertov (since about 1968, anyway), Robert

Bly, William Stafford, and W.S. Merwin. I find these poets efficient but boring. They each write a particular kind of poetry efficiently and conscientiously, but they have nothing much to say to me (this could well be my limitation), and I find little to recommend about them. One thing I am sure of, they are not giants like Eliot or Williams, who were important to you even if they had nothing to say to you personally. But then that could be true of all the people who follow on my list.

Then there's another list, of the bad but interesting. For example Diane di Prima (try Revolutionary Letters), Ginsberg (if you haven't read Planet News you shd read the following poems in it, 'Wales Visitation' and 'Who to be Kind to'), and Kenneth Fields, a rather unpleasant man who teaches at Stanford who is trying to get away from the Winters influence – in what I think is an interesting way, to be traced in two books The Other Walker and Sunbelly. He has tremendous verbal gifts, at least, and that's the one real prerequisite for a poet. (There's also a man called N. Scott Momaday, who has written a short and excellent book, Angle of Geese: he's really a prose writer (and has won a Pulitzer or sumpn), and this is his first and last book of poetry.)

Here's the list.

Snyder you've already read, but he's worth rereading in Riprap, Myths and Texts, and The Back Country. I don't like much [of] what comes after, except the incredibly beautiful and sexy 'Song of the Taste' (from Regarding Wave). Has started to take himself too seriously, and has an enlarged ego, I suspect, from thinking that since he's a Zen priest he's got rid of all those problems. Hope I'm wrong.

Creeley. Came round to him all over again since I went to a wonderful reading of his last year. You could reread For Love again, and move anywhere into his other books from that. But not his prose, that is immensely BORING.

A couple of older ones:

You must read Winters' Collected Earlier Poems, avoid the crotchety introduction at least until you have read the book, but the poetry is fantastic, almost as good as Williams at the time (the twenties), but very different, self-destructive, horribly and dangerously intense.

Robert Duncan: the best way to get into his work, especially since he 'over-publishes' (hate that word so why do I use it?) is to start with the fairly accessible book The Opening of the Field. Then read his prose book The Truth and Life of Myth. (This last might blow your mind more than anything else on this list). As Rexroth said, his subject is love.

A couple around my age:

Michael McClure: I knew him and liked him, then was impatient of his poetry, then didn't think about him for years, then really liked a book that came out in 1970, Star, and an incredible and totally unknown novel The Adept – narcissistic but completely imaginative (so that the narcissism got drowned in imagination) – which are making me go back to his earlier and difficult work.

Edward Dorn: of course you have read, haven't we all, The North Atlantic Turbine and Geography, which are great, nothing really worth reading before these, but try these two – both stunning: By the Sound (Frontier Press), as lovely prose as I have ever read (actually based on something very early, I believe); and (recent, disguised as comic book, published by Turtle Island, certainly available from Kepler's) Recollections of Gran Apacheria – clean and murderous.

Younger:

James Scully, his second book, Avenue of the Americas, a very fine book, very sensitive to the intermittences and changes inside the skull. His first book not too good.

Rod Taylor you have.

Belle Randall you have. She didn't get much reviewed, but seems to be getting a bit of an underground following.

Andrei Codrescu, a Romanian who forfeited his native language to write in American (or so he told me), his License to Carry a Gun and History of the Growth of Heaven. He is mebbe a bit too consciously amoral (tho not pretentiously so) and seems unable to work in long – or even medium-length – forms. But he's exciting.

Then I just listened to Orson Welles' War of the Worlds. I can understand how it flipped them out in 1939!!! I almost believed it myself!!!! Most ALARMING!!!!!!! It was enough for me to grab the cats & the pots of basil in my arms & hide in the store room!!!!!!!!!! GOD!!!!!!!!!! FRITENING STUFF!!!!!!!!!!!!!! SO SEND OUT YOUR MESSENGERS FOR ALL THESE BOOKS OR THE MARTIANS WILL END HUMAN CULTURE FOR EVER.

It is probably up to you alone to continue the grand tradition of Judaeo-Christian from Homer to Jack Straw's Castle. Quick, Teetee, preserve Homer & Bill & Alighieri, & the others, and ME. Oh dear I'd better go to bed. (I now have 7 beers under my belt.) Obviously. Maybe you'd better cross out Shakespeare, so no one will ever know how much better he was than me, & I can reign undisturbed. That wd be the act of a loyal friend. You never knew him, after all. (besoffen)

Next morning: oh dear.
 Love,

 Thom

TO *Tony White*   TLS Tulsa
Thursday 12 December 1974

1216 Cole St., San Francisco,
Calif. 94117, USA

12 Dec 74

Dear Tony,

It's an incredible time since I received your letter, so long in fact that I don't yet dare turn it up, otherwise I will feel so sick with guilt I may not be able to start this. [. . .]

Meanwhile Tony came over and had quite a violent relapse. Marcia also came over, but she hasn't yet deigned to even say hello on the phone, so I have no idea where SHE's at. But TT saw a good head-doctor, stopped seeing him, had a relapse, and finally I bullied him into going to see him regularly. I mean, when you live in the style that the Tanners do, I'm not going to take seriously that he can't afford to see a good shrink when he needs one that badly. Got my pronouns a bit mixed up, but you see what I mean. Actually, that Tanner has a way of being lovable in the midst of misfortunes that in anyone else would be merely boring.

So as far as I know, he's OK in what must be a slightly tentative way. I have had a wonderful six months, unlike the rest of the world: I'm not completely sure why, either. There has been the usual share of disasters, of which more later, but I've had a peculiar sense of having got it together at bottom, as if my understandings of my own contradictions were getting a little greater. Or maybe it's a trust in my own luck. Not altogether sure what I'm speaking about, but in any case it's been my best time since 1968 – and we know what year that was, don't we folks: that was ACID YEAR. All this, anyway, though I was becoming (like many another this year) strikingly impoverished. At one point, I had some readings to do in the East, of which you obtained me one, and couldn't afford to get to them without borrowing from Mike, Tanner, and even Bill. Then one day, when I had $10 in my bank account, I was cleaning out a chest of drawers, and came to this drawer full of old notebooks and shit from "my beginnings" up till about 1967. I had known it was all there, and it all gave me a bored constipated feeling:

I found myself thinking I might as well throw it all away, as it had nothing to do with me any longer and was just an irritant. Then this thought coupled with the thought that I could get MONEY for it if I went to the right place. So the University of Maryland now has it all and gave me $6000 for it, some this year, some next, and some the year after next. I suddenly realized that though I find what most people do with manuscripts most of the time absolutely pointless and silly, I absolutely don't care about it compared with the pleasure of having lots of money! Thus principles vanish, but few can have vanished quite as quickly.

I've been doing quite a deal of writing – I did in the autumn, anyway, and I will send you some of it when Christmas is over. Can't stand the idea of waiting in all those queues at the post office to see what the postage wd be on a fat envelope. – And I've been reading Whitman with great pleasure, more than ever before. It was you that got me to want to read or reread him. There is some of him that I just can't take, like Starting from Paumanok – I just can't help thinking that all the feelings in this poem were achieved at the expense of an awful lot of dead Indians (probably DHL said this first of all), but things like the poem about the little noiseless patient spider, The Sleepers, Spontaneous Me, Of the Terrible Doubt of Appearances, are so good. It is a strange experience reading him, because he is so honest about his feelings that he leaves himself constantly vulnerable. You read a line or two and think – that's a bit silly; you read a little more and think – that's even sillier; then you read a line that is brilliant in itself and also in retrospect makes sense of the lines coming before it. My favorite line – I was sitting on the lavatory at the time I read it and I positively laughed with pleasure it was so good – was 'If you want me again look for me under your boot-soles.' – from the last section of Song of Myself. It is even wonderful that that there is no comma after again.

The only prose book I've read since I came back from England is The Old Wives' Tale. (It looks as good as it did in 1965.) Whether that is a sign of cosmic serenity or of mere senility I don't know.

HOT FLASH. Got a new perm today, my third, actually just a touching up of the last one. I have become very sophisticated since I last saw you, and now have a mass of tight curls. None of that beginner's loose stuff for me any more, I'm doing a real Shirley Temple trip.

[. . .]

Last weekend, Mike and Bill were driving home from a bar, full of a drug called PCP (did you have that while you were here? it's a perfectly nice drug, but assuredly not one to drive on) and they drove the car into a light pole. Bill went mildly into the windshield, Mike went practically through. They got a lift home (it was only a few blocks away), where I was on a totally different drug, having a fine time with a guy I'd just met called Gary. Suddenly from my bedroom I heard Bill giving crazy screams while coming up the stairs, and came out and there was him and there was Mike, and Mike looked like a picture of Jesus in the crown of thorns done by a particularly literal and sadistic Meister of painting in medieval Germany. Blood pouring from his face and head. Well, everybody behaved perfectly: our friends and neighbors upstairs drove Mike to an emergency first aid place close by; Gary drove Bill and me back to the ruined car, and he also got hold of a tow truck service on the phone before we left; and even the cops were completely nice, choosing not to notice that Bill was so stoned. (Had a beer or two, did you, they remarked, and that was all.) Well, the next day Mike went to hospital, and apparently had been in great danger that night of choking on a blood clot, and spent the last three days there under observation. He came out today, and apparently both he and Bill are fine (though they sleep a lot: effects of shock, apparently) and the only scars they will show will possibly be one by M's eyebrow and one on B's chin, like very polite duelling scars and rather romantic in a genteel sort of way.

I went East some time ago, as I said above, and did a reading in Washington, and stayed in NY City during which I did a reading at Bard. Washington was, well, interesting. I'd never been there before, and I was only there two days, during much of which I went gaping around a lot of lousy monumental art like the Supreme Court and the Library of Congress. But that place where they all meet – what on earth is it called, Congress I guess, is really pretty nice. – It suddenly strikes me that you probably saw all of this for yourself when you were here. Anyway, it was all very pleasant, a very unseasonable November sunshine made it seem like a campus between terms, and I really had no time to explore the slums . . .

Bard College was odd. The train trip there was sensational. I'd never realized that landscape like that existed in the East – in fact there was a whole school of 19th century painters called after the Hudson River, which the railway track runs along all the way from NY City. And I can understand why, it is like Victorian illustrations to the Bible, rays due to sun and rain dashing up and down from the dramatic clouds to the dramatic hills, very nice indeed. But in some ways I feel rather glad you were spared the boredom of Bard itself. Like almost every private college I've been to in this country, everybody there seemed a touch complacent, "we are special, after all." Solely on the basis of brief visits, giving poetry readings, I think I prefer State Colleges, or even (lowest of the low) Junior Colleges (only two years to get a degree) where they are much more unsure of themselves and much more

312

interesting. That's why I can't stand Stanford nowadays and still like sloppy outrageous Berkeley (where I'm teaching next term, by the way).

The more beer I consume, the more parentheses, eh?

I did have a fantastic time in New York itself, though. I was staying with this 24 yr old bar tender (sound familiar?),[1] who I finally realized had such good impulses that the only person in the world I could compare him to was Bryan. I mean, flighty, highly strung, at times silly, but so good in every important sense. I said to him once, and it turned out I was right, I bet no one has ever betrayed you, has he? – because his sensitivity to people was so invariably correct that I can't imagine him ever in a position where anything like that cd occur. I'm not in love with him, let me add, though I love him a lot. On the other hand, I think I am in love with his Newfoundland, who grew to like me so much that when I came in would give a bark of greeting that was a kind of yodel of joy (I took her for her walks quite a bit, that explains that).[2]

Mike & Bill send their scarred love.

I'll send you some poems after Xmas.

> Love,
>
> Shirley

1. See TG to White, 17 July 1974, above.
2. See 'Yoko' (*CP* 299–300).

1975

Friday 28 February 1975

1216 Cole Street,
San Francisco,
Calif. 94117

28 Feb 75

Dear John Haffenden,

Thank you for your letter. I'll tell you what I remember, but I suppose this letter will be fairly short, since I was never really close to John Berryman, though we certainly had some good times together. I suspect that Tony Tanner saw a good deal more of him, since he (TT) actually lived in Berkeley, whereas I lived in Oakland.

I don't quite know how it was set up, but I first met him for lunch in Berkeley with Carolyn Kizer. I brought along Tanner, partly for protection I think. I didn't know what I was in for with Berryman, and I've never been good at meeting other poets. I had first met Carolyn only very recently, possibly as recently as the day before. She assumed that Tanner was my boy-friend, I gather; I think Berryman was too sensible to do so: if he did so, he was quickly disabused, since he was to meet the woman Tanner was going around with (& later to marry) very soon after. I remember only two things we talked about. His contempt for certain of the critics who admired him, and his admiration for Elizabeth Bishop's poetry. I knew her poetry very little: that evening he brought me a copy of her 'Roosters' along with my copy of the new Dream Song.

Anyway, Berryman had been asked to Berkeley to teach for the Speech Department, and he felt (I don't know whether rightly) that they had been keeping him to themselves, and not introducing him to people from other departments. And apparently we made him feel very up during that lunch, so Tony and I asked him to come to some movies that evening – we had already decided to go to them and he seemed so lonely we thought he might enjoy them. We were going to meet at a cheap restaurant on Telegraph Avenue called Robbie's. I think he turned up late, and we were already eating, but in any case he was already drunk when he arrived, and he didn't eat, but just went on drinking (it was possible to get beer there). He was very excited, because he had just written the (later rejected) Dream Song you mention, and arrived with a copy for each of us.[2] (It's not too good, and I've always been rather relieved that he didn't publish it.) Anyway, it was all very pleasant, we were all three in high spirits, and then we went across the street to see a double bill of 'I Vitelloni' and 'The Wild One'. Berryman laughed extremely loud at odd moments, not always coinciding with the rest of the audience. He also talked rather loud, and irritated some of the audience. Later he fell into a loudly snoring sleep. It was a loud evening.

There are only three other occasions I remember meeting him, – I didn't like parties too much, especially faculty parties, but I must have run into him a great deal on campus. The first of these occasions was at a poetry reading set up by the Architecture Dept for an Arts Festival they held every year. The poets to read were all teaching on campus, Berryman, Louis Simpson, and me. (Maybe there were others?) Unfortunately somebody had forgotten to advertise the reading, and only about fifteen people turned up. Louis and I decided to make the best of it, but Berryman was in a very bad mood. He had been ill, he told me, of some complaint he had picked up many years before in the Orient. I said I hoped he was better, and I must have asked him what the illness was like. 'Can you imagine,' he said, 'lying in bed unable to move a muscle, for hours on end, not even able to move enough to reach the bottle of medicine standing on the table inches away from you? That's what it's like.' If the tone sounds a bit rhetorical here, then I'm being true to my memory. Incidentally, he seemed drunk this time also, but completely in control. When his turn came to read, he first of all addressed the audience, berating them for being so few. 'Harvard of the West! Harvard of the West!' he said scornfully (of Berkeley). He then read divinely: I think it was the first time that I had heard him read, and it was only from the time of this reading that I began to understand the tone of his poetry.

Then I remember another reading, this one set up by an ex-student of his, Hank Coulette, at Los Angeles State College. Hank was teaching there, and it was to be their first poetry reading ever. The readers were Berryman, Phil Levine, and me. (Again, there may have been other poets.) Each of us was introduced by somebody different, thus I was introduced by Christopher Isherwood, and very flattering that was, I must say. (I already knew CI, and he was teaching that year at LA State.) The audience was very unsophisticated, and insisted on clapping between each poem. (They are now a wonderful, and very experienced audience, one it is a great pleasure to read to – largely due to Hank's influence, I believe.) Berryman again read wonderfully (I suspect he always did.) Later he, Hank, Phil, Christopher and I went to drink at a dark unwindowed cocktail lounge right off that central square in Los Angeles, where the down-&-outs and hustlers hang around. (I remember the darkness because it was so sunny outside.) Was it there, I wonder, in front of Berryman, or on some later occasion that Hank did his uncannily accurate imitation of a Berryman reading? Some time later, maybe on the same day, Christopher told me emphatically how very charming he found Berryman. And he was, that day, he was as good as he had been at that first lunch meeting, it was total charm.[3]

A year or two later, I met him, very briefly at the ceremonies for the National Institute of Arts and Letters. He was receiving a (gold?) medal, which was very prestigious; I was one of several recipients of awards of money. (I believe this was 1963 or 4.) He had grown his famous beard since I previously saw him, and the change was remarkable. (It was before the rest of us grew our beards.) We didn't have time to say much to each other, but I do remember that when I congratulated him on his medal he pointed out in a slightly resentful tone that my award carried more money!

Well, those are the memories. He was always very nice to me indeed, though I believe he didn't have any very high opinion of my poetry. I don't know if the oriental illness was real or another name for alcoholism. (You must know the answer to this.) I always wonder whether he knew that there are two roads in Berkeley right next to each other, one called Henry and the other called Berryman.

Hope this isn't too confused. I admire you for writing a biography, it must be unbelievably complicated squaring people's accounts with each other and then squaring them with your admiration for Berryman.

Best wishes,

Thom Gunn

1. John Haffenden (1945–), literary critic and editor, wrote Berryman's biography: *The Life of John Berryman* (1982)
2. For an extract from the 'Dream Song', see TG to Wilmer, 9 January 1999, below.
3. See Philip Levine, 'A Day in May: Los Angeles, 1960', *Georgia Review* 59, no. 1 (Spring 2005), 60–75.

Wednesday 18 June 1975

> 1216 Cole St.,
> San Francisco,
> Calif. 94117, USA
>
> 18 June 75

Dear Charlotte & Willie,

It's only a little more than a year ago that I was staying with you. That was a lovely day when you both took me out to the beaches near Land's End. None of the thrift seeds I brought back seem to have done anything. Maybe this is an unthrifty country.

I have lots of giant flowers, though – delphiniums and foxgloves all over the place and soon the red-hot pokers and hollyhocks will be flowering. I have a mental picture of myself as being worm-size and reading books in a huge forest of flowers.

Here are some stamps, if you want them. Most of them are American, but there are a few interesting oddities from elsewhere.

My cat Lucy had her spring litter – two blond (beige?), one marmalade, one grey, and one a tortoiseshell like herself. I gave all but the last away, and rather wanted to keep the tortoiseshell – I got very attached to her and called her Dumpling – but I have three adult cats already so I found a wealthy owner for her.

Meanwhile the father of the next litter is pure white. Should have some very interesting results. (Happened yesterday.)

Poor Billy, one of the people who lives with me, has hepatitis – which I had about twelve years ago. He went bright yellow all over, including his eyes. He is much better now, but still has to stay in bed most of the time, though we got him a nice reclining deck chair to sit in the garden, which he does when the fog gives way to sunshine.

His name is not Poor Billy, but Bill. But he's Poor Billy for the time being.

I hope you are up to your usual exciting activities. Don't get thrown over a cliff by any high-spirited horses, Ms. Gunn. Don't get swallowed by any sea-serpents, Mr. Gunn. Give all your friends and relatives a friendly punch from me and tell them to take a swim, as it is the best exercise known to the world, and very cheering besides.

> Love,
>
> Thom

TO *Tony White*   TLS Tulsa
Saturday 28 June 1975

1216 Cole Street,
San Francisco, Calif. 94117

28 June 75

Dear Tony,

I've taken three months or more to answer your lovely long letter, and realize in rereading it what a time I've taken since Sheila and John H and Bryan, who all overlapped, have been gone such a long while. I'm sure you've had detailed accounts from them of all that went on when they were here. It was lovely for us, and I think they had a good time too. JH of course had his terrible trip – we always like to bring at least one day of chaos to the heads of our guests – but he said that SF was an even more attractive city than Prague, which I thought was a charming compliment.

The Tanners continue exuberantly apart, and it does look as if Marsh will continue here. They both are very happy: TT is writing a book he is excited by, on adultery in the Victorian novel, French as well as English,[1] is taking German lessons, bounces with good health, and was so relaxed last time we saw him that I found him literally handsome (physically, I mean) for the first time in my life. I gather, from Marsh, that he is expecting Nadia to join him by and by.[2] The only regret I have is that he comes up very seldom indeed – last saw him down at his place in fact. I don't <u>think</u> it is that he likes us less – I certainly hope not, but suspect that he may associate this house with his dreadful arrival and semi-breakdown of last fall. Boy, that was worrying. He is exuberant now, as I say, but even the extent of his exuberance is a touch suspect: it is such an extreme contrast to the way he was before.

[. . .]

At one point last fall he said that the only time he was happy was when he was swimming, and visualised an ideal world as being a vast swimming pool. I myself do a bit of swimming (originally for that pinched nerve, which now gives me no trouble) and this month when I had about two weeks of acute depression began to agree with him. The depression was most puzzling, it seemed to be caused by nothing at all, I had every reason to be happy but felt rotten. Then, the same morning I had posted the ms for my next book of poems to Charles, I suddenly realised that <u>that</u> was the cause of it.[3] I had been doing minor revisions to poems, and deciding on the order they should take – one would think both satisfying and easy work, giving a feeling of achievement without involving any real labour, but I suppose it gave me the sense of disposing of five years of my life, and what next? A silly way to feel, and one I rather disapprove of, but one doesn't feel the way one does for very good reasons. But I've got over that, and am back to my usual bland and characterless self.

You should have got a book of great opulence written by me and published by Olwyn. – At least, she said she'd send you a copy. All the ten poems in it were written about three or four years ago. (Though you may recognize half of one rather obscure poem as being later used as a section of Jack Straw.⁴) Thank you very kindly for you remarks about that poem, by the way, and also for your help with Yoko. I followed your advice with the latter, and now it reads much better. You have always been so helpful with my poems – nobody else has had the practical insights you have had into what I was doing over the last twenty years, and sometimes I wonder what I would have done without your good sense and penetration to get me out of obscurities and sillinesses. I don't know whether I've ever thanked you adequately for your help. Well, believe me, old thing, it has meant everything to me. And of course you have always been "inspirational" as well.

[. . .]

Bill has been having hepatitis for the last four weeks – I have never seen anybody so yellow – but we nursed him at home (we're very experienced in the whole field of hepatitis you know) and he is far better, on his feet again, though the doctor says he must spend most of the next two weeks resting. We got a marvellous reclining outdoor chair for him in the garden, so his yellowness has merged into an impressive tan. Somewhere about a month before this, he and Mike resolved their worst difficulties I think for good, deciding to go on living together but to have a bit more independence in their sexual lives. Thank god for such sensible and unhistrionic people, who can place the importance of continuing a relationship over the more dramatic and picturesque alternatives. Boy, this letter is full of pithy apothegms, isn't it. Or do I mean aphorisms. Sententiae, let us say.

[. . .]

Bryan came for a few days, as I said. If anything, he improves with the years. I really think that he is the most practical lover of humanity I have ever known. So incredibly generous in spirit, and yet so thoroughly sharp and perceptive.

Got a good letter from Don. He should be back in August. I haven't even seen him in eighteen months. He sounds, as they used to say last year, mellowed out. He said, very sweetly, that he often thinks about my criticisms of him for being such an absolutist and for making snap judgments about people. I guess I get rather hard on him, but the hardness comes from liking him so much. He also said he hoped Tanner would consent to have a beer with him. I think Tanner will. [. . .] Obviously travel has been good for him. Certainly it can't have been good to stay watching television for two years and hardly leaving his room except to go out and buy food.

[. . .]

I read a strange and for me wonderful book called Lilith by George Macdonald (the same one who wrote At the Back of the North Wind). Have you read it? I don't know if you can take fantasy and that sort of thing. I find this book full of images that really stick in the memory, and keep recurring. It is like nothing else I've ever read. At the same time I can imagine someone finding the book completely impossible, being unconnected with any kind of literal reality. I think you'd like it, though, I don't remember us ever disagreeing violently over any book.

Still haven't read The Magus. I find I read more slowly the older I get.

[. . .]

Just about a year and a month since we were in Paris. That was a lovely little trip.

Maybe see you here <u>next</u> year. Bill just said Ringo is doing a song on television, must go. Did I tell you about Bruce SPRINGSTEEN? 2 records, and the best new singer since – who shall I say? Elton John maybe.

       Love,

          Thom

1. Tanner, *Adultery in the Novel: Contract and Transgression* (1979).
2. Nadia Fusini (1946–), Italian writer, academic, and translator of Virginia Woolf. She married Tanner in 1979.
3. *Jack Straw's Castle* (1976).
4. 'Solus Ipse' was published in *Mandrakes* (1974) and became the eighth section of 'Jack Straw's Castle' (*CP* 274–5).

1976

TO *Tony White*   ALS (postcard[1]) Tulsa
Wednesday 14 January 1976

[1216 Cole St.,
San Francisco,
Calif., 94117]

14 Jan 76

Dear Tony,

I suddenly realized you are about to reach my age, so this is the first birthday card I've ever sent you. A happy year from the Pleiades & all in Cole Street! I think of you snug in your cottage listening to the haystack & roof-leveling wind from the Atlantic. Will write you a letter soon, in answer to your long double-letter. I wonder if Olwyn got that copy of my book Mandrakes to you. Big love

X X X X X X X Thom

1. The postcard shows the Pleiades star cluster, also known as the Seven Sisters.

TO *Ander & Margaret Gunn*   ALS Ander Gunn
Monday 19 January 1976

1216 Cole St.,
San Francisco,
Calif. 94117

19 Jan 76

Dear Ander and Margaret,

I don't know if you have heard yet, but I got a letter today with some terrible news – Tony [White] is dead.

He broke his leg about a month ago, playing football, and it seems on Jan 10 suddenly had a heart attack and died very soon afterwards. Apparently a blood clot from his leg.[1]

As John Holmstrom said in his letter to me, he was happy to the end, and it is us we have to feel sorry for. His last letters to me were the happiest I had ever had from him. I cannot believe I shall never go round the pubs with him again. He did mean an awful lot to me – as he did to a lot of other people. He made a better thing of his life than almost anyone else I know.

Sorry about the shortness of this letter, but I don't really feel like writing any more.

Much love,

Thom

1. For the circumstances of White's death, see Sam Miller, *Fathers* (2017), 176–9.

TO *Tony Tanner*   TLS King's

Tuesday 27 January 1976

1216 Cole Street,
San Francisco, Calif. 94117

27 Jan 76

Dear Tony,

sorry not to phone, but I am no good on the phone, always sound different from the way I feel, and I also hear from Marcia that it can put one in the red.

I know you heard about Tony's death, as Marcia phoned me the day you wrote her. John Holmstrom had written me a few days earlier, & I'd been debating whether to phone her about it – then I realized it wd be better for her to hear from you, and you would know how to tell her in the best way. As indeed you did.

There's nothing to say about it, is there? Karl Miller wrote – very sweetly – asking me whether I would contribute to what sounded like a symposium of tributes to be published in the Review. Tony would have hated it, but I figured that if it would help some of his friends deal with their grief I couldn't be against it. At the same time I declined, having nothing to say except banality: e.g. I would love to have a last beer with him at Becky's.[1] And I have a lot of private remembering to do, as do you, and Holmstrom, and Shiela, and a lot of other people, and I'm not ready for him to disappear into literature just yet. I must say I haven't felt a loss like that since my mother died. It is probably worse for you over there, because you were at least in the habit of seeing him every now and again – that old duke of the dark corners;[2] but in any case the world does seem enormously diminished, and

I still can't altogether believe it. As Holmstrom said: it's us we have to feel sorry for. But there's so much to be glad about, that his death was quick, that we'd been lucky to know him for so long, and that he was such a model man. The two people I know who grew into wisdom have been Mike and Tony – and such a flexible and practical wisdom, none of your distant sage about them. Maybe wiseness would be a better word. And maybe it means something that they both dropped out from the world of applause, the world of actors and directors, to be able to become unique. I know he had his own troubles, and they were in some ways extreme ones, but he faced them so honestly. Who else, after all, have I ever heard admitting that he could not relate satisfactorily to any other human being? And yet continuing to relate in some way or other so that his friendship was one of the things we most valued in the world.

Forgive me, I seem to be writing this letter more for my own sake than for yours. I promise you it will be the last time I do that.

Marsh will have told you that we have been having a sensational drought here, sun every day, just the weather that Europeans imagine obtains in California all the time. I'm teaching at Berkeley this term, as will be my custom till 1995, I think the date is, and I must say last week after I heard of Tony's death it was a big help to be teaching rather than to be staying at home. 'Losing oneself in one's work' – I guess even that's a cliché. I doubt if there's anything new to be said. But perhaps that's ultimately a comfort, in a strange kind of way, that you join everybody's situation at certain times in your life.

[. . .] It would be good to hear from you.

> All love, dear Tony,
> X X X X
> Thom

1. Becky's Dive Bar was a real ale pub in the basement of the Hop Exchange in Southwark, a favourite of White's. See White and Martin Green, *Guide to London Pubs* (1965), 34.
2. An allusion to *Measure for Measure* (4.3.152); see also 'Talbot Road' (*CP* 380–5).

Monday 8 March 1976

1216 Cole Street,
San Francisco,
Calif. 94117

8 March 76

Dear Douglas,

[. . .]

I haven't written before because of the great snow storm of student writing that I've been buried in. But this weekend wasn't so bad – a pause between assignments and I had only late ones to grade. So I went to one of the bars on Saturday night and picked myself a great big redhead from L.A., who was a big success. Then Lucy had six kittens on Sunday – an all-star team as usual.

[. . .]

It's rather cold. Went out in my merry greenwoods jacket and bought a toothbrush and a lot of toilet paper. (I hate to run out of toilet paper.) Really looking forward to the end of term, so that I can actually do some reading of books again, instead of students' stories and poetry. Got my proofs from F & F – oh, I guess I told you that on the phone, didn't I? I think Farrar, Straus, & Giroux, have accepted that wonderfully nelly picture that Bill did, to put on the back cover of their edition.

Haven't written anything in ages, either.

> Sitting at my window watching
> the world go by –
> pretties, uglies,
> old and young,
> sometimes I wonder
> what do I here?
> what is the purpose
> of this pageant,
> this tapestry woven
> with both dark and bright threads,
> where I belong not?

There, now I've written something. Gives me such a feeling of achievement.

Well, I have no rule against a sustained sexual relationship. It just seems that sex seems largely promiscuous since living with Mike I get all the love I need. If that sentence makes sense.

Now I must have a bath!

It was lovely having you here, I'm sure you know that. We all enjoyed having you.

> Love,
>
> Thom

---

1. Douglas Chambers (1939–2020), professor of English at Trinity College, University of Toronto. See Glossary of Names.

TO *Tony Tanner* TLS King's

Tuesday 20 April 1976

> 1216 Cole St.,
> San Francisco,
> Calif. 94117,
> USA
>
> 20 April 76

Dear Tony,

I'd like you to meet my new typewriter. It is made of orange plastic, and is called Contessa. A strange name for a typewriter, but then I suppose no stranger than calling a car a Firebird or a Hustler.

Keep getting postcards from the farthest flung places. You sound in a jolly frame of mind. My thoughts have been much on Cambridge recently, for the simple reason that I've been writing a memoir of it 23 years ago for a volume of similar memoirs.[1] It is interesting trying to be objective about such a romantic period of my life, which in some ways I still feel so close to. I did really grow up then from a mental age of fourteen to my real age of 21 – finally. And wonder how I managed to pack so much in.

Speaking of Cambridge I received a copy of Dick Davis' book, as I'm sure you did.[2] I've been reading it, off and on, for the last three months, and even after I sent him a letter about it in answer to his I find myself going back to it.[3] Obviously I'm wrong about there being no good new young English poets, he is of the very best. He says I influenced him, which much flatters me, but I must say I see no signs of the influence in this collection, since he is like nobody else. Even some of the short poems, like the very last, I still haven't got to the end of. Totally uninfluenced by any Americans, I would say (except possibly Winters and Cunningham), and making something of the English tradition – something new – as people like John Fuller and I suspect Geoffrey Hill are not. They are marking time, he is doing something into which he has got the whole of himself. I'm sure he must have offered it to Faber first. What fools they are to have turned it down when they print dreary shit like Alan Dugan and Richard Murphy. Much as I like Monteith, I don't really think he can distinguish good poetry from bad.

San Francisco has gone through a few interesting changes in the new year. We have a new mayor and a new chief of police. You meet people merrily smoking grass on Market Street, I am told there are twice as many hookers on the Tenderloin, and the mayor has assured a gay bar owner I know that the cops will never touch his establishment. In the Sunday paper the chief of police was calling for gay policemen. And you occasionally see women cops on the beat, looking just like miniatures in complete police uniforms, even in pants. Also there is a city strike, involving the buses, so I have been doing a lot of walking – I figure I walked ten miles one day.

I taught my term at Berkeley, a really good term, with a lot of bright students, and I think in a weird way I taught all the better because of Tony's death. Throwing myself into my work and all that. I saw Mark Schorer once or twice, now retired, looking fantastically old and with a face more mottled than any I have seen since Jack Spicer's a short while before his death. Also Henry [Nash Smith] once – he looked old indeed but he also looked as if he had plenty of years left, bless him.

It is strange having somebody die who is both one of one's closest friends but also someone one doesn't see for a few years at a time. It's not as if Tony ever came to Cole Street. I still keep thinking of things I want to tell him and then having to remember he is dead. I suppose his death will hit me afresh when I next go to England, which I certainly hope is not too soon.

[. . .]

Don remains in New York, where I hear he is working as a waiter. It appears he thinks people have expectations of him in SF which he feels he cannot live up to, I can't say I really understand that attitude but Mike says he does.

Went down to the Davies the other day, and had a lovely time, as I always do with them. I think Donald really loves me. I certainly love him. Not that I'm sure how well we really know each other. He wrote me a poem, and I said 'Don't you think you accept me rather too much at face value?'[4] But I think he just considered I was being modest, which I wasn't. I suppose one adopts an attitude implying strength and charm as a way of coping with the world, but I never thought anybody believed that that was where I began and ended. It's a strange feeling when one feels like crying out, 'But I have conflicts and weakness too, don't you see?'

I went down to the Davies to meet Ezra Pound's daughter, the Princess Rachwelz, I think her name may be spelt.[5] Very odd to see that famous face reduced till it is positively petite, and on a woman's body. Also there was Seamus Heaney, a very warm and sweet-hearted man. Wish I could find his poetry a little more interesting. A friend at Cal, where he is teaching for the term, said he always felt in danger of calling him 'Heinous Sheeney'. Strangely enough my experience has been identical.

Also went to dinner with the Dorns. A regrettable drunken evening. Ed and I were strangely aggressive to each other. I feel the worse about it as he has become one of my favorite poets. His collected poems and the complete Gunslinger came out a few months ago, and I must say they are very impressive. Needless to say, there has been almost no comment on them in print. Older people seem to have trouble reading him, but my 19 year old students have no trouble at all. I suspect that he has a puzzling sense of humor to those who grew up thinking of Robert Lowell as king of the cats.

I've only written prose this year, but I suppose the poetry will come when it feels like it. I read Doctorow's Book of Daniel, which I'm sure you know, and was terribly impressed by it, its daring and scope, and its beautiful clean writing too. I'm having a stab at Henry Miller right now, Big Sur and the Oranges etc. His writing reminds me of Reader's Digest more than anything else. I remember The Colossus at Maroussi as being much better.

I'm off to Chicago for a couple of days, and then the University of Kansas for five days, next week. Don't seem to get so far afield as you. It would be nice to hear from you, what's happening internally and externally, i.e. how are your bowels and your fingernails? Do you yet know if you will be coming to Baltimore next year?[6] I feel very out of touch with you, but that is probably my own fault.

Our love to Nadia, if she's still in Cambridge, or for that matter if she's NOT still in Cambridge, and of course to the divine old Tanner.

     X X X X X

     Thom

---

1. See 'Cambridge in the Fifties' (OP 157–68).
2. Dick Davis (1945–), poet and translator. He was a student of Tanner's at Cambridge, where he met – and became friends with – two of Tanner's other students: Robert Wells and Clive Wilmer.
3. TG reviewed Davis's collection In the Distance (1975); see 'Immersions' (OP 138–41).
4. Davie, 'To Thom Gunn in Los Altos, California' (1977).
5. Mary de Rachewiltz (1925–), Italian-American poet and translator.

6. Tanner had long flirted with the idea of moving to the USA. In 1976 he accepted a professorship at Johns Hopkins University, but, struggling with his mental health, returned to his old position at King's in a matter of months. 'I must say,' TG wrote to his Aunt Barbara in December 1976, 'I feel rather as if I have lost two of my best friends this year, not one' (Private collection).

TO *Douglas Chambers*   TLS Toronto
Wednesday 12 May 1976

1216 Cole St.,
San Francisco,
Calif. 94117, USA

12 May 76

Dear Douglas,

I sure hope this <u>does</u> reach you before you leave. You must have realised by now what a terrible letter-writer I am, but apology is no excuse. [. . .]

As you gathered, my mid Western trip was somewhat overhung by that intestinal flu. And intestinal it was, especially for the first two days: I didn't even dare leave my crummy hotel for the Art Institute for fear more fluid would disgracefully pour out from me down their marble steps. Oh well, their Caravaggio is the most boring I've ever seen anyway.[1] – Kansas was much nicer. Certainly the country around Lawrence, where the U o K is, is gorgeous and green. I saw it in all its detail from the little six-seater plane in which I did the last 40 miles of my trip, so close to it I could see where the tractors had turned in plowing the fields.[2] And I must say they didn't make much demands on me at the university – the easiest job I've ever had – so I had a lot of chances to sleep off the end of my flu, and also read Gunslinger as a whole, and reread Emma, and a couple of science fiction novels by the imaginative Philip K. Dick (he specialises in solipsism). A rather pleasantly varied reading list, don't you think? Hadn't read Emma in years. Boy, doesn't that Jane Austen do it well, though? I mean, the sheer technical problems of the novel are solved with such ease, it is just wonderful to see her actually turning them to advantage. And then she's such a tough humane old thing as well.

Yes, I sympathise with your problems with Robert Duncan. For the first few months I knew him well I couldn't stand the nonstop monolog, brilliant and funny though it is. But I came to terms with it, and am now content to just wait till it's my turn. After all, I have so much more to learn from him than he from me – I think he is the most learned person I know, and can put it to such uses for the imagination. Also there is the Shelleyan amplitude (and repetitiousness) of his published work. Yet the good things are so many that they make the labor worth it. I'd stand by stuff as early as the Medieval Scenes and most of Caesar's Gate, let alone lots of The Opening of the Field, and things here and there from the subsequent two books. The Bending of the Bow is a bit unrewarding, but it does contain My Mother was a Falconress, which is . . . well, not to make pompous remarks like 'one of the best poems published in the 1960's', at least I'll say a wonderful poem. Annoying that subsequent work is uncollected, but there's such good stuff there. And a lovely funny poem added to Caesar's Gate in 1972, On Being Tedious, where he is holding forth to people in a bar, and goes off for a piss, and returns to find they are all gone. <u>And</u> it's raining outside. (In his poem.)

But also I'm aware that he has a special place for me, in that he is in many ways my opposite – prophetic, learned, diffuse, Olsonian, – where I am the opposite of all those. So I have a lot to learn from him, I feed on him in a way that I can't feed on somebody I'm much more like, like Donald Davie, whose work I seem to enjoy only where he is being uncharacteristic.

A wonderful book of poetry to get while you're in England, by the way – In The Distance, by Dick Davis (Anvil Press). It has all the virtues RD lacks. DD seems to me as good as any English poet right now – and I intend to say so in print (Gertrude Stein on receiving compliments, when she was famous but still not taken seriously, would answer 'Thank you, but are you prepared to say that in print?'). But he works by modulation, and most readers only want the big flashy effects of Ted Hughes. Don't mistake me, I like TH too, but I wish there were more who could like both him <u>and</u> Dick Davis. You certainly will, anyway.

You should see the garden now. Boy, talk about big flashy effects! It has never looked so good. I think my ultimate ambition is to include one of every plant. Not much room in my back yard for the Garden of Eden, I admit, but I try.

Mike and Bill effected a friendly separation. Billy now living in the front room. [. . .] Difficult times for both of them, anyway, but I'm trusting in their loving natures and their common sense to bring it all around straight in the end.

A side effect of this is that I now have my desk in Bill's old work room, facing out over the garden, in just about the best place I can imagine for a desk – plenty of vegetable activity to pause over, but almost no human activity to distract.

And all I seem to write now is prose.

[. . .] Have a wonderful summer in England, Old Stud, and write when you get a chance. Mike and Bill send their love. And so do I!

X X X X X

O O O O

Thom

1. TG confused the famous painter (Michelangelo Merisi da) Caravaggio with the artist known as Cecco del Caravaggio; the latter's painting, *Resurrection* (1619–20), is held by the Art Institute of Chicago.
2. See 'Small Plane in Kansas' (*CP* 330).

TO *Michael Schmidt*[1]   TLS (aerogramme) Manchester

Wednesday 16 June 1976

1216 Cole St.,
San Francisco,
Calif. 94117

16 June 76

Dear Michael Schmidt,

Thank you very much for your letter, which I have been thinking about for the last week. I have known about Davis, Wilmer and Wells since the publication of their joint book Shade Mariners about six years ago. And I have liked their work a lot. In fact I just wrote, a few weeks ago, a review of Davis' book, In the Distance, which I think will be in the next issue of Thames Poetry. Much as I like to think of them writing about me – I am very flattered – perhaps it would not be a good idea to ask him. Him reviewing me and me reviewing him within just a few months would look a bit like back scratching.

There are difficulties about the piece on Winters, all of them in my own head. I do want to write something about him one day, partly to get everything straight for my own benefit.[2] But I don't see it very clearly as yet. You speak about your ambivalence with Winters: it could not be greater than my own. There was the personal sweetness of the man, and then the public ferocity, and then again the disastrous tendency to confuse a man's personal worth with his poetic worth. Also though there is much I admire about his criticism – and much I have learned from it – it excludes a tremendous amount of what I consider indispensable poetry. His own poetry was fantastic, I agree, and there seems to me no question at all that he is one of the abidingly good poets of the century. Ultimately I suppose, my problem with him was this, and still is: learned and wise as he was, beautiful poet as he was, he felt a distaste for the multitudinous particularity of life, there was a fastidiousness, ultimately perhaps a fear for all the careless thriving <u>detail</u> of everything, a strong tendency – increasing as he got older – to exclude all that could not be transformed to principle. Perhaps the main reason, after all, why he couldn't stand such an obviously great poet as Whitman, was because Whitman was one of the great enjoyers – and in the end I have to admit that because his sympathies were wider than Winters' his understanding was wider too.

But I'm not sure how to go about writing this for a year or two, if ever. Maybe the way to go about it would be to make it an entirely personal and chronological account. But I'll postpone it for now. [. . .]

Best,

Thom Gunn

1. Michael Schmidt (1947–), poet, novelist, general editor of *PN Review*, and founder and managing director of Carcanet Press. This letter was first published in *Letters to an Editor*, ed. Mark Fisher (1989), 82–3.
2. See 'On a Drying Hill: Yvor Winters' (*SL* 197–212).

TO *John Holmstrom*   TLS Texas
Thursday 17 June 1976

1216 Cole Street,
San Francisco,
Calif. 94117, USA

17 June 76

Dear John,

I am a scandalous letter writer, as you by now know. Anyway, I'm now answering your last three letters, each of which gave me great pleasure. Really. You write beautifully, you enlarge my understanding. That sounds a touch 18th century, but it's what I mean.

I wish you were able to come over this year. It is being a surprisingly difficult year for me. I don't know why I say surprisingly, since it opened the way it did. One of the difficulties for <u>me</u> about T's death has been in the very fact that he isn't here in San Francisco in the same way he never was in San Francisco (except for a couple of months a long time ago). I suddenly realized that this is like the situation in Hardy's The Walk: after his wife's death he goes on his familiar walk just as he did when she was still alive, but then she never accompanied him when she was alive:

> 'What difference then?
> Only that underlying sense
> Of the look of a room on returning thence.'

Maybe my 'room', in this situation, is England. (I need some confirmation of Tony's death from it which I haven't yet had.) Anyway I seem to be leading a very 'indeterminate' life: there is every reason why I should be enjoying it – and I am enjoying every enjoyable thing, as it occurs, but once it has stopped occurring I return to the same hungover unease. I don't know why I had assumed this sadness would be less deep after six months, or would resolve itself: loss is loss, and time often only helps to show how deep and wide it is.

I suppose I am trying to 'understand' something which is not to be understood. In any case I don't feel that my loss is worse than yours or other people's.

The garden, on the other hand, has been nothing less than splendid so far. We eat raspberries daily from the seven bushes, canterbury bells have been a most welcome entrant into the annual Flower Beauty Contest, and I am learning from past mistakes so that this year it isn't left bare in patches when one thing stops flourishing and before something takes its place. This would be a good time of year for you to come, by the way, June – no rain at all, and the chance of good sunshine and a light wind all the time. I was so ashamed that you got drenched almost daily when you were here before, I could have bitten myself.

Haven't written a thing since the beginning of the year. I did write five poems last December, did I send you those – 'Hide and Seek', 'Elegy', 'Adultery', etc.? I assume I did, but let me know if I didn't and I'll send them. – they are in free verse, but I have a strong feeling that I want to move back to metre for a while, to do something concentrated and thoroughly unfashionable. You should get a copy of my next book (all of which you have read) when it comes out in September – if by any chance you don't, let me know.

[. . .]

Yes, I know what you mean about Whitman's rhetoric. But it's a period characteristic no worse than the period characteristics of, say, Wordsworth. What I mean is, the rhetoric is either absent or completely translated into something else in his very best, e.g. section 52 of Song of Myself, and I can take it in Crossing Brooklyn Ferry or The Sleepers – because the main strengths of those poems are so secure (rather as we can take a badly written scene in a Shakespeare play in our stride). Then of course there is the sheer shit like Starting from Paumanok. I've been reading a very good book of essays by John Berryman called The Freedom of the Poet (dunno whether it has yet come out in England). And he has a fine account of WW in it. JB is hardly my favorite poet, in fact I find his early work boring and his later work merely peculiar (though occasionally very funny), but this is one of the best books of criticism I've read in a long time. He's excellent on Shakespeare, for instance, and on Marlowe. Wish he could have written poetry that came up to his standards of what it should be like.

Your account of your own attempts, or self-thwarted attempts, at writing are sinister. Did I tell you how Yvor Winters said to me, 'I never write any poems nowadays because whenever I have an idea for one I can see what's wrong with it before I start work on it.' This seems to me roughly what you do, and I don't think you are giving yourself a chance. Most of the best parts of a poem are not explicit in the preliminary conception, they come up in the actual adventure of writing. I'm referring to the poem of "the ethereal vision after the night of indigestion", the one you didn't write. If it moved you enough, then it is a good subject, and it's worth taking the risk.

[. . .]

I'm finishing this next day. I often write such unsatisfactory letters, though sometimes I can write one that says exactly what I want. This is not in the latter class! [. . .]

The other two send greatest love. As does I.

    X X X X

       Thom

TO *Mike Kitay*   TLS Mike Kitay
Tuesday 28 September 1976

1216 Cole Street,
San Francisco,
Calif. 94117

28 Sep 76

It's the middle afternoon, and I should be off swimmin,
Instead of which I'm at my desk to write New Jersey women.
True, it is pouring rain, it's coming down quite steady.
(I'm sure that rooftops on Nob Hill are rainproof, good and ready.)
I thought in any case I'd tell you all my troubles
And do it all in rhyming which you may prefer in doubles.
The form, which certainly I hope improves the pleasure,
Is obsolete (Elizabethan), known as Poulter's Measure.

The Ambush¹ is the place where both Bill S and I go,
But Billy's rather down because he still has impetigo.
Jack Straw is on the way, now you might think that's plenty,
But I myself would like it more if I could write like Dante.
I managed in the end to get ahold of Tanner,
And didn't find much cause to be concerned about his manner.
On Sunday we took speed, and all I say's a pox on
Whatever Peter sold us that he thought to be desoxyn
– In fact I took a second and it didn't make me higher,
And the outdoor art show that we saw seemed not a bit less dire.
Upstairs you might well guess has not been without trouble
Since yesterday when who came back? th'insipid hippy couple.
Sometimes Life seems to be a matter of endurance.
(I'm wondering where to send the policy for Steve's insurance.)

But Michael Tolliver has really cheered your friend up:
He's entering the jockey shorts free contest at the End Up.²

And I say don't feel down, like some downtrodden peon:
Just take some speed and drink a beer and turn the new TV on.

1. The Ambush (1973–86) was a South of Market leather bar, art gallery and informal community centre on Harrison Street, frequented by TG.
2. Michael Tolliver is a major character in Armistead Maupin's *Tales of the City*; the EndUp is a nightclub in San Francisco's South of Market neighbourhood.

TO *Douglas Chambers*   TLS Toronto
Monday 4 October 1976

1216 Cole St.,
San Francisco,
Calif. 94117

4 Oct 76

Dear Douglas,
    Here is that terrible correspondent again. Thank you for your letter of return, and I suppose you are hard at work again by now.
    Interesting what you say about the boys of the thirties, because they were still the main influence on me and my friends when we started at Cambridge in the early fifties. Somehow we couldn't <u>use</u> Dylan Thomas in the same way we could Auden. The great thing about Auden was that he could speak

about absolutely everything, and he made you feel that it was easy. So I owe a great debt to him, and so do a lot of my contemporaries, though it is far from fashionable to praise him. But ultimately my reservations about him are terrific: he talks easily about everything, but so much of it is <u>too</u> easy. The book where he really let go, and the one I still read with most pleasure, is The Orators – which he wouldn't allow to be reprinted until the end of his life, perhaps less for the political reasons he gives in the prefatory note than for the fact that it's a dead give away about his (homo)sexual fantasies. But it is a fascinating book, darling – almost like Cocteau (of all the unlikely people).

Isherwood, in the long run, seems to me to outdistance him. He too has an easy style, but it is not, like A's, mannered, and it allows him to go much deeper into things: I think particularly of the end of A Single Man, and the first few pages of the last Berlin Diary (in Goodbye to Berlin). Boy, that simple prose is doing so much. It has always seemed to me that people have underestimated Isherwood <u>because</u> he is so easy and entertaining to read – you could read one of his shorter books on a plane trip. I have a strong suspicion that his best books are ultimately much better than, say, Faulkner's best books.

I seem to be pontificating.

[. . .]

I will look up the Carruth book.[1] He loathes my work, but that's no reason why I shouldn't like his. Let me recommend a book to you: The Names of the Lost, by Philip Levine (Atheneum, NY). Very recent. He is someone I have known and liked for twenty years, but I found his early poetry rather dull. Recently, though, each book has got better than the last. His style is very bare, beautifully so, but is able to take on ALL the complications of being human. My comment is pompous, but he is not. I wish I could do the kind of thing he can, I feel the tremendous vulnerability of people, but I don't seem to get it into the poetry. (Unlike Yeats, I've always thought 'the poetry is in the pity' a perfectly valid ars poetica.[2]) For example, in a poem like 'Fever' (in To the Air), I wish I could have got under the boy's skin more, let him exist more for his own sake rather than bringing myself in, in relation to him. (He was an imaginary boy, maybe that was one of the troubles.)

[. . .]

Have you read Scott's <u>Old Mortality</u>? It is wonderful, except for its title, which refers to somebody in the <u>introductory</u> matter, not in the novel itself. Right now I'm laboring through <u>Guy Mannering</u>, very dull stuff indeed.

I'll be sending you a copy of my new book soon. I don't know which will reach me first, the English or the American edition. I'm going to be interviewed by 2 gay publications one local (the Sentinel[3]) one national (the Advocate[4]). <u>That</u> will give them something to think about at Berkeley! Actually it won't bother them at all, though it will embarrass the closet cases, of which there are more than a few (strange, at a place so politically liberated as Berkeley is in most other ways).

> Love,
>
> Thom

1. Hayden Carruth, *From Snow and Rock, from Chaos* (1973).
2. 'My subject is war, and the pity of war. The poetry is in the pity' is from Wilfred Owen's preface to his posthumous collection *Poems* (1920). Yeats disagreed. 'I have a distaste for certain poems written in the midst of the Great War,' Yeats wrote, and, without naming Owen, commented that 'passive suffering is not a theme for poetry'. See *The Oxford Book of Modern Verse 1892–1935*, ed. Yeats (1936), xxxiv.
3. Roger Austin, 'Books', *San Francisco Sentinel* 3, no. 21 (7 October 1976), 8, 11.
4. Tony Sarver, 'Thom Gunn', *The Advocate* 220 (27 July 1977), 39–40.

1977

1216 Cole Street,
San Francisco,
Calif. 94117

23 March 77

Dear Douglas,

Yes, I've been terrible not to write, and I would have continued terrible for
at least a week more, but I calculated so well for today that I actually have
a couple of hours free this afternoon before going down to southern Calif
for a reading at 10 a.m. tomorrow morning. I've really had a good term: I
taught well, I was interested in all my students, and they were interested in
me. And of course the beautiful days of our winter drought did no harm to
me either.

[. . .] Apparently (according to my publisher) the NY Times have
commissioned no review, so I guess that means there won't be a review. Oh
well, one shouldn't be concerned about these things.

A rather ghastly Anglo Irish poet called Richard Murphy came through
at the Univ. Ghastly that is both in person and in writing. I asked him (and
he's been here for the last year) what American current poets he likes, and he
said none, really. And most American poets aren't interested in reading any
English poets. No wonder there is so little cross-fertilization if there's simply
no interest.

He was telling me how little Philip Larkin sells over here, which I must
say surprises me. Then he said that L's last book has already sold well over
20,000 in Britain. And I must say I wonder what that says about Britain.
Most of those readers don't like L for the beauty of his form (though that
is what I mainly like about him) – so what do they find attractive about his
most prominent attitudes – his closed mind, his sour & begrudging tone,
his assumption that provinciality is a virtue? I am not putting him down as
much as I seem to – I like him a lot, but when he is untypical, mostly: when
he shows unexpected sympathies or when he writes a marvellously Symbolist

337

ending to the poem High Windows. But I doubt if the majority of those 20,000 read him for those things.

Ah me, the state of poetry. Well, I got The Book of the Green Man yesterday from Serendipity, and also John Heath-Stubbs' Artorius, and look forward to reading them both. Do you know H-S's work? He's one of the best people writing in Britain, though you wouldn't know it from the reviews. I read The Ebony Tower, and am interested in trying something longer by him. At the same time the stories left me uneasy: there is a strangely Jamesian feeling of the craftsman <u>working</u> a subject as far as he can, but his subject doesn't have the rawness that you find in James, the animal passion of Wings of a Dove. I got a sense of (favorite word of the year) manipulation in Fowles. Still, I like him enough to go on.

We had a fine time with visitors this winter. It was just lovely having you here, and I can only hope you enjoyed us half as much as we enjoyed you. Then my friend Allan from NY came for 5 days, and that was pretty exuberant too, though he'd been having all those love troubles.

I finally finished an autobiographical introduction to Hagstrom's bibliography[1] (47 is a little early for an autobiography, I think), and I have certain interesting plans for some prose, a book I think, that I'll tell you about if they start to materialize. It will be a very strange book.

[. . .]

I finish up at school on Monday, and am looking forward to having time for all the things I haven't been able to do – LAUNDRY first of all, there's a tremendous amount to do and we don't have any clean clothes or sheets, and I have a lecture to prepare for Illinois,[2] and then some writing of my own, if you see the distinction, and some reading of my own, and swimming, and catching up with friends I've hardly seen since January. I decided it's going to be a wonderful year, and so it is.

[. . .]

I must get going now. M & B send love
     and so do I
        X X X X
          Thom

1. 'My Life Up to Now' (OP 169–88).
2. TG gave a lecture called 'An Apprenticeship' at Lake Forest College in May 1977. A typescript can be found among TG's papers at the Bancroft Library.

Tuesday 31 May 1977

> 1216 Cole Street,
> San Francisco,
> Calif. 94117
>
> 31 May 77

Dear Douglas,

I am not sure how long I can stand my new reading glasses on the nose I got so sunburned today, but I am consumed by guilt at not having answered your letter of over a month ago, all the more in that Michael Lynch forwarded the copy of Body Politic containing your review [. . .].[1] And tormenting my nose is really to punish my face (and thus redeem any guilt?) since I see from your letter that you must already be in Italy.

But I do want to say how much I appreciate your review. Since you had to de-lineate it and all that you may not think very highly of it yourself, so I want to assure you in complete seriousness that it is the one review of the book (and one of the few reviews I've ever received) that is completely right, i.e. accurate, about my intentions. This is quite apart from the fact that it praises me, though of course I like that, and the particular <u>kind</u> of praise, very much. But you perceive the emphasis made, you <u>describe</u> the book accurately, and very few reviewers seem able to do that, though of course without an accurate description no kind of evaluation is going to be possible. So I thank you very deeply, dear friend (though I realise that the impulse behind the review was something more altruistic than friendship), and the piece makes me more happy than you can have anticipated.

I must say, I love your meeting with Allan Noseworthy. I talked with him on the phone the other day and he seemed as delighted to meet you as you were to meet him. But of course I'm not surprised you got on. The pure of heart always get on well together. (That's a reference to E.M. Forster. I seem to be getting very pompous this evening. You both have a wonderful sense of humor and maybe that is quite as important as p. of heart.) AN was at the Everard Baths in NY the night it burned down (about 10 or more dead & many more injured), but with typical luck got bored & left a few hours before the fire started.

I went as Pert in Residence to a college, Lake Forest, in the second richest district in America. I forget the first, but the second was quite enough. Lake Forest is almost all mansions. The wealthy matrons just love the arts and of course were pierced with joy at a genuine English accent, even one as malformed as mine. The wealthy husbands were drunk or feeble, I heard one rather pathetically telling someone about how he took up the piano after his electric shock treatment. One or two of the husbands were refreshing in an Andrew Undershaft kind of way. – My hotel room had a view of a gas station: with a rather too characteristic Gunnesque sentimentality I treated it as my hold on reality. The hotel itself, which liked to think of itself as very English (though it wouldn't have done too well in the England I remember) catered mainly to the ancient and horribly rich, also. I was crossing the hotel lobby one evening, looking quite like myself but not contemptibly so, when an eighty-year old Lady Britomart remarked in an Edith Evans voice to her companion: There goes one of the great unwashed hordes. So you can see that if I speak of them as if they were caricatures it is because they themselves speak as caricatures. The younger faculty, on the other hand, were just splendid, and not just the English teachers either. And the students were pretty good too, though the girls were still (still) imitating Sylvia Plath. After that, and before a couple of readings in Madison and Cincinnati, I spent two days in Chicago. I went into the famous leather bar on a Saturday evening, and boy was it terrible.[2] Everyone was acting as if they were straight and they had no idea why somebody was looking at them in that faggotty way and smiling. Luckily, just as I was about to deliver the entire Middle West to Dante's hell, a large handsome boy with longish hair and obviously stoned on something clumped in; I sat beside him, and he almost immediately popped some acid in my mouth, and in the night following he managed to be the One Just Man that redeemed about two thousand square miles of this continent for me.[3]

I'm having a shitty time writing. I keep working over three rather trivial poems that I've had around for ages. I am trying something in prose, but it's heavy going, and my comfort is that Flaubert took 9(?) years over MME BO. (That wasn't meant to be in capitals.) Well, I'm probably not really through as a writer, but even if I am I've had a nice long innings, more than many people have.

Well, yes, maybe we should have a talk about authorial intention. Some famous critic (Wimsatt) wrote something about it, didn't he, about the fallacy of intention. I can see how someone could start with a fairly defined conscious intention but unconsciously perceived (or even unperceived) emotions could completely alter it into something else. May well be so of Carnal Knowledge. May well be so of Measure for Measure, for that matter.

[. . .]

I am amenable to the suggestion of resurrecting MORE uncollected poems in 'small-book form', but I can't think which poems would be worth it. The

printed books contain such a lot of ghastly junk, Elvis Presley, Lines for a Book, and such like. I'll have to look up the paraplegic poem, if you like it.
[. . .]
Much love, and also much gratitude for your review,

X X X X X

Thom

1. Chambers reviewed *JSC* in *The Body Politic* 34 (June 1977), 16. Michael Lynch (1944–91) was a gay-rights activist and a pioneer of queer studies in Canadian academia.
2. Chuck Renslow opened the Gold Coast in 1958.
3. Lot is the one just man in Sodom (Genesis 19:1–38).

TO *A. E. Dyson*[1]

TLS Manchester

Monday 15 August 1977

1216 Cole Street,
San Francisco,
Calif. 94117

15 August, 77

Dear Tony,

Yes, indeed it is a long time since we last met. The friend we were with is dead, and no doubt that pub is a very different place. The district certainly is.

I am right behind you with the Manifesto, and will be very glad to sign it.[2] This is the kind of thing that needs to be openly said. When I was at Cambridge as an undergraduate, I remember hearing the most horrifying anti-semitic remarks made quite casually and often in front of Jews: nowadays this would no longer be considered acceptable behavior. So your parallel between homophobia and antisemitism is, I think, a very exact one. Now, as far as the universities I know here go, you would be very unlikely to hear anti-gay remarks from teachers or even from undergraduates. Most of them probably know all about my sexual orientation, and they certainly don't seem troubled about it. However, universities are not the whole of society, and if people in them take a strong enough stand against homophobia, something is bound to leak out into the rest of society. I think it is time that famous people – artists, writers, sportsmen, politicians, journalists – asserted their own homosexuality (as Isherwood has for so many years, and as others are increasingly doing over here), so that people who already admire them will be forced to acknowledge that they have been admiring a homosexual. I wonder if it might not be a good idea, then, to restrict the signers of the

341

Manifesto to homosexuals? I can see obvious objections to such an idea, but it is worth considering.

My only criticism of the Manifesto, and I am sure others have made the same objection, is in the use of the phrase, more than once, "Christian and secular" when you should be saying "religious and secular". I know that in England there is no separation of Church and State, but there <u>are</u> other religions practised there! [. . .]

Congratulations on coming to your twentieth anniversary.[3] Unfortunately, I have nothing to send you, and don't know when I will. I have had an awfully long dry spell since I finished my last book, and feel very unsure about the few poems I <u>have</u> written in the last two years. Boring. Sometimes I wish I was a potter, so that I could always have something to be working on. I am sorry, anyway, as I would have liked to contribute.

   All best wishes,
    Thom
[. . .]

1. Anthony Edward 'Tony' Dyson (1928–2002), literary critic, educational activist and gay-rights campaigner.
2. Dyson's *Towards a Charter of Homosexual Rights* (1978) was co-signed by 174 sponsors including politicians, academics, writers, actors and theologians.
3. Dyson co-founded *Critical Quarterly* with C. B. Cox in 1959.

1978

TO *John Holmstrom*   TLS (aerogramme) Texas
Tuesday 24 October 1978

1216 Cole Street,
San Francisco,
Calif. 94117,
USA

24 Oct 78

Dear John,
   [. . .]
After my nice two days with you things went down. I decided I would be
a model of patience (didn't have much choice) as I listened to the troubles of
relatives and of civilians too. Once I was forced to go into the lavatory and
indulge myself in a series of silent screams (learned from Mother Courage),
but apart from that I behaved moderately well. [. . .]
Then I did spend another six days in London (Hampstead), which I
enjoyed, and was all too short. I had one day which was full of good looking
young Londoners, with that callously friendly face that they possess so well,
and that night went to the two gay bars of Brompton Road.[1] Where I met
the dregs of London. So I remained a nun in England. As a matter of fact,
someone did take me to the William IV in Hampstead, where my mother
and father used to drink, and which struck me as one of the nicest and
most varied gay bars I had ever been in, a bit of everything, even some
heterosexuals but this was the evening before I left and it was too late to do
anything about it then.
Then I went to Canada. Toronto is nice, with all the limitations implicit in
that word. I was at one boring dinner party, when the young woman sitting
next to me turned to me and spoke her first and only words of the evening:
"Do you have a position?" she asked. I wondered whether she meant sexually
or politically, but realized soon that she wanted to know whether I taught.
But I did meet an interesting young man called Lionel. I had always wanted
to have sexual commerce, I mean congress, with someone called Lionel, so I
fulfilled an ambition.

343

I did read one book which impressed me a lot – Don Doody had pushed it into my luggage before I left New York, and his taste is always good – <u>Dog Soldiers</u>, by Robert Stone. Very beautifully written, and really thick with experience, like Dickens. He's not really like Dickens, except that he gets <u>so much</u> in.

Anyway, I'm not displeased to be back in the country of the young. – I hope Paris was fun as well as work. – I did go along Talbot Road once. Instead of the floods of tears I'd expected, I felt very bored, and only just made as far as Kildare Terrace. We all send lots of love.

[. . .]

Love

X X X X

Thom

1. The Coleherne and the Lord Ranelagh were famous London leather bars that TG first visited in the mid-1960s.

1979

TO *Belle Randall*   TLS Bancroft
Tuesday 15 May 1979

1216 Cole Street,
San Francisco,
Calif. 94117

May 15, 79

Dear Belle,

How nice to get your letter. How much nicer it would be if there were any chance of seeing you down here. [. . .]

I'm having a pretty good summer. I too am writing, though with all too familiar difficulty. But it is something to feel that a portion of the work is actually keepable. I swim twice a week and I just shaved off my beard for the summer. And all the seeds I sowed came up (though something or other has eaten all the basil seedlings, as usual). My last year's term at [UC] Davis is paying for having the front of the house shingled and painted. A very nice man, a friend of Billy's, is doing it, and he keeps on giving us snorts of coke. I love it when one's employees treat one like that.

I have been reading two books of James Merrill's – fascinating, all about sessions with the ouija board. He and his friend raise up W.H.Auden, among other people. (<u>Divine Comedies</u> and <u>Mirabell</u>).[1]

[. . .]

I <u>couldn't</u> have said I hadn't had sex in 6 years. We must have been very stoned. No, I don't think promiscuity necessarily involves using people. Short relationships can be just as full of reciprocity as long ones. (Fun's fun, said the Duchess.) But I love what you said that your midnight cowboy would hang around and ask you to do his laundry and listen to his poetry. That happens so often, especially with friends of mine.

Thank you deeply for your remarks about 'Sweet Things' and about my poetry in general. I said to Mike that it made me feel very good when you said that I was yr favorite living poet. Mike said: 'Well, you are mine too.' I said: 'But I'm also the only living poet you have read in about twenty years.' But from you it means a lot more, not just your affection for me.

345

[. . .]

I haven't told anyone else, but I'm trying to write a series of only loosely related poems about Marriage. In my arrogant way, I refer to it in my mind as the Marriage Group, as in Chaucer.[2] It would start with wooing and go through all sorts of marriage (including gay) and separation and end up with Philemon and Baucis. Ambitious, huh?[3] I have much of a novelist's interests in me, but none of a novelist's staying power, I have often thought. This kind of project makes me happy to think about because I can encroach on the territory of you lucky people who deal with human behavior.

I have a hardbound, American published Selected Poems to come out this Fall (nothing new will be in it).[4] I assume that this one too will drop into the still well of the outside world and cause no more ripples than the last one did. Must stop being sorry for myself – I had enough success with the first few books to last anyone a lifetime.

I am going to be 50 at the end of the summer. Not sure whether to ask my 50 best friends to a party or disappear from the city for a few days. My attitude toward being 50 is highly ambivalent. It all seems a bit sudden, as if I were Rip Van Winkle and had just woken up from a nap of about ten years.

I've just read again one of my favorite novels, What Maisie Knew, by Henry James. I think I find it funnier every time I read it. I certainly didn't think of it as being an especially comic novel the first time around. If you haven't read it, I don't recommend it till you have finished your novel as James could be a profoundly corrupting influence on anybody's prose. He is so wonderful that one would be tempted to imitate everything in him. It's OK for a poet in that no one recognises the debt from another genre. (My most Jamesian phrase is from Yoko, when she says of an old turd, 'I can place it finely'.)

Must stop as it's my turn to make dinner.

Love,

Thom

1. See 'A Heroic Enterprise' (*OP* 142–7); TG called *Mirabell* 'the most convincing description I know of a gay marriage'.
2. 'The Marriage Group' in the *Canterbury Tales* includes the Wife of Bath's, the Clerk's, the Merchant's, and the Franklin's tales.
3. The 'Marriage Group' spans TG's last three books; its poems were never collected as a group in print. They include 'Adultery' (*CP* 313–14) and 'His Rooms in College' (*CP* 351) in *PJ*; 'The Hug' (*CP* 407) and 'Philemon and Baucis' (*CP* 416) in *MNS*; and 'Rapallo' and 'In Trust' (*BC* 96–9) in *BC*. See also 'The Married Men', *PN Review* 24 (November 1981), 21; uncollected.
4. *Selected Poems: 1950–1975* (1979).

TO *Douglas Chambers*

TLS Toronto

Sunday 23 December 1979

1216 Cole Street,
San Francisco,
Calif. 94117,
USA

Dec 23, 79

Dear Douglas,

[. . .]

I have been having an autumn of, to put it mildly, great variety and eventfulness. I went to England and did 17 poetry readings – the first 16 in 12 days. I was in parts of Britain I knew nothing about, and was delighted by the beauty of some of them, especially in the North crossing from Manchester through Durham up to Newcastle. I was reading Little Dorrit again, but the journeying was so great that I stared more out of the window than at my book. And oh dear the young men of England – it's only the young ones mostly, they go all wrong after 30 or so – but they are too much, with their air of brutality that so quickly melts into the disarming grin. – The tour was an immense success, but I don't think I'd ever want to do such a thing on that scale again. It was a question of being exhausted or exalted, and luckily I was the latter. The almost three weeks were like living on amphetamines, eventually I realised I was speeding on my own vanity.

I realised afresh, as if I never had before, how I couldn't live in England now and be a poet. As anything else, an ordinary teacher, I could love it – and I had a great time, and loved what was familiar about England as much as what was unfamiliar (you may gather, this was one of my happier visits); but as a poet I am a good deal too famous there to be comfortable. It was certainly something to be stared at in that worshipping way by all those hundreds of good-looking school-children and by their older brothers and sisters and parents at later readings as well; and it was simply ludicrous being introduced to audiences as if I were Yeats, for Christ's sake; and it was fun being a star for a while. But if it had gone on much longer I'd have started to believe it – my greatness, that is – or at least in the possibility of it, and that would make writing (never that easy, after all) that much more difficult. Poor Ted Hughes, meanwhile, is positively beleaguered by celebrity, and in no mere metaphysical sense, either. His fellow farmers see him on TV and think he must be a phoney; and he has to set his whole family around him in positions of sentinels to keep off the Hughes-maniacs and the Plathnecrophiles. So I have been very happy to return to San Francisco, and in the same day (yesterday) get a telegram from my publisher that I've just won the WH.Smith prize of the year for my new Selected in England, and go down to the local bookstore here to observe that the numbers of the same book do not seem to have diminished by even one. It's called having the best of both worlds.

Came back to spend Thanxgiving in NY, but felt strangely tired, and though I had some good times rambling around and talking with Allan (who had just moved back there), I only went to the Mine Shaft twice, which betokens either fatigue or unusual restraint. Came back here and had a violent cold for a week, then developed one of the more dramatic diseaseases of my life, Bell's Palsy, a pretty sounding name for paralysis of one side of your face. I was scared shitless, partly because it could have been a tumor of the brain, and partly because if it was Bell's Palsy then it can sometimes take as much as a year to get your face straight again, or <u>sometimes</u>, for reasons no one understands, the face stays lop sided for ever. I tried to tell myself that maybe I would just have sex in pitch black orgy rooms with other deformed people; I also tried to convince myself that paralysed is punk, and thus fashionable. To tell the truth, I didn't succeed in reassuring myself and I still didn't fancy a future of looking like Vincent Price. But the best happened. After the paralysis had gone about as far as it could go, in the first five days, it started straightening out almost immediately, and now – about ten days after – you wouldn't know I'd ever had it. Or rather, there is a touch of unevenness, but you'd have to study my face for a long time to spot it.

I haven't been able to drink for the last two weeks, but I've been having a wonderful time on grass. I hadn't realised how when I turn on nowadays it is almost always in combination with beer or wine and these last two weeks I have been having the <u>purest</u> highs since 1966! I mean I've been sitting in the kitchen listening to rock and roll late at night and really getting <u>inside</u> the music. (It is true, one time I suddenly realised that the music I was dedicating my entire soul to was the Chipmunks, if you remember them!!)[1] But there is nothing like escaping a disaster narrowly for making me manic, and I have been living in complete euphoria for the last few days. Long may it continue.

I do hope I do see you soon, because I have more to tell you about than I can get into a letter. This year has contained far too many dramatic crises for my liking, most of them not to do with me, let me say, my main wish for 1980 is a Bland New Year. And I met James Purdy. (He's bats, but I still think he writes – and still writes – the best short stories of anybody living.) And I observed the by now probably famous poster in London which advertises meat balls wearing cartoon smiles with the words 'Meet a saucy faggot'. And

I visited Keats House for the first time since my teens, I think, and was very moved. And read the two new up & coming English poets, Craig Raine and Christopher Reid, and found them very English and rather disappointing.[2] It's that kind of Aldous-Huxley sarcasm that gets me (NOT a Swiftian style, let me assure you): they just don't want to acknowledge their feelings, or they don't know what to do with them, or I don't know what. They're both very talented young men in terms of stylistic detail, but they haven't the faintest idea of what they are writing about unless it is something completely outside of themselves (they each have a rather good poem, I would guess done as a joint exercise, about a butcher). Josephine Miles, on the other hand, has just had a good book of poetry out, maybe her best, called Coming to Terms, University of Illinois Press, which I much recommend. She is one of the very few poets I can think of for whom the structure of the poem does more for the poem than the language in it. (If that seems puzzling, think of This is the house that Jack built, where structure is all and language subsidiary).

Also I read a superb novel (in paperbacks everywhere here) by Richard Price called Ladies' Man, which contains the best treatment of gays in a straight novel by a presumably straight novelist. I'd be interested in your opinion of this novel. It's a "best seller", but he seems to me first rate. – [. . .]
     Love,
        Thom

1. A trio of singing anthropomorphic chipmunks created by Ross Bagdasarian Sr. for a novelty record in 1958.
2. Craig Raine (1944–) was poetry editor at Faber & Faber (1981–91); Christopher Reid (1949–) succeeded him (1991–9).

1980

TO *John Holmstrom*   TLS (aerogramme) Texas
Tuesday 22 April 1980

1216 Cole Street,
San Francisco,
Calif. 94117,
USA

22 April 80

Dear John,

Well that was a cool queer stay I had in England last Nov.¹ Actually it was great: but I find it difficult to describe the oddity of both being a half-stranger to a place and yet an ex-inhabitant. There is a touch of the exotic and a touch of the intimately known, so there is both discovery and rediscovery. I don't mean it is necessarily all that wonderful, a typical experience is being in an altogether too familiar British Railways station sipping BR tea and looking out of the window at familiar British weather and yet being in an unfamiliar town.

I had a good time and earned some money, and it was very good seeing you that last day. Your advice on my poetry is very useful to me. I can't always take all of it, but you are the only person alive who is able to get into the subject matter deeply and who also knows about language and rhythms. I continue to write just meter, but more of that later if I have room.

[. . .]

This year I am trying out celosia (cock's comb, which looks weirdly <u>like</u> a cock's comb), which I have as seedlings indoors. What else? A newly developed orange pansy! I have dreams of it, profuse and as orange as oranges. I have been subject to Proustian disillusionments about this kind of thing since I was promised a blue rabbit when I was eight and when it arrived it was just an ordinary old dark grey.

We have decided to take over the top part of the house for ourselves. Lonnie, the responsible one, split up with Michael, the flighty one, and moved out.² Having Michael up there not paying his bills and running through a succession of unsuitable room mates, has helped us to make up our minds.

Then Bill can have a studio and I can have a study that is not a thoroughfare, and we will even have a guest room.

I've been writing with considerable eagerness. I've been trying to continue a kind of series about friends, written in quatrains like two I showed you last Nov.[3] I am trying to make them really fast-moving in their rhythms. Of course, the difficulty is that they may be of interest only to me and a few other friends, but I'm trying to overcome that. I have also, by mixing a theme from Donne with a deliberately Hardyish style, written what I hope people will find the most disgusting poem in the English language, if anybody cares to publish it, that is.[4]

Saw an oldish film, Coppola's first, I think, called <u>The Conversation</u>. If you have never seen it, I recommend it <u>a lot</u>. I'd put it with the best I've seen, on my Top Ten (not that I have any idea what the other nine are). Saw a very old Hitchcock, <u>Spellbound</u>, the other day. A marvellously silly story, but it's always nice to watch the Hitchcock tricks and novelties, often quite superficial, and it was good to see the fashions of our childhood (what funny hats women wore), and the young Gregory Peck and the young Ingrid Bergman were both completely beautiful.

Don's wicked old father is dying. In a few months Don will be rich and can then move to some city in Europe which is equidistant from two opera capitals and has an opera there as well, and can thus cheerfully devote himself to his obsession. At least that is what he once told me he was going to do.

All our love to you, and remember you are more than welcome to come and stay for a long time whenever you can.

SOON.   X X X X X   Thom

1. 'Well, it's a cool queer tale!' – a line from Hardy's 'Her Second Husband Hears Her Story' – is the epigraph to *BC*.
2. Lonnie Leard and Michael Grove lived in the upstairs apartment (1214 Cole) in the 1970s. Leard died of AIDS in 1987 and 'enter[s] less directly' into some of TG's AIDS elegies (*CP* 492).
3. 'Transients and Residents' (*CP* 374–9).
4. 'The Miracle' (*CP* 357) is a poem about ejaculating in the restroom of a McDonald's. See TG to Lux, 26 February 1995, below.

TO *Ted Hughes*¹   TLS Emory
Thursday 24 April 1980

1216 Cole Street,
San Francisco,
Calif. 94117

24 April 80

Dear Ted,

I owe you not only two letters but two lots of thanks, first for your gift of Moortown and second for your kindness in presenting the W. H. Smith Newsboy-of-the-Year Award. They sent me a tape of the luncheon proceedings, but I don't have anything to play it on. Several people however sent me the note in the Guardian summarising your speech, and I must thank you for the extreme generosity of your remarks. (As well as for coming up to London, getting mixed up with literary and semi-literary people, all the pomp and boringness of public occasions. Nice that you got drunk. That at least must have made it easier. One day I may get the chance to do something like that for you.)

Moortown is terrific. But how could it not be, bringing together as it does most of your best work since Crow? Much of it was familiar to me, some from reading (Prometheus, your fine earlier gift to me) and some from hearing you read aloud (Feb 17, Sheep, Birth of Rainbow). Rainbow I admire especially, in that it is such a successful attempt to get away from the Ted Hughes poem. (I think every writer has the same problem of keeping away from self-repetition and self-parody, God knows I've fallen into both often enough myself.) But in getting away from the TH poem you don't stop being TH: Birth of Rainbow is a wonderful new thing for you, I think. Actaeon was new to me, and I like it very much. One thing I admire about your poetry is that the physicality is seldom static – it's not, in fact, merely 'images' that you do so well, but processes. That's one reason I've admired the Prometheus so well these several years – in the last two sections especially, the process of transformation going on both internally and externally. And when I first received the copy of Moortown, I opened it at 'The wood is a struggle – like a wood / Struggling through a wood.' I can't tell you how good I find those two lines. Nobody else has done that kind of thing in that way before – whatever it is you are doing is what Pound called a poetic 'invention' – it is immediately clear and unmistakably right and it is so new that it is like being present at that struggling wood. It's really quite alarming. Or it would be if it weren't so good.

352

Well, forgive this gush.

You say you have come to a standstill in your writing, and certainly you were not happy when we met – the word I would have used of you is 'beleaguered'. That was a week before your trouble with your leg, which sounds dreadful. – Well I've certainly had my dry spells – the last and longest was over 2 years 1976-8. I eventually found myself facing the possibility that maybe there was no more poetry to come from me, and tried to reconcile myself to that fact. But then suddenly, when I'd given up hope, it all came back again, and I was writing with as much eagerness and excitement as when I was 22. I learned nothing from the experience, except that I have become very dependent on the process of writing poetry and that it will probably always return to me; but I learned nothing, I mean, about how to deal with the dry spells, or about what brings them and what ends them.

One thing I find helpful, strangely enough, is teaching one term a year. The very fact of being <u>prevented</u> from writing for 10-12 weeks, because I am too busy, seems to concentrate the faculties. During that term I keep getting marvellous ideas and want to write badly. So once the middle of March comes I have a lot of <u>impetus</u> to write, which I might not have if I'd been completely free.

[. . .]

I have recently invented a secretary called Sharon Worth. This is not a wimsy (whimsy?), but a practical measure. She is going to write letters in green ink to people who ask me to do things I don't want to do, saying things like 'Mr. Gunn is on religious retreat in Idaho' or travelling in Scotland or something like that. I think she looks rather like Shelley Winters. She has taken creative writing classes from me more times than I can remember, she does secretarial work for me free, and she is fiercely loyal. Perhaps one day she will get a poem or two published. (Her poetry will be very derivative from mine.)

My love to you & Carol,[2] and to Robert and to Olwyn when you see them, and my deep thanks again.

      X X X

        Thom

---

1. Ted Hughes (1930–98), poet and contemporary of TG; their work was often paired together, and in 1962 Faber & Faber published their joint *Selected Poems* which sold more than 80,000 copies. With Philip Larkin, they were at the centre of British poetry in the early 1960s: as Edward Lucie-Smith wrote, 'Around 1960, it sometimes seemed as if all the poetry being written in England was being produced by a triple-headed creature called "Larkin–Hughes–Gunn".' See *British Poetry since 1945*, ed. Lucie-Smith (1970).
2. Carol Orchard, Hughes's third wife.

Tuesday 22 July 1980

1216 Cole Street,
San Francisco,
Calif. 94117

July 22, 80

Dear Douglas,

You send me such glamorous postcards: I love the skinheads at the train window that I found waiting on my desk when I got back from Santa Fe. This plain white paper is all you'll find waiting on your desk when you get back from London.

Santa Fe, the DHL Festival that is, was hilarious.[1] I have never been to a Conference before, but I went into it open-eyed, aware that there would be a lot of bullshit. And indeed there was, though I had enough sense to avoid most of the worst, i.e. a trip to the "Shrine" where girls in white dresses strewed white rose-petals on said shrine at sunset, and also the DHLawrence Festival Gala Ball, where people were supposed to appear as a character from one of the books. I toyed with the idea of doing a Jose Ferrer as he appeared as Toulouse L and swinging in on crutches[2] – Sir Clifford himself (do you know by the way that L based Sir C on Osbert Sitwell?). But though some of the conferences were awful, some were good. Richard Hoggart was ultimately the brightest man there, and the only one from whom I learned anything. But it was nice seeing Dan Jacobson, as pleasant as ever, and Stephen Spender elicited a certain respect from me: he spoke to the point, and was really very good. I travelled there and back with Robert Duncan (imagine being talked at for 5½ hours at a stretch, even such good talk), but we already know each other well. I met Ginsberg for the first time, and was hugely impressed: I'd always imagined he might be a bit hysterical, like some of his poetry, but he is sensible, and kind, and takes charge and looks after people in a way I admire. Also Gregory Corso, and we got on well. I was staying in a house with Wm Burroughs and a small entourage of his with which I went around quite a lot, to the conference, to gay bars, on one occasion to Los Alamos, through the most spectacular landscape I'd ever seen, to see what remained of the exclusive but rather spartan boarding school that had been there when WB went there in 1929, at 15.[3] (It was the only thing on that mesa at that time, to be bought up by the govt and of course replaced by a rather shoddy and very depressing little town with streets named like Trinity Drive and Oppenheimer Street.)

To return to the conference, the two villains, for me, were A.Alvarez, who had a kind of negligently patronising manner I found most offensive – he was so obviously there for the money alone; and Keith Sagar, who chose to denounce the world in the tones of not DHL but guess who? I wonder if there was anybody else there besides me who could actually catch the very intonations and physical stance of Leavis as he lectured in the fifties. (Harry T. Moore made me think of a freight train, heavy, inexorable, loaded with facts, and <u>impossible to stop</u>. Dreadfully pompous.) I did have a pretty good time, however, and came back yesterday feeling that five months and not five days had elapsed since I had left San Francisco. Oh yes, I also fell in love with a very glamorous dude from San Francisco who gave me some cocaine the last evening I was there. He is awfully my type, all charm and smiley and good humor, but I don't imagine I am his. Anyway he doesn't return here till mid August so we shall see then.

Do you have any idea, by the way, of when you might come here? Mike and Bob[4] will be away, so there will be heaps of room, even if there are other visitors, as there will be at times. But a date might be of help. If you don't know any dates, that's OK of course.

No, I haven't read the book on the Movement, and don't intend to.[5] I will trust that somebody bright like you will tell me what is good or bad about it. Did I tell you I did read Robt Martin's book, which you refer to.[6] It is brilliant on Whitman, I think; accurate but boring on Crane; and as you say the rest is bunk. And superficial bunk at that. (Though he does make me want to read Alfred Corn, who appears to be completely out of print.)

[. . .] I'm getting a great deal of pleasure from reading W.S.Graham's Collected Poems, which if you don't know them it is best to begin at the end. I've been reading tons and writing tons. I have even promised my next book for delivery to the publishers next June, and if you know how superstitious I am about this sort of thing you will be STRUCK by my confidence. Among other things I have written the poem I have always wanted to write about leather bars, s m games, etc.[7] I was writing about three different poems, and then suddenly realised that they were parts of the same poem, and it is 3 ½ pages long. But otherwise I have the book completed except for an insanely ambitious poem, or rather series of poems, in meter, of which I have still not even started parts six to eleven.[8] I have a terrific title for the book, by the way, The Passages of Joy. (Samuel Johnson, The V of H Wishes: "Time hovers o'er, impatient to destroy,/And shuts up all the Passages of Joy" ..... Nice, since it seems to refer to the ear-hole and the cock-hole and the nose-hole as well as to all the other possible meanings of the word passages.[9])

[. . .]

355

I must hurry off and make dinner for all 5 of us. [. . .]
Much love from us all,
Thom

1. The second New Mexico D. H. Lawrence Festival was held in Santa Fe on 16–20 July.
2. An allusion to *Moulin Rouge* (1952), dir. John Huston.
3. See 'A Drive to Los Alamos' (*CP* 372–3).
4. Bob Bair (1950–). See Glossary of Names.
5. Blake Morrison, *The Movement: English Poetry and Fiction of the 1950s* (1980).
6. Martin, *The Homosexual Tradition in American Poetry* (1979).
7. 'The Menace' (*CP* 337–43).
8. See 'Transients and Residents' (*CP* 374–9). Its subtitle – 'a sequence interrupted' – alludes to TG's original plan for a longer sequence, for which notes and drafts can be found among his papers at the Bancroft Library.
9. Johnson, *The Vanity of Human Wishes* (1749).

TO *John Haffenden*   ALS (postcard[1]) Bancroft
Wednesday 24 November 1980[2]

1216 Cole St.,
San Francisco,
Calif. 94117

Nov 24

Dear John –
    Someone sent me the copious interview in Quarto and it looks very good,[3] though I can't say I care for the pictures (the Lizard Man!).[4] But I want to thank you especially for your historical (and critical) accuracy in dealing with my connection (or lack of it) with the Movement (in PN Review).[5] You have it exactly right about my reservations with New Lines.[6] What is more, I refused to be in the second New Lines unless Ted Hughes was included, if it was really intended to represent the best poetry being written.[7]
                        Best wishes,
                        Thom

1. Ylla [Camilla Koffler], 'Sea Elephant' (*c.* 1950).
2. Date supplied through postmark.

3. 'Experience and Ideas: An Interview with Thom Gunn', *Quarto* 8 (July 1980), 9–11; an expanded version was later published in JH.

4. The 'Lizard Man' photographs were taken by Fay Godwin. TG wrote to Monteith (22 July 1980) to ask that Godwin's photographs not be used for publicity: 'She is a very fine photographer and I hope I am not unduly vain (perhaps I am duly vain, however), but because the lighting was poor when she took them and because I was tired as well they are the most horrifying pictures ever taken of me. As Mike remarked, I look like the Lizard Man' (Faber Archive).

5. Haffenden reviewed Morrison's *The Movement: English Poetry and Fiction of the 1950s* (1980), see 'Well, Yes, The Movement', *PN Review* 16 (November–December 1980), 62–4.

6. See TG to Conquest, 11 March 1955, above.

7. See TG to Conquest, 31 May 1962, above.

TO *Douglas Chambers*   TLS Toronto
Sunday 28 December 1980

1216 Cole Street,
San Francisco,
Calif. 94117,
USA

Dec 28 / 80

Dear Douglas,

We all loved your hearty cowboy card, and have it stuck opposite our dining room table. Your letter was very welcome, but you do seem to be having a dispiriting time this year. Your mother's illness must be immensely worrying, and the slowness of her recovery saddening; but it is amazing how aging people can rally, so I think you can feel a lot of hope. Last fall I visited my first editor, John Lehmann, and found him I thought close to senile: he had just had an operation, he was so deaf he hardly heard anything you said, he really seemed on his last legs. I thought to myself, well, that's the last time I'll ever speak to him. So it was to my great delight and surprise that he turned up in SF in May, staying with some young men of his acquaintance, alert and positively spry, hearing everything that was said to him, etc. – Also you do sound overworked: don't they ever give sabbaticals in Canadian universities?
[. . .]

At first I thought your reaction to Sisson's editorial a bit excessive, though it certainly irritated me a good deal.[1] But I like what you say about colonialism, and I certainly agree for your reasons that American poetry is better than Brit right now. THEN I received issue number 18 a few days ago, and exploded.

Now I have written my own letter of protest to the mag.² It would be nice if they print both letters together. [. . .] Anyway, I was just getting ready to send the PN Review a batch of new poems, since they have always made very kind remarks about my work, but when I got that issue (the issue in which an attempt is made to render the word faggot respectable for straights to use), I decided, fuck it, if they are going to be anti-gay, they don't get this gay's contributions.

I spent it seems ages of uncertainty putting together an article about Yvor Winters, my memories of him and my love for him and my reservations about him.³ Then put it away thinking it very muddled before I went to NY. When I read it on coming back from NY it turned out to be just what I would have wanted it to be, though it will be hated by Winters-disciples and almost equally hated by those who can't stand Winters. That suits me. I'm not in either group.

[. . .]

I like my new workroom, which is comfortable and messy, with pictures stuck all over the wall and a large poster of Sid Vicious in full leather right behind me. It is the room right over my bedroom. Billy's bedroom is the next room. We're all getting on very well. Billy's favorite drug is unobtainable (angel dust) so he is at his best – he hasn't been so happy for several years.

Yes, I know Stanley Spencer's work. I've seen a lot of it, some in I think the Tate.

New York was wonderful. I stayed with Allan and Yoko in SoHo, my favorite part, where I once lived for some months in a loft, spent a good evening at Coleman Dowell's, resumed my acquaintance with Ed White, to whom I feel increasing warmth, met Ned Rorem (a slightly <u>difficult</u> man, who has set an old poem of mine), exhausted myself at the Mine Shaft, re-exhausted myself at another small leather bar which closes its doors (with customers inside) for 3hrs every Tuesday evening (if you are interested & in NY on a Tuesday, it is called <u>Jay's</u>, on Hudson St just off 14th in a triangular shaped building. You get there between 9 & 9:30, pay $5 at the door, & check your pants in at the clothes check. All beer is free.), fell in love for a night, went twice to the St Marks Baths, saw lots of old friends, met two people on separate occasions who seemed to possess unlimited coke, saw a fall of snow the last night I was there, and gave 3 readings (one of which at Harvard). Many funny stories to tell you when I see you: remind me to tell you how I lost the hair on my ass and how Ned Rorem reacts to slang and how a group of literary people almost got beaten up by punks. Tantalising stuff, eh?

[. . .]

I don't understand your remark about Pound's being responsible for the colonialist attitude of Sisson, etc. – I wd have thought just the opposite. Sisson could have written his unimpressive poetry without Pound, but Bunting is unthinkable without Pound (tho I'm beginning to think BB may be EP's equal).

Read Mailer's The Executioner's Song. Boy oh boy that man is impressive. The book has such scope. You start by thinking it is all rather depressing – all the women get married at 16, and had been married several times since, hardly any of the men can handle their drink – but as the mass of material reveals itself, Mailer's immense sympathy (surprise) comes into play, and the depressing stuff becomes meaningful because there is an attempt to put it all into proportion. It is a lovely book, I think his best.

Also read Alfred Corn's latest, very disappointing.[4] Guess I'll review it for the 3d Review.[5] With a very good local poet, Aaron Shurin's <u>Giving Up the Ghost</u> (you may have to go to yr local gay bookstore for that one), and Timothy Steele's <u>Uncertainties and Rest</u> (Louisiana), I think one of the best two first books of poetry in the seventies, and WS Graham, who I find increasingly difficult tho very good.[6]

Everybody in the house has had a terrible form of flu in turn, except me. Mickey has it right now, poor darling.

We do so hope you can make it in Feb. All send their love,

X X X

& me too,

Thom

1. C. H. Sisson, 'Editorial', *PN Review* 12 (March–April 1980), 1–2.
2. See *PN Review* 20 (July–August 1981), 2. Dudley Young had used the word 'faggot' in an article; TG protested that 'faggot is not a "neutral" term. [. . .] The word is used throughout the United States as a term of abuse and contempt.'
3. See TG to Schmidt, 16 June 1976, above.
4. Corn, *The Various Light* (1980).
5. 3d = three pence, in Britain's pre-decimalisation currency.
6. TG reviewed these four collections in 'Playing Politics with Poetry', *Threepenny Review* 6 (Summer 1981), 4–5; uncollected.

1981

1216 Cole Street,
San Francisco,
Calif. 94117,
USA

February 5, 81

Dear Michael,

Thank you for your letter and for your request to reprint the two poems from Inquiry.[2] I am put in a difficult position in answering you, for the very reasons that you suggest.

On the one hand, PN Review is the best poetry magazine that I know: it is interested in poetry in no glib way, it publishes good poems, and it keeps up to date in reviewing new books. Its contributors have also been extremely generous to me.

At the same time, it is not just a poetry magazine. It does seem to me, as it seems to others of my acquaintance, that it has developed an antigay stance that has nothing whatever to do with poetry. (There is Dudley Young's article, which is so outrageous I am surprised it was not accompanied by an editorial disclaimer. There was Sisson's editorial about the word gay, which – trite as it was – showed where his sympathies lay. There is even the ironic distaste showed by the word "evidently" on p.7 of issue 18, if I am not imagining things.) I might point by contrast to the editorial stance of Inquiry.

But I don't really see how I can contribute to a magazine which has the habit of sneering at a segment of the human race of which I am unavoidably and unabashedly a part – a segment which I need hardly remind you contains and has always contained a number of good poets.

I am indeed sorry to find myself writing all this.

    With best wishes,
     Thom

1. This letter was first published in *Letters to an Editor*, ed. Fisher (1989), 161–2.
2. 'The Victim' (*CP* 358) and 'June' (*CP* 352).

TO *Michael Schmidt*[1]   A L S Manchester
Saturday 2 May 1981

Amherst College
but as from 1216 Cole Street,
San Francisco,
Calif. 94117,
USA

May 2, 1981

Dear Michael,

Thank you for your long letter, the contents of which I have turned over in my head a good deal. [. . .]

[. . .] You explain Sisson's article very well indeed, though it does seem to me hard that it is this particular word that always gets complained about when people discuss the losses involved in modern usage. (A local columnist in San Francisco went on about it day after day.) One might, for instance, also complain about the total loss of the original sense of the word faggot – Shakespeare's sense, Chaucer's sense too probably. Though I can't speak Spanish, I'm not entirely convinced that the transformation of the word chicano doesn't involve a loss for those who do speak in Spanish – as well as a gain. Still, I'd rather drop this subject. I agree in principle.

Which leaves the Faggot Article. I too think it was a mischievous production, but I would use the word mischievous in a less light-hearted way than you do. I think it was wrong of you to print it. I applaud your desire to start a debate, but there must be limits to what you decide to print in the interests of controversy, and for me abusive language about a minority rather sharply marks one of those limits.

You say that it is peculiarly English to say "I disagree and so I am not going to speak to you", i.e. boycott PN Review. However, I do not want to be that bland and gentlemanly Englishman who is able to overlook everything, as if words etc. were not important enough to object to. If I consider PN Review to be anti-gay, I have two alternatives: (1) to no more contribute to it than I would join a queerbashing gang, and (2) answer Young's article. Unfortunately I am no good as an arguer or debater, as you are no doubt in the process of observing. (There is the further problem that I'm not sure I

361

have anything to say about Young except that he presents opinions as facts. A small example of his doing so is to be found in his explanation of the etymology of faggot.)

It is true that I have no right to assert that PN Review has an anti-gay policy, since I couldn't possibly know that. Nevertheless, it is the only magazine I have ever come across that has contained both an article attacking the use of the word gay (for whatever reason) and another freely using the word faggot. At the very least I wish to convince you that a very unbalanced effect has been brought about. Maybe a balance can be restored, as you restored it so admirably after being accused of a right-wing bias. If it is not ludicrous to attack gays, then it must be possible to praise them!

As I think I pointed out in my original letter, I am well aware that PN Review has been behind me from its start: I am most grateful. Also, you are one of the last people in the world I would wish to quarrel with. I suppose that if I have got you concerned about the balance and fairness of the PN Review on the subject of homosexuality (a subject that never needed to come up if it hadn't been for Young's foolish and offensive article), I have succeeded in what I was trying to do.

If you still want to use those two poems of mine from Inquiry, you are welcome to. If you don't, I can understand why not.

With sincere respect and good wishes,

Thom

1. This letter was first published in *Letters to an Editor*, ed. Fisher (1989), 162–3.

TO *Clive Wilmer*   TLS Clive Wilmer
Monday 19 October 1981

only till Dec 3
c/o Department of English,
University of Cincinnati,
Cincinnati, Ohio 45221,
USA

19 Oct 81

Dear Clive,

I could be doing other things, should be, in fact, but there's nothing like writing a letter when you feel like it, is there? You may notice from the above that I am for the second time this year doing time at a university rather distant from California. This one is for 10 weeks, and though the work is light, to put it mildly, it is a bit boring and I don't think I'll do it again. (Until I need the money for some emergency to do with the house!) No, ten weeks is too long to be away from one's friends and family. At least I haven't reacted as badly as some of the yearly poets have done to this place. Cincinnati drove poor Robt Lowell batty, but then, so much did anyway. He stayed one week, got committed, never taught any classes at all. Something awful happened with Berryman too; and Phil Levine fell into an acute melancholia, even writing to me at the time, which he does only once every 5 years, his trouble being that he had never spent more than a day or two away from his wife in over 20 years of marriage. John Ashbery spent most of his salary in going back to New York for five days of every week, and Caroline Kizer, that dreadful poet, shut herself in her apartment and was hardly ever seen at all. You notice I have taken full advantage of the department gossip. It's not a very good university, but the city is unusually nice-looking (though v right wing politically and no cinemas to speak of that are easy to get to! that underlining is supposed to be accompanied by a stamp of the foot). Pleasant hills going down to the Ohio River, some of the most distinctive 19th cent domestic architecture in America (influenced, apparently, by riverboat decorations, scrolls and such), two of the most splendid art galleries in the country (Taft money). The first three weeks I felt sorry for myself and lonely and the only times I was happy were when I was lighting up a joint for the last hour or so before going to bed and looking out at the many lanes of traffic outside the window, where I live being one of the few spots that does not have a lovely view. Now I've regained a little bounce, however, but the time certainly has changed when I liked being alone in a strange place, considering it a challenge, and I suspect having a fantasy about myself as a kind of Stendhalian hero to whom heaven knows what may happen any moment.

I committed myself to delivering a lecture about Bunting before the end of the term and actually wrote the first two pages this morning. He is wonderful, but boy he is difficult at times. That's the trouble with all those guys who do that juxtaposing stuff, they never tell you why they're putting the items side by side – because they are like, because they are unlike, or because of some completely different reason. Most of the early stuff is rot, except for 2 versions of Horace – but Chomei and The Spoils and Briggflatts are tremendous, and so are many of the later 'odes' and translations, especially the last version of Horace. I do think that Davie is correct – whatever BB's weaknesses of execution and theory, his actual practice is such as to make him the only poet in England who points a way forward, the grasp on what is important about his life being equalled by a grasp on language and the way it can be made to work rhythmically. So all the time I've been spending on him is time on someone important, tho alas I can't imagine him having much effect on my poetry at this late date. (It always is possible, of course, I'm such an incredibly imitative bugger.)

[. . .]

Glad you liked Night Taxi. It was published in the New Republic and apparently a poetry-reading cab driver in Boston liked it so much he sent it up to the TAXI NEWS ('the voice of the New England taxi industry') who have asked permission to reprint it. I find that very flattering. Now I just need my dog poem to be reprinted in some dog weekly ('the bark of the Ohio pet-food industry').

[. . .]

Yes, F n F plan to bring out our book at the same time as my new book of poems (June, is it?).[1] I can never understand how doing so cd possibly help the sales of either (tho they assure me it will, did with Heaney they say) but I can see how it will help both to get more reviews and longer reviews. I suspect that the prose book will be liked more than it deserves, and the poetry book liked less. But use every man after his deserts, and all that.

[. . .]

Do you ever hear of Tanner, by the way? [. . .] Does he sound in good health, I mean emotionally? I never hear from him, he hasn't answered my letters in years (do I recall American ordeals too vividly?), so I don't know much about him at present. But I still think of him as one of my dearest friends.

No, I didn't mean the tightening of the hands on the wheel (in Night Taxi) to be vaguely emblematic of death. Just precisely indicative of tiredness and tension! I mean, in so far as tired behavior is in a general sense always connected with dying behavior, I suppose it might be, but it wasn't in my mind especially and I don't think symbolic writing like that interests me much nowadays. Did you spot my little theft from Keats at the very end, by the way? He has some bleak elm-tops somewhere in his unrhymed sonnet called I think "What the Thrush Sang" (or What the Thrush Said).[2]

[. . .]

X X

Thom

---

1. Gunn, *The Occasions of Poetry*, ed. Clive Wilmer (1982).
2. 'And the black elm tops 'mong the freezing stars' is from 'What the Thrush Said'.

TO *Mike Kitay, Bill Schuessler and Bob Bair*[1]   TLS Mike Kitay
Wednesday 11 November 1981[2]

[c/o Department of English,
University of Cincinnati]

[. . .]

Yes Kids, it's your favorite uncle, Affluent Gunn. Just gather 'round ole Affie while he tells you the good news: there will be whistling in your house in twenty-two days. I shall be whistling the Affluent Gunn Theme Tune till Bill S stabs me with a roach clip. Yes Sir, I shall be arriving at 5:46 p.m. from Dallas on American #603. (Thurs, Dec 3.)

Thank god for that. Today, the eleventh, was a vacation, but my students wanted a class anyway, and I was delighted to hold it, as I wdn't have known what to do otherwise. Tonight my great standby, the periodicals room, is closed, so I'll go for a walk through the general frigidity which is now the norm in this so-called place.

[. . .]

Next week I give my Basil Bunting lecture, which I have almost finished writing, and also a poetry reading on campus to some kind of teachers' fraternity. The following Sun, Mon, Tues, I go to Bowling Green for a poetry reading. BG is said to be one of the most unattractive towns and campuses in the Mid West. We will see. Then two days after I return it will be Thanksgiving and Don Doody, if I'm lucky, will be here to stay three or four days. If I'm lucky . . . we know how seldom Don does what he announces. (Do you know by the way he plans to spend about six months with us on Cole St next year – half the summer and all the opera season, anyway? Nice if he really does.)

And by that time it will be almost time to return to SF. I don't really think I will ever go away to a college for more than 3 weeks again, the loneliness is much more difficult to bear as one gets older. It's not anything especially <u>poignant</u>, it just makes for such an empty life. Every now and again a faculty person asks me out to lunch or dinner and I am especially lively and animated because at least it is doing something. I didn't get old for this. I just turned down an invite to an international poetry conference in Rome in April, most expenses paid. I'd like to go to Rome again, I guess, but I do not want to be one of those people who go to Poetry Conferences. At least I have <u>some</u> artistic conscience left.

[. . .]

Well NY was a wow. I guess I told M and Bob about it on the phone, but here's for the others. A German movie called TAXI ZUM KLO is a must.

It sounds too trashy even for me, but it is not, it is very sweet and terribly funny and has the most healthy attitude toward gay sex – matter-of-fact in a way that no movie and not many books have been. I believe straights like it a lot as well. – I had a terrific meal at Norm's:[3] lobster quiche (made by Ed White, who was also there), Chickens stuffed with whole garlics – about 100 of them – with some rosemary (one of the best things I have ever eaten in my life), and some wonderful pear tart or something that paled beside the rest. I'm only worried about what kind of dinner I can give Norm when he finally does come to SF. Maybe I cd really surprise him with franks and beans? AN3 was in fine shape.[4] Boy, does he love Mike. (I wonder why.) Yoko reminds me of the ballet-dancing hippos in Fantasia, her great round body moves with surprising grace. She flattered the shit out of me by greeting me with yodels and passionate embraces for about 15 minutes. The lower East Side was just full of gorgeous punks, obviously every art student worth his salt has the punk look now, hope it reaches Berkeley campus by Jan. "Bar", where Don took Mike, is still wonderful, but has become cruisy at nights now, which meant that my night of rest, when I went there simply I thot to have a drink, ended up a night of play.[5] Oh well, that was just as good as rest and much more fun. (The guy's room-mate was one of those girls who let men touch them while jacking off in places around Times Square. Unfortunately I never got to see her. If I had, I wonder if I would have had a spontaneous emission?)

I'm getting on with The Princess Casamassima. I like it a lot now. I think it was only the first 100 pages I didn't like – nobody has a right to go that slow, I say to Mr. James. Considering I have been reading it for seven weeks now, weeks when I have been notoriously unbusy, Mr. James might well respond with the same observation to me.

My god what a big red moon, full it looks, just pushed itself up over the medical center buildings that make my horizon (i.e. beyond the huge parking lot and the intersecting highways with the perpetual ambulances). Mebbe I'll go downtown to the bar. No, it's too cold. Anyway I've started going to bed at eleven and getting up at seven. Makes the evenings shorter. I hope I have by now made you all feel thoroughly sorry for Uncle Affluent [. . .] Well, I guess I know why AN3 loves Mike. You are all so loveable because you cook so well.)

I make my life amusing by using bottled salad dressing. So far, Green Goddess is the best and Yoghurt with Garlic is easily the worst.

Love to all. If they start building that duplex, undo by night what they do by day.

XXXXXXXXXXXXXXXXXXXXXXXXXXXXXXXXXXXXXXXXXXX

Love,

Affluent Gunn

1. For Schuessler and Bair, see Glossary of Names.
2. Date supplied through internal evidence.
3. Norm Rathweg (1950–87), architect, interior designer, and co-founder of the Chelsea Gym with Louis Keith Nelson. Rathweg is the subject of 'Courtesies of the Interregnum' (*CP* 476–7) and 'To the Dead Owner of a Gym' (*CP* 478).
4. AN3 is TG's shorthand for Allan Noseworthy III.
5. Bar, on 2nd Avenue and East 4th, was one of TG's favourite bars in New York City.

1982

TO *Oliver Sacks*
Tuesday 20 April 1982

TLS Sacks Foundation

1216 Cole Street,
San Francisco,
Calif. 94117

April 20, 82

Dear Oliver,

[. . .]

Good news that you are anticipating Quickenings. I always felt thwarted that you denied us a leg to stand on, though perhaps that might yet reach us one day in a revised version.[1] Glad that Awakenings is being revised again. I constantly lend my copy to people I think shd read it: it is a wonderful book, and means a great deal to me.

I am a bit slothful at the moment. My pattern seems to be: a long cessation of any coherent writing after I have completed a ms, then a tentative start followed by, during the next few years, various separate bursts of activity, ending with a sense of the new book as a whole, in which I do make discoveries about my subject(s) that I have never anticipated. It's strange, the psychology of being a writer. But I suppose it's better not to be merely facile – the blocks, the feelings of paralysis, the times when language itself seems dead, these all help me in the end, I think, because when the "quickenings" do come they are all the more energetic by contrast.

[. . .]

      Love,

          Thom

---

1. 'Quickenings' was Sacks's working title for *A Leg to Stand On* (1984).

Friday 23 April 1982

> 1216 Cole Street,
> San Francisco,
> Calif. 94117,
> USA
>
> April 23, 82

Dear Duggle,

[. . .]

My term was tiring, I'm not sure why. I did go off for 4 days in the middle to Northwestern Univ, and the travel exhausted me more than I wd have thot likely, maybe that was it. We had double our usual rainfall but finally we have had a gorgeous week and I have been digging my yard and planting my seeds and feeling like the farmer in WCW's Spring n' All. The last 2 weeks have been very restful and enjoyable in about every way, the gods descended, among them a large blond Pole called Gary, and also among them our wonderful spring birds whose name I don't know but who carry on with dash and vigor and a great variety of warbles and calls every year.

I have now fixed up my work room – my new work room – have you seen it upstairs? I think not – as a guest room as well, and it is so nice I might occupy it myself. I wrote 2 prose pieces on Bunting, one shd be coming out any day from PN Review,[1] and the second will be in the 3P Review,[2] so you'll see them both. I don't say many original things in them, but I like the work I have put into them, I go on reading him almost every day and constantly find new good things. I may write on his Odes and Overdrafts in one essay, and then I may get round to a fourth on The Spoils, which I find his most difficult poem, but it also contains some of his best things.[3] I found that my starting point for the PNR essay, about the fashion for things archaic this century, which I thought obvious but slightly original, had already been made, at greater length and with far gter documentation, by Guy Davenport. Have you read his book of essays, The Geography of the Imagination? It contains some excellent things, a few slightly silly and mannered things, but above all it is <u>useful</u>. For example, his essay on Olson is the only illuminating thing I have ever read on CO. He is of what you might call the Jonathan Williams persuasion, EP, Olson, Williams (J.), Ron Johnson (a couple of good essays on him),[4] Buckminster Fuller, and so on. (Just reread this para: it contains the word <u>things</u> 5 times.)

Mr. Wms did make a triumphal progress thro here, with Tom Meyer, whom I found a sweetie, tho I didn't greatly take to his affected poetry.[5] A slide show, a party, a photography session. A great charming imperturbable impressive and witty man, perhaps impossible to live with, but one loves his love of poetry. One loves also, the way he sets up his own pantheon so determinedly. That is what people shd have the sense to do more. To hell with great traditions – it is good to inspect other people's great traditions and then select what one needs from them (I have always liked EP's anthology From Confucius to Cummings very much) – one's own pantheon. I find people too slavish to English departments. (But, as you wd point out, better to go thro what an English department has to offer, to know what is offered before rejecting some of it. Here we may operate anarchistically but it is with a fair degree of wide reading behind us.)

I'm trying to write a piece on Coleman Dowell that I promised a year ago I wd finish by June.[6] He is a wonderful novelist almost uncommented on, which makes him good to explore without presumptions. (Island People – the masterpiece – is what I'm writing about, though in relation to Mrs October was Here – the failure.)

Haven't written any poetry except a few scraps, fragments that don't lead anywhere, but that's a familiar story after finishing a new book. I refuse to let it depress me. (Tho I do wish my sense of achieving was less tied in with what I write. There shdn't be any connection, and it can't be good for the poems.) I wd like to write a long poem about San Francisco, and have already written a few little incidents that could be part of it, but I wonder if people in London, Toronto, New York – or for that matter, Hebden Bridge, Yorkshire – are really interested in reading about a city they've never visited. Hm.

[. . .]

Well, what else? I made 3 pages of footnotes to Briggflatts for Michael McClure, who asked for them. I can send you a copy, or give it to you when you come here. – I read the 4-novel long Parade's End by Ford Madox Ford. I think it is worthy of standing beside Ulysses – or almost so. So full of surprises. – So, we can expect you here in October, Ace?

Now I must read some of the poetry for the Berkeley poetry prize I'm judging. Luckily it's not one of the more prestigious prizes so I don't have to read endless (a) fashionable poetry and (b) incompetent poetry. Geoffrey Holloway was a sheer delight – we immediately got on well – and I thought his lady was wonderful too, if you'll forgive my 1960s language.

Hope this gets you before you leave.

      Love,

           Thom

[. . .]

P.S. There are some interesting new places here you might like.
> (a) a "performance gallery" that does some good out-of-the-way plays, has poetry readings etc. (J. Wms read there)[7]
> (b) a kind of Mine Shaft West (i.e. with smiles) called the Caldron[8]

1. See 'What the Slowworm Said' *PN Review* 27 (Sept.–Oct. 1982), *SL* 53–65.
2. See 'Wings Deep with Inner Gloss', *Threepenny Review* 10 (Summer 1982), 6–7; uncollected.
3. See 'The Lesson of *The Spoils*', *Parnassus: Poetry in Review* 17, no. 2, and 18, no. 1 (1993), 20–39; uncollected.
4. See TG to Ronald Johnson, 25 November 1995, below.
5. Jonathan Williams (1929–2008), poet and publisher, founded the Jargon Society; Thomas Meyer, also a poet, was his long-time partner.
6. See TG to Dowell, 26 May 1983, below.
7. 544 Natoma Street hosted many gay readings and events in the 1980s.
8. The Caldron, a sex club at 953 Natoma Street, opened in 1980.

TO *Donald Davie*   TLS Yale
Monday 17 May 1982

> 1216 Cole Street,
> San Francisco,
> Calif. 94117
>
> May 17, 82

Dear Donald,

I have delayed answering you so long because I had so much to say; but more turns up to say all the time, so I'd better write now while I still remember the original things I wanted to talk about. [. . .] I did find Cincinnati awfully boring, but it is a pretty place and my one real solace was the presence of Don Bogen and his wife Cathryn, who I'd known when they were graduate students at Berkeley: both generous and lovely people. He is a good poet, a fact I've known some years, and is getting better. Doesn't have a book out yet, tho he has had a ms going the rounds for several years.

Back here I haven't been doing much poetry writing. Fiddling with the unfinishable, mostly, and looking forward to the end of the fallow period. I think I operate on the Three Field System, something I used to diagram pretty slickly when I was seven, for history classes (bet you had to do that too) – I go fallow for about one year in three. So I'm writing lit crit: at least I can write (that sort of) prose by an act of will. Just received the magnificent complete Mina Loy which Jonathan Williams has at last brought out, after it was promised ten years ago.[1] It is absolutely wonderful, and there are poems (late ones) that I never guessed existed. So I want to get round to writing about her later in the year, once I get over the difficult novels of Coleman Dowell (Island People is a masterpiece, and I know almost no one who has read it), which I somehow promised I wd write about. I have a vague idea that I'd like to write a book entirely about really good unread writers, but I'll probably never get round to doing it all.

[. . .]

About the last chapter of your Penguin Pound book. The bit on abortion and creation of poetry / having children is, I thought on both readings, a small irritant in a magnificent book of criticism.[2] Maybe you were simply teasing out the implications of EP's position, but it looks remarkably like an importation of your own opinions into a book that is far from opinionated in every other way. Yes, Pound thought that homosexuality was a form of usury: it is an improper use for one's seed – but then if he was logical he wd have gone on to say that so is contraception. Perhaps he did somewhere. 'Creation' as a term for the production of literature is merely a high falutin metaphor, after all: Pound, you, and I know that whatever we are doing when we write a poem we are not acting like gods. I needn't remind you that there is an even better tradition for calling poets makers.

No, I don't think I've ever thought of you as a scourge of the gays. But perhaps be more careful what you write in private letters to Marjorie Perloff. She shows round her letters (not to me, I hasten to say, since I don't know her). She showed one to Robert Duncan, in which you thank her for her book about O'Hara, and apparently go on to say that you don't think that a homosexual (except, you rather sweetly said, for me) could write good poetry. I've thought about this statement for several years, and I still don't know how you could deny the title of poet to say Marlowe or Whitman. But of course it is unfair for anybody to show around private correspondence, which is intended in a specific context; and also one shouldn't gossip, as I have just done.

I do bring up the letter to Marjorie Perloff not for the purposes of gossip but because it does strengthen my feeling that your writing in that page or so of the Pound book is perhaps more personal than you believe. Might one also hazard a guess that you do not approve of abortion?

The yard is at its best. I have found a flower called nemesia that won't stop flowering for about three months. Probably too late for you this year, but Doreen might try it early next year, if it can stand the heat down there. I'm not sure I have any of the herbs still that she so kindly left at my front door a few days before you left California, but perhaps the rosemary bush (a very sturdy one) comes from a Palo Alto origin. It must have been nice to be one of the contributors to the Georgian anthologies and make up whole stanzas out of the names of flowers.

Lord Annan lectured at Berkeley a month or two ago. It took me back thirty years when he was just Noel Annan. But he <u>should</u> be a lord: he looks like a lord, and he speaks like a lord. And his lectures were as good as ever – they seem like first-rate theatrical entertainment, but after the lecture you find you have learned a lot!

<blockquote>Love to both,
Thom</blockquote>

1. Loy, *The Last Lunar Baedeker*, ed. Roger L. Conover (1982). TG later reviewed Conover's *The Lost Lunar Baedeker: Poems of Mina Loy* (1996) in the *Times Literary Supplement* (30 August 1996), 3–4; uncollected.
2. See Davie, *Pound* (1975), 113–15.

TO *Donald Davie*

TLS Yale

Thursday 29 July 1982

1216 Cole Street,
San Francisco,
Calif. 94117,
USA

July 29, 1982

Dear Donald,

Thank you for your letter and the review.[1] Quite likely I would not have seen the review if you hadn't sent it. I'm sorry if my letter was intemperate and inquisitorial, and I am grateful that you took the claims of friendship as being more important to you than what you found objectionable in the letter. More than grateful, moved. I get defensive on the subject, and I apologise. Yes, my justification does have to be by Enlightenment principles, but then so does the justification for the Bill of Rights and for much else that I (we?) believe in. However, when I say this, please don't think I don't take notice of what you say: I do, and shall go on doing so, in that it strikes me that you and Duncan (utterly different as you are) are about the only contemporaries from whom I have much to learn. – If your letter is generous, your review is princely. Friends in England have sent me a few other reviews, and – quite apart from whether my books were liked or disliked – yours is the only one

373

that addresses itself responsibly to questions of style and subject matter. So I thank you from the bottom of my heart: it may be good to be praised, but it is even better to be taken seriously. Reviewers so much prefer to speak about some earlier book or of something curious but untypical in the book under review – or in England they particularly like to be bitchy. [. . .]

So many points to speak about I'm not sure I can answer them all. [. . .] I don't regret saying what I do about WCW: if anything I wd speak much more highly of Paterson, now that I understand the Cantos better. – I have liked and admired Pound for some time, by the way, certainly since Dekker and you, in books, helped me into the Cantos. I was teaching his Selected Poems, all of them, including the selection of Cantos, to a large and enthusiastic class at Berkeley in 1966. But I think I would still say that his principles for Imagism were (in part) fuzzy. Perhaps that parenthesis 'in part' is what I should have added. But the fuzziness is in the remarks about abstraction. One could point to 'feline leisure' from Canto II as a good counter to 'dim lands of peace'[2] or, nearer in time, to 'the apparition (abstract) of these faces (concrete)'[3] as an example of the way one simply can't talk without abstractions. I'm beginning to sound like YW. And also with the first of the 'Don'ts': an 'intellectual and emotional complex in an instant of time' is not perhaps as clear as it might be – one moment it seems to make sense, the next it doesn't.

. . . Yes, I haven't heard a word of Rod Taylor in years. I find it difficult to believe that he stopped writing poetry altogether. His career as a singer didn't lead anywhere: he simply wasn't much of a singer and his songs were derivative and second-rate.

The subject of camp: whew, you really do take on the big subjects! Well, you're right, somebody has to be daring. I wonder what you think of the relation that Isherwood establishes (or tries to establish) between camp (high camp) and the Baroque in the bit that I quote (in my Ben Jonson essay) from what is admittedly his worst novel.[4] I think it is a connection worth taking seriously, i.e. the idea of 'camp' as play, elaboration.

Pinsky is an interesting case of something.[5] Maybe of my changing my mind about a poet's value. When I first read him I was really excited, but I certainly don't find he wears well on a second reading. He would never believe with Bunting that a poet's best friend is his wastepaper basket. When I get down to it, it really is true that dichten equals condensare as Pound quotes BB in the ABC of Reading. I've just been reading Lorine Niedecker – all of her, I think, unless something posthumous turns up (with appreciation for yr pages on her in the PN Review) – and I am so delighted by her condensations, her lack of verbosity, the way every word or phrase is marvellously framed with margin so that one has to stop and consider.

[. . .] I'm thinking of writing about Mina Loy's poetry and also Janet Lewis' – different articles, of course! The later Mina Loy is something of a revelation. – I'm reading and rereading a lot of Melville these days, finding it interesting how the sheer talent for language emerges in the early books, by its own energy raising itself into life even when he is following the most dreadful models. Your new house sounds great. My best to you and Doreen, and I thank you again for your loving letter.

X X

Thom

1. Davie, 'Looking Up', *London Review of Books* 4, no. 13 (15 July–4 August 1982), 19.
2. See 'A Few Don'ts by an Imagiste' (1913).
3. See 'In a Station of the Metro' (1913).
4. Isherwood, *The World in the Evening* (1954).
5. See TG to Robert Pinsky, 1 June 1989, below.

TO *Ander and Margaret Gunn*   TLS (aerogramme) Ander Gunn
Monday 16 August 1982

1216 Cole Street,
San Francisco,
Calif. 94117,
USA

August 16, 82

Dear Gunnies,

I hear your summer has turned from cold to muggy. Well, ours hasn't been spectacular either. But one result of our having had double the normal amount of rainfall last winter is that the blackberry bushes I am always trying to keep from taking over the yard have had so many berries that we have blackberries on our cereals (those of us as eat cereals – the healthy ones) every day for the last couple of months. [. . .]

You may have noticed that my latest books have ruffled the calm of the London literary establishment, who ranged from snide (Observer)[1] to really vicious (our old friend Ian Hamilton, of course, who seems bent on extending a career founded almost entirely on malice!, in the Times Lit Sup).[2] [. . .] At first I was disappointed at the massacre intended, but then I thought that disappointment is just a sign of vanity: none of the people who attacked me are people whose work I respect or whose opinions mean anything to me.

I have certainly never wanted to be a part of the London literary scene, and if I am being punished by them for not sharing in their preconceptions about poetry and sexuality, then so much the better – I'm in less danger than in being contaminated by their praise.

[. . .]

This govt is completely crazy, working out contingency plans for a nuclear war. New York could be evacuated to the north of New York State, but only if they are given two days warning of a nuclear attack, which warning is, after all, just a touch unlikely. Also plans for mail to be forwarded to your place of evacuation. Old Ronnie is becoming the laughing stock of the nation, but he's none the less dangerous for all that. I always said that Carter didn't look so bad to me. But then he just did things, he didn't have the professional newscaster charm.

If you want to sow seeds that are easy and have wonderfully showy results try Black Eyed Susan: big yellow flowers, most rewarding – and they look like the kind of flower that will reseed itself every year. I sowed foxgloves ten years ago and have never had to resow them again, they just reseed themselves over and over.

[. . .]

X X X X Love to all under your lofty roof!
Thom

1. Peter Porter, 'The Boys in Black Leather', *The Observer* (27 June 1982), 30.
2. Hamilton, 'The Call of the Cool', *Times Literary Supplement* (23 July 1982), 782.

TO *Gregory Woods*[1]   TLS Gregory Woods
Saturday 2 October 1982

1216 Cole Street,
San Francisco,
Calif. 94117, USA

October 2 / 82

Dear Greg Woods,

It was most considerate of you to send me the chapter in your thesis that takes me for its subject. Thank you – I have read it through twice. I don't know if my reaction will surprise you or not, but I think you have got me all wrong. That is, I think your general conclusions about my poetry are inaccurate, and the ingenuity with which you have made my poems lead to those conclusions seems misapplied. I do realise, of course, that as you say in your letter, the chapter is not meant to be 'a complete picture' of my work, that it is only about the sexual side of it – but insofar as the sexual part is an important part of my poetry as a whole a serious misreading is going to be a misreading of all of me. I should perhaps point out that I find you <u>innocently</u> misleading – you are never malicious, just over-ingenious.

I won't go through the chapter instance by instance since doing so wd be largely a matter of saying 'surely this is not so?' time after time. (A major trouble is that you cannot be content with a literal interpretation – everything has to symbolise something else.) What I quarrel with chiefly is the way you have read my (sexual and some other) poetry as pretty well exclusively sadomasochistic in content or implied content. To do so you can argue from only two poems: one, The Beaters, an early and bombastic poem in which I was rather childishly trying to shock, and two, The Menace (which comes, oddly enough, outside your chosen time-limit). What I was trying to do in this second poem was to release leather bars* from the rather crude assumptions made about them by straight people, newspapers, and gays who have either never been in one or have only gone to one to find in it what they expect. The quote from Bateson was all-important, central to my intentions. I was trying to emphasise the importance of improvisation and play. Therefore I am disappointed when you cite articles from newspapers and magazines that rehearse the dreary mythology of s and m, involving as it does all the rigidities of role and routine which I find repulsive. I was <u>not</u> simply trying to embody public assumptions in writing this poem.

However, you do at least, so far, have the justification that these two poems are about the subjects that you say they are about. The connection between yr examination of them and the rest of your argument seems to be found in the following remark: 'In the semiotics of cruising, black leather signals a greater or lesser interest in sadomasochism'. Having said this, you go on to find sadomasochism in every poem in which a soldier or motorcyclist figures. Surely you must know how questionable your generalisation actually is; but even if it were literally true, the semiotics of cruising is not the same as the semiotics of poetry – at least I certainly hope they aren't. I have in fact said something in my prose about possible significance of the soldiers and bikers in my work, and I am really made sad to think of their being seen one and all as sexual sadists. (It might help you to remember that the movie 'The Wild One' came out at the same time as I wrote 'On the Move': I wonder if you are prepared to take this as being a sadomasochistic film?)

Having established your generalisation, you then go on to take poems that are not sexual in content or implication and interpret them as sexual poems, and to take sexual poems and interpret them as sadomasochistic poems. Many of your readings completely astonish me: e.g. snow in one poem and distant smoke in another become semen for you; you see the Unsettled Motorcyclist making an 'anal' descent into the earth; and the poor wolf-boy becomes a 'catamite' at the end of his poem, the blood on his paws becoming the blood from where he has <u>scratched</u> his lover's body (ugh).[2] Come on now: he drops on four feet because he has turned into a wolf, and his paws (only the back ones, I guess) are bleeding because he has been running barefoot through the stubble (the wound he receives in the one life carries through into the other). He has no lover in the poem; it wd be a much happier poem if he had. But to understand this poem – or, I wd say, most poetry – you must possess a firm trust in the literal meaning of language. If you can grasp the literal situation, then my hope is that you might be able to apply it to other similar situations – even though they are not in the poem and the application is your work and not the author's. Thus the wolf-boy's situation fully grasped might be seen to apply to that of anyone else leading a double life – maybe sexually divided, or divided in other ways.

Well, you must realise by now what a risky thing it is to send a poet a critique of his work! As I say, you have got me wrong, but I say so without resentment, and I expect there will be critics who will get me much wronger than you have. You are certainly no Alan Bold: you seem to like my poetry, and you have a lively and intelligent style.[3] I thank you for your sympathy. I expect your chapter will get into print: I'll leave it to someone else to answer it, if there is such a someone.[4]

* Footnote to the other page, where there wasn't room for it. Remember, leather bars don't exist just in the U.S. You don't have to trust an Italian journalist's description of them. You can find one on Old Brompton Road, in London, the Coleherne – it has been there for years. In composition it has always been much like an American leather bar: some there interested in sadomasochistic activities to 'a greater or lesser' degree (though it is doubtful that they wd subscribe to the same mythology or that many wd have fixed roles); some there wd be simply homosexual bikers; a good many fetishists too; but the majority of people wd be there because they are attracted by 'the butch' – or the semblance of it. It is ridiculous to assume as the newspapers do that everybody there is after the same thing: that is melodrama. There are as many different homosexualities inside as there are outside the leather bar.

What a long letter. Best wishes,

Thom Gunn

1. Gregory Woods (1953–), poet and academic.
2. See 'The Unsettled Motorcyclist's Vision of His Death' (*CP* 54–5) and 'The Allegory of the Wolf Boy' (*CP* 61).

3. See Bold, *Thom Gunn and Ted Hughes* (1976).
4. Woods published a revised version of the chapter in *Articulate Flesh: Male Homo-Eroticism and Modern Poetry* (1987), 212–31.

TO *Ted Hughes*   ALS (aerogramme) Emory
Monday 27 December 1982

1216 Cole Street,
San Francisco,
Calif. 94117,
USA

Dec 27, 82

Dear Ted,
     [. . .]
Thank you for your comments on my book.[1] I am overwhelmed by them: I hope they are justified. I like the comparison to Elizabeth Bishop. She lived here for a year – I think 1969 – and I got to know her fairly well, but I could never get close to her poetry, which seemed to me weakened by its constant ironies. It was not until her last, splendid book, Geography III, that I really came round to her, and I could see the ironies in their proper place. That Moose poem is one of the best poems written in our lifetimes – the moose is there, the busload of people is there, she is there, vivid and alive and solid. So thank you again – you are very strengthening, as you have always been.
          Love to you both,
          Thom

1. Hughes's letter (10 December 1982) about *PJ* can be found among TG's papers at the Bancroft Library.

1983

TO *Douglas Chambers*   ALS Toronto
Monday 16 May 1983[1]

> [1216 Cole Street,
> San Francisco,
> CA 94117]
>
> May 16

Dear Duggle –

[. . .] Thank you for your wonderful card of my imaginary nephew (my Nephew-in-God, as it were). I actually got a hard on on receiving it. – So, you're in England already. I met someone the other day, aged about 30, who said he went to England to see what the English punks are up to. – Craig Raine is in SF. Not quite sure what I make of him personally. How could someone as nice and intelligent (or fairly intelligent) as he seems be able to become part of that self-aggrandising London literary drama. I don't know a good poet who'd contemplate it, though I could name several bad ones. Anyway, we are to make a tape together tomorrow – 30 min of raining, 30 min of tommygunning – to be issued as part of a series from F n F this Fall, each tape to be an older poet (or Socrates) on one side, and a younger (or Pathick) on the other.[2] I hope it will be a bit better than my other dismal recordings. I've also recently taped an interview with Michael Schmidt in England (done by phone) for a BBC program about Donald Davie,[3] & on Friday I'm to tape a poem called Bow Down (I assume I showed it to you, it's the last thing I wrote, in August) for a program of poetry ed by Jon Silkin.[4] [. . .] I'm writing essays in prose again, which gives me the feeling of being still a writer and also the chance to exercise my small intelligence. – I try not to go to the Caldron (in fact I go only about twice a month), because of AIDS. I keep thinking I shd make out with less people, but God keeps throwing such wonderful-looking men in my path. Maybe I shd cynically get a lover for the sake of hygiene . . . [. . .]

> Love
>
> Thom

[. . .]

1. Date supplied through internal evidence.
2. *Thom Gunn and Craig Raine: A Faber Poetry Cassette* (1983).
3. 'Nightingales Sang for Me Once: Donald Davie' was broadcast on BBC Radio 3, 22 October 1983.
4. 'Bow Down', *Threepenny Review* 14 (Summer 1983), 3; reprinted in Silkin's literary magazine *Stand* 25, no. 2 (1984); uncollected.

TO *Coleman Dowell*[1]   TLS New York
Thursday 26 May 1983

                                                            1216 Cole Street,
                                                              San Francisco,
                                                                Calif. 94117

                                                                May 26, 83

Dear Coleman,
    I want to thank you very much for the copy of <u>White on Black on White</u>, which I just finished (last night). I once called <u>Island People</u>, with forethought, a masterpiece, and I am sure this is another. I suspect it is even better than the earlier book, though I'm still too close to it to be certain.
    What astonishes me is its range. (What astonishes me, indeed, is the increase in range, book by book, all along for about 15 years.) How can you know so much? Well, I realise even as I ask it, how silly that question is, since the multiplication of experience and research by imagination is like a geometrical progression – with you, anyway: it can make for a life more convincing than my own experience. – It's disturbing all right, and I find it quite wonderful how disturbing you dare to be. You dare not only <u>deal</u> with the problem that most writers, if they touch it at all, treat from safely fixed positions (like some writer in Harpers proving a safely middle-of-the-road thesis), but you <u>enter</u> it. Entering it, experiencing all the abrasions of being black, and of being white too, makes for that kind of ambivalence you are so good at, which finally lights up meaning more than the certainties of any Harpers writer.
    The ambivalence, the abrasiveness, the disturbingness, are what <u>still</u> may keep you from becoming the popular writer you ought to be, but the fact that you insist on them keeps you such a good one! People like to be sure about things, and you don't let them be, but maybe this time people will be more perceptive. It certainly is a wonderful book, and it means a great deal to me.
    [. . .]

Love and admiration,
Thom

1. Coleman Dowell (1925–85), novelist and playwright. TG reviewed Dowell's *Mrs. October Was Here* (1974) and *Island People* (1976) in 'Pushy Jews and aging queens: Imaginary people in two novels by Coleman Dowell', *Review of Contemporary Fiction* 2, no. 3 (Fall 1982), 135–45; uncollected.

TO *Douglas Chambers*
Wednesday 8 June 1983

ALS (postcards[1]) Toronto

[1216 Cole Street,
San Francisco,
Calif. 94117]

June 8 / 83

Dear Duggle,

So! when a character in St-Simon's descriptions of court life wears his bottles for riding, it shd be rendered <u>shit-kickers</u>, I guess. – I loved your remarks about the British press managing to imply that the AIDS diseases are a penalty not only for being gay but for being American as well. That is a <u>mot</u> worthy of Oscar Wilde. – I notice my Caldron membership has run out: well, I haven't been there in some time & I guess I'd better not go there again. What a pity that such a generous place shd come to an end, but it's necessary for all the sex-places to, I guess. I'm trying just to have sex with a few regulars & making it as safe as possible. (Prodding each other with broomsticks held in welding-gloves.) No more "exchange of body fluids," alas. – Every other day I go to see my old friend Clint in hospital – not AIDS, but his second open-heart surgery. It's not a cheerful trip: he's normally a Mark Tapley but he's become a Timon.[2] – I'm trying to revive enough of my highschool Latin – which was very poor – to read Catullus. Quite successfully, really. I've found the best way to understand the scansion is to learn some of it. Learn some of the poetry by heart, I mean. If only they'd given me something like this to read when I was 17 & 18 I'd probably have never stopped. – Also, I'm trying to write an essay about Winters' early poetry. Dick Davis (in his recent book on YW) was excellent on the later poetry, but I thought he didn't completely understand the early.[3] I'm making slow progress. And I meant to go on to my Mina Loy essay afterwards but I guess Mina may have to wait till next year.[4] [. . .] Incidentally, if you want to read a <u>good book</u>, you might try <u>Hart Crane and Yvor Winters, their literary correspondence</u>, by Thomas Parkinson, now in paperback from the U. of Calif Press (I'll send it to you in Canada if you can't get a copy). It is good criticism, good biography, good literary history – it's the best thing written on Winters & also gives one a sense of what it was like to be around in the 1920s. It's true I know the author but then I know the authors of most of the books about Winters. I'm just reading it for the 2nd time. – I guess these 2 cards cover the spectrum? – Are you writing any poetry? I hope I didn't paralyse your writing arm by not understanding the last one you showed me. There are many worse things than obscurity & I am the first person to be baffled by the difficult after all. It's overcast here but the Oriental poppies are coming out! Mike & Bill & Bob all send love, as I do.

X X X X   Thom

1. Postcards: 'Shit-kickers / Bottles', by Reggie Smith (1982); 'Doris Fish, San Francisco's fabulous star of stage and screen' (1981).
2. Mark Tapley is a character in Dickens's *Martin Chuzzlewit* (1844); for Timon, see *Timon of Athens* (1605–6), from which TG derived the title of his long poem 'Misanthropos'.
3. Davis, *Wisdom and Wilderness: The Achievement of Yvor Winters* (1983).
4. See 'Three Hard Women: HD, Marianne Moore, Mina Loy' (*SL* 33–52).

TO *Mary and Catherine Thomson*

TLS (aerogramme) Jenny Fremlin

Thursday 28 July 1983

1216 Cole Street,
San Francisco, Calif. 94117,
USA

July 28, 83

Dear Mary and Catherine,

Thank you for your lovely letter. I think you have been having the same weather as we have: the lousiest spring I remember, followed by the most marvellous July since I've lived here – not a foggy morning, let alone day, until last weekend. The garden flourishes: the lilies are doing a great show-off act right now, and I have just ordered some more to plant this November. My writing has got very stuck, but then it always has from time to time. Gives me a good excuse to complain, when I can't complain about the weather. [. . .] The new neighbors are very quiet (in the back), just renting for the year I believe. However, we have a rather noisy new neighbor on one side of us, in the top apartment. We suspect she is a whore and the man she lives with is her pimp. The whole neighborhood knows a great deal about their private lives because they scream at each other (late at night) with the windows open. One time she spent all the rent money, but that wasn't the time he hit her. She was also very angry when he didn't turn up for 4 days and when he did he was on drugs (about 40 people woke up to hear that one). It gives all of us quiet people an ongoing drama to follow. Little do they know I'll write a poem about them one day!

[. . .]

My old friend Clint, I have known 23 years, had his second open-heart operation. His heart is now in fine shape, but they have somehow managed to ruin his right arm (some drug they gave him during operation to do something to his blood pressure gave him an allergy so bad that it turned the arm poisonous, started destroying tissue and muscle, etc.) He has been in a lot of pain for months now, still in hospital. I have offered to have him here when he comes out, as he'll need a bit of nursing. Don't know whether he'll take me up on that or not.

[. . .]

Well that's good news that you will come and stay with us, Catherine, once you have got Jerusalem out of the way. Perhaps Mary will come too! We will feed you well and try to make you comfortable and perhaps you will end up in the movies like everybody in California is supposed to do. – The political news is depressing isn't it? The real trouble with Reagan is that he has an absolutely fixed mind, and is completely unable to learn from his experience (or for that matter his constituents). Maybe he wants a few military victories before next election so he can get in easily like Mrs Thatcher. Oh well.

Oh, talk of the devil: she just started screaming at him next door.

Much love,

Thom

TG with his mother, Charlotte Gunn, 1930. TG kept a copy of this photograph above his desk at Cole Street.

TG with his father, Herbert Gunn, and brother, Ander, in the mid-1930s.

Ander Gunn and TG in the early 1940s.

TG at Cambridge, 1952.

Mike Kitay at Stanford, 1957.

Tony White as Aufidius
in the Marlowe Society's
production of *Coriolanus*,
Cambridge, March 1951.

TG and Karl Miller in the yard of 2638 West
Craig, San Antonio, Texas, July 1956.

Tony Tanner, Tony White and TG outside King's College, Cambridge, November 1964.

Marcia and Tony Tanner at Stinson Beach, California, August 1967.

Don Doody in Palo Alto, July 1969. The lettering on the car reads: 'The Electric San Francisco Garden of Eden'.

TG to Tony Tanner,
19 December 1966.

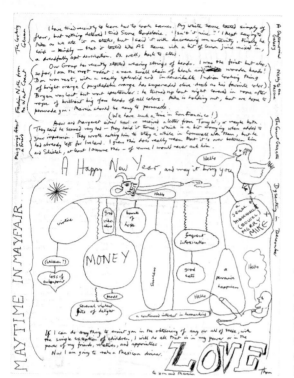

TG to Bill Schuessler,
April 1974. TG, about
to visit England, leaves
instructions for Schuessler
on how to look after and
distribute Lucy's four
kittens.

TG and Ander Gunn with
TG's nephew and niece,
William and Charlotte, in
Cornwall, June 1974.

From left: Mary
Thomson, TG, Jenny
Fremlin, Charlotte Gunn,
Catherine Thomson
and Barbara Godfrey
at Barbara's house in
Highsted Valley, Kent,
November 1979.

From top: Bob Bair, Mike
Kitay, Bill Schuessler and
Jim Lay, *c.* Halloween
1978.

Clockwise from left: Don Doody, Bob Bair,
Amy Kitay, Michael Belot, Bill Schuessler, TG,
Mike Kitay and Martin Rosen in the dining room
at 1216 Cole Street, July 1985.

NIGHTS WITH THE SPEED BROS.

Lovers, not brothers, whatever they might say
That brilliant first night, being equally blond,
Equally catlike as they reached beyond
The tropes of dalliance to the meat of play.

What I still keep from our long lamp-lit climb
Through gallant and uncertain fantasy
Are marginal gaps a window granted me,
When I removed myself from time to time.

I gazed at moonrise over the wide streets,
A movie letting out, a crowd's dilations,
Bars, clocks, the moon ironic at her stations:
By these the window paragraphed our feats.

Then dawn developed in the room, but old.
...I thought (unmitigated restlessness
Clawing its itch): "I gave up sleep for this?"
Brown leaf replaced the secret life of gold.

Note: the window looked out on the entire main block of Castro Street!

Thom Gunn

May 27/91

Dear Douglas —

Did I ever send you this? It's the only poem I have written since last June. Not very good, but it's merit is, that it is all true.

I figure you are at Stonyground now, very far from the decadence of the city & such-like matters. I finished grading exams last week, and am now devouring books like the reverse of that dragon in Spenser (the one that vomits up Popish pamphlets). The Voyage of the Beagle & The Ring and the Book (neither of which I ever read before), & I'm in the middle of rereading Hardy's poetry, & I'm also reading all of Louise Glück. She is good — her best book seems to me the middle one, chronologically, of the five, Descending Figure. (If you can't get it I'll send you a copy.)

I look after the yard & go to movies with Mike and read and at least keep a notebook! Spent Saturday night with my friend Robert. He is very wild, sexually, and I feel flattered he is still interested in me. Mostly this is a sexual affair though we do go to street-fairs and parties together. He's terrific — like the Lamb of God in black leather!

Mikey was just 60. He has grown back his beard — it is all white but strangely enough it makes him look younger. He's at the cabin this weekend.

Are you visiting us this year? We'd love to have you.

xx
Th

TG to Douglas Chambers, 27 May 1991. In the final version of 'Nights with the Speed Bros.' (BC 34), TG replaced 'Brown leaf' with 'Dead leaves' in the last line.

The wall collage in TG's workroom at Cole Street. TG began this in 1980. Famous faces include Basil Bunting, William S. Burroughs, Harrison Ford, Richard Gere, Thomas Hardy, Christopher Isherwood, John Keats, Keanu Reeves, Arthur Rimbaud and Bruce Springsteen.

Above: August Kleinzahler, with Patrick, in his apartment in San Francisco, *c.* 1990.

Above right: 1214–16 Cole Street, San Francisco, June 2019.

Right: Clive Wilmer in Cambridge, late 1990s.

Left: Douglas Chambers at a book launch, Toronto, early 1990s.

Far left: Billy Lux in New York, mid-2000s.

Mike Kitay and TG outside their house on Cole Street, late 1990s.

Thursday 4 August 1983

[1216 Cole Street,
San Francisco,
Calif. 94117]

August 4 / 83

Dear Douglas –

A very nice <u>springy</u> one this – a pity, though, that he looks as if he's only just bought the jock strap. I'll stop writing here, lest it comes thro.

And continue with the home-made. (Obviously.) [. . .] I've been reading Kenner's new book <u>A Colder Eye</u>, about Joyce & Yeats, which I suspect will be a best seller. – I'm having a summer of curious block & sterility. There's nothing like not doing something to make you continue to not do more of it. Poetry seems out of the question – deprived of words (for now, anyway), I am amazed at the extent of their literally magical powers & the fact that those powers spring out of nowhere, with such force, while one takes them for granted. (Rimbaud knew a <u>lot</u>!) – I'm reviewing Creeley's Collected for TLS I think, a nice dry poet, who however is not easy to read in bulk.²

[. . .]

I certainly didn't mean to tell you what <u>you</u> should do for sexual hygiene. In fact I wd think in Venice and Toronto you could do pretty well what <u>you</u> wanted in complete safety – for the time being, anyway. I was just telling you what I'd decided was better for me. As it is, the Caldron was going to close in Sept, but he's going to keep it open another month. – I certainly trick as much as ever, but only one at a time, so as to lessen the odds (considerably).

Robert Wells wrote a beautiful book-length translation of the Georgics last year. Apart from that, he's probably just a slow writer.

There were two Marshalseas, did you know that? I get my information from the notes at the end of the Penguin Classix ed. of <u>Little Dorrit</u>.³ – My understanding is that Becky's Dive is in the original foundations of the <u>older</u> one (not Dickens').⁴ The building over it, built by Woolworths I think, is obviously modern.

Apart from meeting wonderful men, reading Catullus (slowly), enjoying the best summer weather I've ever known here, "fostering" my yard (strawberries in it now), reading Hugh MacDiarmid (not for the first time), etc., I have been growing a double chin, of which I have become very self-conscious since I first greeted it in an unaccustomed mirror with side view. "Who are you?" –

"My name is Double Chin." – "Are you going to be staying long?" – "I am your destiny." – "Oh."

I also had a parasite; or Alien, undoubtedly sexual in origin. Deciding that <u>that</u> was not my destiny too, my dr prescribed pills which I found very depressing.

Did I tell you Craig Raine was here? A most likeable man, whatever his poetry. He is now, for all practical purposes, my editor at F & F, for which I heave a sigh of relief, as I cannot stand my old one, Charles Monteith, who is haughty & megalomaniac. Craig told me that cunt tasted not of fish but of Marmite, a fact I wd like to get into a poem one day if I knew how.

Seamus Heaney was also here, in charge of a creative writing school at a Catholic college. He got me 2 readings there – very nice of him. He is an affable – very warm man. I don't really know how much is Irish mannerism and how much personal, but I like him anyway.

How nice. Two poets running whom I can stand!

Ran against Larry (of my poem 'As Expected') on Sunday. We ran around together for quite a while when he was 21! Now he is over 30, very handsome, & was in full leather. Luckily he is a gerontophile so he spotted my double chin, my hundreds of grey hairs, my craggy face etc. & we had a riotous evening together at home.

Mapplethorpe in London![5] I imagine they'd censor his most extreme stuff. (His extreme stuff is too much even for me, & you know I'm not fastidious. But I love his manner. Nothing cd be more poised. Walking around in broad daylight with dried come all over his leather pants & not caring a damn!)

I must look up Jeremy Prynne. I met him once & he asked me if I thought of my poetry as like toast. (The reader bites the toast; I like the image.) I remember his poetry at that time as being rather like Creeley.

My poor friend Tony Tanner has suffered another gigantic breakdown. This time he tried to kill himself too. You see people disappearing down a whirling funnel and there's nothing you can do to help them.

And I probably told you my brother & his wife have separated after I think 30 years of marriage.

[. . .]

It's an odd year, certainly.

Love,

Your suitor, my Lord,

Wee Tomlet

(like a small tomato omelette)

1. TG often made his own pornographic cards by pasting magazine pictures onto blank postcards.
2. See 'Small Persistent Difficulties: Robert Creeley' (*SL* 87–95).
3. The Marshalsea was a debtors' prison and features in *Little Dorrit*.
4. For Becky's Dive Bar, see TG to Tanner, 27 January 1976, above.
5. The exhibition *Robert Mapplethorpe, 1970–1983* was held at the Institute of Contemporary Arts, London.

TO *J. D. McClatchy*[1]   TLS Yale
Saturday 24 September 1983

1216 Cole Street,
San Francisco,
Calif. 94117

Sep 24, 83

Dear Sandy,

[. . .]

I was rather relieved that I was unable (because of a conflicting date in Ohio) to be at the Dead Auden Conference, because the money was tempting but in all honesty I would have had to be an ungracefully dissenting voice.[2]

So what follows, if you find it worth referring to, is not to be credited. Now, I find I think of Auden very little. The two books that still interest me are the first, in which he was making some very bold and exciting experiments with language and measure, and the second (The Orators), in which he carried the experiments still farther, and which is certainly one of the enduring books of poetry from the 1930s. From then on, a steady and increasing trivialisation takes place, often in the interests of elegance. He is quite simply not a very serious poet – serious in the way that Yeats, Pound, Stevens, or even Williams and Crane were.

This, of course, without reference to him as a man. I would in no way wish to question the testimonies of my friends Oliver Sacks or Christopher Isherwood. He did influence me a lot when I started writing, 1950 to 1953, but not after that really. I am grateful that he made it clear you can write poetry about anything and he showed me the way, or some of the way that Shakespeare and Donne weren't able to show me (because they were of another century).

It may amaze you, but I didn't realise Auden was gay when I first read him. Most of us didn't. Eventually we did hear rumors, of course, but even then we weren't sure that the rumors weren't simply scandal. He did disguise things so very carefully.

Dunno if these notes help any.

[. . .]

Best to Alfred [Corn] and you,
Thom

1. J. D. 'Sandy' McClatchy (1945–2018), poet and literary critic.
2. The 'Dead Auden Conference' refers to the commemoration of the tenth anniversary of W. H. Auden's death, held in New York (17–21 October 1983).

TO *Douglas Chambers*   TLS Toronto

Thursday 29 September 1983

1216 Cole Street,
San Francisco,
Calif. 94117

Sept 29 / 83

Dera duggle,

That's what comes of trying to get a letter started too quickly. One more try:

Dear Duggle,

[. . .]

I've had a good summer. From starting it, if I remember correctly, absolutely unable to touch a book, I've ended it positively immersing myself in different studies, the weather has been better than good, I met a boy called Randy,[1] exactly half my age, with whom I've been making it every weekend for about the last 6 weeks, and I haven't wanted to make it with anybody else, he has been that good. He is also sweet-natured, and – though since he did so many sports at school he is badly undereducated (never opens a book or even a magazine as far as I can tell) – he has his own perceptiveness and intelligence. I know what I see in him; I have no idea what he sees in me, but just bless my luck. Oddly enough, I'm not in love, I'm not sure why.

Reading through Yeats again has been a good experience. Not having done it for about twelve years, I'd only read one of his poems at a time in isolation for a while, and had begun to think of him with irritation – irritation that is at the hectoring tone, the self-dramatisation, the cranky ideas. But he has to be read in a mass, I realise: in the context of the whole heroic career all the individual poems work again, and I come to realise

388

the kind of attention he demands. Which only goes to show how far I have come (to my surprise) from my New Critical beginnings. I particularly love, this time around, An Acre of Green Grass. I've also been reading and rereading some books about him, and I find the best one – best in individual points made and also best and most useful in the general conclusions he comes to, is once again by my 'colleague' Tom Parkinson, WBY, The Later Poetry. Highly rec.

As you may gather, I'm starting to prepare my lecture course for our next gruelling term. Also certain Creative Juices seem to be starting to stir again. Won't have anything to show for many months I'm sure, but I'm working diffidently at a few rhymes. I think I have to get back to meter for a while – to hell with what's fashionable, free verse is too limiting. The only person alive who writes free verse with the qualities I wd want in mine is Basil Bunting, and I don't think I am able to write his kind.

A poet to look up, by the way, young neighbor of mine from New Jersey by way of Canada, is August Kleinzahler, who published a book with the Coach House, Toronto, A Calendar of Airs.[2] (If you can't get it, I know I can buy one from him and send it you.) He has another ms going the rounds, which is even better. He is the ideal heir of WCW, the spoken voice, the humanity, and I think he is better than anybody on this continent of his age (30 or so) that I have read. But his scope, too, is ultimately too confined – I don't see how it can be extended. I have (No, I don't 'have' him, nor do I want to, though he's a nice man) another young poet I am betting on, James Powell,[3] one of whose best poems is in the latest Threepenny Review, no book out yet.

I'm just reading, also, the absolutely amazing correspondence betw Edward Dahlberg and Olson in the first 3 issues of Sulfur (of which I sent for a set – a marvellous mag). Not much Olson and a lot of Dahlberg, who reads like a Dickensian hypocrite – it makes for unintentionally high comedy.

The boys send their love. We have M's niece and nephew staying here right now, and M has come down from the river for a few days ....

X X X X

Thom

1. Randy Glaser is the subject of TG's poem 'Bone' (CP 410).
2. August Kleinzahler (1949–), poet and close friend of TG's. See Glossary of Names.
2. Jim Powell (1951–), poet, translator, and classicist. TG refers to the poem 'Home Free', *Threepenny Review* 15 (Autumn 1983), 8.

1984

TO *Clive Wilmer*   ALS Clive Wilmer

Thursday 5 January 1984

1216 Cole Street,
San Francisco,
Calif. 94117,
USA

Jan 5 / 84

Dear Clive,

Thanks for your card. It is a long time since either of us wrote, and I'm pretty certain that it's I who owe you a letter. Glad you liked my Creeley thing – I wrote it fast on my rebound from being unable to write on early Winters. (I've since realized Kenneth Fields has written better on early W than I could ever manage.[1]) Getting published in the TLS you sure get seen, don't you? I've never had so many people say they'd read something I'd written.

Tony Tanner's second wife, Nadia, was in California but because of the errors of a foolish mailman in Santa Barbara we never did get together, though we both wanted to. So what I know about Tony is from a rather hurried phone call on her last day – he was supposed to accompany her, but instead she put him into some kind of clinic for alcoholism and general distraughtness. He had been turning up drunk to lectures and there had been a suicide attempt: the story was terrible, though it was difficult to tell whether the alcoholism was cause or effect of what seemed to be the worst breakdown of all. I wrote to him, but since he doesn't write back, it is not easy to know what is going on except that it is a sad, sad business.

[. . .]

I'm about to teach a monster course in the "modern" poets from Yeats onward and have done some massive rereadings to prepare my lecture notes. Reading them in bulk makes them far less irritating – particularly Yeats. Doing so, one has to take each poet's work not as a number of separate poems but as a connected career, and seen in that way someone like Yeats is positively heroic. And I can forgive Yeats a lot of silliness when he writes such lines as

"Picture and book remain,
An acre of green grass."   How beautiful![2]

You ask do I have any new poems? Not much, and I too feel about mine (as you say of yours) "they're a bit on the thin side." How I'd like to produce a few chubby poems, positively belching from their repleteness with the morsels of experience. Anyway, your kind question led me to do some retyping, and then some xeroxing, so the ten enclosed are most of what I've done since my last book, apart from my piece of melodramatic modernism called "Bow Down", which I think you've seen. The only one I <u>know</u> is good is "Skateboard", & that is certainly frail enough. It is supposed to go with "Well Dennis O'Grady" and "Outside the Diner" as a sort of dwarfish triptych of the streets. If you get time, I would like to know what you think of the structure of "To a Friend in Time of Trouble" which at times I think silly and at other times supremely sensible! Any opinions of the others would be a help, as no one has seen most of them & I'm very unsure of them.[3] "The Stylist" is supposed to be funny.[4] I'm not sure that it is.
Happy New Year and love to all,
Thom

1. Fields, 'The Free Verse of Yvor Winters and William Carlos Williams', *Southern Review* 3, no. 3 (July 1967), 764–75.
2. Yeats, 'An Acre of Grass' (1938).
3. The five unnamed poems are 'The Hug' (*CP* 407) and 'Bone' (*CP* 410) from *MNS*; 'The Best Secret' and 'These Minute Designs' from the pamphlet *Sidewalks* (1985); 'The Kitchen Table' is unpublished (Bancroft).
4. 'The Stylist', *A Just God* 1, no. 1 (November 1982), 91; uncollected.

TO *Douglas Chambers*   TLS Toronto
Wednesday 30 May 1984

1216 Cole Street,
San Francisco,
Calif. 94117,
USA

May 30, 84

Dear Douglas,
    It is a terribly long time since I received your letter, and now the fine quartet of postcards from Europe. No of course I'm not pissed off at anything: if I was I'd write and tell you, I'm not a reticent person, but I can't imagine being

pissed at you, so dismiss that possibility permanently. When I don't write it is from having no time or else from negligence: in this case it is the former.

A fifteen week term is, yes, very different from a ten week term. In the eleventh week an alarm started going in the heads of me and all my students: term should be over, it shrieked. We all got very restless. But I taught pretty well this term, just the same. I think I got them enthusiastic about Pound, Williams, and Bunting. Another term I would introduce Mina Loy, whom I'm beginning to think very important indeed. I would not introduce HD, though she is so in nowadays: unlike many of my friends, I think her talent was really very slender, at the end as at the beginning. Unfortunately, they don't want me to teach the course again, just yet anyway: it is not a course for which English majors can get the credit toward their major, just a course for which they can get general English credits, so I had only 25 people in it toward the end. It's really what I most want to teach though, literature – it's lovely forcing oneself into close reading about which one has to be explicit in a class. It was flattering, though, I had several graduate students auditing the course right to the end.

[. . .]

We have Allan (of Allan and Yoko) staying here as of the last few weeks. He has AIDS, kaposi sarcoma, is rather thin, and stays very tired. He will probably stay here quite a while, either till he gets a remission, or has to go to hospital, or dies. But it is a pleasure being a help to him: he is not self-pitying or pushily stoical – I must say I would like to act like him if I find myself with the condition. (As, after all, I well may.) And I am proud that Mike and Bob welcomed him just as much as I did, more generously, really.

Duncan has had a total collapse of the kidneys – that was in February – but is having dialysis (my medical spellings are not of the greatest) three times a week, and by August expects to be in better health than ever. He is incredibly cheerful and chatters as much and as ramblingly as ever.

My friend August K introduced me to Clayton Eshleman last week, editor of the wonderful, long-defunct Caterpillar, and now of the very classy Sulfur. He wants me to contribute to the latter. I would love to be in it, but can't quite imagine myself there. He was a slightly trying person, I found. In so much of our conversation he seemed to be trying to find out if my enemies list was the same as his. But I'm not sure I have an enemies list. He seems like one of those people, with a genuine love of poetry, whose main energies are spent on the politics of poetry. Maybe that's what makes him a good editor.

I am to have a poem in some hundreds of busses (here) in July! An old one, at least three years old, 'Well Dennis O'Grady'. I am rather pleased, as it is about a bus stop. I am still writing quite a bit, will send you a bunch of poems one of these days. Funny you liked 'Bone': I have had such a revulsion against Randy, the subject of it, that I can't look at the poem except as a piece of elegant self-delusion. I have tried to be more clear-sighted in a quite long poem to the wonderful (and difficult) Charlie.[1]

Explanation of 'Bow Down': at school we had a folk-song to sing that started:

> A farmer he lived in the West country
> Bow down, bow down
> A farmer he lived in the West country
> And he had daughters one two three
> Singing I will be true unto my love
> If my love will be true unto me

It was a version of the Binnorie story, with the youngest sister being killed by the other two, and has no relevance to my poem, but I have always been interested by the second line, a regular refrain, which obviously indicated a dance performed while the song was sung.[2]

I am at last getting round to weeding my yard, which is gorgeous this cloudless and fogless summer, just bursting with flowers and herbs and strawberries. I go regularly to the gym, and my ambition is to look like Popeye (old face on young body): I get a lot of pleasure from it anyway. Also I have come across a very fine Latin primer, and since I didn't really do very well with Catullus last year I have decided to relearn Latin from the start so that I can read the Latin poets with some ease. I learn most of it in the toilet, whenever I go there. Charlie tells me that one day I will sit down and read some Latin in a library and will start shitting from sheer association. Be that as it may, I have much more appreciation for the powerful condensations of the language than I ever did in high school, where it was one of my least favorite subjects. The primer is so great because it has extracts from all the Latin authors (also from the Vulgate) except Caesar, so I'm reading them already. Of course the declensions and conjugations were there all the time in my head – I'm amazed – so it's not exactly hard work. I like Terence on taking the bull by the horns: auribus teneo lupum. I shall now sprinkle my letters with Latin maxims, like some pedant in Shakespeare.

Just about to read through Parkman's seven histories of exploration.[3]

How nice (I think) to be teaching a course on Contemp Poetry. Ours here has got swallowed up in the generalised Modern Poetry which I just taught. I've been thinking who I would include in it. First, the poets influenced ultimately by the Pisan Cantos: Olson (though I can't stand him, he is important for his effect on others), early Levertov, the Duncan of The

Opening of the Field, perhaps early Snyder, Creeley certainly, 'Gunslinger'. Next, Winters in America and in England: Bowers, perhaps Turner Cassity, Alan Stephens, Momaday perhaps, and Dick Davis, Wells, and Wilmer. British establishment: Hughes up to Crow, Hill (esp Mercian Hymns and Peguy), Tomlinson in rigorous selection, and – well Heaney or not? I'm really not sure Heaney is that good: I think he was invented by a committee of teachers with a sense of high fashion. (A very genial <u>man</u> though.) American establishment: early Lowell and late Bishop. (No Berryman.) Perhaps 'Ariel' which is good in spite of its influence. (No Merrill or any other poet who admits to going to the opera. No writer of dramatic monologs but Lowell – I am convinced that the form is the shallowest ever invented.) Impossible to classify: Bunting; W.S. Graham; Lorine Niedecker; Roy Fisher. A course on those four alone would be an education in itself!

[. . .]

Love

Thom

P.S. I understand Bunting (at 84) wowed 'em at the Albert Hall a month or two ago.

P.P.S. I did like the movie Betrayal, which you probably saw ages ago.

P.P.P.S. We have Allan's boyfriend (of the last 12 months) Richard Locke staying with us this week. The famous porn star of the Joe Gage movies. He is a remarkable-looking man & I have finally decided he is very nice, but I do not find him sexy! (Just as well, considering.)

1. 'The Differences' (CP 413–14) is about Charlie Hinkle (1957–87). See Glossary of Names.
2. The Binnorie story is a variant of the ballad 'The Twa Sisters'.
3. Francis Parkman, *France and England in North America*, 7 vols (1865–92).

TO *Oliver Sacks*   TLS (aerogramme) Sacks Foundation

Monday 4 June 1984

1216 Cole Street,
San Francisco,
Calif. 94117

June 4, 84

Dear Ollie,

I'm writing to you in London because you sent me your book when you were just about to fly there, and that was only the end of May. At last, the

Leg Book, which contained many a good surprise (considering I had already read a shortened version) and was well worth waiting for.[1] Different from your other books, not only in subject matter, but different in kind <u>because</u> of the subject matter. Personal and at times subjective – but that is much of the point of the book, isn't it? One of the most marvellous passages is the description of the migrainous scotoma on p.69, into which Nurse Sulu enters, or in a sense disappears. This is not only exquisitely written but it forms an essential link in the chain of your small realisations that add up to the larger understanding. (And I seem to remember that it was not there in your short version, the London Review of Books article that I can't lay my hands on at present,[2] living as I do in a state of perpetual disorganisation that looks like organisation – as opposed to yours, which looks honestly like disorganisation, I think, remembering your room on Christopher Street). Another exceptional passage is on pp.46-7, the explanation of proprioception. And of course the last chapter, which pulls everything together beautifully. At times, in the more ecstatic parts of the book, you read like Melville, and I admire Melville enormously, having read and reread him all through two years ago: it involves going forward for stretches on your nerve alone and is responsible for M at his best and worst (best Moby Dick and worst Pierre). It is a great risk-taking, a kind of effusion. I think there are two small weaknesses in the book, both due to a momentary loss of control; first with the first description of the bull on page 5, where you use the word huge(r) four times, and also stupendous, enormous, vast, and great. By the time I get to the last sentence ('It became, first a monster, and now the Devil') I have a sense of leaving the clear-cut reality of the mountain and of being led into a thicket of rhetoric. And yet a central sentence is absolutely right: 'It sat unmoved by my appearance, exceedingly calm, except that it turned its vast white face up towards me.' <u>That</u> is startlingly right, but then we get into language for its own sake, it seems to me. On the other hand, when the bull returns in your dream, it is very real, distorted monster as it was. The other passage I don't like is on pp.130-131, the part about the 'sweet haven', <u>too</u> effusive. Maybe I am wrong about these two passages, anyway, and forgive me for mentioning them: because they certainly don't harm the book as a whole (any more than occasional effusiveness in Melville or Dickens harms their best books as wholes), which is sturdy and astonishingly varied in texture and tone – a very rich work indeed! Perhaps it's because of this richness and variety, in fact, that the book can accommodate what I take to be a couple of weaknesses. – I feel properly honored that such a fine book takes my name as its first two words – thank you![3] And I enjoyed it, and learned from it, as I always do with your writing. I hope to see you here in July.

Love,

Thom

P.S. Reading through this note, I am not sure I make it clear on what level I am criticising your book. I consider you literally of Dickens and Melville level – up there, indeed, with them! It is not interesting to me just because it is written by a perceptive friend: it is "classic" in its importance.

1. Sacks, *A Leg to Stand On* (1984); see TG to Sacks, 20 April 1982, above.
2. Sacks, 'The Leg', *London Review of Books* 4, no. 11 (17 June 1982), 3–5.
3. The preface to *A Leg to Stand On* begins with the sentence, 'Thom Gunn has written powerfully of the "occasions" of poetry.'

TO *Barbara Godfrey*[1]

ALS (aerogramme) Jenny Fremlin

Thursday 14 June 1984

1216 Cole Street,
San Francisco,
Calif. 94117
USA

June 14, 84

Dear Barbara,

I'm afraid it is a dreadfully long time since I last wrote, I hope it was this year but I'm not even sure of that. My term ended a month ago, and it was very good really – all my classes went well – but it didn't leave me time for anything. No sooner was term ended – the day I finished marking exams, in fact – than [Allan Noseworthy] living in the desert phoned saying he was ill and could he come here to get treatment. Of course we encouraged him to come here, and it was good to feel we could do something for him, but about ten days ago he developed an abominable form of pneumonia. We took him to the emergency room at the hospital about midnight – poor man, you get so depressed and irritable when there is not enough oxygen in your blood (as if being ill wasn't depressing enough), and two days later he was in a breathing machine, with a tube going down to his lung. He cannot speak, because in some way the tube prevents the vocal cords from working, just writes notes on a pad. I realized yesterday that it's almost impossible he will make it now, he seems unable to keep any food in him, and his face and body are so wasted he looks like someone from Auschwitz. So it has been a sad month for us, and it's getting sadder. There is theoretically a small chance that he will survive, and it will be wonderful if he does, but if he does die in about 10 days time then it seems hard that his life has been prolonged for such a length of time when at this stage it is nothing but continuous pain.

I am sorry to start off with such unhappy things, but it seems to be something I can't get away from. I have about 6 phone calls a day from his friends in the East, a friend in the desert, his mother (who is coming out next week), etc., and there's usually lots of tears on the phone. Well, you can imagine.

The summer will end better, anyway. Ander is coming for 3 weeks of September and Thérèse for two weeks of October. That should be fun: I'm never quite sure what people want to see here, but I can always find out. Of course, we have the Democratic Convention starting here on Monday (today is Thurs), and I imagine the streets and busses will be full of people in funny hats.

[. . .]

I had very little time to put into the garden this spring, but it did wonderfully anyway. Everything from the previous year just came up again. I had added some lilies – wonderful red ones, I forget the name; and my strawberry friend gave me a few extra strawberry plants, since his multiply so fast; and the Oriental poppies etc spread very nicely without much help. I think foxgloves are almost the best flower of all – they are so generous, they give so much flower for so little. I only needed to buy foxglove seeds once, my first year here, and they have kept going by vigorously seeding themselves (bounteously, I should say) ever since.

[. . .]

Well, I must go off to the gym to exercise my almost-55 year old body. I'm all into health and Latin these days (I would have been shocked if I could have foreseen that at 25!). Then to see poor Allan at the hospital.

I hope you have a wonderful summer, dear Babs!

        Love X X X X X X
        Thom

1. Barbara Godfrey, née Thomson (1898–1989), TG's eldest aunt. See Glossary of Names.

Monday 2 July 1984

> 1216 Cole Street,
> San Francisco,
> Calif. 94117,
> USA
>
> July 2, 84

Dear Douglas,

Many thanks for your letter. June was a terrible month, in that Allan died of pneumocystis in hospital. He was in pain, I should think, the whole time. He had a fucking great tube down his throat or his nose to his lung for almost all of 2 weeks. But we got his family out here, and that was some comfort to him. He made funny little remarks to the end, writing on a pad since he couldn't talk. Apparently he was reconciled to his father, with tears and embraces, after several years of estrangement, and his nurse, a Philippine woman who had become quite knowledgable in working with AIDS patients, asked Allan if this was his "special friend"! But it was terrible, and shocking, and very painful. I suppose people at other times in history went through this kind of thing frequently, but we have become soft. Anyway, I shall miss Allan a great deal, he was very important to me.

Thank you for the reviews of Oliver Sacks' book, which I had already read. It is a good book, though not so good as the previous one – as I have told him, I found it too effusive in places. Even to the point of unctuousness (query: can one get away with the rhetorical "Nay" in the 20th cent? I think not.) I've read Heaney's Sweeney book and think it stinks, I wonder what you think.[1] I'm halfway through Alfred Corn's <u>Notes from a Child of Paradise</u> (only half way because I had an attack of sinus over the weekend which prevented me from doing anything except feel sorry for myself), and much recommend it to you. It is an aut [autobiographical?] narrative in meter. Some parts are quite magnificent, others embarrassing – but the good bits easily outweigh the bad. When he has a subject that boy can really write, there's no doubt about that. (But I do not understand his metrics at their most loose – I suspect they are just sloppy, but there just might be a theory behind them I suppose). Yes, I too wish I could like Fenton's poetry, especially as I am to read with him in NY this fall.

Certainly you shall meet August when you are here next. A most agreeable, nay, lovable, man. Bright and very funny, too.

I met Jon Silkin some time, and we got on very well. Hearing me read Bow Down, he asked if he could use it in Stand so I was delighted to say yes. Stand is better than the London Mag, after all, and I've contributed to that plenty. A mag by the way that I find contemptible is Grand Street, they sent me a copy full of Richard Ugh Murphy, (Murf the Smurf) and Amy Clampitt of the refined emotions, this plus an offer of $800 was supposed to make me want to write for them on Kipling's poetry. I've wanted to write about Kipling for some time, but I wanted more to make the gesture of turning down $800. (And I pretend not to be theatrical!)

I realise I have probably not shown you the enclosed poems. As you will see from the one to my brother I have now written a poem with both a father and a grandfather, perhaps for all I know uncles and great-grandfathers too.[2] – The mention of Adrienne Rich in the first line of another presents a pretty problem.[3] Most readers wd take the unqualified reference to be a mark of approval, but actually I don't like her stridency & her poetry bores me. On the other hand, I think the incident points to something quite charming in the character (Charlie) reciting her, and the fact that it is a male doing it, etc. As for Charlie, we are no longer boyfriends but are still friends (as you might be able to tell from the regretful tone of that poem – I could tell we were near an end!) I still find him wonderful, but I think for the first time in my life the age difference has got to me: we were always wanting to do different things. Well anyway, I'm glad to still know him.

[. . .]

Now for your questions about pictures. With some of them I feel highly defensive, feeling that if it is your business to track down my sources then it [is] my business to cover up my tracks. But the pictures you ask about are in two categories, I'd say, those that are acknowledged to be part of the poem's subject and those that aren't. I take them in your order. Caravaggio is obviously in the first category, and it is very proper of you to refer back to the picture itself.[4] I wrote the poem in Calif, but I referred back to reproductions (would I had read a little farther than Vasari, in my library work!) Anything you can find to illustrate images in the Bewick poem wd be in the same category, and obviously the pix in Positives are even more to the point, since the verses were written mostly about them. Mapplethorpe I have little opinion about: I am not sure which of his pictures would not interfere with the comparative generality of the poem.[5] (After all, it is dedicated to him because I had the idea for it while he was photographing me). The Little Jew is also in the first category, but I'm damned if I know how you cd lay your hands on it. I think I saw it reproduced in an English Sunday Supplement (Observer or Sunday Times) between about Sept 1954 and April 1955 (the poem was published in May), and I had seen the picture at least twice before (it was taken in Warsaw, I think, if that's any help).[6] VERY clever of you to find what certainly looks like the right Madonna and Child, though when I saw it in the Chicago Art Institute the ascription I think was anonymous: but that certainly looks like a curl in the middle of the baby's forehead, doesn't it?[7] The Carl Timner picture: he is now famous, I understand, in Germany (I knew him in Rome, when we were in our early 20s). I don't know what the picture would be called, but it was painted in 1954, about Carnival time.[8] He was amused by my poem, because he had intended one of the 2 figures in it to be female but I (typically) took them both to be male (and there were other figures lurking about in the background, too). I'll keep this letter open and see if Billy has a photo of his self-portrait (this seems to me to come somewhere between the two categories, in that his pictures could never be part of the common knowledge of the common reader, but are part of the overt subject of the poem).[9] The remaining two examples come in the second category, i.e. the reader of my poem was not supposed to be capable of referring back to an available artefact. 'Bravery' is a trivial poem, anyway, but the original painting entered my imagination and came out other than what it was: I knew the painting wd remain unknown and the ref to C Arnett was in the nature of a mystification, like Ramon Fernandez in The Idea of Order at Key West, for example. (Only I know where this picture is now, and I don't believe you have ever seen it!)[10] – The Snail is in the same class, really. You only know that my poem started from a picture because I was unwise enough to tell you. I probably wouldn't recognise the picture if I saw it now: I saw it when I was waiting for a friend at Stanford (about 1957?) and was leafing through a book of reproductions – but let me say at the risk of pretentiousness that I remade it so thoroughly in my imagination that I suspect what I saw was entirely different from the way I now remember it. Very unKlee-ish, in any case.[11] (Hope this para doesn't seem Hostile!)

Got to the end of a page, nothing more to say.

Love,

Thom

1. Heaney, *Sweeney Astray* (1983).
2. 'An Invitation' (*CP* 411–12).
3. See 'The Differences' (*CP* 413–14).
4. Caravaggio, *Conversion of St Paul* (1601); see 'In Santa Maria del Popolo' (*CP* 93–4).
5. 'Song of a Camera' (*CP* 347–8) is dedicated to Mapplethorpe.
6. The iconic photograph of the Warsaw Ghetto uprising (1943); see 'Confessions of the Life Artist' (*CP* 162).

7. Probably the anonymous *Virgin and Child* (*c.* 1265–75) at the Art Institute of Chicago; see 'Expression' (*CP* 321).

8. Timner's painting *Vier Tänzer* ('Four Dancers', 1954); see 'Before the Carnival' (*CP* 44–5).

9. See 'Selves' (*CP* 322–4).

10. TG owned Arnett's painting of a man wearing a leather jacket; see 'Bravery' (*T* 16–17).

11. Likely Paul Klee's watercolour *Snail* (1924); see 'Considering the Snail' (*CP* 117).

TO *Tony Tanner*   TLS King's

Monday 30 July 1984

1216 Cole Street,
San Francisco,
Calif. 94117,
USA

July 30, 84

Dear Duke,

Haven't heard from you for many a twelvemonth but one gets used to that sort of thing nowadays, and I have certainly been wondering how the Ducal palace – and the Ducal passions – have been getting on. Heard nothing of you since my phone call from Nadia last year. Clive and I keep in touch, but it seems that you and he never run into each other.

The household here keeps pretty much together, in fact things are a bit better this year than in recent years, in that certain alcoholic and drug habits are better in control. Bill is something of a concern at times, Mike is exemplary while remaining human! Don said of Mike that he loves him because he always tries so hard to live a good life. Not the good life, you notice, but a good life. I think that's well put. Don astonished everybody for the last year by having a heavy sexual relation with a girl we have all known for some twelve or more years. And I always thought his bisexuality was bullshit. And for him to be heavily sexual in any way but through the mind was also a surprise. It is wonderful that people can still go on changing. Not sure that I change much – though I have certainly surprised myself in one or two minor ways. [. . .] I not only gave up smoking again last October but have been going to a gym since last November: this also astonishes me by giving me a great deal of pleasure. In fact my life seems to be led, these days, in a condition of Whitmanian astonishment. Not that my poetry is very whitmanian at the moment: I have been writing quite a lot this last nine months, a lot for me, anyway, and it is severely metrical, almost all of it. I'm pleased to be writing again, since as usual I'd written very little since the publication of my last book, 1982. Happens every time – I publish a new book, and I have great difficulty in writing for the next two years. Thinking about how to deal with this publication-jinx, I proposed to myself the following plan. I would settle on an arbitrary date – 1992 – for the publication of my next book. By that time, in all probability, I will have completed at least one and a half books, so possibly with half of an unpublished book still in my drawer I won't feel that drained sense that I have nothing left to give anyone in 1992. I will have something left – half a book! Of course things don't always work out quite as logically as all that.

Actually the summer had a terrible start. Just as term was ending (I was marking exams) a friend, Allan, phoned me from Palm Springs where he had been living with his lover, and said he had AIDS and had decided he ought to come to SF or NY for treatment, so I said come stay with us and gave him my room. He was one of my best friends, since 1974, and we have always been very close. Two weeks after he came to stay with us he developed the abominable form of pneumonia that is one of the most common of killers in that condition (he already had the skin cancer), and we took him in to the emergency room one midnight. Two and a half weeks later he was dead. It was all awful, and I was quite shaken. I suppose that until about 50 years ago everybody went through this kind of thing pretty frequently – watching people dear to them dying young, but modern medicine has kept us so fenced off from such arduous experiences. I can't believe he died only June 21, I seem to have been through a year of sadness since then.

I am to be in Cambridge (England not Mass.) next June, did you know? They are paying my fare to be part of the Cambridge Poetry Festival – there is going to be a bizarre collection of poets there, I can tell you. I don't imagine you will want a further complication to your life (which I assume will still be complicated) by having a guest, so I'll get the festival people to put me up in a hotel, as they are willing to do. But I do look forward to seeing you – as much as possible. I am pretty grey-haired these days, but still something of the live wire. Did you read Rob Wells' wonderful translation of the Georgix.[1] Clive is good (very good) and Dick too, but that achievement is beyond the reach of either of them I think. Also of me, for that matter. I'm reading all of Francis Parkman's histories right now, they give me a certain melancholy satisfaction that comes from well-written history. It's like Gibbon – a lot of wickedness and cruelty, but admirably laid before one by a mind that set store by accuracy and balance.[2] I suppose it almost implies that balance and accuracy are virtues that can, if not do battle with the wickedness and cruelty, at least offset them. Enuf of this turgid moralising. [. . .]

Much love, and to Nadia too if she is there,

Thom

1. Virgil, *The Georgics*, trans. Wells (1982).
2. Edward Gibbon, *The History of the Decline and Fall of the Roman Empire*, 6 vols (1776–89).

TO *Douglas Chambers*   TLS Toronto

Tuesday 9 October 1984

1216 Cole Street,
San Francisco,
Calif. 94117

Oct 9, 84

Dear Ole Thing,

   [. . .]

I did see Oliver, on one of his lightning visits here, and he was bubbling over with his peculiar kind of worried energy which I love so much in him but could so easily find irritating. I doubt if I'll have time to visit him in NY. I'm going to be there for 8 days, staying with people I've never stayed with before, and feel I should spend some time visiting Allan's friends in turn. This will take up my entire time, so far as I can see, what with a draggy poetry reading at the YMHA as reason for being there.

My garden has been looking quite <u>specious</u>, in Ben Jonson's sense! Cosmos bigger than I've ever seen them before, etc. Also, at THE GYM (temple of the ego) my pecs and biceps are bigger than I've ever seen them before. A little late in life but you can always teach an old dog new tricks. I had one remarkable meeting with two guys, lovers, one of whom I'd made it with last year, very happily, and the other was his half-brother who he'd not known till they were adults: very beautiful guys, anyway, who suggested we go home, and as we were leaving the bar remarked, 'we have some speed', and we then had sex for fifteen hours. Fifteen! Of course I was strung out for half a week after that, but it was worth it. Then my brother came for 3 weeks, with whom I have a different kind of relation than the Speed Bros with each other.[1] Then I had another session with the S B. Only 12 hrs that time. I think I'd better stop doing it with them or I'll have a stroke or a coronary or sumpn . . . My brother's visit was terrific, we had a few arguments, but got on very well, especially considering we have not spent 3 weeks (or 3 days, probably) perpetually in each other's company since well before the age of 20. All my friends liked him, and he liked all my friends.

[. . .]

I note your exasperated comments on your students. Well, it's a problem, isn't it. But I still genuinely prefer teaching the relatively untouched (by education) to those who have been around Eng Depts long enough to speak about resonance in poetry (Did you see Educating Rita, the reference is to that if you don't recognize it). This goes for poetry writing classes as well. Perhaps it is just a sign of my own self-conceit, that I like to have an effect on those who are more easily impressed.

I found – still find – the most necessary thing with almost all undergraduates is to show them a) that they already like/appreciate poetry, poetries, they do not think of as being such, anything rhythmical, for instance, all this leading to b) the emphasis on the variety of poetry that is there for them to read. This is where I have to avoid the theories of not just Winters but any critic: they must see first how it's all poetry, including stuff I personally don't much like, Vachel Lindsay, perhaps, or Life Studies. I see the teacher's earliest duty as being to introduce the student less to quality than to the mixed richness and trash of a whole genre. Though naturally I have always emphasised what I thot good (I'd be less human if I didn't). I did for many years, probably would still if I taught freshmen – good lord yes I did it this very year with juniors and seniors now I come to think of it . . . . (resume sentence:) I did for many years find IA Richards' four kinds of meaning (sense, intention, feeling, tone) very useful for undergraduates trying to speak about poetry, as pegs to hang thr reactions on. Of course, they are pretty crude pegs: intention especially doesn't hold up to sophisticated examination, but the terms are useful for what they can do at a relatively early stage.

This is why I find it difficult to deal with what you say, argumentatively enough, about 'statement v. enactment.' The opposition is a fruitful one for the elementary student (any undergraduate, nowadays), but whereas statement (sententiae, italicized in Macbeth in the Folio, for example) remains a pretty clear category to me, 'enactment' as a category has become more imprecise as I have read more: it's a catch-all term, so that almost anything one likes, stylistically, can be called enactment, from The Congo to one's favorite passages in Shakespeare. So I certainly agree with the way you are opening the eyes of your undergraduates to possibilities, but you can't speak the same way to me!

As for Winters. Well, he needs reading in toto and you need to read him for what he can give you, otherwise you get bogged down in your own irritations.

He has nothing to tell you about Milton but a lot about Emily Dickinson. At his worst he is ungenerous and bad-tempered, and it is necessary to read him with greater generosity and good temper than he seems to be prepared to give you. This is difficult, no doubt, but he has a lot to give in other ways.

I myself <u>am</u> finally if not an absolute Wintersian then at least a fairly consistent fellow-traveller. That's a wishy-washy thing to be no doubt, but I have my reasons for not going along with him completely. Of course I wouldn't want to appear anybody's disciple in public because that is the first way to be misread. But I do have genuine and long-last disagreements with him on many important matters – on what Jonas Barish calls his 'prejudice against drama', on his misreading of the 18th century (Pope, anyway), on his lumping together British and American romanticism as if they were the same thing (he understood the American type very well), and on numerous of his exclusions, which became greater with age. However, I essentially agree with his definition of poetry – I do think he grasps the solid core of it (as <u>I</u> understand it), and he has said more meaningful things about poems and poetry than any other critic I know (of course, his book about the American novel is a masterpiece, but that's not what we're talking about).[2] He opened my eyes to the virtues of more good poems than I can begin to remember, the virtues of which have remained strong and sustaining to me through thirty years. (I think for example of Bridges' 'Eros', which I wouldn't know if it weren't for him: Bridges isn't even <u>represented</u> in the <u>Norton Anth of Ptry</u>.) Where he and I wd not agree in general is that I think great talent can not only on occasion overcome 'faulty' principles but turn them into poetry as good as if it were written on 'sound' principles – hence I can admire Pound and Bunting and Rimbaud as much as I do, heroic adventurers who succeed most of the time, and since they succeed in the main thing then it must be a good thing to be somewhat unprincipled!!!!

W's great core of prose, for me, remains: <u>Primitivism and Decadence</u>; the essay on 16th century poetry (in its original form as reprinted in Paul Alpers' anthology of essays on Elizabethan poetry);[3] and various other essays, especially from <u>The Anatomy of Nonsense</u>; and even selected pages from <u>Forms of Discovery</u>, tho that book as a whole is very uneven and riddled with the irritations of a man dying of cancer.

All this prompted by certain very off-hand remarks of yours. Poor Douglas! But I thought I ought to come clean.

To change the subject to a poet Winters loathed (and who loathes him) have you seen Duncan's much awaited book?[4] Pretty good, with some wonderful surprises, especially the last poem, which he said in a recent reading is really as series of disconnected poems (whew, that was a relief, I'd been trying to connect them someway), 'Circulations of the Song'. He looked much better during the reading (last month) than for a long time, I guess I told you he almost died – complete kidney blowout – in Feb, and has been on dialysis ever since. Is still. Must stop.

Excuse <u>terrible</u> typing & haste –

Love –

I like to think of you on your Sabine farm[5]

This letter is so long because I am not teaching –

Love from all

Th

P.S. We look forward to February (let me know the dates when you next write, so I can avoid having too much to grade that week – if I can).

P.P.S. I have in mind a very <u>nasty</u> poem about Philemon & Baucis. That <u>must</u> be a first: whoever could want to be nasty about such a nice old couple!

1. See 'Nights with the Speed Bros.' (*BC* 34).

2. Winters, *Maule's Curse: Seven Studies in the History of American Obscurantism* (1938). Winters's compendium *In Defense of Reason* (1947) comprises three short books – *Primitivism and Decadence*, *Maule's Curse*, and *The Anatomy of Nonsense* – and a long essay, 'The Significance of *The Bridge* by Hart Crane'.

3. Winters, 'The 16th Century Lyric in England: A Critical and Historical Reinterpretation', in *Elizabethan Poetry: Modern Essays in Criticism*, ed. Alpers (1967), 93–125.

4. Duncan, *Ground Work: Before the War* (1984).

5. A reference to Horace's farm in the Roman Campagna, mentioned often in his *Odes*. Chambers was a great gardener and wrote about gardens in literature: see *The Planters of the English Landscape Garden: Botany, Trees, and the Georgics* (1993), and *Stonyground: The Making of a Canadian Garden* (1996), about his familial home near Walkerton, Ontario.

ALS Sacks Foundation

1216 Cole Street,
San Francisco,
Calif. 94117

Nov 23, 84

Dear Ollie,

Here is the poem you asked for.[1] I saw the human perception of the plant as inviting mixed metaphors. With "a thicket of lances" what I really wanted to name was those spiky assemblages which guard the exits to parking lots – if you try to <u>enter</u> that way they will mangle your tires. But I don't know what they are called.

How good to see you, o saffron-handed one![2] I may have seemed in a doze of antihistamine, but I was attentive and interested at the center. I have thought about what you said of anecdotes & narratives. I think we all live a series of anecdotes, but some power put to use early on permits or compels us to <u>connect</u> them into narratives (usually picaresque): thus – this anecdote happened and <u>then</u> this anecdote happened <u>so that</u> this anecdote happened <u>until</u> . . . etc. We (most of us) <u>compose</u> our lives into narratives.

We also <u>compose</u> our facial expressions. Someone with Down's Syndrome, for example, does not. If we didn't compose our faces, we too would let our lower lips hang down, become vacant-eyed, instead of keeping our mouths firmly closed and making sure our eyes carry some kind of expression others will read as meaning something or maybe just as meaning we are in control.

I wonder what the origin is of the urge to "compose" oneself. Is it something taught us and learned (social)? Or is it inherent to being an average human with an unharmed brain? Hm.

Love,

Thom

1. 'Yellow Pitcher Plant' (*CP* 439–40).
2. Sacks writes about this meeting – 'the curry blew up, and I got covered with yellow powder' – in 'A Symposium on Thom Gunn', *Threepenny Review* 102 (Summer 2005), 7.

TO *Mary and Catherine Thomson*

TLS (aerogramme) Jenny Fremlin
Friday 14 December 1984

1216 Cole Street,
San Francisco,
Calif. 94117,
USA

Dec 14, 84

Dear Mim and Kay,
    [. . .]
    Yes we took [Ander] to the cabin at Russian River, which Mike and Bob (Mike under Bob's direction) have transformed in the last three summers from a rotting old shed into a pleasure palace for the townies. Ander loved it, as he did pretty well everything else.
    When did I complain about my parents, as you say in yr letter? I try not to complain about anything. ('Try'). In any case I wouldn't have wanted different parents.
    I went to New York for a week. Saw your friend Oliver Sacks there, but unfortunately had had an attack of sinus the night before and had had to take so much antihistamine that I wasn't very alert. However he spoke all the time, and as usual gave me a lot to think about afterwards, telling me all about his patients and the problems he is working on now, while we ate the filthiest (I don't mean dirty, just awful-tasting) Indian meal I had ever touched. He had fish and I had chicken but my chicken tasted of his fish. But he ate all his fish and then all my chicken, he has huge appetites and does everything, including talking, on an enormous scale. It was wonderful seeing him, anyway. Saw various other friends, going back to my friend Ted Tayler from Stanford thirty years ago, now on his third wife but apart from his marriages a wonderfully wise (and funny) man, and author of an exceptional book on Milton (who he points out was also married three times).[1] However I got more and more depressed in NY: it was very sad without poor Allan, who I usually stayed with. I went to see his neighbors and the man who rented his apartment: all his things were still there, including some quite valuable stuff and they didn't know what to do with them, so I am writing to his brother. I did notice that he had kept every letter, it looked like, that had ever been written to him, so I located an enormous bundle by myself and dropped them in a dustbin outside. As a friend said who had to clear

out Sylvia Plath's flat after her suicide: 'The dead leave everything behind.' Don't they just.

San Francisco is not the happiest of places now. I know a lot of people who have died of AIDS. As everybody says, it is like the Plague – you don't know who is going to get it next but it's going to get a lot more people before it is finished. They now think the germ has an incubation period of up to five years. And it is always – eventually – fatal. Just recently the straight people have started to get it, so it's going to sweep right across the population – in Europe too. We keep hearing of cases like this one (my barber told me this). Someone told his parents in the Mid West he has AIDS. They said they would send money, but he was not to come home to die, as it was God's judgment on him for being gay. (I said I hope he accepted the money.)

[. . .]

Well I was already reconciled to having that asshole in the White House in Nov. But naturally I was not happy. The trouble is the rich and the middle classes go around in cars and do not see how the poor and homeless and (in various ways) helpless are living on the streets in large numbers now. I see this because I <u>walk</u>. Also I still think that one of the few duties a govt has is to look after the helpless. [. . .]

   Love,

    Nephew

[. . .]

---

1. Edward W. Tayler, *Milton's Poetry: Its Development in Time* (1979). Tayler (1931–2018) was a scholar of Shakespeare and Milton at Columbia University. He and TG were graduate students together at Stanford in the late 1950s, and TG has remarked that Tayler was instrumental in teaching him how to teach.

1985

Thursday 3 January 1985¹

> 1216 Cole Street,
> San Francisco,
> Calif. 94117
>
> Jan 3, 84²

Dear Sex Kitten,

I'm assuming that you're back on this continent and suffering the cold that the early settlers and missionaries underwent that I've just finished reading about in the seven vols of Parkman.

[. . .]

Well, now that you've read Station Island, what do you think of it, I wonder? The middle part, the sections of the title poem, I mean. It's terrific, in many ways, the best thing SH has done, I think.³ A constant happiness of phrase, as when he refers to the young priest in his soutane on his bicycle, being 'glossy as a blackbird' – beautiful, enviable! And yet I have my usual trouble with the work as a whole – perhaps even more than usual. As there has always [been] an earlier presence lurking stylistically behind the poetry – whether Lowell or Yeats, here the whole thing is haunted – not by Dante, as is Heaney's intention, but by Dante through Eliot, which I assume is unintentional. The influence especially is of the blitz ghost appearing in imitation terza rima in Little Gidding, one of the few passages in TSE that I really love. From that passage Heaney borrows a whole general tone and feeling, besides many stylistic characteristics. I can't help feeling that he is borrowing too much from Eliot stylistically, and not really making it his own. It's all very puzzling – I can hardly believe he doesn't know what he is doing, but if he is why is he doing it this way!

[. . .]

All send their love – I must stop and get an F bus.

X X
Uncle Thom

1. Date supplied through internal evidence.
2. TG misdated the letter.
3. Heaney, *Station Island* (1984).

TO *Mary and Catherine Thomson*   TLS Jenny Fremlin
Wednesday 30 January 1985

1216 Cole Street,
San Francisco,
Calif. 94117,
USA

Jan 30, 85

Dear M & C,
    We are having an unusually cold winter, like everybody else, so I am glad I
haven't put in the new strawberry plants – it is supposed to be frosty for the
next 3 nights. When you say in your letter about its being so cold with you,
I so well remember that depressing winter of 1947-8, going to get our coal,
Jenny with whooping cough, etc. (One of these days I shall replace Barbara
as chief rememberer of 40 year old facts.) But how kind you were to have
your awkward nephew live with you.
    [. . .]
    All the more as I'm writing this short letter to say that I am not coming to
England this year after all. I have cancelled my trip, and have already written
to the two festival committees in London and Cambridge telling them not
to expect me. They will probably be very annoyed with me – everybody
will probably be annoyed with me – but it can't be helped. Under Reagan –
or rather in his second term – the sexual bigotry that is usually not far
beneath the surface of any immigration official at airports and 'points of
entry' has indeed surfaced, and immigration is giving a hard time to foreign
homosexuals entering the country. Worse than hard time, I should say –
turning them back. So I would run the risk of not being able to get back
here, my own home. There is nothing to worry about if I don't leave the
country and then try to get back in, but there is if I do! So I have decided
to wait until there is some test case that gets things decided in the courts
(I hope I don't have to wait until there is a new president), but have no wish
to be a martyr and the subject of the test case. Wouldn't be able to afford
the lawyers, anyway. I am sorry to disappoint you and particularly sorry I
shall not see Bar (I hope to get Ander and his buxom widow Bette over here
this summer), but I can't really say I am sorry not to be doing the readings

411

in England.¹ I have really got rather tired of travelling, and I have got VERY tired of big celebrity readings. I have no wish to be famous, and I am working (successfully, it seems) at stopping being famous.

Term has started and I have lots of new students. I hurt my back <u>again</u> last Saturday – not in the gym, I think, and am having long soaks in hot baths, which I hate! It is getting better. I suppose I just have to be very careful about lifting things for the rest of my life. Mike is watching a long long serial on TV (English) about Anglo-India, Peggy Ashcroft etc, called The Jewel in the Crown, I think. About the only thing I watch on TV is the music videos, i.e. short films made of popular songs and singers. They are popular with seventeen-year olds and me.

Catherine sent me the prettiest xmas card this year, and Mary's was a hoot! I loved the infant Jesus laughing at the pie throwing. I showed it to people, and they couldn't believe it had been sent to me by my 70 year old aunt . . .

Much love, and I hope it all thaws soon, also Margaret Thatcher's icy heart,

X X X   Th

1. Ander and Margaret separated in 1984. Ander and Bett Berwitz were together from around 1984 until Bett's death in March 2018.

TO *Robert Conquest*   ALS (postcard¹) Elizabeth Neece Conquest
c. Wednesday 6 March 1985²

[1216 Cole Street,
San Francisco, CA 94117]

Dear Bob –

Or rather <u>you</u> sent <u>me</u> Ted's poem – thank you very much. I wouldn't have seen it otherwise. He is an idiot to have accepted the job, though: he can never resign from it, and is condemned for the rest of his life to write about the <u>weather</u> of royal funerals births, marriages, etc.³ Hot weather, snow, variable overcasts, sporadic showers, rain alternating with sleet, high winds in the coastal regions, perhaps there is plenty of subject matter left for him after all.

Thom

1. Postcard is Poetry Comicard 2: 'Song: to Celia', by Ben Jonson; from *Poetry Comics! A Cartooniverse of Poems*, by Dave Morice (1982).
2. Date supplied by postmark.

3. Hughes was appointed Poet Laureate of the UK in December 1984, then an appointment for life. The poem Conquest sent TG was probably Hughes's first Laureate poem, 'Rain-Charm for the Duchy', written for the christening of Prince Harry and published in *The Observer* on 23 December 1984.

TO *Tony Tanner*   TLS King's
Friday 17 May 1985

                                                    1216 Cole Street,
                                                    San Francisco,
                                                    Calif. 94117,
                                                    USA

                                                    May 17, 85

Dear Tony,

Here at last is the letter I have owed you for some months. As a man grows older, or anyway as I grow older, I find that teaching, when I am doing it, takes up more and more of my attention and time. Not that I teach any better – in fact this last term I didn't teach very well – but it certainly sets me back in my correspondence. Now at last I am through, and I can write you and weed my yard, and get down to some interesting reading. I'm delighted that I'm NOT coming to England this summer – I'd probably already be on my way, and having to deal with air travel and time changes and customs and then the incredibly phony world of big name poetry readings, where people are really more interested in your personality than in the poetry that is frankly rather difficult to follow and where you are doing it for the money or the glamor but for anything but the poetry itself. The reason I'm not coming though is that under Reagan the immigration people have been giving a hard time to gays entering this country, and since I would be a British national returning to this country but still without any special status I would risk not being able to come back to what is after all my home. And I couldn't very well lie, after all my frankness in print! [. . .]

I feel much oppressed by deaths. First two of my three favorite living poets died within a couple of months of each other, J.V. Cunningham and Basil Bunting. The third is Robert Duncan, who is barely alive. Then Jo Miles died last Sunday – a release as they say: when I last saw her, a week or so before her death, she could not finish a simple sentence, and she was aware that she couldn't, and she minded.[1] Then about three weeks ago our terrific dog died – easily the best dog I have ever known, large, handsome, generous and intelligent, liked even by dog-haters like my Aunt Catherine and my boyfriend of last year Charlie. And of course, AIDS is ongoing: a friend went into hospital a few days ago who we had long suspected had it, and this letter was just interrupted by a phone call from the above-mentioned Charlie who told me that one of the guys he shares with has a biopsy scheduled and they suspect the kind of skin cancer (which we airily refer to as "k.s" as if it were a Texas magnate on a soap opera) associated with the disease.[2]

Don was round yesterday. He is a constant delight to us – to all of us, I think. He is one of those people whose very silliness is endearing. I guess that implies that he has 'mellowed' – yes, I suppose he has. But he also remains one of the brightest and kindest people I know: there are limitations to that brightness and that kindness, but they are limitations that serve to concentrate.

[. . .]

I hope you are well, and better. How was teaching again? Are you exercising yourself still? Exercise is important to all of us, as a man grows older, indeed! I go to the local gym three times a week, as I am sure I have told you several times already, and will tell you several times more. I bore everybody new that I meet by trying to persuade them to join a gym and learn Latin.

I did read a lot of James Baldwin this spring and was very impressed by Another Country. It had its best-sellerish moments, but then so does Mailer, and I thought it better than anything by Mailer (except perhaps The Executioner's Song, but then that's not really a novel). Baldwin does seem peculiarly neglected, for someone so good. Have you ever written anything on him? Have you read Coleman Dowell's White on Black on White? Another great book, I think – largely unreviewed and so largely unknown – which also deals with black-white and hetero-homo relationships in almost every conceivable different combination.

Mike sends his love and so does Billy – Mike is now a very handsome grey-haired man with the body of an 18-year old. Billy is pretty well bald and is excited about taking a three-day train trip to Wisconsin to see his parents. [. . .] Since I have given you a survey of changing hair styles I should complete it by saying that my own hair is perfect! No, it is very grey in a kind of neutral varying way, and I am looking rather sagging in general (all except my chest and biceps, which appear to belong to a younger man!) and am fast approaching that look of the armored reptile behind which the old man's eyes dart furtively, seeking refuge . . .

That seems a good place to stop. Forgive me for having taken so long to write, and write and tell me how you are.

XXXXXXXXXXXXXX ← kisses to your body in general
XXXXXXXX ← kisses to your buttocks and private parts
XX ← a kiss on each closed eyelid, like a thought from one of
the Angels
X ← a kiss to that holiest of tabernacles, your pretty little
navel

       Love,
          Thom

1. TG wrote Miles's obituary in *California Monthly* 95, no. 6 (June–July 1985), 29.
2. Kaposi's sarcoma, a type of skin cancer associated with advanced HIV. The character J. R. Ewing in the TV series *Dallas* (1978–91) was referred to simply as J. R.

TO *Mary and Catherine Thomson*

TLS (aerogramme) Jenny Fremlin

Tuesday 23 July 1985

1216 Cole Street,
San Francisco,
Calif. 94117,
USA

July 23 / 85

Dear Mary and Catherine,

No, I'm not dead, though it is so long since I wrote that you might well have been wondering. I am enjoying a quiet summer, a contrast to last year, when Allan died. It is more of a typical summer for the weather too, overcast but fairly warm most of the time, which I really do prefer: it makes it much easier to stay at my desk. I'm preparing my lectures on 400 years of English poetry: just finished writing the one on Elizabethan songs today, so you see I have quite a way to go yet, even though the course doesn't start until January.

I can see the humming birds dashing about, from my upper window: they live on sugar (nectar) so they have terrific vigor. Very aggressive to each other, too, they will charge each other in mid air. Ander really liked seeing them dart around last summer. My raspberries <u>finally</u> justified themselves – we kept picking them week after week through the whole of June and July. However, the strawberries are behaving most oddly: they seem more bent on survival than on producing fruit, sending runners all over everywhere to create new plants. Maybe they know something that I don't, that is sending them into a panic.

I loved Isherwood's comment on his eighty years, which he is certainly beginning to show: "yes, I'm afraid the entire East Wing has gone dark." I think it is wonderful that he can joke like that about his failing powers: I certainly have good models to follow in my life!!

[. . .]

I finally became a capitalist and invested some money. In very safe bonds. So safe that they won't bring me much when I retire. But it will be something, and it will be all I have to live on besides a) what I get from rents from the house (which will be paid off in about 10 years) and b) what I get from my books, but that is never much. I have no pension coming from the university because I teach only half-time. Not that I worry about it. I imagine my needs will not be many: we all get free medical insurance at the age of 65, and I shall no longer wish to dress like a fashionable dandy. (That was a joke.)

[. . .]

I saw five hours of the fifteen hour Live AID concert, for the starving Africans. It was wonderful, the kind of thing television does well, very exciting and moving.

I am reading Horace, a project that will take me several years. Don't say Horace Who? (That's what a character in one of Shaw's plays said to an elder statesman when she asked him his favorite poet and he said Horace. But he's much too good for an elder statesman.) Also reading The Mill on the Floss in between times, for the first time since my teens.

Thérèse still doesn't know if she is going to visit this year, after having cancelled last year. I wonder if she is ill? – I am having some friends to dinner tonight: strawberries for pudding (not from the yard, there are only about two ripe), and a tomato salad to start with, and a lamb stew. I have recently found an easy way to make lamb stew.

I hope Mary is going fruit picking again this year with her bawdy hard-drinking friends; and Catherine will be off to China perhaps, or somewhere equally exotic. I plan on going down to the grocer's at the corner some time – but not for several weeks, and then only for a very short visit.

No you were very generous and kind to me in my teens. I often think of how disruptive I must have been to your lives in the 1940s, and I count myself lucky to have aunts who took me in so selflessly. Orphans are always a bore – but particularly in their teens.

I must go to the gym and improve my health.

     Love,

       Thom

TO *Douglas Chambers*   ALS (cards[1]) Toronto
Thursday 26 September 1985[2]

[1216 Cole Street,
San Francisco,
CA 94117]

Sep 26

Dear Duggle –
    This is a crappy card, & I do not mean it, nor do I find the wings in the pic attractive. But I am at a loose end & feel internally vigorous but outwardly sick – it's OK, <u>not</u> "AIDS-related": an intermittent toothache preparatory to root canal work, a back "put-out" yet again so I can only walk slowly & in a 90-year old fashion, etc. etc. Just all the ills that flesh is heir to.
    A really nice nothing-summer. Overcast a lot of the time – even our Indian Summer, now, is not its usual self – but I have applied myself to the English poets in sequence, which as I've already told you several times is a pleasure (just moving from Gray to Burns). I'd forgotten how <u>good</u> FRL was in Revaluation, esp. on Pope, & on, for example, a comparison between the verse movement of Shelley & Wordsworth. His later books [are] taken up with wars in the University Grub Streets, but he did start so well . . . I'm reading a splendid book by M.H. Abrams, <u>Supernatural Naturalism</u>, which I'm sure you must know. He writes so well – so clearly, I mean, & the stuff is all so interesting.
    I wonder if I can start to like Shelley better. I would so like to. I'll find out next month!
    Every now and again I have sex – <u>always</u> "safe", I may say – but not as often as I could. Lots of people here are still nuts, & the bathhouses that are still open have reverted to what they were. People find it very difficult to stop doing what they like best, which I completely understand – but you'd think they'd try to [modify?] it when it will lead almost certainly to a painful and drawn-out death. Promiscuous sex is no longer political, just suicide.
    [. . .]
    I told you, didn't I, we invented a National Poetry Prize & awarded it to Duncan. He had peritonitis so couldn't come for the award, & then shingles and so couldn't come for the press conference 10 days later, but he sounded terrific on the phone a few days ago, & I couldn't stop him talking. [. . .]
    Saw a divinely funny English movie last night, called <u>A Private Function</u>, about kidnapping a pig with diarrhoea – just my kind of subject, as you can imagine. I hurt my already bad back with laughing – & very much liked

most of <u>The Return of the Soldier</u>, its acting & direction, until the ending, which posed too easy an R.D. Laing choice between a healthy insanity & an unhealthy sanity. But still very good. – If you haven't seen it, don't bother to see <u>The Kiss of the Spider Woman</u>, which I found grossly sentimental & rather boring & with an ending neither I nor anybody I have spoken to can figure out.

I have written only one real poem this year. No, Andrew Hudson is not that guy who does soft porn pix of bricklayers & athletes undressing – tho I know who you mean. He does decorative, rather 'in' artistic jokes, but some of his work would make terrific illustrations & I think it may be a lovely booklet, & he also (from his letters) seems a warm & sweet man.[3]

I must soak my pore back in a hot bath then go to Berkeley for a ridiculous committee meeting.

> Love to Michael,[4]
> + to yourself – you are going to England <u>now</u>? – I don't understand –
> X X X X   Thom

I think my handwriting is even worse than yours – at least yours is decorative. Sorry, I'll type next time.

1. The two greeting cards show leather-jacketed men wearing dark sunglasses.
2. Date supplied through internal evidence.
3. TG's pamphlet *The Hurtless Trees* (1986) includes illustrations by Hudson.
4. Michael Wade (1960–90), Chambers's on/off lover.

TO *Ander Gunn*   ALS (aerogramme) Ander Gunn
Thursday 28 November 1985

> 1216 Cole Street,
> San Francisco,
> CA 94117,
> USA

> November 28 / 85

Dear Ander,

Thanksgiving day today. I am cooking the turkey, since I seem to get up early these days. So I just put it on, with an onion, a carrot, & an apple inside to join the dressing later on, & I also put on the neck in some water etc. to make some broth for the gravy. Yum yum. The turkey was 22 lbs, & there are only 9 of us to eat it, so there will be leftovers for days. Now I don't have

418

any responsibilities left until 5, except to look at the rain & gossip & <u>baste the turkey</u> constantly!

[. . .]

A warning: I was given an answering machine for my birthday. This hooks on to the phone, & since I (a) hate having to stay in for a promised phone call that may never be made anyway (e.g. roofer says "I'll call you Thurs afternoon" & calls Fri morning instead) and (b) often hate answering the phone even when I am in, it is a wonderfully convenient gadget to have. BUT that means you shouldn't ever phone me unexpectedly from England (not that you ever have done, except for a couple of times), otherwise you could lose your money and your patience.

Poor Gary died (guy with AIDS whose immense house Don was staying in – you saw the house but didn't meet Gary).[1] Don left, but returned to nurse him through the last few weeks. He is terrific in that way – as in so many others – when real need occurs, he will just turn over his life to help a friend. So Gary died, without a will and without relatives (he was an orphan) and a huge house full of treasures. Don decided that it was a waste for the State to get all this & is selling off all the treasures as fast as he can, so as to distribute the money among G's best friends. And Don is such that you can be sure none of this is for himself, though he is risking jail by doing it. (But something about Don loves the drama of risk.) – Every time he comes to see us, you may be sure he is loaded with bizarre gifts.

[. . .]

(Baste turkey now.)

Have you ever read <u>Huckleberry Finn</u>? I just read it, first time since 1954, and it really is one of the great enjoyable books. You would love it. It is not a children's book by any means, though Mark Twain started it with that in mind.

My friend Oliver Sacks has just published a new book <u>The Man Who Mistook his Wife for a Hat</u> which I like very well & I hope is a great success. A collection of case histories mainly to do with altered perceptions.

Didn't write a poem from January till the end of October, though it was not from want of trying! Finally I am writing again, which makes me happy, always in an odd kind of way – not happy euphoric, but it is good to be at work on something you can do well. I think of poetry as being like carpentry, or clothes design, or architecture, or something else of that practical sort. I am not more perceptive about the emotions, or more <u>feeling</u>, than anybody else, but I <u>am</u> better with words. I said 'in an odd kind of way' above, and it was in that odd kind of way that I actually got a kind of satisfaction from writing that long poem about Allan's death: I thought of myself as fashioning a kind of monument for him, and using all my skill at its most elaborate – even showing off with it – so as to make that monument worthy of him.

– Do you remember how our socialist Mayor and a gay city councillor were murdered by another councillor, Dan White, in 1978, and DW got a very low sentence of manslaughter? Well, he was released last year, eventually returned to his family here, & the other day killed himself. It was somehow a great relief. As somebody said, "Now we don't have to think about him any more."

I made about 15 lbs of quince marmalade the other day. Perhaps there will still be some when you and Bett come to stay, though I am giving away a good deal of it to the people who are always giving us the cookies (Martin) and pickles (another friend) they make.[2] <u>Pretty</u> good quince marmalade, though I have certainly had better in England. I think I know how to improve it next time I make it (it took me 2 days to make it).

Well, I must shave my grey bristles and then BASTE the BIRD again. We are having cold weather: I am wearing more layers of clothing & having more layers on my bed than ever before in SF. Of course, maybe as well as the cold being worse than usual, I feel it more because of my age. Ah the trials of the body!

Love   X X X X X X X X X   Th

1. Gary White (1932–85) was a chemist who supplied sugar-cube acid in the 1960s. 'For our acid parties,' remembers Mike Caffee, 'he would bring us carefully diluted bottles of pure LSD that we would dose onto sugar cubes or bits of blotter paper using eye-droppers.' TG's prose poem 'The Colour Machine' (*CP* 205–6) is written for Caffee; it is about a light-sculpture box that Caffee built to accompany music.

2. For Martin Rosen, see TG to Ander Gunn, 9 September 1991, below. The other friend is Louis Bryan, Allen Day's lover (see TG to Ander Gunn, 31 August 1987, below). Bryan met TG in July 1974 and became a friend of the Cole Street house, supplying them with jams and pickles for many years. 'Thom was a sweetheart,' Bryan remarked: 'He intuited that in those days I didn't have a lot of money, and that it would be a big help to me if he returned the empty jars.'

1986

TO *John Holmstrom*   TLS (aerogramme) Texas
Monday 20 January 1986

1216 Cole Street,
San Francisco,
CA 94117,
USA

Jan 20, 86

Dear John,

It is so long, several years, since I last wrote, that I hardly know how to start up again. Little pieces of news would be unconnected with other little pieces of news from 1985 or 1984. Or, for that matter, maybe the previous two years as well. We are all much as we were, except that we have spread over the whole house now, and Michael Grove, whom we hardly ever see, lives somewhere else. Bill lives upstairs, where I have a work room now, with a friend whom he steadfastly refuses to call a lover, and I live downstairs with Mike who has a lover called Bob. So we are Mike, Bob, Bill, Jim,[1] Thom – what anonymous names. None of us has AIDS, though one of my best friends died of it, violently and suddenly, eighteen months ago, and Bill is now visiting daily a friend who has had it a couple of years and has only about a month of life left. Of course we have known plenty of others, acquaintances, who have died of it in the last year or two: it puts us out of the rather privileged life we have all led since the discovery of antibiotics and returns us to the kind of existence we would have had at the turn of the century, when the young died as much as the middle-aged or old.

[. . .]

We saw Sasha last year, as you probably know, and hope to see her here again soon, if she still plans to come over. It was wonderful to meet her again after all these years – she had grown older so intelligently and open-mindedly, just the way we always hope to ourselves.

       X X X   Thom

---

1. Jim Lay (1939–86) was Bill Schuessler's lover from the late 1970s until his death.

TO *Clive Wilmer*   TLS (aerogramme) Clive Wilmer
Saturday 1 March 1986

1216 Cole Street,
San Francisco,
CA 94117,
USA

March 1, 86

Dear Clive,
    [. . .]
    I have just published my first unpleasant review in about 20 years, about
Helen Vendler's awful anthology, which there is no reason you should have
seen. She is a big power, so is worth the trouble. It is in tandem with an
appreciative review of a new book by August Kleinzahler, a new poet.[1] I'll
send you a copy – or show you one – when you're here. Now, about [Robert]
Bridges. Reading some Samuel Daniel a few days back, and hating him, I
had to admit that what I was hating was just the quality I have been finding
in Bridges. It's a kind of awful, correct, suit-and-tie blandness. Bridges, like
Daniel, doesn't want to engage passion and so keeps at a gentlemanly distance
from it though he knows by the tradition he respects so superstitiously that
one is after all supposed to pay it proper respect. What gives "Eros" its power
is that in it he is passionate about his terror of passion, and so he does come
through for once into absolutely wonderful utterance – the poor old gent
taking on considerable nobility when terrified out of his wits. But it is unique,
so far as I can tell. I moderately like a few others, not as wholes, but for the
occasional line or group of lines. What I'm saying is that I don't think all this
forms a good enough basis for an essay. I can't write the whole thing about
one short poem, and for the rest, no one needs yet another recital of RB's
faults. I'm sorry. I seem to consistently let you down with prose, don't I?[2]
                            [. . .]
        X X X
                    Thom
[. . .]

1. See 'Responsibilities: Contemporary Poetry and August Kleinzahler' (*SL* 22–32).
2. TG had agreed to write an assessment of Bridges for *Numbers*, a magazine Wilmer
co-edited with John Alexander, Alison Rimmer and Peter Robinson.

Tuesday 3 June 1986

1216 Cole Street,
San Francisco,
CA 94117
June 3, 86

Dear Tony,

[...]

I was delighted to get your letter at the end of March. Forgive me for not having answered sooner. I really work very hard while I'm teaching these days, even though I do so only one semester a year. This time I had one course on Eng poetry from 1500 to 1900: it was wonderful, I wish I could teach it every year. I was flattered that though it was an undergraduate course I was regularly audited by about ten graduates. I was trying to show them the richness and range of it all, an obvious endeavor of course, but got so carried away by [my] own enthusiasm and the enthusiasm of some of them that I spent the last month of term in a terrific euphoria. Euphoria came to an end when I put my back out last week AGAIN – first time this year, but just from reaching down to pick up a book I'd been reading while sitting on the toilet. Thus from tiny actions can arise mighty pains.[1] Well, at least it is going away, hot baths etc. Some people love soaking in hot baths, but I don't.

I am to be 57 in August, but apart from back trouble, which is VERY occasional I feel splendid. I probably told you, I go to a gym 3 times a week – it is only 2 blocks down the street. My love life has declined somewhat – I had a kind of affair for most of 1984 with a wonderful blond 27 year old called Charlie, very bright, working in a warehouse at the time, and a poet – but something was never right about it, we were never close in the right way. I think it was for me, the first time January was in love with May:[2] I think it was that he had a 27 year old restlessness and I was too old for him, though he was a genuine gerontophile! Well, we are still very fond of each other – I don't let people go, as you know – but he is now in Rio, before going back to school to do graduate work in Portuguese. Also, I suspect, and obviously so does he, that he is now an ARC case. Have you in England got sophisticated enough in plague terminology to know that that means Aids Related Condition? Which may <u>become</u> AIDS in another year or two or may stay on all his life as ill-health. I have another friend in NY who has this, ARC I mean, who actually suffered from TB last winter: he is coming to stay here in July because it may be his last chance to do so.

Talking of staying here brings me to Clive, who will be here for next week. As you know he has been in Sta Barbara teaching, but I talked with him for an hour on the phone some time ago and look forward to his being here. He is starting up a new mag this fall – much needed I'd say, tho I suspect his range of poetic sympathies is a bit too narrow for it to be an ideal magazine. Both here and in UK the traditionalists and the avant garde refuse to see good in each other. It's a rare person who can see both: but it's only in someone who can that there is going to be any future. What a stuffy letter this is becoming. But that's the trouble with not having seen you face to face in so long.

You sounded so happy in your letter, I was happy for you. God nose you have earned a bit of happiness. I was prepared for it of course by Jack [Collins]'s account of you. The sound of a book on Venice in Ruskin, Proust & James is enough to make a man think he is in Heaven already.[3] I do look forward to it. I only recently read any Ruskin, for the first time, in Clive's Penguin selection, and of course it was you who got C onto Ruskin in the first place, as he is fond of remembering.[4] The fourth writer who made so much of Venice was Pound, but I can understand why you're not including him too: he would need a whole volume in himself.

I have just been reading Barbara Guest's life of HD.[5] It is fascinating; partly because so badly written and partly because it is the only biography I have ever read where the author obviously hates her subject (though unaware of doing so).

I still write poetry. I have terrible periods when I can't write at all, when all language seems without life, a world without words, but I know by now, however long those times may last, it will always come back to me again. Recently I have been writing almost entirely metrical stuff: I gather that for those of the young who do read me here this makes me considered "audacious" (the word one of them used) to the point of being avant garde.

[. . .] Yes, of course Bill still lives here: he is part of the family. Don lives nearby: the life he chooses to live contains more difficulties every year, but he enjoys that, he enjoys the attempt (almost always doomed) to help other people in the most bizarre of situations, he likes a hard life. I once pointed this out in a poem I wrote about him (Crosswords) in my last book. He hates the poem, I think more because he dislikes praise as such (which for him is necessarily insincere, tho he feels at liberty to praise others, me for instance), but maybe he thinks it inaccurate too.

[. . .]

It is ten years since Tony died, as you must have thought. It doesn't seem a long time or a short time, just a much harder time than it would have been if he were still with us.

424

XXXXXXXXXXXXXXXXXXXXXXXXXXXXXXXXXXXXXXXXXXXXXX
Mike especially sends love
Thom

1. 'What dire offence from am'rous causes springs, / What mighty contests rise from trivial things' is the opening couplet of Pope's *The Rape of the Lock* (1714).
2. An allusion to Chaucer's 'The Merchant's Tale'.
3. Tanner had started work on the monograph that became *Venice Desired* (1992).
4. Ruskin, *Unto This Last and Other Writings*, ed. Wilmer (1985).
5. Guest, *Herself Defined: The Poet H.D. and Her World* (1984).

TO *August Kleinzahler*[1]   ALS Yale
Saturday 28 June 1986

1216 Cole Street,
San Francisco,
CA 94117

June 28

Auguste –
I have more notes, xeroxed reviews, books etc. to thank you for than I can keep count of. Thank you! and thank you again, thank you individually for each one. I have had a fine lazy month, so lazy that I made a list for next month (list of things to do) headed Dynamic July. Reading <u>Ulysses</u> again is very good – it is great that there is not yet an edition with notes, otherwise I'd be having to look everything up. As it is, when there is something I don't understand, I either stop and puzzle it out for myself or figure I'll get it <u>next</u> time I read the book. Was reading the <u>lunch</u> chapter today: what a vision of greasy hoggishness – I'd forgotten how good it is, better than Pound in Hell (or <u>on</u> Hell, I should say).
I persist with H.D. – she is a peculiarly resistant poet. There is a high finish to her poetry, her early poetry anyway, which <u>resists</u> the reader. This is interesting, since most of her subject matter (maybe all of it) is her own vulnerability. I have to practically get a poem by heart before I can enter it. (Nothing wrong with that.) Some of the poems I now like <u>a lot</u>, to my surprise.
Richard Yates. I'm very grateful for your persisting in recommending him. The story that sticks most in my mind is "Judy Rolled the Bones",[2] but maybe that's because the sergeant in it so much resembles the sergeant under whom <u>I</u> went basic training (but <u>his</u> story is even more dramatic). <u>The Easter Parade</u>

425

is very fine but I think falters at the end – seeing Emily go downhill reminds me of seeing Balzac's heroines (& heroes) go downhill, also whatshername in The House of Mirth.[3] I have the sense that he doesn't quite know what to do with her at the end of the book. But until then every character is (usually dreadfully) unforgettable – the awful English husband, the father, the mother (who must be Yates' mother, because she comes in stories too), the dreadful males Emily takes up with, both sisters . . . . RY is a bit like Isherwood in one respect: you figure someone that easy to read, that much fun, can't be "great", because surely "the great" are difficult! Then you realize what a snob you are to have that thought.

[. . .] One thing nobody mentions about Niedecker, whom I'm still reading, is the way she plays with the cute. Cuteness of rhymes, tone, etc., sometimes subject matter too. It's a considerable risk she takes, which largely pays off: most of the time a certain toughness keeps the poems from being cute, but I think occasionally she is just cute (e.g. in parts of that disorganised mess For Paul (the mess being Bertholf's not LN's) in part 2 of the Jargon ed).[4] Not often though. But she is unusual, like nobody else, as I thought when I first read her.

I hope things are well with you, you are eating, etc., writing. I am writing 2 poems that are going nowhere. Gestation is such a bore.

       Love,

          Thom

1. August Kleinzahler (1949–), poet and music critic. See Glossary of Names.
2. See Yates's collection of short stories *Eleven Kinds of Loneliness* (1962).
3. 'Whatshername' is Lily Bart in Edith Wharton's *The House of Mirth* (1905).
4. *From This Condensery: The Complete Writing of Lorine Niedecker*, ed. Robert J. Bertholf (1985).

TO *Douglas Chambers*

TLS Toronto

Wednesday 16 July 1986

1216 Cole Street,
San Francisco,
CA 94117

July 16, 86

Dear Little Friend,

Thanks for your letter. I'm just about to go to Seattle for 5 days, to take part in some miserable "writing conference", i.e. give hurried advice to credulous students on how to write, in three mornings. From what I've seen of their work, some of them already know how to write, without my help, and the others will never know. As you may infer, I don't much approve of such affairs, but I have always wanted to see Seattle, and now I can do it for free, and it is also a chance to see my favorite ex-student, a poet called Belle Randall.

Otherwise my summer has been singularly empty. I was all poised to write my head off, but somehow none of the planned poems is working out. The returns certainly get sparser with age, I'm finding, though of course there were some like Tennyson who went on grinding it out till the end. It is a question of the imagination's flagging energy, it seems; however it still has its moments, and I trust it will continue to have them until the end: I want to publish at least two more collections in my life. Actually the empty summer is very nice: lots of reading, lots of movies, occasional sex (the cock's energy flags a little too). Rereading Ulysses, and it is wonderful to be embarked on all that exuberance again. That's what it is, exuberance: that's why it is so much more than the principles of Flaubert projected to an extreme. It is gorgeous and irritating and brilliant and unstoppable. And read Hero and Leander again, CM's part, that is: it really forms a kind of standard of poetry which historically makes all the other Elizabethans irrelevant, if that makes sense: I mean, if Shakespeare, Sidney, Greville, and Donne had never written, most of the lessons of good poetry are already there to be learned from Chris. Of course there are OTHER (& important) things to be learned from them, and I'd never dispute that Shakespeare and Donne are better, and probably Sidney too. – Currently reading The Dunciad and finding it remarkably heavy going. I must have read it before, in fact I know I have, but I simply forget it, and I think I can see why: it seems to me more abusive than witty, and the central theme was covered with vastly more vigor by Dryden in MacFlecknoe. I do like Popey – the imitations of Horace & of course Dr Arbuthnot mean a great deal to me, but all this shit-diving is a bit too much even for my fetid mind. . . . . . I saw Kagemusha (by Kurosawa, you probably know it well) and find it probably the best movie I ever saw, much better than Ran: a clean unconfused narrative packed with the maximum energy of skill and inventiveness.

[. . .] Had a wonderful visit, tho only 5 days, from Clive Wilmer last month – he is a delight to be around. [. . .] Which brings me to asking if you might want to come here this summer instead of next Feb, since I'm free now and will be teaching then. Say September? You may gather from this that the typewriter became aware of the end of the page before I did. – Trollope doesn't even come in the same class as Dickens or George Eliot but he's much better than Thackeray: The Way We Live Now is his best book, I think, but his characters are so dreadfully plausible – he would have been incapable of imagining an exceptional person, and that is a terrible weakness.

Love to Michael and to you!   Thom

TO *Douglas Chambers*   ALS (postcards¹) Toronto
Friday 24 October 1986²

1216 Cole Street,
San Francisco,
CA 94117

Oct 24

Dear Unwithered Dug,

How nice to hear from you! But how sad about Dinos.³ I don't see any reasons for secrecy about AIDS <u>after</u> death, I must say – as for secrecy during illness, I think Billy & Jim just feel they have enough to fill their time and minds already and are afraid of people being solicitous. It's not altogether unreasonable: I can think of several specific acquaintances (among them one of Bill's employers) who wd, from the best of motives, just be a lot of extra trouble to deal with. I really can't say what I'd do if I got AIDS. I certainly won't give speeches from a float in the Gay Parade, though! I guess we all have to deal with it differently. A trite but true axiom, that.

I'm meanwhile just suffering from my back trouble. Fucking bore!

Told you, I guess, that I was reading and annotating M. Moore – a great delight. I can't stand her goody-goody later poems (some of them) like In District of Merits, but the stuff up to 1935 seems more splendid the deeper I get into it. I even bought my most expensive book, which I couldn't afford at all, her 1921 Poems, a pretty pamphlet, unauthorized by her, brought out by HD and Bryher. It contains things you can't get hold of now.

I'm also reading George Herbert, and of course it's no surprise liking him. To dislike <u>him</u> would be like disliking Mozart or the early Beatles. And also James' most perverse novel, <u>The Sacred Fount</u>, which I enjoy so much, in its unforgivable obscurity that I guess this makes me a literary pervert as well as a sexual one. Also Flaubert's Education Sentimentale to keep up my French – I like it better than Mme. B anyway, always have, just as I've always preferred The Magnificent Ambersons to Citizen Kane. I'm full of strange analogies today, it must be the influence of M. Moore.

How brave of you to be teaching Dorn. A wonderful poet and a nasty homophobe. But admirable – I'm not being ironic – to teach him to yr students. In doing so you're bringing them right up against the problems & delights of reading the alternative poetic tradition. I bet no one else (East of Vancouver) besides you dares teach him in Canada.

[. . .]

I'm writing too, though I don't much know what to make of what I'm doing. I'll send you some xeroxes if you want.

[. . .]

                    X X
                    Thom

1. This letter consists of three postcards: a John Johnson photograph from *Playgirl*; a male model by Fisher Ross; and one of TG's homemade pornographic cards.
2. Date supplied through internal evidence.
3. C. A. 'Dinos' Patrides (1930–86), a distinguished scholar of Renaissance literature, was TG's colleague at UC Berkeley in the early 1960s.

TO *Douglas Chambers*   ALS (postcards¹) Toronto
Tuesday 16 December 1986

                              1216 Cole Street,
                              San Francisco,
                              CA 94117

                              Dec 16 / 86

Dear Douglas,

[. . .] I know you aren't in Canada, but I want to thank you for the beautiful present while I still have time to, term coming up and all! It is very goodlooking, & when I get round to reading Parkman again I'll start it in this edition! I came back from August's hiding it under my coat, because rain was pouring down. Almost as soon as I got in I got a call that a young friend was dying in hospital, of AIDS of course. This was a guy called Larry I'd first met in 1972, meeting him in a leather bar on his 21st birthday! (I wrote a poem about him called AS EXPECTED.) When I got to the hospital next day he was already out of it, skin green, the now-familiar respiratory tube filling his mouth & throat (how that monstrous choker scares me, I must admit!), and with ½ an hour to live. It was tough. Considering our affair was many years ago, and I really only saw him about once a year these days, I was surprised how stricken I have felt. Then I had to go to NY and there was a memorial service for him when I got back. I knew enough not to go "view" his embalmed body & cosmeticized face (friends told me that nothing about him looked right), but I could see his poor dead nose sticking up out of the coffin where he lay behind the speakers, all the time I was there.

NY was great. I was there only 5 days, the first day was for the prizegiving for the General Electric Awards – I ended up at Elaine's (!) as part of George Plimpton's party (!!),[2] hadn't met him in 33 years. – It snowed one day, & that was just what I wanted. – My host, Norm Rathweg, has had AIDS for a year, & is holding up pretty well, considering. He eats 3 or 4 hot meals a day and does his best to continue enjoying his life (though I think it is sometimes an effort), tries to help other people with AIDS, sees his friends etc (he'd insisted I stay with him & his family), just gets tired rather a lot. A real "role model" for me if I go down with it!! (He's the big beautiful blond who owns the Chelsea Gym. Still fairly beautiful, I must say.)

Meanwhile Jim, here, eats almost nothing & hasn't left his bed in so long I can't remember when I last saw him on his feet. I don't know how he is still alive, since he is virtually starving himself to death.

[. . .]

I've written a bit, scraps of stuff, dunno what they amount to.

[. . .]

I'm committed to the TLS to do a monster review on Marianne Moore. I'm much regretting it – haven't even started the review yet – haven't even read the main book in fact.[3]

At least the fact that I almost never go to bars means I read more books in the evening. I'm reading The Golden Bowl again, this time loving it. Also Edwin Denby's poetry with (limited but real) appreciation.

Happy New Year, Ace!

X X Th

P.S. Love to Michael

1. Four postcards: a Max Warner photograph from *Playgirl*; a photograph of the Sisters of Perpetual Indulgence; an advert for the Brig, a leather bar on Folsom; and one of TG's homemade pornographic cards.
2. Elaine's (1963–2011) was a famous restaurant on the corner of 2nd Avenue and East 88th popular with actors and writers. George Plimpton (1927–2003) was a founding editor of the *Paris Review*.
3. 'Observations of the Octopus-mountain', *Times Literary Supplement* (6 February 1987), 127–8; uncollected.

TO *Ander and Bett Gunn*   ALS (card[1]) Ander Gunn
Tuesday 30 December 1986

1216 Cole Street,
San Francisco,
Calif. 94117,
USA

Dec 30, 86

Dear Ander and Bett –

Thank you very much for both your letters. [. . .] Thank you, Ander, for the enormous number of beautiful photographs. You certainly make me look as good as conceivably possible without my turning my back on the camera – and they are terrific pix in themselves. The picture of Bill I still think is the best that will ever be taken of him – it is full of his warmth and goodness and intelligence.

Bill isn't particularly thinking about pictures of himself right now, since he had to deal with the last days of Jim, whom he nursed.[2] It was an ordeal for all of us – most of all of course poor Jim, who shrank and shrank till he was about 3 stone, all bone, poor baby, couldn't eat and the last three days couldn't even swallow liquids. We squeezed wet sponges on the roof of his mouth to moisten it. But it was Bill who did everything, & hardly slept those last 4 or 5 weeks, because Jim always seemed to wake up for the night & needed constant changing and attentions. A nurse came in about twice a week, and an "attendant" (who was very good), but Jim mostly slept during their spells. Finally he died about 8pm on Christmas Day, and now we've been looking after Bill. He was dreadfully uncontrolled at first but has been getting very sensible: I took him to lunch on the revolving restaurant of the Hyatt Regency (on Embarcadero) on Boxing Day because he said he'd like to do 'something grand.' (I thought it was a very healthy thing for him to say).
[. . .]
We all wish you both a happy new year! It's going to be a marvellous one! no deaths, lots of happiness!!!

X X X   Love   Thom

Mike just said an extra hello! & love!
[. . .]

1. Red Grooms, *Red Star* (1980).
2. Jim Lay (1939–86) was Bill Schuessler's lover from the late 1970s until his death. TG refers to Lay in his poems 'Terminal' (*CP* 469), 'Words for Some Ash' (*CP* 472), and 'Sequel' (*BC* 37–8).

431

1987

TO *Donald Davie*   TLS Yale
Saturday 14 March 1987

1216 Cole Street,
San Francisco,
CA 94117

March 14 / 87

Dear Donald,

Thank you so much for your article in The Journal, and for the Milosz book.[1] I read the first at once, and haven't had time for the second – and won't I think until the end of term. I have time for little besides my students during the term I'm teaching, the work seems to grow greater, not less, but at least it's all interesting, and I can't imagine liking a university more than I do Berkeley. I do think the cleverest thing I ever did was to give up my tenure here in 1966, and teach here only one semester a year – I don't think I'd be writing poetry otherwise – even though I shall have no retirement when I "retire" in nine years time. But sufficient for the day etc! Meanwhile I'm glad I still do have these bursts. I have almost enough for another book, but since I have a tendency to dry up for a couple of years on the publication of a collection, I'm going to just put it away till 1992 (ten years from my last, arbitrarily chosen date), and hope that I can cheat the tendency in that way! We'll see.

Thank you for your kind words about my Vendler review – you will no doubt be thoroughly tired of the damn thing by now, having seen it reprinted in both Scripsi and the PN Review. And indeed I saw yours and was delighted that we were saying the same thing.[2] (I also liked your little point about the word poetess!) Yes, it is all very tiring, the lack of comprehension that the British have, on the whole, and most of the East Coasters here, that there has been a larger world of poetry than their own comfortable little one, Auden, and Kipling, Anthony Hecht (the modern American, poor man, that the English dote on), and crumpets for tea. And perhaps one, but no more than one, token Modernist. The worst thing of all, I suspect, is the continued neglect of Bunting. The British pay him lip-service, but it's clear that they would sooner read James Fenton – and do! The Americans mostly haven't heard of him, or if they have they are committed Poundians or whatever, and think he was doing the same kind of thing as Charles Olson, whose work he apparently greatly disliked! Well, one could go on for ever like this.

My great delight this last year has been to discover how very good Marianne Moore is, once you have separated her early work (<u>Observations</u>) from the later. You probably knew this years ago! (To do Vendler justice, she once wrote a good essay on MM – at a time before her, Vendler's, style had yet been corrupted by high-minded thoughts about Keats and Stevens.[3])

Poor Duncan had a complete kidney failure 3 years ago, and has dialysis 4 times a day. He is amazingly alert and perceptive in mind, but his work is over – he'll never write another poem, the poor man cannot even finish reading a real book any longer, he who once said that he read as other people are gluttonous over food! I go to see him, take him for walks when he is strong enough, and I must say I admire his tremendous cheerfulness – he is still <u>good company</u> – because he has nothing to live for besides the brute fact of life. But he could go on like this, probably, for years. And I suppose life can still be enjoyed in such circumstances.

I can't believe you are retiring. But then I can't believe my own age, either! (I'll be 58 this year.) And I find it difficult to imagine you living full-time in England. But Devon is beautiful – I once stayed overnight with kind Ted Hughes, 1974, I think – and I have never seen a lusher English landscape – and I imagine you and Doreen could have a very good time down there. And you would be free to write all the books you haven't had time for yet!

I must stop – I have papers to grade, as usual.

Love to Doreen and yourself,

Thom

1. Davie, *Czeslaw Milosz and the Insufficiency of Lyric* (1986).
2. Davie, 'Keeping out the Redskin Poets', *The Guardian* (12 December 1986), 13.
3. Vendler, *Part of Nature, Part of Us: Modern American Poets* (1980), 59–76.

1216 Cole Street,
San Francisco,
CA 94117

March 23 87

Dear Belle,

At last I get round to answering your letter. I find teaching more and more absorbing – not what I expected – but also it takes up more and more of my time. So I waited until this wonderful new institution: Spring Break. [. . .]

Interestingly enough, I don't remember our exchange about poetry and getting high – but I'd say the same if we had it now! Not that I don't value getting high: I do still smoke grass, though I don't know many others who do, and I even take a bit of acid every now and then. Both activities take me to places I like being in, and places that I can still learn from, even places that may be a source of poetry – after all I did write a whole volume of poetry based on acid experience. But as a source it is only one of many sources, surely. I was speaking literally when I said that poetry was language, and also quoting a famous anecdote. (Degas: I always think I could write poetry if only I had the ideas. Mallarmé (I think): Poetry isn't ideas, it is words.) But it would seem to me that if you say something like 'perhaps there is more poetry in getting high than on the printed page', you at least SEEM to be claiming that the poetry of fantasy is more poetry than all the other kinds, that Christina Rossetti's 'Goblin Market' (which I adore, and I think is one of the best poems of the 19th cent) is more the real thing than Pope's satires or George Herbert's devotional poetry or Little Gidding or for that matter the Ballad of Hattie Carroll.[1] Maybe you are not making such a claim, and I am just inferring it. But in any case, you end your paragraph saying 'the poetry, for me, is not so much in the language as in something prior, that which inspires it'. A very interesting statement, and one which I can only respect, while saying that I simply disagree with it on the basis of my experience as both reader and writer: the poetry, for me, is in the working out of that something prior through words, the poem being for me always, I think, an intimation fully realised in language, and thus developed, strengthened, altered almost out of recognition. It seems we have a philosophical disagreement!

I may be attributing ideas to you that you don't really have.

[. . .]

I tried reading Merrill's Recitative, and did get bored. Maybe I should have another try – I'll wait for your review. I haven't read the Burroughs essays, though it must be the one book by him I have not read:[2] for me he is one of the two prose geniuses around (the other being Robert Stone, very different). Naked Lunch and Cities of the Red Night are two books I came back to again and again.

I've made friends with Donald Davie again. Also, I have been asked to write an essay for a Festschrift when he retires – I plan to call it Three Hard Women, implicitly calling his attention to three modernist poets he has – so far as I can remember – never referred to – HD, M Moore, and Mina Loy.[3] I'll concentrate on their EARLY work: HD I am afraid bores me to tears after about 1920 (I realise what an unpopular thing that is to say nowadays) – just a big old whiner; M Moore I like Moore and Moore, particularly her early work; and Mina Loy is neglected by almost everybody – I dunno why, when you think how early she insisted on the importance of female experience as material for her poetry (Parturition, for example). Should be complicated, and fun, to write.

[. . .]

Now I must go to the gym!
        Love to Joe,[4]
               x x x to yourself
                 Th

1. Bob Dylan, 'The Lonesome Death of Hattie Carroll' (1964).
2. William S. Burroughs, *The Adding Machine: Collected Essays* (1985).
3. 'Three Hard Women: HD, Marianne Moore, Mina Loy' (*SL* 33–52).
4. Randall's husband.

TO *Douglas Chambers*   ALS (postcards[1]) Toronto
Monday 29 June 1987

                         1216 Cole Street,
                          San Francisco,
                          CA 94117

                          June 29 / 87

Dear Duggle –
   Richard and Chris are a bit too cute, aren't they, for all their leather & tattoos. Both of which, along with legendary pecs and outstanding biceps, were much to be seen at yesterday's marvellous gay parade. It really is the

best day of the year – everybody is so nice to each other – even I realize that I am a look-snob and am very nice to the uglies, as the beauties are to me! Also, I like the way the lesbians are at last standing up for themselves in great numbers, and now almost half the audience & marchers are dykes. They are so sweet really: my awkwardness around them makes me realize how they must feel around me.

I had a nasty flu – a coughing type, which was going round. I actually had a day of distorted vision, a bit like acid – things wobbled, things seethed. I went to bed & read Philip K. Dick. Otherwise I have read a vol of Post-Structuralist essays by different folks, for my own education.² A few were really good – Geoffrey Hartman is fun, a "colleague" of mine Frances Fergusson was splendid on the Ancient Mariner (I don't even know what she looks like), Harold Bloom is at least lively. Others were full of nonsensical jargon. And the pomposity. Also reread Conrad's Victory & didn't like it nearly so much as I used. The main man is such a bore. But it is very amusingly sexist and racist. I did like Typhoon when I read it last year, tho.

The best news is that Billy came back from his 6 weeks in Paris perky and happy. It took him out of himself just as it is meant to do. He has stayed off the dreaded angel dust & has been loving and happy – so far – we all touch wood!!! It's nice to have the old Billy back, even for a while. I thought I'd never see him again.

Every now and again I have Sensational Safe Sex. (Not often enough.)

[. . .] I am writing (poetry) a bit. I think by the end of this year I'll have a new book completed. Round the end of '88 maybe I'll xerox it up in about 10 copies & send you one. It will be called The Man with Night Sweats, as I probably told you. I am just finishing a poem about an otter's genitals.³ (Really.)

My sick friends are exemplary. There do seem an awful lot of them to visit, and some of them are so weak you can't stay long – but they are on the whole so brave, so cheerful, so courteous – almost as if they are afraid of making you feel bad. I'm sure I'd bitch all the time – disagreeable old woman that I am. The most difficult one to deal with is my dear feisty Charlie – my love of 2 years ago – he is blind in one eye now and the other eye is going. I don't know how he can stand it. He is 30. – Still, we (I think I speak for San Francisco) have got out of our state of shock (I think) and are trying to be practical in helping people. Of course, none of us can be confident that we won't get it ourselves, but there's no point in dwelling on our fear. 'If it be now, 'tis not to come,' etc.

[. . .]

I hope you didn't think too badly of me for that boring poem about hitchhiking I had in the TLS. I didn't realize till after it was accepted how boring it is: a case of a poem with all the life worked out of it. The only bit with any life left is the last few lines.[4]

Oh, you are in London now! With the selfish English.

It has been wonderfully overcast lately – I can see the hummingbirds giving blowjobs (actually they are <u>catheterizing</u> them) to the fuchsias from my windows. My yard has been so good this year & I have done very little work on it: the rewards of age, they call it. You wither up, the young laugh at you, you write nonsense, you dabble in your shit & require a nurse to clean your piss off the furniture, you live in a shroud of your own mucous, but AT LEAST YOU HAVE A GOOD GARDEN. In that ease you will have the richest old age of all.

X X   Thom

1. Four postcards: 'Richard and Chris', a tattoo by Alan Oversby; 'The lone ranger', a tattoo by Chris Wroblewski; and two of TG's homemade pornographic cards.
2. *Post-Structuralist Readings of English*, ed. Machin and Norris (1987).
3. 'The Life of the Otter' (*CP* 429–30).
4. 'South', *Times Literary Supplement* (12 June 1987), 633; uncollected. This poem is about the hitchhiking trip TG made through France in the summer of 1951, during which he 'experienced a revelation of physical and spiritual freedom that I still refer to in my thoughts as the Revelation' (*OP* 159).

TO *Donald Davie*

ALS Yale

Wednesday 1 July 1987

1216 Cole Street,
San Francisco,
CA 94117

July 1 / 87

Dear Donald –

You probably found it difficult to believe me when I said I didn't have time to read the short book you so kindly sent me, but it was true: I <u>like</u> my large classes at Berkeley, but keeping up with them takes all my time during the semester.[1] Anyway, I am glad I was able to take my time over reading it, in June, impolite as I may have seemed, and reading it too slowly. It is marvellous, like so much of what you do, because it brings up important matters that few other critics even recognize as being there, they are so

437

confined by the assumptions of their time. It is a book I found possible to engage with and learn from while knowing little of Milosz's work – and if I now make two reservations they are less of things I think wrong than of things I think need expansion, further discussion, for clarification. (1) 'The insufficiency of' your <u>definition</u> of the lyric! When you speak of the lyric in this book you usually refer to the Romantic meditation, but surely by disregarding the Romans and the Eliz-Jacobeans, you are treating it as too narrow a form. The statements made in the poetry of Horace and of Herbert were fully supported by their prose selves, we may be sure – even though the viewpoint of the one could often be called pastoral, and the other's attitude to God could often be called Protestantly personal, neither viewpoint nor attitude weaken the general validity of the statements made. – Horace and Herbert wrote a long time back, no doubt, but it is as easy to consider going <u>behind</u> the Romantic tradition as to consider going back <u>within</u> it: Jonson and Catullus don't seem to me (or you, I'm sure) any more inaccessible than Rimbaud or Burns. – In any case, I think you make the lyric seem a slighter and narrower thing, in this book, than it really is.

(2) I am interested in what you say about Milosz and Whitman, p.49, sentence starting "It is worth reflecting . . ." (and also wonder how this fits in with your implied condemnation of Whitman in your article on Williams this year). But the whole question of the sufficiency or insufficiency of the lyric could be seen to hinge on how general or idiosyncratically personal the "I" of the lyric is. The first person in Thomas Hardy or in Sappho (not that I can read Greek) is not the same as the first person in Robert Lowell or in the Shakespeare of the Sonnets.

– Anyway, it is a book every poet writing should read, and it has put me in mind that I should overcome my distrust of (or boredom with) translations and work my way through Milosz, in whom you have thoroughly interested me.

[. . .]

Love to yourself and Doreen,
Thom

1. See TG to Davie, 14 March 1987, above.

TLS Ander Gunn

1216 Cole Street,
San Francisco,
CA 94117

August 31, 87

Dear Ander,

Thank you for your terrific letter. I was thinking only the other day how lucky I am to have a brother like you. [. . .] Not only did you forward me Mary's letter, but I received one too, with completely different news. Well, I'm now 58, and it feels the same as ever. I went into the local liquor store yesterday, to greet my friend – even older than me – who works there, and whose birthday is the day before mine. And there was this old lady who has lived on the street for 60 years, who said, "Your birthday? What are you, twenty-one? I always celebrate my birthday for three days. You should too. Always celebrate your birthday for three days." So I did. She was sipping wine at the time: how they get away with that I don't know: surely it's against the law to drink in <u>any</u> store.

It has been a difficult August. First my friend Norm in NY died, my friend who owned a gym. Then, on the same day, Allen Day[1] and Lonnie Leard. You should especially have met Lonnie – great friend of Don's and of all of us. I met him first, 21 years ago, and introduced him to everybody else when he was a shy young teacher from S. California. Charlotte met him when she was here, and he put on a special dinner for Catherine in 78 or 79 so that she could try a range of American foods. A very generous man, in fact, and we shall all miss him very much. He lived in the country the last few years, that's why you & Bett didn't meet him, I suppose. (You will notice I have a new typewriter – a splendid $200 Smith Corona I bought from the typewriter dealer I used to take the old one in to for repair. His greeting, "Well what's wrong with that piece of shit now?" gave me confidence in his judgment. The old one was $500 in 1981. A new typewriter, and very satisfactory, but unfortunately my typing is very uncontrolled today.) And we shall be losing Charlie very soon, he is in hospital, shockingly thin, and gone blind, poor baby. It seems sadder to die at 30, as he is, than at my age. I have done so many things that I wanted to, and have had such a full life, and he's still only at the start of it. You must remember him from 84, short blond. He taught himself Portuguese after leaving the university – so well that when he applied to graduate school several years later, he impressed all six universities he tried, by his proficiency in telephone interviews, that they all offered him grants. Well, it's all sad, and there's nothing to do about it. You must be getting tired of my moaning in letters.

[. . .]

We have a friendly cat named Ida, though I often refer to her as the Big Bopper, and sometimes as Stupid. She is young, large, and boisterous. Her favorite game is Ambush the Passing Foot, and twice has almost knocked me down, yesterday when I was carrying dishes from the table. She generously gave me a dead lizard on my birthday, so she is thoughtful too.

[. . .]

All send love. Don Doody has been away for about ten months but returns to the district next week. The Pope will also be visiting, but I doubt that he will look in on us. Still, we are hoping, and will keep the place well-vacuumed just in case. (Actually, it should be interesting. Numerous Gay protests have been planned because of said Pope's intolerant attitude to us. Some men dressed as nuns plan a relay race between two points of his proposed route.)

I visit New York for 2 days this week. [. . .] With Allan Noseworthy dead in 84 and Norm Rathweg dead this month I don't have anybody left there I am fond of enough to visit. Perhaps I will just go to the museums in my spare time.

> Love to you, love to Bett,
> don't get too dry, don't get too wet,
> if you keep yourself powdered wherever you're put,
> you'll never suffer from athlete's foot.   (a T.G. "original")

XX   Th

1. Allen Day (1941–87), erotic artist under the pseudonym 'Strider'. Friend of TG from 1975. Day's letters to TG can be found among TG's papers at the Bancroft Library.

TO *Belle Randall*

TLS Bancroft

Friday 9 October 1987

1216 Cole Street,
San Francisco,
CA 94117

Oct 9 / 87

Dear Belle,

There's no date on your last letter, but I know I have owed you an answer for a long time, maybe even since last year. First it was teaching that kept me from answering you, and then a summer that was too full of heavy concerns. By this time maybe you have your second child: I hope so – it is good to think of you and Joe with two children, making the decision to be a stable unit of family and succeeding in being so. Hurrah! I was touched by your letter, which was loving and reassuring. No, I don't have AIDS, and appear to be in splendid health, as does every surviving member of the house. I say surviving, because we did lose Jim, whom quite possibly you never met – he lived upstairs but ate with the rest of us, for about ten years, but died last Christmas Day.[1] It was a horrible illness and a painful death (at home), but I am beginning to realise that death (not just from AIDS) is almost always painful and difficult, and that the image that us sheltered children have always had of dying sweetly in one's sleep is one most seldom realised in experience. I have had other friends die at other times, but the very worst was from August 8 to September 9, during which time I lost four friends – friends not acquaintances – two of them on the same day. After the first three I thought I was holding up surprisingly well, but the fourth one – poor Charlie who was only thirty, and so full of promise – really did me in. So I have been having a rather hard time, which I tell you about not so you should feel sorry for me but so you may know what has been happening to me and also the reason for my silence!

At this rate, our discussion about the subject matter of poetry will drag on into the next century. I suspect that what you may be speaking about is inspiration? Or not? Let me expand on my "position": I think there are no appropriate subjects for poetry PER SE. What is appropriate for you or Duncan to write about is the matters that move you. I can't tell either of you what they are because I can't tell you what moves YOU; nor can you tell me because you can't tell what moves ME. Maybe a better phrase than "what moves me" would be "what stirs my imagination into producing poetry"? Thus a good subject for Ben Jonson might be a court marriage between two nobles he barely knows; for John Ashbery it is tone of voice; for Emily Dickinson it was death beds, and more death beds; for you it is God speaking cryptically (and I like very much that part of your letter where you give examples from your poetry – if you remember what you wrote so long ago!). Favorite subject matter for Elizabethans: the month of May. Favorite subject matters in the 19th century, nuns, "easeful death", being free as the wind. Favorite subject matter in this century, waste lands, garbage heaps, the city dump, one-night cheap hotels, uncertainty of purpose. You and I have each tried in our time to redeem some of these subjects from cliché – it is always worth trying. But what I want to emphasize is that from my observation the inherently poetic varies from person to person. I probably reacted defensively about the whole business because I suspect that I have been trying to get into my poetry a lot of little stories and anecdotes that most people would put into short stories and novels and essays nowadays.

I'll throw in some poetry with this letter.[2] I sure have been writing a lot of it this last year. Death has a way of concentrating the imagination, certainly. Don't feel you should comment on them unless you are moved to; you have quite enough poetry to comment on for your classes. And just think, maybe your children will start writing it one of these days.

I am reading Rilke, the Duino Elegies especially, in Stephen Mitchell's wonderful translation – good poetry AND I know enough German from high school to tell from the opposite pages how accurate the translation is – Rilke's Selected Poetry.[3] I get round to reading everybody in the end, I find. I always wonder if I shall finally read Goethe, whom I find a most unattractive-sounding writer. (Well, I did read a novel by him.)

I am to teach a course about poetry next term to a class estimated at 240 students – and at the same time educate several [teaching assistants] who will be taking some of them off into separate sections for two extra units. AND I'll be teaching two other courses. So after the misfortunes of the summer I am hurrying to get my 45 new lectures written.

Have you come across an Englishman called Paul Giles I think new on faculty at UW?

I'm going to Boston for a week next month to do a few readings in the cold weather to the highly educated!

[. . .]

> Love to Joe
> Love to you
>> Thom

Bill & Mike send love too.

[. . .]

---

1. See TG to Ander Gunn, 30 December 1986, above.
2. The enclosed poems are no longer with the letter, but likely included 'Words for Some Ash' (CP 472), 'Sacred Heart' (CP 473–4), and 'Her Pet' (CP 474–5).
3. *The Selected Poetry of Rainer Maria Rilke*, trans. Mitchell (1981).

1988

Friday 1 January 1988

1216 Cole Street,
San Francisco,
CA 94117

Jan 1 / 88

Dear Tony,

It is New Year's Day, but any day is a good day to write to one's Tanner.
Lovely to hear from you I think about six months ago. [. . .] It has been
a year very much oppressed by the worries of the disease, first trying to
help Billy out of the sheer awfulness of losing his lover of 10 years – who
lived here and died last Xmas Day (I mean 1986), and then of friends who
are sick. Billy has emerged wonderfully, a tribute to his built-in sanity.
The worst month of the year for me was August, when in a month I lost
four friends, including the last person I was ever in love with (cf poem The
Differences [. . .]). It was rough, but Mike especially helped me a lot. I have
written an awful lot about death – at times I have thought I must be getting
monotonous, but then I think of Emily D who seemed to write ONLY well
about death, so I suppose it's a good large subject, about which there's an
awful lot to be said. I have rather few friends left, but a greatly increased
wardrobe. That seems to be the legacy of AIDS, the survivors do end up
with heaps of shirts! Don did some heroic nursing – everything he does has
to be on a heroic scale – otherwise he is a pleasure to have around, though
as quirky as ever, and possessing an immense pot belly, the result of drinking
brandy every day.

[. . .]

I have been reading E.M. Forster through again. The surprise is that the
only book I really like is Maurice, just the one that when it came out we
all said isn't up to the rest of Forster. It is more energetic than any of the
others and is mostly untouched by a kind of tic of easy irony that I find just
dreadfully irritating even in P to India.

I shall be 60 in a year and a half! Amazing, I think. Not that I look any younger than I am. I'm just so surprised that I'm almost there already. The years do flash by like a strobe light don't they [. . .].

I haven't been in England since 1979. Perhaps I'll visit again in the year I publish my next book, 1992. I have to stay here to grow my flowers. Perhaps you will decide to visit us before that time and we can show you that San Francisco is still City of Orgies, as Whitman rather oddly called Washington while he was making it with his bus conductor. I don't feel much – at all – tempted to come over, as you guess. I don't know why, apart from an irrational terror that I might die there.

The cold and damp seep through our thin walls, and it rains almost every day. An old man needs a good electric blanket, I find, since he doesn't drink anything like he used to. I certainly hope you have one too – it must be terrible keeping the breath of the Fens away from your rooms up those stone staircases. I did love your account of travels, Greece, Israel and Egypt. I hope your wonderful-sounding book on Venice is taking shape as you want it to. Something to look forward to is what I call that.

[. . .]

Bill & Mike especially send you tumultuous surges of love, as do I!

        X X X X X X X   Th

TO *Gregory Woods*

TLS Gregory Woods

Saturday 27 February 1988

1216 Cole Street,
San Francisco,
CA 94117

Feb 27, 88

Dear GW.

[. . .]

I received your letter yesterday, and you say you need to hear from me by the end of the month. Well, it will be March before you get this, but I hope it will not be too late. One day I want to write more fully about Duncan, both about his importance as a poet, which is not generally recognized in Britain or on the East Coast here, and about him as a man (which might well be another article). Meanwhile here are some notes I made on him between classes yesterday. You can print them as they stand or cannibalize them (i.e. quote any bits that suit you) as you please.[1]

Robert Duncan's poetry is important to me in three ways.

1. As one of the two most talented heirs of the Modernist Revolution he managed to combine Modernism with the Romantic tradition, which always seemed diametrically opposed to each other.[2] The other heir, the other great post-Poundian poet, Bunting, could acknowledge both Pound and Wordsworth as ancestors; Duncan with his terrific eclecticism claimed not only Pound and H.D. but Shelley and Blake as his. Bunting's "Briggflatts" and Duncan's Opening of the Field are moreover the only poetic events of central importance to have happened since World War II in English.

2. He turned the dry and barely coherent theory of Olson into poetry living, exciting, and alert. Olson's poetics of "projective verse" (or open poetry) are nowhere more satisfactorily realised than in Duncan's poetry. "Composing the field" is illustrated on a minute scale in "Childhood's Retreat" on p.49 of Groundwork I: the real adventure takes place during the writing of his poetry, which he appears to have never revised.

3. He wrote magnificent gay poetry, I think as good as "Hero and Leander" and "The Sleepers". He considered the mutual love of men as proper and beautiful as any other branch of Love, and wrote about it in all its variety (the kind of variety denied by those who parrot the phrase "the homosexual life style", as if there were many "life styles" for heterosexuals and only one for us!). He did not believe, I think, in the gay sensibility: he believed in anything but specialisation, and aspired to as inclusive a sensibility as any poet this century. (The desire for inclusiveness sometimes led to inflated writing as it did in Whitman. That is the risk taken.) I say this in spite of his having linked the irregularity of his sexual inclinations with the irregularity of his writing poetry. To have a talent lacking to others makes anyone irregular in a regular world. Bunting too was irregular. (Larkin by contrast was only too regular.)
    [. . .]

       Best wishes,
         Thom

---

1. See, 'Robert Duncan's Romantic Modernism', *European Gay Review* 4 (1989), 54–5; uncollected.
2. TG later examined this idea at length in 'Adventurous Song: Robert Duncan as Romantic Modernist' (*SL* 143–70).

Saturday 9 April 1988[2]

1216 Cole Street,
San Francisco,
CA 94117

April 9

Hello Steve –

As you can see from the enclosed, I wrote a poem about you.[3] It is accurate as far as I can make it – except it was not a #6 bus but the U.C. shuttle, which seemed too complicated to put into a poem where it was just a detail.

Anyway. I am sending it to you not for your appreciation but to find out from you whether you would mind my publishing it. Perhaps I am violating a confidence, perhaps I am making something public you do not want to be public. Or whatever.

If you want, I could change a detail or two where possible. Or if you want, I will simply not publish it.

I'm not sure if it's finished yet. The title seems silly (I imagine it as the last poem in a book) – perhaps there are things that need rewriting.[4]

In any case, I'll be grateful if you could let me know – phone or send a note.

With my continued admiration, "sturdy looking" hunk that you are –

Thom

1. Steven Fritsch Rudser (1955–), sign-language interpreter and teacher. He adopted a three-year-old boy in 1987.
2. Date supplied through internal evidence.
3. 'A Blank' (CP 487–8).
4. Its original title was 'The Last Poem'.

TO *Clive Wilmer*   TLS Clive Wilmer

Monday 30 May 1988

1216 Cole Street,
San Francisco,
CA 94117

May 30, 88

Light of my life:

You wrote me Feb 22, and look how long I have been in answering. The fact is, the last term has been a very hard-working one – mere quantity of work rather than extra hardships! In fact, it went reasonably well, apart from my not having time to see my friends or do anything for myself. Augie [Kleinzahler] will tell you he hardly saw me, other friends no doubt forgot there was someone of my name among their acquaintance. There was a wonderful week off at Easter, and I actually wrote a poem I had been wanting to write since January.[1] (That's the way writers are supposed to go about it.) All this by way of apology.

[...]

Interesting what you say about Pessoa. Yes, I too, by dint of piecing out some Portuguese on pages facing bad English translations, had also gathered that there seems to be a lot there. – I have been reading Lorca's Poet in New York in a new translation since term ended about ten days ago (I know no more Spanish than I do Portuguese, by the way, but again you can gather quite a lot from the opposite pages if you have a bit of Romance knowledge). He is a good poet, though it is interesting to see how much tiresomeness, Bly-ery and Merwinese, originates from him. Someone should write (maybe someone has written) an essay on the importance of DIMINUTIVES in surrealist poetry. Inside say a horse's skull you imagine a tiny military academy, inside a crocodile's eye a little universe where planets go around a sun, these are made-up examples, but my point is that in such poetry there is a tendency to make the whole world a collection of things that in the poet's imagination are all dolls' houses inside: metaphor as miniaturisation. This is a sweeping and unfair comment, and there is a great deal besides that I find exuberant and delightful in Lorca.

I know what you mean about the amount of sheer exposition necessary when lecturing about Pound. Yes, as you say, it is amazing how many of the students haven't even read the Odyssey: I would have thought they'd have come across it in comic book or Italian-muscle-movie form if no other way. (I was teaching him this term.) I would love to be present at your lectures. At the same time, why do all of "you English" have to apologise for him at the same time as you praise him? You say "yet as a whole it is such a disaster" when speaking about the cantos. That strikes me about as unnecessary and somehow as misleading as saying that The Fairie Queene or the Canterbury Tales are disasters too: they are also unfinished, and in them too there are stretches (necessitated by the nature of the enterprise) of writing fully as boring as the Chinese cantos: but no one bothers to point this out.

In fact, we don't think of them as disasters, do we? We think of them as defining a new sense of form. What needs emphasizing is that the best of the cantos are as solid as writing can get, for example, I don't see how Canto 47 could be better, in any way, and many other cantos and parts of Cantos. There are terrible stretches of fragmentariness, but I don't know that these as such are worse than the Parson's tale or great stretches of dull melodious stuff in Spenser. All three works are deficient compared with the perfect over-all form of Dante or Milton, but that's obvious and not worth saying – it is like saying that Dostoievsky can't hold things together in the way Jane Austen can.

I haven't seen or really corresponded with Davie in years. I do admire him, but he is a changeable and difficult man, and I can't really deal with him as a friend. (At the same time, I remind myself, it was all my fault that he and I had a disagreement a few years ago, from which we never really recovered.[2]) Ultimately, for all his conservativism, he likes to surprise too much and he is too inconsistent. Or maybe those are the sources of his virtues! [. . .] I enclose some poems I have written in the past year [. . .].[3]

[. . .]

Much love – I'll write more promptly next time –
Th

1. See TG to Fritsch Rudser, 9 April 1988, above.
2. See TG to Davie, 17 May and 29 July 1982, above.
3. TG enclosed 'The Reassurance' (*CP* 471), 'Words for Some Ash' (*CP* 472), 'Sacred Heart' (*CP* 473–4), 'Her Pet' (*CP* 475), 'To the Dead Owner of a Gym' (*CP* 478), 'Memory Unsettled' (*CP* 479), 'To a Dead Graduate Student' (*CP* 482), 'The Missing' (*CP* 483–4), 'Death's Door' (*CP* 485–6) and 'A Blank' (*CP* 487–8).

Sunday 5 June 1988

> 1216 Cole Street,
> San Francisco,
> CA 94117
>
> June 5 / 88

Dear Greg:

About 30 years ago, I was speaking to Isherwood about Auden. We agreed that someone would one day write a great study of him showing how the role of the communist spy he found so attractive was just as much that of sexual spy (often sexual spy <u>pretending</u> to be communist spy) and that this was the REAL key to Auden.

Well, you have done not only that but you've done an exemplary study of the whole subject.¹ You said some months ago that your book has not been widely noticed in straight publications – I hope this is not still so but I'll bet it is. However, it is such an obviously superior work that intelligent readers and scholars will find it one by one, and in a few years it will be taken for granted that this is an indispensable book. It is <u>sturdy</u>: alert, courageous, thorough-going, logical, sympathetic. It does its work so well that it contains certain essays on associated subjects – for example on the connection between obscurity of poetry by gay poets and their sexuality – that are not your central concern. The book is so immensely more perceptive than anything I already know on the subject, for example Robert Martin,² I can't imagine it being better.

I especially like the energetic and persistent fairness of your mind – for example as it turns up in the chapters on Ginsberg and on Auden, on loneliness in Auden and the whole wonderful introduction to Ginsberg ("Indiscretion"). I am indeed happy with your treatment of me – you have done me more than justice, perhaps. It's as well to remember how much easier history has been for my generation to live through than it was for Auden's. And then he was a guilt-ridden Christian as well, which made it that much more difficult for him to extricate himself from the whole mixed mess of class and sex and religion and morality, in the way that Isherwood did, indeed. But even as the atheist I am, I wonder if I could have matched the splendid clean candor of Isherwood if I had been that generation rather than one still young enough to feel the freedom of Stonewall and after. When you note Auden's writing to Duncan (another exemplary hero, indeed) that he hopes he won't publish the study he contemplates because he won't be able to get a teaching job if his gay identity is identified too explicitly, it certainly recalls to me the fact that I would have never been able to get into this country or to stay here if I had been more publicly honest about myself than I was in the 1950s. Not I think that you are unfair to Auden: you are hard on him, but rightly so, and you make up for such hardness fully and even compassionately in yr conclusion to that chapter.

[. . .]

Best,

Thom

1. Woods, *Articulate Flesh: Male Homo-Eroticism and Modern Poetry* (1987).
2. See TG to Chambers, 22 July 1980, n. 6, above.

TO *Lee Smith*[1]   TLS Morgan

Tuesday 21 June 1988

1216 Cole Street

San Francisco, CA 94117

June 21/88

Dear Lee Smith,

It is almost two months since your letter. The first month I was too busy with school work to answer, and the second I guess I have been too lazy. However, I have thought about it.

Using Winters is not, of course, an easy matter. He was, to paraphrase Robt Pinsky, an accurate critic but an ungenerous one, so one applauds the rightness but is chilled by the lack of generosity. At first when I was in my twenties I was of course tremendously influenced by him, then I tried to distance myself from the influence, but in recent years I have had to realise that he was the best and steadiest guide I could possibly have had for my writing life, and that without him I might well have simply blown this way and that before the winds of fashion. He has given me a strength which I do not in fact have – it is borrowed. It is not obvious to people how much it is borrowed because I do not find the material that presses most upon me – (sensual material, gay, my implicitly optimistic view that the affections may constitute a pretty sure guide, etc. etc) – at odds with the practice of those he identifies as the masters – for example Jonson, Baudelaire, Dickinson. People think of him as having turned his admiration of such poets into a kind of rigid orthodoxy, but anything but that is true. The admiration and what he

450

deduced from their practice is finally for a very warm state of emotion ~~even if one~~ all the more living for being largely regulated by the structure of the whole poem.

So I have found him – and still find him – a fruitful and relatively flexible influence. It must therefore be possible for others to use him in the same way. The trouble goes deeper than the immediate question of YW, though: there is almost no recognition on the part of talented writers that the use of fixed meter can be used for the improvisatory and up-to-date subject matter that properly form their main interest. You can't simply say Read Winters! to them; they have to <u>want</u> to write in meter and rhyme, used with a certain consistency, and to believe that it is possible to speak about important and living concerns by such means. To ask for such a conversion in assumptions is to ask for a great deal: it means, I suspect, that the people who are going to grow up into poets should start reading metrical and rhyming poetry, and start caring about it, at an age a good deal before they ever think of the university.

At this point it is relevant to take a look at English/British poetry of the last thirty years. <u>They</u> are still largely interested in such traditionalism of form, but apparently without wanting to combine it with the energy of the Modernists, so their use of rhyme and meter comes over as good mannered trifling.

I find one poetic work of unquestioned greatness published in English since say 1945, and that is Bunting's <u>Briggflatts</u>. It puts everything by Duncan, Olson, Larkin, Lowell, and certainly myself in the shade – and makes everything I have said in this letter rather abstract and beside the point. So it may well be that what we are really waiting for is someone who has enough talent to make the cultural moment his own. If, indeed, that last sentence means anything; but if Bunting could write something so brilliant by a kind of digestion of Pound with the Norse epics and perhaps a bit of Wordsworth as well, then the influence of Winters has nothing much to do with it all.

I am fascinated by the letter from W that you found in the files. You have to remember that he was by then much tired out with operations on his cancer, and that he was always of a despondent turn. You ask what sort of a teacher he was: I wrote an account of him as teacher in an essay included in my book Occasions of Poetry – expanded edition of this book only, as published by North Point Press (not the British edition).[2]

Thank you, anyway, for your kind letter. It was good talking to you after the reading too.

best,

Thom Gunn

P. S. On reading it through, I don't find this letter that coherent, but I'll send it anyway.

1. Lee Smith (1962–), author and journalist, wrote to TG having read Winters's letters in the archive of the *Hudson Review*, for which he worked in the mid-1980s.
2. See 'On a Drying Hill: Yvor Winters' (*SL* 197–212).

TO *Jack Hagstrom*[1]   ALS (postcards[2]) Amherst
Sunday 17 July 1988[3]

> 1216 Cole Street,
> San Francisco,
> CA 94117
>
> July 17

Dear Jack –

Glad you liked Charlie's Poems – they do look very good, I think, nice and firm in print.[4] I was very lucky in having to deal with such a wonderful printing firm: all women (at first I thought they were lesbians, but they weren't – but I liked them a lot anyway!). One of them, a woman I know only as Amy, did the illustration, and I think it is terrific. – Of course, the irony is that I think I am doing this for Charlie, and I am really doing it for myself. Charlie couldn't be more indifferent to this kind of thing where he is now. And perhaps I'm trying to make myself more comfortable that I didn't do more for him when he was alive.

I have sent you some copies. You can have more if you wish, I have heaps left. I think I shall put a personals ad in the gay press here one week so any of CH's friends I didn't know may receive copies. – Charlie's friend in D.C. is looking after people at Wesleyan, etc. No, C never knew Wilbur: I know exactly who he knew & didn't know at Wesleyan!!!

[. . .] Have you seen the quilt yet?[5] If it has yet to come to NY, you might devote an hour or two to it when it does. It is very moving, you will probably see panels for several lost friends, from Liberace to some attractive bartender – but you will be impressed by the solidarity, and by the feelings expressed which tend to a gentle almost teasing wit rather than solemnity. My favorite was for John Ponyman, a not very successful but very handsome actor I knew, who died early 1984 – on his panel: "From Dust to Sawdust to Stardust."

Billy who lives here did a panel for his dead lover Jim, and is combining a visit to his folks in Milwaukee right now with a visit to the quilt in Chicago to see the panel in context.

452

At one Gay Parade last month when the Names Project came by, they had five panels carried as specimens: I knew the names on the first two, one of them a very old friend, Chuck Arnett (subject of a poem I once wrote called 'Crystal')! [. . .]

Meanwhile I have been all alone in the house for the last week. I don't normally like this, but it makes a change. Mike & Bob at Guerneville, Bill in Milwaukee, just me & the cat. I'm just about finished with the ms for my next book, I think (which will now rest in a drawer for a year or two). And I've been writing an article on Ginsberg, who I must say I have to conclude is the best living poet (in English) since the deaths of Bunting and Duncan.[6] His Collected Poems can be read like an autobiography, & nobody alive has written better poems than 'Many Loves,' 'Aunt Rose,' or 'Mugging.'

> Best,
>
> Th

1. Jack W. C. Hagstrom (1933–2019) compiled two volumes of TG's bibliography: the first with George Bixby, the second with Joshua Odell.
2. Two postcards: a male nude by Fisher Ross; Roy Lichtenstein, *I Love Liberty* (1982).
3. Date supplied through internal evidence.
4. TG edited Hinkle's *Poems* (1988) with the writer and journalist William McPherson (1933–2017). *Poems* was designed and printed by Eos Press.
5. The NAMES Project AIDS Memorial Quilt was first displayed in October 1987. To commemorate those who died from AIDS-related causes, their friends and families made fabric panels that formed the patchwork quilt.
6. See 'A Record: Allen Ginsberg's Poetry' (*SL* 102–15).

TO *Clive Wilmer*   TLS Clive Wilmer

Thursday 28 July 1988

1216 Cole Street,
San Francisco,
CA 94117

July 28 / 88

Dear Clive,

[. . . August] had a very good time in England, was treated very well there, grateful for all your efforts, and when he told me his reading at Cambridge had been during exam weeks, I said 'Well I wouldn't have gone to a reading by Wm Shakespeare during exams!' I like his Pig Press book a good deal too.[1] I tell him the title poem is an instant anthology piece.

[. . .]

'1975' is really about cruising the corridors of a bath house: I can understand how it would seem rather obscure if you didn't realise that.[2] In 'Her Pet', 'pounced' refers forward to 'it'. In the graduate student poem – about my poor friend Charlie, who was also the subject of 'The Differences' some years ago and then later of the one you don't much like 'Memory Unsettled' – the fourth line scans thus:

To a / unique / promise / –   checked / at ran/dom

It does seem to me legitimate to ask the reader here to allow a pause on the dash, equivalent to an unspoken syllable. Such demands are tricky, I am aware.

[. . .]

. . . There are 2 Niedecker books, as you probably know. One is a selected, which actually contains pretty well everything anybody would ever want by her: nicely produced, excellent text, well edited, also quite inexpensive: The Granite Pail (which refers to a seaside pail for making sandcastles, ask American friends for gloss on phrase) – I am thinking of using it as a text in a class I teach next spring. – The other edition LN is the complete poems: From This Condensary. It is a fat book, and the text is so loaded down with alternative versions that it is (as George Butterick pointed out in a review) almost impossible for the reader to use: I know, I tried reading it through. It is scholarship (not even good scholarship) out of control ...... All this by way of explaining why I am sending you a Selected rather than Collected Poems.

POUND. What you said was that Pound is so fatally flawed, and I said why do you always bring this up when so many other poets are also fatally flawed, e.g. Edmund Spenser with his atrocious and unacceptable politics, and unfinished poem. Now you seem to equate (or confuse) political wrongness (which you call wickedness, word that certainly doesn't help us to keep our heads clear) with poor writing, and saying that you just can't disentangle the two as you can disentangle The Parson's Tale from The Pardoner's Tale. Well, I beg your pardon, but I can! Canto 47 can most certainly be taken by itself, it forms a detachable and complete poem, I think it probably contains as exquisite poetry as you are likely to find this century, and it is thoroughly sexist but makes sexism acceptable in rather the way that Shakespeare makes Henry V heroic. To take a VERY interesting example, I would say, moreover, that Canto 51 contains some pretty 'wicked' implications (quoting Rudolph Hess with approval, and you can be pretty certain those Regents are Jews with Fagin-like noses), but it shows EP's writing close to his best. On the other hand, the Chinese cantos are about as unwicked as you could possibly want, but they are of an accumulating boredom difficult to parallel, and I certainly hope never to have to read them again (like The Parson's Tale, for example). To say that the Cantos as conceived are merely a ragbag, a container, is only to repeat what EP himself said in the Urcantos, and what later Winters, Tate, etc, repeated. You certainly might show SOME awareness that there is a tendency among American poets and critics to claim that Pound created a new form (I think he did, but I differ from them in that I think he <u>stumbled</u> on it). Sure, his politics were lousy, but so were those of certain left wing writers – and I don't see Stalin's death camps as being inferior to Hitler's – but when people discuss Brecht (a great dramatist) they don't speak about his art as 'fatally flawed' by his politics, I notice, though there is much to say on the subject, with <u>Mother Courage</u> if with nothing else. In a hundred years time I don't think people will view Pound as being more wrong than Brecht, though he was a good deal more idealistic, a good deal less slippery, and a good deal more unlucky.

NO! your letter was not boring, as witness this LIVELY response to it. I hope I am not being obnoxious, you know how I depend on your friendship, I hope. [. . .] I am having a tranquil hard-working summer, irrationally happy, I think it is because I don't have to visit friends in hospital this year, as I no longer have any close friends with the plague. And the sheer contrast to the painfulness of last July-August-September: I hope I shall never have to live through a time like that again, but I probably shall.

You must be in Greece now. Welcome back to Cambridge when you return. I gave a bright graduate student your address, JOSHUA WEINER,[3] but he probably won't look you up. He is also a student of Pinsky's, my admirable colleague, but admires Bunting, as Pinsky does not.

      Love,

        Thom

1. Kleinzahler, *On Johnny's Time* (1988).
2. See '1975' (*CP* 397), which corresponds with another of TG's bathhouse poems, set in 1975, 'Saturday Night' (*BC* 45–6).
3. See TG to Weiner, 18 July 1995, below.

Tuesday 2 August 1988

1216 Cole Street,
San Francisco,
CA 94117

August 2 / 88

Dear Duggle,

[. . .] I enclose a picture of myself and the new body I bought in the gym;
I am carrying two of my heaviest poems with me, just about to show them
to my garage buddies.[1] Thank you for your response to my poems: I am
especially grateful for your criticism of those two lines in 'Her Pet', no one else
had the sense to tell me that, yet I had a feel of their awkwardness: of course,
they can be omitted all together, I mean altogether, as you recommend.[2] Since
you kindly said that my poems make you happy, I enclose some more, which
are <u>bound</u> to make you miserable. I don't think there will be many after
these, as I do feel sucked dry as an old Dug after these. The J Car poem is of
Charlie, the Courtesies poem of my friend the gym-owner Norm.[3] No need
to comment on them if you don't feel like it. [. . .]

How terrific that you still have elms. I don't in truth know the difference
between English and American elms, but the English ones were very
impressive – the next most impressive trees of my childhood, to the horse
chestnuts, I think.

[. . .]

Of 'The Missing' yes the imagery came out of studying a reproduction of
Michelangelo's unfinished statues. Of the 'Ash' poem,[4] I was trying at last
to use that 7-syllable line Sidney brought into English which was especially
popular among the Eliz-jacs: I don't know that Michael wasn't right in his
reading of the last words: I mean Jim had been an extremely argumentative
man, but also any extra meanings of argument probably seem appropriate.

I was reading not Martial but Baudelaire again – going through the
Tableaux Parisians section of Les F du M makes me realise how much he is
still my master – the master of all of us: he appraises the sensual so ruthlessly
while at the same time never denying the way he has relished it, and so it
still retains, in the writing of the poem anyway, its relish, and so there is a
continual drama set up between the judgement and the senses. I was also
reading – made myself read – Enid Starkie's life of B: my what a boring
and pious work, and what a dumb woman that Oxford professor is.[5] Now
by contrast I am reading Bald's Life of Donne: much more scholarly, and

paradoxically much more readable – the Melbourne professor who risks pedantry is a far better writer than the Oxford professor.[6] I met a nice tall boy called Tim, 28 years old, with whom I have rather perverted sex every weekend. I don't know what he sees in me, but I know what I see in him.

What else? [. . .] Was very touched by Jesse Jackson's speech at the Demo convention in which he mentioned not only people with AIDS but also Gays and Lesbians as part of the people of this country for whom there should be hope. Nobody else who has run for president has ever REFERRED to us before. I wish he could be president: but of course he is far too much aware of real injustice, being black, to ever appeal to our white Wonderbread population who have the real power.

[. . .]

Wondering what poets to end up my Freshman course 'Introduction to Poetry' next year – I work up through the Ages in an anthology, then end with four poets in bulk, two of whom are Whitman and Dickinson, and the other two are changeable, last year they were E. Bishop (Geography III) and Kleinzahler – I decided to take a plunge and teach Lorine Niedecker's Granite Pail and Snyder's Myths and Texts, which latter I still find very solid after all these years (though I find his poetry since 1970 to consist largely of Buddhist bumper stickers). I thought of teaching one of Ginsberg's individual books, but the trouble with them is that though each one contains some wonderful poetry, it also contains some trash which is just what I'd want my students NOT to think poetry should be. I have no particular plans for all the rest of the year, except to reach the age of 59 (in a few weeks), and do a lot more reading, write a couple of articles, and if possible write some more perms. I think I have just about reached the end of my next pertry book: 'A Blank' wd look good as last poem.

A large embrace to youse,

a large embrace to Michael,

Th

1. A reference to a favourite TG postcard: Herb Ritts, *Fred with Tires, Hollywood* (1984).

2. Chambers thought that the following two lines in 'Her Pet' were unnecessary: '(Much as I read the shrunk face of the friend / I visited today in hospital)', which followed 'She went through to get here, to shake it all' in TG's original draft. In cutting the lines, TG turned the poem into a pair of sonnets. 'Her Pet' belongs to the AIDS sequence but is not, on the surface, about AIDS; rather, it alludes to or echoes the other poems, whereas the cut lines refer specifically to his hospital visits. Chambers's letter to TG (7 June 1988) can be found among his papers at the Thomas Fisher Library.

3. 'The J Car' (*CP* 480–1) and 'Courtesies of the Interregnum' (*CP* 476–7).

4. 'Words for Some Ash' (*CP* 472).
5. Starkie, *Baudelaire* (1933).
6. R. C. Bald, *John Donne: A Life* (1970).

TO *Donald Davie*

TLS Yale

Wednesday 10 August 1988

1216 Cole Street,
San Francisco,
CA 94117,
USA

August 10, 88

Dear Donald,

My brother retired to a certain Daisy Cottage somewhere in Cornwall, and you just about the same time to Silverton in Devon. Well, if I had to choose I'd certainly prefer the soft bosomy landscapes of Devon to the dour windswept Cornwall. I wonder how it feels to retire: I would imagine that the first reaction is as after the second part of the Tripos: "Oh dear, do I have to start something all over again now?" But you must have got over that, if indeed you ever felt it, and are probably back delightedly writing poetry and prose with less pressure behind you.

[. . .]

No your treatment of Williams didn't <u>offend</u> me.[1] I didn't agree, but I thought you put the case well and only overstated a few times (notably about absence of punctuation – everybody wrote without punctuation at that time, it was a fad), and I thought your point about his using his charm a most telling one. You are certainly right about that damn plums poem – that is not the Williams I value, and that is unfortunately the side of Williams that has been of most influence. But your article annoyed me, in quite a healthy way: I hope we shall remain vigorous enough in intellect for many years (I'm going to be 59 this month) to annoy the world at large, as well as each other, mildly, by our enthusiasms and exclusions.

Meanwhile I must thank you for the second great gift you have given me. The first was Bunting, when you and Doreen presented me with a copy of The Spoils, many years ago when you were still at Stanford; and the second is Milosz, whose work I only started to come to grips with after reading your wonderful book.[2] All that you say of M seems true, but I am still exploring . . .

458

My other belated discovery was of Rilke last year. I had tried reading him (in translation, because my German is rudimentary) since I was fifteen or something, but never got anywhere until the Stephen Mitchell translations (Selected Poems) which actually sound like good English poetry. I am very interested in the way his long sentences seem to touch some point from which the imagination and the literal experience are both accessible simultaneously. I'm not sure that that last sentence means anything, but perhaps you can see what I am trying to say.

[. . .] I am delighted you liked the Dejection poem, and interested when you speak of Milosz in connection with it.[3] Actually, one English friend, whose childhood books were evidently different from mine, and who disliked the poem a good deal, said the poem sounded like Eeyore speaking. I think there is a touch of Whitman behind the poem, & a touch of the Bible (remember, I may be unreligious, but I went to an English school, so I know the Authorized Version pretty well). Also there is an outright steal from the first pages of Great Expectations – of Cooling Churchyard, where Pip meets Magwitch.[4] I am writing of <u>those</u> marshes, the North of Kent, though Dickens calls them Essex, and know all those little churchyards pretty well. If you look up Great Expectations and compare it to my poem, though, my poem seems very barren in invention by comparison, and you can't help realising what a tremendous poet Dickens would have made if he had seen the kind of thing that could go into poetry. But he thought a poem was bumpety-bump and so all he wrote in verse are those interminable songs that he fits into Pickwick. But he could be a great stylist – and I know you know this already, I know how you admire him. Anyway, as I say, the best things in my poem are stolen. No need to thank me for these pamphlets!

I'm trying to persuade Faber to bring out Marianne Moore's <u>Observations,</u> a duplicate of the 1st edition, but I'm sure they won't.[5] It is the only way for anyone to understand what she was like before she turned into a fussy eccentric in a tricorne, – what Eliot and Winters and Pound and Williams saw in her: to isolate that good early stuff from the New Yorkerish trivia she wrote afterwards, at the same time revising half the virtue out of her early work. I'm getting incoherent!

Anyway, my warmest love to you both on High Street, Silverton,

Thom

1. Davie reviewed *The Collected Poems of William Carlos Williams, Volume One: 1909–1939* (1986); see 'A Demurral', *New Republic* (20 April 1987), 34–8.
2. See TG to Davie, 14 March and 1 July 1987, above.
3. 'A Sketch of the Great Dejection' (*CP* 423–4).

4. 'At such a time I found out for certain, that this bleak place overgrown with nettles was the churchyard,' Dickens writes; compare with TG's 'little churchyard clogged with nettles' in 'A Sketch of the Great Dejection'.
5. TG wrote to Craig Raine (26 July 1988) emphasising the need for Moore's *Observations* (1924) to be reissued (Faber Archive).

TO *Douglas Chambers*   TLS Toronto
Wednesday 7 September 1988

1216 Cole Street,
San Francisco,
CA 94117

Sep 7 / 88

Ravishing Creature,
    [. . .]
    Any chance of seeing you guys during this year, by which I mean academic year? Sure would be nice for ME. I won't be quite so fearfully busy this next spring as last year, as I shall be teaching one course less than I was then, though of course that's quite enough to keep this lad busy. This has been a pretty nice summer compared with last year, as I'm sure I've already told you. Not the least good thing has been in my writing so much. I thought when I reached my 'cut-off poem' for The Man with Night Sweats that there I would stay for a while. But no, I went and wrote a longish poem about a gay street fair in the Folsom area:[1] a poem I'd been wanting to write for years, either about this street fair or another, and finally I combined a description of the event with a tribute to Duncan's Opening of the Field I'd just been rereading. It is to be out in one of our local gay papers in October (the Sentinel) at least so they tell me, and I'll send you a copy when it does. It is written in a deliberately Whitmanian line for all its references to Jacobean masques, i.e. it's in a completely different style from what I've been doing this last fourteen months or so. My inconsistencies trouble a lot of critics, I know, e.g. John Bayley, who sez I have no personality;[2] one friendly critic calls me post-modernist because I am so derivative (– and I LOVE that: don't we all want to be included in the latest list of fashionables?);[3] but the truth is, when I first started learning from Auden (little as his work attracts me nowadays) one thing I learned for good was that the style was not the man, and I went on to get confirmed in this belief by what I read of the Eliz-Jacks, the style may vary depending on what you are up to in the poem. And so what may

seem multiple schizophrenia, The Hundred Faces of Thom, is really simply baroque superficiality.

[. . .]

I'm just reading a really superb book, Renaissance Self-Fashioning, by Stephen Greenblatt, whom I know very slightly indeed since he teaches at Berkeley. It is so good, and so wonderfully bright, that I can't put it down. I am, however, working myself up to writing an article on Robert Duncan – not a memoir, not yet, anyway, but more of a review of his last collection – I should be able to do this easily, you might think, but he is not always easy to put your finger on – some of that poetry in the two weaker books, Roots and Branches & The Bending of the Bow, is pretty turgid stuff, like the worst of Blake's prophetic boox.[4]

I had a terrific Labor Day weekend, just over. Sex, drink, drugs, the lot. Us old men do have to catch up with a lot of sleep though, after doing that kind of thing these days.

A couple of raccoons came in through the cat door to eat some leftover dog food last night. When the dog (she is fairly new, an elegant and athletic Husky) came into the kitchen today, she pissed all over the corner where they had been. Very understandable!

We had two French friends of Bill's here for some weeks, very nice men. Bill was showing them round the Folsom one of their last nights here, and some man was so taken with him that he followed them back to the car where they sat talking, Billy in the driver's seat, and started rapping imperiously on the closed window at Bill's side, but rapping with his hard cock. Bang bang bang, but Bill wouldn't open up. The next day there was an elongated smudged imprint visible on the glass, which Bill said looked a bit like the Shroud of Turin.

[. . .]

Now I must go over to Berkeley to do a few errands and go to a meeting. I am being very responsible because there is talk of giving me 'security of employment' – if they do I shan't have to teach 3 courses a term any more but 2, like the rest of the department. I may have trouble locating the English Department, however, as they discovered just before term started last week that the whole of Wheeler Hall (that immense building containing the whole of the Eng Dept plus at least two other departments) is so contaminated with asbestos that is must be completely abandoned for at least 12 months AT ONCE. Sounds like something of a horror situation.

So long Farmer Chambers,
and love to Michael Poet,
Th

1. 'At the Barriers' (*CP* 399–402).
2. See Bayley, 'Castles and Communes', *Times Literary Supplement* (24 September 1976), 1194.
3. See Paul Giles, 'Landscapes of repetition: the self-parodic nature of Thom Gunn's later poetry', *Critical Quarterly* 29, no. 2 (June 1987), 85–99.
4. See 'The High Road: A Last Collection' (*SL* 129–42).

TO *Clive Wilmer*   TLS Clive Wilmer

Monday 14 November 1988

1216 Cole Street,
San Francisco,
CA 94117

Nov 14 / 88

Dear Clive,

I felt fearfully guilty when I started reading your letter – guilty at my lack of tact, at my having overstated my criticisms, etc. – and was much relieved when I got to the part where you returned to reading my letter and found that I had not criticised you nearly so harshly as you remembered ("5 rounds with Mike Tyson"!). Please believe me, anyway, when I say that (specifically) you have written some of the poems that give me most continuing satisfaction – poems that I would with confidence include in an anthology of personal favorites – and that when I do go on about what seem to me weaknesses in poems you send me, it is because I am judging them by the high standards you have set yourself, in my mind; and that I see no signs of a decline in your talent, even though you are going through a period during which you are finding it difficult to concentrate on what you want to say – difficult to know what you want to say: but that happens to everyone (happened to me specifically at the beginning of the 1960s, after My Sad Captains, and at the beginning of the eighties, after The Passages of Joy – and also other times: it is impossible to write with uniform ease and energy, and sometimes one simply writes at half strength). Better to do so and keep in practice.

What a breathless and peculiar sentence that was! Glad I wormed my way out of it. More generally – as if I have not been general enough already – it is important to remember when you ask anybody's opinion about your work that YOU probably know more about what you are doing than they can know. You know what you are aiming at, and sometimes they can't even guess, if you have written at less than your best. Also, they may be wrong.

You are simply asking for <u>advice</u>, after all, and people who ask for advice can take it or leave it. [. . .]

Now to Ezra Pound. You are right, we can't go on like this, writing each other a paragraph on our disagreement over him, every three or four months. So let me say, concisely(!!), that I don't agree with you that his technique is, before <u>Rock Drill</u>, necessarily connected with sloppy thinking. What's wrong with Fascism is probably not bad thinking so much as bad feeling – or perhaps it is bad thinking to be racist and inhumane, etc: bad thinking not to <u>take account of</u> feeling. As for the connection of usury with Jews and homosexuals the one is based on poor statistics rather than on poor thinking, and the other is based on a perfectly clear medieval analogy that he assumes, with justice, we already know about (probably comes in Aquinas). No, Pound's Cantos do <u>not</u> have "a structure like a Bach fugue", nor does any other work of literature I know of: and if it did I would hate it, I suspect. It is a rich associationist work, tremendously innovative and risky in its structure, tremendously exciting as such, based on ideas I find on the whole perfectly <u>logically</u> thought-out and largely distasteful – but then I am used to finding the politics and religious ideas of authors I admire distasteful – Dante's are pretty unpalatable, and so are Shakespeare's, not to speak of Fulke Greville's. And so on. I promise I will say no more.

[. . .]

Glad you are in love. Don't worry about your writing: just let nothing discourage you into thinking you are no poet, after all – it's just all there, biding its time, and it will spring out when it is ready.

Excuse the haste of this terribly sloppily written letter –

Love,

Thom

1989

TO *Clive Wilmer*   TLS Clive Wilmer
Tuesday 28 February 1989

1216 Cole Street,
San Francisco,
CA 94117

Feb 28 / 89

Dear Clive,

A delight to receive yr letter. I must answer it now, as on Friday I get in written work from two classes and I won't have time to write to you for weeks after that! [. . .]

Dick just sent me <u>his</u> recent Barth book, which I am sure to enjoy.[1] I haven't yet seen his Omar Khayyam, but I plan to buy it when I do, and it is sure to be available here.[2] I finally got round to reading Rob's Theocritus, and I was delighted and enlighted at the same time, planning numerous imitations which will probably never get written.[3] I love the style he uses, between formal and colloquial – admire it tremendously, knowing how difficult that is, even when one is not translating. What a wonderfully talented man he is!

I have had annihilating writing blocks myself. I remember in about 1978 saying to a friend "I haven't written a poem in 2½ years and I have had to reconcile myself to the fact that I shall probably never write another", because I also remember his sweet answer: "Well, I'm not sure <u>I</u> can reconcile myself to it." And then it did eventually come back, I don't know why or how. All you can do is ride it out, start on your notebooks as soon as you can, and meanwhile keep yourself busy with prose, if you can. I know how awful it is: it is not exactly as if you were suddenly in a world without words, but rather as if you had become largely though not entirely deaf. Maybe fate has in mind for you to return to poetry with a JOLT, like Edgar [Bowers], or indeed Paul [Valéry . . .].

Speaking of Edgar, I was one of the judges for the Bollingen Award (that's the one which started with the furore over Pound's Pisan Cantos) and I was happy that we ended by choosing Edgar for it. I have to admit though that the idea was John Hollander's – he is a GREAT admirer of EB's. [. . .]

I have been reading through the ms for EB's next collection.[4] [. . .] I had been impressed by individual poems, but had not realised quite how good they would all look together: I think the book will maybe be even better than his first. I don't know what YW would have made of it, not nearly enough stoical gloom for the old man, I suspect. He was always deeply suspicious of happiness – and that is perhaps the great reservation, finally, to be made about Winters.

Thank you for your kind remarks about the poems in the TLS. The imagery IS tough in "A System", I am aware. So is his state of mind: he has been isolated like someone in an empty building, which is first a boarded-up department store, and then a prison, which is all like a maze, "laced up with passage ways." If he <u>did</u> unpick the ties to his isolation, though, the whole structure of his life would come apart (based as it is on the use of this drug) and he would end up with a tangle like the tangle in that string-drawer that is to be found in every household. And so on, I'm not sure that that elucidates it.

I am delighted and flattered, you may be sure, by the attention promised for my 60th birthday.[5] I would have thought you had become a little tired of my work by now: you have always been so extraordinarily kind to me in the past, and I am well aware that what stature I am considered to have is really the result of our living in a time in which achievement is mostly very low. In a village of mudhuts, a two-storey building looms like a skyscraper, indeed. You say you would like a batch of poems from me. I wonder what your deadline for these will be. I have nothing I could give you at the moment, and the first ½ of the year is not a good time for me to compose, I am so busy teaching, but I'll let you have what I can when I do write! [. . .]

I would be happy to be interviewed by Jim Powell.[6] He has some kind of an underpaid fellowship at Reed College (Portland, Oregon), where he is teaching now, with he tells me not enough money to buy himself a pair of new jeans. He will undoubtedly be down here for the summer (starting in mid-May, I imagine), possibly might get down here on visits before then. [. . .]

Augie did interview me, and the result was pretty good: it has been on the point of publication in the (Australian) SCRIPSI, for about a year now.[7] If Jim doesn't work out, I don't know who, but I think he will.

Have anyone write on me that you want. There are some people who admire me whose admiration is so qualified by prejudice that they make me squirm, but poets should have to squirm every now again, it helps to keep them from complacency. My only suggestion is Robert Pinsky, who would undoubtedly do a very fine article if persuaded. He is very funny about what he calls my "almost clinical sympathy" for people. He likes my recent work, which not everybody does. At the same time, I'd hate it to seem that I was asking him to do this out of personal affection to me, so if you do write to him, please don't put it as a favor to me, and make it easy for him to refuse with grace. He has been (personally) extremely kind to me in the past (until recently a "colleague"), and he is a busy man.

[. . .]

Anyway, thank you very much. Of course I have read Wendy Cope (she wrote <u>Preparing a Fix for Rudyard Kipling</u>, or was it <u>Sharing a Toke with Ian Fleming</u>?) and find her wonderfully funny.[8] She must be one of those people who is terrific to know.

[. . .]

Much love,

Thom

1. Davis, *Let Them Be Changed: Poems from the Persian* (1989).
2. Edward FitzGerald, *Rubáiyát of Omar Khayyám*, ed. Davis (1989).
3. Robert Wells, *The Idylls of Theocritus* (1988).
4. Edgar Bowers, *For Louis Pasteur* (1989).
5. Wilmer edited the 'Thom Gunn at Sixty' supplement in *PN Review* 70 (November–December 1989), 25–56.
6. See 'An Anglo-American Poet: Interview with Jim Powell' (*SL* 218–30).
7. August Kleinzahler and John Tranter, 'An Interview with Thom Gunn', *Scripsi* 5, no. 3 (April 1989), 173–94.
8. Cope, *Making Cocoa for Kingsley Amis* (1986).

TO *Robert Pinsky*[1]   TLS Stanford

Thursday 1 June 1989

1216 Cole Street,
San Francisco,
CA 94117

June 1, 89

Dear Robert,

[. . .]

Thank you for your suggestions about the order of my book.[2] I had meanwhile done some reordering of my own: if my original list seemed odd it was because I was playing with an idea of a largely chronological order, which I now realize simply doesn't work. However, your suggestions are extremely useful to me, and you have certainly got rid of one of my assumptions, that all the free verse poems HAVE to go together. You are right, some of them indeed belong with the metrical ones. Anyway, it's all in flux right now, but I am taking a great deal of notice of your list and of the rationale for it.

Just been reading Ashbery's latest book, April Galleons. Now I don't suppose HE ever has any difficulty in placing his poems in an order: even passages within poems could be changed around. But it is difficult to object to a poet who can write the line, "Isn't that your son's tibia in the pilaf?" And the book does make me laugh a lot.

I did find a wonderful poem by Wordsworth I'd never read before, "St Pauls", written 1808, not published till 1947. (You have probably known it for years.) I have never really been able to figure W out. I'd sooner read Geoffrey Hartman on The Prelude than The Prelude itself, and the Lucy poems leave me feeling that it's possible to be too artless (Peggy Lee: Is that all there is?). And then Wordsworth sneaks up on me and I find things by him as good as Shakespeare, e.g. in Resolution and Independence and the lines on Hogg's death and in the second half of Mutability – no doubt there are other great poems I haven't read. I know how Keats' worst poetry is connected to his best (it would be possible to make a kind of spectrum), but I don't know how W goes from his worst (or even his average) to his best. It's as if, once in an age, he is suddenly able to find a tune which matches his complete intentness of feeling. As in this poem. It is wonderful being bowled over by a Wordsworth poem, anyway.

When you are here, I'd love to see you for a meal, for a talk, or if you have only time for a cup of coffee I would gladly cross Bay Bridge on my knees. I know you'll be here such a short time.

I'm writing an article for Janet's 90th birthday.[3] Boy is she a good poet. She seems better every time I read her through.

X

Thom

1. Robert Pinsky (1940–), poet, literary critic and academic; he was TG's colleague at UC Berkeley (1980–9).
2. TG wrote to Pinsky (3 May 1989) asking for his opinion about the order of poems for *MNS*. This letter can be found among Pinsky's papers at Stanford.
3. 'As If Startled Awake: The Poetry of Janet Lewis' (*SL* 66–73).

TO *Clive Wilmer*   TLS Clive Wilmer

Monday 25 September 1989

1216 Cole Street,
San Francisco,
CA 94117

Sep 25 / 89

Dear Clive,

I was dazzled by the supplement to the PN Review, and I only hope it doesn't go to my head and I start imagining I am a living classic.[1] I suppose I was <u>most</u> pleased by your poem and by Davie's prose piece: it is not just the praise, but the fact that the praise is so persuasive, being in each case from such a fine mind – it is <u>worth</u> being praised in such terms, I feel. (I have made fun of DD's excesses in the past, and no doubt will again. Nevertheless even his excesses are worth considering: as with Winters' it is always possible he might be right.) I am awed as well by the range of people here: Ted, Augie (2 of his best poems), Pinsky, Dick, Janet, good lord, how wonderful – and the interview is, no question, the best I have ever had, probably the only printed interview that would be worth reprinting. [. . .]

Literally, I can't thank you enough: whether I deserve it or not, the whole collection of kind people make it seem as though the subject of it all should be read, and even have his books bought!

[. . .]

I should have thanked you before for Stephen Romer's <u>Idols</u>. He is very good, very distinctive: beginning a poem by him I am not only interested, I have no idea where it will end. (I wonder if this might not be a good test of poetry nowadays.) It will not end in a nicely rounded way, like Winters or Larkin or alas me. Nor will it end in an undeterminate way, like Whitman or Duncan or O'Hara. His (apparent) mix of influences is fascinating – English at times for that kind of frank relaxed domestic tone which is perhaps the distinctive gift of the English poets since 1945 – but there is a desolated Frenchness of tone available also – and also a wide range of <u>interests</u> which opens up the imagination to mythologies of the mind (Joyce, Rilke, Corbière). As you can see, I haven't got him completely figured out yet, but I do admire him a lot.

I have at last written a long letter to Craig Raine, trying to be friendly but covering every grievance I have with F & F, including some you know nothing of.[2] I have among other things tried to open up the possibility of your critical book again (probably you wouldn't want to write it now), but I

468

thought I should let him know what I expect of a publisher's loyalty.³ Faber should pay more attention to loyalties and less to royalties. Good slogan!

Glad you like Jim's book. I enclose a copy of the review I wrote.⁴

[. . .]

I certainly didn't notice you being nervous that day we did the recordings.⁵ It was such a pleasure to see you again. I must apologise for having said that my only criterion for good films was to be given an erection: I was victim of a rather Nazi-like impulse because I was so irritated by all the mention of movie-as-art [. . .]. I suppose I just have a rather nasty side that everybody was too kind to mention in the PNR!!

I am sweating out a review for the TLS of some books about Whitman.⁶ WW is a strange one – one of those poets whose best is superb and whose worst is devoid of even minor talent. But that's the Romantic syndrome, I guess – the same can be said about DHL and Wordsworth.

[. . .]

Do thank Wendy Cope – deeply – on my behalf for her intervention in getting Faber to buy that ¼ page of advertisement from PN Review for my books. I am very grateful for her altruism and generosity.

                & love to you

                      & unspeakable gratitude

                    Thom

1. See TG to Wilmer, 28 February 1989, above.

2. TG's letter (21 September 1989) can be found in the Faber Archive.

3. Faber had recently published short critical introductions to Philip Larkin and Seamus Heaney. Wilmer wrote to Raine with a proposal for a similar book on TG and was told there was not enough interest in TG to justify it.

4. Powell, *It Was Fever That Made the World* (1989); see 'Fever in the Morning: Jim Powell' (*SL* 121–5).

5. Wilmer interviewed TG for the BBC; see *Poets Talking: The Poet of the Month Interviews from BBC Radio 3*, ed. Wilmer (1994), 1–7.

6. See 'Forays against the Republic: Whitman' (*SL* 15–21).

TO *Clive Wilmer*   TLS Clive Wilmer
Sunday 12 November 1989

1216 Cole Street,
San Francisco,
CA 94117

Nov 12 / 89

Dear Clive,

Well, all in all, I'd prefer 15 seconds of earthquake to 15 seconds of living
in Lebanon – at least you know it's going to stop. I jumped into a doorway,
where I was bounced about a bit, and a few things fell down on the floor, but
very little was broken, and the house is OK too, and we were very lucky.[1] We
are built on rock that goes right down to Hell, as the man once told me about
New York City. All the places that suffered were on fill, whether coastal or
dried-up ponds and lakes. Bob, who is the boss in a warehouse, was 2 blocks
from the worst part of it all, in Oakland, where the top deck of a freeway
fell down on the one below, & he couldn't get home that night. (Bay Bridge
is still unusable, but there is the subway.) It was wonderful, he said, people
brought extension ladders from their backyards, and ropes, and saved people
from the freeway, even though the cops tried to stop them from doing so
because it was unsafe.

Just went down to Los Angeles to give two readings, staying there with
the Steeles, who were very kind. Went and returned by train – now, that's
the best way of seeing California – oh, I'd forgotten, that is the way you
have already seen it. Most of the other people on the train were young men
and old ladies, in which latter category I count myself nowadays. What I
liked most about LA was the Getty Museum – did you go there? It is an
extraordinary place, and I'd like to spend a week or two going there for a
couple of hours every day then going to the beach in the afternoons. It is in
structure an exact replica of a Roman villa in Herculaneum – and really I
found myself thinking, conspicuous consumption in Malibu = consp. cons. in
Herculaneum, or, the very rich = the very rich, in each case buying their art
from the best sources. But it is stunning statuary, etc.[2]

[. . .] Thank you [. . .] for having the BBC send me the tape, which arrived
Saturday and I listened to it last night. You are a very good interviewer, and
your voice is just the right degree of honesty, eloquence, steadiness, etc. My
own varied between pompous fussiness at the opening to the beginnings of
humanity at the end. Mike said this was because at the start I was speaking
to the mike (& nervous becos of that audience out there) instead of to you,

470

which is a fair enough comment. I was relieved that I sounded like a real person in my readings of self and Whitman, on the other hand. But what I said in the interview was nothing to be ashamed of, and I attribute all that to you. Thank you again.

[. . .]

I shall give the Faber question a rest. What I do think I shall press for, though, is this. If they don't have more of my books in print by the time my next collection comes out, I shall ask them to do a Collected. At least I shall be able to check easily on whether the whole lot of me is available or not. Sorry about all this egotism. I do thank you, however, for having alerted me to Faber's varied kinds of neglect.

[. . .]

Edgar B is living up here for a few months, is thinking of buying a house – perhaps one quite near me – now that he is semi-retired. We had lunch a couple of weeks ago, & shall be reading together at Berkeley soon. He hopes his new book will be out before then. He is an admirable man, but I find it difficult to imagine being intimate with him. He seems to lack silliness, and that unnerves me a bit. Maybe I am wrong. I have found that nowadays I take longer to like people.

Still haven't written any poetry since the one to Helena Shire,[3] but I did a quite good article about Donald Hall and his new (best) book[4] (poor guy, then I heard he has cancer of the colon), and am writing one, perhaps quite long, on Isherwood, which I promised the Threepenny Review two years ago.[5] I have had a great idea for an essay contrasting two types of poetry – better than the Open and the Closed – YW called poetry an exploration, Duncan spoke of it as an adventure, and the contrast between explorations and adventures strikes me as being very illuminating.[6]

[. . .]

We have had the sunniest autumn I remember here in years. Today seems like – finally – the first day of winter, with all the melancholy and that sad feeling of helplessness that it brings. I'm looking out of my window now and seeing the leaves being blown on the wind like pages from the calendar in a 1940s Hollywood movie – gee, do you think I could write a John Ashbery poem after all?

Love,

Th

1. A reference to the Loma Prieta earthquake (17 October 1989).
2. See 'Herculaneum', *Conjunctions* 19 (November 1992), 139–41; uncollected.
3. 'The Antagonism' (*BC* 5–6).

4. See 'Living the Present: Donald Hall' (*SL* 96–101).
5. 'Christopher Isherwood: Getting Things Right' (*SL* 173–96).
6. See TG to Woods, 27 February 1988, above.

TO *A. E. Dyson*   TLS (aerogramme) Manchester
Tuesday 21 November 1989

1216 Cole Street,
San Francisco,
CA 94117,
USA

Nov 21, 89

Dear Tony,

[. . .] Well, no, if you are expecting San Francisco to be like Venice, you'll really be disappointed. I'd say more like Copenhagen – a pretty city rather than a beautiful one. A friend said SF was second only to Prague in his eyes, but I've never been <u>there</u>. There are almost no really beautiful buildings, but there is a general impression of prettiness – the houses are mostly of white or pastel-colored wood, the natural situation (sea, Bay, and hills), is stunning, and the people are still ready to grin a greeting to you. [. . .]

I am happy indeed about the casebook.[1] Perhaps <u>this</u> will take the place of Alan Bold's book, which I am distressed to see is still used.[2] Clive Wilmer and also Neil Powell[3] each wanted to write books about my poetry, but Fabers decided they were not famous enough, and of course no other publisher is willing to underwrite the immense costs of quotations from Fabers poetry! No, I <u>now</u> like Greg Woods' book very much – it was his first version of the chapter on my work which troubled me a good deal, <u>everything</u> being treated sexually.[4] For example, a red-coat soldier comes to the "mouth" of a cave, and this was treated as fellatio! But after he sent me his original version of the chapter, I wrote him my criticisms, and he took notice of them all, and I now consider it a very good study of myself <u>as a sexual poet only</u>. As I have told him. I also like his chapter on Ginsberg, very much indeed.

No, I am not very worried about the Germans of today. I'm more worried about American foreign policy right now. How could you doubt that I am a socialist? Well, I guess it doesn't show much in my poetry. But socialism, despite perversions, still strikes me as having a concept of <u>fairness</u> behind it, and capitalism seems to me more and more to be based on simple greed and selfishness, however they may become softened.

It is interesting to read what you say about the importance of sexual desire for oneself, or for a poet or novelist's writing. I agree, especially since I have written a short article on Whitman (for the TLS) and am just about to start a longish one on Isherwood, this year. It is still important to stress it about Whitman because there was 100 years of pretense that he wasn't talking about what he was talking about; it is less important to make the point with Isherwood since he himself forced the emphasis so admirably for the last twenty years or so of his life. I am very happy with Greg's treatment of me now it has been shorn of its inaccuracies and its over-large generalisations – because my sexuality HAS been of prime importance to me even when I seem to be speaking of something else. Nevertheless I am not only a sexual poet any more than Whitman or Isherwood are only sexual writers. Sexuality is often only the most noticeable of the kinds of impulse for which we require the freedom of exercise. It HAS been so repressed that it often takes on a symbolic importance, symbolic that is of all repression. But with talk about repression and symbols I'm slipping into a kind of jargon of which I ought to be more wary. Nevertheless it would certainly be possible to read a lot of my poems and understand them fully without knowing I am gay. The same might be said of Goodbye to Berlin and even of most of "Song of Myself". – Yes, I agree about James Baldwin – I discovered him only in the last 10 years. Another Country is extraordinarily good; more than half of Just Above My Head is too (but Giovanni's Room dates very badly). – I have grouched about Larkin in the 70th issue of the PN Review, and grouched too much no doubt: I think that he is an exquisite poet, stylistically far better than Ted and me, for example, but disastrously limited by his choice of subject matter – finally that choice has the effect of a kind of cowardice. [. . .]

     Love,

       Thom

1. *Three Contemporary Poets: Thom Gunn, Ted Hughes & R. S. Thomas*, ed. Dyson (1990).
2. Bold, *Thom Gunn and Ted Hughes* (1976).
3. Neil Powell (1948–), poet and biographer.
4. See TG to Woods, 2 October 1982 and 5 June 1988, above.

TO *Douglas Chambers*   TLS Toronto
Friday 1 December 1989

1216 Cole Street,
San Francisco,
CA 94117

December 1, 89

Dear Douglas, Stud and Professor,

[...]

Well, Bob moved out of the house a couple of weeks ago, after twelve years with us. He and Mike were simply getting on too badly, and his presence was bad for Mike, so they agreed he should leave. [...] I still <u>feel</u> he is a member of the family. Maybe I should treat it not as a loss but as a situation analogous to when one's son goes to college! It is a great pity, though.

[...]

I have written – still – only one poem this year.[1] But I've written a lot of literary journalism!!! Which keeps this old man off the streets. Just got my proofs of Whitman article from TLS: in the course of it I remarked (not cynically) that the origin of Whitman's love of humanity seemed to be in his love "for hunky working men", a phrase I found amusing. They changed it to "for well-built working men". I don't know [if it was] because they thought the British wouldn't understand the word – U.S. slang, or because they thought I was enjoying myself too obviously. I didn't question it, their alteration, anyway. It gave me encouragement seeing it at last in proof, and helped me go on with my monster essay on Isherwood that I'm all in the middle of. I have such difficulty connecting my thoughts – my sentences. Always have, it's nothing to do with my age. It is so wonderful when I can write good clear connected prose on a first draft, but it has happened so seldom. Also one does wonder if what one has to say may not simply be obvious, and the fact that no one else has said it is because it was assumed everybody knew it anyway! Well, you know all about such problems. Everybody does.

[...]

I have met several wonderful young men in the last few months, must have reached a new stage of hoary gerontophile-attracting wrinkledness. The best, 2 weekends ago, suddenly said in the middle of sex, "What's your last name?" and when I told him said "Oh, I like your poetry", and marvellously didn't even refer to the matter again during the entire night. I love not being liked for my poetry but for my dreadful old body.

[. . .]

X X X X X X X X X X X X X X X X X X X X X X X X
X X X X X X X X X X X X X X X X X X X X X X X
X X X X X X X X X X

Thom

1. 'The Antagonism' (*BC* 5–6).

1990

TO *Ander Gunn*   TLS Ander Gunn
Tuesday 2 January 1990

> 1216 Cole Street,
> San Francisco,
> CA 94117,
> USA
>
> Jan 2 / 90

Dear Ander,

I'm sure you know that Jenny phoned me about Barbara's death, as she must have phoned you as well.[1] I didn't feel nearly as sad as I had on hearing about her first attack of angina over twenty years ago. Till she was about seventy she was such a splendid woman, not an ounce of selfishness in her. I think of her remembering how she had bicycled all the way from Higham in to Strood to see Mother when she (Mother) was first married. Quite a few miles, that. "What energy I must have had then," she said – but she still had terrific energy when she was telling me about it. I love to think of the young Barbara pink-faced and pedalling and long-haired on her bicycle.

The last ten years sound more like a gradual fading-out.

Oh, I hadn't intended to leave such a significant looking space, but let it stand. We'll hint at significance where we can. I didn't spend that great a New Year – that is, not till Mike grabbed me and took me out to the movies. I was thinking about what an awful decade it really has been. You know how the papers love to make lists of the ten best or worst films, books, etc etc of the decade. Well I thought of the ten most important things in my own life for the decade, and the only really good thing among them all was you and Bett getting married. So there's one positive among all the loss and death![2]

We loved your sensational card of the sun above the fog-bank, but couldn't make out if it was of the Californian or Cornish coast. I thought it was of here, and then I realized there was no reason I could remember that it might not be there. It <u>is</u> a good picture, and I was impressed, as I have been by a lot

476

of your recent work. (I don't mean that as patronizingly as it sounds. Real admiration, dude!)

It really is as if no American president can really feel he has balls until he has invaded some minute country, isn't it?[3]

As usual, we are not getting enough rain. I seem to have written that in every letter I've sent you for the last five years. We had not a drop in December, when we are supposed to get several sizable storms. Then we had a few showers yesterday, but it was nothing. I can't stand it if we go right back on water rationing. One comfort at least, it looks like our roof is leaking, so if it doesn't rain much before next summer we won't have to set out the buckets.

Well this is just a note to wish you happy new year, in spite of everything!!!!!!!! [. . .] I am sorry to tell you that Ida the cat appears to have turned into a male. We are astonished and rather shocked. Should I write up to the Draft Board, I wonder, or just wait until the census people come round? And do we tell the neighbors or just hope they don't notice? Ida certainly doesn't seem to mind.

Much love to Bett and you,

Th

1. Barbara Godfrey died on 11 December 1989, aged 91.
2. TG recorded the list in his diary:
   'thinking of what happened to me in the eighties – ten-things list like the papers.
   1. AIDS invented itself
   2. Jim died
   3. Billy got AIDS (ARC)
   4. Allan died
   5. I met Charlie, and he died of AIDS
   6. others died of it, in 1987, Allen Day, Norm, & Lonnie, as well as Charlie, all died in one month
   7. I didn't go to England; & I stopped holidaying in NY after Allan & Norm's deaths
   8. Mike & Bob split up; Mike is sad all the time; Bob moved out, effectively ending the idea of the family
   9. In England, Barbara dies at 91; and Ander remarries (and that's good).
   10. I wrote a lot of good poetry, which is the only other good thing that happened, of importance.'
3. The USA invaded Panama in mid-December 1989 to depose Panama's military dictator Manuel Noriega.

TO *Tony Tanner*   TLS King's

Sunday 7 January 1990

1216 Cole Street,
San Francisco,
CA 94117

Jan 7 / 90

Dear Tansy,

I cannot tell you how happy it made me to get your letter. And also happy that you are living a full life indeed, and relishing it, what with your wife, and stepdaughter, and lovers, and books, and work. [. . .] Our family has contracted to the size it was when you last saw us, except we fill the whole house now, just Mike and Billy and me. Well it's satisfactory that we at least are still alive.

Don's life is really far too complicated to catch you up on. In a sense he is a middle-aged male Joan of Arc, one damn cause after another. I love him, but he also irritates the hell out of me, and he does smell rather too much for my bourgeois nose, since he seldom washes. He is quite portly, or was when we last saw him, about a year ago, being a perpetual sipper of brandy. That seems to me a rather attractive habit, though not for me. I wish he was here (though not living in this house, maybe), since he is one of the few people in the world I can talk to with pleasure (of course you are another). My friend Allan was another, but you never knew him, though I knew him for ten years, and alas now he is dead.

Someone I knew much less was Charlie, a handsome and fearfully intelligent young man – a dazzler in fact – I mean I knew him less long, and indeed the course of our love was far from smooth, and we had ended up as sexual friends more than anything else, and then HE died, which was also very painful – the more painful since he was only 30, and one was aware of such potential – as a writer, as a teacher, as a lover – and he hadn't done anything to speak of yet. An Old Man's Love, I used to mutter to myself.[1] And indeed since then, Sept of 87, I haven't found myself close to falling for anybody. Exhaustion, perhaps.

[. . .]

Mike is quite a considerable source of happiness to me, and I am pretty lucky that we have been able to live together most of the last forty years (38 more like, but I love a round number). He is the most astonishing malade imaginaire I have ever known:[2] he knows it too, but he says being aware you are a hypochondriac doesn't make you feel any the better. (It's like the

478

saying that even paranoids have enemies.) Every now and again we spend a wonderful time together, as for example New Year's Eve, and I know I must have somehow done the right things all along after all, and the rest is just bad luck and good luck over which I didn't have much power.

It was really a pleasure to see Clive for a few days again this summer. I realise to my astonishment what a solidly good person he is. He is never bitchy, he is really trustworthy, he is "good". Though I have to admit that when I told him the story of how I told you "I made Wesley Trimpi cry at a poetry reading I gave" and you said "Good! Good!!! He has made me cry often!" (i.e. from boredom), Clive – who had just stayed with the Trimpis for three days – did start to giggle uncontrollably. He tells me that Mrs T (by far the nicer of the two) has split with Wes, who was – surprise of all surprises – quite a philanderer with his female students.

[. . .]

Jack Collins has been made the head of the first Gay-Lesbian Department in the country (at least I think it is).[3] I find him alternately endearing and maddening (probably all these people find ME maddening also, I should remember). He is the most genuinely sentimental person I have ever met, I mean he brings it to positively Rousseau-esque levels. Once he was telling me about a student in a class who burst into tears: "He cried, I cried, we all cried . . ." But it is guileless, he is about as generous as they come, and every now and again you do feel of him that, yes, it is the right way for him to be, and that this way of feeling through everything, of the professeur larmoyant, is perhaps as good a way as any other to get through to people. But of course it grates on a Shavian rationalist like me (I do think that's where it all comes from with me, I educated myself on Shaw when I was about 13, not that I ever read him now).

A very nice man from I think Sussex University, Alan Sinfield, was at Berkeley for the Spring. We got on well, in fact he interviewed me for the (London) Gay Times.[4] He has just written a very dashing book on Politics and Culture and Literature in Postwar Britain, which will probably disturb some of the young codgers who write for the TLS etc.[5] Anyway, he said he'd never met you, so look out for him when your paths cross, as they are bound to do some day. He is fun as well as bright, bright as well as fun.

Do you really want to know what I think of the Venice Poem (by [Duncan])? I haven't reread it in quite a while. For RD it was the great break through into something of his own, and I think it really was too. There's a good deal of Edith Sitwell baroquerie hanging around in it, but on the other hand the queer bits are immensely strong: "Men fuck men by audacity" I remember that without even looking it up. I admired it, and took note, but on the

479

other hand it doesn't seem to me to show his talent at full stretch, nor does anything before 1959.

[. . .]

High blood pressure, eh? Pooh, I say. I have had high blood pressure since I was 49! What you can do is to get your doctor to prescribe a little pill that you take at bed time: that brings your blood pressure back to normal, so you have both "high" and "normal" blood pressure, neither of them <u>really</u> real, as who should say. There is one pill that makes you piss a lot & makes it difficult to get erections. Avoid this pill. But there is another, here under the tradename of LO-PRESSOR, which does not have these quite depressing effects. If you are curious, I can find out what chemicals it contains.

[. . .]

Well, it is raining (the rain is about as welcome as it is at the end of the Waste Land, Da, datta, etc, we are having quite a drought), and it is time for the first of my glasses of wine. I normally have only 2 glasses of wine a day, but abnormal situations are always coming up, thank god.

XXXXXXXXXXXXXXXXXXXXXXXX

Mike and Bill send love too, and Don does too, since
I spoke with him on the phone a week or two ago,
or anyway subsequent to yr letter,
Love to the big boy,
from his admiring friend
Th

1. Trollope's last novel, *An Old Man's Love* (1884); see also 'Lines for My 55th Birthday' (*CP* 415).
2. An allusion to Molière's play *Le Malade imaginaire* (1673).
3. Jack Collins (1948–) was a graduate student at Stanford in the 1970s, during which time he spent two years at King's College, Cambridge, where Tanner was his director of studies. Tanner later introduced Collins to TG in San Francisco in 1974 and they became friends. Collins established the first Department of Gay and Lesbian Studies in the United States, at City College, San Francisco.
4. Sinfield, 'Thom Gunn at Sixty', *Gay Times* 131 (August 1989), 26–9.
5. Sinfield, *Literature, Politics and Culture in Postwar Britain* (1989).

Saturday 3 February 1990

1216 Cole Street,
San Francisco,
CA 94117

Feb 3 / 90

Dear Ted,

[. . .]

I think you are just sixty yourself now, aren't you? Well, welcome into the sixties. Soon we shall be so old that nobody will say anything nasty about us in print any more, but just give us meaningless respect and remain amazed that anyone could be as old as we are and still writing (but I hope we shall both beat Thomas Hardy and Sophocles to it, into our nineties that is). I do wish I were more interested though in what the young of both our countries are writing: every now and then I see a glimmer, but it does seem as if Larkin was a malign influence on the British, encouraging a kind of pusillanimity that takes from them any chance of the imagination (I suppose the attraction of him is that he deals with the everyday), and as for the Americans, most of the best of the younger ones are <u>bold</u> enough, but boldly interested in kinds of experiment where the verbal has cut its connections with experience. Perhaps this is just the sourness of age. I do like August Kleinzahler's and Jim Powell's poetry over here, at least.

I haven't been to England since I last saw you, 1979, at that big reading. I just decided, today, that I think I will come over and do some readings and see some relatives in 1992, and told the people at South Bank I would (they were actually asking me for <u>this</u> year).

<u>Wolfwatching</u> is wonderful, it is as if I am reading you for the first time, and it seems to me your best book. I love the way you take a strangeness and <u>use</u> it – not like the surrealists, for whom strangeness is an end in itself, – <u>you</u> make unexpected meaning out of it (the Christmas stocking of "On the Reservation", for example). The energy of your poetry is famous of course, and I think all of us envy you a bit for it, but it wouldn't count if it weren't matched and in a sense defined by your delicacy. Just now, reading "A Dove" again, I first questioned line 3, "wings snickering", but then I heard the dove's wings in my mind doing just that. For its rightness, it reminds me of the phrase I have liked so many years of your gnats "scribbling" on the air. So accurate, such phrases, that they seem obvious, and yet no one ever said them before you.

I also admire especially all the poems in the book about (presumably) relatives, and the Black Rhino, and "Us He Devours" (a poem you have been preparing for some thirty-five years). I like this collection so much because it combines the strength of your first three books with the strength of your subsequent books, the deliberated with the impromptu, the literal with the imagined. Saying all that is to simplify, but I have to in speaking about poetry for which the preparations have been so complicated and so drawn-out and probably so unconscious. All I can see is the results, and guess at what made them so.

My love to you – and also to Carol & to Olwyn –

[. . .]

X   Thom

TO *Glenn Jordan*[1]   ALS Glenn Jordan
Friday 9 February 1990[2]

[1216 Cole Street,
San Francisco,
CA 94117]

Feb 9

Dear Glenn –

I sure like this blue paper, don't you? You ask me what I think of Cynthia Ozick's article on TSE.[3] Well, it's slick and magaziney, but it's essentially accurate in its facts and judgments (except in one respect). I mean, Eliot was king of the world when we were at our universities, wasn't he? and he was both a symbol of experiment and in all his tendencies essentially conservative. In her summaries of his biographies, she gets it pretty well right, though she certainly doesn't make any allowances for him. He hardly embodied any of the characteristics, as a person, that would qualify him for a friend of mine. And boy, was he a hair-raising bigot – though a genteel bigot, but I'm not sure that that makes it any better.

She does however speak as if his poetry (except for Prufrock) is now largely unread and unappreciated, and that's simply untrue. Perhaps, rather, it has fallen into a more proper perspective. I teach him as one of 5 or 6 poets in a course called "Modern Poetry" (ha ha) every few years, and the other people who teach it have invariably included him – however could they not? I don't, actually, like his poetry that much – though I admit its power. But an interesting thing happens when we come to The Waste Land in the course –

every time. I like Pound better as a poet, and people such as W.C. Williams, Stevens, Basil Bunting, even Marianne Moore mean a great deal more to me than he does, but I try to be fair to him, since I figure it is my job to spread enthusiasm & understanding of poetry – and the majority of the class goes wild over The Waste Land (I am talking about 100 students), though I don't. I think it is because at the age of 20 one is so excited by the possibilities (and the compatibilities) of self-dramatization – that is why they like Sylvia Plath (who was good too) so <u>inordinately</u>: sarcastic gloom, full of resonant self-deflations, is exactly up the alley of a 20 year old, it certainly was up mine. So C.O. is wrong about that, and I imagine will continue to be. But I'm glad that poets I think as good or better than he have begun to be taken more seriously in recent years: in a small way I think I have helped to bring their elevation about. I have certainly tried for it.

It's all been a bit sad since Bob moved out. But we hold ourselves together, the three of us still here, and no doubt things will get happier soon. I've been writing heaps of criticism recently – the last thing I wrote and I think the longest thing I ever did, on Isherwood, it will be out in June in the <u>Threepenny Review</u>. Writing poetry now, though.

      Love,

         Thom

1. Glenn Jordan (1936–), television director and producer, met TG and MK in Palo Alto in 1958.
2. Date supplied through internal evidence.
3. Ozick, 'T. S. Eliot at 101', *New Yorker* (20 November 1989), 119–54.

TO *Clive Wilmer*

TLS Clive Wilmer

Tuesday 20 February 1990

> 1216 Cole Street,
> San Francisco,
> CA 94117,
> USA

> Feb 20, 1990

Dear Clive,

Thank you for your terrific letter, full of good things. (I suppose terrific is spelled some other way, after all. Do you know Douglas Chambers has a spelling-correcting typewriter: when he writes to me it corrects my name, which is obviously wrong, to Thor, thus "Dear Thor". There are few gods I feel less in common with.) I did like what you said about Yeats, because that was very much the experience I went through with him in about 1972 or so. In memory, he exasperates, but in the actual rereading you are dazzled by what you accurately call his courage. No, not dazzled, because being dazzled implies that you can't see detail, and it is precisely in all his detail that Y's courage becomes so evident. Anyway, I had hardly written a poem for a year for the previous three years, but reading him for a course I was about to teach – studying the entire body of his work, and then coming across a reference to the fact that he would often write out the plot for a poem in prose and then versify it, line by line, I thought "what do I have to lose?" and taking a prose outline for a poem I'd made out about nine months before I spent several days doing exactly that, versifying it. I remember it all clearly, reading Yeats and working in snatches on this poem ("To a Friend in Time of Trouble") under a big tree which at one stage sheltered me from some freak summer shower, at Russian River, the place the poem is about. So there's a very personal gratitude mixed in with the more general renewal of my admiration.

[. . .]

A colleague of mine, a man I have always liked but I never thought much of his poetry before now, has astonished me and many others by bringing out a very fine book-length poem from New Directions. His name is Peter Dale Scott and the book is called Coming to Jakarta. It is really surprising for two other reasons, 1) that it is a good political poem, and 2) that he successfully uses the method (roughly) of the Cantos, and is thus yet another leftwing heir to the fascist Pound. (Not, as I've been trying to explain to my students, that EP was exactly rightwing in the modern sense – he admired Mussolini because he was anti-capitalist among other things – but let's not get into that again).

[. . .]

The new poem Douglas mentioned must be "The Antagonism", which I'm sure I sent you, it's the one I wrote for Helena Shire. It's the only poem I wrote last year, except a prose poem that I'm not sure about.[1] I include three poems I wrote these last two months. The short one took place in Snodland, Kent, about 1946. I remember my aunt telling us about what "the Russell girl" had been doing, and then saying in a very doubtful tone: "She says she is doing it to punish them."[2] The longish poem borrowed its form from Herrick's On His Winding Sheet, probably unsuccessfully, but HE does use it splendidly.[3]

I'm reading Tony T's collection of essays Scenes of Nature, Signs of Man. The one on James and Adams is him at his best, but the book does seem to suffer from being a slightly miscellaneous collection. I do have such high standards for him! I went the other day to hear a lecture by Frank Kermode on Value and Literature. He took an hour to tell us that there are two kinds of value: intrinsic value and attributed value. This was hardly news to us. Really he is a most disappointing lecturer – I once heard him before at Princeton 20 years ago. He is elegant and obvious: not illuminating at all. I do still like his first book, Romantic Image, very much, but that was about 1955, and he has run through many professorships since then.

I'm glad you are seeing Tony. I heard from him over Christmas, finally, and he sounded probably as really contented as he wanted me to think him.

[. . .]

      Love,

          Th

[. . .]

1. 'The Deeper', *Threepenny Review* 43 (Fall 1990), 32; uncollected.
2. 'After the War', *Times Literary Supplement* (5–11 October 1990), 1060; uncollected.
3. The 'longish poem' is 'An Operation' (*BC* 20–2); 'The Problem' (*BC* 23–4) is the other enclosure.

TO *Craig Raine*[1]   TLS Faber
Monday 26 March 1990

1216 Cole Street,
San Francisco,
CA 94117

March 26 / 90

Dear Craig,

I have told everybody for some time now that I'll be publishing my next book in 1992, and so this is probably the right time to send it to you to see if you want to do it, as I remember that Fabers usually takes two years to get a book out. It is enclosed, and I hope you like it.

I know that you like suggestions for front cover illustrations, so I also enclose a photo-copy of something that I think would go quite marvellously with my title, René de Châlons' skin peeling off his skeleton resembling liquid as it does, and thus sweat.[2] (What he is offering God in his uplifted hand is his heart, by the way, but you probably knew that already.) The problem is that your regular format presumably wouldn't have enough room for a figure this size. If you didn't want to alter the format for the front cover, it would always be possible to make a kind of medallion out of the head, chest, and hand (Even though that would miss out the skin effect). See what you think – or the people in charge of the cover. After all, you may not want to do the book.

I'm sending a copy of this manuscript to Jonathan Galassi by this same post.[3]

[. . .]

> Best,
> Thom

1. Craig Raine (1944–), poet; poetry editor at Faber & Faber (1981–91).
2. Ligier Richier, att., *Cadaver Tomb of René de Châlons* (*c.* 1544–7).
3. Jonathan Galassi (1949–), publisher and poet, in 1990 editor-in-chief at Farrar, Straus & Giroux.

TO *Donald Davie*

TLS Yale

Saturday 19 May 1990

> 1216 Cole Street,
> San Francisco,
> CA 94117
>
> May 19 / 90

Dear Donald,

You will think me very backward in not having written to you before about Under Briggflatts, but in fact I couldn't get hold of the book until quite recently (very handsome in its Chicago edition).[1] I read it right away, but then found myself eye-deep in end-of-term papers, and immediately after in final exams, from which I have only just gotten myself free. You remember how it is. Anyway, now that I am free, I want to thank you for the essays about my poetry, which I find all the more flattering because I approve so of the premises from which they come – if I don't share all of those premises, I at least understand them and consider them important ones. And to thank you also for your fairmindedness. I don't know if you believe me, or put it down to the inflations of gratitude, but I have said in the past, and continue to say, that what you say about my poetry matters to me, as almost no one's critical remarks (kind or unkind) matter to me, and that it is with you in mind that I often find myself writing. In a sense, my next book is an attempt to answer the reservations of your second essay – an attempt to write a gay poetry as solid and as central to what we (you and I) would consider the tradition as any heterosexual poetry could be. The "next book" has at last been sent off and I suppose will be out in about 18 months.

[. . .]

I was also very pleased to see you spending so much time on Kenneth Cox, who has for long been one of the relatively few critics who has a lot to say to me.[2] I agree with you about the fact that Larkin's influence has been baleful because completely limiting (Pinsky called much of his poetry 'sour'. An appropriate word, I think.) I have got a volume of Ivor Gurney, and his poetry is going to come first in my June reading. I am only sorry you didn't find a place in your book for your essay on how NOT to read Briggflatts, which as I have told you before I think one of the best essays ever written [. . .].[3]

[. . .]

Robert Pinsky has a new book out (The Want Bone) which seems to me by far his best. In it he is doing exactly what I was speaking about in that last para – by transforming his technique he has also changed the subject matter of his poetry.

I have just been reading Boswell's Tour to the Hebrides and take the following as offering a tip on how to get out of an awkward situation:

> "Lady Errol had given each of us a copy of an ode by Beattie, on the birth of her son, Lord Hay. Mr Boyd asked Dr Johnson, how he liked it. Dr Johnson, who did not admire it, got off very well, by taking it out, and reading the second and third stanzas of it with much melody. This, without saying a word, pleased Mr. Boyd."

So, if I ever meet Douglas Dunn [. . .] or Stanley Plumly, and they show me a recent poem by themselves, I shall read a passage from it "with much melody." Thanx for the tip, Doc!

I might just see you in 1992. I might come over then (haven't been in Britain since 1979), & visit you on the way to my brother, who lives in Cornwall. My love to you and Doreen.

　　　X X

　　　　Thom

1. Davie, *Under Briggflatts: A History of Poetry in Great Britain, 1960–1988* (1989).
2. Kenneth Cox (1916–2005), critic, essayist and translator. TG provided a blurb for Cox's *Collected Studies in the Use of English* (2001), writing: 'I have learned more from Kenneth Cox's essays than from any other living critic of twentieth century poetry. He writes with masterly directness about the masters of indirection, and his summarizing power rivals that of Samuel Johnson.'

3. Davie, 'One Way to Misread Briggflatts', in *Basil Bunting: Man and Poet*, ed. Terrell (1981), 161–8.

TO *Robert Pinsky*   TLS Stanford
Thursday 16 August 1990

1216 Cole Street,
San Francisco,
CA 94117

August 16 / 90

Dear Robert,

I have felt lethargic all this week. It's the time of year, I imagine, high fog and all that, which I say I like, and <u>do</u> like, but, after a week or two of it, it would be nice to have a day of sunshine, wouldn't it. (So don't get too nostalgic for the West Coast.) I get up, have breakfast, and then go back to bed where I can read a book of Paradise Lost each morning. That over, I can't think of anything to do.

[. . .]

I saw "Drugstore Cowboy" (from about 2 years ago). It is VERY good. The only movie where people on drugs actually resemble real people on drugs. It sounds boring and depressing, when you hear about its story, but it isn't at all. One of those artefacts so good that you are happy to be a member of the human race that produced it. That sounds pompous, but is true. You probably saw it already.

Well yes, I <u>was</u> heavily influenced by Yeats, you are right, but my first published stuff was more from reading Donne and Shakespeare and Auden (THAT mix!) – then Yeats entered the picture and shortly Winters, and they fought it out inside of me, as it were. Imagine Goofy, and on one shoulder there is a little Goofy with wings and halo saying "Write like me, Goofy", and on the other shoulder a little Goofy with horns and trident saying the same. That's how it was with me in my first year at Stanford, I guess.

Here is a poem I wrote a couple of months ago.[1] It is in my Elizabethan dumpling manner – compressed and plain – and <u>I</u> am quite pleased with it, but I have a suspicion that the circumstances of the story being told might be so much labor for a reader to make out that it might not finally be worth "his or her" trouble.

We have had lots of guests staying – from New York and from Paris – <u>that</u> must be why I'm so exhausted!

Love,

Thom

1. 'Sequel' (*BC* 37–8).

TO *Douglas Chambers*

TLS Toronto

Wednesday 19 September 1990

1216 Cole Street,
San Francisco,
CA 94117

Sep 19 / 90

My dear old girl,

You must be firmly back in Toronto by now, and I hope you are a little happier, and the place doesn't carry you back too vividly to Michael's death.[1] If it does, remember the obvious – no less true for being trite: it does take some time to get over death; if in the end some strength, some innate impulse toward health, toward looking after yourself, does burgeon, it really can't be forced; but it will come, and you will be amazed at your own comfort and selfishness and hopefulness about your own life. I'm not sure that this is exactly reassuring, the way I have put it, but it will be.

I've been having a quiet summer – June, July, and this month very sweet and slow. (August, depressing and TOO slow.) I get through some of the things I meant to do – wrote an essay on Eliz Bishop (for which I got more fan-mail than for anything except my bitch-piece on pore ol Vendler) in the TLS[2] and am now in the complicated toils of a longer essay on Pound and Duncan, that is getting longer by the minute.[3] [. . .]

You will be pleased and proud: I read Paradise Lost again for the first time in years, and I liked it! I mean I really enjoyed it, all except the summary of the OT in the last two books, which seems to me below the standards of the rest. I think I've finally got my dislike of Christianity out of my system – my prejudice against it, perhaps (though I'm still not crazy about it). Where did it come from, I wonder? Having to go to boring services at the boarding school I was rushed off to on the outbreak of war in 1939? (I giggled one Sunday in church, and was punished by having to go to bed at 5 in the afternoon for four days.) Those dreadful Church Parades in the army? A lingering hatred of what I called to myself "Victorianism" – which was still real enough in the 1930s in England? I don't really know: it's not as if religion was ever treated in my home with anything but a robust disregard . . . And also my prejudice again Milton's Latinism. I know where that came from, of course: FRL. Now, I can admire the compression – a ferocious compression, indeed – of Milton's Latinist English, even liking "what redounds, transpires" in a kind of comic-affectionate way, the same way I like James when his style starts to caricature itself in the last novels or Hardy doing the same thing in his poetry. I love the creation of the lion, anyway, almost getting stuck as it gets born from the earth, and freeing its haunches as (presumably) a chick frees itself from the egg. And so on. . . . Then I went back to Comus, and didn't like it as much as I remembered. And then to Lycidas, which was one of my first big poems, and of which I had whole stretches by heart when I was a melancholy 16 or 17, and it is FUCKIN FAR OUT, as we used to say. Lycidas is half way between the marriage poems of Spenser and Briggflatts. ("Music.")

I must have mentioned my young friend Robert – several times, probably, in an unbearably boasting kind of way.[4] He is 36, a handsome Indian in his looks, though Spanish in his name, rides me around on his motorcycle, is very appreciative of my physical attributes (as I am of his), and a lot of fun to be with. He is careful, I have noticed, to space out our times together: if I try to get him to come over more often, I don't succeed. That's OK: he has established, and I have agreed, that we are "boy-friends and not lovers". He is coolly adult, unlike yours truly (I would be capable of falling in love with George Bush if he came on to me in the right way (well, not Bush, – say Oliver North)). Well, that seems OK to me – I am lucky to have him, and the whole thing will last much longer this way!

Did I ever tell you Duncan's definition of the Romantic movement: "the intellectual adventure of not knowing."[5] (Any help with the puzzle of was it Clare's rejection of the scientific terms for plants?) It seems to me an extraordinarily brilliant summation. Of course it leaves stuff out. But it does explain why a late Romantic like Yeats could use the word "ignorant" as a term of admiration; it explains something of the resonance to "I cannot tell what flowers are at my feet";[6] it refers to negative capability, the love of impulse ("there is a pleasure in the pathless woods"[7]), the interest in spontaneity, etc. Duncan was a stunning thinker.

Needless to say, this has a place in my large rambling essay about Duncan.

I want to write a book about what came after Modernism, which would direct itself toward "Briggflatts" and "A Poem Beginning With A Line By Pindar" which both use Modernist methods and Romantic content (BB goes back to Wordsworth & RD goes back to Blake+Whitman). And that is what makes them both so good, so much better than any of the rest of us, that they were prepared to seek out the potential of the greatest innovations of the last 200 years.

I do go on, don't I? Forgive my elderly wanderings . . .

Oct 10 I go down to S.Calif by train to give a couple of underpaid readings and stay with the sweet man Robert Peters and his equally sweet lover;[8] and the last week of October I go to NY to give an overpaid reading. That will be strange. Both my former hosts being dead now. Last time I was in NY I had a bad time because of all that, I'll see if I cope better with it now.

[. . .]

Love,

Thom

[. . .]

PPPPS. Augie's new poetry is better than ever. Clive Wilmer recently wrote what may be his best poem ever ("Contemptus Mundi" is its name).[9] Edgar Bowers is nice, isn't he? (But his presence always make me feel I'm rather unweighty, even frivolous.)

1. Chambers's lover, Michael Wade, died of AIDS on 8 June 1990.
2. See 'Out of the Box: Elizabeth Bishop' (*SL* 77–86).
3. See TG to Wilmer, 12 November 1989, above.
4. Robert Gallegos (1954–2012) is the subject of 'American Boy' (*BC* 47–8).
5. See Duncan's essay, 'The Truth and Life of Myth: An Essay in Essential Autobiography' (1968), in *Collected Essays and Other Prose*, ed. Maynard (2014), 139–94.
6. 'I cannot see what flowers are at my feet' is from Keats's 'Ode to a Nightingale' (1819).
7. 'There is a pleasure in the pathless woods' is from the fourth canto of Byron's *Childe Harold's Pilgrimage* (1812–18).
8. Paul Trachtenberg (1948–), poet and Peters's long-time partner.
9. The title 'Contemptus Mundi' was later changed to 'To a Poet from Eastern Europe, 1988'. It appears under that title in Wilmer's collection *Of Earthly Paradise* (1992).

1216 Cole Street,
San Francisco,
CA 94117
Dec 29 / 90

Dear Michael –

Thank you for the lecture/essay on Duncan and Moly.[2] I thought it accurate
and suggestive and interesting, and I'm very glad you did it.

One interesting aspect of the whole subject is this – in addition, I mean:
I still do not think that my Moly poems, whether the ones Duncan chose
to concentrate on[3] or the whole book, are particularly sexual in content
or implication. The book was supposed to be about psychedelia and
metamorphosis (Moly = LSD in this book, in fact). "Rites of Passage" is
spoken by a boy at puberty in a sexual defiance of his father, it is true, but it's
about as homosexual as Jim Morrison's "The End," to which it bears some
resemblance. "Moly" itself doesn't seem either homosexual or sexual to me.
I mean, there may be implicitly gay content to these poems, but it does not
seem more so than in much of what I'd written before the book. Duncan in
fact chose to interpret these as gay poems, and I'm grateful indeed considering
the richness of his poems that resulted. (My Hermes was a teenage boy, in the
epigraph to the book, because it was in that guise he appeared to Odysseus
when he gave him the herb: I found this appropriate because the drug-dealers
on the city streets in those days were so often teenage boys, see my poem
'Street Song' in Moly.)

When you publish your essay – and I hope you do – I think you might take
note of this, that Duncan is deliberately (and probably consciously) diverting
my subject-matter into another channel. Great that he did!

Best wishes and happy new year,
Thom

1. Michael Davidson (1944–), poet and professor of American literature.
2. Davidson, 'Marginality in the Margins: Robert Duncan's Textual Politics',
Contemporary Literature 33, no. 2 (Summer 1992), 275–301.
3. Robert Duncan, *Poems from the Margin of Thom Gunn's "Moly"* (1972).

Saturday 29 December 1990

> 1216 Cole Street,
> San Francisco,
> CA 94117,
> USA
>
> Dec 29, 90

Dear Tony,

I received the Casebook yesterday, and am delighted with it. At last elementary school teachers and any others who need guidance (as well as grown-ups who can think for themselves, that is!) will have somewhere to look besides Alan Bold's obnoxious book.[1] The whole section on myself, and especially your essay, does give me, finally, a sense that I have done something publicly with my life, that I am responsible for some sort of achievement in the material way. Most of the time I tell myself that this kind of thing doesn't matter, but it is good to feel it – like Keats, I always had a hankering to be admitted to the company of English poets, and the first third of your book, with its range of appreciative reactions, certainly makes me feel I am munching some sandwich at their picnic.[2]

So, my dear Tony, I do thank you from the bottom of my heart. And, as you already know, I thank you especially for your essay on my last book, which was dismissed so contemptuously by Peter Porter and Ian Hamilton and all the other powers – or almost all of them – in the literary journals.[3] I am grateful to you for recognizing what I was trying to do (especially in 'The Menace' – exactly that!) and for valuing it so highly. Though I must say, when I read of you being 'haunted' by my lines, I have a flash of modesty all at once (who am I to haunt the waking hours of others?).

All I could think of to express my gratitude was to send you the manuscript of my next book, which will be out, I hope, just over a year from now. Please don't feel I am fishing for more compliments, or even for any comments at all. It's just something you might want to dip into from time to time before the book itself comes out. Also, as an afterthought, I enclose a small book of poems by Charlie Hinkle, which I and another friend of his put together after his death at the age of 30. I quote some lines from it at the beginning of the 4th section of this new book.[4]

[. . .]

At 18 I went into the army, and though it was almost unbearable it somehow woke me up to myself and I began to enjoy the company of friends

493

etc etc. By 22 I was at Cambridge and (it now seems to me) excited by my life all the time – and it was at this age that my writing somehow started to be finished enough to publish, in university magazines, and I believed in myself as a poet, all of a sudden.

You ask about "The Missing", why "image" and not "touch" in line 12? Well, I mean image almost in the sense of emblem or symbol. Yes, the unfinished statues are by Michelangelo, I had been looking at his half-done statues of "Slaves" in reproduction shortly before writing the poem.

[. . .]

Hadn't written any poetry for five months – that's always been common for me, those long gaps with nothing done – then wrote two short ones in December, but looking at them now I see they are so bad that maybe I should go another 5 months. I so envy Yeats that he could reach a level where he was always writing at a certain intensity – it wasn't all great, but it was up there, connected with greatness, by the 1920s and 1930s: I just go back to the starting point again and it seems as if I know nothing. And that brings me round to my gratitude again for your book, since I am reminded that I have done something, so I must know something too – you have given me proof of it. Thank you, very much, again.

And a happy new year!

Thom

[. . .]

1. See TG to Dyson, 21 November 1989, above.
2. 'I think I shall be among the English Poets after my death', wrote Keats to George and Georgiana Keats, 14–31 October 1818 (*Selected Letters*, ed. Gittings [2002], 151).
3. See TG to Ander and Margaret Gunn, 16 August 1982, above.
4. TG quotes Hinkle's 'Rain' at the beginning of the elegies section of *MNS*.

1991

TO *Mary and Catherine Thomson*
                                    TLS (aerogramme) Jenny Fremlin
Sunday 6 January 1991

1216 Cole Street,
San Francisco,
CA 94117,
USA

Jan 6 / 91

Dear Girls,

Happy new year and thank you for your lovely letters and cards! I do remember bits and pieces of that Christmas at Pit Cottage, but didn't remember all the adults eating goose and me & A eating beef stew. (I must tell Ander about that, as all he seems to have is younger-brother memories, about things I could do and he couldn't!)

I made a turkey as usual this Christmas (20lbs), with a good stuffing and everybody made everything else (two people made brussels sprouts, due to lack of proper organization! Mike's were much better than the other lot). And as usual we insisted on Bill making bourbon on a cloud, which is like a huge blancmange made in a circular mould, and I think the ingredients are just bourbon (whiskey) and lots of heavy cream and some gelatine and I think eggs, or perhaps just whites of eggs. The reason I'm not surer about what's in it is that though he makes it every Christmas I've never watched him do so, because I'm so busy basting turkey etc in the downstairs kitchen (yes indeed, it is a grand life when you have two kitchens).

We have had terrible arctic cold, the papers call it the Yukon Express, and I'm wondering how many plants in the garden have survived . . . certainly part of the bougainvillea has been killed, but it looks as if the part against the house is still alive. We too have lots of people sleeping on the streets, have since Reagan's time, when he let all the people out of the mental hospitals to be cared for "by the community". Since the community had no money to look after them, that meant they slept in parks and doorways. It has been a terrible season for them this year. The cat gets under our electric blanket and

495

purrs smugly (he doesn't care about others at all). He is the one who used to be Ida, but is now Linc (a very American cat, short for Lincoln, we got the name from a film on TV, but it enables me to make poor jokes about the missing link, etc).

For some reason I have kept thinking these last few months of that time, about 1947, when Jenny first saw a black man – crossing Maidstone Bridge, she couldn't take her eyes off him, kept looking back, and trying to attract Catherine's attention, trying to stop her to attend to this strange phenomenon: "MOTHER!" – I was just telling someone last night, another story, in an attempt to explain "our" attitude to religion. Jenny came in to the kitchen from playing with her little friends (Christine, etc.): "Mother, what do we think about God?" And Catherine answered briskly, "We think God is silly." So Jenny went back to her friends to report that we think God is silly . . . I have always been rather proud of that answer.[1] Most other people have mealy-mouthed aunts, after all. It proves to me that I was brought up in a way I approve of! (As if I didn't know.)

[. . .]

Just about to start teaching again in a couple of weeks. It's so nice to be subjected to a schedule that is not of my own choosing, I find – though I quickly get tired of it, and am delighted to return to my own plans by the middle of the year. Six months in an institution, six months on my own, that suits me fine. (Well, of course, institution sounds strange, doesn't it? I haven't gone round the bend yet, all I meant was the university!) But also I think having to do with all those young people helps to keep my own mind from getting stale – they're good for me, anyway, asking me difficult questions and challenging my assumptions and figuratively speaking giving the elderly Englishman a kick in the balls.

We also have been having an appalling drought (as well as the big frost) – the drought is the worst so far of the last 4 (dry) winters. Perhaps everybody will have to leave California except me and my family because there isn't enough water for them.

Hope it is too cold for the children to hammer on your fence.

     Love,

       Thom

---

1. See 'The little cousin dashed in' (BC 65).

TO *Mary and Catherine Thomson*

TLS (aerogramme) Jenny Fremlin

Sunday 24 February 1991[1]

1216 Cole Street,
San Francisco,
CA 94117,
USA

Feb 24

Dear Girls,

Thank you for the picture of the acrobatic pussies.

We are having wonderful sunshine now – just what we don't need, since this is the fifth and worst winter of our drought: we are supposed to have over 20 inches of rain in the winter and so far we have had under five – and the rainy season is almost over. The papers say we will soon be cut by another 50% of our water allowance (we are already being rationed). So it will be goodbye garden for this year, though I shall certainly make moonlight visits to my favorites with teacups of water. And for us it looks like a summer of whore's baths (That's what a friend of mine calls washing at a sink with a flannel) and San Francisco smelling like Paris when they still had outdoor urinals.

[...]

You remember my friend Oliver Sacks and his wonderful book called Awakenings, which Barbara liked so much (I was always so pleased Bar could really enjoy a book by one of my friends as I never felt she could like mine except from loyalty)? It has been made into a film. The film is really rather soppy (the book wasn't, and that was one of the terrific things about it), but there IS a very fine performance by Robt De Niro of the main patient which makes it all worth seeing. Mike and I went to see it last week. I mean I cried all the way through, but I cry in movies anyway, it has nothing to do with its being any good: when the little boy is reunited with his loyal puppy at the end of Lassie Come Home, the lights always go up to find me speechless with sobs. I can cry at anything on the screen.

Talking of NOT crying: Ander wrote me that Olive died last December.[2] Unpleasant man that I am, I let out a whoop of delight. One less hard, cynical, unloving bastard in the world (Hell would be too kind to her).

(There's sincere hatred for you!)

Did I tell you I am going bald? I have a big round bald patch, a good deal too symmetrical for my taste (it looks like a friar's tonsure). I also have a vitreous detachment in my left eye (dramatic flashes, but not at all serious –

497

I just like to complain), high blood pressure (like half the rest of the world), back trouble (like everybody over five foot ten), and a lot of other ailments I can't remember unless I write them down. Looks like I'll last till about 95, a foul old bore everybody will wish would stop talking, stop making unfunny jokes, and stop publishing.

With that I shall leave you,
wishing you heaps of hugs,
Th

P.S. It was good talking to you on the phone!

1. Date supplied from postmark.
2. HG's second wife, Olive, was TG's and Ander's stepmother. 'I told [Charlotte, his niece] to be careful with Olive,' TG wrote his Aunt Barbara (15 December 1976), 'since she eats boys and girls live for breakfast every day' (Private collection).

TO *Jon Silkin*[1]   TLS (aerogramme) Leeds
Tuesday 9 April 1991

1216 Cole Street,
San Francisco,
CA 94117

April 9 / 91

Dear Jon,

Thank you for your letter. It is good to know you are over here for a while, and being looked after, I suppose! I have no poetry to send you, I'm afraid, not having written any since about last June. There are times when I just dry up for a while, you must too, I can only hope the hiatus isn't too lengthy this time (I always think of Coleridge's Dejection Ode when that happens, there seems to be no life to things, and it's the life in them that meets <u>my</u> life in language). But I can do a piece on syllabics for you.[2]

The subject of your book is fascinating. I'm particularly interested in the way Blake invented his free verse from imitating Ossian, how Whitman invented his from someone called Thomas Tupper[3] whom I've never looked up (but Whitman's is so wonderful, so varied, constantly verging on Victorian anapaestic lines while remaining true free verse), and most of all how the early Pound developed his different kinds of free verse from The Seafarer through Canto I to Canto II, from prose for the Cathay poems, and so on. It seems to me we have reached an impasse right now, and there IS an urgent need to reconcile meter and free verse, if that is possible, because meter is getting starved without the improvisational powers, and free verse simply turns to very dull prose without any connections to song. There have been times when I have thought that such a reconciliation is impossible, as if to mix urban and rural landscapes, but I think the work to deserve your very careful scrutiny is your old neighbor's <u>Briggflatts</u> which does seem to hover in a wonderful area between free verse and meter without ever losing its tightness of diction, it stays springy and alive at every point. The other most successful I would say is the late Eliz Bishop (I mean in poems like The Moose): I believe <u>she</u> thought she was just loosening up the iambic line a bit, as Eliot did in Gerontion, but it seems to me she is doing more than that: you keep feeling where TSE is messing something up metrically, whereas you feel that her rhythms are adequate in themselves. I think I am too old to invent myself afresh: I taught myself syllabics so as to free myself from meter into free verse, and I did – so that now I can write free verse OR metrical, but I can't somehow do my best in a rhythm that partakes of both.

[. . .]

Yes I agree, the New Formalists are talentless slime. And I don't like their politics, either. (They seem to be <u>reactionary</u> slime.) Fortunately, none of them seem to have any ability to write, so it doesn't really matter.

Love,

Thom

1. Jon Silkin (1930–97), poet, academic and founding editor of the magazine *Stand*.
2. See TG's essay on 'Syllabics', in *The Life of Metrical and Free Verse in Twentieth-Century Poetry*, ed. Silkin (1997), 374–6.
3. Martin Farquhar Tupper (1810–89), prolific poet and prose writer best known for *Proverbial Philosophy* (1840), a book of essays written in free verse.

TO *Ted Hughes*[1]   TLS (aerogramme) Emory

Sunday 14 April 1991

1216 Cole Street,
San Francisco,
CA 94117,
USA

April 14 / 91

Dear Ted –

[. . .] I know how you feel about not having written any poetry in 18 months. My entire writing career has been a series of feasts and famines;

and I rather suspect I am in a famine too right now, only having written one silly little thing since last June. [. . .] Meanwhile I agree, if you can't write poetry, write prose, and I look forward greatly to your expanded study of Shakespeare.[2]

I don't know how you have been able to bear all the posthumous nonsense you have had to take since S.P.'s death. As she got made more and more a symbol of whatever the reader needed, you got made into one too, but of the opposite to what the reader thought he (or more likely she) needed. It does strike me that there is less sheer <u>nonsense</u> – both naive and sophisticated – about her over here nowadays than there was, but then I have never kept up very systematically with the great world of lit crit, but in any case my commiserations with you over your recent tribulations. Ronald Hayman I remember all too clearly as slimy – ingratiating in an awful way that never succeeded, and determined to use people to the utmost. Yes, I noticed that he had appointed himself biographer of every writer a bright undergraduate might be likely to read. Clever fellow – and <u>of course</u> S.P. was bound to be the latest. I must admit that my antipathy to him has prevented me from ever looking into his books.

I certainly would encourage you to print whatever you have written about S.P. and that you should add to these pieces anything needed to make the story complete. I imagine you are speaking about a short book, but obviously even if it is a very short book, less than 100 pages say, it would be published because of the extreme interest of its subject and author.[3]

I agree that such a book would be good for the record and also good for your own well-being. It is a help to one's mental health to stand up for oneself, after all, but at the same time it might be best if you did not go overtly on the defensive. You would be defending yourself implicitly, in fact, by giving for example the reasons you adopted a certain order in the Ariel poems (if you did), without directly answering the accusations you tell me about. You would also be helping everybody if you were to include such material as the story of the jugged hare, which I well remember you telling me when I stayed with you in Devon. And you could include the fact that you read whatever mss were submitted to you so as to spare Aurelia such references as to the jellyfish (if I have got that right). I have no doubt that it would be a fine book in itself as well as a piece of history and a necessary document. And you could feel that you had stood up to the slanders of Slimy Hayman and the political ladies. And the 1990s would probably be exactly the right time – 30 years after – to publish such a book.

    Best,

       Thom

1. Hughes had written to TG (25 January 1991) asking for advice about publishing work he had accumulated about Plath and her death. This work was later collected in *Birthday Letters* (1998). Hughes's letter is with TG's papers in the Bancroft Library.
2. Hughes, *Shakespeare and the Goddess of Complete Being* (1992).
3. See Hughes, *Birthday Letters* (1998).

TO *Mike Kitay*

ALS (card[1]) Mike Kitay

c. Tuesday 21 May 1991[2]

> [1216 Cole Street,
> San Francisco,
> CA 94117]

When you finally get to the age of sixty
You have fluttered a lot of hearts and dicks (T
Gunn's among them), but isn't it weird
How handsome you are with your new white beard,
Rounding your chin, and your still-blue eyes, ek-
zactly like Linc[3] crossed with Chris Isaak.

Happy sixtieth,
Handsome!
Th

1. Wayne Thiebaud, *Boston Cremes* (1970).
2. Date supplied through internal evidence.
3. See TG to Mary and Catherine Thomson, 6 January 1991, above.

TO *Ander Gunn*

TLS Ander Gunn

Friday 24 May 1991

> 1216 Cole Street,
> San Francisco,
> CA 94117,
> USA
>
> May 24 / 91

Dear Ander,

[. . .]

Mike was 60 two days ago. Looks much the same <u>so far</u>. We first met 38 years ago, wonder if we'll make it to 40. As I said to him the other day, whichever of us survives the other is going to have a very hard time, but I suppose it's pointless to think about such things, especially as we may both last until our 90s and then die in the same bomb blast. Anyway Billy and I cooked an absolutely splendid meal for him, and we were nine at the table. His niece was there: she lives in SF now, and has gone from absolutely unbearable to more or less all right. She will probably get even better. Mike has that effect on people. They like him so much that they start learning from him.

[. . .]

A month or two ago some people turned up with a lot of signs and started picketing a neighbor's home. I asked them why they were doing it, and one of them said "your neighbor is an abortion doctor!" So I said, "we need more of those. My mother had an abortion." I was so angry that they were invading the privacy of this poor man's family that I went home, wrote a note saying that we were 100% behind him, got the rest of the house to sign it too, before mailing it through his mail slot. Then I got into an argument with the picketers, teasing them and being really obnoxious. It had been wet earlier that day, and I ended up saying, "Well, I hope your God rains on you and soaks you to the skin." Our discussion was conducted on that level. Then I got together with some of my other neighbors taunting them. I am proud of my left-wing neighborhood. The picketers left saying defiantly that they would return, but they never did. The doctor and family must have been forewarned because they were all away for the day. The funny thing is that I don't even like them.

We had a nice odd-job man to mend our refrigerator. His name is René and we have used him before. He is from a Latin American country and speaks little English. While he was replacing the old fan, I was chatting with him, when he suddenly said, "Mr. Gunn do you believe in Jesus Christ?" – "Let's not talk about that," I said briskly. It turned out he is a Jehovah's Witness. Luckily his English is so bad that it was easy to deflect his further attempts to talk about religion.

Yes, Mary writes very little. I have the impression she is feeling her age nowadays. No, I have forgotten their birthdays, July and November, I suspect. You'd have to ask Jenny.

[. . .]

Th

[. . .]

TO *Clive Wilmer*
Tuesday 28 May 1991

TLS Clive Wilmer

1216 Cole Street,
San Francisco,
CA 94117,
USA

May 28 / 91

Dear Clive,
[. . .]
I got my last exams marked last Monday and started reading Darwin's
Voyage of the Beagle at once. It is a lovely book, not only because he notices
so much that is interesting (that goes without saying), but that he writes so
well and also has a very pleasant personality – generous and discriminating
in a way that is completely connected with his fine way of speculating and
drawing conclusions when he can. I haven't finished it yet, but I'm also in
the middle of reading, more unexpectedly, Browning's Ring and the Book –
I was straightening some books on shelf and thought, I've had this for ages
and I've never read it, opened it, started reading, and felt like going on
until I had finished Book I! It's certainly a good read, but I must say I find
Browning's poetry as prosy as Charles Olson's. I know that has been said
before (Oscar Wilde said it in fact): what happens is the same thing (with
only idiosyncratic differences) that happens in the dreadful Aurora Leigh –
the verse is determinedly influenced by Shakespeare, metaphors dutifully
brought in to do a lot of noticeable work, clots of consonants to show us that
life ain't too easy, and a garrulity that recalls the First and Second Gentlemen
of Two Noble Kinsmen. The style at its very worst is found in the epigraphs
that George Eliot thought up at the start of chapters in novels: the Victorian
idea of Shakespeare ("An if i' th' adage, Sir, your scullion thus / Accosts your
lord, thus, well, fuck me" that kind of thing).
   I'm also reading Thomas Hardy's collected again, and I'm in the middle
of Louise Glück's five books: my impression is that her Descending Figure is
the best. She has a very interesting way of bringing in the discursive into what
seem virtually imagistic poems. At her best she really is wonderful.
   So you see I am like the dragon in Spenser, but in reverse. It threw up all
sorts of books, but I devour them.[1] I wrote only one poem since last June, as
I'm sure I told you, but one of my resolves is to try to catch the brain fever
essential to writing again. I will study my way into it, I hope.
   [. . .]

503

Yes, you are right, people <u>don't</u> speak enough about contrast between style and subject (and yes, it IS one of the key poetic experiences). Most people speak as if style at its best is always mimetic. I'd like to see someone discuss the two experiences in relation to one another, the mimetic style and the completely unmimetic style.

I see Augie quite a bit. He is a marvellous neighbour to have, and so sustaining. He is desperately poor, has a job filling medical records at the hospital at the top of the hill – but he's a regular Mark Tapley to the old, staid, gloomy Gunn. I taught his friend Deb he lives with, in a course at Berkeley last term.[2] She certainly is a quiet one. She was also the best student in the class.

[. . .] The trouble with [Peter Porter] is that he thinks <u>Auden</u> of all people was the poet for memorable lines. Poor Auden is responsible for so much slick writing in the present – take him away from Porter and there's nothing left: what's more, take him away from Ashbery and Fenton, and there isn't a great deal left. (I think Fenton hates Ashbery because they share the same literary father, it's Cain and Abel).

[. . .]

I have no news but internal news, as you can see. [. . .] Did I say that I am almost certainly going to visit England in July of 92? Old codgers like me lay our plans v-e-r-y carefully, years ahead, when it comes to such violent matters as getting on a plane and then getting off again somewhere else.

   Love,

    Thom

P.S. Of the enclosure: I like a tiger who has read Joyce.[3]

---

1. A reference to Spenser's *The Fairie Queene* (1590). When the hero of the first book, the Redcrosse Knight, attempts to choke the dragon, 'Her vomit full of books and papers was.'
2. Deborah Treisman (1970–) became fiction editor of the *New Yorker* in 2003.
3. TG enclosed a *Calvin and Hobbes* cartoon in which Hobbes (a toy tiger) says to Calvin (his owner): 'Being with you, it's just one epiphany after another.'

Wednesday 31 July 1991

1216 Cole Street,
San Francisco,
CA 94117

July 31 / 91

Dear Peter,

or P.L.S. as the outside of your envelope said mysteriously and modestly. Thank you for your letter. I hear of you from time to time when Augie tells me he has spoken with you on the phone. What kind things you say in your letter about my influence on you – surprising too, since I always figured your talent was different though not antagonistic to mine. I still remember my admiration for the scope and detail of one of your poems, something about being in the Berkeley (or Oakland) palace of justice or whatever it might be called. Do you know the one I mean? When I say scope, I mean it had a grown-up poet's way of dealing with its subject that I'd probably never come across in somebody as young as you were then.

I like yr description of life on the Lower East Side. I hope you do still write. You say "at this stage of the game, it's all imitation anyhow": sure, I imitate poems/poets I admire too, but what makes them mine in the end is my inability to do an efficient imitation.

I see a lot of Augie, who lives only a couple of streets away, and his friend Deb, who is quiet, beautiful, forceful, and I'd say rather sexy, insofar as I can judge of women. His poetry seems to get better and better. I was afraid about 3 years ago that he was stuck inside a Kleinzahler formula, but as soon as I started thinking that I found he was changing. He is a great reassurance to me, in every way. A darling.

Jim P, as you know, has been very troubled. I have seen him a few times in the year he has been back here, but we are no longer very close, and it is difficult to get on with him. I am very sorry about that, because I had started to think of him as a close friend, and probably no one had so much good sense to tell me about poetry since I knew Yvor Winters. Well, maybe we'll get closer again. Meanwhile he slaves away at his thesis, which is also his book of criticism, which Robt Pinsky once said to me with guarded enthusiasm "will be a very good, possibly great book."

I am amused by what you say about the poems in "The Missed Beat": viz. "I like the poems in it a lot, but not that much!" Nor do I: they were all poems which for one reason or another had not appeared in a book (or even

505

in print) at the time they were written. So by definition there was something wrong with them.² Still, the printing is pretty. [. . .]

> Love,
> Thom

1. Peter Spagnuolo (1965–), poet; student of TG and Jim Powell in the 1980s.
2. *The Missed Beat* (Newark, VT: Janus Press; Sidcot: Gruffyground Press, 1976) is a pamphlet of seven poems TG deemed not quite good enough to be included in his major collections. The poems are 'The Soldier', 'Light Sleeping', 'Excursion', 'From an Asian Tent'*, 'The Clock'*, 'Aqueduct'*, and 'The Missed Beat'. However, TG later included the three asterisked poems in the 'Poems from the 1960s' section of *CP*.

TO *A. E. Dyson*   TLS Manchester
Sunday 8 September 1991

> 1216 Cole Street,
> San Francisco,
> CA 94117,
> USA
>
> Sept 8 / 91

Dear Tony,

I did not mean to overwhelm you by sending you that manuscript.¹ In fact, it was itself a thank you gift, for the book you had put together about the three of us, and especially for the essay you wrote about P of Joy. But your long response of course has made me very happy. You get my points so well, the ones I am afraid I haven't made sufficiently clearly. You realize as a matter of course, for example, that I have framed the whole by the familial in the first and last poems. That for me is important (the last poem I think of as the Rashomon effect: it's an obvious device having a new life come in at the end, but an important one for me). Your careful and complex and inclusive reactions are very valuable, and I can't tell you how grateful I am for them.

I am above all grateful that you say my writing has been "a liberation". When my dead friend Robert Duncan was once asked the seemingly impossible question of "Who is your ideal reader?" he said – an older woman, a fat jolly woman rather like the best sort of aunt, I should think, in a flowered frock, who is faintly scandalized by his work and at the same time enjoys being scandalized by it, and says as she takes up his new book, "Now what has that boy been up to now?" She was so vivid that I speculated for the first time who my ideal reader was, and I realized it was my 20 year old self, or a simulacrum

506

of him, full of dread about the future, and particularly of the future in store for the sexuality he has only just fully recognized, and that much of my poetry has been written as a kind of signal to him that "it's really all right, you know." So I think one of the impulses behind my writing has been to reassure – my past self, even my present self, and anybody else who needs the reassurance.[2]

How will the book be received, you wonder? And of course I can't help wondering myself, but I am past caring in a sense. I hope a lot of people like it, but it won't matter too much if they don't, and I shall be a bit worried if the critics who have disliked me so much in the past (Ian Hamilton, Peter Porter) should admire this one, because surely that would mean I had been inconsistent in some way?

Various responses to your responses (this kind of thing could go on for ever):

You are clever to say that "The Sketch of Great Dejection" must have Bunyan behind it. Yes, of course it must, but I don't think I knew it till you said it. I was too aware of its having so much Dickens in it, to the point of borrowed phrases from the first pages of Great Expectations. I know those marshes so well, even the church yard with the little gravestones, so I felt perfectly honest in stealing them (I felt that CD and I were collaborating).[3] Also I thought they were thefts so easy to detect that that made them less like theft. I find it interesting that you detect "poverty" as being an ongoing pre-occupation of the whole book: yes it is, but I hadn't known it until you said it.

In "Patchwork" I recollect what Duncan said about his being a "derivative" poet (with pride, or at least defiance), I think that we are all in some respect derivative poets, I imitate Keats and Shelley and many others in speaking of a bird as a poet, so my mocking bird (based on a magnificent one, just as I describe) is a derivative poet! It is a poet just as my Nasturtium is also, even closer to the surface, a pretty streetboy. (Someone even asked is the streetboy topped with a DA haircut, like the back of the nasturtium described.)

"The Stealer". You ask (rhetorically) the approach of what? Yes, I wanted that kind of reading. I don't think of love as being like death, it seems, but on the evidence of this and the Isherwood poem I must think of as death as being like love.

What you say about Yeats and me makes me uneasy. In the 1950s Yeats was too much of an influence on me (though I hope I never printed the poems in which sounding like him became a positive infatuation), and he has hung over me all my life: I don't like him but I love him, and I can't get him out of my system as people can't seem to recover from some early unhappy love affair. Reading him liberated me into a life-long oppression, you might say, he was so important for me at that particular moment of discovery. Only the other day a poem of mine about the excavations of Herculaneum turned out unexpectedly to be full of echoes from "Sailing to Byzantium" I think the poem got quite derailed.[4] I'll try to get it back to something of my own, but I'm not sure I can.

[. . .]

Anyway, thank you very much for all the pains you have taken. I hope you will be in London for some of next July, as I will be myself, and will I am sure be staying just round the corner from you again.

       Love,

         Th

1. See TG to Dyson, 29 December 1990, above.
2. See 'Talbot Road': 'In my hilarity, in my luck, / I forgave myself for having had a youth' (*CP* 383).
3. On this poem, see also TG to Davie, 10 August 1988, above.
4. 'Herculaneum', *Conjunctions* 19 (November 1992), 139–41; uncollected.

TO *Ander Gunn*

Monday 9 September 1991

          1216 Cole Street,
          San Francisco,
          CA 94117,
          USA

          Sept 9 / 91

Dear Ander,

First I should thank you for the card and the pencil. The picture on the card was wonderful: you seem to be constantly exploring new kinds of semi-abstraction – really sensational, that hole in the clouds, I still have it propped up in front of me on my desk. [. . .] As for the gold plated Parker pencil, just what I needed! At the beginning of the year I was given, as part of a prize, a Waterman ballpoint and fountain pen. I never use the fountain pen, being a late-century man myself, but I use the ballpoint all the time – and I shall now use the Parker pencil whenever I need a pencil, which is often. So thank you very much for your generosity and thoughtfulness, neither of which I deserve.

Enclosed is a poem I wrote this summer which might be of interest to you.[1] The trouble is that it is not 48 but 47 years – but next year it <u>will</u> be accurate! (I calculated it wrong.) The other trouble is that I am not sure how many people younger than we are know what a gas poker is: no American seems ever to have seen one (maybe they already had central heating when it was invented). I hope I describe it accurately enough to visualize, in the last stanza, but it may need a note, which I regret, as I hate notes.

[. . .]

We have had a damp foggy summer with almost no sun (or rain for that matter, to relieve the drought), but to tell the truth I have rather liked it. I have stayed indoors a lot and have written an incredible amount. So it has been a pleasant summer. A few of the usual crises, of course, but it wouldn't be life without a few crises. I lead a lucky life.

For my 62nd birthday, Mike cooked me a fantastic beef + carrots + tomatoes + black olives dish (makes my mouth water just to mention it) and a zucchini soup and an antipasto of sliced avocado and mushrooms. Bob came over and cooked mashed potatoes, all he had time to do after work. Martin made a raspberry cheese cake,[2] and best of all Billy made strawberry shortcake (at my request), but it was so rich, and there was so much whipped cream, that is was more like strawberry éclairs.

On Labor Day [we had] a picnic on Angel Island (Labor Day was Sep 2). I hadn't been there in 20 or 21 years: last time a large party of us had found an empty beach, stripped off all our clothes and taken acid (Mike ended up with the worst sunburn of his life that time). How times change! Just a picnic and wine drinking this time. But Angel Island is a fabulously beautiful place – like some island in a children's adventure story – reached by a ferry. No one is allowed to <u>live</u> there except the Rangers (who look after the trees etc, & police the island) – but you can camp overnight, I believe. Next time you and Bett visit you must come picnic there: it is so much better than Tiburon or Sausalito, in that there is an actual place enjoyable in itself at the end of the boat ride (not some silly shopping center). It was a very good day (and also one of our few sunny days).

I have 9 sunflowers in the yard. They are all about 4 feet tall, except one, which is almost 9 feet tall, and this one has a face about 2 feet across. When I show it to my friends, they gasp! I am very proud of it, and would like to write a poem about it, but William Blake already wrote the best sunflower poem I can imagine, so instead I strut around feeling obscurely that it is a kind of tribute to my virility to have grown it. (More likely superior drainage in that part of the garden.)

[. . .]

So, Russia, huh? Well, it sounds promising, at least. The poor dears haven't had a very good time ever, it seems. Maybe things will start looking up for them. Just let's hope that bureaucratic greed isn't simply replaced by big business greed. But it must certainly be good meanwhile to get rid of all that state puritanism, which must be worse than anything. I imagine that if I had been born in Russia I'd have spent all of my life in concentration camps for sexual deviants!

[. . .]

I have tried all techniques with Jehovah Witnesses. They are usually rather nice people, I find, so it is difficult to be rude to them. The one I use now is to smile warmly and say as I close the door: "No, thank you, I don't want to talk to you." One youngish woman when I did that said, hoping to engage me in further conversation (which could possibly end in my conversion); "What, you close the door on me?" so I said "No I'm not closing the door on you, I'm closing the door on God." [. . .]

Love to you and Bett,

Th

1. 'The Gas-poker' (BC 10–11) is about their mother's suicide.
2. Martin Rosen (1950–) met TG in 1977 through Don Doody, with whom he shared an apartment in New York. He later moved to San Francisco, where he and his partner, Michael Coughlin, were regular guests at Cole Street.

TO *Donald Hall*   TLS New Hampshire

Tuesday 29 October 1991

1216 Cole Street,
San Francisco,
CA 94117

Oct 29 / 91

Dear Don,

Yes, I remember Major Hoople – you have to remember that my brother and I saw the American comics pretty regularly because our papa was a newspaper editor and had them forwarded to us. (Our mother didn't approve of comics, and so our father took good pains to make sure we saw them!) You are right about Marianne Moore using the Babu style too, and James, who was obviously her chief influence, as I expect she said herself. They both enjoyed it because they loved indirection and elaboration for their own sake. It seems to me that Pound and Eliot use it more as parody: that wonderfully fussy voice that Eliot uses at points of the Journey of the Magi (which he later uses in complete seriousness in parts of the 4 Quartets), or Pound in Propertius – they seem to be using it as part of a pompous persona. My problem with Homage to S P is that I've never understood why EP picks on Propertius, of all people, to make him speak this way. Maybe random comedy is not a bad thing at all – make fun of <u>everybody</u>, like Dickens or Joyce! – maybe it's not necessary to decide why you are or seem to be targeting one person rather than another. (Come to think of it, it may be connected with Dickens' polysyllabic humor.)[1]

[. . .]

Your comments on my poems were helpful. I liked you saying of "A Home" that it is "excellent, merely excellent". Yes, I agree that that <u>is</u> its trouble. – As for "Gas Poker": I couldn't have written it in first person, and I think I ought to be faithful to what enabled me to write the poem in the first place, the sudden realization (obvious though it was) that it could be written in third person.

I enclose the speedy answer I received from my new editor, who seems both friendly and efficient, Chris(topher) Reid. What I suggest is this: I enclose a list of proposed contents to give you some idea of what it might contain. (Of course, I realize that it's unlikely you would have read most of the essays listed, or, if you have read them, that you'd necessarily remember them.) I would expect the book to run between 60,000 and 70,000 words, but it could always be shorter.[2] Did you want it to include an interview? You mentioned something like that, and I have only done one interview I'm proud of.[3]

[. . .]

Yes, I thought I would have told you, I do have a book of poetry due from Fabers in Feb and from FS&G in April. <u>The Man with Night Sweats</u>, it will be called: it <u>will</u> include the Boston cafeteria poem, but I think that will be the most recent one included.[4] I have already got one third to one half of a subsequent book of poems done. From this I get a feeling of security, which is indefensible and absurd (it's as bad, I sometimes think, as the father of a friend of mine who before going to sleep at night always worked out how many dollars he was worth before he could have a peaceful night) – but at least I don't have to worry all the time about going dry – a worry that at times, I am convinced, has actually <u>made</u> me dry up for years on end, especially after publishing a book.

[. . .]

      Love

          Thom

[. . .]

---

1. Babu English, associated with the educated middle class in imperial India and other British colonies, is a pompous, polysyllabic English in which indirectness, poetic aspiration and heightened diction lead to unintentional humour. TG was likely thinking of Davie's account of 'Homage to Sextus Propertius' in *Pound* (1975), 56–61. Davie argues that Pound's poem is obliquely concerned with the declining British Empire.

2. This book became TG's *Shelf Life: Essays, Memoirs, and an Interview* (Ann Arbor: University of Michigan Press, 1993; London: Faber & Faber, 1994).
3. See 'An Anglo-American Poet: Interview with Jim Powell' (*SL* 218–30).
4. 'Cafeteria in Boston' (*CP* 452–3).

TO *Clive Wilmer*   ALS Clive Wilmer
Wednesday 4 December 1991[1]

[1216 Cole Street,
San Francisco,
CA 94117]

Dec 4

I went away for the first time this year – to Washington for 5 days – it was wonderful, 70° though in November. I saw the enclosed picture,[2] some other wonderful Titians, a handful of Turners, & had a good time at the Phillips Collection too – I felt a bit like those poor girls after they've eaten the fruit in Goblin Market – oil paint dribbling down over my lascivious chin! All those governmental buildings are a bit much: like a bunch of banks, but the early 19th century houses (even 18th century, perhaps) are very pretty, & I enjoyed eating crab cakes. I was giving a reading sponsored by Joseph Brodsky – to my surprise I found him a sweet harassed man, ruefully unsurprised that everything goes wrong – I hate his poetry & his essays still, but persuaded him to give EP another chance (cunningly told him Auden liked Canto 47, which is true). What else – I read A.S. Byatt's Possession, an inconceivably awful book I assume is so popular because so many people nowadays have degrees in English. I read Martin Amis' London Fields which I liked little better (a little, perhaps, because it was so robustly nasty – he's even nastier than his dad!). But both Byatt & M. Amis are so impressed by their own cleverness, it seems. I really should stick to reading poetry.

I've been writing a long, long essay on Bunting's The Spoils for many months now. I don't believe it's much good, my essay I mean, but I can't tell at this stage.[3]

The answer to my question about Wilfred Owen's use of wooer is that he prepares the reader for its slight oddity of pronunciation by using the word wooed earlier in the same line. I, alas, do not. I have tried to change my line, over & over, but every revision makes it worse.[4]

Merry   X
             X
             X   Thom

1. Date supplied through internal evidence.

2. A postcard of Titian's *Venus and Adonis* (*c.* 1560–5) from the National Gallery of Art, Washington, on which TG wrote: 'Clive / This is the kind of Christmas you are going to have! New Year as well. xxx'.

3. See TG to Chambers, 23 April 1982, n. 3, above.

4. See 'In the Post Office': 'But this time for your – friend, roommate, or wooer? / I seek a neutral term where I'm unsure' (*BC* 13–15).

TO *Douglas Chambers*   ALS Toronto

Sunday 8 December 1991

> [1216 Cole Street,
> San Francisco,
> CA 94117]
>
> Dec 8 / 91

Just a note from the weathered to the unwithered.

I did go to Washington – 5 days – the only times this year I have not slept at Cole St. It was 70° (in November!), & I walked along the great avenues in shirt sleeves – what a pretty place it seems – though I could have done with a few less columns & domes. I went into the Washington Eagle on Saturday afternoon – 8 customers <u>older than me</u> raised their eyes to me when I came in, but the bartender (who told me he was also a firefighter) was very nice, & I started a conversation by saying "Well, <u>those</u> are biceps to die for, aren't they?" He overlooked the Mae West aspect of my remark, seemed pleased, & we gossiped for a couple of hours (that was all, I had so many beers in my excitement I had to take a taxi back to my hotel).

Having dinner with my friend the novelist we were reminiscing about dead Charlie. He told me how Charlie had anal gonorrhoea while a student at Wesleyan. At the infirmary, while getting examined by a (good-looking) doctor, Charlie remarked: "One more inch, Doctor, and we're engaged!"

At the moment I heard this, I caught the eye of the male half of a very stuffy young couple at the next table: he had heard the story as distinctly as I had. It was wonderful, a joke within a joke, the horror on his face.

[. . .]

Look forward to seeing you in the unThatchered England of July (I shall be there the whole month) –

> Love,
>
>   Th

1992

TO *Gareth Twose*[1]
Saturday 25 January 1992

TLS (aerogramme, photocopy) Amherst

> 1216 Cole Street,
> San Francisco,
> CA 94117,
> USA
>
> Jan 25 / 92

Dear Gareth Twose – Thank you for your letter. Let's see if I can get this all onto one letter-form. Otherwise I'll flow on to a second. I'll make a general statement first, and then pick up any of your questions that it has not covered.

In general, I do not set much store by reviews, since the majority are hasty and ill-informed, beside the point, and have little useful to tell me. I would happily read none of them, but unfortunately am too curious to prevent myself from reading them. I never keep them. Of course, I'm glad to get the attention, and even more the publicity, since naturally I want to be bought and read. I have recd a greater number of friendly than unfriendly reviews, but often find I am being liked for the wrong reasons, e.g. because I write in meter, because I'm queer, because I have made it (been in the right anthologies), etc. <u>Unfriendly</u> reviewers often seem to view the writing of poetry as a field of competition, in which they (or thr champions) are pitted against me. At times there seems to be a malice present which is positively personal, tho I'm unable to account for it. (Did I once kick Ian Hamilton's dog?)

Of course, there are exceptional reviews, when I feel the reviewer has given me a fair reading (and not necessarily favorable). They are few. Donald Davie is the principal of these exceptions: in his review of <u>Passages</u>, he gave me something to think about for my next (present) book. I hope my new book will show him something he didn't believe possible, a gay poetry firmly grounded in the past![2]

Why have my later books been liked less than my earlier ones? 1) At least one of them is rather poor (<u>Touch</u>). 2) You grow up, but people want you to

stay the original enthusiastic boy-poet. 3) Moving to America seems like a betrayal. 4) Experimenting with verse-forms is likewise considered unEnglish and improper. 5) Homosexuality is all very well for dead poets, and all very well in the abstract, but people don't want to read about it in poetry being written today. (People hated Passages, which I am sure is a pretty good collection, because it was full of queer stuff and much of it was in free verse.)
[...]

        Good luck,
            Thom Gunn

1. Gareth Twose (1960–), poet and teacher, was a graduate student at the University of Manchester when he wrote to TG as part of a project about the impact and value of reviews.
2. See TG to Davie, 29 July 1982, above.

TO *Tony Tanner*   TLS (aerogramme) King's
Thursday 26 March 1992[1]

[1216 Cole Street,
San Francisco,
CA 94117]

Dear Tony,

[...] I have been inconsiderate in not saying before when I would like to stay at Cambridge (you are MORE than kind to offer to put me up), and I am proposing, then, to arrive on Monday, July 6, and leave on Friday morning, July 10. I will therefore burden you for four nights with my fantastic fornications (not really – I am a very mild and timid old man now, with a rapidly spreading bald spot and a succession of timid smiles).

[...]

Trinity College sent me their annual record, as they always do, and I found among the obituaries the name of my roommate in my first year at Cambridge, Mark Myers, who did well, apparently, having ended up as "His Honor Mark Myers, Q.C." I am glad, he was a sweet man, whom I'd known in the army and even hitched with a bit through the Auvergne: he was very hard-working, no doubt found me rather trying to room with, very ambitious, it is delightful that a Jew who looked so much like Julius Streicher's conception of a Jew should have gone clear to the center of the Anglo establishment, but though we always greeted one another with fondness hardly saw each other after that first year. But reading of his death has <u>flooded</u> me with memories of that year, which I normally never think of, because in a sense nothing happened in it, I didn't know anybody who later became my friend, publishing my first poem and meeting Tony W only in the last days of the third term. And yet I realise, as detail after detail comes back to me, <u>everything</u> really happened then: I was a country mouse of no great development thrust right in the center of – power, we would now say, but then I would have said tradition (in both the TSE and British Empire senses), of which the characteristics were both beauty <u>and</u> power. I mean reading all of Chaucer, sharing a room with someone who was all set to be a Queen's Counsel, being made to feel that all this exquisite architecture was part of <u>my</u> possession now, drinking wine with some handsome young man whose brother was at Sandhurst. It's amazing I didn't become a conservative and an obnoxious snob. I had for a long time felt so out of it (didn't we all, in National Service?), and now I was so flatteringly invited to be thoroughly in it. I'm sorry to bore you with all this, but it has been so strange to retrieve all those specifics with such vividness!

We get on pretty well over here meanwhile. I think Mike and I make each other very happy. Don stayed with us for a few weeks over Christmas: he has become one of the most eccentric people I have ever known: endearing quite as much as irritating, though. [. . .] I am teaching a class of 150 freshmen, and find them all delightful – intelligent, charming, funny, appreciative of the points I try to impress on them about poetry. I've taught this class before, but never with such a sense of hidden amusement. The amusement is from the fact that to people of about 18 someone of 62 is about as human as an iguana, and I remember this vividly, but at the same time behind the iguanaian exterior is someone rather like them except vastly better-informed. [. . .] Look forward enormously to seeing you – it is 13 years, you know.

> Love,
>
> Thom

P.S. Have you seen <u>Angels in America</u>? We were lucky enough to see it here last year in a very unprovincial production, since it was in fact commissioned by a theater in SF. It is stunningly good. The author writes as well as a poet – I mean not poetically, but with that kind of concentration and suggestiveness.

---

1. Date supplied from postmark.

Mary and Catherine Thomson

TLS (aerogramme) Jenny Fremlin

Tuesday 4 August 1992

> 1216 Cole Street,
> San Francisco,
> CA 94117,
> USA
>
> August 4 / 92

Dear Aunts,

Finally I got home, after a trip almost as bad as the last one. I don't want to feel sorry for myself, but it did take 22 hours in all. Nobody's fault – the fire at Kennedy, an incredible storm over New York – but I got a kind of constipation of the brain, I'm getting too old for that kind of thing. To think I used to travel on the Italian railways smoking cigarettes because I couldn't afford food!

The Lighthouse reading was wonderful. The place itself was great – they have a cafeteria open to the public (it's one of their ways of raising money), and you can eat in the gardens there. The BBC filmed the whole thing and I suppose will show extracts from it on one of their Cultural programmes! A friend from Cambridge days brought her daughter, who was very pretty and had a butterfly tattooed on her shoulder. I kissed the mother on the face, the daughter on the shoulder.

The day before, I had gone to dinner with Sasha. Married to Lord Young – the <u>good</u> Lord Young, a Labour Lord in fact.[1] Various other Cambridge friends were there, also the son Toby Young, who writes for the Guardian I notice. But poor Sasha, she told me she may have to go into hospital again (she was the one who had ovarian cancer).

There were also two parties, one in the third largest garden in Highgate (!), full of poets I had met and poets I hadn't met, and one held just for me, where there was at least one slimy author, Ronald Hayman I knew at Cambridge, I had hoped I would never meet again. It was all fun, anyway, and I love the new English "Mediterranean" climate.

[. . .]

I found that fifteen pounds, Catherine, and thank you very much! Up to your sly tricks again! You shouldn't have done so, but you are a darling anyway.

My life became much too concentrated during July. Now I shall have to dilute it a bit. The cat was delighted to see me. The people were not unpleased either.

Thank you for a lovely pair of half-weeks that I spent with you. I hope I hold up to my eighties as well as you do.

Love,

Thom

1. Michael Young, Lord Young of Dartington (1915–2002), sociologist.

TO *Hugh Haughton*[1]   TLS (aerogramme) Hugh Haughton
Friday 7 August 1992

> 1216 Cole Street,
> San Francisco,
> CA 94117,
> USA
>
> August 7 / 92

Dear Hugh Haughton,

This is just a note, and a very belated one, to thank you for your generous and perceptive review of my book in the TLS.[2] I would have written before, but either Douglas Chambers gave me your address and I lost it or he forgot to give it to me. I do want you to know that yours was the review that gave me great pleasure. It is quite something to find my book appreciated not only for the things I knew I was putting into it but for a consistency I hadn't been aware of, a consistency that is not of intentions but of the mind. I suppose everybody's mind returns again and again to images, concepts, themes, without being completely conscious that it does so and that a certain word or image is charged with meaning: that's the stuff dreams are made of after all. But I really hadn't known that the book was held together by all those appeals to the embrace. And of course you are right, you spell it all out so admirably, I cannot imagine a more satisfactory exposition than yours. My unawareness of something so obvious certainly makes me realise, not for the first time, that some of the poets we have been reading all our lives might have been similarly unconscious of some of the larger patterns in their work. I really do believe that Shakespeare didn't realize that he used imagery of loose clothes so consistently in Macbeth; and it's perfectly possible that the early Marvell didn't know that "green" was a favorite word. I suppose most people are naturally so intent on immediate patterns, for example in the poem being written or the dream being dreamt, that they miss out the larger patterns. Just as well, perhaps: less sense of contrivance.

Anyway, thank you for a wonderful review. Everybody should have that kind of thing written about him once in his life!

Best wishes,

Thom Gunn

1. Hugh Haughton (1948–), academic, author, and editor.
2. Haughton, 'An Unlimited Embrace', *Times Literary Supplement* (1 May 1992), 12–13.

TO *Wendy Lesser*[1]   TLS *Threepenny Review*
Thursday 13 August 1992[2]

1216 Cole Street,
San Francisco,
CA 94117

August 13

Dear Girl,

Your essay is good, but the opening is a little dutiful.[3] Couldn't you start with something a bit snappier? Like . . .

Drat!

Wendy stood up, wiping her grease-stained hands on her old "U.C." overalls. The third time today!

Another disc had blown in her Introduction!

Rolling herself a cigarette with one hand, she thumbed through the tattered pages of her Essay Manual with the other, her dog-eared copy of which she had used for fifty issues now, since the days when she first started out on the punishing byways of magazine-country.

James . . . Japanoiserie . . . Jargon . . . Would nothing answer her problem? Then . . . Bingo! . . . of course, Jarrell![4]

Leaning her trim but shapely editorial haunches against the battered fender of her grounded Introduction, she thoughtfully struck a match on her semi-traditional boots, hungrily inhaled the fag, and settled down to what the trusty manual had to tell her . . .

Well, perhaps not exactly like that. Your main point is a marvellous one, about the window that may be looked through both ways! But I would most like to see you being <u>much</u> more personal yourself: rather than starting off dutiful and general (about the nature of the essay), start off by telling us about what interests us most (and perhaps you too) – what it's like to be an editor, how you chose essays, etc., etc., – the kind of thing you do end up the Introduction with, but more of it, and in greater detail. (You of course suggest doing this yourself). THEN lead into Jarrell (if you must, I find his large statements a little pompous – and all that stuff about awe and terror – don't awe and terror preclude just that wonderfully gossipy curiosity that makes for most good essay-writing?) and your really dandy bit about Montaigne.

Forgive all this carping, but I do think your first page is such that many a reader will want to skip it.

Talking about biography, remind me to tell you about Philip Larkin's childhood on Tuesday. Really sensational stuff.

Looking forward,
Th

1. Wendy Lesser (1952–), writer and founding editor of the *Threepenny Review*. See Glossary of Names.
2. Date supplied from postmark.
3. A draft of Lesser's introduction to the essay collection *Hiding in Plain Sight: Essays in Criticism and Autobiography*, ed. Lesser (1993).
4. Randall Jarrell (1914–65), poet, critic and essayist.

TO *Douglas Chambers*   TLS Toronto
Monday 5 October 1992

1216 Cole Street,
San Francisco,
CA 94117

Oct 5 / 92

Dear Douglas,

[. . .]

I'm reading <u>The Brothers Karamazov</u> again, in the new translation (in Viking books). It is simply the best novel of all, better than Melville, better than Proust, better than Dickens, better than Stendhal or Flaubert. (The only possible rival is War and Peace, but then the last third of that is cotton wool.) It seems to me the best novel for the same reason that <u>King Lear</u> is the best play: it just gets into farther reaches, is more comprehensive than anything else. How funny that when I first came to America Dostoevsky was being acclaimed as an existentialist (Camus thought he was too): he is a Christian, and I must say he makes Christianity more attractive than any other writer ever. Quite makes me wish I had an atom of religious potential in me. It's quite wonderful, as you can tell, and in this new translation there are even some parts that translate as good comedy in English.

[. . .] Did I tell you I am to have a Collected Poems out next Fall, also a new collection of prose essays [. . .]? Probably. (I can't stop boasting.) I haven't written a poem since August '91, though. Right now I am being saved by a kind of commission: I am among various writers who have been asked to provide poems (for a book) based on Ovid's Metamorphoses. So that is getting me composing again, though with a terrible straining and creaking of the joints. I chose Arethusa and Arachne for my two.[1] (Do you know Shelley wrote a lovely poem called "Arethusa". Dreadful meter (you can see where Poe learned his sins), but beautiful imagery: he speaks about A passing under the sea "through the coral woods / of the weltering floods", for example. Then Duncan tried rewriting it in a kind of free verse in Roots and Branches, not very successfully, I think.)

Sandy McClatchy, whom you mention, is a difficult person for me to deal with. I do think he has more power – over the choosing of people to get awards and prizes, as an anthologist, as editor, as reviewer, as informal adviser to heaps of people who organise poetry series – than any other poetry critic in America except Vendler. As a critic, he is dreadful; as an anthologist, not at all bad; as a poet, boring. My problem with all this is that he likes me too much, and it is an embarrassment. I am not one of his school (poets who write elegantly about opera). I am to read with him in NJ at the beginning of December, and I think he offered to drive me to my next reading, at Yale, where he edits the Yale Review, so this is going to be touchy for me. Shall I be honest with him, and suggest he change his life? Shall I reproach him for calling Allen Ginsberg "tacky" in print? I hate being honest, I do it so ungracefully. Certainly I can't tell him his poetry bores me – you can't do that to a man (or woman!).

Yesterday, the Castro Street Fair. Jolly. I brought home a steel-worker from Salt Lake City, a really nice boy here for a few days, gave him some acid, and introduced him to some other things too, all of which he responded to with huge enthusiasm. That seems to be my new role: sexual educator to wonderful gerontophiles from out of town.

[. . .]

Well no, you probably won't ever get over your sadness about Michael [. . .]. But isn't that wonderful, in a way, that your feeling can be that strong that it doesn't get blunted by time? It is a kind of memorial to Michael, the fact that he should be remembered that long and that clearly. Hardy wrote a poem (I can't remember the name, it isn't one of the famous ones) about people's ghosts surviving only so long as they are remembered, and "dying" only when the last rememberer himself dies (or herself!).

[. . .]

I think Robert [Gallegos] is losing interest in me sexually, perhaps has lost. I don't blame him, I wouldn't even touch an old educator of 63. We still go out and have fun together, though, like going to dinner and orgies and movies together.

Don't I gabble on, old turkey that I am.

    X X X

       Th

---

1. See 'Arethusa Saved' (BC 25–7) and 'Arachne' (BC 30).

TO *Robert Wells*[1]   TLS (aerogramme) Robert Wells
Wednesday 7 October 1992

> 1216 Cole Street,
> San Francisco,
> CA 94117,
> USA
>
> Oct 7 / 92

Dear Rob,

I should have written to you long before this. It was a very great pleasure being in your company those times in England, and talking with you and Clive, and drinking and eating with you, and perhaps most of all going to Kettle's Yard – which was new to me because it wasn't yet there (or open anyway) when I was an undergraduate.[2] Last time I saw you was at the magnificent pastoral party in Highgate, being slightly harassed by Heath-Stubbs.

England was perplexing and exciting. I tried to fit in too much – I tried to fit in everything, after all, following a 13 year absence. My image for the month is of the tube trains, being on them reminding me, strangely, of when my family moved back to London when I was 8, and the efficiency and glamor of the tubes was for me a summation of the wonderful promiscuous mingling of multitudes that I took London to be. What a little Whitman I must have been! But going on them so much this time made me jump at the intervening 54 years to my first feelings.

Clive was tremendously reassuring – that someone can simply carry that much talent in conjunction with that much good sense so modestly and unfailingly IS reassuring, isn't it? It is amazing in a way that I can feel Clive is one of my best friends when we have lived on separate continents for most of our adult lives. – Tony on the other hand, was tremendously disturbing. Of course, I hadn't seen him since his balance became impaired, but it wasn't just that: he kept on telling me how happy he was, and he was clearly unhappy and lonely and terribly hampered by his condition.[3]

I must thank you a lot for having given me the Michael Longley book.[4] You were right, he was somebody I should know, for my education if nothing else. I love the way his poetry seems to be condensed until it is all <u>things</u> – or rather, words with the solid slightly-resistant, knobbly presence of things. I envy him the stroke of adapting Homer into poems spaced out like markers along the collection, I envy him the collection itself. (He seems to me much better than Heaney, by the way, though I did like <u>Station Island</u> a lot.)

[. . .]

And looking back on your letter, I want to thank you for your comments on my book. Hope I see you again soon – I wonder when and where!

My love to your family

& you,

Th

1. Robert Wells (1947–), poet and translator.
2. Kettle's Yard was the Cambridge home of the collector and connoisseur H. S. (Jim) Ede (1895–1990). It houses Ede's idiosyncratic collection of (mainly) twentieth-century art, including many works by the French sculptor Henri Gaudier-Brzeska.
3. Tanner first suffered problems with his balance in 1977, when his depression forced him to resign from Johns Hopkins and return to Cambridge. In the 1980s he continued to suffer from depression and his drinking severely affected his balance. By the time TG saw him in 1992, he was unable to walk without two sticks.
4. Longley, *Gorse Fires* (1991).

TO *Robert Pinsky*   TLS Stanford
Friday 23 October 1992

                                                        1216 Cole Street,
                                                         San Francisco,
                                                            CA 94117

                                                          Oct 23 / 92

Dear Robert,
    Very happy to get your letter, with the excellent version of Canto XXV
in it,[1] just right for Hallowe'en which is coming up soon. I shall search for
snake masks (I've already seen two ends of a plastic snake that you can insert
so that it seems to be coming out of one ear – that's its head, I forgot where its
tail is supposed to stick out.) I liked it a lot, the passage I admired most was
the one about the flame in the process of burning paper. [. . .]
    The house is being painted outside. I keep going into new rooms to get
alone, and a painter's head pops up outside. The colours will be Mahogany,
Birch, Newport Gray, and something else equally yuppie-sounding. It
will look wonderful when finished, as mouth-watering as Ben and Jerry's
icecream – which I like not because I am politically correct (though I am) but
because it is like taste-heaven. If one could combine such an icecream with
sexual intercourse ......! But the mind shrinks back, astonished at its own
appreciation of the sheer perversity of its fantasies ......
    [. . .]
    I went to England for all July, as I probably told you I was going to. It
was unsettling in many ways. One of my aunts – now 85 – now drips poison
(I mean verbally) about every 20 minutes: I don't think she realizes how
awful she is being (comments on relatives, and at one point she came right
up to my face, like the aged Bette Davis in one of her late horror movies, and
told me (because I wouldn't take sides between my brother's first wife and his
second) "You're WEAK, you're WEAK"). That was difficult, and also it was
difficult to find that one of my oldest friends can now only walk with the help
of 2 sticks (I knew about this, but it was much more shocking to see than to
hear about):[2] he gets no exercise, drinks an appalling amount, and is badly
neglected by his wife, who was in Italy when I was visiting him. However,
I had a great visit with my brother: he came to one of my readings in London
with his wife, and then drove us down to where they live in Cornwall taking
two days over it. It was all very theme-park-y Britain, Hardy country and all
that, but was very pleasant, and my brother and I failed altogether to have
our routine quarrel during the five days I spent there. Also, London was a

524

hoot. To my guilty surprise, I found it was fun to be Little Mr Celebrity for a month. I met the Venerable Sisson at a magnificent party in a huge garden in Highgate given for I think the 21st birthday of Carcanet Press . . . Michael Schmidt had told me, at lunch that day (when I met him for the first time), that Sisson had read my book and had found positively distasteful the line "So when you gnawed my armpits, I gnawed yours".[3] When I was introduced to him, I am sure it was not my imagination that the reason he turned away as soon as was compatible with politeness was that he detected – or thought he detected – a really rotten armpit-smell on my breath.

I hope you finish your poem to Davie, and I think he will be delighted if you send it to him. I spent a night at his place – his wife looks younger than ever, but Donald is fat and scant of breath, and I wonder how long he has left.[4] He was very cheerful, very hospitable, and didn't mind at all when I kidded him about religion and such. However, he had the last laugh, I suppose, since the last thing before going to bed was a discussion of "heresies". (At least, I remember the <u>fact</u> of this, but I don't remember what the heresies were, or what either of us said.) It was a cheerful little stay.

[. . .]

What is it like to have a friend and colleague who is a Nobel laureate? I'm sure Derek carries it very well – as if it had never happened.[5]

     Love,

        Th

1. See *The Inferno of Dante: A New Verse Translation*, trans. Pinsky (1994).
2. See TG to Wells, 7 October 1992, above.
3. See 'The Differences' (*CP* 413–14).
4. An allusion to *Hamlet* (5.2.240).
5. Derek Walcott (1930–2017) received the 1992 Nobel Prize in Literature.

1993

TLS Clive Wilmer

1216 Cole Street,
San Francisco,
CA 94117,
USA

Jan 5 / 93

Dear Clive,

Many thanks for your long letter. I have so much in it to answer and so many things to tell you, I probably won't remember half of them. Before I forget, though, I want to say how very much I admire your interview with Ted – you really know how to bring out the best in him, as you do with everybody you interview [. . .]. His last paragraph is quite magnificent, and such a new way of putting it – poetry as part of the psyche's immune system – that it is a new explanation.[1] I think perhaps it explains some of my last book, for example.

Did I tell you I was coming to England – just to London – for 4 days to receive that prize?[2] It was at the beginning of December, I was put up (by Faber) at Hazlitt's Hotel, an old and expensive hotel near Soho Square, and I met all sorts of people. I liked Simon Armitage a lot, at one point he turned to me with a kind of friendly drunkenness, and said conversationally, "Do you know any good jokes?" (So I told him Tanner's joke about the private on church parade, where the sergeant hisses "take your cap off in the house of the Lord . . . cunt!") On the other hand, Christopher Logue disliked me a lot: I am not sure I have ever had anyone come on so strong with a lot of aggressive categorical opinions, so that after ten minutes of this (the others at the lunch table stunned) I said "you're bullying me" and turned away. I think he must have been drunk. I also met Andrew Motion, much more winning than his poetry, and Michael Hofmann, with whom I'd have liked to talk longer. Anyway, it was fun to get all that money to put in savings for my retirement.

I've been reading Skelton and Housman. Skelton ("Speke Parrot") is much more interesting than I ever dreamed, or rather than I ever dreamed before the new Oxford Book put me on to him[3] there's a good deal more to him than Skeltonics. I had never read Housman all the way through before, but I wanted to now mainly because Rob so clearly admires him: it's certainly not difficult, but in the end it's a bit like eating candy, he has his cloying moments. He also has his fantastic moments: I'd give my eyeteeth to have written "The night is freezing fast" ("Prompt hand and headpiece clever" is like the best of Hardy). I could make a selection of six poems – not the anthologized ones either – that would make him look as good as Marvell or Tennyson, though he isn't.

I agree with Dick and Rob that your recent book is your best, as you may have gathered.[4] I hope you know that our friendship has nothing to do with my notice of it in the TLS.[5] Conversely, by the way, I hope you don't feel any pressure from our friendship to write the book about my poetry (if the whole thing comes off): of course I would like you to do it, and I think you have more insight into what I'm aiming at than anybody else, but I can just imagine the awkward position you would think yourself in if you decided the whole idea had gone off the boil but you felt in loyalty to me you had to go on with it. Please don't. You are overworked as it is, and I wouldn't have the least resentment if you threw the whole thing up.

[. . .]

Thank you for all your detailed criticisms of the two poems. What you did with Arethusa part 2 is in some ways the most useful response that can be made: I have used about half your suggestions – but the whole context is changed, as I have eliminated Parts 1 and 3, and now part 2 IS the whole poem, somewhat altered, and with a few introductory lines.[6] (I was trying to be Dryden – the Dryden of the Tales – in part 1, and god nose who in part 3, HD perhaps.) So now there is not such a mixture of different manners, and part 2 has a chance (without such complicating contexts) to be more defiantly itself. You were, as always, a great deal of help.

Not that the poems led anywhere. I keep writing very nice little prose notes for poems, but they don't develop into poems. Oh well, it'll be all the same 100 years from now.

[. . .]

I also saw the fearfully jolly Seamus and Marie Heaney for an hour or so in London – they also were staying at the hotel, obviously THE place for the rich poets (Wm Hazlitt died there, Mozart is commemorated along the street by a blue plaque, he lived in Frith St. while being exploited by his father as a child I suppose). .... It is very cold and we are about to get what is predicted as the biggest storm of the season – it has stormed all the last four weeks and I suspect our 6 year drought is over.

Love

Th

[. . .]

1. See *Poets Talking: The Poet of the Month Interviews from BBC Radio 3*, ed. Wilmer (1994), 146–51.
2. TG received the inaugural Forward Poetry Prize for Best Collection in 1992 for *MNS*.
3. *The New Oxford Book of Sixteenth Century Verse*, ed. Emrys Jones (1991). See 'Enmeshed with Time: The Sixteenth Century' (*SL* 3–14).
4. Wilmer, *Of Earthly Paradise* (1992).
5. See 'International Books of the Year', *Times Literary Supplement* (4 December 1992), 9–13.
6. 'Arethusa Saved' (*BC* 25–7).

TO *Howard Moore*[1]   TLS (aerogramme, photocopy) Jago Lee

Thursday 11 February 1993

1216 Cole Street,
San Francisco,
CA 94117,
USA

Feb 11 / 93

Dear Howard Moore,

I do want to thank you and Jago Lee[2] for the fine article in The Gower.[3] As I expect you realise (but he may not), the interview is a good deal more intelligent and better put together than most adult professional efforts that are published in national periodicals. It is well-researched, lively, interesting, and honest, and I hope you will be able to tell him so when he returns from travelling round the world (that, at least, is what he told me he planned on doing this year).

I must say my visit to the school and this issue of The Gower, show me how UCS has changed – and all for the better. There does seem, now, a far greater openness, encouragement of informality, and opportunity for experience as well as for breadth of learning. Much as I liked UCS in my time there, the years 1938–47 do seem, from this distance, like the tail-end of the Victorian era. We knew one another by sirnames only, and no one mentioned "The

Miller's Tale", let alone published poems about it in the school magazine. (As a matter of fact, though, I was introduced to that work in the school library. I remember, when I was about 14, a boy beckoning to me mysteriously to point out a passage in it – so I sat down and read it then and there.)

Thank you again,

And best wishes,

Thom Gunn

1. Howard Moore taught classics at University College School (1988–94) and edited the school magazine, *The Gower*.

2. Jago Lee, a television and film producer, was a student of University College School (1985–92).

3. Lee, 'Thom Gunn (1942–47): The Laundromat Cowboy', *The Gower* 52, no. 3 (December 1992), 16–18.

TO *Douglas Chambers*   ALS (card[1]) Toronto
Monday 15 February 1993[2]

[1216 Cole Street,
San Francisco,
CA 94117]

Feb 15

My Boy –

If you have troubles, let them rest on the broad shoulders of Tyler or Jake, or they would be pleased to take you on both at once (see reverse for identification).

I expect to arrive Thursday, March 25, at 2:14 p.m. (US AIR # 270, from Philadelphia). If you have a class then, just tell me how to get to your place. Alternatively you could let that leather-punk student you told me of meet me. But I really don't want to disrupt your life. I'll be leaving 3 o'clock Sunday afternoon, by which time you will be tired of me throwing up on your carpets, etc. ("I wish you fellows wouldn't leave come on the blankets," says one of the young explorer-heroes on the boat bound for South America, in Burroughs' Cities of the Red Night, I think.) throwing up on your carpets, leaving come on your blankets, sulking in the kitchen, and barricading the bathroom.

[. . .]

There is a terrific new leather bar here, called the Jackhammer.[3] Robert & I went there Sunday afternoon (today's a holiday!), & the standard of looks

529

was very high. There are now 4 leather bars in the Castro (there used to be none), but this is the only one that's any good.

[. . .]

I have <u>finally</u> started to like C.K. Williams' poetry. It took me ten years. A group of poems about jealousy in the latest book won me over.[4]

I do go on. I can't stop. It's like multiple orgasm, that is something to envy women for, I think I experienced something LIKE it with mda a few times, but maybe I only imagined it. Isn't the imagination wonderful? On the other hand, so is the cock. I hope I never have to choose between having an imagination and having a cock, the two work so well together, rather like the two horses of the soul in Plato. Have I got that right? How could the soul have two horses? On the other hand, have you ever tried putting a cock ring around your imagination? And with that important question, I must leave you.

X X X X X Th

1. Greeting card: David Sprigle, *Tyler and Jake, Philadelphia* (1992); two men embracing, one wearing just a baseball cap, the other a bandana and jeans.
2. Date supplied through internal evidence.
3. The Jackhammer, at 290 Sanchez Street, opened in December 1992.
4. C. K. Williams, *A Dream of Mind: Poems* (1992). TG refers to 'Some of the Forms of Jealousy'.

TO *Clive Wilmer* TLS Clive Wilmer
Thursday 15–Saturday 17 April 1993[1]

1216 Cole Street,
San Francisco,
CA 94117

15 April

Dear Clive,

Very good to get your letter the other day. I know what it's like when teaching doesn't leave you time even for correspondence. A particularly vile form of flu has been around, which I managed to bring back after a visit to the east, and gave to Mike, who has had it even more lingeringly than I. I could retire next year, when I am 65, and, starting off the day with the remnants of flu, I keep thinking maybe it would be a good idea. Except that it wouldn't be, at all. I need to have a rigorous outside body (i.e. the university) give me a schedule that has nothing to do with my own choice – mainly to get me out of a solipsistic existence at my own interior desk, I think. Also, because of my really unusual and inconsistent career at Berkeley, I would have only a minute pension to live on – which is why the Forward Prize was so useful to me, I put everything like that into savings to live off whenever I do retire.

[. . .]

But recently I have suffered a great attack of modesty. I have been reading the proofs of my collected poems, 500 pages of them, TWICE, looking for errors and all I have been able to see in forty years of poetry is pretentiousness, datedness, and boredom, boredom, boredom. I got up every day an hour early to proof read for several weeks, and felt about as kindly to the poetry in front of me as if I was Ian Hamilton. I think it will be out in September. I'm not sure when the prose book will be out, perhaps about the same time, but that at least will make for better reading.

April 17

Teaching "Resolution and Independence" yesterday, a poem I don't even remember reading as an undergraduate but which I now like more and more for its controlled eloquence. It seems to me a kind of climax of Wordsworth's reaction against Augustan declamation, plain in language, in image, in incident, almost – but not quite – unbearably drawn-out. I must say, I do keep wondering if Bunting was right about WW being the best comic poet in the English language since Chaucer. "The Idiot Boy" becomes a riot if read as such. And Wordsworth's small talk about the weather to the leech gatherer could be heard as hilarious: This morning gives us promise of a glorious day! It's somehow a wonderful poem whether or not it contains pockets of laughter.

During our week off – our Spring Break – I went off to give a reading at Harvard and two in Toronto. Met all sorts of old friends at Harvard, the genial Seamus H introduced me, the genial Nobel Prize Winner of this year [Derek Walcott] was in the audience. After the reception it started to snow heavily. Two boys offered to show me the hot spots of Cambridge, Mass., and I unwisely, having drunk a lot of wine, thought that would be a lark. They kept feeding me whiskey, which I don't normally drink, so quite soon I was falling-down-drunk in the snow. Luckily they were responsible enough to bring me home. Toronto was absolutely wonderful for 4 days, spring weather, staying with Douglas Chambers (an admirer of yours as you no doubt know), meeting his agreeable friends, etc.

[. . .]

I feel oddly defensive of Larkin in the dispute about his letters.[2] It was already going on when I was in London those four days of December. Of course he was a nasty old sod: that's hardly a surprise. But I certainly

wouldn't want <u>my</u> letters to be published immediately after my death, or ever, making sarcastic references to people I haven't even met. (If there hadn't been a Seamus Heaney, the critics would have had to invent one. – I once said that to you.) It still doesn't take from the limited worth of Larkin's best poetry, and you know that it isn't precisely the most important poetry of our time, in my opinion. Writers are a strange lot, or do I mean simply that people are a strange lot, but I don't expect my poetry to be judged by my private life and I wouldn't do that to Larkin. (I WAS raised on the New Criticism, after all!)
[. . .]
The nice man and at times good poet, Charles Gullans, died the other day I have heard, I think of a heart attack (I know he had one before: he came to with a handsome paramedic blowing into his mouth, and thought he had died and gone to heaven: I hope heaven really does turn out like that for him, he deserves it).

        Love,

           Thom

[. . .]

---

1. Date supplied through internal evidence.
2. Larkin's reputation was damaged by the publication of his *Selected Letters* (1992), which revealed his many reactionary prejudices.

TO *Peter Spagnuolo*   TLS Peter Spagnuolo
Thursday 3 June 1993

                              1216 Cole Street,
                              San Francisco,
                              CA 94117

                              June 3 / 93

Dear Peter,
    I was very happy to get your letter and poems, and am sorry I have taken so long to answer. Due to going away for a week, to Boston and Toronto, getting flu, racing to keep up with the work in my classes, and then weeks of nervousness about the Commencement speech I was to make in the Greek Theater (I must have arrived!), I was behind with everything. Now term is over, my garden is full of weeds, I keep meeting hedonistic young men on speed, I read book after book, and I have started on a song-cycle about Jeffrey Dahmer (the necrophiliac cannibal). Each time I've met Jim [Powell],

he has been cross and silly. One exception, the English poet Roy Fisher visited – who used to work as a jazz pianist – and after the reading Jim was lucid and sensible, and turned out to know a great deal about jazz musicians I had barely heard of, and even about their instruments. But otherwise he is darkly obsessional: he has informed Augie that he (AK) has joined the culture Nazis, whoever they are, and though he still I think likes my poetry, I know he despises me as a person . . . . I had lunch with Augie yesterday. He doesn't say so directly, but he still hasn't gotten over Deb. I think he would much like to receive a batch of poems from you.

I am surprised you apologize for being drunk that night. All the bad behavior was mine. You were delightful, and funny, and long-suffering. I should be careful, I do tend to get too drunk after a reading: the tension broken, etc. I should know myself by now.

I have been reading and enjoying C. K. Williams' <u>Flesh and Blood</u>, a book of several years back. I find his line interesting, how it IS identifiably a line and how he does do a lot with it, though it is not a line to learn from, it's his exclusively; but even more I am interested in the way he finds subject-matter <u>anywhere</u>, especially on the street or on public transport. If you're in a bookstore, look up the sequence (of six poems, I think), at the start of Part II, each entitled "Reading".

I like all of your poems a lot, except "Down with the Time Sickness", which is a complete unconscious borrowing from AK. His idiom suffuses the whole, and even the images, one by one, derive from poem after poem by him. I could specify, but why bother. I'm sure you learned a lot from writing it! . . . I think "Alyosha and the Boys" is a sound and bold poem.[1] And very moving. I regret the experience that it derives from (being in jail, I mean), but at least this poem is one good thing you got out of it. No, it is not sentimental – you are making no claim to have found the one sweet moment, the sustaining memory, in your past. There are only two slight changes I would want to suggest, both in the last two lines – if you could omit "only" before "boys" and replace it with something with no emotional only factual content, and change "this" to "the" (too much like that Dinah Washington title, "This Bitter World", wasn't it?[2]). Both matters of emphasis. It is a fine poem, and don't let anybody persuade you otherwise.

[. . .]

> I must stop now. These four or five poems should be printed. Take Steps. Take care. I remember lino printing from school. Fun, huh?
>> XXXXXXXX best
>> Th

1. Spagnuolo's poem 'Alyosha and the Boys' is unpublished.
2. Washington, 'This Bitter Earth' (1960).

TO *Douglas Chambers*   TLS Toronto
Friday 3 September 1993

1216 Cole Street,
San Francisco,
CA 94117

Sep 3 / 93

Dear Douglas,

Thank you for your letter which you end by saying you must make lunch for gardener Tim. That is a sexy ending – sandwiches for the sunburned reaper. And thank you again for all the kind and <u>effectively</u> flattering things you say about my recent poems. Yes, I'd love it if you sent Lukacs my Athens poem.[1] [. . .] I enclose a copy in which I spell his last name correctly. I now think "Love and Friendship" terrible – I try rough meter again and again, but I seem to be only able to do neat meter properly.[2] And enclosed two new poems, the last for a while I suspect: "Enough" is about Mike's ex-sister-in-law's futon, as described by her daughter. I have no idea if "Clean Clothes" works or not.[3] Probably just trivial.

My 64th birthday was a hoot. I went with Robert, ex-fuck-buddy, to dinner with friends rather early (it was a Sunday), so that the hosts could go to bed early for the next day. So Robert & I were left to our own devices about 9:00 that evening. I suggested we go for a drink to our most glamorous leather bar, the JACKHAMMER. Well, half an hour later, Robert and I were chatting flirtatiously with three rather sturdy looking guys and I said "How about an orgy at my place?" and everybody said yes, but the last one said, "why not at my place, I live only 3 blocks away". And it was absolutely brilliant – a five-way on my 64th birthday. Age is apparently exactly like youth. How reassuring!

A few days afterward I went to the Farmers Market at Civic Center to buy cheap overripe tomatoes for a few gallons of tomato soup. It was great being around all those real vegetables, ripened on farms just north of Golden Gate Bridge – rather than gassed to look perfect but have no taste, like the fruit and veg we get in regular markets – but actually looking pretty splendid anyway, a few flaws just making them a bit more real. (An analogy is approaching.) It reminded me of Sunday night – I mean I got the same feeling, and then had to decide why I had the same feeling. Something about it's all being genuine

534

unforced pleasure, and "natural", as opposed to what kind of sex Safeway considers will do for me. I don't think it would be possible to get such a frail analogy into a poem without its being terribly strained, but I'm sure YOU understand.[4]

[. . .]

One day, please tell me what you did to make that sautéed leek so terrific. Did you blanch it first, or sumpn? When I sautéed it, it was tough, unattractive. Teach me, mentor-sweets.

Passionately,

Th

1. 'A Wood Near Athens' (*BC* 105–7). Attila Richard Lukacs (1962–), artist whose work often depicts overtly homoerotic subjects. A painting from Lukacs's installation piece *True North* (1991) is the cover image of the American edition of *BC*.
2. Revised and retitled as 'Coffee Shop' (*BC* 95).
3. 'Clean Clothes: A Soldier's Song', in *Re/mapping the Occident*, ed. Malessa and Mitchell (1995), 132; uncollected.
4. 'Market' is unpublished (Bancroft).

TO *Tony Tanner*   TLS (aerogramme) King's
Friday 10 September 1993

1216 Cole Street,
San Francisco,
CA 94117,
USA

Sep 10 / 93

Dear Tony Tan, The Cambridge Man,

You are probably still in Italy, but must be in the way of returning, so here's a letter for your return. It is only a year and two months since I stayed with you, savoring your grand hospitality, but it seems like twenty. Oh, but we do get old. My old friend, contemporary at Cambridge, Sasha ("Lady Young"), one of the best ever, just died of cancer,[1] another – Margie Baron that was – stayed with us a few days, unrecognizable, and Karl Miller has written what sounds like a strange book of memoirs.[2] I just turned 64. Well, I'm grateful for the best of lives – I can hardly imagine it better. But, strangely, I've been drinking far too much this last year: I must do something about it, I can't take these hangovers. At least I have been writing a lot of poetry. As always, it comes and goes, but this summer, it came.

The Cambridge Man is NO relation to the Cambridge Teddybear, that awful shop on King's Parade. You are an example of what people should be, IT is an example of . . . ugh, I don't want to think.

I got, did you hear, the ultimate prize, short I suppose of the Nobel Prize, a MacArthur Fellowship.[3] Untold wealth. Very timely, as it will give me something to retire on, whenever I do that (not too soon, my semester a year keeps me going, I sometimes think: teaching, which I used to find drudgery, I now find a joy). But before I invest and save said wealth, I am taking some off the top to take Mike and myself to Prague and Venice. We have never been to Prague, so it will be a terrific adventure: somehow my travel agent has got us a <u>flat</u>, central, near the Old Town, apparently where we want to be, costing much less than a hotel to stay in. I imagine the young men of Prague will set the tone of my sexual fantasies from now until my death. So long as it is nothing like the most boring movie I ever saw, the Unbearable Lightness (and Lengthiness) of Being. And of course Venice. Your wonderful, and overlooked, book [*Venice Desired*] will be constantly in our thoughts, but we have been there before – last in the snow of 1953–4. We spent New Year's Eve there: at the next table, Mike told me, were two lesbians. <u>How do you know</u>? I asked.

All this in about three weeks time. (Of course, I need the money for retirement because so much of my employment at Berkeley has been casual, and so I was not doing anything toward a retirement fund. "My public will look after me," I said grandly.)

[. . .]

I'm reading Virginia Woolf, for the first time since my teens. To my astonishment, I do still like <u>Mrs D</u> a lot. It's all whimsical and flighty and sensitive (don't tell anybody of the female persuasion I said this), but it is so <u>well done</u>. <u>To the L</u> is probably better, but less fun (in the same way <u>The Ambassadors</u> is better than <u>Maisie</u>, but less fun). <u>The Waves</u> I shall never open again, I remember the deep atrophy it sent me into when I tried to get through it last time.

[. . .]

Well, dear friend, I hope things are well with you. That's not a question, some questions are unanswerable, as when my charming grocer from perhaps Iraq or somewhere similar said the other day, "well, what do you think of what's happening in the Middle East?". To say I'm <u>glad</u> doesn't seem quite up to the question. [. . .]

Thom X X X

1. Miller wrote Moorsom Young's obituary for *The Independent* (25 June 1993); TG wrote a letter in her memory. See *The Independent* (1 July 1993), 26.
2. See next letter.
3. MacArthur Fellowships – or 'Genius Grants' – are awarded annually to between twenty and thirty individuals by the John D. and Catherine T. MacArthur Foundation. The amount of TG's award was $369,000, distributed over five years. '[I'm] finding it rather difficult to handle, really,' TG remarked. 'I mean the idea of suddenly getting this award. Not the money. That I can handle quite easily.' See Hamlin, 'Gunn Gets Used to Genius Label', *San Francisco Chronicle* (15 June 1993), D2.

TO *Karl Miller*   TLS Emory

Tuesday 21 September 1993

1216 Cole Street,
San Francisco,
CA 94117

Sep 21 / 93

Dear Karl,

Thank you indeed for Rebecca's Vest. I am glad I was so pushy as to ask you to send me a copy. It arrived Saturday, I started it Sunday morning and finished it Sunday evening. It is amazingly inclusive, especially considering its length. Something to do with your technique for bringing footnote- and parenthesis-material successfully into the main body of the text, a complicated style from a complicated man, but never unclear. It will be of interest, for a long time I think, to readers not of our generation, but of course it is of especial interest to me: you have said more about my life, by speaking of yours, than I could have said myself. For one thing, we read most of the same books in our teens, my favorite film was Les Enfants du Paradis, I too liked Boyd's sonnet (see enclosed),[1] I started my interest in Greville from reading the epigraph to Point Counterpoint, I too was a literary mass (and mess) of introspection. And then you sum up National Service, Cambridge, Leavis, our specific obstacles, etc. so well. I am particularly moved by the honesty and sweetness of your remarks about marriage on p.170. It may surprise you that I can say the same about my own.[2]

I am grateful for what you say about me. The sentence about "He came to know there . . ." is true, but I hadn't realised that anybody knew how fully true it was besides myself . . .[3] About self-pity, my need to denounce it came partly directly from Leavis's lectures and partly in the attempt to rise above what by then seemed to me the puling self-conceit of adolescence. But you are completely correct in what you say on page 180 – I am not sure that anyone has said this. I wrote a poem called "Self Pity" in the late 1980s, but was persuaded (rightly, I think) to change it (it is now "The Missing"). It is still about that subject, however.

I hope you can see that I find your book 100% admirable! It is truthful and subtle and moving, and I shall read it several more times in the next few years.

[. . .] No need to answer this, or we would be answering one another's answers for years to come. My love to Jane,

and you,

Th

1. 'Boyd's Sonnet', *PN Review* 88 (November–December, 1992), 26–7; uncollected.
2. 'To be married at a time when principles of independence gained ground was to discover that a relationship which has always been difficult for some could become more difficult than before,' Miller writes. 'Another way of expressing some of this would be to say that my youth has remained with me, as youths do, but that the regard for marriage which came with a new sense of the claims on my mind of people other than myself has remained with me too.'
3. Miller writes of TG, 'At Cambridge he found himself, body and soul. He came to know there what he was, and to know that he wished to be what he was. This was to mean, for his poems of the time, that while gentleness had its place, self-pity was out' (134).

TO *Ander Gunn*   TLS (aerogramme) Ander Gunn
Wednesday 27 October 1993

1216 Cole Street,
San Francisco,
CA 94117

Oct 27 / 93

Dear Ander,
It must be a long time since I last wrote. Your wonderful electric shaver accompanied me to Prague and Venice and Chicago, the fabled jaunt that Mike and I went on and only returned from ten days ago, and it (shaver) was indispensable, and I use nothing else nowadays. Prague was a most extraordinary delight: not too expensive (compared with London and Venice), sunshine in October, an apartment to stay in, nice people, slightly old-fashioned on their emergence from fifty years of first Nazi and then

Communist confinement, and the city itself! It was especially fun that we had heard of nothing that was there, none of "Oh you must see this statue by Michelangelo", so we walked and walked, and round every corner there was something new and beautiful. It was as beautiful as Venice, where we had both been before. The food was a bit rich (duck, ham, sausages, dumplings, whipped cream), but the draught beer was the best I have ever tasted. And so I tasted a lot of it. Mike and I had a terrific time, as you can tell. It was the first time we had gone anywhere together in I don't know how long – probably 1960 or so, when we started not getting on very well for about 5 years. It was also very exhausting, all those cobbled streets, all that walking and climbing, all that eating and drinking, all that traveling, for your decrepit 64-year old brother. (Actually, that is sheer self-pity: it was all very good for my body and mind.)

We had the painter in today, a wonderfully honest and good-natured man we had paint the outside of the house last year. He is to start painting the downstairs apartment TOMORROW. (The upstairs apartment will wait till next summer.) You can imagine the hysteria, Mike's advertising signs etc ......[1] I say that we must treat it as an <u>adventure</u>! The others are not completely convinced.

[. . .]

We have had the best year for weather. A good wet spring and a good sunny summer – both quite unusual for here. We are having so much hot and dry weather at the moment that they are worried about fires in the hills. There are always some nutty arsonists around, and right now they have been setting fires in S. California. Oh well, ho ho. The skyscrapers in Chicago are very fine, and slightly easier to see from a distance than those in NY. Venice was a hoot, of course. But our best day was when we went to Torcello, the island with the best Byzantine church in the world, and boy is it impressive with its huge saints on wall-mosaics swimming in seas of gold: we had lunch at an outdoor restaurant, and the island is full of wild cats, the cats hustle you for scraps – looking longingly into your face – like sparrows at some outdoor café elsewhere.[2]

Love to both,
Thom

1. See TG to Tanner, 27 September 1971, n. 1, above.
2. See 'Cat Island' (*BC* 32–3).

TO *Clive Wilmer*   TLS Clive Wilmer
Saturday 6 November 1993

1216 Cole Street,
San Francisco,
CA 94117,
USA

Nov 6 / 93

Dear Lad (a Housmanic opening),

Lad of the Fens, there's a lot to tell you and answer, so I'll make a start on this now and finish it tomorrow. I've been reading George Oppen lately – or rather, making another stab at him. I can't help admiring him, but just what I do admire, that uncompromising austerity, is just what puts me off. I know that Keats can get a bit much, but really there's nothing wrong with <u>enjoying</u> language. He is like Olson for me in one respect – I willingly admit that he is important, and even good, but I can't ever work up any enthusiasm for him.

John Ash is around for a while (living on my street). He is really a good deal too Firbankian for me, languid-languid. I liked him on our first meeting, in New York, now he just bores me. Went to a poetry reading by him: it is strange how a poetry reading, especially well done, can make up your mind about someone's poetry. (I always liked Merwin's stuff pretty well until I heard him read.) Similarly with John – it seems awfully trivial and repetitious stuff. Mind you, he has a few poems he <u>didn't</u> read that I still rather like.

About Goblin Market. I admit the problems while dismissing them! Let me explain. It seems to me that much of the strength of the poem comes from the fact that CR is messing with matters of which she cannot have been fully (or perhaps even partially) aware. It is good primarily for the obvious reason that she is telling a very weird fable with fearless literalness, and so is not being evasive of matters <u>suggested</u> by the story, of which she would be horrified if they were pointed out to her. Surely there are probable biographical (or historical) reasons for stepping very lightly around those matters. What well-brought-up young Victorian lady (even a sister of DGR) would have <u>heard</u> about lesbians or would <u>dream</u> of writing about menstruation, etc? For that matter, was there a way of thinking about poetry available to her by which she might have realised she was "really" writing about herself and the sister who helped her out of the despair occasioned by the breakdown of her engagement from that young man of insecure religious opinions? (Just think of her insistence on religious orthodoxy in that instance!) Lots of writers, even today, are immensely literal about what they write (e.g. Tolkien), saying, for example, "this is just a fairy story", and a lot of the power of that writing comes from their not being conscious of the source of the emotions evoked by things not in the forefront of their minds; and I think a lot of <u>her</u> power comes from the fact that she is not conscious of some of the things suggested by her story. Specifically, I don't think she could have written "suck my juices" if she had had even remote thoughts of oral sex between lesbian incestuous sisters in her mind. I'm not even completely sure that she had thoughts of the fruit of the Tree of Knowledge in her mind.

A lot of the power of a work of art, I'd venture to say, comes from the artist's unawareness of the full network of associations that it produces. Probably this applies as much to the visual arts as to the literary . . . (I'm repeating myself.) Anyway, since you ask me, I'd say almost anything your student cares to bring up may legitimately be suggested by the poem: lesbians, oral sex, incest, etc. but it will not form any neat or clear-cut pattern. Only the story is neat.

It all comes back to intentions. Who was it, Wimsatt, who spoke of the fallacy of intention? How ridiculous, as if this wasn't one of the things the reader had to deal with in understanding a piece of writing? I.A. Richards knew that, and Empson heroically reasserted it, in the name of a beautiful sensibleness, after Wimsatt had made his pronouncements. But the recent critics are as bad as Wimsatt (one of the New Critics they supposedly hate) in their insistence on the impossibility of ascertaining (or the irrelevance of) a writer's intentions.

[. . .]

I know what Rob means about the poetry kit. A friend, Tom Parkinson, once wrote a good article about Gary Snyder, on his early poetry.[1] In it he said that there was already a danger that GS would write a "Gary Snyder poem", i.e. rewrite poems he had written before. Snyder didn't take the remark too kindly, I understand. And of course he's written little else but the Gary Snyder poem since about 1970. Alas. But it's a danger all of us are liable to – even Shakespeare wrote "the late Shakespeare scene" several times in his parts of The Two Noble Kinsmen. (And I can't believe anybody else did it instead of him. It's self-parody, not another's parody.) You're right about "Clean Clothes", anyway, it is "the Gunn poem" I'm rewriting in it. Glad you like "Enough": I do, too, and one reason is that it is so unlike me. I'll think about your suggestions for "Coffee Shop": clearly, I like some of it so much that I don't want to abandon it. Right now I have ambitious thoughts of some poems about David, the O.T. King, I mean: I Michal and David. II Bathsheba and David (the treatment of Uriah deserves Shakespeare, of course) and III David and Abishag. Wonder if I'm up to them? Not sure how to go about the whole thing yet, probably have to let the stories stew for a few months.

[. . .]

I gather you have some Rexroth already, but not the Complete Shorter Poems.[2] Two I especially admire are "Strength Through Joy" (the Nazi reference is of course deliberate) and "The Signature of All Things" (the latter is a miracle). Perhaps you know them both already, in which case forgive me for being patronising. There's also a lot of muck by him, since he could not (for all his early friendship with YW) ever cope with poetry of statement: in his hands it became merely brutal assertion (though he finds ways of coping with it wonderfully in both the above mentioned poems!)

[. . .]

Love,

Th

[. . .]

1. Parkinson, 'The Poetry of Gary Snyder', *Southern Review* 4, no. 3 (Summer 1968), 616–32.
2. Kenneth Rexroth, *Collected Shorter Poems* (1966).

TO *Douglas Chambers*   TLS Toronto
Friday 24 December 1993

1216 Cole Street,
San Francisco,
CA 94117,
USA

Dec 24 / 93

Dear Douglas the Perfect,

[. . .]

I have published a new book of prose (in the U.S.) which eventually I'll get round to sending you. It is a pretty-looking book, and I feel pleased about its contents. The Americans are more likely to praise it than the English, for whom I suspect it is too catholic.

[. . .]

I had an <u>extraordinary</u> three-way with two guys I met in a bar one Saturday afternoon (<u>they</u> had never met before, either): we carried on from 3 p.m. until midnight. Nothing was left undone, and a few extra things also. At the end, one of them said it was the best day of his life! I have to admit, we snorted a great deal of speed (which seems to be the drug of next year – again), and I had a horrifying hangover until at least the next Thursday. I'll probably kill myself doing this kind of thing one of these days. Still, it's worth it: such a fulness of pleasure could convert anybody into a panting young Romantic in a moment. One of these guys phoned me and asked me if I was doing anything over Christmas? I detailed my turkey duties and intentions. "Pity," he said, "I wanted to introduce you to my friend Patrick, we intend to party from Christmas Eve right through Christmas." Well, I can always meet Patrick some other time, if he survives!

You ask difficult questions about scansion. Regardless of whether "Coffee Shop" comes off or not (and I am such a clumsy writer that it probably doesn't), what I was doing in those irregular lines was to employ substitution. "A terrible childbed hast thou had, my dear."[1] The second foot substitutes an anapaest for the expected iamb. Of course, the extra syllable is so light as to be practically elidable. I was trying to do the same thing in a line you find awkward, "They know they'll never be bored again." (I'm doing it in the third foot, however, a harder place to get away with substitution, I think, and the extra syllable – whichever it is – is less light. So it's probably an awful line. Clive thinks it is too.) As the result of the examples of Eliot (eg. "Gerontion") and Yeats (all the later work) and the confusion some people have between the rules of accentual-syllabic and the rules of accentual verse, the whole business is rather screwed up nowadays, and people like me write a poem like this where the meter is just bumps and grinds, and doesn't really come off, but hope they can get away with it.

You knew that already, didn't you? You were just being polite.

The lemon Mickey grew from a seed about 25 years ago, on the kitchen table of our old apartment on Filbert Street, is now a tree with 23 bright yellow lemons on it. Isn't Nature wonderful? Or rather, isn't California wonderful? (But it has got cold recently.) The one thing about age I notice is that you feel the cold worse.

Next term I volunteered to teach a "freshman seminar" in addition to my other courses. The subject is to be Shakespeare's Sonnets – all of them – and boy have I taken on a handful. (Did I tell you all this last summer?) For one thing, there's so much there. For another, whatever the true story of the sonnets may be, it is now completely clear to me that WS was a fag like us, an extremely renaissance fag indeed, the kind that led a highly idealised but I am sure sexually consummated love-life with men, and considered women good for nothing but sex alone. Nevertheless, he went into the psychology of it, he broached the subject. I also read a book by Bruce R. Smith, whose opinions I have just summarized, but I think I would have been forced to the same conclusion by myself.² Talk about the scales falling from the eyes. Why was I earlier taken in by the grave scholarly assertions that Elizabethan men spoke of passion and merely meant what <u>we</u> would call friendship? The difficulty with all this is that freshmen will, I think, be less receptive of such an interpretation than upper division students ...... Oh well, I can always retire ...... Any thoughts you have on all this gratefully pondered.

[. . .]

Love,

Thom

[. . .]

1. See *Pericles* (3.2.55).
2. Smith, *Homosexual Desire in Shakespeare's England* (1991).

1994

TO *Tony Tanner*   TLS King's
Saturday 1 January 1994

> 1216 Cole Street,
> San Francisco,
> CA 94117,
> USA
>
> Jan 1 / 94

My Dear Young Man,

Yes indeed I received your letter, and it gave me much delight and many a laugh, though at the same time I cannot imagine a communication more impersonal. Warm, but impersonal.

Anyway, it is New Year's Day and I didn't get drunk last night, so what better occupation than write to Tan the Man. 1993 started me out in a state of exceptional depression. I am always depressed in January, and it was only a few months ago I figured it out. My mother killed herself on Dec 29, 1944, and I think I set my moods an annual pattern from that. Also, I started 1993 with scabies, also an affair was falling apart (no connection, oddly enough), also, I couldn't write. Also Mike was away the whole month, his mother being operated on for cancer, and the only other person in the house was Billy [. . .]. I was, you see, sorry for myself for several reasons. There were others, but I forget them now.

I was fascinated by Karl Miller's book, which you may have read. It was in so many ways my teenage history as well. I too read Aldous Huxley and so on (I don't suppose they do nowadays at all), and all the business of acne and the army, about which latter I find him enormously funny. And then of course it becomes literally an overlap with my history when it gets to the Cambridge section. And I am struck by his subtext, and my text indeed, in the letter he quotes from me, which is about self-pity.[1] People from Downing made us feel that it was the worst sin in the world, and yet that is exactly the feeling twenty-year-olds are so subject to. It's an interesting question, and much of our responses to it may have been governed not only by Leavis but by a kind of reminiscence of Victorian public school values that we thought we had rejected very thoroughly. So, repressing it, we tried to translate it; hence the brutality of Amis and Larkin, etc., a rather refreshing brutality in some ways, when he recognizes, acknowledges, and accepts self-pity as something that's a part of us anyway. But rejection of it sure was an important feature of our generation in England, and I'm not sure anyone else has mentioned it.

Anyway the year got better. I was given prizes that positively glutted me, so much so that I just turned down the Queen's Gold Medal for Poetry (silly old Queen), actually on the grounds that it is an inappropriate award for an absentee like me. Ted Hughes says I must be the first person ever to refuse it.[2] Obviously I take far greater pleasure in being able to tell you about this than if I had accepted it. I also turned down an offer to teach at Naropa, Colorado, at the Jack Kerouac School of Disembodied Poetics, where they have summer schools and are very serious about writing for the breath. That was also quite easy to refuse, given that I never teach at summer schools, being far too lazy.

[. . .]

I did have lunch with Tony Kushner [. . .] (he wrote those two great plays, Angels in America), and found him just as bright and sympathetic as I could have wished. In NY recently I saw the second play, and I must say I don't know how he does it. There I also had lunch with Don Doody, taking him to a place I love and discovered by chance last year, a restaurant in one of the great balconies of Grand Central Station. Don has actually made a down payment on the condo his flat is being turned into – can you imagine? never has he before made the least move toward settling down anywhere. He is happy with the regularity of his routine: "On Mondays I play bridge, on Tuesdays I have Shelley over (old woman friend from I think Tulane days) and we watch a movie on the VCR, on Wednesdays . . ." and so on through the week. He smokes defiantly, can walk no more than a block because of some obscure and apparently undiagnosible injury, has most recently developed a series of double chins running in a kind of sequence of foothills to join the formidable mountain of his stomach. He watches TV most of the time and drinks a lot, which means that he never reads books at all. This strikes me as a waste of a keen mind, if a peculiar one, however to each his own way of dispersing his potential, I suppose. He does have a lovely apartment, overlooking the edge of Central Park (north part) and a big wooded stretch containing a pond covered in ducks . . . .

[. . .]

I am 65 next year, but by law they can't make you retire (I now have something called "security of employment"), and I will go on teaching till I go gaga – at least four more years! – as I can't deal with twelve months of unscheduled leisure. I know, I've tried it. And I need to deal with all those fresh-cheeked young minds to keep a measure of mental health in me (I don't want to get like Don Doody, after all).

        Love,
              from us all,
                    and a FABULOUS new year,
                          Th
P.S. I don't mean to imply that DD is near death. It's more likely he'll survive me – and I intend to live to 90.

1. See TG to Miller, 21 September 1993, above.
2. The Queen's Gold Medal for Poetry is awarded to poets from the UK and Commonwealth. A committee of scholars and authors, chaired by the Poet Laureate, makes a recommendation to the Queen. See Hughes to TG (16 December 1993) in *Letters of Ted Hughes*, ed. Reid (2007), 652–4.

TO *Donald Hall*   TLS New Hampshire
Monday 30 May 1994

                                        1216 Cole Street,
                                        San Francisco,
                                        CA 94117

                                        May 30 / 94

Dear Don,

I was in NY for a day earlier this month, and I heard there about Jane's illness.[1] I never met her – I could have when you last read here, but I foolishly threw away the chance – but I want to convey something of my feeling for both of you in this time. It is so difficult – all three of us live by words, but we find them finally better for indirect communication than direct. All I can say is that I think of her whom I don't know and of you whom I do know, often and with love, in this time of pain and danger. I suppose the fact that I write is my real message.

[. . .]

Term is just over, and I'm reading Brad Gooch's life of O'Hara, which I've been promising myself for a year.[2] It's wonderfully interesting (a little too detailed in recording trivia but not nearly so bad as Paul Mariani's endless WCW a few years ago, in which the reader was apprised of every dentist appointment kept and every lamb chop eaten[3]) – and I'm much struck by your kindness and fairness when you are quoted. It's a strange feeling, isn't it, seeing yourself drop into history like this – it happens to us literary folk more and more often as we get older. (I met Sylvia Plath only once, for lunch with Ted,[4] but I have a recurring daymare of appearing, grossly rendered, in the background of some awful movie about her life.) What I do want to say here is that you have not only been important for your poetry (and you know what I think about that – and I know more about poetry than a hack academic like David Perkins), but you have also been important, historically, for connecting things, and above all for bringing people together. Take just me, for example: you brought me to Oxford, where I met people like Geoffrey Hill; you encouraged me to apply to Stanford; you invited me to Massachusetts, and introduced me to Lowell, etc.; and to Michigan, where I met Ted Berrigan; – and you have done as much for heaps of other people, and you have done it for poets, for poetry, not for yourself, with true generosity and selflessness.

This seems a bit like a Vale letter, doesn't it, and I expect we shall all go on for ever, but I thought I might express a bit of this kind of gratitude in case it is too late tomorrow. We've never lived close together, but your example and your disinterested help have meant an awful lot to me since we first met.

Meanwhile I wish you both strength and luck

(no need to answer, of course)

with love,

Thom

1. Jane Kenyon (1947–95), poet and translator, who married Hall in 1972.
2. Gooch, *City Poet: The Life and Times of Frank O'Hara* (1993).
3. Mariani, *William Carlos Williams: A New World Naked* (1981).
4. See Plath to Aurelia Schober Plath (10 January 1961) in *The Letters of Sylvia Plath*, Volume II: *1956–1963*, ed. Steinberg and Kukil (2018), 569.

TO *Douglas Chambers*   TLS Toronto
Wednesday 8 June 1994

1216 Cole Street,
San Francisco,
CA 94117,
USA

June 8 / 94

My charmer,

I am having a difficult year and I don't even know why. I'm beginning to think it is a reaction to the symbolic importance of completing my 65th year, traditional time of retirement. I have really no good reason to feel uneasy – I get more applause than one man needs, I do not run completely dry of ideas for poems, I couldn't be more contented with my household, I make out sexually pretty well for my age, and startlingly gorgeous men keep turning up at my gym. But I feel tired and discontented much of the time. Oh well, there are two new movies starring Keanu Reeves in town and they are bound to set everything right. Meanwhile the last B.A.R. (do you remember the local queer sheet?) referred to me last week in its gossip column as "nouveau riche leather-man Thom Gunn", which I adore.[1]

[. . .]

I do have a certain difficulty with [John] Clare [. . .] and I'm not sure I have ever admitted it to you. He is such an impromptu writer that he fills out a lot of paper with what I can only call padding. At his best he is a marvellous writer, but his best is often only an isolated line or passage here and there in a wilderness of flatness. Many <u>poems</u> have one great stanza. I love the often anthologized "Badger" – I wish there were more like this where the interesting writing is sustained. (Well, isn't this the kind of complaint Keats made of him, now I think?) You should make a selection of his forty best poems one day when you have time.

[. . .].

Enclosed three poems I have been agonizing over.[2] I think of them, though different in number, as forming a parallel to the Dahmer poems.[3] That is, starting with a poem rather rooted in convention (for Dahmer, an Eliz poem about love at first sight; for David, the Psalms), but from that poem all the later weirdness grows. I have terrible doubts about the first two poems. Isn't the first poem too long? (Maybe it should consist only of the second half.) Isn't the second poem too cut and dried? (Though my intention was to make it part of a feeling mixed with regret.) The third poem I like much better –

very much an old poet's subject matter, the young body laid on top of the withered and cold body of the old man. I have my doubts that I can get away with "gat", though, which I use purely for COLOR. What do you think?

I have been reading Brad Gooch's City Poet (life of Frank O'Hara), and found it absolutely brilliant. Partly because it is full of great gossip, and that's appropriate because you can hardly separate O'H's poetry from gossip; partly because it is full of implicit but quietly firm judgments of the most intelligent kind; partly because it shows a poet at work in the most interesting way. The fact that his way of working is about as far from mine as I can imagine only ADDS to the interest. It is a very enjoyable book and I recommend it!!!!

Jack Hagstrom here last week, told me poor James Merrill has AIDS. I hope you can get enough money together soon to publish your Horace book.[4] If you're not careful I'll set up as a publisher and do it myself. And here is one of the great themes of our time: which to choose, West Coast Cock or Eurocock? Of course, Toronto Style Cock is nothing to sneeze at, it's one of my favorites.

And so ....

Love,

Thom

1. Kevin Davis, 'Out There', *Bay Area Reporter* (2 June 1994), 34.
2. See 'Dancing David' (*BC* 110–14).
3. 'Troubadour' (*BC* 87–94).
4. Chambers's translations of Horace were never collected as a book.

TO *A. E. Dyson*   TLS Manchester
Friday 15 July 1994

1216 Cole Street,
San Francisco,
CA 94117,
USA

July 15 / 94

Dear Tony,

I think I must have already owed you a letter when I received yours of last month. I can both imagine and not imagine how you feel about losing Cliff.[1] I barely met him, as you know, but I could feel what you meant to one another by the very comfortableness I could discern – it was a taking-for-granted in the best way that both the straight and the gay might envy. You are right, it is in such marriages that the really meaningful lives are lived, but for many people the public stuff (gay politics) must be worth while so as to give them the confidence to essay such a relation. We can both remember the time, only too well, when so many homosexuals accepted the straight world's evaluation of them. I never could believe that I was wrong, or unnatural, or sick: I remember having an argument with a friend of a friend, a gay doctor, in the 1950s about precisely that. Anyway, you do have my sympathy, for what it is worth, but I haven't had the experience of loss on that scale, and can't help hoping, in full selfishness, that I never do. Now, in my 65th year, I am beginning to feel awfully tired, but that may be due to the symbolic nature of the year (the year at which people for so long traditionally retired). I hate easy symbols, but the old unconscious apparently loves them.

Yes, I know about Ruth [Townsend], and try to send some helpful noises, but I have never known anybody with multiple sclerosis. I have known her longer than anybody in my life, outside of family – she was the girl next door, on Frognal, in 1938. In a certain sense, though, I know her only as if she were family – from sharing so many experiences – rather than as a friend, from sharing feelings and ideas.

I'm enclosing what I have written since my last book. It doesn't shape up as a book, even though so much of it has accumulated. The David poems are from this summer, and are designed to balance the Dahmer poems of last summer. There are probably poems that I would omit when it does eventually come down to a book. – Please don't feel that I am asking you for comments: I'm just enclosing this since you have always showed such interest and kindness. [. . .]

I'm amused at you rereading the William books at bedtime.[2] I did that with all the E. Nesbit books, a few years ago: she was, I have always realised, of the greatest importance to me, confirming, creating "values" that moved into adult ones . . . .[3] Yes, the difficulty of telling what is parody or not. A graduate gave me an essay on Wallace Stevens I <u>hoped</u> was a parody, but alas it was not.

> Love
>
> Thom

1. Dyson's partner was Cliff Tucker (1912–93), a Labour Party councillor and gay-rights campaigner.
2. The thirty-nine books of Richmal Crompton's *Just William* series (1922–70) chronicle the adventures of the mischievous British schoolboy William Brown.
3. Edith Nesbit (1858–1924) published books for children under the name E. Nesbit and was one of TG's favourite childhood authors. 'The books that meant most to me,' TG wrote of his childhood, 'were prose romances – George Macdonald's and John

Masefield's books for children, and all the novels of that sensible and imaginative woman E. Nesbit' (*OP* 171).

TO *Clive Wilmer*

TL Clive Wilmer

Tuesday 23–Thursday 25 August 1994

1216 Cole Street,
San Francisco,
CA 94117

August 23 / 94

Dear Clive,

Many thanks for your splendidly lengthy letter(s), and this will be the first instalment to my answer, which I shall continue tomorrow. Ron Johnson's big work is finally to be published in the Fall of this year, so I shall send you a copy then (not sure which month).[1] It is a splendidly perverse and yet not-perverse-at-all, thorough-goingly Poundian and yet first-phase-of-the-Romantic, almost graspable, learned yet simple work. Winters would have hated it, yet have loved it as an example of a technique taken to its extreme. It certainly has its admirers, not only Guy Davenport, but also Duncan, Ken Fields, and me. I haven't read the whole thing, I should say, but doubt if doing so would chasten my liking for it at all. . . . I have known RJ <u>to an extent</u> for about 25 years, or perhaps more, certainly since he came to this city. I have never known him well, and don't want to: he is a generous dinner-giver (though deeply poor, so poor that he had to go back to Kansas for a year, but is now living here again, having been saved by a term of teaching at Berkeley), quite funny to talk to, has always been kind to me and about me, and I hope the publication of ARK will make him as famous and eventually as incomed as he has always deserved to be. On the other hand he has always been a bit <u>grand</u> in manner when sober, and is I have heard too often a mean spiteful drunk. So, something balances out, I suppose. I am fascinated by your interest in him, though. [. . .]

I enclose a lot of nonsense, in the hope that some of it might prove useful to you one day. Or maybe none of it. Throw it away if not interesting. The Shakespeare talk was this year, the commencement speech was May 1993. Commencement is graduation day, I gave it from the depths of a gown to about 5000 people, mainly students graduating in English and their parents. I was extremely anxious for six months, thinking of those five thousand having their big day turn sour because of my truisms. The day itself, the students were passing bottles of champagne from row to row, the parents were clearly relieved and delighted that it had all finally happened, and nobody listened to me anyway: I was in heaven as a result, and probably delivered fairly well after all.

I also send you the balance of unpublished poems since TMWNS,[2] which I call, for lack of a better title, Preliminaries 2. My new favourite title for next book is a quotation from Mina Loy's "Love Songs" – SUSPECT PLACES. Nobody will recognize where it comes from, of course, since nobody reads ML. The whole bunch of poems I have written the last 6 years does not look like a book yet, some poems will be omitted, but even so only the love poems seem to stick together, but you can look on this lot and the last as some of the ingredients.

You will notice that I have revised the poem called "Bathsheba". I showed it to you, Augie, and Robert Pinsky (in Boston nowadays). None of you liked it much, but RP pointed out it is necessary to my scheme, which it certainly is; so I have to make it better. One thing I envisioned it as being is a not very sympathetic poem, somewhat summarizing in a way I associate (perhaps unfairly) with John Crowe Ransom, a poet I have never much liked. I also borrow a little of the tone, perhaps, of YW's "Sir Gawayne". Anyway, you pointed out the ineffective order of the second stanza and Pinsky pointed out the complete lack of precision to the romantic uplift of the penultimate line: "For from our wide ecstatic need . . ." (He used kinder language.) I have now altered both, I hope for the better. But how lucky I am to have friends who do me the honor of letting me know when I have written badly. You, of course, have been making helpful suggestions to me for I suppose something like 30 years now. Well, let me be formal enough for a moment to say thank you for all your good offices.

More tomorrow or the next day !!!!!!!!!!!!!!!!!!!!!!!!!!!

August 25

And now what I am bracing myself to do is give you the reading list you ask for . . . but at this point I am not sure what it should contain. I have been influenced by everyone I have ever read, I suspect (hasn't everybody else also?), but usually I can't tell in what ways, from E. Nesbit and H.G. Wells to whatever I read last week. At least it is simplified by the fact that, from the time you and I became friends, we have shared a lot of enthusiasms. Before then . . . .

The ellipses of doubt . . . . . .

In the late spring, 1950, in Paris between the army and university, I read two books that separately and cumulatively made a tremendous effect on me. My reaction to them was of release! They were Stendhal's Charterhouse, and

553

King Lear. I can't attempt to describe exactly their effect or why they meant so much to me, after 44 years, but I think it had something to do with the idea that one could contain romantic incident (dream, adventure, excitement of childhood game in adult life) in one's experience so long as it was sharp-edged, defined, and (in what I was to know later as FRL's term) "realized" – through language and tone. Think of the trumpets in Lear, think of Fabrice hiding out in caves from his wicked elder brother – the stuff of fairytale and of pirate story. But of course there is also the hilarious account of Waterloo – I've just been reading it again – where Fabrice is almost like Chaplin, a lucky fool, constantly saved by his sheer unawareness of the dangers surrounding him. In any case, whether I describe it rightly or wrongly, these two works together gave me an extraordinary sense of possibilities.

Ho hum. So I went to Cambridge, I was reading Baudelaire already, I was crazy about Auden all this first year 1950-1 (he was the modern idiom for me at that time, he was the one who made modern subject matter seem possible), and the other two important things that happened were that I discovered Donne in the middle of the year and I read all Shakespeare in the summer vacation, between a job working on a farm and hitching through France. My images were heroic – I saw Shakespeare plays and other such done by the ADC and the Marlowe, etc.

Next year I really started reading and learning from Yeats in earnest. Probably I started reading Sartre around now – especially the plays, I never had much time for his fiction, and especially a lecture published as a short book called something like "L'existentialisme est un humanisme" or was it the opposite (n'est pas un h???!!!) Later Iris Murdoch's little book of Sartre was one I studied intensely,[3] and Camus became important for me also.

One could make too much of all this, of course, but I think I was, almost consciously, trying to provide myself with some philosophical grounding to my poems – an existential raison d'être for the highborn Elizabethan heroes who filled my imagination, or Roman too: je le suis, je veux l'être – I am it, I WILL myself to be it – I will be the high ideal I am. God knows what I had in mind. I had read some Racine & Corneille at school then more for "Tragedy" paper (part 2 of Tripos!). A locus: the last speeches at the end of Sartre's Le Diable et le Bon Dieu.

While this was all happening, of course, I went to America, so even while I was still drenched with the waves of Shakespeare and Donne and Yeats and Sartre – the next waves, the colossal waves of modern American poetry, broke over my head . . . . The Yanks were tremendously good for me, I think, all except Stevens. This is not to take from Stevens as a poet – his best might well be the best of the lot – but I never knew how to use him, and where I tried to make use of him I got into strange obscurities (at the worst as in "Berlin in Ruins", at the best as in the first poem of "Misanthropos").

None of this is probably much help to you, I am afraid. But how would you describe your lifetime of reading? You read everything you can lay your hands on, and since reading is a part of your life, it is all very difficult to detach from anything homegrown (if anything IS homegrown, after all.)

[. . .]

Yes, I know what you mean about not writing poetry from the will. But when desperate, we have the will to make use of. I wanted badly to write the poem that became The Blank, but term was coming up and I knew I needed several clear days to write it in, so I let it go. Then about 10 weeks later we had our week off (Spring Break), and I thought, "I'll make myself write it, a few lines a day, until I have a first draft: after all, what do I have to lose? And if I don't try to write it this way, it will never get written."

[. . .]

1. Ronald Johnson, *ARK* (1996).
2. TG enclosed 'A Young Novelist' (*BC* 12), 'Arethusa Raped' (*BC* 28–9), 'Arachne' (*BC* 30), 'Enough' (*BC* 31), 'Troubadour' (*BC* 87–94), 'Coffee Shop' (*BC* 95), 'A Wood Near Athens' (*BC* 105–7), 'Dancing David' (*BC* 110–14) and 'A Freedom' (unpublished; Bancroft).
3. See TG to White, 24 January 1955, above.

TO *Ander and Bett Gunn*   TLS (aerogramme) Ander Gunn
Friday 2 September 1994

1216 Cole Street,
San Francisco,
CA 94117,
USA

Sep 2 / 94

Dear Gunns,

I have mislaid Ander's last letter, but I don't think you are moving till the start of next month, so I'm sending this to the North. Good luck with it, I don't think I'd be up to it myself, but we all specialize in different things. Me: laziness; you, moving house; Hitler, violence, etc. [. . .]

I was hysterical all this year, unsettled, unhappy for no good reason, never at my best, and then suddenly I think my actual 65th birthday broke the jynx. Well, that's a relief. How hard I must work to seem a simple and uncomplicated person! I realize this from a long profile of me [. . .] in the Los Angeles Times Sunday Magazine.[1] I have no complaints about it, it is complimentary throughout: I seem a person without a trouble in the world and someone who never uttered an unkind word to anyone. It did make me realize how we all, while being less than half-aware of it, work continually at projecting a personality. And then something like this is published, and you see what you have been doing all along!

It is odd. Suddenly, after all these years I have become famous. But of course, only an idiot wants to become famous. It may well have its conveniences – though I suspect they are more in the nature of unguents, soothing lotions for the irritated spirit; but it is of course completely irrelevant, and always has been.

[. . .]

Catherine's birthday is September 22, when she is 85. How strange to think that she was only 20 when I was born, no wonder she and Mary seemed so jolly when we were children. "We're going down to Covey [Hall] to see the Girls," Mother would say. Not so jolly now: I found Mary a bit like Bette Davis in a horror film the last time I was down there. As I said at the time, I don't think I could ever deal with her again, so wicked and spiteful. Oh dear, that will probably be me in 20 years time, won't it? Evil Captain Gunn of Cole Street, who gives all the children poisoned apples and bad advice.

Well, good luck with your move, and I wish you lasting happiness in your new place. And you must never complain about the weather again: you <u>know</u> you are moving back into the Wet Riviera. [. . .]

Much love to both,

X X X X X X X   Thom

1. Wendy Lesser, 'Thom Gunn's Sense of Movement', *Los Angeles Times Magazine* (14 August 1994), 16–18, 36–8.

556

1216 Cole Street,
San Francisco,
CA 94117
Sep 26 / 94

Hello Homo,

Or rather Sep 27. And even as I write, I realise I shall not be able to send it until I have been over to Berkeley this weekend and picked up my meter sheets. Which are not worth much, I think. I hate theory, even this kind of theory. But I must try to work out a metrical theory loose enough to accommodate both what I wrote in those sheets and the possibility of a simultaneous syllabic theory so that a poem like "At the round earth's imagined corners" can fit either at the same time – it works with the ear, but "how and why" is the question? with all those stressed syllables jammed together so wonderfully?

I am going over to Berkeley one time with Mike and Bob to see Mark Morris' Allegro thing, the other time to attend a meeting of Morris, Greenblatt, various dance critics, etc., who will speak about Milton 'n' Handel 'n' Morris. Should be interesting. Of course, Mike and Bob know far more than I do about dance and about ballet, for that matter, my own interest being rather recent. (I'm SO butch.) I have been reading a splendid book by Joan Acocella called <u>Mark Morris</u>. It's the kind of book I hope might one day be written about my poetry, maybe in A.D. 2094, really bright and perceptive about causes as well as about results. Apparently she was a student of mine 30 years ago – but I don't remember anyone I taught from that far back![1] But then I come to a passage like this one, and my first thought is, I wish I had written that, so maybe there is some connection after all:

> Why do people prize clear structure? Because they like to understand what they are seeing (seeing in dance, that is) and because this makes them feel that life is understandable. There is another, well-known reason: structure gives them freedom. The clearer the rules, the more flexible the situation. One can test the rules, bend them, even break them, without having to worry that the whole thing is going to fall apart.[2]

I need hardly tell you why I like that. It may be <u>well-known</u>, but I wonder how many of my students even guess at it nowadays. Mebbe I'll start a class with this epigraph next term, and later get them to write an essay applying it.

Well, lucky you, being sexually harassed by a cute student. I recently met a New Yorker here for "Leather Week" who was a thorough delight. He had the wonderfully ethnic name of Terence Sullivan. I never once felt like saying "Terence, this is stupid stuff." (First line of a famous poem.[3] Can I catch you out on this? YOU get me stumped, mate, when you speak of my "reworking of that trope of Auden's about Yeats.") The last lines of "Breaking Ground" are from Ralegh's "The Ocean to Cynthia", but I'm sure you got that![4]

[. . .]

Well, about death ....

You wonder at my resilience through the long stupor of the world of Night Sweats. I think it was not resilience, but rather that writing the poetry was what helped me (though I must say Charley's death brought me as close to a breakdown as I have ever been): and why writing poetry should have helped me I shall not even speculate, since I have no wish to puddle up this letter with bathetic triteness. But I do think we – our generation on, that is – have had it unnaturally easy for most of our lives. ALWAYS people have experienced lots of death near at hand until the discovery of antibiotics in WWII – my parents had schoolfriends die, one of my mother's sisters died of TB while young, both my grandmothers died before I was born. But we knew hardly anyone dying – if they died, it was of old age or through accident – so we forgot that if we were born to seek out happiness we were also born subject to disease. I'm getting sententious, aren't I? But it has taken AIDS to remind us of what every previous generation was familiar with, and to be aware that if we personally live to an advanced age, we shall be out there alone and in the cold. (So here's hoping I don't last more than another 10 years. I certainly don't want to outlast Mike. I may not mention him often in my letters, but I would find it very difficult surviving his death.)

And now for a few funny stories. This you have probably heard: Jeffrey Dahmer to Mrs Bobbitt: "You are not going to leave that, are you?"

(I wonder if I got that right.)

Norman Mailer turns up at Yale, having prepared no talk, probably a bit drunk, sits on floor before audience, takes off tie, asks for questions. A long silence. Finally a young man says: "Mr. Mailer, how much do you weigh?"

[. . .]

Folsom Street Fair on Sunday. The biggest Californian event after

    (a) the SF Gay Parade

    (b) the Rose Bowl Parade.

Isn't that wonderful. There were 30,000 people, mainly young men in black leather pants. I did not fall in love more than 500 times, though.

And the rains are coming early this year. It almost rained Sunday.

Love

X X X

Th

1. Joan Acocella (1945–), journalist and dance critic, took TG's English 100 course at UC Berkeley in 1965.
2. Acocella, *Mark Morris* (1993), 166.
3. The penultimate poem of Housman's *A Shropshire Lad* (1896).
4. See 'Breaking Ground' (*CP* 305): 'Shee / is gonn, Shee is lost, / She is found, shee / is ever faire.'

TO *Clive Wilmer*   TLS (aerogramme) Clive Wilmer

Monday 10 October 1994

1216 Cole Street,
San Francisco,
CA 94117,
USA

Oct 10 / 94

Dear Wilmie,

Bet you've never been called THAT before. I was made very happy by your post script about Tony. He keeps such a determinedly jocular surface over his letters that I find it difficult to know if he is really happy or just wants me to think he is happy. He is brave by contrast to me, I just spill out all my discontents and in doing so mitigate them . . . . I keep having poignant thoughts about growing old: I was hugely amused by your identifying with Old Capulet last time you read R n' J . . . Woke today realising I already have memories of WWII that a majority of people were born too late for: the sight of lorry convoys winding down the residential roads, people asleep on bunks in the tube stations, a dogfight over Liverpool Street Station (that was my first visit to Cambridge, after which I <u>knew</u> I must go there later as a student). I found myself thinking like the robot dying on the roof at the end of <u>Blade Runner</u> "the things I have seen".

[. . .]

I really find it hard to speak about "influence". I am, as a matter of fact, rereading the two big novels by Stendhal this year, on the last 100 pp. of <u>La Chartreuse</u> right now, and loving it as much as ever. But what, really, carried over into my poetry from it? I first read it, in Paris, before going

559

to Cambridge, right next to my first reading of <u>King Lear</u> (that would be 1950). They knocked my socks off, Shakespeare knocked one sock off, Stendhal looked after the other. So my memories of them are not precisely distinct. Yet my sense of the novel was a great feeling of release, as if anything were possible (surely contradicted by <u>Lear</u>, and yet of course the <u>language</u> of <u>Lear</u> demonstrates just the kind of possibility, and individual power to shape experience that its plot appears to deny). Yes, didn't someone entitle an essay "Stendhal, or the cult of energy"? And he establishes the primacy of energy so cleverly by disarming the intelligent reader through irony (at times making fun of the hero's naïveté) and through the rational speculations of the characters. I suppose that kind of carried over into my writing later, though the combination of passion + rationality most clearly used as model was Dr. Donne's! . . . Even more difficult is it to speak about E. Nesbit as influence. <u>Five Children and It</u>, <u>The Would-Be-Goods</u>, <u>The Railway Children</u> – these are three of the best. What makes these so rich and <u>Swallows and Amazons</u> so impoverished? E.N. is a <u>generous</u> as well as imaginative writer (she was an early Fabian, you know), she is fun, she is <u>fair</u>, etc. No, you don't need to read her.

You ask what I think of Alvarez' piece.[1] Well, I'm grateful for the attention, of course, but I can hardly take seriously the assertion that good poetry has to come out of unhappiness. Bang goes Sunday Morning, bang goes the Grecian Urn, bang goes To Penshurst and MacFlecknoe. It may well be that my own poetry is boring, but his assumptions are as naïve as those of any teenage romantic. <u>Of course</u> poetry may be written out of other feelings than misery. Poetry may come from anything, I suspect, even economics or methods of guano farming.

[. . .] I'm writing nuffink, but one day it will all come back. Meanwhile I get wonderful ideas that won't get into words. [. . .]

Much love –   Thom

1. Alvarez reviewed *CP*: 'Marvell and Motorcycles', *New Yorker* (1 August 1994), 77–80.

Tuesday 8 November 1994

1216 Cole Street,
San Francisco,
CA 94117,
USA

Nov 8 / 94

Dear Ander,

This will be a short one, but I wanted to say congratulations on your new house, which sounds a dandy, and I hope you will both be so happy there that you will never want to move. [. . .]

I went down to Los Angeles for five days to give two readings, being put up in first one hotel, then another. The weather was divine, unlike the horror-smog of that visit we made together. The first two days I stayed only a walking distance from the famous Venice Beach, called Venice because in 1920 or so an enterprising real estate man thought the area would be more attractive if he dug a few canals. And it is charming. Ugly as most of Los Angeles is, the beaches are the best in the world – that is for sand and sun and ocean and for perpetual good weather and pretty young people playing games. I walked down there and found a hamburger place with friendly young men and women working there and sat drinking wine and looking at the waves (and finally had a meal). Also there was that slightly greasy and cheap atmosphere that I find essential to my enjoyment (a touch of Southend added to the high-class effects put there by Nature). Next day a woman I know who was part of the project I was there for (she was to interview me on stage after the reading) came down from the North and I took her to the same place, where we BOTH sipped wine and ate omelettes. I'm always so sorry you and Bett saw only the worst side of California when it really is, I think, the most beautiful place in the world. (Well, maybe the Himalayas . . .)

Glad you liked Shelf Life. [. . .] I am <u>delighted</u> by its cover – the first time since 1982 that I have actually preferred the English to the American cover. I love Diebenkorn because his painting is so pretty. Their first suggestion was a picture by David Hockney (people always want to put me with him, because we are both queer and both went to live in California), and I said "No, no, no, he is <u>Southern</u> California, he always does swimming pools, and almost no one up here has swimming pools, it is too cold." So they chose this picture, and I am very satisfied.[1]

[. . .] I'm doing fine, for 65, though I certainly sleep longer at nights. Mike gave me a very warm "comforter" (a bit like what we used to call an eiderdown), which the cat likes a lot (he inserts himself into it when it is folded up on a chair in the corner, and looks out of it like the filling in a sandwich), and I have now abandoned my electric blanket because I am superstitious about all those electric currents running through my body and causing unknown diseases. (It has got cold the last few days.) We had a great 3 day storm over the weekend, with another predicted for tomorrow – so we hope this will finally do for all the droughts.

[. . .]

Love,

Thom

& love to Bett & to the dogs.

1. The Faber edition of *SL* features a detail from Richard Diebenkorn's *Ocean Park #105* (1978).

TO *Tony Tanner*   TLS King's
Wednesday 9 November 1994

1216 Cole Street,
San Francisco,
CA 94117,
USA

Nov 9 / 94

Dear Tony,

I was delighted by your letter and brief mention of obviously happy travelling (no longer impersonal) here and there, many more theres than I would choose to leave here for. The world is so full of a number of things / That I'm sure we should all be as happy as kings. When I found those lines in my Child's Garden of Verses, little goody-goody Thom ran to show it to his mother, who was cooking, saying something like "Isn't that true, Mother?" She surprised me by telling me she thought it was complete nonsense. So I gradually got educated . . . .¹ (She must have thought, "Have I given birth to a complete prig?") Back to travel: Mike and I are going no farther than New York this year, but I think of Perigord and a little Italy for next year. It's largely England I can't take much of – nothing to do with you, of course, but maybe I could do it without seeing relatives or publishers.

Here's a story about karma. Alan Shapiro, a nice and good poet of my acquaintance, had just ended his first year at Brandeis, and was at a family barbecue, the barbecue being executed by an uncle, who hasted to ask him if he was getting any (sex, that is). In fact Alan hadn't been, and said that he wasn't in love. The uncle said he wasn't speaking about love but about sex. Alan said that for his generation (it was the late 60s) sex without love was considered bad karma. The uncle turned to him, pointing a hot dog on the end of a fork, "Well <u>Mr Brandeis</u>," he said, "better bad karma than no karma at all!"

Talking of which (actually this hasn't the faintest relevance), it did strike me the other day that Charles Manson was the first of the completely subjective critics. Remember his interpretations of the songs on the White Album, "Piggies", "Helter Skelter", and "Blackbird"? Post modernist that he was, he did not subscribe to any intentionalist fallacy. But at least he really <u>believed</u> the meanings he read into the songs, which is better than some critics I can think of. (Sour crusty old man I'm becoming.)

I gave a reading in L.A. recently, and afterwards three women came up to me. One of them said: "You probably don't remember, but I asked you to eat at my sorority house at Berkeley in 1961." – "Oh yes, I do," I said, "the helpings were much too small for a young male like myself." The second came up and said, "You probably don't remember, but you gave a reading at Southern Methodist University in 1971, and you were the first person who ever gave me a joint to smoke." I didn't remember, but was I think justifiably proud that I had been so completely fulfilling my ambition of corrupting the youth. The third woman was much more interesting. I had read out three new poems about (King) David, one of them about Michal's shock that he should have danced before the Ark "uncovered".[2] But he was wearing an ephod (a short priestly tunic, I had found), so what was so shocking about that? Ah, she told me, it was made of transparent material, so everybody could see his manhood. (I like the word manhood.) And she had just come back from Israel, and with reference to the last of my three poems, she took from her bag and gave me a small bottle of perfume, called "Abishag". You remember her? She was the beautiful young virgin they used as a hot water bottle for the dying David when they could not warm his body.[3] So the perfume is essence of young girl. Abishag is really an old man's subject, though no doubt some queer critics will take me to task for betraying the cause.

I just read Alan Sinfield's book <u>Cultural politics – Queer reading</u>. I think it's pretty good, though I can spot an undefined term or two. But I like his general direction politically. Of course I am tickled to bits to be used as the climax of his argument. I am always flattered to be used as anybody's climax.

(I know you have no time for him, consider him brash, are glad that he broke up with his lover, but I got on with him rather well when he was here, & thought him likable, unstuffy, very funny at times.)

I've been reading a lot, a LOT, of J.G. Ballard recently. There is nobody quite like him, Poe writes about obsession too, but so appallingly, Burroughs has his own angle on it of course, but he's essentially a stylistic experimenter. One thing that interests me about Ballard is that he is so little attracted to such experiment. (He has tried it, in an absolutely unreadable book called The Atrocity Exhibition, but mostly he is a beautiful very rational stylist.) Three books I adore, the famous Crash, which I find hysterically funny (I always wonder, does JGB mean it to be quite this funny?), The Unlimited Dream Company and The Day of Creation. I've read a few others, but he has written scores of books, and I have several more to go yet.

Do you ever go to the movies, I wonder? There is a new one, an absolute dandy, the best I've seen in 5 years, called Pulp Fiction. It is a bit as if Henry James were to write a treatment of Titus Andronicus. (Now, I wonder what you will make of Titus in your Everyman intro?[4] My impression is that WS is deliberately trying to do a Friday the 13th, and outdo it, and at the same time have fun by taking it so far. "Enter Titus with bloody stump" indeed. Enter Bobbitt with bloody stump.)

One aspect of this movie that interests me is the method of narration, which I relate to Shakespeare's chronicles. I also admire Tony Kushner's plays greatly. Don Doody hates them and tells me (on the phone) that they are like comic strips. But so are Shakespeare's history plays (and others, e.g. Ant & Cleo), and so is Mother Courage. It's the only way to cover a lot of ground fast, and now quite a popular film and play are doing it, almost as if it were a new method of narration.

Well, Mr. Kings! My summer hysteria seems to have cooled down. (65 isn't so bad after all.) Billy has got better, and I hope has learned something. I am amused to be famous this year, but doubt if I shall be next year. There is a wonderful mag for the early twenties called SPIN (largely about very up to date rock and roll): you can imagine how pleased I was that they included half a page about my Collected (probably sold two copies at least),[5] and they asked me (among plenty of others, I think) to name my best book of the year.[6] Also, young men have started coming up to me after poetry readings and giving me their phone numbers. (I do not let it go to my head.)

We had a half-term election yesterday. As you've probably read it was appalling. There's a lot of the Christian right behind the republican successes. Christians were nothing but trouble all through history and the fuckers haven't stopped yet. But we have a big storm today, and maybe that will wash all the Republicans away. On which note the wild wicked old man will stop .... (You notice I flatter myself. But so did Yeats, didn't he?)

X X X

Th

1. Robert Louis Stevenson, 'Happy Thought', in *A Child's Garden of Verses* (1885).
2. For 'God' (*CP* 110–11) see 2 Samuel 6:14–16, 18, 20–3.
3. For 'Abishag' (*CP* 114) see 1 Kings 1:1–4, 15–17.
4. Tanner was writing introductions to the seven-volume Everyman edition of Shakespeare. These are collected in *Prefaces to Shakespeare* (2010).
5. Dale Tucker, 'Out for Justice', *Spin* 10, no. 2 (May 1994), 36.
6. TG responded to the question 'What were your favorite books published in 1994?' in *Spin* 10, no. 9 (December 1994), 118. TG chose *Perestroika*, the second half of Kushner's *Angels in America*, calling it 'the best American epic since Moby Dick.'

TO *Billy Lux*[1]   TLS Billy Lux

Monday 12 December 1994

1216 Cole Street,
San Francisco,
CA 94117

Dec 12 / 94

Dear Billy Lux,

Thank you for the letter and the set of pictures, which were tremendous.[2] In answer to your question, there are over thirty new poems not included in the Collected, A Home and Rapallo among them: all of them were written subsequent to The Man with Night Sweats and will eventually be part of my next book, whenever that will be.

The photographs were moving and sensual. I think I always find sensuality moving, as such. They are very fine, especially the nude boxer (?) in the mirror, the jack-off shot, and the sleeper. Caravaggio kid.

Someone I scarcely remember otherwise once said to me, "I was raised in a home." And the tone in which he said it remained in my memory when I had forgotten his features. The poem is all made up from my imagination, but I guess much of the detail is from everybody's experience of going to school but taken farther.

About Wrestling. Reading it through yesterday, I realise it IS a rather obscure poem.[3] It is based on the story of Jacob wrestling with the angel. The angels in the Old Testament are not beautiful renaissance creatures with wings. Angel means Messenger both in Greek and Hebrew, I am told.

565

So the angel just looked like a human, I would like to think a powerful and sexy stranger. Anyway, about my use of the story: I take the physical connection between human and divine to be part of a discourse – experience + understanding which is at the same time of the supernatural and of the natural.

I am not religious, but this is what a religious belief would be like if I were.

The discourse about the universe is both transparent and complicated like a palimpsest on an old manuscript, where on the parchment the supposedly erased writing is still visible through the unerased writing.

The statements made here are big, I suspect too big, but they all have to do with the facts that bodily contact suggests so much more than it says, and also that wrestling and embracing so often can look the same (do you know Tintoretto's Cain and Abel, which I never saw before last year?). And imagine what it would be like to have bodily contact with an angel!

If you ever have time to write again, tell me what are the letters tattooed on Don's knuckles.

Thank you again, Billy Lux!
Thom

1. Billy Lux (1958–), writer and photographer. See Glossary of Names.
2. Lux had enclosed photographs of his friend Don, some of which appeared in two German magazines: 'Don NYC', *Männer aktuell* 10 (October 1993), and 'Don Called', *Euros* 18 (1993).
3. 'Wrestling' (*CP* 260–2).

1995

TO *Billy Lux*   TLS Billy Lux
Sunday 26 February 1995

1216 Cole Street,
San Francisco,
CA 94117

Feb 26 / 95

Dear Billy,

I think I must owe you four letters by now, but you must forgive me. I've been busy with school, nice courses, nice students, but they take up time. I enjoy your letters – they are quietly interesting, and funny, and sexy. It is interesting that you have not done much writing (and shocking that that bastard teaching you at Austin scared you off writing like that) because you write so well, and I was wondering what you had written outside of letters.

I was overjoyed about the Miracle boy in MacDonald's. Actually, I didn't know they had toilets either, but I guess they have to, by law. The poem was based on, simply, my saying to someone of a mutual trick who had announced that he was moving to Portland, "has X left San Francisco yet?" and he said, "yes, last week, I drove him to the airport. Boy he's hot, isn't he. We stopped off on the way to the airport and I blew him in a toilet." Having them in a MacDonald's was just because I wanted to make it even funnier. I wanted the poem to be grotesquely funny like Hardy's late poem "Her Second Husband hears the Story", but it has turned out to be my most disliked poem, comments ranging from "obscene" to "mawkish". I continue to reprint it from defiance, and feel amply justified now that you have proved that art is just as true as life.[1]

The come on the toe is based on one time I was in a Christopher Street bar about 10-15 years ago, one Sunday afternoon. Somebody who lived only a block away asked me back, and once up there he told me that it was just a quickie because he had to go to work in twenty minutes. So I got him to come on my boot, and didn't wipe it off, and returned to the bar bearing it like a badge, and was really very popular.

The bit about renewing it like a saint's blood just comes from my own grotesque mind.

[. . .]

"Brown leaf" in the Speed Bros, yes I can see why you thought it was a drug.[2] All I meant to refer to was fairy gold, as in I think Irish folktales, which looks like gold in the evening but next morning turns out to be just dead leaves. (Boy, I'm typing today like a dyslexic.) Maybe I should change the wording to "dead leaves."

I love your pen-pal questions. I am neither neat nor messy: or rather, my awareness of how disorganized I <u>can</u> be, and have been, makes me rather neat. Somebody once told me this was because I am a Virgo (remember signs?), and then he more interestingly connected it with the way I write in rhyme and meter.

Do I have a favorite opera? Sometimes I hate opera, or rather I hate the connection with being queer – is it just an adjunct of homosexuality like teddy bears? Why do so many of my friends make such a <u>thing</u> about it? I really prefer movies and plays. But I was considerably bowled over by a production I once saw here, of Electra, and I love Mozart (everybody loves Mozart, like everybody used to like the Beatles), though I'd sooner hear him on tape than watch him again.

An epigram: teddy bears are the poor faggot's opera.

Maybe that could be put better. My favorite epigram, ever, is one I read in an obituary of Francis Bacon, the painter I mean. "I give champagne to my real friends and real pain to my sham friends." Now, I could think for two years and not think up anything as clever as that. I wonder if I would have liked Bacon. I have always thought it was courageous of him to boo Princess Margaret at some party where she was boring everybody to death with her renditions of Cole Porter songs.

"Love without shadows" comes from "The Descent", I just looked it up, a latish poem by WCW.[3] Yes, I like him a lot, he has meant a great deal to me, but I have come to prefer the early Williams, hard and rather fierce to the late more fuzzy and sometimes sentimental Williams.

[. . .]

When we die and go to Homo Heaven, you will get all the young ones and I will get the thirty year olds. I think we'll both be happy that way, though we could always share borderline cases.

I can't find your pen-pal questions letter right now, so I can't remember the others that you asked. I should ask you some:

Do you eat big breakfasts or just snatch some coffee? What is your favorite movie star (for sexiness)? (for talent)? Are you circumsized?

This is out of nowhere: I realize every now and again that I am head over heels in love with some poem – I mean irrationally and for ever. One of these has been, for a long time, Ralegh's "Walsinghame" ("As you came from the holy land") – perhaps because I misread the last part (which must be about religion) as being about love for a human; and then, a few years back, Hardy's "I say I'll seek her" (which is surely the only poem ever written about not keeping a date that is spoken by the person not keeping it without really knowing why). And then I realized the other day that Campion's "My sweetest Lesbia" is another. I can't stop repeating bits of it. I've always liked it, but I was teaching it the other day, and click that was it. (Elegant defiance.)

One thing I like about you from your letters is that you are such a thorough romantic and yet so cool (in the regular sense) about it. Obsessed but observing yourself with detachment, like a character in Stendhal.

I'm rambling. I am somewhat <u>uncentered</u> these days from not having written anything since May and no poem even in sight.

X
Th

1. 'The Miracle' (*CP* 357).
2. 'Nights with the Speed Bros.' (*BC* 34).
3. An epigraph to 'Philemon and Baucis' (*CP* 416).

TO *Billy Lux*   TLS Billy Lux
Thursday 6 April 1995

1216 Cole Street,
San Francisco,
CA 94117

April 6 / 95

Dear Billy,

Writing to thank you especially for the great glossy of Don's cock still hard under the cuffs. <u>That</u> is one that has gone on the wall by my desk. Thank you for your friend Arthur's book, it is funny and energetic.[1] Interested in your answers to pen-pal questions. A "turtleneck" certainly sounds distinguished. No, I never traced my cock on a blank page and mailed it, but once I did receive a letter containing an empty condom from a sex-buddy in S. California, asking me to return it, used. So I did. I like to oblige the handsome. You didn't ask, but I eat muesli for breakfast (!), am circumcised, and my favorite actor for sexiness is Keanu Reeves (even as far back as The River's Edge).

My friend Norm, who died several years ago, a blond giant who thought it his duty to ask me to dinner with every celebrity he knew, once had me meet Bruce Mailman (Mehlman?), owner of the St. Mark's Baths. I couldn't stand Bruce, no sympathy, no sense of humor, nothing there. I never knew he had hopes of reopening the Baths. It would need Burroughs to do justice to the ghosts found in ruined bath houses, wouldn't it? Or maybe it could be done as a movie. [. . .]

No, I haven't seen, or even heard of SUPER 8 ½, but I'm sure I would be one of those who laughed at it. I even laughed at Bad Lieutenant. I loved it when he was smoking crack or whatever off aluminium foil and an aged woman in black, a great aunt perhaps, passed by the doorway and gave him a brief reproachful look.

Well, I'm sure you'd be a hit in the escort service. What I wouldn't be able to stand about hustling would be that so many of the johns would be the last people you'd ever choose to have sex with. Still, I suppose you could just shut your eyes and think of America.

I finally made it with a guy I've been after for months. I think he must live in my favorite bar: he is good-looking, long-haired, sweet-natured, and sleeps in someone's truck. He has no job, appears to live on nothing (the occasional job, helping someone haul stuff, helping out at the bar). He is about 35, is slim though he lives largely on beer, and he doesn't appear to have a thought go through his head. I almost thought he might ask me for money, but no. [. . .] But I guess he must think about sex quite a lot because he was terrifically imaginative and exciting all night. I still glow with it, and that was a couple of weeks ago.

That's the only thing that has interested me lately, the rest has been teaching and constant rain. The back yard is lush and beautiful, it couldn't look better if I had weeded it. I love the enclosed fantasy of the Greek army someone sent me.[2] Or maybe the Greek army really is shirtless. I find that back and neck and ass deeply sexy.

It is great receiving your letters, I have never done this kind of thing before.

Thom

1. Arthur Nersesian, *New York Complaints and Other Poems* (1993).
2. A still from the film *Evdokia*, dir. Alexis Damianos (1971).

Sunday 7 May 1995

1216 Cole Street,
San Francisco,
CA 94117

May 7 / 95

Dear Billy,

I've let another batch of your letters accumulate. Well, they were coming
at the rate of one a day. Not that I complain, I am glad that such a handsome
man should have me on his mind – in any way. You speak about yourself
"commending the poetry in such an unlearned way", but don't you realize,
that's why I write – not for the people who have to review or teach poetry for
a living, but for people who read it because it means something to them. (It's
true, there may be an overlap.) In any case, having you come up to me after
that reading made my heart beat fast.

When I said I've never done this before, I must have been speaking about
having a pen pal. I never believed in such things. But you make me laugh and
get a hard on at the same time: now, that is CHARM. Don't think about it,
you have it without trying.

No, my tattoo, a panther, is not on my right lower calf – it wouldn't have
showed beneath my black motorcycle boots, which you noticed so accurately:
it is on my right forearm. And I have had it since 1962, before tattoos were
fashionable, and about six years before Janis Joplin had <u>her</u> tattoos done by
the same tattooist, Lyle Tuttle, thus making him famous, and sought after on
talk shows. Her tattoos were small flowers, I think, done on her "chest" and
"inner thigh".

[. . .]

I am overworked, end of term. My students from one class want to have a
drinking party tomorrow, but there are still exams ahead for another class.
Haven't been out, haven't done anything sexual for it seems like a century,
actually it's only two weeks, but when it's all over I intend to buy some speed
and share it for a whole horny night with the first attractive man I meet, and
we can be Bad Lieutenants together. Well, I hope we can have a good deal
better time than <u>that</u>.

[. . .] I am sorry you are having second thoughts about photography. I love
photographs – I have probably said this before, haven't I? – they are bits of
excitement captured from experience, captures of the genuine stuff, in the
same way as I think poems are. [. . .] Thank you for the wrestling pictures –

I like them all, and they are very hot – those wonderfully muscled guys closing in on each other with what looks like mean sexual intentions! I was going to single out the one I like the best, but I can't choose.

And I loved the stories about wrestlers. Especially: "I got really aroused thinking about [his] hot tears splashing on my hard cock while he sucked it. Is that normal?" I think you have the same sort of mind-set that I do: sex that is a) complicated and b) funny is definitely normal in my fantasies, and always was – I mean back to when I started to jack off when I was 11. Like you I had a non-existent sex life in my teens. I don't count sex-games with boys at school and in any case I never got to do it with the boys I most wanted, just the ones who were available.

[. . .]

Pen Pal Questions Corner: (these will be disappointing)

No, I have not been in Asia. I usually get up at 7:30 when working: I have my muesli right after I feed the cat. I wear a jockstrap or nothing. I wear a jockstrap not because it serves any particular function, besides I guess catching the odd drop of piss, but because it is sexy, and reminds me of other guys wearing jockstraps. I like to wear a cockring (leather strap kind) under the jockstrap sometimes. Using public transport with the cock parcelled up like that can be a good feeling. I was at home the day Moscone and Milk got shot – I remember one of my housemates coming in and telling us.

No, I don't do crossword puzzles, having no talent for them, though most poets are said to be good at them, and most of my friends like doing them. I met Robert Opel about a week before he was shot, in his gallery, shot over some very obscure business, it was always assumed a drug deal. He seemed pleased to meet me, as I knew several of his friends quite well (that means sexually). We didn't really talk, as this took place at his gallery, The Fey Way Gallery, which was that kind of porn-art gallery that was really big in the seventies – or it might have been early eighties – and this particular night was the opening of an exhibit, which consisted as I remember of such things as Tom of Finland pictures, tied up men (real ones I mean), Mapplethorpe photographs, and various good and bad erotic drawings and sculptures and photographs. It was a strange time, I remember seeing a production of Midsummer Night's Dream advertised – it was an all-male version in leather called Dream, maybe a musical. I didn't bother to see it, but I rather wish I had now.

I like that remark someone made about Tom of Finland that he was the gay Norman Rockwell.

Pen Pal Questions Corner, part 2: do you wear underwear? do you wear underwear when sleeping alone? do you wear a cockring when you have no immediate expectations of sexual congress? do you go to any gay bars in NY? (on receipt of answer to this one, I will tell you my favorite gay bar in NY, few New Yorkers have heard of it) what is your favorite alcoholic drink (if any)? what is your favorite drug (if any; if there are several, list in order of preference)? do you like Indian food? (I had to blandify the list a bit, it was getting too much).

Thank you for the picture of Matt Dillon, it is very early, must date from On the Edge or thereabouts.[1] I would still sooner <u>take</u> Keanu in <u>his</u> first movie, The River's Edge (maybe The Edge of the River). He had a great line of dialog in that I like to think was his own, speaking to his mother's obnoxious boyfriend, he says, stomping up the stairs: "All you ever do is fuck my mother and eat her food. Motherfucker! . . . FOODEATER!!"

I find the English actor Tim Roth sexy, I'm not sure why: he was the guy with Amanda Plummer at the start of Pulp Fiction. He also played the lead in a TV movie of Heart of Darkness, the only movie I ever liked made by Nicholas Roeg. . . . I have never heard of Witold Gombrowicz, but will keep an eye out for his books. Now I will go back reluctantly to grading student essays. Tell me how the escort service worked out, if at all. In your last you had so far not answered the phone to them.

[. . .]

X

Thom

1. *Over the Edge*, dir. Jonathan Kaplan (1979).

TO *Douglas Chambers*   TLS Toronto
Monday 22 May 1995[1]

1216 Cole Street,
San Francisco,
CA 94117

May 22, perhaps

Dear Wild Boar

Well, I'd rather say Wild Interesting. Now it's MY turn to celebrate the end of term, which I did in my own way. I went round on Saturday afternoon, to take some speed to one of my favorite young men (young in this case being 37), and we carried on for a good many hours, there was another (really) young man as a separate course for a couple of hours, there were videos, there were toys. Now I can spend the rest of the year thinking about it!

I had one of my best three classes ever. I mean not for the way I taught it but for the people in it. We all became friends (it was a small class) and were all sorry to see one another go (most of them graduating right now). So I turn to pastoral matters. Or rather I don't turn. I swoon with admiration at your foresight, energy, and industry but I've got so tired of cultivating my tiny patch of ground that I've decided to convert it to a bush, shrub, and small-tree garden, much easier to keep up.

I had my picture taken by Arthur Tress (for Enitharmon pamphlet, to replace what would have been Attila R L's irreplaceable contribution).[2] He is, somehow predictably, a nice little queen looking like the old idea of a bank clerk (the NEW idea of a bank clerk being a buffed leatherman), sweet-natured and funny. He took some grotesque pictures of me, and fell for Billy's black flatmate Joe, who had never heard of him . . . .

[. . .] You probably don't care what Tony Kushner says, but telling me about the new opera that has been made about Harvey Milk, he said it was SO BAD that it made him feel <u>ashamed</u> of being gay. (True gossip: he had to make the terrible decision between <u>his</u> choice to play the lead (the guy with AIDS) – the original very good actor, Stephen Spinelli, in the movie of <u>Angels</u> being made by Altman – and Brad Pitt, who wants badly to play the part. Of course he remained faithful to the original and better actor, but what a wrenching decision to have to make! Brad Pitt being one of the most gorgeous men in the world, though of course highly unsuitable.) By the way, you would love a wonderful movie called <u>Priest</u> we saw recently. Good, even though it is British. I would never have gone to it without the company I was in, i.e. Mike and Bob, because it sounded so religiose, and like you I hate religion as much as British movies (unlike you). It is tremendous, a good gay movie: I love it, the priest gets so frustrated by the Church he throws on his leather jacket and bicycles out to the Liverpool gay bar where he picks up a splendid tough little guy. You should see what said tough little guy does with his tongue later in the movie when he is asking for communion.

Mike was 64 yesterday. [. . .] We are planning to go to Spain in September. I've never been there. I hope it is like Almódovar's movies (which are about as realistic as A Midsummer Night's Dream.) It will be an adventure anyway. [. . .]

                            & love to you,
                                Uncle Th

1. Date supplied through internal evidence.
2. *In the Twilight Slot* (1995).

Monday 26 June 1995

1216 Cole Street,
San Francisco,
CA 94117

June 26 / 95

Dear Billy,
I have been a long time answering your letter and there is a lot to answer
in it. The most astonishing part is the last sentence, where you say "There's a
bathhouse I go to in my dreams, but it doesn't correspond much to any real
ones I've been to." Me too! It is always the same place, the same floorplan,
and all on one floor, quite simply, but not like any real bathhouse – they
were all on several floors. What has puzzled me is that I think I have seldom
or never dreamt of imaginary places – imaginary people, often, imaginary
content, naturally, but in real places I have lived in, real houses and real
towns, however distorted and changed – at least I think so – and my dream
bathhouse doesn't even seem based on a real one. I almost am tempted to
say, let's make a date to meet there one night (very Borgesian thought, that),
but it would be pretty difficult to co-ordinate, I guess. Next time one of us
is there, we could leave some sign for the other one to find (a used condom,
a discarded sneaker, a cock pump), but I suppose those damn dream towel-
boys would have cleaned up before the other one of us got there.
      [. . .]
My Favorite Bar (an essay, like What I Did in My Vacation): It is actually
quite well-known, I suppose, except no New Yorker I take there has ever been
there before. It is the bar called "Bar" on the corner of Second Avenue and
Fourth Street. I have always found it friendly and sexy – relaxed. Once, it was
apparently used to film the bar scenes of that movie Cruising (terrible movie,
but Al Pacino was cute in those days, and looked glamorous in leather), but
that was before I knew it. I used to chat with a rather overpowering ex-speed
freak there called J. J. Mitchell: he was friendly, but wouldn't let you go, and
I never remembered where I'd first met him. The last time I talked with him
there he told me he had been Frank O'Hara's last lover. (It was true.)[1] He
died of AIDS that year. One of the bartenders was the porn actor Scorpio
(I guess he's dead too).[2] But I have had a great deal of success introducing
people to that bar, anyway. It does not specialize.
      I think you were right to stop drinking and smoking grass because you were
depressed. I drink too much, but it is always wine or beer; if I drink liquor

I get like a queer Senator Packwood – unappetising to witness, I imagine. I also take too much speed, though this is only the last year. I love taking it with somebody for sex, and we have infinite cockplay without coming. It is wonderful to both be on the edge of orgasm for 12 hours or more. And then, of course, I can't sleep for days and get a terrible hangover and it can't be good for the presumably very few brain cells I have remaining to me at this age . . . I never did heroin, can't afford coke, and ALL downers send me right off to sleep (though I like grass a lot). But the times I'd get into bed with some guy and he'd persuade me to try quaaludes again, and in 20 minutes I'd be off to one of the soundest sleeps I'd had in my life!

"I enjoy writing you letters and don't expect any sort of tit for that." (That's you.) My definition of tit for tat: You lick my tattoo while I handle your nipple.

I am noted for my unfunny jokes.

(Unfunny, maybe, but sexy.)

[. . .]

Maybe I said this before, but the photographer who most affected me was Robert Frank, the Robert Frank of The Americans, which I bought, remaindered, about 1 or 2 years after it came out. I know he is an obvious choice, but he caught a rough-housing, sweet-natured, sexy side of America (also a lot more too) nobody had before. Arthur Tress deals only in theatrical production – that's OK, of course, but it doesn't move me like the other thing does. Incidentally, in some of the enclosed pictures I was trying to be Keanu Reeves in Little Buddha! Somehow, I didn't quite succeed. Don't bother to see Johnny Mnemonic, by the way: he is a complete darling, as usual, but he is really rather bad in a bad picture.

[. . .]

Uncle-like advice: 1) If you want to read Stendhal, start with The Charter-house at Parma. It has (I think) the sexiest hero in fiction. 2) If you wear a cockring, it is probably better to wear one of those leather straps than the metal ones. I have heard of cases where the metal ones had to be taken off with metal clippers (the cock swells and all the blood gets trapped on the wrong side of the ring . . .). 3) Never correspond with convicts. They always end up first killing you and then making off with your savings – or the other way round.

Let's have a South Indian meal together when we meet in NY in October. That is, if you are in NY then, and want to meet.

Otherwise we can have some South Indian food sent in at the dream bathhouse.

My favorite bartender in my favorite bar here – who was enormously flattering when we first met, and whom I still find very exciting, has completely cast me off because I apparently didn't notice him in the bar one time. Not that we ever made it, would that we had, but he has a sexy blond beard and used to give me strenuous gropes in the back of the bar – he also took a picture of my cock in the bar on his Polaroid camera, and it has joined about 100 similar pictures.

Got your postcard from Illinois. I know what you mean. But it would be a lucky Illinois farmboy to chance across you walking down Main Street.

X

Th

1. 'Famous Friends' (*BC* 53–4).
2. 'Classics' (*BC* 66).

TO *Joshua Weiner*[1]   TLS Joshua Weiner
Tuesday 18 July 1995

1216 Cole Street,
San Francisco,
CA 94117

July 18 / 95

Dear Josh,

Our latest heatwave has dissolved in fog, so I can <u>think</u> again (no doubt you wish the same for yourself) – and though I have an intimidating list of letters to write, yours was so much the most interesting and welcome letter than any of the others I have to answer that I start off with it. What a wonderful care package it was part of too! My musical education continued (haven't had time to listen to the tape, but it will be ideal in the shuttle for drowning out the Rush Limbaugh station that our driver favors) [. . .] and best of all the poems. Pete [Spagnuolo] has become heroic, a man of destiny, I almost feel a good subject for a poem: I could see him entering this role when we all met after the reading last Fall. But I don't know how to go about it, there would be such a temptation to do some kind of Yeatsian falsification. So I continue to make excuses for not writing anything. In an act of pure madness the other day, I promised an English publisher I would write a short book of introduction to Bunting's poetry.[2] I, who take six months to write a twenty-page essay! I'll regret <u>that</u> moment pretty thoroughly, I wean. (And I also wager, as soon as I tire of weaning.)

[. . .]

Brian [Bouldrey] reported you as saying I had been brutally dismissive of your thesis chapter last spring. Was I really, or were you (or was he) just joking? It was certainly not bad work at all, but I do believe that you have the power to write the very best book on [Mina Loy] that anybody alive can do, and so my standards for you are stringently high.

Your account of the conferences is hilarious. (Yes: "there's always another Hardy poem one hasn't seen before" – do you know "I say I'll seek her", spoken by someone failing to keep a date who doesn't know why he is thus paralysed, a grotesque subject, and one of the most beautiful poems I know?) And even worse, the second conference.

[. . .]

Mina Loy: "Islands in the Air" sounds like a gift – and it's all yours! – an ideal way to approach what has always struck me as a fascinating but very incomplete work. Since "Love Poems" and "Hot Cross Bums" are so different in intent and structure, there is surely no pressing necessity to consider them in the same chapter as "AM and the Rose", but it might just be fruitful to consider them (structurally) in relation to one another. The only way I can read "HCBums" is as a series of linked short poems: I actually had to mark the divisions between them in my text. I wonder if she had thought much about rationales for a long poem? Quite likely the three poems, in their different ways, just accumulated.

I finally read Louise Gluck's last book, The Wild Iris. It amazes me how she brings it off – neither of the last two collections have come close to The Triumph of Achilles – and every poem she has ever written consists of whining – and yet it is the Higher Whining, and it almost always comes off, she is unquestionably one of the best poets around (even though personally I didn't like her at all). She is incredibly sensitive to the rhythms of thought and feeling, that's it, so that even when you think the person speaking is a selfish piece of shit, the utterance is always fully and complicatedly alive. So it was good being freshly amazed at her quality.

[. . .]

Augie Kleinzahler's new book is splendid, I think, especially the poems of direct or indirect mourning for the end of his affair with Deb.[3]

I haven't seen Batman Forever yet, but will because I love Val Kilmer's lips – and they will always show even when he has his bathood on. [. . .]

Love to both,
Th

---

1. Joshua Weiner (1963–), poet and academic. Weiner was the only graduate student TG supervised; he wrote his thesis on Mina Loy.

2. TG promised William Cookson he would write a monograph on Bunting for Agenda Editions; he never completed it.

3. Kleinzahler, *Red Sauce, Whiskey and Snow* (1995); see TG to Wilmer, 28 May 1991, above.

TO *Clive Wilmer*   TLS Clive Wilmer

Friday 29 September 1995

1216 Cole Street,
San Francisco,
CA 94117,
USA

Sep 29 / 95

Honeybunch,

I just looked up vagary in the dictionary, and it has two pronunciations, of which yours is listed first, and so must be the more common. My apologies . . . I never even dreamt. We learn, even when we have reached the age of 66, which I hope can qualify as two-thirds the number of the Beast. As for the rest of my critique of your poem a) remember, you can only use what is useful in what your friends tell you about what you have written: <u>you</u> know your intentions best; (b) where it is like Lament, I am nothing but flattered (my own poem is like other poems too, after all); (c) I have noticed sometimes, for example when seeing a film, that I can sometimes be exceptionally disgruntled or exceptionally receptive to the work in question. Perhaps when I wrote, what's more, I was envious of your fluency when I have been so long at a standstill. My continued apologies . . . Go by the consensus. Donald Davie was, after all, difficult to please.

I read about Donald's death in the Guardian I bought at the Barcelona airport,[1] waiting for the plane to the U.S. Of course I felt the loss, though I had been aware that he was ailing, and in fact I was struck by his signs of age when I stayed with him in 1992. He meant a lot to me: he was a <u>lovable</u> man, and, though he could be crusty, intemperate, and just plain wrong, his was the only body of criticism by a contemporary that meant anything to me in terms of my own practice. His books helped me with Pound, he personally introduced me to Bunting's poetry, and so on. Not his early criticism, I didn't read that at the time it was written, but everything later. As for his poetry, I admire it more than you think. It presents a difficulty: <u>most</u> of it seems to me pretty undistinguished, but there is a large handful of poems that are brilliant – you and I agree on the names, I think – and which make him, I think, superior to the more famous among my contemporaries. (For me, the greatest concentration of good poems is in A Winter Talent, and the most startling recovery in the sequence A Stopping Train.) [. . .]

Spain was very enjoyable. Madrid was perhaps a mistake, but we had fun, in spite of the fact that most of the city seemed to be Beaux Arts bank architecture. But we tired ourselves out walking from place to place, seeing the Goyas in the Prado was really a kind of education you seldom are able to get with a painter, and I think if I had stayed much longer in Spain I would have ended up a slimy old pedophile – NEVER have I found underage boys sexually attractive before! As for Barcelona, it was wonderful in every way. Where else would you find, within a cathedral precincts, a pond containing twenty exuberant and noisy geese?

I too was very happy indeed with the Paris Review interview.[2] I must thank you for the immense amount of work you put into it, and also I think your very presence and the pertinacity of your questions and probably the sweetness of your disposition must have brought out the best in me. The things I say in it seem better and brighter than the things I normally say. [. . .]

I have just been reading Briggflatts again (I will be saying something about it in Georgetown University next week): I just can't get over it, it is so good. I don't understand why everybody else doesn't see that too!!!!!

[. . .]

I have revised my ideas about what it is necessary to carry around in a wallet . . . The sunflowers ended by dwarfing any mere human . . . I would love to write some sort of poem about Donald, as you can well imagine, and as you would probably like to yourself. Well, that kind of thing comes or it doesn't.[3] [. . .] I've been reading Dostoievsky's Possessed recently, a new translation, under the name of DEMONS. I find him enormously satisfying, in the same way as something like King Lear. For all my lack of spiritual need, D is so good that he rips me out of my own context and shows me, by putting me into it, how much bigger and more important his is than mine . . . . Did I ever show you a poem about Rimbaud I wrote called "Shit"? I wrote it six years ago, and gave it in desperation to the compilers of a rather bad Faber Festschrift for Ted's 65th birthday, edition of only 300 copies so I doubt if you can get it. I'll send it to you if you are interested. It is very smart-ass. Not like me, like a thoroughly tasteless bit of versified literary history written in imitation of Mauberley. Still, reading it alongside all the other contributions to that sorry volume, I don't find it that bad any longer! Must stop, the typing is getting worse and worse.

[. . .]

Universal love,
and for you, the special kind
reserved for literary comrades,

The Beast
66
Thom

P.S. Congratulations on your coming Selected Poems. Something like an Apotheosis by Rubens, I think, you being wafted up to a ceiling by fleshly maidens of the Carcanet persuasion.

1. Frank Kermode, 'Poet of harsh eloquence', *The Guardian* (21 September 1995), 15.
2. Clive Wilmer, 'Thom Gunn: The Art of Poetry LXXII', *Paris Review* 135 (Summer 1995), 142–89.
3. See 'To Donald Davie in Heaven' (*BC* 59–60).

TO *Mary and Catherine Thomson*

TLS (aerogramme) Jenny Fremlin

Monday 2 October 1995

1216 Cole Street,
San Francisco,
CA 94117,
USA

October 2 / 95

Dear Mary and Catherine,
    [. . .]
    Spain was lovely, especially Barcelona. I don't like sherry, so didn't try it, but the ordinary wine was dreadful, worse than cheapest California wine. However the beer was magnificent – strange for a Mediterranean country. We were right above the market, the Ramblas, a long street with stalls, etc. We had a reservation in a hotel which couldn't take us, so they arranged for us to stay at the same price at a much better hotel ("four star"), in a wonderful room overlooking the Ramblas four floors down. The last evening we were there, there was an extraordinary storm we watched from above, I had never seen anything like it, lightning for an hour almost continuously, like a storm in a horror film – they said not uncommon in this coastal town. [. . .]
    The best food of all was "Tomato bread". You slightly warm in the oven some thick slices of French bread brushed with olive oil, then take a ripe

tomato and cut in halves (cherry tomatoes will do, too) – and <u>rub</u> over the bread till it is good and pink.[1] I make it every day, though of course soon the tomato season will be over, and we will have beautiful-looking tasteless tomatoes gassed in Holland, no good at all for anything.

Thérèse said in 1992, that she was afraid she wouldn't live to see another Labour Govt and that made her so sad. But it looks as if she will be proved wrong . . . <u>We</u> don't have an election until next year. It is difficult to like Clinton (though I do admire his wife), but I hope he has a chance of getting in again instead of one of those Republican shits, hardly one of whom is worthy of respect. I mean, there <u>are</u> some Republicans with principles, but I don't think any of them will get the nomination.

You say there are all those people you know with barns, and you wonder why. Well, I remember what people were <u>supposed</u> to do in barns, though it was probably just sexual lore, – and anyway we're all getting a little old for that kind of thing nowadays . . .

As I remember, there were always a lot of Jehovah Witnesses in Snodland – also a bit of every other denomination you could think of – even Ebenezer people – which I never came across again until California. I think of California as in some ways the Snodland of the USA.

I am off again in two days to do a mini reading tour – to Washington and New York and Chicago, then not to stir outside the front door again for the next few months, and after that only to go to work.

Meanwhile it's a sunny day and I must go to the gym and then perhaps ————— tomato bread for lunch!

Love,

Th

1. TG provides the recipe in *Food for Life . . . and Other Dish*, ed. Schimel (1996), 34. 'It is from Catalonia,' he writes, 'and would be perfect to attract that Catalan highway patrolman you have been after for so long.'

1216 Cole Street,
San Francisco,
CA 94117,
USA

Nov 2 / 95

Dear John,

I have been tormenting myself with guilt thinking I have owed you a letter for several years, and now I look up your last, the one that enclosed the aerial view of what you call so nicely the Property (we all examined it together one night at the dinner table), I see I am only ten months late. Not at all bad by my standards. Not that I have much to tell. I haven't written any poetry since May of last year; Mike and I visited Madrid and Barcelona; I have managed to get Bob interested in the garden [. . .]. Barcelona was absolutely wonderful, and of course all the adolescents were extraordinary-looking, as in Italy. Somehow they go from perfect babes to perfect boys to perfect adolescents to perfect young men, without any of that awkwardness, that terrible graceless self-consciousness, that afflicts the young in northern Europe and America. But at 30, suddenly all attractiveness vanishes, and the wonderful golden boy has become pudgy paterfamilias.

[. . .]

We would really like it a lot if you could come and stay with us before we, and I suppose you, die. Otherwise it would be too supernatural a get-together to be fun. Any second half of a year would be great – that is, between July and early January because I teach every spring and can't cope with much outside of teaching at this age. Though I think I will retire in 1999, after which you could come and stay any time at all. It's worth thinking about, though I'm sure you have everything very well arranged on your comely Property. But think how good it would be to leave the chaos of Cole Street to return to Geuffordd.[1] It really would be fun to have you here for a while!

The last things I wrote were three poems about David (of the O.T.). I kept on feeling that they in some way balance the Dahmer poems, though I didn't know why, and mentioned this to a friend, a poet, Robert Pinsky. "It's obvious," he said, "they would both kill for a fuck." A great explanation, but it didn't satisfy an audience I was reading to in Chicago last month – about ten old ladies rose and left after I read the Dahmer poems. "You

583

wouldn't be leaving if I'd written some poems about Napoleon or Julius Caesar, Ladies," I said to their retreating back, "and they both killed many more people." Understand, I said this in a friendly voice, not derisively, but none of them turned or answered. But I suppose it was the masturbatory bits that really got to them!

Thank you for the nice things you say about the poems, anyway. Your reaction is just exactly what I would want, "nearly but not quite making you laugh." No, I have as great a distaste for what Dahmer actually did with his passions as you do – I hate the very idea of mutilation, though cannibalism strikes me as less repulsive, perhaps because less common. But of course I have always taken a certain pleasure in shocking people. (I know it is childish, but there you are.)

The poem "A Wood Near Athens". I was trying to do a TSE-or EP-like collage, in a mild, probably rather genteel way. That is, instead of putting in connecting phrases like "for example" or "that brings to mind the fact that even in Old Testament times, in the Holy Land itself, people were most confused in dealing with their sexual desires", leaving them out and just putting in the examples, so that the reader could make the connections. Collage, in fact. Well, it was an idea . . .

I read about Toby Young's complicated editorial adventures (how unkind those girls were to deride his baldness), and I read the occasional dry and funny review by Karl, and I got a mad letter or two from Margie, but I don't keep up with anybody. Is John Coleman still alive, I wonder? People do die, don't they? I wish they'd let me do it first and then they could do it any time they please. . . . There must be lots I'm missing out, but we are all in good health [. . .]. And all send their love. As I do

X X   Th

---

1. Geuffordd was the name of Holmstrom's new house near Pen-y-Bont-Fawr, Wales.

Wednesday 15 November 1995

1216 Cole Street,
San Francisco,
CA 94117

Nov 15 / 95

Dear Belle,

[. . .]

I read an obituary for Donald in the Barcelona airport coming home from a holiday with Mike.¹ No one can be spared as little: he was a fault-finder in the best way, because the fault-finding was allied to a complete openness to whatever talent was there, regardless of the politics of the owner of that talent. And the number of people he celebrated: Gurney, Scott, Dorn, Niedecker! He's right about Mrs. Hemans, of course. He tended to be right in his literary tastes – and it was always helpful to <u>disagree</u> with him, since it would have been impossible to agree with him about everything.

His best poems were extraordinary: I would say they are few but very solid – the odd thing is that they emerge from a desert of (to be honest) mediocre poetry. But the best ones are <u>there</u>, and they stay there for rereading.

And of course he was an immensely lovable man, and it is impossible to detach his lovableness from the literary part of him. It must, by the way, give you an odd comfort that the letter to you must surely be the last work of his to be published in his lifetime.² Of course I had read the letters when the issue came out. Your letter is good, and he takes it in good part. But I do rather agree with what <u>he</u> says about hierarchies in the canon.

I note the reference to myself, and find the religious extensions a bit mind-boggling, to tell the truth.³ I'd say that the canon emerges largely through luck – the luck of posterity containing the rare taste of a Donald insisting that we pay attention to some neglected poet, for example. Of course, I don't rate LUCK or POSTERITY any more highly than you or he would. It's a chancy business, and I am certain heaps of great talents <u>have</u> gotten lost for ever. The concept of a heavenly court arbitrating literary taste charms me: it is very Platonic, and I am certain it is a major heresy: but I suppose if God looks after sparrows worth a farthing each, then he may plausibly pay attention to the literary fame of Lady Pembroke too.

When he speaks about egalitarianism as the U.S. vice and bad faith as the British, I must say, he hits a couple of nails very well on their heads. It's a succinct truth. Every generation makes its own mess, I suppose, but who wd have thought that this one would have made these messes!

[. . .]

Otherwise, what? I haven't written anything since May of 1994. Well, after 500 pages of a Collected Poems, I shouldn't feel bad about that, but I don't usually feel fully alive unless I am in the middle of writing. That sounds pretentious, I am sure, but you must know what I mean: it's not a question of happiness, or of achievement, but of the satisfaction that comes from being able to speak about something as well as experiencing it.

[. . .]

I have signed a contract to write a short book about Bunting. I must be mad. A book?!⁴ Florence (the person I mean, not the city), when last encountered, was beyond Florence: Ophelia would be more like it.⁵ Nothing else to report, I think!

Love,

Thom

Did I send you the last thing I wrote, 3 love songs by King David?!

1. See TG to Wilmer, 29 September 1995, above.
2. Randall's letter, and Davie's response, were published in *PN Review* 105 (September–October 1995), 2–3. Randall wrote to *PN Review* about Davie's essay 'The Canon: Values and Heritage', *PN Review* 103 (May–June 1995), 12–15.
3. 'Whether we know it or not,' Davie writes in *PN Review* 105, 'we are appealing to, and trusting, something other than "posterity", that blank and rubbery check. In this, as I'm sure you perceive, I'm at odds with Thom Gunn, our mutual friend whose trust (apparently) in posterity depends upon a trust in unredeemed humanity – such as I cannot share.'
4. See TG to Weiner, 18 July 1995, above.
5. Florence Elon, TG's long-time colleague at UC Berkeley, is the subject of 'Jamesian' (*CP* 450).

TO *Ronald Johnson*¹

TLS Kansas

c. Saturday 25 November 1995²

1216 Cole Street,
San Francisco,
CA 94117

Dear Ron,

A pleasure to hear from you, and an equal pleasure to read your prose.³ It is succinct and studied, and I think really pretty useful, especially for the young poets for whom it is intended. Very few criticisms, but here they are. You may not feel they are advice worth taking.

"Measure" is a vexed word, especially as WCW uses it. It is perhaps a pity that you have to start with him. It is actually an exact synonym for "meter", but WCW's pronouncements about the variable foot are confusing and contradictory. (A man called Cushman – I think Stephen Cushman – wrote a very good book called The Meaning of Measure, all about WCW's definitions.) Someone once said that to speak about the variable foot is like speaking about the elastic inch. My own feeling is that Williams found the tripartite line looked good on the page, but there were actually no rules at all, and he really just proceeded by ear, as he had always done. In any case, your third paragraph is the least helpful one in the essay.

In answer to your question, I do like your use of the word Protestant, and I think it is helpful indeed. The US was founded by Protestants, of course, but what you seem to mean by it is this: Protestants broke away in the first place because they did not believe in learning about God from an outside institution: you had to listen for him as a voice inside you. From that it was a small step to finding the Muse inside you. Your Muse, your Protestant Muse, your American Muse, your quirkily individual Muse, your Muse.

I personally hate the usage "his/her" – it is clumsy and cowardly. If you think it sexist to use "his" as a generalizing term for both sexes, use "her", which I have come to like a good deal! (both funny and politically correct.)

"Like Pound, at first it's best to read about him rather than him." I know what you mean, but not necessarily. I tried with Pound (also with Stevens) for years before seeing the genius. Mostly with early poems (attractive, but many of them pretty dated), and with early Cantos, which I don't now understand I didn't take to more. Then I came across Canto XLVII printed by itself (I think) in Auden's Faber Book of American Poetry.[4] (WHA was a magnificent anthologist.) Thus encouraged to take it as a self-sufficient poem I read it with amazement, for the first time, fell in love, and came to read the rest. Of course it's anything but a self-sufficient poem, but it worked as a great introduction (as "Sunday Morning" did to Stevens).

And what's more, I have found many students whom you can turn on to Pound by means of this Canto. Others tell of getting into Pound through the Pisan Cantos when they first came out, but that was a little before my time, and they seem to me to constitute a much more difficult initiation.

[. . .]

But I am getting dogmatic. Congratulations on getting to 60. I'm 66, and the decade seems ok, except maybe symbolically. But I've never been one for symbols. Fetishes, yes, but not symbols. When Gus [Blaisdell] finally gets it together enough to bring out ARK, I think you will be at last famous. The Chicago Review doing a special issue on you,[5] reviews all over the place, plowboys in Tennessee reading you and hitching to KS in the hope of sucking your cock, that kind of thing.

Love,

Th

1. Ronald Johnson (1935–98), poet known for his major work *ARK* (1996).
2. Date supplied through internal evidence.
3. See Johnson's two-part essay 'Hurrah for Euphony': 'Part I' – written for his poetry students – was published in *Re/mapping the Occident*, ed. Malessa and Mitchell (1995), 49–50; 'Part II' was published in *Chicago Review* 42, no. 1 (1996), 25–31.
4. *The Faber Book of Modern American Verse*, ed. Auden (1956).
5. TG contributed to this special issue; see 'Starting to read *ARK*', *Chicago Review* 42, no. 1 (1996), 21–2; uncollected.

TO *August Kleinzahler*   TLS Yale

c. Saturday 25 November 1995[1]

1216 Cole Street,
San Francisco,
CA 94117

Augury of Innocence!

Yes the Ganders are quite a pair.[2] Forrest Gander sounds like an airport. He was very lovable, I thought, though in confidence I must confess I thought his poetry didn't know where it was. I am sorry I told his sister that "oh, women don't matter", but it was the Kingsley Amis in me, and the shock my remark registered was amply worth the untruth. (Of course women matter: they cook us cakes, don't they?) Actually, the movie she thought was anti-woman wasn't so – it was enormously funny, and I think you would laugh your head off (Clueless, at the Balboa, but probably not much longer. I don't think you would like the movie on with it.) Did I tell you how good I found To Die For and The Usual Suspects?

John Bayley, a real old codger now retired from Oxford, and I suppose something of an influence in English letters, though I find him pretty slippery, is reviewing Helen Vendler's two new books in the TLS. In one (or both?) of them, our Irish girl has taken up the Kleinzahler case, it appears. I am very much afraid that all he is referring to here is her odd little guess that you are a drink-besodden little elf in the Polo Grounds was it? However, the gist of his review is that he fairly much approves of the academic colleen because she does after all help us understand the more inaccessible (but <u>important</u>) practitioners of the Orphean art like "Ashbery, Berryman, August Kleinzahler, Jorie Graham, Rita Dove", on whom she "is really good." (Thank God, at last I shall have some guidance in disentangling the gnarled intricacies of Rita Dove, whom surely <u>no-one</u> could read without help.) (Joke.)

[. . .]

Your "Sunday Morning Downtown" is as good as it sounded in your reading – observant, original, interesting – just right, with an exquisite control over tone while never letting in a Kleinzahler mannerism to spoil it. Lines 22-3 are an example of the just-rightness. Another poet would have ruined the spontaneity by changing the order of these 3 sentences. It is one of your best poems ever, I am sure of it, and really contains far more numerous implications, humane, civic, etc., than a reader wd at first have thought possible. The only possible thing I could say against it is that its title is like so many others of yours that you're going to run out of this sort of thing one day (a poem about being bitten by a poisonous snake in the Tucson desert called "Tuesday Afternoon in the Desert", for example).

[. . .]

When Bunting prints his "Three Michaelmas daisies" or WCW his "This is just to say", what makes them effective, really, is simply that they got published as poems among so many more considerable poems. "Hey, these are part of me too!" Well, that's nice, Basil and Bill, but we did assume that, you know. (Creeley is the worst offender for printing pages and pages from his notebook.)

I'm at least struggling away in <u>my</u> notebook – better than nothing after all – but I can't say the results amount to anything yet. A poem about David with his cock in Bathsheba's hand,[3] one about literary critics being like Charles Manson,[4] one about overhearing a wedding-dinner next door ten years ago.[5] That kind of thing. I see Wendy on Friday: I gather she got pretty sick of England. GOOD.

I did have a wonderful time in New York. Sometimes I think I ought to live there. But I oughtn't really.

My young friend Robert [Gallegos] is about to go to France for a month. I am trying to think up suitable small talk for him to learn, "J'aimerais te sucer la queue," that sort of thing.

[. . .]

Might you be around to address a huge class (100-150) of freshmen who have been reading your book – Monday April 29, say, if you can look that far ahead. I'll pay you something, but it's unlikely to be much over $100. (I'll see what I can get, closer to the date.) But think of the copies you'll sell!

Yours, in Orphic Chimes,

Senator Packwood

1. Date supplied through internal evidence.
2. Poets Forrest Gander (1956–) and C. D. Wright (1949–2016) married in 1983.
3. 'First Song' (*BC* 108–9).
4. 'A Few Critics' is unpublished (Bancroft).
5. 'To Cupid' (*BC* 100–1).

TO *Tony Tanner*   ALS (card) King's

c. November 1995[1]

[1216 Cole St.,

San Francisco, CA 94117]

End of November

Dear Tony,

[. . .]

I do love Ford's Tietjens novels – enormously – I think they are as much an achievement as JJ's Ulysses – though of course <u>different</u> – but with an equal emphasis on style.[2] The great difference perhaps is that Joyce depends almost entirely on improvisation (I can't prove that, but I am sure of it) and Ford's book is worked out in astonishing detail beforehand.

[. . .]

I thought I'd retire in 1999. Teaching is delightful – in fact it makes life worth living – but I'm not as good at it as I was. (I think I peaked in the late 1980s!) Some students think my approach old-fashioned. (It is: I am not interested in interpreting the art of another time by my own politics, but I am very interested in scansion!) Some students think I am harsh (I probably am).

One day you will come here and meet Bob, who has lived with us about 12 years now, and my great friend & neighbour August Kleinzahler, whom I've known some 15 years.

Oh, my book on Bunting. I must start writing that some time. Nice of you to look forward to it, though. I do myself.

Happy Christmas & everything you want the New Year to be, dear wag, x from us all x Th

[. . .]

1. Date supplied through internal evidence.
2. Ford Madox Ford, *Parade's End* (1924–8).

TO *Ander Gunn*   TLS Ander Gunn
Thursday 28 December 1995

                                                      1216 Cole Street,
                                                      San Francisco,
                                                      CA 94117

                                                      Dec 28 / 95

Dear Ander,

Typing that date, I realise it is 51 years since the event that altered our lives. Well, it did, but I can't say my subsequent life has been the worse for it. What I mean is, disasters try you, but usually if they don't wipe you out you find ways of coping which may make you stronger. Well, that IS a cliché, isn't it, and of course it can only be partly true. But I can hardly imagine a life more to my taste than mine.

[. . .]

I finally started writing again in November. Hadn't finished a thing since May of 1994. What a relief. Of course, I'm always going through spells when I can't write (the longest was 2½ years), but I'm happier when I'm writing, when I'm plugged into the computer of existence, as it were!

We had a storm to end all storms about two weeks ago. Winds 100 mph all night (higher speeds were recorded), keeping everybody awake banging at doors and breaking windows. A family I know near the beach had all their windows blown in. Across the street the best tree on the block snapped in two, the big half falling on a parked car. In the park, 1000 old and big trees were torn up. And there were numerous big potholes appeared – into the biggest a whole mansion slipped, very dramatic, we watched it on the news. I have never seen a storm like that before, and hope I don't again.

[. . .]

                    And a happy new year to both of you
                              + love from all of us
                                    Thom

1996

Wednesday 10 January 1996

1216 Cole Street,
San Francisco,
CA 94117

Jan 10 / 96

Dear Forrest,

I can't tell you what a kick I got from your letter.[2] When I first saw you I thought, a poet in boots is well grounded. I also thought, a man in boots is likely to know what he wants. (Much later I thought, young Goodman Arkansaw should have a full-length picture on the back of his book.) But I thought at the same time I must be deluding myself. Then in the bar I was bowled over by our conversation, short as it was. I didn't say anything I didn't mean (I'm not especially honest, but I find it time-consuming to be dishonest, so I have gotten in the habit of telling the truth by default). I have certainly thought about you a good deal since then. I bet you have a leather jacket too. If you don't I would like to wrap you up in one of mine.

On the cover of a magazine called BAM I saw a picture of a singer wearing two leather jackets, one over the other, and thought . . . interestingly excessive! His songs are not good (Glenn Danzig of the band Danzig) but his band all wear biker jackets and have obsessive cock-sucking stares, which must be a good influence, in the long run, on the youth of America.

Aren't I a dumb romantic? Well, that's OK, I'm glad I am. I would like to sit down and talk with you for days. Another thing, I would like to get in a room with you, and lick you all over for days. Or whatever.

I liked your description of the Ozarks in your letter. I have been there, but only going through, and that was years ago. You had a much healthier vacation than I did. I made a fruit cake, which not only contained bourbon, but had to have bourbon "dribbled over" it while it was "ripening", every two days for two weeks. That success, and Christmas, behind me, I took a bit of speed with some unscrupulous but attractive people I came across, but didn't sleep for three nights. Then I slept through New Year's Eve. Now I'm preparing classes.

I admire all of your Wesleyan book,[3] but the parts I was uncontrollably moved by were, first, the Prelude, beautifully regulated and unregulated at the same time, and also the Librettos for Eros, which I still read again and again. And this is nothing to do with your looks – I am glad that your looks made me seek out your poetry – but as you must know, the poetry would move me if you were Quasimodo. Patterns of Unsettlement I am going to xerox for a class – it has something going for it I can't track down – you read it that night and it constantly grows on me: I can't understand why the last two lines almost break me apart. For the rest, I can't get over the Librettos. A Table Laid with Horrors I resisted at first but now I get it. It is simply what the title states, and has its place. I take it Final Testament is spoken by a God. The others, what can I say – the occasion of the poem is loss – and in the seven poems you move from complete excessive presence to complete desolation, and it is all intimate horror but in a way that it is a human necessity to deal with. I only half understand the means by which you bring it all about, and that delights me, because I know it is all so good and you have really, I think, in Pound's term, committed an invention. I would give anything to write something this good.

You probably don't have time to answer all this. I hope you do, but if not let's wait till we run into one another again. I hope it's soon, my friend.

Th

1. Forrest Gander (1956–), poet. TG and Gander read together, with C. D. Wright and August Kleinzahler, at Intersection in San Francisco on 17 October 1995. 'Eve reading . . . Forrest Gander, a poet in cowboy boots I was much taken with, as he was with me. We had a sweet little interlude alone at the bar near the Roxie before the others joined us.'
2. Gander's letter to TG (29 December 1995) can be found among TG's papers at the Bancroft Library.
3. Gander, *Deeds of Utmost Kindness* (Wesleyan University Press, 1994).

TO *Clive Wilmer*   TLS Clive Wilmer
Thursday 18 January 1996

1216 Cole Street,
San Francisco,
CA 94117
Jan 18 / 96

Dear Clive,

Got your wonderfully encouraging and helpful letter a few days ago, and answer now partly because I am so full of myself, and partly to supply another poem.[1] [. . .]

Anyway, I want first to tell you about the Makin book you so kindly sent me.[2] I assume you have maybe read it, but perhaps not. I was both delighted and dismayed by it – delighted because it is SO good – it is probably the best book of criticism I've read since Stephen Greenblatt's Renaissance Self-Fashioning, I mean he has not only a lot to say about Bunting but he also has a well-worked out attitude to poetry, and that attitude is also an attitude to living a life. That's rare: Davie had it, Winters had it, FRL (for better and worse) had it. Few critics write as if their subject matter is THAT important. And I was dismayed, of course, because his book leaves me with little to do, and is already better than what I can do. Well, I'm committed to writing it, and I'll find something. (Plenty of time left.) (Maybe I'll be dead before the deadline.) (Etc.)

"Cat Island" is Torcello, not Venice. The remark about the Byzantine church was made by John Ash, who should know. Revised version enclosed. – Yr remarks about "To Cupid" were especially welcome: I'd been trying with it for over a year. First it was in rhyming quatrains, but they were too smart-ass, for some reason. Then I tried it in short free verse lines, then in long free verse lines – or was it the other way round? Finally got it to work in blank verse – which is at this stage perhaps a bit too silkily smooth for its I hope troubled subject, but I won't be able to judge that for some time. I'm delighted you thought Cupid was based on a real man. He wasn't, but I wanted to make him seem so. – I wonder if you like the epigrams because they are so purely mean-spirited, and thus more like BJ and JVC!![3]

[. . .]

No, I won't be making it to the Davie memorial. I don't even like to travel as far as San Jose during the semester nowadays. If you want a suggestion of a good Davie poem to read, take a look at the original "Mushroom Gatherers" on p.11 of A Winter Talent (not the later rewrite).

The frenum is that little band that joins the foreskin to the shaft of the cock, just under the head – even in circumcised people like King David and the present writer. I have also just found in the dictionary that it is the same kind of flesh under the tongue. Well, that would be ludicrous – it is all right to have Bathsheba leading David around by his cock, but hardly his TONGUE![4]

My idea behind this poem is: The story of David in the O.T. starts with a legendary character, he is equally out of fairy tales, the youngest son, a shepherd who becomes king, Jack the Giant Killer. At the start then, he is without individuality, he is multiple (like the member of the primitive village who is every other member too), he is generic (like a baby). Then, how interesting, he becomes an individual – his story is told in such detail that there is conjecture it might have been written by a member of his court. He becomes specific, complicated, singular. He moves with a tread only his own, not to be confused with that of the generic hero-poet-shepherd boy-giant killer.

But maybe it doesn't work anyway!

Of course I agree with you about originality. Poems are based on poems – as Pound knew, as Bunting and Duncan knew, as Winters knew. But evoking the name of Winters, I have to make a reservation: we shouldn't be obsessed with originality (to use yr phrase), but we shouldn't forget it also. I have risked total unoriginality in two poems – consciously, I mean – 'Words for some Ash' and the first Dahmer poem – hoping that I was writing with such vigor (!) that they would come off – but it WAS a risk, in any case. I think of all the bad verse published that came from trusting in Winters' belief that it was sufficient to keep within such bounds that originality could be kept down completely. I think, typically, of Wesley Trimpi's poetry. Well, of course, maybe ole Wes never had any talent of the sort, but it might have been of some interest if he had assayed an original image, an original turn of phrase, an original way of putting a poem together. Originality is opposed to cliché as well as to tradition.

I've gone on too long. Forgive this self-absorbed letter. Happy birthday, youngster!

     Love,

        Th

P.S. I was asked to dinner with Salmon Rushdie but I'd never read anything by him so I said I couldn't. I suppose it could have been rather exciting. They did say "Don't mention this to anyone."

1. 'A Los Angeles Childhood' (BC 61–2).
2. Peter Makin, Bunting: The Shaping of His Verse (1982).
3. Poets Ben Jonson (1572–1637) and J. V. Cunningham (1911–85).
4. See 'First Song' (BC 108–9).

TO *Billy Lux*   ALS Billy Lux
Tuesday 23 January 1996

1216 Cole Street,
San Francisco,
CA 94117
Jan 23 / 96

Dear Mr. Billy –
    I felt rather guilty about not writing to you before, getting your letter
yesterday. But I know you don't want me to feel guilty, so I won't.
    I have been writing some poetry [. . .] & also doing admirable things to
the sexual organs of various young men. (Some were in their forties, but
when you are 66, men in their forties are just sexy kids.) I met one of my
great crushes on Saturday afternoon in a bar – he was a bartender in another
bar for 2 years – but a bartender in a busy bar, at work, is a difficult man to
attract the attention of – and this was the first time I had seen him among
"the public".¹ He was tired and had to go home but gave me his number;
I phoned him next day & he sounded ridiculously enthusiastic (must be a
geriatric specialist, I suppose), & we made a date, talking for a long time. (He
had a bare chest under his jacket in the bar, and he had the longest and most
beautiful nipples I ever saw. He told me he used to wrap rubber bands around
them to stretch them, because when he worked as a bartender he had to give
the customers something to look at. So on Sunday evening I tried wrapping
rubber bands around my own nipples – I do try to keep up! – but it was very
difficult and not really worth it in my case, I decided.)
    New York sounds a bit bleak. Cruising in the snow does tend to shrink
the cock and the enthusiasm, I have found. But I'm surprised you didn't
find some hot young scab-janitor to make it with in one of those deserted
bathrooms with no industrial soap or paper towels. The first man I had a
crush on in the U.S., in 1954, was a beautiful black-Irish janitor who cleaned
the toilets at Stanford. I used to have long pointless boring conversations
with him which got me nowhere. I was young & shy then.
    [. . .]
    Thank you for your letter – you manage to make even a janitors' strike
funny. You are a lovely writer.

                                        X   Th

1. Robert Prager (1955–2014), writer and bartender. See Glossary of Names.

Tuesday 20 February 1996

1216 Cole Street,
San Francisco,
CA 94117

Feb 20 / 96

Dear Forrest,

You see I have restrained myself from answering your letter for one month. I am in danger of coming on too strong, aren't I? I was always rather obvious, and your answer to my last was kind in the extreme. I was delighted to receive the copy of Lynchburg, because I had been searching for it, and not finding it.[1] I enjoy it, and am especially interested in the libretto for Robert Johnson as a predecessor for Librettos for Eros, a series of poems I simply cannot get over.[2] I have told a lot of people about the Wesleyan book (I have not told them I have met you). I love the way you can move into Biblical archaism (the Gander special effect) and make a triumph of it. Best of all, maybe, at the end of Land Surveyor. I sent you my book because I wanted you to have something by me, though completely aware that you may have already read it.

I also read your Nasty Worm story in an old Conjunctions. If I'd been there, I'd have dealt with it before it could do anything to you. Signed, Your Protector. Then we'd be alone together in a sealed room and I have no idea how we could pass the time.

[. . .]

I love your penpal questions! My favorite photographer is very obvious, Robert Frank, whose pictures I first saw in 1959, I think, and have meant a lot to me. I love their ease and warmth and populism. I don't like Mapplethorpe's, in spite of the fact that he took my picture on the cover of my Collected, because he is all the opposite, all theatrical distance and carefulness.

I have been trying to think up answers to the questions about favorite body of water and street, and I can't. At one time, Talbot Road, but it got ruined by being half pulled-down. At one time Third Avenue, but years ago it was ruined by having so much money poured into it. At one time Prince Street (NY) when it was still Little Italy and not SoHo (I lived on it several months in someone else's loft). I love streets where I can watch people.

I keep thinking of your phrase (when driving through the Ozarks) "hawks gleaming in the naked trees". That is very Gander.

We have storm after storm, but who am I to complain about the weather to an Easterner, especially this winter? I too have spent days grading endless miles of papers, but then I wasn't too good at that kind of writing when I was the age of my students, either.

Have you ever read Peter Everwine's poetry? The first poem I ever read by him was called "Desire": it was in a magazine I read in a supermarket. I at once had to read both his books.[3]

Later I met him, and he told me he doesn't write any more. Some of your poems in Lynchburg are a bit similar to his, the way you do everything through unexpected images. (I don't mean derivative.)

I would come to give a reading at Iowa, as you suggest, but I think you will find they don't want me, as I went there to read only two and a half years ago. I will be in Chicago in the middle of October, for certain, which is not too distant. I would read for nothing. Also, I suspect that Jori Graham ended up by not liking me much. She gave me to her husband to look after (a sweet man, you will find, if you don't already know them).

[. . .]

               Your friend,

                  Thom

P.S. Was this letter less outrageous?

P.P.S. I hope you know you can always stay here. I have a large bed, and I have never found wolf spider or beggar tick in it.

1. Gander, *Lynchburg* (1993).
2. The renowned blues guitarist Robert Johnson (1911–38) is the subject of Gander's 'Life of Johnson Upside Your Head: A Libretto'.
3. Everwine, *Collecting the Animals* (1972) and *Keeping the Night* (1977).

TO *Douglas Chambers*   TLS Toronto

Saturday 20 April 1996[1]

                                   1216 Cole Street,

                                   San Francisco,

                                   CA 94117

                                Saturday, April

Dear Douglas Darling,

Thank you very much for Stonyground: the Orgasm [. . .].[2] I won't have time to read the book for a few weeks, the end of term pending (you know all about that), but look forward to it very much. Congratulations on it, anyway! Is this the book you started one morning when I was staying with you in 1992 or 1993, sleeping late, the first day of Toronto spring?

Oh yes, I see Augie constantly. He is visiting my classes on Monday. They adore his poetry, when they can grasp it. It is very interesting, and not I think a reflection on my teaching. I decided to teach Lycidas, as I probably told you at the time, as I took weeks preparing the class. (This was to freshmen.) Since they like me, they tried to like it, to respond to my enthusiasm. Other poems, of course, went completely dead on them. Then there were true surprises: several of them went out of their way to tell me how they liked the Epistle to Dr. Arbuthnot. (Interesting, don't you find?) Meanwhile, I was having my own problems (everything possible was in this course, entitled Introduction to Poetry): for the first time since I was 14, I began to rather dislike Keats. And disliking Keats is like disliking Mozart or the Beatles – nobody dislikes them. Bright Star seemed about as gratuitous as a Mars Bar. Anyway, they like AK's poetry so much that they are pointing [out] its virtues to me. Good for them. Students today seem much more bright than my generation was, but then I am lucky to be teaching at Berkeley.

More about poets. I was deliberately withholding from you the fact that Forrest Gander is such a great beauty, because I was afraid that you would think my judgment of his poetry was addled by my appreciation of his looks. Actually, his Librettos for Eros is so good I find it difficult to think of anything since Briggflatts that can equal it. Maybe you saw his picture on the back of his second book, Lynchburg, which isn't that terrifically good. That book, I mean. OK, but period style. He's the real thing. (He lives with a woman by the way, and they have a young son.)

I think you should publish the Horace poems on your own, and if you need financial help (viz. money) from me, I will be happy to supply it.[3] In these MacArthur years I can make such offers. (I have given several lumps of money to poor young poets, two of whom I don't even like personally – so for you! you only have to ask).

[. . .] I am really sorry I sent you that poem "What Humans Do".[4] When Augie commented on it, he said two things: a) it is an awful poem (awful was his exact word) b) birds do it also, bees do it, even educated fleas, etc. He was right on both counts. Well, we all make mistakes. Enclosed a few new ones. Actually I've done quite a few new things this year. You will undoubtedly get all the references in Famous Friends; the quotes and semi-quotes in DD in Heaven come from the Paradiso, but I guess anybody could guess that.[5] [. . .]

What else? I'm reading Maria Edgworth's Belinda. It's a hoot. The only person I know who has read it is the head of my department. Have you? The other day I met a bookstore clerk who is extraordinarily handsome, is only

25 (a bit young for me), loves having sex in leather, went out of his way to seduce me (I was flattered), and introduced me to a new drug (it wasn't wildly exciting, but he was, and we are going to see each other next weekend again). I always hoped success would be like this!

A month ago I met this utterly handsome boy in a bar, also of that absurdly young age (I really prefer them a little older), who was living on the streets, & was ridiculously a) naif, b) honest, and c) dirty. We solved the whole problem by my buying some speed and him having a shower when we got home. Next day I gave him some clean clothes. I said to him: you know you are the most restless person I have ever slept with, and I've slept with some restless people. He said: When you go to sleep in a doorway, you have to remain alert. Well, I see what he means.

Anyway, my life remains curiously interesting.

Bill is in superlative shape, making it with drab black men, himself happy and witty and handsome. Mike seems a little tired, doesn't seem to have sex with anyone, but we are wonderfully close these last few years. Bob must be having sex with somebody or other, but never at home. I wonder why not? Of course, I am the W of Babylon herself, but you always knew that. We've had a wet cold spring, but not nearly as bad as the rest of the country or "Europe" let alone "Canada". [. . .]
                    X X X
                            Th
[. . .]

1. Date supplied through internal evidence.
2. See TG to Chambers, 9 October 1984, n. 5, above.
3. For Chambers's translations of Horace see TG to Chambers, 8 June 1994, above.
4. 'What Humans Do' is unpublished (Bancroft).
5. 'To Donald Davie in Heaven' (*BC* 59–60).

Friday 24 May 1996

[1216 Cole Street,
San Francisco,
CA 94117]

May 24 / 96

Dear Billy,

I have been criminally neglectful of you this year. I received your friend's wonderful piece on Keanu, and the advertising-card you so kindly got for me from the Transit Authority, and your letter, and your postcards, but have written very few letters to anyone. But now term is over. During the final exam I finally let my eye examine the 82 freshmen for sexual characteristics. About half were unfortunately but inevitably women – all very well in their way of course, but it is their way, or rather their way, not mine. Of the rest, there were four knockouts – one sturdy boy-next-door, like a blond G.I. of 1945,[1] – and one Keanu, dark, tall, boyish, with a winning smile (he wants to be a fireman) – and two others, handsome and sexy in less classifiable ways. I hope they all came to know each other through the class and celebrated the end of term together with elaborate wrestling contests (amusing sexual penalties for the losers – "Hey guys, that's not fair, I won the last three times!").

[. . .]

Now a big holiday weekend in which I plan to continuously outrage my body and mind into complete exhaustion by Monday night. After all, hasn't a 66 year old earned the right to act as if he was 21?

[. . .]

I had occasion to look up something in my diary of 1978 (I write about two lines almost every day), and started reading, and couldn't stop. The number of people I made it with (I have forgotten almost all of them), and the amount of drugs ingested – not only by me but by the rest of the family! We'd have people to dinner, and then pass around drugs, then I'd take another drug to go out to a bar, and then, as often as not, I'd meet someone who'd take me home and share yet a third drug. They had names like "curly Jeff", "disappointing Brad", "charming and good-looking (but a bit nelly) Doug", "Jim", "leather buck-teethed Carl", "stunning redhead Jim" . . . then suddenly I'm in New York, where I meet an interesting number called Jim Leaffe. I do remember him: he had a most unusual sexual fantasy, that he was Ishmael in Moby Dick. "And you are Captain Ahab," he said. "No,"

601

I said, "I'm <u>not</u> Ahab, but I'll be Queequeg if you like." (I always try to be accommodating.)

Yes, I liked your last postcard of the wrestlers from 1912, and the big toe is heartbreakingly touching, because its owner must surely be dead by now. "Touching": Ed White wrote a blurb about Dale Peck, author of a novel I hated called I think <u>Martin and John</u>, referring to him as "touchingly young." Bizarre compliment. And <u>I</u>'m touchingly old, I suppose.

You can tell my mind is jumping all over. I hope you are taking a few photographs – your talent is too great to go dormant. Forgive me for not writing in such a touchingly long time. I am (touchingly) yours,

Thom

1. A reference to 'A GI in 1943' (*BC* 55–6).

TO *August Kleinzahler*   TLS Yale
Friday 4 October 1996

1216 Cole Street,
San Francisco,
CA 94117

Oct 4 / 96

Dear Augie,

Well, we certainly miss you around here, and from what Simone[1] told me today we'll be missing you even longer next year, when you go to Iowa. Iowa knows what's good for them, apparently. Anyway, your invitation to stay here remains permanently open (we can give you a nonChristian Christmas, for example), and this house is going to have the foundations BOLTED (what to, I have little idea) next month, so it will be very safe, and if there is an earthquake, we can stand firm while the city disappears around us in brittle shards.

We're all doing fine. Bill continues doing art work [. . .] and I can't tell you how happy it makes me to have him back again, 100%, after all these years. Mike remains sensible, ein feste Burg,[2] and Bob wonderful [. . .]. I went to NY, and that was a delight. Once I got out from under the FS&G festivities, which were not at all bad, really, parties, champagne, marble bathrooms, contemptuous doormen, stupid fans who want to discuss my poetry without ever having read any of it. Susan Sontag has to <u>kiss</u> me – why? Alfred Corn wants to <u>kiss</u> me – why? I hate kissing people when I'm not horny. I think it's an irritating habit of elderly New Yorkers, much preferring a Prussian-type handshake myself, or even a stoned and nonchalant wave of the hand. Hi there, stud, I'd sooner say to SS. Anyway, we got through all that, and I behaved fairly well toward almost everybody. (I gave away my 2 comps for the prose reading to a good-looking boy who kept on lurking around me during the intermission of the poetry reading. "This is exactly the reason I moved here from Kentucky," he said, "for readings like this." You poor sucker, I thought, you really moved to NY so you could go to readings by establishment poets? – and gave him my tickets. I wasn't going to disillusion him. I also wasn't going to endure the terrible boredom of another such self-congratulatory evening in the Town Hall.)

Blimpies have gone down in quality, I think. Or is it just that my standards are higher these days?

Once I HAD got through the readings and the grand hotel and the dinner (very good) and the party in the NY Public Library, with 800 guests (I met Wallace Shawn and have a dreadful sense that I may have patronised him, I had drunken conversations with James Fenton and though I don't like his poetry too much, he is rather a sweetheart, I managed to amuse him, that is. (It isn't everyone who has met Pol Pot's brother.)),[3] I moved to a cheaper hotel, and then was shown around by a young man who writes film scripts and is as enchanted by me as I am by him.[4] It's all platonic, and I guess will remain so, but he makes me laugh all the time, and he shows me around parts of NY I'd never know about from somebody older. When I revisit the haunts of twenty years, it's like entering a geriatric ward: in certain bars I am the youngest customer! But this guy takes me to inexpensive restaurants and wonderful bars and music places in the extreme East Village, and is incredibly generous with his time and attention. I went with him to a poetry reading his wrestling-trainer was giving in some cellar beneath St. Mark's Place, and it was more fun than the business at the Town Hall a few days earlier.

Gave a reading at SF State yesterday, nice audience. (I have found there is always one extremely hot man in every poetry reading I give and on every plane I board – but I seldom manage to speak to either. Good to look at, though.) Simone was there, with all the Stanford fellows, and Brighde [Mullins]. She smiled beautifully through the whole reading, and we had a great chat afterward. I said several nasty things about Jorie Graham to her before finding out they were great friends. She very kindly did not punch me on the nose.

[. . .]

Oh yes, Forrest came through to give a reading, wrote an enthusiastic note saying he wanted to take me out to lunch and get me drunk on martinis. That sounded all right, though the idea of a bullet through the head from his wife during a martini hangover might have been less than all right. But we failed to connect (I was still in NY when he gave his reading here), and that was probably just as well. It was all a great change in tactic for him, by the way. That young man sure is changeable. On the other hand he can be a beautiful poet.

Thank you so much for TRAINSPOTTING. We have all read it. Mike & I say things to each other like "Get ootay here, plukey-faced doss cunt." (Literary talk.)

> Much love, and remember – once you've made it through to Thanksgiving the rest of the year is easy –
> X
> Th

1. W. S. Di Piero (1945–), poet, essayist and translator, taught at Stanford for many years. He, TG and Kleinzahler were friends and lived in the same neighbourhood.
2. 'Ein feste Burg ist unser Gott' is a hymn by Martin Luther, notably set by J. S. Bach. In Thomas Carlyle's translation, the hymn begins 'A safe stronghold our God is still'.
3. Fenton's journalism from Cambodia, the Philippines, South Korea and Vietnam is collected in *All the Wrong Places* (1988).
4. See also next letter.

TO *Douglas Chambers*   TLS Toronto

Monday 7 October 1996

[1216 Cole Street,
San Francisco,
CA 94117]

October 7 / 96

Dear Dug-Boy,

Got back recently from NY, where I had a good and varied time. All that grandness connected with my publishers' 50th birthday – marble bathrooms, contemptuous doormen, champagne all over the place, etc. [. . .] Went to the Frick with Pinsky and Bidart, both of whom I love (they would never kiss me), and the wife of our editor, Susan Galassi, who works there, showed us all the top two floors, which are closed to the public. But the collection itself, I had forgotten, is breathtaking. Poor Mrs. Gardiner, in Boston, could only afford the third-rate, but wicked Mr. Frick could afford the best on the market. I love Whistler's portrait of M. de Charlus, I didn't remember it was there – also Titian's wonderful young man, and even the Fragonards.

Then I moved to a cheaper hotel and spent much of the rest of the week with darling Billy Lux, a would-be movie script-writer and wrestler and poetry-reader – we have intense feelings of mutual love which I suspect will always remain platonic – who showed me round cheap restaurants and bars and even poetry readings in the extreme East Village as only a young person could. [. . .] I also had a cheerful lunch with Ollie Sacks where he plied me with salmon eggs, periwinkle eggs, cuttlefish eggs, and was it flying fish eggs? They were delicious. I'm reading his new book in proof right now, and it is as good as ever.[1] I remember when he was in his 20s and he said his ambition was to write scientific books that were also decent literature (forbidden word now?), like Darwin, Freud, etc. Well, he did succeed, didn't he.

[. . .]

I keep hearing of more and more people with HIV who do better and better over the years – they retire, they spend all their money, and their T-cell count goes nicely up and what are they supposed to do? A guy in NY who retired 15 years ago is now wondering what to do with the rest of his life, a strange and awkward decision to have to make in his late forties or early fifties. And Bill, who has had it longer than anyone I know, has invented a new art form.

Well, I didn't invent a new art-form, but I invented a great title for my little free verse poems on conversational subjects, <u>Gossip</u>, as I'm sure I told you several times [. . .]. I plan to go up to twenty or so, and to make it the middle section of my next book. My next book – I keep feeling it may be my last (few poets go on writing after 70), and keep it around, while it gets longer and longer.

I got 86ed[2] from my favourite bar after the Folsom Street Fair, really quite justifiably – this other guy and I had both our cocks out, in one another's slimy paws. The Fair itself was wonderful – 10,000 men in leather pants, all seemingly on speed. Well, maybe not going to the Hole in the Wall will help me to cut down on my consumption of speed, it really can't be good for a 67 year old with high blood pressure.[3]

Come on, honey, you really can't consider The Crab a good poem.[4] All it had, for a while, was a certain boldness of subject matter, but hardly even that nowadays.

I agree with Craig[5] that Clueless is marvellously faithful to Emma, though I couldn't bring myself to see any of the direct Jane Austen movies. It's not snobbery on my part, I just love her books too much as they are, and prefer a complete modernisation. And I have always loved the Fantastic Voyage. When Duncan was still with us, but already years into his kidney trouble, he one day had a calcium deficiency which made him mildly crazy: I visited him in hospital while they were trying to figure out what was wrong with him, and his fancy was that dialysis was the same as the Fantastic Voyage, but I was the only one who knew the movie well enough to catch what he was talking about. I must stop.

Love,

Th

1. Sacks, *The Island of the Colorblind* (1997).
2. 86ed is an American slang term for refusing service or ejecting someone from a bar or restaurant until further notice.
3. The Hole in the Wall Saloon opened on 8th Street in 1994 and quickly became TG's favourite South of Market bar.
4. See TG to Tanner, 31 July 1961, above.
5. Craig Patterson (1961–), professor of English, met Chambers at Trinity College, University of Toronto, in 1980 where they began a friendship that lasted forty years.

TO *Billy Lux*   TLS Billy Lux
Wednesday 30 October 1996

1216 Cole Street,
San Francisco,
CA 94117

Oct 30 / 96

Dear Billy,

I haven't written to you in so long I almost stop feeling guilty, but I was reading over some of your old letters to me today, and admiring the way you put things and you have been a lot in my mind. Your last letter was the best of all, the one that ended "forget pee-shy, I got pee catatonia", witty and sexy at the same time. That's what I'd like to be. I was trying to turn it and selected passages from others of your letters into a kind of collage-poem for my series (does that make you feel used?), but I don't think I can do it, your prose rhythms are so good. I thought, if I could arrange someone's conversation into "A Los Angeles Childhood", why couldn't I take bits of someone's letters to make up "Letters from Manhattan"?[1] I'll go on trying, though.

[. . .]

I went to Chicago for the MacArthur Fellows' Reunion, which is more fun than it might sound. People give papers, some of which are fascinating – Bill T. Jones on his ideas for directing The Bacchae, a scientist on singing caterpillars, I gave a poetry reading, and we all had a big dinner at a museum of Natural History, under statues of elephants and a big dinosaur skeleton.

There I met a very sweet movie director called Allison Anders, who told me she knows both Madonna and Martin Scorsese (I was very impressed, as she meant me to be). Later I found out her major achievement was a section of Four Rooms, which nobody I know has seen. But she did tell me that Madonna's handsome boyfriend is not only the sperm donor father of the daughter but in fact a genuine fucker/impregnator father.

[. . .]

I then returned and got a big cold, so I have spent the last week being a phlegm-factory and have had time for little else. On the other hand, it's really good to be home and not sit on planes watching Michael Keaton in movies I'd never dream of going to otherwise: more fun to take Nyquil and wake coughing.

[. . .]

I sent Tim a letter about his poetry, which I found I liked even more to read than hear, and he reads well too.[2] I told him I like his short poems best of all, and also said I think he writes better about sex than about love – I suspect he will not like either of these comments, but they are actually high praise.

X   Thom

1. See 'Letters from Manhattan' (BC 71–2).
2. Timothy Gerken (1962–), writer and photographer, Lux's former wrestling coach.

TO *August Kleinzahler*   TLS Yale
Thursday 31 October 1996

1216 Cole Street,

San Francisco,

CA 94117

Oct 31 / 96

Dear Aug,

It was a delight to get your letter, and I'm sorry I've taken so long to answer it. I was away in Chicago and then in Buffalo, briefly but too long, to read poetry and speak to a minuscule class. Buffalo is the most godforsaken place in the world, REALLY ugly, and the new university is only matched for bleakness by the buildings at York University in Toronto for a kind of wind-swept desperate utilitarianism. The people nice, however, a slightly eccentric English faculty who were proud of having much truck with Olson and Duncan while they lived. Creeley didn't come to my reading, but then, why should he?

[. . .]

Well, I don't teach graduate students poetry-writing. I think it's entirely possible to teach undergraduates, provided they start with some talent in the first place. Bunting taught you a lot, didn't he, in this way or that? I figure it's like freshman English: they hand you in something, and you give them some idea of how it could be better written. That way you're helping them in the long run with their writing and their reading and with relating their perceptions of their lives to their language. It's called education. I don't teach graduate students because by then they have gotten too sophisticated for anyone like ME to help them. They're off on their own pretentious trips, they are imitating Ashbery or someone like that, they have read obscure French critics. No, I don't believe in MFAs either, maybe I'm just being conservative and saying, If I did without an MFA, then they should be able to as well. (Me and Chaucer, you understand.)

Oh dear, the 27 year old does sound like trouble. Be VERY careful. In 1958, when I started teaching, Ian Watt (who was sweetly enough acting as a kind of mentor to the new teacher at Berkeley) said: during conferences ALWAYS keep your office door open. (So no girl can accuse you of sexual advances, etc.) So I always have, and refuse to close it, even on request!!! Naturally I was quite surprised that the propositions started coming in from the occasional girl, and even once or twice from some boy. (I was young then.)

I have finally started work on the Bunting book, but chapter one is pretty easy, "a life" which is just my digest of bits of Sister Forde and Peter Makin.[1] I have discovered one amusing detail: you remember the bared breast in Kleinfeldt's (Briggflatts)? Of course you do. The place was a bar in Soho, and the breast belonged to an apparently rather poor but lovably eccentric painter and drunk called Nina Hamnett. In her old age she said "Modigliani used to say I had the best tits in Europe", she used to go to this pub with Bunting who was her drinking buddy (or more?), and her affectation was to hang one breast out. I'm beginning to feel like a scholar, for having discovered this.

Everybody was saying in NY that Bob Hass's nosepicking poem was the first thing of his they had liked in years.[2] Me too: it's not pretentious for once, but simply funny. As I've always said, I can forgive anybody a lot if he makes me laugh. (I mean "he/she" . . .)

Your comments were very useful to me indeed, and I thank you deeply. It amazes me that I am so poor at self-criticism: I really couldn't guess which was my best and worst poem in the three I sent you – but I guess that's the point of showing each other poems: you get so absorbed in the experience of writing the poem, and take the occasional risk you hope is worth it – no, that's wrong, you take constant risks, every line is a risk, and the personal investment is so great you finally have little idea of what you've done. You are invaluable to me as a critic, I hope you know that. I have never before had a friend who was at the same time a real friend and a poet I admire. Well, let's hope you are able to come back here and live.

[. . .]

So, you are reading the Charterhouse, one of my favorite three or four novels. What I've always loved about it is that the critics go on about its being in the tradition of the French psychological novel – and they are right – but it is also a kind of Rafael Sabatini adventure novel, and it is quite marvellous how dumb Fabrice is allowed to be, which makes you like him all the more. I first read it when I was almost 21, the summer before I went to college, around the time I first read King Lear. Jesus knows they are dissimilar enough, but each gave me a tremendous (and inexplicable) feeling of triumphant freedom – perhaps only because it turned out to be rather good, after all, living in a world where such wonderful things could be written.

[. . .]

What's Coover like? He was a great friend of 2 English friends of mine, but when I met him once, briefly, he didn't seem very interested in speaking to me. He did write a tremendously funny novella once called Spanking the Maid (great title): it was apparently intended as an experimental parody of porn, but you wouldn't have known it from the real thing!

We had our first rain the other day.

X

Thom

1. Victoria Forde, The Poetry of Basil Bunting (1991); for Makin see TG to Wilmer, 18 January 1996, above.
2. Hass, 'Shame: An Aria' (1996).

TO *Douglas Chambers*   TLS Toronto

Friday 15 November 1996

1216 Cole Street,
San Francisco,
CA 94117,
USA

Nov 15 / 96

Dear Sigil –

I know you don't care for diminutives, but maybe we could settle for Sig
or even Siggy.

Pretty chilly today, I suppose winter has started, but who am I to tell a
Torontoan about chill and winter? We are having our house <u>bolted</u> to the
foundations, a good thing to do in earthquake country. Our contractor is
a very dashing fairly young man with a ponytail and an enormous Harley-
Davidson, quite a romantic character to have around: he is straight but rather
flatteringly has told us he considers us to be family, in that he does messy and
complicated jobs for us that he won't do for many of his clients. Anyway our
house is going to stand, and stand proud, for the next earthquake.

[. . .] I've written some other bits for Gossip. I've realised my form for this
usually involves a little turn at the end, and that this was originally modelled
on the turn at the end of Augie's "Show Business" – do you remember
that, three books back? I have tried to vary it, though, like the couplet in a
Shakespeare sonnet. But my main object with the Gossip series is to make
them fun to write. Well, they <u>are</u> fun, maybe not much good, and really no
easier to do than the other kinds, but fun, anyway. I enclose three: "Letters
from Manhattan" is entirely made up of bits from my movie-script-writing
poetry-reading friend Billy Lux, so it can hardly be said to be written by me.
Not sure it works – Mike says it's too prosy and random. "Bravado" is a
composite portrait – I did <u>see</u> that tattoo once, though I never spoke to the
guy.[1] I wonder if he knew what bravado means, or if he thought it was just a
word for bravery? Do you recognize "He waits and looks around him"? It's
from one of my favorite poems. (E. A. Robinson "Eros Turannos")[2]

I got this from an interview with Kenneth Koch: apparently Virgil Thomson
rather wonderfully said that opera is all about saying goodbye and ballet is
all about saying hello. It's true, when you think about it.

O. Sacks' new book is called The Island of the Colorblind, and that's what
it's about. It's very good, of course. I know his title is based on that of H.G.
Wells' short story The Country of the Blind. He and I apparently shared a

passion for H.G. Wells' short stories – for each of us it was the real move into adult reading, round about 11 or 12. (They are still wonderful short stories.) For me it went: E. Nesbit > Conan Doyle + Rider Haggard + A.E.W. Mason > H.G. Wells short stories and Science fiction > H.G. Wells Kipps and Mr Polly and then suddenly I was there, a grown up reading grown up books. (I omitted Dumas: he came in there right after E. Nesbit.) I remember when I went to boarding school (a nice progressive school) during the blitz, there were various private study periods we had to spend in the library. My bay of the library was for books by authors beginning with I or J. Noticing all the books by Ibsen, of whom I'd never heard (I was 11), I started to read him – but not the famous Ibsen, I read Brand and a long strange romantic play about Julian the Apostate called Emperor or Galilean, I think.³ I must have been a strange child. I'm certainly a strange adult.

I really miss Augie, as I've probably told you, and wonder if he will ever come back to live here. He seems to enjoy teaching at Brown, and in fact must be a marvellous teacher, but he'll never get a job here.

[. . .]

A nice new teacher at Berkeley, he is 29, called Chris Nealon, and his specialty is Queer Studies. I find him absolutely charming: we had lunch yesterday, but not sexually. I don't mean we didn't sexually have lunch, though we didn't do that either . . . oh well, you know what I mean. I'm nevertheless running across a new difficulty: when I do meet someone I like, and they have read me and liked my poetry, I get a sense of their liking me too easily, of giving me too much credit. It's a bit like having the looks of Montgomery Clift; I have a weird puritanical sense that friendship involves earning and shouldn't be so easy. Well, that's perverse, isn't it, and maybe I don't really mean it.

I'll close before I write any more nonsense.

Oh yes, I had an interview in a local gay paper, where I said of a certain bar I go to, that I'd discovered that about half the clientele is homeless.⁴ A friend phoned me and said, it's more like a twentieth than a half: what you meant, he said, is that half the people you are attracted by turn out to be homeless. How right he was.

Love   Thom

1. See '7 a.m. in the bar' (BC 67).
2. See TG to Tanner, 10 June 1966, n. 2, above.
3. Ibsen, Emperor and Galilean (1873); see TG to White, 24 January 1955, above.
4. Austin Lewis, 'Poet Thom Gunn Shoots off His Mouth', San Francisco Frontiers Newsmagazine 15, no. 14 (7 November 1996), 19–20.

[1216 Cole Street,
San Francisco,
CA 94117]

Dear Stud,

(Elaine Feinstein was amused when I pushed past her burly husband at some literary party saying "Excuse me, Stud". "You have me thinking of him in a completely new way!", she said.)

I think, I hope, I answered your last, but just felt like writing, also to enclose stuff. You have been through hard times this year, and that's been tough to take. When sorrows come, they come not single spies, but in battalions. I always wonder how Sh could have given such good lines to Claudius. Perhaps (a) they aren't really that good, but I'm just a sucker for cliché, or (b) they are part of Claudius's complicated duplicity, his silver tongue.

I have finally started on my Basil Bunting book. Am I up to it? Not really. What I can do is write a dry but accurate little introduction which will have deserved the £200 advance I received. One page a day, I say to myself, like a recovering alcoholic, but I doubt if I can finish it by the end of next summer as I promised. It is interesting though, isn't it, how much more you penetrate a work once you have to write about it. For example, it wasn't until I had to write about Pinsky that I found the weakness to his poetry is in its high sense of civic responsibility and total lack of the personal – finally it is goody-goody, though in a pretty inventive way.² And writing about Chomei at Toyama I find myself wondering whether there is not too much improvised in the tone once BB has decided to make him a cynical agnostic rather than the most devout Buddhist he is in the original.

Three more little instalments in the Gossip series.³ I write them because I wanted to do something that is fun. (Not that they come any the faster for that.) I sent a bunch to the Sunday Times (UK, I mean), and they were slightly appalled by the words like fuck and nipple and so on. I had forgotten, I thought we lived in the 1990s. [. . .] In "Bravado", the bar is full of people who have been kept awake on drugs all night (all true). [. . .] Poor young men who possess beepers are either drug dealers or male whores, part of the showiness of what they conceive of romantically as an outlaw profession. I may have sent you "Classics" before. Maybe nobody could like such poems except their mother, but I'm their mother. I must close this.

Love,

Thom

1. Date supplied through internal evidence.
2. See 'Inclusions', *Agni* 44 (1996), 214–21; uncollected. TG reviewed Pinsky's *The Figured Wheel: New and Collected Poems 1966–1996* (1996).
3. The third 'Gossip' poem TG enclosed was 'Hi' (*BC* 68).

TO *Billy Lux*   ALS (card) Billy Lux
Wednesday 4 December 1996[1]

[1216 Cole Street,
San Francisco,
CA 94117]

Dec 4

Dear Young Stud –
     [. . .]
     Yes! come and stay next summer – as long as you want. July, August the best months. My brother & sister-in-law will probably be here in June & I may go somewhere like Venice with Mike in September. I will give you my room to sleep in & so you can bring back 2 tricks a day if you want. I'll sleep in my work-room. It will be fun having you here. I think you will love my favorite bar. (I am reinstated there. The owner did not remember 86ing me.) I will take you to some other bars too. You won't need to drink or accept the drugs offered you, just appreciate the rich variety of men who will want to tuck you under their skinny arms. (We will also feed you.)
     [. . .]
     You would look good in a pea coat. I hope you found one. I always thought them very sexy, especially when I was adolescent & found everybody in his late teens & early twenties sexy (i.e. especially American servicemen in London). But then I suppose I still do, find I mean. Mike once said I was so like Will Rogers, who never met a man he didn't like.
     Haven't seen a movie in ages. On TV, <u>EZ Streets</u> was too good to last – it was marvellous, even had two cute leads, & direction & photography such as you <u>never</u> see on TV. Saw Jurassic Park again (on TV), surprised I liked it so much. It is terrible I guess, but compared to Independence Day it seems like Pirandello.
     Yes, MacDowell must be cocksuckers, you are right. But think how you would go out of your mind with sexual frustration if <u>none</u> of the other artists were attractive – highly probable – just cabin after cabin full of good grey-haired liberal men & women without any sense of humor or zest for cock. And without zest for cock, really, where are we darling? Nowhere.

On that note I must end,
                    X
                         Th
[. . .]

1. Date supplied through internal evidence.

TO *Douglas Chambers*   ALS Toronto
Saturday 21 December 1996[1]

                                            [1216 Cole Street,
                                              San Francisco,
                                                CA 94117]

Dear Doug "Cuddles" Chambers,
    Yes, Billy Lux really did talk about Plato. I kind of slid by him at Cambridge
– read part of the Republic & pretended to read the rest, never understood
Nietzsche. He really does read them. I love associating with young men who
are horny & educated & with young men who are horny and uneducated.
When I say young I seem to mean in thirties or early forties. Billy Lux is very
attractive & a great pleasure to be with & he makes me laugh a lot – we have
never made it, & actually I don't care, I want to do what he wants. (That's
the language of love, I know, but though I adore him I'm not in love with
him. I don't seem to get uncontrollable crushes any more. Thank god.) He's
in NY & I hope will be staying here this summer. Meanwhile here: there's
New Robert (not Robert Gallegos, who's still a friend, but Robert Prager,
ex bartender, ex graduate instructor, now 41)[2] – we first made it last March,
I think, & we do have very prolonged drug & sex experiences every now and
again. He charms me partly because he's a bit difficult by temperament. He
seems to have been fired from every job he ever had, & the reasons are always
too difficult for me to understand. He has the biggest male nipples I have ever
seen (he trains them with rubber bands), & he has such a wide disinterested
knowledge of pornography I tell him he should be back in Academe, teaching
Queer Studies. George Oppen on old age: "what a strange thing to happen to
a little boy." TG on his youngish friends: "What a lucky thing to happen
to an old man." We plan on a drug marathon to bring in the New Year. That's
what I did last new years, for 3 days, but I didn't know RP then. If I get a
heart attack, tell them all I died smiling.
    We're all happy here, except the cat, who is having a very troubled old
age. I think of him as being King Lear, Billy S. is the Fool, Bob is Kent, Mike

& me Regan and Goneril, and the dear dog Alice as Cordelia. (A certain thieving friend of Bill's could be Edmund & I completely forget who we cast as Edgar.) Perhaps Mike & I could leave the cat out in a storm on the heath of Golden Gate Park? – About pneumonia. Billy has had it twice in the 18 years he has been positive. He dreads getting a cold in the winter. [. . .] Due to the new medicines it is quite extraordinary how the obituary pages in our weekly paper (remember B.A.R.?) have been reduced from an average of 2 pages to half a page, week after week now for about three months. I think maybe the breakthru happened without my fully noticing it.

[. . .]

I'm still suffering now writing the third of eight chapters on Bunting. These are just drafts, of course. Then do another three or 4 once school's out & then the next year finish it & revise the lot. It's not going to be that good a book – not so good as Shelf Life, I think. I'm just laboring to get it down, it will be a text book with the occasional stylish phrase.

Augie is coming back for a few days at Christmas. I realized last week I think he is the best poet writing in the language (who for example could be better? Louise Gluck is perhaps almost as good, but she passed her peak with The Triumph of Achilles, & every poem she writes is a whine – but she whines extremely well). Robert Prager will also be at Xmas dinner + sundry straight people + eccentrics – maybe it will all go as well as Thanksgiving.

[. . .]

Happy New Year at the Red Home. Sounds like you have a sabbatical. We saw the Australian TAP DOGS, which was wonderfully enjoyable. I'm reading SABBATH's THEATER, which is wonderfully <u>dirty</u>.

Love to you, also to Brian,[3]

Thom

1. Date supplied through internal evidence.
2. See TG to Lux, 23 January 1996, above.
3. Brian Norbury (1938–2017), British civil servant and Chambers's partner for almost fifty years. Chambers, although based in Canada, usually spent several months of the year with Norbury in London.

1997

TO *August Kleinzahler*   TLS Yale
Tuesday 4 February 1997

1216 Cole Street,
San Francisco,
CA 94117
Feb 4 / 97

Hi there, Sport!

Feeling rather diffident today, about everything. Diffident about poetry, about teaching, about having got out of bed in the first place. Maybe I should set up a relationship with some god or other? Well with me, I'd get the wrong god – oops, sorry Shiva, didn't mean to step on your tail. (The missing footage now restored to Star Wars consists, apparently, of Han Solo treading on Jabba the Hut's tail: that's why he gets turned into a wall-plaque in part 3.) I probably shouldn't have got up, but then I'd be warmer but bored. I'm writing this letter so as to avoid working on the notes for tomorrow's lecture on Pound. I have of course lots of angel-faced students, and they are very pleasing here, I must say, the undergrads anyway – in that they are really interested and do a successful struggle with the poetry and do go away with something in their handsome little heads. There do seem to be more dykes than heretofore – or am I just getting deceived by the haircuts and all those heavy chins?

You must just have about recovered from the familial beating-up by now. Probably you are sallying out to NYC to beat up people who misbehave in poetry readings. (I harp on this because I admire it, I hope you know!)

I think "Late Autumn Afternoons" works very well. You have cut down the first two stanzas in just the right way. It's all beautifully full of things and stressed syllables close together (which are like things, kind of), so that when we get to the stacks and the flashing crowns there is already a good place waiting for them. And as for the last two stanzas, I always admired those, as you know. – Looking at it as soberly as I can, I do think that the real subject should become apparent to a reader who is a stranger to your life. I mean such a reader would surely take proper notice of "no one saw. No one knows" and "the drawn shades." – And then there is the extra-literary concern about discretion. What I would do is publish it in some incredibly obscure magazine in Scotland or Romania where none of my friends will have a chance to read it. That way, if you suddenly dropped dead, the scholars would at last find it, and the rest of us, Bill Corbett as well as me, will have long crossed Acheron.[1] And if you don't drop dead (as of course you won't) you could publish it in your next book, and we will hope that the whole thing will have resolved itself and la petite amie's husband will read it and say jocularly over breakfast to her, "so that's what all the trouble was about four years ago, dearest chuck."

("Dearest chuck" you will recognize as what Macbeth calls Lady M. Ha ha.)[2]

I was reading Isaac Babel's Collected Stories and very splendid they are. The accuracy, the kidding rhetoric, as well as the appalling violence. In my naivete I thought, I've GOT to tell Augie about these, they are so HIM. But of course, looking back to the epigraph of I think A C of Airs there I find the Jewish Cossack himself waiting for me in an epigraph.[3] So – another of your influences! Completely Kleinzahlerized, of course, but the kidding rhetoric is also very you, once I think about it. He is terrific, of course. I am especially sorry he never was able to go on with the Odessa Stories, because in some ways they are the best of the lot. He does have a wonderful way of hiding the point of the story in a casual last paragraph which at first sight might read like – oh, a descriptive conclusion to some genre study (as in "The roar in the boiler house. / The drawn shades.") and is anything but.[4]

I've written a couple of pieces of trivia to add to my series, but about them too I feel diffident and won't send them to you until I have something to put with them.

My poem about Fabrice, which the N Yorker accepted over a year ago, may at last be published there on Valentine's Day.[5]

Well I'm glad you had a fairly good time Christmas Day. It was good seeing you. It does seem a long time to have to wait until about a year from now before you are living on Frederick again.

Timothy Liu arrived (Holloway Poet) from Iowa, with greetings, "love", rather, from Forrest, and "this is my partner", a pleasant looking sandy-haired man.[6] Actually T.L. seems very nice – and flattering, auditing all my lectures in the Modern Poetry course (Pound to Bunting). But he started in the front row and is gradually working back – could it be that he is bored and is really working his way out of visibility and the room itself? Can't blame him. (I haven't read any of his poetry yet.)

Hope Lynchburg turns out spectacular. Perhaps you'll meet a minister's ex-wife in a luncheonette and show her new ways of appreciating the Lynchburg body of desire.

That sort of thing.

Love to all,

Th

1. William Corbett (1942–2018), poet, essayist, and editor.
2. 'Be innocent of knowledge, dearest chuck', *Macbeth* (3.2.46).
3. Kleinzahler, *A Calendar of Airs* (1978). The epigraph is from Babel's story 'Guy de Maupassant'.
4. The concluding lines of Kleinzahler's 'Late Autumn Afternoons'.
5. 'To Cupid' (*BC* 100–1).
6. Timothy Liu (1965–) was the visiting Holloway Lecturer at UC Berkeley; see TG to Gander, 25 November 1997, below.

TO *Billy Lux*

TLS Billy Lux

Monday 17 February 1997

1216 Cole Street,
San Francisco,
CA 94117

February 17 / 97

Sweet Lad,

Enough of watching Sesame Street, which I was just watching for the first time this Presidents' Day afternoon with Billy Schuessler, my long-time housemate. Well, everything happens at the wrong time in my life, doesn't it? I was heartily amused and at last learned to count.

[. . .]

I am feeling very guilty about not having written to you in so long. I feel like I have USEd you. I got all those great letters from you, and then you were so kind to me in NY and showed me all those places in the East Village I would never have found on my own, and then I even got a dubious poem out of your wonderful letters, and then I seemingly dropped you .... but I DIDN'T REALLY!!!!!!!!!!

[. . .] We had a wet winter, but this being SF, we've had sun the last couple of days, and I've been grading my students' papers in the back yard. My students this term seem hotter than ever (women excepted, of course), but luckily that weird paternal instinct makes them merely theoretical to me. I do tend to treat them as being just about the same age as me, as friends I suppose, but maybe that's just as well ...... Last night, Bob, another housemate, got the video of Strange Days, so I saw it again. I love Ralph Fiennes, he is so terrific at being unreliable, I think he is one of the hottest actors – I can see from his movie how good he must have been as Hamlet on the stage. And of course, it doesn't hurt that he wears leather all through the movie, which is really ME in many ways, sci fi, drugs, rock and roll, general sexual shoddiness, etc.

My friend (poet) Robert Pinsky, asked me to send him poetry for an on-line literary mag called Slate, so I sent him the only two poems I was ready to let go of right now: one was "Classics", about bartenders' tits, if you remember, the other was "Letters from Manhattan". He took the first, but his reaction to the second was unexpected: he thought it was all about my experiences in Manhattan, and didn't like it because it seemed like "the gay poet" kind of dipping his wick into Manhattan then boasting about it, at age 67. Yes, I can see why he would dislike it – it is charming and sexy when you say it, but if the reader thought I said it, and was pretending to be a wrestler, what's more, it could seem patronising and gross. I'm not sure what to do about it: one thing is I could start it with a salutation, like "Dear TG" or I could junk it. I do love those bits I quote from your letters. But in any case I'll find another way one of these days of paying proper literary tribute to your wonderfully healthy and attractive constant horniness.

I'm still horny all the time, but I try to push it down. For one thing, I'm no Keanu or Billy L, for another, at 67, one might disappoint. ON the other hand, I go to the Hole in the Wall (Hole i' th' Wall, would make it sound more Shakespearean), and I meet people who, because of the drugs I offer them and because of the poor lighting, come back with me for an extraordinary night or so. Weekend of last week I met this 46-year old biker who said he hadn't had sex for six months because he was breaking up with his lover, Juan, and so I thought it my duty to comfort him, which I did. He comforted me too, though I was comfortable enough to start with. But it got better as the night went on.

Well, how about this for resolutions? No more speed after the age of 70, no more alcohol after 75, no more sex after 80 (probably not much more available at that age anyway), and die at 85, the last years being full of really good meals and lots of jokes.

You can push me around in my black leather wheel chair when I am in New York, occasionally abandoning me in the middle of a block at midnight from sheer exasperation. THAT will be the cue for all the young wolves to rush over from the shadows, leap on my body, and force me to come against my will.

Please.

I have written a few more "Gossips" but I'll send you them along when I'm more sure of them. [. . .]

Please also send me an account of everything sexual you have done in the last two months. I am a vampire, it will keep me young to read about it. Pinsky said of the last few lines, about the Rambles and snow-shovelling – "Great, simple, economical, all that Pound says an image should be." And of course, as I wrote back to tell him, it was my glamorous friend in New York who wrote every word of that poem. Mebbe you should write poetry as well as movie scripts.

Didn't you get either of the writers' colony grants? The insensitive cuntlappers! [. . .]

The blossom is out, Linc the cat's skin condition has been cured through a change of food, I have two hot dates promised, one with the forlorn biker for next weekend and the other with my speedfreak friend with different colored pupils for a few weekends after that. All's right with the world!

                    Love,

          Th

---

1. See 'Blues for the New Year, 1997', about Robert Prager: 'He has different- / colored eyes and nothing / about him quite matches' (*BC* 76–7).

TO *Billy Lux*   TLS Billy Lux
Tuesday 10 June 1997

                                        1216 Cole Street,
                                        San Francisco,
                                        CA 94117

                                        June 10 / 97

Dear Billy,

What a delight to get your letter and also find your voice on my answering machine. I liked your account of being an extra for Godzilla, very much, and also your review. Terrific picture of you in army uniform (you should try wearing it to the Lure) – oh yes and Keanu too. That was from Point Break, was it called? I am beginning to think that Keanu doesn't really care about his career at all, he's looking for someone like me but can't find him. Hey Keanu, I'm here! HERE! If you ring my doorbell I'll show you all round the house!

I read out the swimming pool episode to my people ("my people"! sounds like I'm Moses), and it was savoured by all.

The first two weeks of September will be perfect. (I must go to Houston on Sep 23, so I do mean the first two weeks). You are more than welcome to stay here the whole time and not feel you have to go off to inconveniently straight friends. You and my "people" (since I seem to have opted to call them that) are sure to like each other, I will give you my bedroom so that you can bring back anyone you want for the night, and I will leave you alone or not just any way you want. (I didn't mean this to sound like I was going to thrust myself between you & your companion as you wanted, I meant in general, like I could show you a bar or two or you could go out on your own.) (Of course, if you do decide to stay a few days in North Beach or Berkeley, I shall not feel hurt, but don't feel you SHOULD, see what I mean.)

Enclosed another of my little series of miscellaneous gossip-poems.[1] It's on one of the forbidden subjects (sex with students), though I manage to side-step the whole thing quite neatly, as I do in real life.

I met an alarmingly sexy New Yorker over the weekend, with the amazing name of D-L Alvarez (you call him "D"), an artist with a show on here (it hasn't opened yet).[2] He has a Mohawk, and I have to admit it's my first Mohawk. (Actually my second, but the other was purple, so didn't seem serious.) I really don't need another fetish, but he makes a very nice punk at 34 years old. We had a tremendous time, and it is just as well that he doesn't live here or I would get to be a nuisance and keep demanding more tremendous times.

Talking of fetishes, I got a letter from a nineteen year old freshman at Columbus, MO, which is half about how he used to keep a copy of my poem Black Jackets in his locker at high school, and half about how he always liked the belt I was wearing in some picture of me he saw. I answered the letter.[3] (Nineteen! I should hand him over to you. I think I prefer men in their thirties or forties.)

I am rather irritated with New Robert, the guy on the Tenderloin mattress. He is SO strung out these days. After about ten days of speeding, his conversation is so dislocated you can't make anything of it. I wonder if I'm addicted? he says. The answer would appear to be yes. Not that he remembers having had the conversation when you speak to him next day. We did spend a good night together a few weeks ago, and he can be very funny. Example of New Robert's wit: someone came up to him in a bar (unattractive) and grabbed his cock: "please take your hand away," he said, adding "It's personal." (As opposed to "nothing personal".)

Yes, well of course one of the reasons you and I get on so well is that I too am a Slave to Cock. One slavery for another, it's really a very sensible and enjoyable station to have. Do you remember that character in Sammie and Rosie Get Laid, who said that he was always getting dragged around by his cock like someone getting dragged around by a big dog. Well it's not just my cock, it's the other guy's even more. And each new cock has its own extraordinary individuality – they're as different as snowflakes. (Did I ever tell you my story about cocks in NY's own Pleasure Chest? Probably not, I don't tell many people. I'll tell you when you are here. The story is bizarre, kinky, and very enjoyable. The experience was like being in somebody else's fantasy. Preview for September: your Leather Sheherezade will keep you awake with his tales.)

I haven't seen many movies recently, and half the time went to movies someone else wanted to see, and I knew I wouldn't like that much, e.g. Waiting for Guffman, and the Woody Allen musical – but I did like Donnie Brasco VERY much. Johnny Depp I used to watch at first on that terrible TV show[4] mainly for his cheekbones and motorcycle boots, but he really has turned into a lovely actor by now, and somehow Al Pacino works well with him, becoming maybe a little more restrained than sometimes (of course he is good, but there are times when he has acted so hard). It's funny about Mafia movies, isn't it – it's like the Mafia has become movie territory, like the Wars of the Roses was play territory in Shakespeare's time.

But I ramble.

Love,

Thom

1. 'Office Hours' (BC 80–1).
2. D-L Alvarez (1965–), conceptual artist.
3. A fan letter referring to 'Black Jackets' can be found among TG's papers at the Bancroft Library; it is uncertain whether TG's response survives.
4. Depp played Officer Tom Hanson in the police procedural 21 Jump Street.

TO *Billy Lux*   ALS (postcards[1]) Billy Lux
Friday 20 June 1997[2]

1216 Cole Street,
San Francisco,
CA 94117

June 20

Dear Billy –

Well maybe I won't give your mail carrier ideas & I will put these in an envelope. Do you like slicked back hair like this? It can be powerfully attractive. Inevitably it comes to mind that before he came out this guy's best five buddies played circle jerk until they had provided him with enough come to comb his hair back (poor boy, he can't afford Brylcreem). Looks best on dark hair. I once came across a guy from NY who liked slicking back my hair & his with some really old-fashioned over-perfumed guck (named after some flower) which greatly excited him. I hated the scent but his excitement excited me. His name was Joe & he had at one time been door man for the Mine Shaft.

I just had lunch with Augie K, coming from lunch I saw this young dark smoldering firefighter taking a covered cup of coffee back to where his friends were waiting for him in the fire-truck. "Wow, I'd trade in Keanu for him," I remarked to Augie. (Hope nobody tells Keanu.)

Then I had an errand to do on Haight Street & saw three punky beggars who wore their biker jackets very well. One was ugly, one was handsome, one was in between. In a quandary, I gave some change to In-Between. All were sexy.

Coming back, I saw at a bus-stop a dark young Billy Lux type lolling on a seat. [. . .]

Lucky I have a date tonight.

Your card was uncharacteristically obscure. "Must have pic of young poet from 'Show Me' state." Maybe Show Me State is the name of a local college?[3] – The SF Film Festival is showing a movie called Leather Jacket Love Story about a young poet from the country who comes to L.A. and is lucky enough to get taken up by a "gentle" construction worker – he buys his first leather jacket for a poetry reading. I wonder if I wrote the script. It sounds terrible, but I love the description.

I did love "Billy Lux is Available at Bloomingdale's 7th Floor Men's Room." The things you boys get up to!

Well what do you want to know about Alcibiades? He was a gorgeous young man, clearly, & Socrates in the Symposium claims a lot of credit for having slept beside him a whole night & not touched him. Or is it Alcibiades who claims the same thing for not touching somebody whose wisdom he loves so much?[4]

Then – see any standard history of Greece, but especially a 19th century one where there would be more attention to personalities. As I remember it: A was an outstanding soldier, later on, in defending Athens against Sparta, but felt badly betrayed by Athens (got voted out of power or something) so changed over to the Spartans & led the conquering ships & soldiers to the sack of Athens. He was obviously one of the great bisexual spoiled beauties of all time (let's hope queer & not bi) & is featured in a minor part in

Shakespeare's Timon of Athens & in two lines of Gunn's poem Adolescence.
But I really prefer street boys & firefighters to aristocrats nowadays.
[. . .]
I met a visiting New Yorker called "D". He was dark, sexy, had a mohawk
& a wicked sexual imagination, is an artist (here for a show), & his full name
is "D—L Alvarez" (spelt like that). I went to his show afterwards & thought
it was just plain silly – a pile of pebbles with "cinnamon & blood" on it, etc.
I preferred his <u>sexual</u> imagination.

X X X X   Th

P.S. Can I enrol in a freshman class at Show Me State?

1. Three postcards: Ralph Gibson, from *Quadrants* (1975); 'Tom of Finland drawing'
(1962); and 'Bernard (Tattoo by Mr. Ronald, Amsterdam)', from *Tattoo* (1985).
2. Date supplied through internal evidence.
3. Missouri is sometimes known as the 'Show Me' state.
4. Socrates slept beside Alcibiades all night without touching him.

TO *Tony Tanner*   TLS (aerogramme) King's
Wednesday 2 July 1997

1216 Cole Street,

San Francisco,

CA 94117,

USA

July 2 / 97

Dear Tony,
    It's an incredibly hot day, and only the end of the morning, but I've
already done two good things, viz. booked Mike's and my tickets to Venice
in October and been to the Farmer's Market at Civic Center, which always
raises my spirits, the sight of all those tomatoes and nectarines and ears of
corn and arugula etc so bright and ripe and delicious. I have tried to write
a poem about it all, but have never succeeded: there doesn't seem to be the
vocabulary. Have to fall back on Goblin Market, I guess.
    I should really be starting the big chapter in the book I am trying to write
about my hero Bunting, but I keep finding excuses for postponing it, day
after day, even though I know what I want to say. But this is a better impulse,
to write to you. I think of you more often than I write, you know that, I hope,
and one thing brings you very much to mind, though it may surprise you that
it does.

That is, Don Doody, who has had emphysema for some time, apparently is in quite considerable pain, and I suppose is dying. I heard this from a letter written by a woman-friend who sees him every week. They have been discussing Shakespeare's plays every Thursday for several years. She wrote that he can barely walk to his mailbox in his building, and "there is no doubt in my mind that he is in far more distress than he can acknowledge." He lives in New York, with a cat and a straight flat-mate he seldom sees, and has kept hardly any books and no records, except for Shakespeare's plays and copies of videos of all the English TV versions of the plays (sooner him than me, I hate most of those productions). I phoned him yesterday, and he sounded pleased to hear from me – we chatted for half an hour but he wouldn't admit to any pain though acknowledging the limitations on his activity. Scrappy to the end! Actually, he was charming. Ever the bully, I told him he ought to see a doctor if only for medication to help pain.

I have no idea how you feel about him nowadays, but if you did feel like writing to him, his address is: [. . .]. Of course it would be hypocritical to write if you still feel about him as you did in the early 1970s.[1]

My own tendency is to be cheerful, to be evasive about ugly things and about my own troubles, to avoid talking about unhappinesses as if to disregard them would be to banish them, and I think you share something of the same tendency, though heaven knows you had had a Packard's van load more of misfortunes than I have had. What I have had to learn from Don is that the abrasiveness and difficultness he exemplifies so often is also a good and truthful way of dealing with one's life. I think he tells the truth a lot more than I do (though he often gets it wrong, due to a liking for conspiracy theory) and I know he has far more courage. When once I wrote a poem about him, called Crosswords, I mentioned how when I sat down on the sofa on which he lived and slept when he lived on 22nd St (NY) I found it wasn't soft at all, but just a plank covered in a blanket. He has always been unwilling to see possibilities in softness, and has always seen it as proper to opt for hardness. Though I have often thought him wrong in his judgments (at least half the time), I respect the fact that he has always refused to take easy ways. Anyway, I feel for him in his pain, admire his stoicism, and already miss him.

Difficult to follow this with small talk.

All my love,

Thom

1. See TG to Tanner, 3 June 1971, n. 1, above.

Saturday 11 October 1997

> 1216 Cole Street,
> San Francisco,
> CA 94117
>
> Oct 11 / 97

Dear Commodore,

A male porn magazine ran a page in which they had asked various people, indicated only by their initials "What do you like to be called during sex?" Among various endearing names, like "Sir", "Sweetheart", and "Sluthole", came "Commodore or Commandant". Too much Star Trek, no doubt. But anyone who called me that at the moment of orgasm would receive my (at least verbal) back of the hand.

Well, Mike and I are off to Venice on Tuesday, I think more because I feel I ought to do something grandiose with him every year with the MacArthur loot than because we actually want to go to Venice again. Well, yes, we are looking forward to it. Anyway, I am trying madly to get a draft of my essay about Rochester, the lord not the city, ready to at least revise on my return.[1] Difficult not to like a man to whom the following could be attributed (it's considered of doubtful authorship):

THE WISH

Oh that I now could by some Chymic Art
To Sperm convert my Vitals and my Heart,
That at one Thrust I might my Soul translate,
And in the Womb myself regenerate:
There Steep'd in Lust, nine months I would remain
Then boldly fuck my Passage out again.

Even having such a poem attributed to one would redound to one's credit. And the other thing is to answer your TWO letters, which put me to shame. I note your growing acceptance of and perhaps even liking for teaching. I figure it's an honorable job, unlike strip-mining, and quite possibly useful, if you can be as good as your best teachers. Anybody who introduces me to some good poems I didn't know before has my deepest gratitude. Also a great deal about poetry can be taught even to those who can't write it. The other thing I notice is that Jorie, far from being the villainous bitch you were afraid she'd be, has turned out to be a faintly comic character you even have a certain fondness for. But she's still unreadable, isn't she?

Yes, I once met Donald Justice. He subrented our place in North Beach for 1964-5, but rapidly underwent a complete breakdown, poor devil, and had to be carried away, thus un-sub-renting it. He heard the tramp of the murderous G.I. boots on the front steps and thought a lot about H-bombs. This was at the time of the Vietnam war starting to escalate. He writes sweet poetry. (Mildly sweet.)

I went down to Houston to give a wonderfully overpaid reading there. It rained all the time so I spent my first day and night reading in my hotel room. It was nice seeing the Levines & Cynthia Macdonald, and meeting Ed Hirsch, whom I found genial and funny and unpretentious. An attractive NY accent too. It does look like an awful city, though.

I am having an affair, or whatever you may want to call it, with a wonderful 41-year old hunk called Bruce. All you need to know about him is that he has a red truck and has no idea that I am a minor celebrity, nor would he be especially interested if he did have one, an idea I mean. Thus, oh glory, I am treated as a sex object. I always envied Marilyn Monroe, as every man did.

[. . .]

I am to read at the U of Utah in December, but I know how to handle those Mormons (I hope). Just don't read poetry about coffee or tea. I am to read with Donald Hall at the Herbst Theater here in January and that quite unnerves me. He was quite a (literary) friend to me in my 20s, and was very generous. I liked his long poem, which came much later, but his poetry of the last few years has been, well, deplorable, all about his sainted wife, Jane Kenyon, who is dead. Acc to Simone, much of the audience who come to hear him nowadays comes to hear about her. An example of his poems about her is to be found in the last Threepenny Review – look no further. I think I will ask if I can go first, and read nothing but ribald Rochesterian poems. R ends a drinking song

> With wine I wash away my cares,
> And then to cunt again.

Tim Liu is as you say a pleasant man and a boring poet. Ric Caddell (talking of boring poets) has published a profusely illustrated 64-page life of BB called A Northern Life. It looks like the kind of thing you buy at the gift shop counter of the Bunting Institute in Durham. Maybe I'll say that in the review the TLS want me to write.[2] But RC is making a bit of a, er, career out of Bunting, isn't he?

Well, enough of malice. I have written nothing, prose or verse, since April, but I probably told you that before and it might be a good idea for the world to stop being afflicted by my production. So, Commander, tell me when you expect to come here, the two weeks, and remember, I can always lend you my room and sleep in my work room.

Love,

Th

1. 'St John the Rake: Rochester's Poetry', in *Green Thoughts, Green Shades: Essays by Contemporary Poets on the Early Modern Lyric*, ed. Post (2002), 242–56; uncollected.
2. TG reviewed *Basil Bunting: A Northern Life* (1997) in the *Times Literary Supplement* (26 December 1997), 24; uncollected.

TO *Clive Wilmer*

TLS Clive Wilmer

Sunday 16 November 1997

1216 Cole Street,
San Francisco,
CA 94117

Nov 16 / 97

Dear Clive,

Thank you for your two letters, and also for the version of Horace. This has for some time been one of my favorite poems by him, and I once even fantasized about doing a version of it myself. I love Milton's absurdly latinate version, for reasons I can't well explain to myself (how about "always vacant always amiable"?).[1] I think yours is greatly superior to his and an almost complete success. The beginning is especially successful, I think you deal well with simplex munditiis (which implies careless without quite saying it) and I find your ending funny and apt – slightly Poundian (I mean the Pound of Sextus Propertius). I'm not always sure about it metrically – do you think of it as being accentual, by any chance? But the first three lines are regular iambics, I'd say ("down there" a trochee). Two lines that trouble me rhythmically are 4 and 15. Would it be possible to say "braid blond hair" for "braid your blond hair" and "charges heavy premiums" for "charges a heavy premium". It is a splendid poem, the way you have rendered it, and completely avoids the grandiloquence of The Falls.

[. . .]

We stayed in Venice that whole two weeks and walked steadily every day. Mike found what I'd been telling him for a couple of years is true, that I'm much slower than I was. "Walking with you is like walking with my mother," he said, his mother being 93. Yes, TG, the young gazelle, now walks old. Not Mike though, only 2 years younger than I. But we did get about,

628

and maybe this time we saw everything – except the glass-blowing, since neither of us cares much for Venetian glass. But we even went to Giudecca this time, to Torcello again of course (I'm afraid a Holocaust has taken the wild cats), and saw the baroquest altar ever in SS. Giovanni and Paolo. And saw the handsomest young firemen ever, lolling around at the bottom of some palatial staircase in a building that must have been a fire station – we glimpsed them through an open door one dark evening – I suggested they must have been discussing beauty treatments. We also identified the Palazzo where the Wings of a Dove is supposed to end. One day we chanced across S. Maria dei Miracoli, which we had missed before. All marble, and inside, as if that wasn't enough, it was <u>lined</u> with marble. There was a cordon across the bottom of the steps to the altar, thus preventing us from getting a close look at the mermaids twining up with the putti. I wasn't sure whether to offer money to the grumpy old verger to get a closer look, but just then he retired for a minute to some inner room – maybe to have a piss – so I jumped over and got my closer look before he had returned.

We were in the Accademia hotel, no longer cheap but wonderful, on a junction of the Grand Canal and two smaller canals had a good time on the vaporettos, loved the Carpaccios again, and the two Giorgiones, had probably the best pesto ever, and I conceived a distaste for spaghetti with cuttlefish and ink. The trip returning was awfully tiring – everything went well, it was on time, and the Lufthansa food is still pretty good, but such a long journey makes me feel my age and I wonder if I'll ever feel up to doing it again!

[. . .]

Augie is still away but I believe is coming back here to live when his term at Iowa is over – to live here for at least 6 months. He does have a problem with not being able to get any job except linoleum-laying locally.

I have written a few extra instalments of Gossip, but they are too trivial to send you, whether successful or not. I think I should finish that off by the end of next year, and then send the book to Faber. Probably my last book? But I have always thought each book was my last.

The only trouble with Venice is that a certain tiredness with Tintoretto does tend to set in. All those saintly heads seen in free fall from odd angles. You start longing for Carpaccio's little dog regarding Saint Jerome. Still, better the whole of the Scuola di San Rocco than even ONE Tiepolo.

[. . .]

    Love,
        Th

1. Wilmer's poem 'To Pyrrha' is a translation of Horace's Ode 1.5. Milton's translation begins, 'What slender youth bedew'd with liquid odours'.

TO *Forrest Gander*   ALS (postcard[1]) Yale

Tuesday 25 November 1997

1216 Cole St.,

San Francisco, CA 94117

Nov 25 / 97

Dear Forrest,

Don't know if I ever thanked you for taking my poems for the Colorado Review.[2] Anyway, I do. [. . .]

Something, however, I <u>don't</u> have to thank you for. Tim Liu tells people you said that I have AIDS. Not true. I'm more cautious than I may seem. Let me say I don't consider it dishonorable to be sick, but I get the test once a year, the last one as it happened in October, and as usual I was HIV negative. So – one romance for another: if anybody else says you have told them this, I'll say I got it from you!

Happy Thanksgiving (two days away)

Thom

1. C. E. Redman, *The Westerner Lodge* (1940s).
2. 'The Artist as an Old Man' (*BC* 63–4); 'Letters from Manhattan' (*BC* 71–2); and 'Blues for the New Year, 1997' (*BC* 76–7).

1998

TO *Billy Lux*   TLS Billy Lux

Sunday 11 January 1998[1]

1216 Cole Street,

San Francisco,

CA 94117

Jan 11 maybe

Dear Billy –

[. . .]

I'm really snuggling down into the wonderful wrestler's sweatshirt you
gave me, in this continuously rainy weather, much appreciating its built-in
muff where the hands can meet and grope each other for warmth. I was also
wearing the Yankees cap you gave me, yesterday, and went to the Hole in
the Wall. There I met the Gunn-type, or certainly one of the Gunn major
types. Pat, just hitched from New Orleans, in a biker jacket, long haired, not
dangerous, too unfocused to be that, certainly hustling for a place to have sex
and stay the night, good-natured (you want to feel my cock? Here . . . . it was
already out of his pants), so I thought he deserved a beer, and <u>didn't</u> bring
him home. [. . .] Someone I <u>did</u> bring home, for the whole works, for three
weekends, was Tony the ex-Marine, who mostly sleeps outside and spends all
his welfare money on speed. Tony is very fine looking, claims to be bisexual
but despises women (like Shakespeare in the Sonnets he thinks of women as
simply sexual holes for seminal deposit), but as far as he can lives on speed
so is unreliable and would probably sell his grandmother for a gram of the
drug (that's better than some people I've come across, who would sell their
grandmother for a quarter of it – Price Granma High, boys!). I had someone
over for the night on Friday, a nice middle-class young man, the sex seemed
a bit empty without ANY drugs at all (!), somehow a bit flat, like Near Beer,
but it was nice hugging him all night while the heavy rain fell outside.

[. . .]

I used to keep my beard dark, as the white crept in, with Miss Clairol.
There is now something much easier to use called Just For Men, even a
special kind for use on moustache and beard, which is marvellous because it

leaves enough grey hairs to look realistic. (I use it on my hair, sybaritic self-abuser that I am.) [. . .]

Oh yes, Venice. [. . .] You would have agreed with us in being bowled over by the Venetian boys, 18-30, perfect, gorgeous, sexy, and ALWAYS joshing and horseplaying with one another. We passed a large castellated building on one of our walks, & at that moment a motorboat drew up with five handsome young men on it. Then they got off, and it was four cops & their handcuffed prisoner. They marched him into the building & they & their prisoner were all joking and laughing like old friends reunited. Maybe they were. I would have loved to have witnessed the orgy that should have taken place when they got inside. There were two, probably 18 years old, who'd just got daring punk haircuts, beside us on a vaporetto, playing Tic-tac-toe, on their way home to one of the islands. [. . .]

I must stop. My typing has gotten chaotic.
[. . .]

Love,

Thom

1. Date supplied through internal evidence.

TO *Mary and Catherine Thomson*

TLS (aerogramme) Jenny Fremlin

Monday 22 June 1998

1216 Cole Street,
San Francisco,
CA 94117

June 22 / 98

Dear Aunts,

Ander said you wrote saying you don't get many letters from me nowadays, so I'll try to write more often. The last term was very busy for me, partly because I get tired more easily, partly because I offered to teach an extra course which had suddenly been left teacherless at the start of term (showing off to myself, which I came to regret!), so I was running to catch up with myself all term. It all went off well, I get on well with my students, and I must say the older I get the more I feed off their youth and energy, like a wicked old vampire. Then at the end of term, the day after, I had to go to New York, which was the last thing I needed to do, to be presented a Medal of Merit from the American Academy of Arts and Letters. (!) It sounds like a Boy Scout medal, but it was actually for poetry. [. . .] Back to San Francisco, and Ander came to stay for ten days. The weather was appalling, damp mist and overcast, until the day he left, when suddenly the summer weather started. However, he didn't mind, and walked day after day up the highest hills, and I think enjoyed himself. We were sorry Bett couldn't come with him this time – her broken spine of 20 years ago making it difficult for her to travel these days – but they spoke every day on the phone, which I thought was sweet, like young lovers. I am glad he found someone to love him at last. [. . .]

Like the rest of the world, we had a strange winter. It took the form of constant rain – storm succeeding storm sometimes immediately. The newspaper was amused to report when it got to 40 days and 40 nights, but it went way over that. We ended up with the highest rainfall (double our usual) in over 100 years. And to think that sometimes we have droughts where we have to avoid flushing lavatories.

Mike's birthday a few weeks ago, I made two beautiful roast chickens for 8 people. The secret of a perfect chicken is obvious, though it took me a while to learn it. You baste with butter every ten minutes, so how can anybody fail when what you end up with is chicken meat soaked with butter? There were also two homemade cakes.

We grow every herb you can think of (except basil, which the snails like as much as we do), also sorrel, for soups, and raspberries, which are having a bumper year – I suppose due to all that rain.

Much love, and to Jenny & Joe as well,
Thom

TO *Clive Wilmer*   TLS Clive Wilmer
Monday 14 September 1998

1216 Cole Street,
San Francisco,
CA 94117

Sep 14 / 98

Dear Clive,
    It is certainly a long time since I wrote, I think partly because I have written so very little poetry this year. Our friendship is a friendship of all sorts I hope by now, and yet it was originally just a literary friendship (from which everything else sprang) and I still feel that when I have nothing to show you

by way of composition I am not worth your consideration. That is nonsense, of course, and I must get rid of that sense of inadequacy, especially if this is merely a prelude to the last barrenness which most writers enter a good time before dying. Ho hum. It has been a strange year in every way, but then isn't EVERY year a strange year, really? I went the other day, with Augie, as result of his repeated urgings, to the Palace of the Legion of Honor to see a huge show of Stanley Spencer. He dotes on SS, but even though I found the retrospective wonderfully interesting as a kind of narrative, I can't like him much. Another friend, Simone Di Piero, says of SS that all the excitement is in his subject matter and not in the execution, which I find a deeply perceptive comment. Anyway, I kept thinking of the time you and I went up there, to the same place I mean, by bus – and whether we went inside or not I can't remember, but we then went beyond the golf course to an idyllic early summer tangle of wild flowers and escaped garden flowers gone wild, and trees on precipitous paths down the slopes of Land's End above the rocks and exploding waves. I was so proud of it all, because this was what I love about California.

[. . .] As for the Bunting book, as soon as I said it was off to Wm [Cookson], suddenly it began to seem a possibility again, ideas started to take shape, and maybe I will write it one of these days after all. No, I really can't write the review of Davie that you ask for – I am sorry, and in another year I would delight in making such a review a place for setting down my thoughts about Donald and his importance, but the whole thought of writing a review – any review – is somehow repellent to me, and in any case I am to be traveling giving self-important poetry readings at self-important places – and what time I shall have to work at my desk will have to be devoted to preparing my courses for next term.

[. . .]

Wm Cookson tells me that you are organizing a 70th birthday celebration among the watercolorist pages of his nowadays rather uninteresting magazine.[1] Well, thank you – you are as usual too kind, and isn't it rather soon after the last one? I am flattered, but you are going to get increasingly weary of this sort of thing at my 80th, 90th, and maybe 100th birthdays. Maybe we should be organizing a celebration for you.

Do you know James Campbell? He visited here last year, and I gt on with him so well that I sent him round to Augie and to Wendy Lesser, both of whom liked him too and he them. He is the author of a truly splendid life of James Baldwin and is also "J.C." who is unkind and sarcastic about a lot of people I don't like and a few I do in the TLS every week.[2] He wants to do a series of four 20 minute interviews of me for the BBC.[3] It is still just a proposal, but I said yes, stipulating that he study your Paris Review interview, and also meaning (and fully meaning) that he's going to have to think hard to ask me about anything I haven't talked about before. But he is a nice and articulate man, and my contention is that it's the good interviewer who makes a good interview, so it should be OK, if it all comes off. (But as you know, I'm not exactly a Gore Vidal when it comes to conversation.) Maybe you might be interested in some transcriptions for the Agenda issue, who knows.

I have been reading Oblomov, as it is about someone like me, terminally lazy and unproductive.

I have also been reading 90 (yes 90) books of poetry as one of the 3 judges for a big poetry award. I thought it should go to a poet called Tom Sleigh, for a splendid book called THE CHAIN, but the other two judges ganged up on me and it will go to Frank Bidart. I like Frank's odd poetry, but not this book, DESIRE, which seems to me easily his worst. Still, I am only too easy to bully. Louise Gluck, one of the other judges, said of the long poem in this book: "I found it thrilling." Well, I found it boring, but was too polite to say so.

So, you penetrated the center of the Lawrence tabernacle! You are right about his stories – the best of them are among the best ever written. I adore 'Samson and Delilah', a seldom mentioned one. On the other hand 'The Horse Dealer's Daughter' at its worst moments is what we used to call like a bad novelette 'the kind of thing the servant classes might like'. I can't read his novels any more, but I still love a lot of the stories and poems. I'm going to teach the poems next term, for the first time in years.

[. . .]

Still, I'm a bitter old asshole, sitting under my umbrella in the yard and jealous of all the people who publish a new book every two years. My next book, probably my last, will go off to the publishers the day I retire, and so come out at the end of 99 or the beginning of the millennium.

[. . .]

Enough, from your favorite aunt,

Th

1. See 'Thom Gunn at Seventy', *Agenda* 37, no. 2–3 (Autumn–Winter 1999), 7–122.
2. Campbell, *Talking at the Gates: A Life of James Baldwin* (1991).
3. 'Between Air and Moving Ocean', a series of five conversations between TG and Campbell, was broadcast on BBC Radio 3 in May 1999 and published as *Thom Gunn in Conversation with James Campbell* (2000).

Sunday 18 October 1998

1216 Cole Street,
San Francisco,
CA 94117
October 18 / 98

Dear Tony,

I just came back from a tour of my Eastern dominions, actually giving poetry readings as excuse and looking up friends for fun, to find a letter from Clive telling me about your illness. He said you were about to go into hospital for a biopsy of the liver. Well, I imagine the results of that have been given to you by now, and I hope they are the best. Though I fear they seldom are. You must be feeling terrible – you are still a vibrant young man, after all – and I am sure you have some difficult times ahead. Radiotherapy can hardly be fun, any more than operations and things like that. But you have always been a man of tremendous strength. You probably don't think that yourself, since people tend to emphasize their own weaknesses, but when you think what you went through before with the depression and the incapacitation and the subsequently limited life you have been forced to lead, it is certainly your strength in face of all that that [is] apparent. When I think how little I would have been up to all that! I'd have been reduced to a huge quivering jelly of self-pity and wept myself into extinction. I say all this, not to cheer you up (though of course I do want to cheer you up) but to remind you what huge resources you should know you have. I am no Christian Scientist, but I do believe that it's some kind of faith in the combination of body and mind that brings us through most of the time.

I also must say that you have been without question one of the friends who has meant most to me in my life. I know it is difficult to keep up the full vitality of a friendship when separated by 6000 miles, but you have always been and will go on being a reference point and a reminder to me not only of affection but of the way to lead a life. Doesn't that sound pompous? But I mean it: I think of things you have said, jokes you have made, quotations, judgments, conclusions, funny stories, and they constantly recur to me as reference points as they do from Mike, my mother, Tony White and I am not sure anybody else in such profusion. I'll bet that many of your students would say the same thing, apart from friends who were not your students in the first place.

One of the people I looked up in New York was of course Don. It's difficult to know how he is, since he is unfailingly stoical and will not admit to any pain of any sort. He tends to sleep more and more, it appears, doesn't read, drinks brandy, smokes defiantly, sees no doctor, enjoys your prefaces to Shakespeare, has a complete set of videos of the (I think lamentable) BBC productions of Shakespeare, and was surprised and overjoyed to get your letter. "Guess who I heard from?" he said over the phone. I said I couldn't guess, of course.

Our house holds together solidly enough. It does seem to have been a good idea to assemble a family in which the children will not disappear into college or marriage. My recent trip was invigorating: somehow doing a bunch of readings for enthusiastic strangers got me writing poetry again – which I hadn't been able to do since last February. I'm now getting my courses ready for what will be my last semester before I retire: I think it's a good idea to retire while you're still on top of things, having had enough doddering teachers in my past to choose not to be among them . . .

Well dear friend, be strong, get well, be patient with your errant body!

Mike sends his love especially, and so do I –

& love to Nadia

X X X X

Thom

TO *Douglas Chambers*   TLS Toronto
Tuesday 20 October 1998[1]

[1216 Cole Street,
San Francisco,
CA 94117]

Dear Douglas,

[. . .] I am selfishly sorry you are giving up your place in Cabbage Town, where I had at least two maybe three gorgeous visits, but I am unselfishly glad that you are changing to the life you most want to lead. Also among my mail were a letter from Clive Wilmer and two new poems from Jim Powell. The letter from Clive told me that our friend Tony Tanner has cancer of the prostate, kidney, and liver, which doesn't leave much room for hope, I suppose. He was one of my closest friends for quite a few years, but 6000 miles and very brief visits on my part certainly dilute a friendship. He is a wonderful man, with his own kind of vitality, from whom I have learned so much. Meanwhile I visited Don Doody in New York, and the effects of emphysema were more apparent. Clint Cline I first met as a jolly little ex-sailor died early this year. This is a new kind of death – my contemporaries, not my juniors and not from AIDS. I bounce along meanwhile in dreadfully good health, as full of sexual greed as ever and it seems usually getting what I want. [. . .] I got such a wonderful reception at Yale, my first stop, about 200 students, who all apparently read me in their freshman year. I hadn't written a thing since February, or even wanted to, except in a kind of abstract way that never leads anywhere, but all this informed attention flattered me in to playing around in my notebook. New York was almost nonstop fun, looking up all my friends, and then I went into a bar on Christopher Street, which is much less depressing now than it was last year, and there one Saturday afternoon was this gorgeous Puerto Rican biker-bartender – he propositioned me, and at 8 o'clock I took him back to my hotel for the night, and it turned out he had a lot of cocaine on him, with which he was very generous, so we practiced homosexualist perversions till after dawn, and he was as sweet-natured as he was sexy. I never thought I'd be that lucky at 69. On another occasion, in a bar, a guy said if I came back with him, we could take some viagra together!!!!! Well, that's a first, but he was unappealing in all sorts of ways and I was untempted. But I was amused. New York was sunny and friendly and full of small excitements. I saw two terrific movies, you may yourself have seen, There's Something About Mary and The Opposite of Sex, both similar in one way – a brilliant kind of well-written and acted farce venturing into a largely taboo subjects. By farce I mean a bit like early Shaw (You Never Can Tell, etc.), smart and daring.

After two weeks, to Washington to read at the L of Congress with David Ferry, an awfully fine poet (though his Horace is disappointing). I really think Imperial Rome must have looked like this – lots of grandiose new marble, all designed to impress with scale and power. I had a fairly good time the one full day there, walked around in the sun, and dipped into the National Gallery where I became very attached to the Vuillards, and started the enclosed poem on the steps in front.[2] It's obviously a good Fall for me! The other poem tells its own story. Andy is my big new crush, and every word of the poem is literally true.[3]

Well, don't you think that Coleridge thought Keats lower-class, "ill-dressed", wasn't it? Byron also sneered at him as a Cockney and so did the Quarterlies. Classes are not distinguished by dress nowadays, but they sure were until 50 years ago. Keats at one stage "dressed like a sailor" – & I don't believe that means cute!

LOVE

Thom

[. . .]

1. Date supplied through internal evidence.
2. 'Painting by Vuillard' (*BC* 49).
3. 'Front Door Man' (*BC* 102–4).

1999

TO *Clive Wilmer*

Saturday 9 January 1999

TLS Clive Wilmer

1216 Cole Street,
San Francisco,
CA 94117
USA

Jan 9 / 99

Dear Clive,

I owe you many thanks, not only for letters, but for your envelope full of clippings of obituaries, and also for the book by Romer, which was full of nice dry short poems – I liked the dryness and the shortness.[1] Your obits were splendid, but the one I most liked was Colin MacCabe's, who no doubt is famous, but is just a name to me: I liked the way he included such a frank account of Tony's troubles.[2] Yes, I miss Tony, but only as one misses someone who hasn't been here; for you obviously the loss is the more poignant in that he was a part of your daily life and is now a gap. We corresponded pretty regularly for years, I seem to remember, but after his worst breakdown at Johns Hopkins, where I did visit him for a day and a night, he didn't seem able to write to me much. I think I was part of America, and America was associated with all the worst things that had happened to him. I remember one occasion after that when he actually astonished me by saying, "You know, I hate America," a remark on which I felt unable to comment. We wrote to one another very little after that, and I found him evasive, as he probably found me intrusive. As for his comments on my writing, where he was of the greatest help was while I was writing "Misanthropos" – that was the year I was in England. I sent him draft after draft of the many sections of it, and must have bored him to death.

I do remember his giving a party at Kings (I think you were there) and putting on a record, then new, of Tom Jones' "It's not unusual / to be in love with anyone," and as the first line was sung saying to himself, but audibly, "it is, actually". He was rejoicing in Marcia being there and I suppose of their marriage being assured. He was very happy that year.

[. . .]

I was very proud to have his first book dedicated to me.[3]

We first met when I was a young teacher at Berkeley and he was doing graduate work there, being close in age. We met at dinner given by [F. W.] Bateson and his wife, and immediately took to one another hugely. After that we went everywhere together, like Two Musketeers. (He gave me my first joint. It had no effect.) When John Berryman, teaching at the university, wanted to meet me and wrote suggesting lunch, I brought along Tony.[4] Berryman was delighted, and even wrote a (later rejected) Dream Song, beginning:

> Gunn and Tanner, Tanner and Gunn
> Made things easier in the sun,
> The California Spring sun . . .

(You can see why he rejected it!)

I doubt if there is anything you can use for your article on the dear man, but my memories of him are primarily of an enjoyer of life, who loved drinking and telling jokes and reading books and knowing people – not really characteristic, perhaps of one who had so many mishaps.[5]

[. . .]

Oh yes, I forgot to tell you that I (re)read With the Grain, really a very good book.[6] But one thing about DD (not at all true of TT) was that he could only seldom write, however much to praise somebody, without also scolding somebody else in the process. That is part of the dreaded Leavis-Winters Syndrome: must get some scolding in! However, he was always more than kind to me – all the more amazing when you consider how different he and I always were.

I must finish,

Love

Thom

1. Stephen Romer, *Tribute* (1998).
2. MacCabe, 'Obituary: Professor Tony Tanner', *The Independent* (9 December 1998), 7.
3. See TG to Tanner, 31 August 1963, above.
4. See TG to Haffenden, 28 February 1975, above.
5. Wilmer, 'Tony Tanner (1935–1998), A Memoir and a Tribute', *PN Review* 127 (May–June 1999), 10–12.
6. Davie, *With the Grain: Essays on Thomas Hardy and Modern British Poetry*, ed. Wilmer (1998).

1216 Cole Street,
San Francisco,
CA 94117

Feb 28 / 99

Dear Augie,
I have so many things to be grateful to you for – shuttle tickets, letter, and the book. I'm especially delighted with the book, as he, Johnson, is such an uninteresting poet I'd never have guessed he wrote such neatly phrased prose.[1] I love Jesus' Son – it's not quite the American Trainspotting, but in some ways better. "The sky was as blue and brainless as the love of God" – now if I could write such a sentence, I'd blow my brains out with satisfaction, knowing I could never do such a thing again. I love the way the book has so many drugs, bars, car wrecks, and unsatisfactory couplings.

Today I'm taking Billy Lux to Wendy's book party in North Beach. [. . .] He is having a great time in SF, subletting an apartment as I suppose you know, giving daily blow jobs to our youth in Buena Vista Park, and paying pretty steady attention to a Mexican waiter he has met. I have yet to come across evidence that BL can lose his temper over anything or be mean to people. This makes him very comfortable to be around, especially because he says so many things that make me laugh.

As for me, I had a 36 hour sexual epiphany with a certain John Ambrioso[2] two weeks ago. I love saying his name because it is so like ambrosia. His name is Sicilian and his parents are Cuban, but he was born and raised in Kentucky. Lucky Kentucky! Of course, like so many of my partners these days, he is a drug addict killing himself with excess because he knows he is dying of AIDS anyway. He has great verve and energy and good looks coupled with a puzzling low esteem for himself. I will make it my ambition to increase said esteem, since I can think of several reasons why anyone would want to be John Ambrioso.

I am bored with teaching and am not teaching especially well, so I will be pretty glad to retire at the end of term. People say, "What will you do when you retire?" (I used to say that, and I realise how patronising it must have sounded, as if one wasn't good for anything but teaching) and I say, "when I wake up and I hear the rain on the window pane, I'll simply turn over and go back to sleep". But of course I am well trained for numerous second careers, for example a drinking career, a sexual career (surely there might be a demand for seventy-year old prostitutes), and a lazy career.

I saw <u>Shakespeare in Love</u> – I thought I'd be too hardened to like it – but even give the fact that its basic premise is ridiculous and that it's pure fantasy and surely Shakespeare was really on the homely side, found it deeply charming and clever. ("As if charm could be deep.")[3]

Glad that things seem all right in Austin. Must be some pleasant cowgirls among your students. If you DO get into the country around there, remember it is infested with rattlesnakes. Watch out for the dust storms. Glad you are seeing [Christopher] Middleton. I can't help feeling slightly sorry for the graduate student who lives across the street "with his sweet nurse wife": he doesn't know yet about you and the nurses. Not surprised that Mark Doty has a lot of charm – you can tell that from his poetry, that's its trouble. Yes, I wonder who'll be in charge of us after Christopher Reid, maybe Jane Feavor on her own. In a couple of months you'll be taking 2 showers a day, to cool off, & the drink will become iced tea.

X X X

Th

1. Denis Johnson, *Jesus' Son* (1992).
2. For John Ambrioso, see next letter and Glossary of Names.
3. See 'Hi' (*BC* 68).

TO *John Ambrioso*[1]   ALS (postcard[2]) John Ambrioso
Saturday 27 March 1999[3]

[1216 Cole Street,
San Francisco,
CA 94117]

Saturday

Hi John,

I'm writing really just to say hello, and to say that our 2 times together were out of this world, and thank you! I have never been so high in my life as this last time, & it was all great – you are the best, my friend. Sleeping in your wooden bed that 2nd night was in a way as good as anything. You are as generous and as hospitable as you are hot.

I'm sorry I will not be available for serious sex before the end of May – it's my job, I take so long to come down from drugs – but I warn you that at that time your ass & cock will be liable to major violations. That is a promise.

[. . .]

[Robert Prager] tells me you have had a bad cold this last week, & have been laid up. Be careful – you've got a body that should be looked after, in every possible way. It should also be given every pleasure you want. [. . .]

I have been thinking about you quite a bit & I have been doing John-influenced things when I jack off. (I didn't come till Wednesday, but I did a lot of trying.) John-influenced: by that I mean latex, butt plugs, etc. Otherwise I got in a lot of sleep all week.

Some time when you are hungry, I'd like to take you out to dinner – probably a weekend would be best. I want to keep your body in shape for my sexual exploitation. (I don't need to tell you how my body enjoys your sexual exploitation.)

Your friend for ever,
Thom

1. John Ambrioso (1962–), late boyfriend of TG. See Glossary of Names.
2. One postcard: two baby pigs (unattributed); one pornographic illustration showing four hypermasculine leathermen fistfucking each other.
3. Date supplied through internal evidence.

TO *Elaine Feinstein*[1]   TLS Manchester
Tuesday 3 August 1999

1216 Cole Street,
San Francisco,
CA 94117

August 3, 99

Dear Elaine,

Well, the surprise is that Ted and I didn't know one another at Cambridge. He was a year or two behind me, but we did overlap. I'm not sure that I had even heard of him when I was there, the reason being that he didn't, I believe, publish any poetry until I had left: probably the first I read of him was in Karl Miller's anthology Poetry from Cambridge, which didn't impress me, and then The Hawk in the Rain, which dazzled me with its fearless energy. We didn't meet until our publisher Charles Monteith took us both out to lunch in 1960, when I was briefly in England. His purpose was to suggest (a) the Selected Poems by both of us which was to come out in the next year or two (it was no collaboration, being a selection from previously published work), (b) a Faber Book of English Verse (edited by both of us: we wrote a lot of letters to each other about this, but we never got it done because we decided we had to read everything, <u>everything</u> ever written in English poetry, and I haven't really got to the end of that yet), and (c) the Five American Poets we did actually publish in the early sixties. I had lunch with Ted and Sylvia (I was meeting her for the first time), shortly after, and then I had to return to California to start the new term, so anyway I never knew him pre-Sylvia. He and I always had good, but hardly close relations, and came to realize soon that our lives were widely different projects, though we wrote appreciative letters to one another every few years.

Somebody you ought to contact if possible is Tony Dyson. I believe he is ill, and sees almost no one, but someone he does see is Brian Cox. You might try through him. Dyson has a lot of fascinating facts about both Ted and Sylvia, who confided in him at least as much as in Alvarez, and maybe his memory is more modest. He's a nice man, too, as you probably know.

> Good luck with your book,
> Thom

1. Elaine Feinstein (1930–2019), poet, novelist and biographer. Ted Hughes had died in 1998 and Feinstein was writing a biography: *Ted Hughes: The Life of a Poet* (2001).

TO *John Ambrioso*   ALS (postcard[1]) John Ambrioso
c. September 1999[2]

> [1216 Cole Street,
> San Francisco,
> CA 94117]

Hello John –

This must mean I am thinking of you, as usual. – Difficult to have to wait to the middle of November, but there it is. (I get back from 10 days in New York late Tuesday Nov 16 – pretty well any time after that!)

So – tell me – what toy do I NOT have you would like me to get? A twisty dildo, some monstrous new kind of cock ring, <u>professional</u> tit clamps, a <u>real long</u> ball-stretcher, industrial hoods (I made that up), police-gloves (heavy & gauntleted) handcuffs suitable for enclosing a big cock like yours as in picture, or any of the many other complicated & nasty toys that the angels of sex have invented for us. Let me know, & it will give me something to do in October to obtain it for you, Big Twisted Stud!

> Best wishes,
> Twisted Thom

P.S. phone me or visit me with your answer.

1. Postcard shows a naked man using metal handcuffs as a cock ring, by Tom Mayes (1996).
2. Date estimated through internal evidence.

TO *Ander Gunn*   TLS (aerogramme) Ander Gunn
Monday 1 November 1999

1216 Cole Street,
San Francisco,
CA 94117
USA

Nov 1 / 99

Dear Ander,

They arrived looking like Michelin men, but slimmed down (not much) to the Tweedledum and Tweedledee of marmalade. Very fine, perfectly packed, and Mike and I will enjoy them beyond measure.

[. . .]

Well, Mary ...... As a matter of fact, Mary is the main reason I don't visit England. How could I visit England and not visit Snodland? And it's not as though I could come across the ocean secretly, see you and give a few readings, and return here without them finding out. They were wonderful, loving, and generous in taking me in in my teens. But those were the worst years of my life (I wouldn't say that to anybody but you, or I guess Mike), and I only felt good during the school weeks when staying with Thérèse. And my last visit to Snodland was so downright awful I decided even gratitude would never induce me to go there again. I'm truly sorry she has noticed it has been 8 years since I was there – but does she forget how she spoke to me? (I'm sure I told you.)

She is now 92, Catherine 90, Thérèse 93.

No, I'm hardly rich, but I could afford to make the trip!

If I'm lucky, New York will have warm weather like this (it's usually good in the autumn), and I will stroll the streets between my very few readings, and go to movies and eat enormous meals etc.

[. . .]

Love to both,

I liked your reference to my private jet HA! HA!

Th

TO *Peter Spagnuolo*   TLS Peter Spagnuolo

c. November 1999[1]

[1216 Cole Street,
San Francisco,
CA 94117]

Dear Pete,

Very good to hear from you![2] Well, it was an equal pleasure teaching you, I assure you. Teaching a good student is more like a collaboration, in that each points out things to the other, each stimulates the other. Yes, I retired, and now have a license to be lazy – the "celebration" that U.C. held for me was less embarrassing than I thought it would be, and Jim [Powell]'s reading (which was part of it) was wonderful.[3] His new poetry tends to be didactic, but when it is not bullyingly so it is as good as ever. We are all very pleased that he is writing again.

Thank you for the two sonnets.[4] The concept of each poem is original and striking and most of the language is very strong. But the rhythms! I think you might work toward a more regular iambic line and toward eliminating so many violent runovers (too many simply make for monotony, and the form gets lost). Sometimes a few slight changes are all that is needed. In "The Raptor's Return", for example, in line 5, if you insert the word "this" before "panic", you transform a line of uncertain scansion into a perfectly regular one. Similarly, the last line "On air she begins her work with the eyes" (a tetrameter), if you change it to something like "Through air she starts her work upon the eyes" you have a pentameter which only adds to the deadly regularity (for the hawk) of her occupation. The other poem, similarly, could start with the line "We two were brothers then in all we made".

I don't know if you really wanted my criticisms, but the teacher in me still longs to set the world right! Let me say, I think both poems are so good, they deserve the extra work.

Best,

Thom

1. Date estimated from internal evidence.
2. Spagnuolo's letter (4 November 1999) can be found among TG's papers at the Bancroft Library.
3. TG's colleague John Niles organised 'The Poet's Eye: A Symposium and Celebration in Honor of Thom Gunn' at UC Berkeley to mark TG's retirement.
4. 'The Carpenter's Left Hand Complains', *Threepenny Review* 87 (Autumn 2001), 17; 'The Raptor's Return to Tompkins Square Park' is unpublished.

2000

TO *Douglas Chambers*   TLS Toronto

Friday 21 January 2000[1]

1216 Cole Street,
San Francisco,
CA 94117
USA

Jan 21 / 99[2]

Dear Douglas,

I've postponed writing to thank you for your contribution to Agenda till the end, after all the other gentlemanly little notes that I wrote to the others, because I want this to be a letter, which I am sure I owe you anyway. I'm not sure if you went to the U of London Event itself – I hope it was fun, most of the people there I have never met, and I'm glad it ended up with a lot of drinking, as Anita Money, the secretary of Agenda, told me.[3] Thank you indeed for your exploration of my disgustingness.[4] (I'm not being ironical.) Very interesting that I seem to have been so fascinated by snails and slugs. Well, they are . . . gooey, aren't they? Though I do like eating them with a good butter and garlic sauce. The only exception I can take is to your calling that man three lines from the end of your essay a "lover" when he was only a trick. But such terms are difficult, and you have already used the phrase sexual partner. Otherwise, I humbly and gratefully applaud your directness and common sense.

No, it's true I'm not that much influenced by Stevens. I admire him, and he often bores me – rather like Wordsworth. Every now and again I realise how something I haven't properly taken account of, like the Leech Gatherer or "The River of Rivers in Connecticut", is as great as Shakespeare (Winters was right – WS was the greatest poet of the century). I came to both of these poems after having become irritated by the tedious old men, to find that suddenly out of Polonius has emerged a Hamlet.

[. . .]

Anyway, it is fun not teaching. I guess you have retired too, now? I enjoyed teaching so much I was afraid I would miss it, but I don't. I get up, have breakfast, and go back to bed for a nap, in winter time anyway. Most afternoons I sit with the cat on my lap and a glass or two of wine, thinking about John Ambrioso, and take another nap. I write nothing, no poetry, anyway, and it will be a wrench when I am able to write again – if I ever do. (Maybe I have done enough mischief already.)

Have you come across a book called <u>Times Square Red, Times Square Blue</u>, by Samuel R. Delany? I recommend it highly, it is about how richly democratic cruising the movie houses used to be. [. . .]

I mentioned John A. Yes, we still have fabulous times together, and I have even got me a VCR and a small collection of really good porn videos for him to look at when he gets tired of looking at the seventy-[year-]old. I have absolutely no idea what he thinks of me – it is either a lot of very subtle stuff or maybe nothing at all – but his energy and sexual imagination are without comparison, and I am happy with them. If he is using me, well then I am using him also, and that doesn't seem to me at all a bad thing. (Women don't like being treated as sexual objects, but men do!) There was a time when I would have fallen in love with him if he had let me, but he very sensibly didn't.

I have probably boasted that my next book is to have a jacket based on a picture by Lucian Freud in England and on another by Attila Richard Lukacs in the USA.[5] The latter is so hot that I imagine queers will buy the book to possess the cover, even if they loathe the thought of poetry. I believe the book will be out in March over there and April here. Also a bunch of BBC interviews done with the admirable Jim Campbell will come out as a book in England around the same time, and a little selection of Pound's poems with an introduction from Faber only, in maybe May.[6] All pretty exciting for a country boy like myself who was kidnapped four years ago by a motorcycle gang and imprisoned in their club-house for their continual exploitation. Well, at least all thirty of them are good-looking and their come is so nutritious that I have need of no other food. But it's an uneventful life, just sex, drugs, and excitement.

[. . .]

My NY friend Billy Lux has moved here, which is a great delight. He cruises Buena Vista Park every day (he lives only a block from there), and is liked by everyone I live with. (They don't like all my friends, and thoroughly disapprove of John A, considering him a bad influence on me. As he is. They are too nice to say anything against him, but I know what they think.)

You are probably in England now, fisting Princess Margaret just as you did in the wild 1950s.

Love,

Thom

1. Date supplied from internal evidence.
2. TG misdated this letter.
3. The conference 'Thom Gunn at Seventy' was held at the Institute of English Studies, University of London, on 22 October 1999 to coincide with the special issue of *Agenda* celebrating TG's seventieth birthday.
4. Chambers, 'Between That Disgust and This', *Agenda* 37, no. 2–3 (Autumn–Winter 1999), 102–6.
5. The Faber edition of *BC* features Freud's *Interior with Hand Mirror* (self-portrait) (1967); for Lukacs see TG to Chambers, 3 September 1993, n. 1, above.
6. *Ezra Pound: Poems Selected by Thom Gunn* (2000). The book includes TG's short introduction to his choice of Pound's work.

TO *Robert Conquest*   ALS (postcard[1]) Elizabeth Neece Conquest
c. January 2000[2]

[1216 Cole Street,
San Francisco, CA 94117]

Dear Bob –

Yes: the best of Bennett is so good that I plan one day to try VW's other villain, Galsworthy – but then I remember listening to the 3rd Program's (interminable) dramatization of the Forsyte Saga, & once again put it off.[3] Woolf had two good novels, I think (<u>Mrs D</u> & <u>To the Lighthouse</u>), the rest either trivial (<u>Orlando</u>) or abysmal (<u>The Waves, The Years</u>). Her trouble was she couldn't imagine people who were not rich and vague.

You will be vexed at me, I suspect, that I have a <u>Selected Ezra</u> coming out soon. I find he gets better and better. His difficulty of reference is hard to excuse, his politics monstrous, but so much of his poetry is so enjoyable. I'll send you a copy.

Best,

Thom

1. Postcard, 'Penny Arcade Display Advertisement, Vending Machine' (*c.* 1930–40). The cartoon image shows a suited man running away from a woman in a polka-dot bikini.
2. Date estimated from postmark and internal evidence.
3. An allusion to Virginia Woolf's essay 'Modern Fiction' (1925), in which she criticises writers of the previous generation, including Arnold Bennett, John Galsworthy and H. G. Wells.

TO *Clive Wilmer*   TLS (aerogramme) Clive Wilmer
Friday 11 February 2000

1216 Cole Street,
San Francisco,
CA 94117
USA

Feb 11, 00

Dear Clive,

It is a long time since I last wrote to you. And ironically you are the last person I am writing thank you to for the essay you had in that Agenda issue. Ironically in that it is clearly the best and most insightful piece in the issue, though it seems like self-flattery when I say so. I am praising your mind and the way it makes connections. So thank you, however belatedly.[1]

I love your remark that "poetry, at its most intense, charges the irreducibly particular with the general." You suggest that I make this statement, but it's you, and it is an important and original thing to say. [. . .] A man from England visited me this last week, and told me that your Paris Review interview is so good because you ask exactly the right questions.

But enough of all these compliments to you that imply compliments to myself. I returned from giving a reading in Dallas the other day, becoming steadily more aware during the first plane ride (by a very fat man) and then the four hour stopover in Las Vegas, and then during the mercifully shorter plane ride to – finally – San Francisco that I was getting flu. Dallas was just boring (nowhere to walk), but the plane ride belonged somewhere in Dante. I arrived home to find a note from Helen Trimpi saying Edgar [Bowers] was very ill. Next morning, first thing, I was phoned by a journalist telling me that Edgar had just died. The strange thing so Helen told me when I called her back was that Edgar's companion (by which I suppose I understand his lover) had died just the night before, I think during an operation. Neither knew of the other's death. This I take to be a wonderful stroke of good fortune – isn't it what we would all choose if we could, to die at the same time as the one we most love? – It does show me, however, how little I knew Edgar. I had no idea – did you? – that he had had a lover for the last 35 years. [. . .] My guess is that he was a bit like Mike, pleased about the poetry and the respect it brought but bored by literary chitchat.

Reading through some of Edgar's poetry in the days since then – well, since just a week ago, I realise I want to write some little essay about Edgar's achievement, before the year is out. It is so good, and so modest in its claims, that it needs a few voices on its behalf to remain current. I was always rather proud that he thanked me for a blurb I wrote on behalf of his Collected, saying I was the only one among the blurbers who seemed to have actually read the book![2]

And when he published the book For Louis Pasteur, I wrote him a letter querying him about a few details that had puzzled me.[3] He was obviously delighted that anybody should take him seriously enough to do so. It is easy for me, who gets reviewed everywhere because of my delight in sensationalist subject matter, to forget how unread such a great poet must feel, when he almost never gets any printed notice except from pedantic friends, almost never gets a poetry reading, almost never gets letters from fans.

I should tell you, just in case you hear about it, that the publisher of your next short book (he was one of the contributors to Agenda) asked me to write a foreword to it. I refused (as I once refused Michael Schmidt to write a foreword to Edgar's book) in that I think to do so is a patronising act, and in a sense intruding literally on another's territory (a blurb is on the dust-jacket, which can be discarded). So I hope you don't, or didn't, take my refusal as constituting a lack of admiration for your poetry. I do admire it, very much.

It rains all the time. I have discovered that old people feel the cold far more than they used to. After breakfast I often go back to bed to read. (Of course sometimes I fall asleep, forming a kind of practice for the mid-afternoon nap, which I take with a glass or two of cheap wine with my filthy cat in my lap. Old cats often can't be bothered to keep themselves clean.)

Love,

Thom

1. Wilmer, '"Those Wounds Heal Ill": Thom Gunn in 1954 and 1992', Agenda 37, no. 2–3 (Autumn–Winter 1999), 13–21.
2. Bowers, Collected Poems (1997).
3. This letter is lost.

TLS (aerogramme) Ander Gunn

1216 Cole Street,
San Francisco,
CA 94117
USA

March 3 / 00

BORN TO RETIRE

Dear Ander,

I toy with the idea of getting the above tattooed somewhere on myself. Not, you notice, Born to Lose, Born to Raise Hell, Born to Surf, but Born to Retire.[1] My life is so full of trivial jobs, or maybe just thinking about them, that I don't know how I ever had the time to hold down a real job, let alone write books.

We are having a wet spring, as I probably told you before. Well, we are still having a wet spring. Last weekend, we had a joint birthday dinner for Bob and our friend Martin whom you must have met. I made the easier things, like a leg of lamb (among the best I've ever tasted), the white onion sauce, and asparagus (who knows where from, in February?) – Mike made a cake, his wonderful avocado and mushroom salad, a dish of potato and onion and tomato, and best of all kugel (which is a Jewish potato dish – baked minced potato and egg and so on), and Billy made another cake. The trouble with eating so heavily these days is that it drives me to bed early – it's not the wine (though no doubt that helps) but all the rich food.

The next day two people from my English publisher took me out to lunch with my friend and neighbor (who is also published by them) Augie. This was pleasant, but I cannot stand it when people are so deferential. I reacted by switching the focus on to poor Augie, who is always fun and has no reverence.

[. . .]

You know I said that San Francisco is becoming a city of the rich and the homeless, with no room for anybody else in between? Well, our district is changing even more rapidly. Practically every house on the other side of the street has recently been sold, and we and our black neighbors stand out as the poor trash. Houses about the same size as ours but considerably tarted up are selling, a few blocks away, for just under a million dollars. Let us say, $989,000. To think that when we bought this house in 1971, the $33,000 seemed so steep to us! What causes all the demand is the young incredibly rich couples from Silicone Valley, about 30 miles to the south, who think SF would be a nice place for them to raise their families, and have largely taken it away from the working class – and SF <u>was</u> a blue collar town when we first came here to live. Well, I suppose we were part of the change, but at least we weren't rich. The one advantage of gentrification that I can see is that our newspaper is never stolen from our porch any more (the rich don't need to steal!). But of course we have no intention of moving or selling. We'll just try to <u>bring the neighborhood down</u> in our vulgar way.

[. . .]

I got Bob (at his request) an electric waffle-maker for his birthday. Now we expect delicious waffles to be made at least once a week (hasn't happened yet).

Love to both,
Thom

1. See 'Black Jackets' (*CP* 108–9): 'For on his shoulders they had put tattoos: / The group's name on the left, The Knights, / And on the right the slogan Born to Lose.'

TO *John Holmstrom*   TLS (aerogramme) Texas
Sunday 21 May 2000

1216 Cole Street,
San Francisco,
CA 94117
USA

May 21 / 00

Dear John,

It's Mike's 69th birthday today, so we have a big meal and other festivities planned, and it is a heat wave to boot, which is very pleasant after our rather chilly and wet spring. Mike is at his best, though he visits his 96 year old mother four times a year, and she can't even remember his visits a week after he has come back here. Bob who you never met is the sweetest of men, and of course Billy has a new lover as of the last two years none of us like much, but we are trying to educate him. We all wish you'd come and stay again, it has been far too long since last time. I, of course, am 70, and retired from teaching last year and – you never told me how wonderful retirement is. [. . .] Every afternoon I have a glass of wine, the cat jumps on my lap, and both the cat and I have a most refreshing nap. I haven't written a poem since November, 1998, and don't see much prospect of doing any more in that line. [. . .] I use what is left of my youthful juices on a disarming and reckless young man (well, he is 37 and that seems young to someone from this distance), a man born of Cuban parents whose name is John Ambrioso (think of ambrosia!), with whom I do an absurd amount of drugs, who is a constant delight. Without previous announcement, he decided to take my anal education in hand, and the second time we were together he got me so high that I suddenly found he had stuck a rather large dildo up my ass – and I was liking it. We have so much to learn from the young, I find.

My housemates rather disapprove of him, because I suppose they consider he is a bad influence on me. And he is. All this speed at my age will probably kill me soon. But I cannot resist someone I find so disarmingly attractive.

You should have received a copy of my new (and last) book by now. [. . .] Nice cover, eh? But the American edition has an even better one, of Boss Cupid himself, a sexy but far from handsome skinhead looking brutally indifferent to the havoc he causes. The book has received many favorable reviews, which I suppose is what you get anyway when you have been around so long that they are all bored with you.

Among poets your side of the water, I like Michael Longley a lot (GORSE FIRES), and also Rob Wells (LUSUS). I think you would like them too. My tastes are as austere as my life is not.

[. . .] I am wild about an English novelist called James Buchan (James, not John).

XXXXX   Th

TO *Clive Wilmer*   TLS Clive Wilmer

Thursday 20 July 2000

1216 Cole Street,
San Francisco,
CA 94117
USA

July 20 / 00

Dear Clive,

I shall not apologise, because my apologies are so frequent they can mean nothing. Though it has been only about six weeks this time. You do sound active! The Cotswolds, Russia, Switzerland . . . Whereas I get up, have some breakfast, find it too cold to stay up, go back to bed for the rest of the morning, wonder whether I should rejoin the gym one day, read a chapter of some book by a worthless fraud called Sebald (worthless but <u>fashionable</u>), sit in some sun in the afternoon, if there is any sun, watch Mike do some gardening, express my approval to him ("Well done, thou good and faithful servant"[1]), feel depressed that it is my turn to cook for us all today, MAKE A LIST of things to do on other days, and start on the wine. You will note there is no trace of literary activity, except for my glance at the fashionable fraud. Well, that's retirement for you. Actually, right now I've put some dirty clothes in the washer, and I'm watching the cute Latino workmen in the next yard that the rich yuppies have got enlarging their deck. (Our neighborhood has been swamped by the rich. Houses like mine have been selling for a million dollars. We stay on, to bring down the newcomers' spirits with our indefatigably bad behavior (Eat the Rich! Piss on their Doorsteps! Ravish their Sons! Dye their Pets Purple!!).)

[. . .]

I am going to St Louis, a university there, for three weeks, this Fall, and Augie is going to Berlin (far more interesting). I told him I expect he will return with a German wife (married to annoy his and her parents). You may see him, I imagine – lucky Augie! Berlin was a beautiful place in 1960, I imagine even better now.

I should have thanked you a long time back for <u>The Falls</u>. I like the type and layout a lot, emphasizing the quality of the poetry, inviting me to take seriously the spaces between the words. Your writing is as usual pure, direct, and simplified, sparing of ornament, and very compelling in the rhythms, in which I detect the influence of Pound, from whom you have profited, I think, more than anybody else since Bunting. I think I have commented before on all of these poems, but seeing them together, I am impressed by the range of feeling and type of subject matter, extending all the way from the first poem to, for example, A Vision. Bravo on the whole book, it is very lovely and, as is right, more than the sum of its parts.

No, I'm not doing any work on the Bunting book. Never will. (Actually one of the <u>Anglo</u> workmen has spectacularly nice haunches, I just noticed.) The energy for it has gotten lost somewhere on the way. You know what I mean.

I must have told you about John, the Cuban-American. He, in the words of the poet, rends the dark like lightning, and doesn't even know it.[2]

Love,

Thom

1. Matthew 25:21.

2. A reference to Wilmer's 'Visitation' in *The Falls* (2000): 'You rend the dark like lightning, leaving day / solemn with ravage, yet / bright with the evidence / of visitation.'

TO *Ander Gunn*   TLS Ander Gunn

Tuesday 5 September 2000

1216 Cole Street,

San Francisco,

CA 94117

Sep 5 / 00

Dear Ander,

Many thanks for the ceramic birthday card – and also, in advance, for the marmalade, my lifeline to civilisation. I'm very glad to hear that you're in touch with Will again. I often wonder if either of us would have been on speaking terms with our mother after the age of 20! We would have had different reasons, maybe, but she might have seemed like our enemy.

So, you know the news about the Covey Hall Girls. Mary, rather unexpectedly, sent me a book (<u>Cider with Rosie</u>) for a birthday present. Also a used birthday card. The author of the book, Laurie Lee, was the lover of the mother of an old school friend of mine, Michael Wishart.[1] She later, round about that time, became the lover of the 20-year old Lucian Freud. I met them both, and I do remember wondering if the mother and Lucian Freud were sleeping together (even though MW had informed me that LL was the lover). Wasn't I sophisticated for a thirteen year old? I also met the mother, when I stayed down in Sussex with the Wishart family, and also the father, who was a famous Communist publisher (the firm still exists, I believe: Lawrence and Wishart). I never saw Michael after about the age of 15: he became a painter, not a very successful one I believe, and died a year or two ago, poor guy, of bone cancer.

Catherine also writes me, and I have had accounts of all that from three viewpoints, one being Mary, who does not really refer to it, and one being Jenny, always the voice of sanity in that family, to whom I had sent some money for them, since obviously the new way of life had become more expensive than before. Apparently, M and C had had a quarrel more severe than usual, and Mary was also jealous of Catherine's walking frame, like a child wanting a toy that the other had. Catherine <u>needs</u> it, and she can't negotiate the stairs. Mary doesn't even need the one stick that she uses. Mary always took refuge in her bed, anyway, since she had severe cases of post menstrual syndrome – though it didn't have a name in those days. . . . Those Thomson girls, who taught them, I wonder, that you can die just when you want to? Our mother actually carried it out, much to the inconvenience of about twenty other people, Barbara tried, briefly and unsuccessfully, to starve herself to death, and now Mary thinks that, just by taking to her bed, she can die by being tired of it all. Actually, I like going back to bed after breakfast, but I don't expect to die there.

Mary was always a bit mad, and probably just has gotten a bit madder. Jenny compares the situation to the story of the film <u>Whatever Happened to Baby Jane?</u> which I had done to myself once or twice, and if you ever saw it you will laugh, because of the resemblance of Mary to the ancient Bette Davis.

Glad to hear about your new puppy. I have the enormous dog of a friend sometimes staying here. She used to have four legs, now has three. One was amputated because she got a cancerous growth on it (she is only 5), which we are hoping has not metastasized. Meanwhile, she has adapted with supreme cheerfulness, hopping around with a big smile and lots of energy.

Her only source of grief was the cat, Linc, who however had mellowed a lot in old age, but we had to have him given the fatal injection because <u>he</u> had cancer of the mouth. I was unexpectedly broken up about his death. Wicked and selfish old pirate that he was, he loved taking an afternoon nap on my lap, and to the end had the loudest purr I have ever heard.

We have decided that when we are ready, we will get a kitten and a puppy together, so they can grow up together, and (hopefully) grow up friends. Linc was a dreadful racist when it came to all dogs.

[. . .]

I now have a VCR of my own, but show only pornography on it. (Horrible huge cocks up to no good.) My housemates despise my obvious tastes. They think I am tasteless. (I am.)

[. . .]

X X

Thom

1. See TG to Mary Thomson, 10 February 1945, above.

Tuesday 19 September 2000

1216 Cole Street,
San Francisco,
CA 94117

Sep 19 / 00

Dear John,

Well, my, we get a little heated in our expression of distaste. I love the cover because it illustrates the title so well: Tyrannic Love, or "Eros Turannos" (title of one of my favorite poems, by Edwin Arlington Robinson – bet you don't know it!)[1] Cupid is a mean little bully, without honor, without consistency, without truthfulness. That is the point, not only of my title, or some of the contents of my book, but of Ralegh, when he says;

> Know that love is a careless child,
> And forgets promise past, etc[2]

Cupid is not a cute little Valentine baby [. . .] but an obsessive force, neither for good or evil.

In my book, I refuse to sentimentalize, I hope, see my two poems to Mike for example (In Trust, Rapallo). We all have sexual fantasies [. . .] but all sexual fantasies are sentimental. Forgive me if this sounds hard-hearted.

I don't write poetry nowadays, not having much left to write about. Run out of subject matter. But that doesn't seem to matter too much. I have a good life, even though I get rather tired much of the time. My cat died recently, and I miss him (another selfish little bully, by the way) purring on my lap every afternoon.

I doubt if I'll get to England again. Your invitation is kind, but I am bored by the country, even here, and prefer the rancid dirt of the city and the arranged dirt of the suburbs. [. . .]

Love,

Thom

1. See TG to Holmstrom, 21 May 2000, above.
2. Walter Ralegh, 'Walsinghame' (1593).

TO *Clive Wilmer* ALS Clive Wilmer

Tuesday 3 October 2000

St Louis

Oct 3 / oo

Dear Clive,

I had thought to start this letter with the usual apologies for lateness, but I'm not as late as I thought – you wrote to me only a month ago – and so I'll complain instead. Actually, there is little to complain about that I couldn't have foretold: they are paying me a disproportionate sum of money to be here for three weeks, but I have few duties to perform, and it does not appear to be a city with good public transport. It seems very BIG, anyway. I have been here only a few days, though, and there is a splendid poet who has been generously showing me around, Carl Phillips. He wanted to be a vet, studied Greek & Latin at Harvard, taught high school Latin ten years, never wrote any poetry till a few years ago when he met Pinsky, and almost simultaneously decided he was queer & separated from his wife. [. . .] He has published three or four books now, and is only 41. He lives with a lover, who is away & I have not met. His poetry is remarkable – like nobody else's – full of wonderful detail, beautiful rhythmically, & with a structural strength I suppose must come from his classical studies. Still, I have been alone all today, and as it is 91°, a heatwave, haven't been out at all. I travel these days with more & more reluctance – I felt disconsolately lonely on arrival, in spite of Carl's taking me out to dinner with a couple who worship Richard Murphy (!) & Medh McGukhian (I give up in my attempt to spell her, but I dislike her poetry worse than Murphy's, which I find simply boring).

Ho hum, then. When I was <u>young</u>, I could simply pop out the door in a strange town, go to a queer bar & go to bed with a comely stranger or three, but that's not so easily done at the age of 71, when it's only a hardened gerontophile who will so much as look at me . . . So I have spent today rereading Pickwick Papers & starting Holmes' life of Coleridge.[1]

I had a clever thought – the likeness of <u>P.P.</u> with <u>Bouvard & Pécuchet</u>, the subject being in each case an earnestly misguided middle-class quest for universal knowledge. Of course, the obvious difference is between Dickens' & Flaubert's attitude to all that, so maybe I'm not so clever after all.

My predecessor here was a novelist called Richard Ford, who suddenly drove off after six days, by no means lasting his 3 weeks. They are still speculating about the cause (I have heard 3 different theories already), but I think it was <u>boredom</u>.

660

The nicest thing said to me here was from a student who drives me to get supplies from the supermarket. I must have sounded sad that my ancient pirate of a cat had died in San Francisco, but she actually offered to lend me her cat while I am here. I was touched, but refused because the cat would feel even more disconsolate than I at being used.

[. . .]

If I seem hard to please, put it down to my having just finished an advanced copy of Bob Barth's Selected Letters of Yvor Winters. For all his great virtues, YW seems to have lived all his life on the edge of exasperation. Not that I'm exasperated by your poems.

Sorry about Sebald. Maybe I'm wrong – plenty of critics have liked him.

Much love,

Th

1. Richard Holmes, *Coleridge: Early Visions* (1989) and *Darker Reflections* (1998).

TO *Douglas Chambers*   ALS Toronto
Thursday 5 October 2000

St Louis

October 5 / 00

Dear Duggle,

Fresh intelligence after a long gap. I hope you are pleased with your new life, & don't regret giving up the city. Not that it is really a new life – it's just that I have never seen you there, in the cunt-ry, only in the city crowded with glamorous youth. It's a courageous choice – more activity than ever – now you are the plowboy who whistle o'er the lea, whatever a lea may be;[1] as opposed to my choice, which was apparently of complete inactivity: my cat got cancer and had to be euthanized, poor old pirate, so I have no one to instigate my afternoon naps. I have written nothing since Boss Cupid, but that's normal after a publication, as you know. I have a kind of feeling that there will be nothing ever again (I am 71, after all), but if the poetic faculties spring to life again, naturally I shall be grateful. I am fairly pleased by BC – I think it's pretty hard and factual and clear, and those are all virtues in my mind. Mike is well, and the sole source of common sense in our house, Bob is well, and works too hard, and Bill is well, and continues to tolerate his stupid, ugly, unfriendly, ungrateful lover Ralph, though with many a shouting match (of course at night, waking the house up). As for me, I continue to indulge in behavior regretted by the whole house, & somehow continue having a great time with the dashing John – every time we're together it's an adventure – who is bound to let me down big time one day, everybody assumes but me. He's an addict, a reckless biker, never reads, never thinks, is only marginally honest (though he has never cheated me), is over-emotional, the best sex I've ever had, and at the same time strangely intelligent in a specialized way. Anyway, he's more fun than I have any right to expect at this age.

So, unlike you, I didn't retire to a life of hard physical work, but to a life of sloth and total self-indulgence. Mike has taken over the yard, and it looks lushly beautiful for the first time; I got bored with the gym; and I start drinking cheap wine in the afternoon. (But somehow, I'm not really a lush, probably because it is such bad wine.) My wants are very few: drink, drugs, a mad biker with an imaginative cock and an infinitely hungry hole, a loving family and a fairly warm climate. Very Horatian!

[. . .]

There is at last a good anthology of queer poetry – Word of Mouth (Talisman Press) ed by Timothy Liu. Liu is a conniving creep, and a boring poet, but he has read widely and intelligently, & it's a good book (though why anybody should need any anthology, except for classroom use, I don't know). I took part in a reading at a bookstore in Berkeley, to advertise its contents, & met there a handsome, fortyish contributor called Tom Carey, who turned out to be the "Tom" of James Schuyler's late poetry who had always sounded so effortlessly sexy. Nice to meet a friendly dude.

[. . .]

A metaphysical speculation: why are the dildoes used in porn movies always black?

(Well, I can speculate about the reason.)

[. . .]

X X X X X

Th

P.S. As you may guess, I have no typewriter here.
Hope you can read this filthy scrawl.

---

1. An allusion to 'The Plough Boy', a ballad from John O'Keefe's comic opera *The Farmer* (1787).

2001

TO *Ander Gunn*

Wednesday 7 February 2001

ALS (aerogramme) Ander Gunn

1216 Cole Street,
San Francisco,
CA 94117

Feb 7 / 01

Dear Ander –

Well, what hi jinx we've been having back here since I last wrote. We have got a very beautiful, but heartless, kitten called Lola, who seems to like me less than anyone else. I'll show her. (I'll feed her.) She is 6 months old, and was raised with two Labs, which may explain her aggressiveness.

But my friend John broke his collarbone and I gave him my bedroom to sleep in for a week (he couldn't even dress himself at first). Lola slept on his bed every night, & they'd never even been introduced! Now I'm back in my own bed & she avoids it, and me. (Mike just now had to tip her out of <u>his</u> room, saying "No hard feelings, darling!") Well – I guess it's true, you don't get loved by the one you want to be loved by.

I will right this wrong.

About 2 weeks ago I was sitting reading late one afternoon when I suddenly started to feel pains in my upper left arm & eventually my neck! I thought, <u>arthritis</u>, well I am 71! But as the pain got worse (I started lying on the floor, but that didn't help), I then thought, <u>heart attack</u>, I'm 71! So I took 2 aspirins (which is what you are supposed to do) & after 2 hours of all this got Mike to drive me to the Emergency Room up the hill. This was 7 in the evening & I didn't get released from the ER until 11a.m. next day. I must say all the interns and nurses were marvellously attentive & reassuring, giving me every conceivable test at once (nothing wrong with my heart, so it may have been arthritis), but I was on a gurney in the main passage way until I got moved to a more private spot, curtained off and called "a room", at 4 in the morning, so I saw <u>everything</u>. And everything was dramatic. If it hadn't been so awful it would have been fascinating. Actually, it <u>was</u> fascinating. One mountainous black woman being wheeled toward me in <u>her</u> gurney being copiously sick into a plastic basin as she passed me (withdrawal from heroin, explained a friendly nurse), an old white man who seemed as well as I was wandering around boring everybody with questions, a two year old baby brought in by his parents, and it died during the night, etc. etc. Of course, I am so intimidated by the nurses I do everything they say, so they always love me & tell me I am a good sport.

I was rather glad to be out of there, though, & told them I'd write a TV series about it all one day. (The joke being there is already a popular series called "ER", which probably shows in Britain as well.)

Yesterday I had my last test, with a Spanish doctor, the "treadmill test." They have treadmills in gyms nowadays. Do you know that the treadmill was a legal punishment in the 18th & 19th centuries? (The poor must have had very healthy hearts.)

[. . .]

Love to both!

Th

P.S. Sorry about the handwriting but I'm doing this on my knee.

TO *Douglas Chambers*   TLS Toronto

c. Friday 18 May 2001[1]

1216 Cole Street,
San Francisco,
CA 94117

Dear Duggle,

I owe you a letter, or letters, from countless seasons back, and have no excuses, really. Is it because I feel like a non-person when I can't write poetry? Is it because I am so sunk in my retired indolence that I cannot even get down to writing anybody? Well, I don't know. I gather that you work harder than ever, got to get back in time for the bedding season, etc. Well, the only kind of bedding yrs truly knows about is something entirely different heh heh.

Anyway, it's a lovely day, I am stumblingly laboring through draft after draft of a new poem, one addressed to my sweetie, John, the addicted daredevil of my dreams, hated by Mike unfortunately, the sex instructor who took my education in hand and compressed a lifetime of practice and information into a mere two years.[2] He's so outrageously handsome and at the same time self-indulgent that I could forgive him anything if there were anything to forgive. His total depravity is like a huge sweet cake iced with charm. And you know how it is with charm – the more you distrust it the more it excites you.

Well, how are the rest of them? Mike is to be 70 in a few days, still handsome, still wise and wonderful except in that one respect. Bill has emerged from his problems with first PCP and then crack into a mere addiction to gin. He has installed a horrible black giant upstairs whom we all dislike and seems to give <u>him</u> little enough happiness, godd nose sic. He is still handsome, though well into his fifties. I call him my Bernard Berenson of porno videos, he brings me back second-hand videos from his place of work, and I guess that makes me the Isabella Gardner of porn, which I collect, I tell myself, to keep John interested. We have no regrets about living with Bob, either: generous, unselfish, practical, he works too hard during the weeks and at weekends works too hard making useful devices for the house. None of them seems to have much sex with anybody, or maybe that's just because they never seem to bring anybody back.

I bring anybody back.

Did a kind of reading tour, for the paperback of Boss Cupid, that is to NY, Northwestern, and Miami University (Ohio), earlier this year. I was somewhat bored and uneasy the whole time, and had my greatest pleasure going to movies I could just as well have gone to in SF. (the best of them, by far, was MEMENTO – I recommend it without reservation.) I'm going to Chicago for 4 days next month, but don't expect much fun: I used to love Chicago, but I don't recognize it nowadays, and the people I knew there thirty years ago have either died or moved away.

[. . .]

Did you read Frank Kermode's book on <u>Shakespeare's Language</u>? Very fine, very modest, very perceptive – told me new things about something I thought I knew backwards.

Write me and tell me about your hopes, your dreams, your fears.

[. . .]

Here's an idea for a bumper-sticker:

BED MEN, NOT TULIPS

[. . .]

> Overpowering love,
> from
> your
> Little Thom

1. Date estimated from internal evidence.
2. 'A Gratitude' is unpublished (various drafts are at Bancroft and Stanford). In a letter to Billy Lux (16 July 2002) TG writes: 'John seems very touched, showed it to the

first speed dealer we visited. I don't really know what to do about John emotionally: well, why do I need to do that? Well, I guess I am on the verge of just becoming a sugar daddy, which I don't want to be from vanity' (Private collection).

TO *Ander Gunn*   TLS (aerogramme) Ander Gunn
Thursday 13 September 2001

1216 Cole Street,
San Francisco,
CA 94117
USA

Sep 13 / 01

Dear Ander,
    Yes it is true that I write less often now I am retired. I do less of everything now I am retired – especially of those things I used to find time for between, after, and before bits of real work. My retired butcher has the same experience, he says. [. . .]
    Well, the time is full of tension. The terrorist acts are deeply shocking. Our young carpenter is from Brooklyn, and is currently replacing most of our back stairs (dry rot), and two of his uncles are missing – firemen ("They were helping people!"). One of the men who deflected the fourth plane's attack and made it crash in Pennsylvania was apparently a neighbor of ours, or almost one, the paper says (not that I knew him). We are bombarded by TV day and night, people are putting out flags and are being rude to people who look like Arabs, and wondering if this is going to lead us into the third World War. I am so tired of all this kind of thing, as I'm sure you are.
    Our president does not inspire confidence, either. Not a very capable man.
    Then there was the saga of Ralph and Bill. Forget where the story had got to when I last wrote. They had not spoken for four months, and Bill was trying to evict Ralph from the apartment. When a straight couple get divorced, nobody expects them to go on living together – but this is San Francisco, where the laws are biased in favor of the tenant, and it is very difficult to evict. (And I'm proud that we are so enlightened here!) But Ralph likes his big room here, and even more the fact that I charge what must be the lowest rent in the city, since the idea is that I rent to my friends, not to make money. I got Bill a lawyer (her WONDERFUL NAME BEING Dolores Chong), but she was not hopeful we could succeed in getting him out. Then Ralph did a foolish thing, maybe because he had been smoking crack all night, Bill tells me. Bill was moving a few small wooden boxes outside the

closed door of Ralph's room, when suddenly the door opened, and Ralph rushed out, shouting and picking up one of the boxes – about 2 feet square – and threw it at Bill. Bill meanwhile having been beaten up a couple of times about a year before by Ralph, had fled to the other end of the corridor, but the box hit him in the hand where it made a small scratch with a satisfactorily large flow of blood. He had told R that if he ever showed violence again he'd make an emergency call to the police and get a restraining order against him. I had rushed upstairs, hearing the noise and having experience of Ralph's vile temper; the police arrived, and were very good. I was delighted to see them lead off Ralph in handcuffs. To our surprise they put Ralph in jail, where he still is, after about two weeks. It was a very small wound, but we conjecture that Ralph may have prior arrests for domestic violence before he left New York. So it looks like we shall get him out of the house after all: and Bill is not in danger since he got the restraining order, which says that he is not to come within 100 feet of Bill and not even phone him. We changed the locks yesterday! Of course, if Ralph is really crazy, he might take no notice of the order and murder Bill, but we are hoping for the best. I had a feeling that he was a confidence man from the start, four years ago. Poor Billy really was in love: I said "Don't look at him in court, or you'll just start crying." But I think he will cry anyway.

When I was little I hoped to have a really dramatic life, but Mother's suicide changed all that. I suppose I got my wish anyway.

[. . .]

> Much love to both of you,
> X X   Thom

Excuse the exceptionally bad typing.

TO *Clive Wilmer*   ALS (aerogramme) Clive Wilmer
Tuesday 20 November 2001

> 1216 Cole Street,
> San Francisco,
> CA 94117
>
> Nov 20 / 01

Dear Clive,

I neglect you horribly, I know, and the fact that I neglect everyone else doesn't excuse me. Thank you for your letter. You are a kind young man to write me at all.

You are not to feel guilty, as I suspect you do, for not writing a book about me. There was a time when I hinted and nagged and nudged you about it, given you had said you'd like to do it. But that was when I still felt raw from the injustice of Alan Bold, and I suspected every elementary school teacher who wanted a bit of help with teaching the Gunn–Hughes set book was going to his terrible little handbook for help. Obviously, having you write about me was a bit like having Tolstoy or Ruskin do so, but the whole business of getting permission to quote dragged out so long (and Craig Raine was so ungenerous) that it all lost impetus, and I doubt if you will ever get the impetus or the desire to do it again.[1] It doesn't matter. You don't owe me anything, & I am not owed anything by anyone. I have been treated with extraordinary generosity, on the whole, & your wonderful essay about me – which is better than I deserve – has been reprinted several times – to my great delight.[2] I expect nothing from you, or from anyone else. (I think there was a time, anyway, when I exaggerated my deserts.)

The effects of September 11 have been, on the whole, depressing, though they could be more so. One of my 90-year old aunts showed an unseemly glee about it all: capitalist America being punched on the nose and all that. I had to write to her that bin Laden is a millionaire & that the thousands who got killed in the Trade Center were the working poor – maintenance people, cleaners, waiters, etc., just the same kind of people she used to serve milk to on her milk-round.

It probably means something that I reread books, mainly, nowadays – all Jane Austen, a lot of Henry James, & so on. The whole system is slowing down – as Isherwood said to a friend, of himself in his last years, "Yes, I'm afraid the whole East Wing has gone dark." You are more than kind to suggest ideas & subjects that might get me going again, but my trouble is not a lack of those. I get marvellous ideas for poems, but I don't have the juice. I have, actually, written three poems in the last couple of years, but they were no good – not worth publishing – because usually what is supposed to happen is that you start with a great idea & when you start working on it all sorts of wonderful things you never anticipated move into it, and you finish it thinking, in all modesty, what an astonishing poem for me to have ended up writing, it's so much better than I planned. No surprises with these three poems, I'm afraid – exactly as planned, rather thin and boring in the fact. That doesn't mean that I don't have faint hopes of resuming things one day, but they do remain pretty faint.

I get so easily tired walking these days, & I suspect that may have something to do with it. I used to walk like a demon, & a lot of my poeticizing took place while walking: the physical energy was somehow connected with the imaginative energy: now I get tired just walking to Haight Street & back.

But my health remains excellent, & I have no doubt that I will continue boring the shit out of the young for many years yet, & I do still love my life, which I suppose is the main thing.

I hope you know that we would love to have you stay a few weeks, whenever you wanted. You would not only be my guest but the whole household's – they all liked you a lot and would enjoy your stay almost as much as I would. [. . .] We all consider heterosexuals a lot of fun and love to get drunk with them, and we'd promise not to describe our own filthy habits (at dinner, anyway).

> X   Love! Admiration!
> Respect! Friendship!
> Thom

1. See TG to Wilmer, 25 September 1989, above.
2. Wilmer, 'Definition and Flow: Thom Gunn in the 1970s', in *British Poetry since 1970: A Critical Survey*, ed. Jones and Schmidt (1980), 64–74.

2002

TO *Ander Gunn*   TLS (aerogramme) Ander Gunn
Sunday 12 May 2002[1]

1216 Cole Street,
San Francisco,
CA 94117

Dear Gunn D.A.,

We are all going to the theater soon, and I have just time to write this. We go about once a year – what goes on on the stages of the district is certainly better than it was fifty years ago, but it is still not very good – however, this is the new Tony Kushner play (the new Shaw) and it is said to be among his best.[2]

I was delighted by the picture you sent me. I remember the occasion very well, and I believe I may have others from the same set. They were taken by a photographer who worked for Father's paper, at Father's flat in Knightsbridge, though he wasn't there at that hour.[3] Mike said when I showed it to him, My, your mother was chic, wasn't she? She was a bit too chic for us. We disliked it so much when she looked so different from the other (drab) parents on Prize Day that she let us choose what she should wear then – and we would select her most anonymous outfit. Nice of her, really.

What we didn't like was that she looked <u>different</u> from the other parents. And there am I, the prig and future poet, looking as intense and poetic as I could. And there are you, "insouciant", showing all the careless charm that made everybody like you so much, rightly. My guess at the year would be 1943.

[. . .]

Our friend John, whom you have not met, after busting both a collar bone and leg (replaced by a metal rod) in separate accidents on his motorcycle, has given up the motorcycle in favor of a most charming dog, a country girl of a year old and a mix of Airedale and shepherd – looking more like an Airedale. I am glad to say that she likes me, and licks my face whenever she meets me. She has a more affectionate nature than our cat (Psychokitty a.k.a. Rose a.k.a. Rosatia) who USES my lap by day and my feet by night, to sleep on, and whose form of affection is as likely to be a bite as a licking, apparently not knowing the difference. But I suppose being used so is a kind of affection. I certainly hope so.

[. . .]

I'm wondering if I will ever feel like travelling again. In April I went to give a reading in Massachusetts, then four days doing nothing in New York, then a few days doing things for a small college in Laramie, Wyoming. In the East, there was a heatwave, in Wyoming it snowed. Also, Laramie, which is a mile + 2,000 feet above sea level, I almost fainted once or twice, was constantly tired and dehydrated (because of the elevation, babies are born jaundiced there) but thought it a rather beautiful small town. I saw herds of antelope, but no mooses (I had been promised a moose or two), and various other groups of deer in the flat countryside that stops at the Rockies. It was all rather strangely attractive: I especially liked the big old bar I was taken to where there was a bullet hole in the big mirror behind the bar itself.

[. . .]

Love to both,
Th

1. Date supplied by postmark.
2. Kushner, *Homebody/Kabul* (2001).
3. This photograph is reproduced alongside Wilmer's article 'Poor Lovely Statue!' *Times Literary Supplement* (23 June 2017), 17–18.

2003

TO *Douglas Chambers*   TLS Toronto

Monday 10 February 2003

1216 Cole Street,
San Francisco,
CA 94117

Feb 10 / 03

Dear Douglas,

Late as I am, owing you three letters or so, I don't as usual know where I should be sending this. [. . .]

Nothing happens much, though I lead a somewhat enjoyable life, being one of those pigs not only greedy but easily satisfied. "Feed the fellow a meal of chaff" Mr F's Aunt would say.[1] I'm happy as always with my house-mates, who are very forbearing with me. Mike does all the gardening now, for many hours a week. Bill is in Florida, visiting his mother for 3 weeks, his T cell count being alarmingly down, but we hope that not drinking gin and being free of his awful lover Ralph (I must have told you THAT saga), and being peacefully bored will bring it back to normal (that is, if no Florida alligator takes a fancy to him). Are you ever going to be able to visit us, what with plantings and tours and garnerings and seasonal duties?

I still have fun with John, who is truly an enlivening man I am lucky to know. I no longer hope in a net to catch the wind, but just take what is granted me with gratitude. And what is granted is a large volume of fun.

I don't miss teaching, as I thought I might, but I have accepted an offer to teach at Stanford this Fall, for the grotesque sum of $80,000 dollars (for one hour a week, on any subject I like, for ten weeks). I was offered this first a year ago, and rejected it, knowing I would have accepted it from greed alone. This year, though, when offered it again, greed prevailed. I will probably be a bad teacher, as it is not easy to lay off for a few years and then return as good as before. [. . .] The slickness and the confidence are all slipped down the drain.

[. . .]

I have selected a Selected Poems of Yvor Winters for the Library of America. The editors are not happy with my introduction. Nor am I, as it happens. I don't do anything well these days, though I do take drugs excellently. I have written only two poems since my last book. Not much chance of any surprises there, I'd say.

[. . .]

Do you watch porn movies? If so, I highly recommend Tulsa County Line, very high degree of inventiveness and country cock. Made by Joe Gage, we all assumed must be dead.

I suddenly find that I'll be in London for a week at the end of March. I've been given a nice prize (all prizes are nice) & they want me to be there to receive it.[2] I suppose you won't be there then? But if you are, let me know.

                          Love
                              Thom

1. A reference to *Little Dorrit* (1857).
2. TG and Beryl Bainbridge were awarded the David Cohen Prize for Literature in 2003.

TO *Ander Gunn*   TLS Ander Gunn
Thursday 24 July 2003

                                    1216 Cole Street,
                                    San Francisco,
                                    CA 94117

                                    July 24 I think / 03

Dear Ander,
    Already it's the end of July and I haven't thanked you for your letter and the marmalade shipment. For both, continuing thanks: Mike and I eat like the luckiest of English lords because of you. Americans do not even try to make marmalade with Seville oranges, thus they can only make a sweet orange jam. Not the same thing at all. Bill and Bob do not seem to have the same cravings Mike and I do. (All the more for us!)
    Two days ago, I went with a friend to have lunch at the Boat Ramp, which is on a deck on China Bay, right next to that place where we went for at least one sunny afternoon, Mission Rock, with Don Doody, etc., sweating out the beer in the sunshine as we drank beer after beer. Never go there now – it's begun to get cheaply touristic, instead of being the resort of fishermen and

workers on boats and owners of small boats. Time flashes by so fast when you are old, and I reluctantly admit that we ARE old, though thank god as silly as ever – at least I am, and you just get more sensible. I often think about what Catherine must feel, the only one of her generation left alive (even Margot's John Corbett died during the last year). But Snodland was always such a wretched place, with its grey terraces and cheap sweet shops, etc, and its farms hidden away between the housing developments. Catherine seems pretty resilient, is lively and forthcoming, but of course is very slow in movement, getting around on her Zimmer Frame, but (like Don) now what Americans call a shut-in, not able to go outside any more than climb the stairs. How strange to live 95 years in the same house, that is not true of anyone else I know or maybe have heard of. Well, I have now lived in this house for 32 years, which is a record for me. But when I dream at night, the most common location for my dreams is not here but 110 Frognal, where after all we lived only a few years (1938–1945). By the way, we are having an unconventional year for weather. Maybe everywhere is. Hardly any sun until July (usually May and October are the best months of the year) – but this year we have been having a welcome heat wave for the last few weeks, just when the summer fogs usually begin (you have experienced those). So nothing is predictable. Mike took charge of the garden now, as well as the garden at the cabin: he has got it looking far more wonderful than it ever looked during my incompetent reign: now flowers I've hardly even heard of overlap and make wonderful contrasts in color and size. You have no need to apologize about not coming up to London in March – I completely understand, my visit took place at very short notice, in any case. When I returned, I had almost flattened out my poor little buttocks on plane seats, and as I probably told you had already promised to go to Maryland and Washington DC on the East Coast. At least once there I was with my poet and neighbor friend August, to do readings and meetings with students, but even a little travel was hardly bearable, and I am very thankful that I have nothing of that sort scheduled for the rest of this year. I am to teach at Stanford University ten weeks of the Fall, but that is fairly close, and I am doing it because I am being offered so much more money than I can be possibly worth. I stop writing poetry, I get prizes and absurd job offers. So THAT's the way it's done!!!

My friend John has a wonderful dog half Airedale and half shepherd, she is beautiful and always licks my hand by way of a greeting. I ask John why, & he says that means she thinks of me as a member of her pack. I feel privileged, especially as our cat, Rose (or Rosacea) doesn't really like me or anybody much. She is apt to lick your hand then bite it, like it is a piece of foodstuff. Mixed messages! Poor thing, she is very beautiful but more than a little stupid.

Much love to both of you,

X X X

Thom

TO *Clive Wilmer* TLS Clive Wilmer

c. November 2003[1]

1216 Cole Street

San Francisco

CA 94117

Dear Clive,

Just a note, even though I must owe you real letters. I'm becoming a lazy old man, drinking too much, writing nothing, even neglecting my friends. [. . .] The answer to your question, which I had unexpectedly trouble finding, is to be found on page 186 of The Occasions of Poetry [. . .] and I think nowhere else. What I mean by this sentence may not be at all what TSE meant: I may not be a modest person, but I do believe in modesty in poetry.[2] They will never want to make a movie about me, I hope. I hate the Sylvia and Iris shit, by which the literary work becomes subordinated to the People Magazine personality.[3] It's true, really started to get deeply interested in poetry when I read André Maurois' Ariel at the age of about 13, but that kind of thing is probably unavoidable.[4] I got more sensible later on and am still a kind of unregenerate New Critic, which I am sure is no surprise to you. I will never see the movie about Sylvia and Ted, the very thought of it turns my stomach.

You can quote any of this letter, if you find it worth quoting. Of course some of a writer's personality comes through anyway – when Kyd said that Marlowe had a cruel heart, that comes as no surprise. But we can try to emphasize subject over self-dramatization, and try again. I would like to be like Edgar Bowers, but I'm a bit of a childish show-off and can't always help it . . .

I hope this letter is not confusing.

It is raining, nobody loves me, and I

hate the world. My Daddy was Hitler,

and I am a Jew in a concentration camp.

(See? it's easy!)

Love,

Thom

1. Date estimated from internal evidence.
2. 'Moreover, it has not been of primary interest to develop a unique poetic personality, and I rejoice in Eliot's lovely remark that art is the escape from personality. This lack in me has troubled some readers' (*OP* 186).
3. TG refers to *Sylvia*, dir. Christine Jeffs (2003) and *Iris*, dir. Richard Eyre (2001).
4. André Maurois, *Ariel: The Life of Shelley*, trans. Ella D'Arcy (1924).

2004

TLS Ander Gunn

1216 Cole Street
San Francisco
CA 94117
Feb 20 / 04

Dear Ander,

"Sometimes we see a cloud that's dragonish." (Hamlet)[1] That was certainly the most dragonish of clouds on your Christmas card, marvellously so. You may have missed the eclipse, but you had a good dragonish cloud that more than compensates for it. Thank you too, a thousand times, for the tawny marmalade. It must be getting close to a thousand jars of that. No, that's all we want – it's the best and we want to go on getting it as long as you have life and strength to send it to us.

Thérèse died at Christmas – of pneumonia, and in her sleep. She was always wonderful to me, considerate and sweet, and treated me better than her own sons, I thought. Her weakness, which irritated Mother, was in being a lion-hunter – she loved celebrities quite shamelessly. So I was rather pleased that I became a minor celebrity, and was in a sense able to pay her back through her glee at that. Ted, the younger son, sent me a copy of a picture of her on the honeymoon of her first marriage in Florence in 1933. She met her first husband in Berlin. 1933 was a very good year for a Jew to be getting out of Berlin, where she had been living for a few years before that.

Jenny is retiring next year so as to take better care of Catherine, who is practically immobilized these days. What a good daughter. And it does make me feel old, doesn't it you?

I had an interesting medical procedure the other day. Day one, I had to totally fast, not eating or drinking anything but clear liquids and jelly, and taking two laxatives. Unbearable! Then day two I went to a hospital, where the doctor was to do a colonoscopy on me, that is, give me some anaesthetic and put a huge cobra of a black rubber pipe up my arse – actually a kind of periscope to look around and photograph any growths and so on. The anaesthetic was so good that I didn't even notice when it took place. I was chattering away to the doctor but he said that I had been silent for about five minutes. (I had one (benign) polyp, so that's all right.) I have my cataract out next week, and that I hope will be all the doctoring I get this year.

You have no doubt read in the paper that our new mayor decided as his first act to authorize the issuance of marriage licenses to people of the same sex, and so far there have been about 3000 gay marriages. Mike and I are already registered as "domestic partners" with the State of California, which means that whoever dies first the house remains [the surviving partner's], and I have not observed much about marriage that makes me respect it that much (I think you are one of the few people I know who is happily married), but here there is much euphoria in the air, and it is always nice to cock a snook at President Bush. I am proud of living in San Francisco!

We have been having an exceptionally cold and wet winter – cold for us, that is, but it didn't go as low as freezing point and all the weeds are nice and green in the next yard. I sleep a lot these days, but that can be attributed to the cat, who likes to take frequent naps in my lap, and to the amount of cheap wine that I drink. I have a friend who lives about two blocks away, Augie (a very good poet); every couple of weeks we meet for lunch and then a movie, and then we have a couple of martinis, which make our memories of the movie very good indeed.

And with that I say, love & goodbye,

Th!

1. *Antony and Cleopatra* (4.15.2).

GLOSSARY OF NAMES

John Ambrioso (1962–): TG's regular trick in the late 1990s and early 2000s, from Kentucky. They were introduced by Robert Prager, Ambrioso's ex-boyfriend, at the Hole in the Wall Saloon in San Francisco in December 1998. Prager and Ambrioso were part of the methamphetamine scene that TG became involved in after his retirement from teaching in May 1999. 'John Ambrioso struck me as the Lou Andreas-Salomé of that set,' one gay writer has remarked, 'i.e. the object of desire for these artists/intellectuals.' Ambrioso lived in various small apartments in San Francisco, first on Leavenworth, in the Tenderloin, and later on Geary and at Fillmore Center, with his three-legged dog called Mika. Ambrioso rode motorcycles and would often 'kidnap' TG and drive him out to Bodega Bay or Half Moon Bay. Of their first sexual encounter in February 1999 TG wrote: 'Handsome, articulate & melancholy hero: we got on wonderfully & fantastic sex'; 'John Ambrioso is an ultimate, living & dying for sex [. . .] probably as selfish as beautiful, but sunny-natured & gives as much as he takes sexually. A guy cd get obsessed with him, (as R[obert] P[rager] did some years ago).' TG helped Ambrioso financially, with money for rent and drugs. They last saw each other shortly before TG's death, when TG introduced Ambrioso to his new boyfriend, Phil Monsky, who was staying at Cole Street. The two did not get along. 'There are good people and they're a little hard to find,' Ambrioso remarked. 'Thom was very central to my stability, my mentality. [. . .] He was so supportive in so many ways.'

Chuck Arnett (1928–88): artist and ballet dancer from Louisiana. Arnett moved to San Francisco in the early 1960s and became well known in the leather scene for his Tool Box mural and his decorations for Saturnalia parties at the Stud. His association with leather bars continued at the No-Name, the Red Star Saloon and the Ambush. In 1961 Arnett passed through San Francisco on the first national tour of *Bye Bye Birdie*; he met TG in a leather bar called Crossroads, behind the Embarcadero YMCA. They tricked several times, including at Arnett's place on Pierce Street after he moved permanently to San Francisco. TG's poem 'Pierce Street' (*CP* 177–8) focuses on one of Arnett's murals; 'Bravery' (*T* 16–17) describes Arnett's portrait of TG; and 'Crystal' (*CP* 375–6) is about Arnett's later life as a drug dealer. 'I admire people who are stronger than me, in fact,' TG said of Arnett, 'and although I may appear like a strong person, I appear to myself as a weak person so I'm always attracted by the strong.'

Bob Bair (1950–): American artist and craftsman from Mansfield, Ohio. Bair came to California in his mid-twenties, via construction work in Colorado. He met Kitay in the Stud in 1977 and they began a relationship. Bair moved into the Cole Street house the following year and, with the exception of a short period (1989–93), has lived there ever since. At the time he met Kitay, Bair was a zookeeper in Oakland and had previously worked as a stablehand in the Berkeley Hills. In 1980, Bair and Kitay bought and renovated a cabin in the gay resort of Guerneville, Russian River, which they kept for twenty-six years. They spent the summers there: TG's 'To a Friend in Time of Trouble' (*CP* 408–9) is about the cabin, and 'In Trust' (*BC* 98–9) alludes to Kitay's absence from Cole Street. For Bair, TG and Kitay's domestic relationship was a revelation. 'Maybe one of the reasons that [the house on Cole Street] has meant so much to me is because it became my family,' he has said, 'which is what happens with gay people. They have to create families wherever they can find them.'

Douglas Chambers (1939–2020): Canadian professor of English at Trinity College, University of Toronto, where TG met him in October 1975. Chambers was a specialist in seventeenth-century literature and published widely on Marvell, Milton and Traherne. He was also a garden historian, and his book *Stonyground: The Making of a Canadian Garden* (1996) examines his own creation of a *ferme ornée* on his ancestral farm in Ontario. TG and Chambers tricked when they first met in Canada and established a firm friendship that they maintained through visits and letters. Chambers compiled a festschrift for TG's sixtieth birthday, *A Few Friends* (1989). In it he writes that out of TG's humane temperament 'has come all his later poetry with its astonishing breadth of prosody. Out of it too has come an affirmation of the physical world in all its sexy randomness and, latterly, its painful loss.'

Robert Conquest (1917–2015): British historian and poet. Conquest's best-known work is *The Great Terror: Stalin's Purge of the Thirties* (1968) and he was a long-time fellow at Stanford University's Hoover Institution. Conquest edited the first *New Lines* poetry anthology in 1956 and asked TG to contribute, thus beginning a correspondence that lasted, on and off, until TG's death. Their letters include discussions of *New Lines* and the Movement, as well as 1950s literary gossip, and contain comments and suggestions about each other's poems. According to Conquest's widow, Elizabeth Neece Conquest, during their thirty-six-year marriage Conquest only went to three poetry readings: one in London, one in San Francisco, one at Stanford. All were TG's. Elizabeth Conquest writes: 'On the way to the first of these, Bob said "Thom's the only poet I know who can read his poems without making a nuisance of himself."'

Donald Davie (1922–95): poet, literary critic and teacher. Davie was educated at Cambridge and held a creative writing fellowship at Stanford, a fellowship at Gonville and Caius College, Cambridge, and a lectureship at Cambridge. He taught at Trinity College, Dublin, and the University of California, Santa Barbara, and held professorial appointments at Essex (1964–8), Stanford (1968–78) and Vanderbilt (1978–88). Davie was associated with the poets of the Movement in the 1950s, and both his poetry and critical work demonstrate an interest in modernist themes and techniques. He read Yvor Winters's work with enthusiasm and got to know him after writing him a fan letter. Davie's first critical book, *Purity of Diction in English Verse* (1952), reveals his concern with 'chaste diction' – as in late Augustan poetry – and with the moral and social implications of its subject matter, interests that would dominate his critical and creative work for the rest of his life. Davie met TG at Stanford in the late 1950s and they remained friends until Davie's death in 1995. It was an unusual friendship: TG was open, liberal, progressive in his attitudes; Davie, on the other hand, was homophobic, conservative and Christian. Their correspondence is at once warm and gently chiding. TG was impressed by Davie's openness to experimental poetry, particularly in America. In a review of *The Passages of Joy*, Davie implied that being open about his homosexuality had diminished TG's poetry. 'I'm terrifically grateful for that essay and for everything Donald has written about me. I think it has been consistently insightful,' TG responded (PR 180): 'I don't think he'll any longer be able to make that connection in light of *The Man with Night Sweats*. Let me say that I also respect Donald so much that something that was in my mind the whole time I was writing this new book was: how can I show him that he's wrong?!' TG's poem in memory of Davie – 'To Donald Davie in Heaven' (*BC* 59–60) – is lightly teasing, picturing Davie in Dante's *Paradiso*, 'But maybe less druggy, / a bit plainer, / more Protestant.'

Don Doody (1931–2006): TG's friend for more than forty years. Born and raised in Chicago, Doody had an itinerant academic career, attending Georgetown and Syracuse before transferring to Tulane, where he majored in anthropology. Doody stayed on at Tulane, gaining a law degree in 1961 and an MA in English the following year, when he defended a thesis on 'Shakespeare and Opera'. Between law school and his MA, Doody visited San Francisco on holiday, where by chance he met TG in a North Beach bar and restaurant called Gordon's. TG had recently moved to an apartment on Filbert, in the same neighbourhood. Their initial sexual relationship turned into a solid friendship, and while Doody was completing his MA at Tulane, Gunn recommended him for the PhD programme at UC Berkeley. 'His effusive letter of recommendation got me into Berkeley,' Doody recalled. 'My grades didn't really deserve it.' Doody moved to San Francisco in 1962 and, to make ends meet, began bartending at the Tool Box. 'Thom was at that point very romantically interested in me, so he used to come to the bar every night,' Doody told Edward Guthmann: 'He would come alone. And he would drink a lot. He would drink a lot of beer. And I got in the habit of driving him home, not staying with him but driving him home.' In 1963, during his recovery from hepatitis, TG stayed with Doody and Bryan Condon at 1045 Fell Street. There he read all of Thomas Mann and planned his long poem 'Misanthropos'. 'Many of the themes and ideas in the poem originated in, or were at least helped along by, the wide-ranging discussions between my friends Don Doody and Tony Tanner, some of them across the bed of my recuperation,' TG wrote (OP 180). He dedicated the poem to Doody and Tanner.

Doody is best remembered for managing the Stud, an ailing biker bar that he transformed into a druggy dance bar in the late sixties. For two years, on 17 December, the Stud hosted Saturnalia parties modelled on Ken Kesey's acid tests: Doody gave everyone acid – supplied by his friend Gary White – and had Chuck Arnett design elaborate, psychedelic decorations for the bar. Doody introduced TG to LSD and was influential in many of the experiences behind TG's *Moly* poems. 'Thom somehow thought of Doody as this kind of guru,' Marcia Tanner remarked, 'this shaman wisdom leader.' When TG, Kitay and Schuessler moved to Cole Street in 1971, Doody and his Stud entourage lived in the upstairs apartment for several years. He had a reputation for being confrontational, restless and highly strung, often quarrelling with, and alienating himself from, friends. TG's poem 'Crosswords' (*CP* 376–8) is about Doody:

> Obsessive and detached, ardent and cool,
> You make me think of rock thrown free to turn
> At the globe's side, both with and not with us,
> Keeping yourself in a companionable,
> Chilled orbit by the simultaneous
> Repulsion and attraction to it all.

Doody returned to San Francisco several times in the 1980s and 1990s but settled in New York, where he died in 2006.

Robert Duncan (1919–88): American poet and key figure in both the Black Mountain school of poetry and the San Francisco Renaissance, born in Oakland, California. TG admired Duncan for his open acknowledgement of his homosexuality: Duncan's essay 'The Homosexual in Society' appeared in the journal *Politics* in 1944. His poetry collections include *The Opening of the Field* (1960), *Roots and Branches* (1964), and the two influential *Ground Work* volumes: *Before the War* (1984) and *In the Dark* (1987). Although TG and Duncan had known of each other for about a decade, it was not until September 1968 that they became properly acquainted: TG began to attend Duncan's poetry workshop and they saw each other socially. 'He was an amazing person,' TG said: 'Talking with him was, by all accounts, like talking with Coleridge' (JC 36). TG called Duncan 'a tremendously fertilizing influence' on his poetry and noted how Duncan's ideas about poetry as process shaped his own writing practice from the late 1960s onwards (PR 171). 'He meant a great deal to me,' TG reflected: 'Besides Winters he's probably the poet who meant most to me in my life' (JC 37). TG wrote three poems about or addressed to Duncan – 'Wrestling' (*CP* 260–2), 'At the Barriers' (*CP* 399–402) and 'Duncan' (*BC* 3–4) – and three major essays: 'Homosexuality in Robert Duncan's Poetry' (*OP* 118–34), 'The High Road: A Last Collection' (*SL* 129–42) and 'Adventurous Song: Robert Duncan as Romantic Modernist' (*SL* 143–70).

Jere Fransway (1928–96): friend of TG from Wisconsin who settled in San Francisco in the early 1960s. He was part of the same circle of gay hippies that included Chuck Arnett and Don Doody, and would often take part in their trips to Golden Gate Park and further afield to take acid. TG's poem 'The Fair in the Woods' (*CP* 209–10) is addressed to Fransway, who organised an outing to the Renaissance Fair in San Rafael on which the poem is based.

Fransway had a coterie of young men living in a house on Clara Street, South of Market, 'goodlooking but untrustworthy' as TG calls them in 'Falstaff', the poem he wrote about Fransway (*CP* 374–5). Clara Street was also Fransway's drug sales headquarters. TG was a frequent visitor to Clara Street, where he bought acid and marijuana.

Fransway's ethic was to look after people. TG writes in 'Falstaff':

> You cooked each evening for some twenty heads,
> Not just for streetboys then, for everyone
> Who came in want of food or drugs or beds.

Fransway later ran a store called the Handmakers at California and Polk, where craftsmen made and sold wares, and parties were held in the back rooms. In the 1970s Fransway lived on and off with his entourage in the upstairs apartment at Cole Street. 'He was the character; you might say he was a leader of people,' Schuessler reflected: 'He influenced people in being more druggy, more into free lifestyle and everything. He was a huge man and he commanded the scene, just when he walked into a room.' Fransway led an itinerant life and often disappeared for several months at a time only to reappear as if nothing had happened. TG saw him for the last time in 1985.

Barbara Godfrey, née Thomson (1898–1989): TG's eldest aunt. Barbara was a nurse in the First World War, during which she met her husband, Frank Godfrey. Frank was the headmaster of a small school in Allhallows, near Rochester, in Kent, and he and Barbara lived in a cottage on the school grounds. After his mother's death, TG would stay with Barbara and Frank during school and university holidays. 'I have kept thinking recently about how I used to work at your dining table at All Hallows in the vacations from Cambridge,' TG wrote to her in 1987, 'and you always used to bring me coffee and biscuits in mid morning. You were so kind, making room for me and then keeping my energy level up!' After Frank retired, they moved to Highsted Valley, a village outside Sittingbourne in Kent: TG wrote 'The Cherry Tree' (*CP* 294–6) about a neighbouring garden. Much of their correspondence consists of TG's gardening news, the state of his health, and family and literary gossip. The last time TG saw Barbara was during his visit to England in 1979. She died in 1989 from a lung infection, aged ninety-one.

Ander Gunn (1932–): TG's brother, born Dougal Alexander Gunn but known as Ander. After their mother's death in December 1944, TG and Ander lived in Hampstead for a further six months under the supervision of the Corbetts – their cousin Margot and her husband John.

Afterwards, however, TG went to live with their mother's friend, Thérèse Megaw, nearby in Hampstead, while Ander moved across London to live in Chelsea with their father and his second wife, Olive. Thus they were separated early in their lives and did not see each other very often, especially after TG moved to California in 1954. Ander did two years of national service, some of it in Malta, and returned to London where he took up photography. He later worked in television, buying props for several stations. In the early sixties, Ander and his first wife, Margaret, had two children, William (1961–) and Charlotte (1962–). William is the subject of 'Slow Waker' (*CP* 363–4);

Charlotte visited TG in San Francisco in 1982. When TG visited London in the mid-sixties, he and Ander collaborated on *Positives* (1966): Ander's photographs 'made a good starting point for my imagination', TG wrote (*OP* 181). On his trips to England, TG always visited Ander and his family, who lived in various places in London, Cornwall and Yorkshire. TG often invited Ander to visit him in San Francisco – see his poem 'An Invitation' (*CP* 411–12) – which he did, several times, in the eighties and nineties. They maintained a lifelong correspondence: TG's tone as an older brother can be somewhat bullying and chiding. Towards the end of his life, TG wrote more frequently to his brother and would often reflect on their childhood more than was typical in his earlier letters.

Ann Charlotte Gunn, née Thomson (1903–44): TG's mother, one of seven sisters born in Snodland, Kent, to Alexander Thomson and Daisy (née Collings). After leaving school she worked as a trainee journalist on the *Kent Messenger*, where she met the worldly and charming Herbert Gunn. They married in 1925 and had two sons, TG and Ander. CT was the source of TG's enthusiasm for literature; he remarked of her in later life that 'from her I absorbed the idea of books as a part of life, not merely a commentary on it' (WS 7). CT encouraged TG to read, and his childhood was full of books such as Beatrix Potter's *The Tale of Samuel Whiskers*, George MacDonald's *At the Back of the North Wind* and Robert Louis Stevenson's *A Child's Garden of Verses*. Above all, TG loved the novels of E. Nesbit. As Wilmer notes, 'It is my private suspicion that he associated Nesbit . . . with his mother, who shared Nesbit's utopian politics and her sense of the practical value of literature' (*SP* xxiii). CT was politically left wing and inclined to be unconventional, from her political beliefs to the way she dressed: in one letter to Ander, TG recalls, 'We disliked it so much when she looked so different from the other (drab) parents on Prize Day that she let us choose what she should wear then – and we would select her most anonymous outfit.' TG cherished her memory throughout his life and his final collection contains two poems directly addressed to her: 'My Mother's Pride' (*BC* 9) and 'The Gas-poker' (*BC* 10–11). When CT and HG divorced, CT quickly re-married. Her second husband was Ronald 'Joe' Hyde (1912–95), a friend of HG's from the *Evening Standard*, where he was news editor for more than thirty years. Like CT's marriage to HG, it was a tumultuous relationship. Hyde left CT several times, the last time shortly before she died by suicide in December 1944. In TG's diary, four days after his mother's death, he writes, 'It was Joe perhaps who caused your death. [. . .] Oh mother, you could have called him back, but you knew we didn't like him! But we would rather you had 10,000 Joes in our house, rather than you had killed yourself' (*SP* 272). In TG's papers at the Bancroft Library there is an unfinished draft poem from 1978 in which he addresses his mother, reminding her of when they had visitors staying: 'I was turfed / out of my bed for whoever it was, / & slept the night, with you, in yours. / When I reached puberty / I was embarrassed – what / if I got an erection / in my sleep? . . . Yet / of course, we were lovers. / Who could equal you, dazzling / contradictory woman? If it is true / to say that you made me queer, / it is equally true / to say you made me a poet.'

Herbert Gunn (1903–62): TG's father. Born in Gravesend, Kent, to Herbert Gunn and Alice Eliza Smith, originally from Scotland. HG began his training as a reporter on the *Kent Messenger* in 1920, where he met Ann Charlotte Thomson. They married in 1925 and had two sons, TG and Ander. After a short spell as the first northern editor of the *Daily Express* in Manchester, HG moved the family back to London in 1938 where he became assistant editor, and later managing editor, of the *Daily Express*. Later he edited the *Evening Standard* (1944–50), the *Daily Sketch* (1953–9) and the *Sunday Dispatch* (1959–61). His former colleague Charles Wintour has described him as 'a superb newspaper craftsman whose technical abilities were not always matched by editorial judgement'. HG was a Fleet Street man of his day. Wintour continued: 'He smoked too much, drank too much, slept very little, yet had amazing energy.' When he and CT separated, HG had several affairs, most notably with the war journalist Hilde Marchant, his colleague at the *Express*, and the Irish film actress Valerie Hobson. TG had a difficult relationship with his father: Ander remembers an occasion during their teenage years when HG described TG as a 'pansy'. Reflecting on his father in an interview, TG remarked: 'He raised the circulation [of the *Daily Sketch*] to over a million by the familiar expedient of treating his readers with more or less total contempt. But personally he was a very charming man with lots of friends. The house was always full of people when I was a child – every weekend seemed like a party' (WS 7). HG was diagnosed with cancer in 1961 and was forced to retire from the Associated Newspaper Group. He died at his home in March 1962, aged fifty-eight.

Donald Hall (1928–2018): poet, editor, literary critic and Poet Laureate of the United States (2006–7). Hall studied at Oxford while TG was at Cambridge. He invited TG to a party to meet other Oxford poets such as Geoffrey Hill and Elizabeth Jennings. He was influential in connecting TG with Oscar Mellor's Fantasy Press, which published TG's first pamphlet and collection, *Fighting Terms* (1954). Hall was also the first poetry editor of the *Paris Review* (1953–61), in which several of TG's early poems were published. He also encouraged TG to apply for creative writing fellowships in the USA; Hall was a creative writing fellow at Stanford – under Yvor Winters – the year before TG became a fellow on the same programme. While Hall and TG saw each other infrequently, they wrote regularly in the fifties and early sixties. Although their correspondence waned, they remained warm and encouraging: TG wrote to Hall in 1994, 'You have also been important, historically, for connecting things, and bringing people together. [. . .] You have done it for poets, for poetry, not for yourself, with true generosity and selflessness.'

Charlie Hinkle (1957–87): boyfriend and friend of TG in the 1980s. Hinkle studied literature and history at Wesleyan University, where he began writing poetry, and graduated in 1981. In 1985 he visited Brazil and the following year became a graduate student in Latin American Studies at Tulane, where he was offered a fellowship, a teaching assistantship and a travel grant for the next academic year. Hinkle met TG on Boxing Day 1983. 'I go to Trax,' TG wrote in his diary, 'see what I take to be a hustler – rather long hair, blond, stocky, & the kind of face that slays me – playing pool & video machines. [. . .] He comes over, & says "You're hot." I bring him back [to Cole Street] for a GOOD night of coke & leather & love.' They saw each other regularly in 1984 and 1985, and Kitay described Hinkle as his only real 'rival' for TG's love. Their sexual relationship evolved into friendship by the time Hinkle left for Brazil. Hinkle returned to San Francisco in 1987 after he developed AIDS and was in and out of hospital for several months with failing eyesight. He died on 9 September 1987, and his death hit TG hard: Hinkle was TG's fifth friend to die from AIDS in five weeks. Hinkle is the subject of 'The Differences' (*CP* 413–14), 'Memory Unsettled' (*CP* 479), 'The J Car' (*CP* 480–1), 'To a Dead Graduate Student' (*CP* 482), 'In the Post Office' (*BC* 13–15) and 'Postscript: The Panel' (*BC* 16–17). With the novelist and journalist William McPherson, TG co-edited a small, posthumous volume of Hinkle's poetry in 1988. A handful of Hinkle's letters can be found among TG's papers at the Bancroft Library. It is thought that TG's letters to Hinkle are lost.

John Holmstrom (1927–2013): studied at King's College, Cambridge, where he was president of the Marlowe Society (1949). Holmstrom preceded TG at Cambridge and was later introduced to him by their mutual friend Tony White. Holmstrom was one of TG's earliest gay friends, and TG felt comfortable confiding in him. He joined the BBC Third Programme in 1951; he later rejoined the BBC as an announcer and member of the Test Match Special team after stints as a theatre critic for the *New Statesman* and literary editor at the Royal Shakespeare Company. He was also a shopkeeper, founding Colts of Hampstead in the late sixties, a clothing shop for school-age boys. Later he compiled an encyclopaedia of child film actors, *The Moving Picture Boy* (1996). Post-Cambridge, his literary and theatrical activities included writing the scandalous play *Quaint Honour* (1958), under the pseudonym Roger Gellert, in which a house prefect is challenged to seduce another boy. The play was produced at the Arts Theatre Club in London, a private club beyond the jurisdiction of the Lord Chamberlain's Office, which held the power to censor plays until the role of official censor was abolished in 1968.

Larry Hoyt (1951–86): friend of TG from Santa Rosa. Hoyt was a conscientious objector during the Vietnam War and worked with young men with special needs at the Sonoma State Hospital. He later taught children with special needs at public schools in Oakland and Berkeley, and teenagers with learning difficulties in the San Francisco Unified School District. His work with special needs persons is the subject of 'As Expected' (*CP* 335–6) and he is the subject of the elegy 'Still Life' (*CP* 470). TG met Hoyt in a leather bar called the Ramrod in April 1972. For a time they were regular tricks and visited the Geysers together that summer. 'He is 21, and a good deal more stable (and more worldly) than I was at 21,' TG wrote to White. Hoyt died of an AIDS-related respiratory complaint in December 1986.

Mike Kitay (1931–): TG's life partner, from Kearny, New Jersey. An actor and theatre director, Kitay was educated at Rutgers University and received a two-year Woodrow Wilson Fellowship to study at Cambridge. There he joined the Amateur Dramatic Club (ADC) and appeared in productions including *Cyrano de Bergerac* and *Love's Labour's Lost*. At the cast party for *Cyrano* in December 1952 he was introduced to TG. They quickly fell in love and TG followed Kitay to the USA in 1954, where Kitay was completing national service in the Air Force in San Antonio, Texas. Kitay began graduate work at Stanford University in 1957; at the same he became involved in amateur theatre along the San Francisco Peninsula, directing plays such as *The Chalk Garden*, *Huis Clos* and *An Italian Straw Hat*. Kitay spent the late fifties and the sixties working in various theatre and television roles in New York and San Francisco, living between the two cities. Kitay returned permanently to San Francisco in 1968, at which time his relationship with TG expanded to include other men. First, Kitay began a relationship with Bill Schuessler in 1969: Schuessler moved in with TG and Kitay that year, and moved with them to Cole Street in 1971. When Kitay and Schuessler split up in 1975, they both stayed in the Cole Street house. In time they brought in new partners. Kitay met Bob Bair in 1977 and Schuessler met Jim Lay around the same time: those four plus TG became the largest and most stable iteration of the Cole Street family, until Lay's death in 1986.

TG describes Kitay as 'the leading influence on my life, and thus on my poetry,' and writes of their complex relationship that Kitay's example was 'of the searching worrying improvising intelligence playing upon the emotions which in turn reflect back on the intelligence. It was an example at times as rawly passionate as only Henry James can dare to be' (*OP* 175). As Wilmer writes, 'They must have looked like complementary opposites: Kitay emotionally open, affectionate, a little needy; Gunn inclined to solitude, inwardly vulnerable, armoured against such feelings as might wound him. My metaphors in that last clause are Gunn's, of course' (*SP* xxvii). Kitay is the addressee of many TG poems, notably 'Tamer and Hawk' (*CP* 29), 'The Hug' (*CP* 407), 'To a Friend in Time of Trouble' (*CP* 408–9) and 'In Trust' (*BC* 98–9).

August Kleinzahler (1949–): American poet, essayist and music critic raised in Fort Lee, New Jersey. Kleinzahler moved to San Francisco in 1981; he met TG the following year and they became close friends. They were neighbours in the Upper Haight, now known as Cole Valley; their correspondence is the result of Kleinzahler taking visiting teaching positions at several universities in the 1990s. Kleinzahler described TG's influence on his poetry as 'the honest treatment of the poetic material at hand, not slipping into rhetorical or poetic postures, inflating subject matter or dodging difficulty'. Kleinzahler studied first at the University of Wisconsin–Madison, then the University of Victoria, British Columbia, where he joined a creative writing course taught by Basil Bunting. For a number of years Kleinzahler wrote a music column for the *San Diego Reader*; many of his pieces were collected in *Music: I–LXXIV* (2009). His poetry collections include *Red Sauce, Whiskey and Snow* (1995) and *Sleeping it Off in Rapid City* (2008), and he has published two collections of essays, *Cutty, One Rock* (2005) and *Sallies, Romps, Portraits, and Send-Offs* (2017). He is now one of Gunn's literary executors, alongside Clive Wilmer.

John Lehmann (1907–87): English poet and editor. Lehmann founded the *London Magazine* in 1954 and remained editor until 1961. TG contributed many poems and reviews to the *London Magazine* during Lehmann's editorship, and several of his early poems also appeared on Lehmann's BBC radio programme *New Soundings* in the early fifties.

Wendy Lesser (1952–): American critic, writer and editor. Lesser is the editor of the *Threepenny Review*, a Bay Area arts journal she founded in 1980 while a graduate student at UC Berkeley. She earned her PhD in 1982 and is the author of several books including the novel *The Pagoda in the Garden* (2005), the non-fiction book *Why I Read* (2014) and *You Say to Brick* (2017), a biography of the architect Louis Kahn. TG met Lesser in 1980 and they became close friends. TG began contributing poetry and prose to *Threepenny* in the early eighties and also acted informally as a consulting editor for poetry submissions. Some of TG's most important late work first appeared in *Threepenny*, including his essay 'Christopher Isherwood: Getting Things Right' (*SL* 173–96) and the sequences 'Troubadour' (*BC* 87–94) and 'Dancing David' (*BC* 110–14).

Janet Lewis (1899–1998): American novelist and poet. Lewis attended the University of Chicago where she met her future husband, the poet and literary critic Yvor Winters. By the time she published her first poetry collection, *The Indians in the Woods* (1922), she was gravely ill with tuberculosis. She spent five years in a New Mexico sanatorium; Winters also suffered from TB and their shared suffering drew them closer together. They married after Lewis's recovery in 1927. TG first met Lewis when he came to Stanford in 1954 to study under Winters, and they remained friends after Winters's death in 1968. TG greatly admired Lewis's novels and poems. In 'As If Startled Awake' (*SL* 66–73), he celebrates 'the body's generous consciousness of itself [. . .] at the heart of both Lewis's poetry and her fiction'. Her poetry collections include *The Ancient Ones* (1979), *Late Offerings* (1988) and *The Dear Past* (1994).

Billy Lux (1958–): Lux introduced himself to TG after TG gave a reading at the New School, New York, in December 1994. Lux had first encountered TG's work in Rome ten years earlier, when his then-boyfriend introduced him to Caravaggio's *Conversion of Saint Paul* (1601) and TG's poem about that painting, 'In Santa Maria del Popolo' (*CP* 93–4). Shortly before the New School reading, Lux had seen TG's poem 'A Home' (*BC* 7–8) in the *New Yorker* while he was working on a photographic essay about a teenage hustler. The poem chimed with the tenderness beneath the toughness that Lux wanted to portray in his photographs. After the reading TG and Lux became pen pals and developed a close friendship. TG often visited Lux in New York, and in the late nineties Lux came to live in San Francisco. TG's poem 'Letters from Manhattan' (*BC* 71–2) is composed of extracts from Lux's letters.

Thérèse Megaw (1906–2004): close friend and neighbour of TG's mother. After CT's death in 1944, TG was first looked after by his cousin Margot and her husband John. Then, from autumn 1945, TG stayed in the basement of Thérèse's house in Hampstead, where she lived with her two sons, Vincent and Edward. 'She was always wonderful to me, considerate and sweet, and treated me better than her own sons, I thought,' TG reflected late in life.

This arrangement allowed him to continue at the nearby University College School. At weekends and during school holidays TG would stay with his aunts, Mary and Catherine, in Snodland. While TG stayed with Thérèse, Ander went to live with HG and his stepmother Olive in Chelsea. It is thought that TG's poor relationship with HG in part necessitated the arrangement with Thérèse. In later visits to England, TG often stayed with Thérèse in London. TG's letters to Thérèse are held in a private collection.

Karl Miller (1931–2014): Scottish editor, literary critic and writer. Miller was educated at Downing College, Cambridge. They met in Miller's first year, TG's second. They soon became best friends and ran the University English Club together. TG gave Miller newly written poems for criticism, 'and he would pin [them] to the wall above his desk for several days before he told me what he thought of [them . . .]. He matured my mind amazingly, and I learned from his habit of questioning, of questioning everything' (*OP* 161). Despite this, TG and Miller drifted apart for reasons that seemed to do with TG's homosexuality; Miller felt excluded as TG devoted more time to his new relationship with Kitay. After Cambridge, Miller became literary editor of *The Spectator* and *New Statesman*, then editor of *The Listener*: TG had poems published in each of these magazines. Miller then founded the *London Review of Books* in 1979 and edited it until 1992, while a professor of English at University College London. TG's correspondence with Miller was sporadic after the early sixties, though they exchanged warm letters when Miller published a memoir, *Rebecca's Vest* (1993).

Charles Monteith (1921–95): publisher and editor. Born in Lisburn, Co. Antrim, Monteith was awarded a scholarship to Magdalen College, Oxford, where he earned a double first in English and Law. He qualified as a barrister at Gray's Inn in 1949 but did not practise law for very long; in 1954, Geoffrey Faber asked Monteith to join the board of Faber and Faber, where he served as a director for two decades before becoming Vice-Chairman in 1974, Chairman in 1977 and Senior Editorial Consultant from 1981 until his death in 1995. Monteith developed a strong list at Faber and is perhaps best remembered for publishing William Golding's *Lord of the Flies*

(1954), whose potential he saw despite other publishers having rejected the manuscript. Monteith's notable authors included Golding, Seamus Heaney, Ted Hughes, Paul Muldoon and John Osborne. TG submitted the manuscript of *The Sense of Movement*, his second collection, to Faber in May 1956 and it was accepted two months later. Monteith was TG's editor at Faber until Craig Raine became Poetry Editor in 1981.

Allan Noseworthy III (1950–84): met TG in New York in April 1974, when he was a doorman at Ty's, a leather bar on Christopher Street. They began a sexual relationship that developed into a close friendship. One evening in June 1974, TG wrote in his diary: 'Spend eve drinking with Allan, & then back for night. We take Placidyl & he asks me "Are you in love with me?" & falls asleep before I have time to answer.' TG often stayed with Noseworthy when he visited New York, which he did almost every year during the seventies and eighties. Noseworthy's Newfoundland dog is the subject of TG's poem 'Yoko' (*CP* 299–300). Noseworthy moved briefly to San Francisco in the late seventies, where he was involved with the Creative Power Foundation's large 'disco-visual-entertainment' parties. At the time of his AIDS diagnosis in 1984, Noseworthy was living in Palm Springs with his on/off boyfriend, the porn star Richard Locke. Noseworthy moved to San Francisco so he could receive treatment, and stayed with TG's family at Cole Street: in his diary TG called 5 May–21 June the 'last days of Allan'. Noseworthy's death is the subject of 'Lament' (*CP* 465–8), the first of TG's AIDS elegies. 'The Reassurance' (*CP* 471), written later, is also about Noseworthy. The day after Noseworthy's death TG wrote in his diary, 'I feel as if I have been a rocket going through a tunnel at supersonic speeds for the last month & now I am suddenly – too suddenly – come to a dead stop in my back yard, surrounded by a stagnant heat.'

Robert Prager (1955–2014): independent scholar, writer and bartender from Detroit, Michigan. Prager studied at Wayne State University (1973–5, 1979–80) and was briefly a graduate student in American literature at Syracuse (1992–3). He became interested in gay literature and began corresponding with gay writers such as Andrew Holleran, Dirk Vanden and Edmund White. Prager made several forays to San Francisco before moving there permanently in November 1994 with his long-time partner Gordon Schneemann. During two of these forays he was roommates with the Beat writer Harold Norse on 17th Street and worked at the South of Market bar My Place, known principally for its backroom sex scene. When Prager and Schneemann split up, Prager moved to a studio in the Tenderloin, then to a subsidised high-rise on Perry Street, next to the freeway overpass. He met TG in TG's favourite bar, the Hole in the Wall, in January 1996 and they began a mutually beneficial sexual friendship: Prager liked TG because he was a gay poet, TG liked Prager because he was handsome and took a lot of speed. 'He is a very interesting slightly odd guy,' TG wrote in his diary, 'v. unexpectedly attractive, his eyes different colors.' For many years Prager worked on a never-completed biography of TG's friend Chuck Arnett; to this end, he conducted two interviews with TG in 1996 and 2002, transcripts of which can be found in Prager's papers at the GLBT Historical Society in San Francisco. Prager is the subject of 'Blues for the New Year, 1997' (*BC* 76–7) and 'Aubade' (*BC* 78); his thoughts on the poetry of gay personal ads probably informed 'The Search' (*BC* 79). Prager was one of several men TG helped to support financially in the last decade of his life.

Belle Randall (1940–): American poet born in Washington and raised in California. Randall studied at UC Berkeley and Stanford. TG was Randall's freshman English teacher at Berkeley, and he later remarked that she was the best student he ever taught. Having read his early poems and seen a photograph of him straddling a motorcycle, Randall had a crush on TG before she met him. 'It would be years before I fully grasped that the friendship he offered wasn't something second best,' Randall wrote, 'but deeper and more lasting than the love affair I imagined could ever have been – a romance in its own right.' Randall was a Stegner Fellow at Stanford (1969–70), where she later taught. In 1973 she published her first collection, *101 Different Ways of Playing Solitaire and Other Poems*, followed in 2010 by *The Coast Starlight*. In 1983 she wrote a spirited defence of TG's work in the *PN Review* in response to the general critical dismissal of *The Passages of Joy* and *The Occasions of Poetry*.

Oliver Wolf Sacks (1933–2015): British neurologist, naturalist, historian of science and author. Born in London, Sacks spent much of his life in the United States. He earned his medical degree at Queen's College, Oxford, and completed residences and fellowship work at Mount Zion Hospital in San Francisco and at UCLA. In 1965 he moved to New York where he worked as a neurologist and author until his death in 2015. When he arrived in San Francisco in 1960, he looked up TG, whose work he had first read two years earlier when theatre director Jonathan Miller gave him a copy of *The Sense of Movement*. They met for the first time in Jack's on the Waterfront, a leather-friendly bar on the Embarcadero, in early 1961. When Sacks undertook a motorcycle tour of the USA later that year, TG suggested he keep a diary; Sacks mailed these extensive diaries to TG during his travels, and TG acted as an early mentor to Sacks's writing. TG encouraged Sacks to become more sympathetic towards other people – 'Your deficiency of sympathy made for a limitation of your observation,' TG wrote to Sacks about his early writing – and was delighted to see how that quality became central to Sacks's first book, *Awakenings* (1973). With TG's encouragement, Sacks became a prolific writer about contemporary medicine: his books include *A Leg to Stand On* (1984), *The Man Who Mistook His Wife for a Hat* (1985) and *The Island of the Colorblind* (1997). Sacks reflected on his friendship with TG in his memoir *On the Move: A Life* (2015), named after TG's early poem (*CP* 39–40). Lawrence Weschler, *And How Are You, Dr. Sacks? A Biographical Memoir of Oliver Sacks* (2019), includes an edited transcript of an interview Weschler conducted with TG about Sacks.

Bill Schuessler (1946–): American artist from Sheboygan, Wisconsin. Schuessler came to San Francisco in 1967 for the Summer of Love and met TG in the Tool Box. They kept in touch when Schuessler returned to Wisconsin that autumn. He came back to San Francisco in early 1969 and TG introduced him to Kitay, with whom Schuessler began a relationship that lasted until 1975. Schuessler moved into the apartment TG and Kitay shared on Filbert Street and moved with them to Cole Street in 1971. 'It was the happiest time of my life, really. It was a wonderful time to be alive in San Francisco,' Schuessler remarked. 'But it was more than that: I was wildly in love with Mickey. And Thom became almost like a father figure to me because he was always looking out for me. Which was incredibly strange – or nice – given that Mickey was his lover. It sounds like incest, but we all got along together.' After Schuessler and Kitay split up, Schuessler began a relationship with Jim Lay, who worked at the nearby University of California Medical Center. Lay was HIV-positive and died on Christmas Day 1986; Schuessler nursed him at Cole Street in his final months. This period of their relationship is the subject of TG's elegies 'Terminal' (*CP* 469) and 'Words for Some Ash' (*CP* 472). A painter and visual artist, Schuessler illustrated two chapbooks by TG: *Sidewalks* (1984) and *Lament* (1987). He is also the addressee of several poems by TG: 'Selves' (*CP* 322–4) is about Schuessler's break-up with Kitay; 'A System' (*BC* 35–6) and 'Sequel' (*BC* 37–8) are about the aftermath of Lay's death.

Helena Mennie Shire (1912–91): Scottish scholar of medieval literature. Her field of expertise was Scottish court poetry and culture, and its relationship to English, French and Italian court cultures. Shire began lecturing at

Cambridge in 1935 and held short appointments during the Second World War at Queen Mary College, London, and the London School of Economics, which were evacuated to Cambridge. After the war, Shire supervised for several Cambridge colleges. TG went up to Cambridge in 1950 and Shire was his main supervisor. Shire 'worked me hard', TG wrote, 'and I liked her very much' (*OP* 158). According to Wilmer, 'She adored him and he thought her the best teacher he had encountered at Cambridge.' During TG's first summer vacation from Cambridge he read the whole of Shakespeare: 'and doing that, Helena Shire later remarked, adds a cubit to anybody's stature' (*OP* 159). Shire was a supportive early mentor for TG. He was quick to confide in her, writing her long letters during his early years in California. TG wrote the poem 'The Antagonism' (*BC* 5–6) for Shire's festschrift, shortly before her death.

Marcia Tanner (1940–): American curator and writer, former director of the San Jose Institute of Contemporary Art. Born Marcia Koenigsberg in Brooklyn, New York, her mother changed her name to Marcia Kane when she absconded with her to Los Angeles. She married Norman W. Albright two days before her seventeenth birthday; though they subsequently divorced, she was known as Marcia Albright during her time at UC Berkeley, where she majored in English. There, in 1960, she met Tony Tanner: they began a relationship and she joined Tanner in Cambridge in April 1964. Later that year she got a job as an editorial assistant at *Encounter*, where she worked with Stephen Spender, the literary editor, and his assistants John Gross and John Mander. The Tanners married in August 1965 and travelled back and forth between Cambridge and the USA for the next decade, while Tony held visiting teaching and research positions at several universities. They separated during Tony's stint as a visiting fellow at the Center for Advanced Study in the Behavioral Sciences at Stanford in 1975. Tony returned to Cambridge, where he would remain with the exception of a brief stint at Johns Hopkins University, Baltimore (1976–7), and Marcia relocated to San Francisco, where she worked for the Exploratorium museum.

Tony Tanner (1935–98): literary critic and pioneering figure in the study of American literature. Tanner was a fellow of King's College, Cambridge, where he studied and taught from 1960 – with visiting positions at various American universities – until his death. Tanner won a Harkness Fellowship (1958–60) to UC Berkeley, where he encountered post-war American literature and culture, and conducted research on the Transcendentalists. His work culminated in a doctoral thesis and his first book, *The Reign of*

Wonder: Naivety and Reality in American Literature (1965). At Berkeley he met his first wife, Marcia Albright, and TG, who was at that time an assistant professor. He and TG became close friends and saw much of each other in the sixties, with TG visiting England and Tanner moving back and forth across the Atlantic. They revelled in their joint passion for the Beatles and Rolling Stones, and TG introduced Tanner to hallucinogenic drugs: Tanner recounts one such trip in his essay 'A Night on Peyotl'. TG's long poem 'Misanthropos' is dedicated to Tanner, to whom he showed innumerable drafts from its conception during his recovery from hepatitis in 1963 until its publication two years later. Tanner flirted with moving permanently to the USA, but by the time he went to Johns Hopkins in 1976 the moment had passed: his marriage to Marcia had ended, and on his arrival in Baltimore he became deeply depressed. He spent that Christmas with TG at Cole Street, and went back to Cambridge in early 1977; he would never return to the USA. He took up his old job at King's and married the Italian writer and translator Nadia Fusini. From that time his friendship with TG became primarily one of correspondence: TG made only three more visits to England (1978, 1979 and 1992) in Tanner's lifetime. He died in December 1998, aged sixty-three.

Mary (1907–2001) and **Catherine Thomson** (1909–2012): TG's youngest aunts, to whom he was closest. Mary and Catherine lived their entire lives together in the Thomson family farmhouse, Covey Hall, in Snodland, Kent. Their father Alexander Thomson (1869–1939) – TG's grandfather – took over the Covey Hall farm in the late nineteenth century and ran it until his retirement in 1939. While the farm buildings and machinery were sold off, Mary and Catherine took over the milk round, which they continued until their retirement in the seventies. They maintained a lifelong correspondence with TG, and he would stay with them while visiting England. Catherine visited TG in San Francisco in October 1979.

Tony White (1930–76): actor, writer and translator, born to an English father and French mother, and educated at Downing College, Cambridge. At Cambridge, White took up acting and performed classic roles such as Aufidius, Cyrano, Gaveston and Romeo in the style of a tough romantic hero; what TG described as a 'romantic-existentialist'. They met at the end of TG's second year at Cambridge and became close friends, borrowing the word 'panache' from *Cyrano* to characterise their 'home-made philosophy, the mélange of Rostand, Stendhal, Shakespeare and Camus' (*OP* 164). After Cambridge, White joined the Old Vic theatre company and spent two years playing lesser roles in classic plays, such as Cassio to Richard Burton's

Othello. He abruptly gave up the theatre in 1956 and became a lamplighter in the East End of London. His other jobs in the sixties and seventies included translating French novels, writing a guide to London pubs and becoming a builder and handyman. White began to spend time in Cleggan, a fishing village on the Galway coast, where he was a foreman at a lobster farm and began to write. He completed a television play and a short story, though the play was never performed and the story was never published. Later he bought a cottage in Cleggan and moved there in late 1975. That December, he broke his leg playing football. A blood clot travelled from his leg to his lung, and in January 1976 he collapsed and died. His death at the age of forty-five hit TG incredibly hard. 'I cannot believe I will never see him again,' he wrote in his diary the day he heard the news. In notes for 'Letter to the Dead', an unfinished prose piece, TG writes of White after his death: 'Different stages of understanding him. There were strange levels to our friendship. You played invulnerable, particularly before me (at Cambridge), because you knew (whether consciously or not) you were my subject matter.' Once TG left for California in 1954, they saw each other infrequently, most notably during the 1964–5 academic year that TG spent on sabbatical in London. They were neighbours and spent most of their time together. TG's poem 'Talbot Road' (*CP* 380–5) is both an elegy for White and a memorial of that year. White was one of the most important people in TG's life: 'He seemed to articulate in a bolder way than I ever could the kind of personal freedom that I had glimpsed on the road in France: he was a model as well as a friend' (*OP* 163). He was also one of TG's most important confidants regarding new poems and ideas, as TG's letters to White reflect, especially in the fifties and sixties.

Clive Wilmer (1945–): poet, critic, translator and lecturer. Wilmer was educated at King's College, Cambridge, where he was taught by Tony Tanner in the mid-sixties. At Tanner's invitation, Wilmer attended TG's reading at Cambridge in late 1964. They met again during TG's year in England. In the following decades they developed a good friendship based primarily on correspondence and punctuated by transatlantic visits. Wilmer has been one of TG's most perceptive critics, writing foundational essays and reviews of TG's work from the late sixties onwards. In 1982 he edited TG's *The Occasions of Poetry*, which brings together many of his critical and autobiographical essays, and in 2017 his posthumous *Selected Poems*. Their friends in common included Tanner and Donald Davie; Wilmer also edited Davie's essays in *With the Grain: Essays on Thomas Hardy and Modern British Poetry* (1998) and *Modernist Essays: Yeats, Pound, Eliot* (2004). Wilmer has also edited selections from the work of William Morris, Dante

Gabriel Rossetti and John Ruskin. His poetry collections include *New and Collected Poems* (2012), as well as many translations from Hungarian poets in collaboration with George Gömöri. TG has had an important influence on Wilmer's poetry; his work, Wilmer wrote, 'has meant more to me than that of any of our contemporaries'. Wilmer is an Emeritus Fellow at Sidney Sussex College, Cambridge, and has held various teaching positions across Italy, in Florence, Verona, Padua and Venice. Alongside August Kleinzahler, he is one of TG's literary executors.

Yvor Winters (1900–68): poet, critic and teacher from Chicago, Illinois. Winters studied at the University of Chicago (1917–18) until he was diagnosed with tuberculosis. He then spent three years at a sanatorium in Santa Fe, New Mexico, where he immersed himself in contemporary poems in journals and little magazines such as *Poetry*. In 1927 he married the poet and novelist Janet Lewis, and he began graduate work in English at Stanford University the following year. Winters's early poems were typically in free verse and followed imagist principles; his subsequent work – both poetry and criticism – was more rationalist, moral and traditional. Winters championed the 'plain style' of sixteenth-century poets such as George Gascoigne and Fulke Greville, turned to traditional rhyme and metre in his own poems, and remained a strong advocate of rational judgement in life and art. When TG was at Stanford on a creative writing fellowship (1954–5) Winters was his principal teacher and proved an abiding influence on his work. 'I think it would be fair enough to say that his definition of a poem is essentially my definition of a poem,' TG remarked, '"a statement in words about a human experience" – which is rather large, but he meant "with moral import"' (PR 159–60). Winters's first three critical books are collected in one volume, *In Defence of Reason* (1947). TG wrote his poem 'To Yvor Winters, 1955' (CP 69–70) in Winters's style, and one of his best critical and reflective essays is 'On a Drying Hill: Yvor Winters,' an account of his time as Winters's student and about Winters in general as a teacher and critic (SL 197–212). In 2003 TG edited Winters's *Selected Poems* for the Library of America.

INDEX OF RECIPIENTS

GENERAL INDEX

Auden, W. H. (*cont.*)
death 300
TG and 41–2, 43, 284, 300–1, 460
and gay identity 335, 387–8, 449–50
influence 504
influence on TG 20, 21, 334–5, 387,
488, 554
Isherwood and 224
and Pound 512
and spying 449
The Age of Anxiety 87
Homage to Clio 120–1
Letters from Iceland 140
'Miss Gee' 226
The Orators 87, 335, 387
'Petition' 119
'Under Which Lyre' 43
Augie/August *see* Kleinzahler, August
Austen, Jane 206, 448, 668
Emma 5, 328, 605
Mansfield Park 206, 208, 260
Sense and Sensibility 260
authorial intention 340, 541
Awakenings (film) 497

Babel, Isaac 617
Bach, J. S. 463
Bachardy, Don 147
Bacon, Francis (painter) 230, 568
Bacon, Francis (writer) 23
Bad Lieutenant (film) 570
Baez, Joan 184
Bair, Bob 680, 392, 470, 474, 483, 509,
557, 574, 583, 590, 600, 619, 654,
661, 665
cabin at Guerneville, Russian River
408, 453, 484, 674, 680
on gays as family 680
and Mike Kitay 408, 421, 453, 474,
477, 557
Bald, R. C. 456–7
Baldwin, James 414, 473, 634
ballads 256, 393
Ballantine, Sheila 186, 196, 199, 302,
318, 322

Ballard, J. G. 564
Balzac, Honoré de 37, 106, 113, 426
La Comédie Humaine 115
B.A.R. 549, 615
Barbara (TG's aunt) *see* Godfrey, Barbara
Barcelona 580, 581, 583
Bard College 312
Barish, Jonas 405
Barker, George 54, 84, 85, 100
Baron, Margaret 15, 16, 22, 535, 584
Barracks bathhouse 290, 303
Barrett Browning, Elizabeth 165
Aurora Leigh 503
bars 47, 58, 125, 206, 233, 285, 326,
340, 343, 366, 575, 605, 613
leather bars 161, 334, 340, 344, 358,
377, 378, 430, 529–30
Barth, John 203, 282
Barth, R. L. 661
Barton, John 18, 91, 214, 215, 260
Baskin, Leonard 284, 287
Bateson, F. W. 119, 641
Bateson, Gregory 377
Bateson, Jan 641
bathhouses 303, 575
Batman Forever (film) 578
Batman (US TV series) 196
Baudelaire, Charles 51, 53, 87, 89, 100,
272, 554
influence on TG 232, 456
Winters and 450
Bay Area Reporter 549, 615
Bayley, John 90, 460, 588–9
BBC 68, 70, 303, 634–5
Beat Generation 104, 172
The Beatles 187, 195, 206, 209, 219,
224, 227, 235, 428, 599
interpretations of songs 563
'Long, Long, Long' 252, 255
Song Book 256
Beaton, Cecil 174
Beckett, Samuel 70, 141
Becky's Dive Bar 322, 385
Bedales 5, 611
Beddoes, Thomas Lovell 166, 252, 305

702

Frank, Robert 576, 597
Fransway, Jere **683–4**, 231, 237, 285, 292
Fraser, G. S. 25, 28, 43, 45, 46, 193
Free Speech Movement 186
Fremlin, Jenny 5, 6, 7, 296, 411, 476, 496, 657, 658, 677
Freud, Lucian 649, 657
Freud, Sigmund 238, 300
Frost, Robert 44, 166
fugue 463
Fuller, John 325
Fuller, R. Buckminster 369
Fuller, Roy 84, 87, 242–3
Fusini (Tanner), Nadia 318, 390, 401, 524, 696

Gaddis, William, *The Recognitions* 282
Gage, Joe 394, 673
Galassi, Jonathan 486
Galassi, Susan 604
Gallegos, Robert 490, 522, 589, 614
Galsworthy, John 650
Gander, Carolyn D. *see* Wright, Carolyn D.
Gander, Forrest 588, 599, 603–4, 617
    Deeds of Utmost Kindness 593, 597
    'Librettos for Eros' 593, 597, 599
    Lynchburg 597, 598, 599
García Lorca, Federico 447
García Márquez, Gabriel
    A Hundred Years of Solitude 295
Garden House case 280
Gardner, Ava 215
Garland, Judy 158
Garman Wishart, Lorna 657
Gascoigne, George 65, 187
Gascoyne, David 30, 84, 87
Gaudier-Brzeska, Henri 249–50, 252
Gay and Lesbian Studies 479
gay anthologies 288, 662
gay bars *see* bars
gay marriage 678
gay newspapers/magazines 335–6, 339, 460, 479, 549, 611, 615

gay parades 428, 435–6, 453, 558
gay poets 356, 372, 449–50, 662
gay rights campaigning 216, 225, 306, 341–2, 440
    see also homophobia and oppression of homosexuals
Gee, Tom 155, 157, 159–61, 162, 206
Gellert, Roger *see* Holmstrom, John
Genet, Jean 141
George VI 7
George, Stefan 30
Gerken, Tim 607
the Geysers 279–80, 289
Gibbon, Edward 402
Giles, Paul 442, 462
Gill, Frederick C. 44
Ginsberg, Allen 100, 236, 267, 308, 449, 453, 521
    TG meets 354
    Howl 100, 257
    Planet News 243, 257, 308
Giroux, Robert 297
Giuliano, Salvatore 82
Glaser, Randy 388, 393
GLBT Historical Society 47
Glück, Louise 503, 578, 615, 635
Go-Go Boys 191
Godfrey, Barbara **684**, 13, 39, 56, 411, 476, 497, 658
Godfrey, Frank 684
Godwin, Fay 357
Goethe, J. W. von 442
    The Sorrows of Young Werther 51, 442
Golding, William 82
Gombrowicz, Witold 573
Goncharov, Ivan
    Oblomov 635
Gooch, Brad 547, 550
Googe, Barnabe 65
Gorky, Maxim 295
gossip 35, 363, 372, 408–9, 531–2
Gottlieb, Robert 30
Graham, Jorie 589, 598, 603, 626
Graham, W. S. 355, 359, 394
Grand Street 399

GUNN, THOM (*cont.*)
back pain 412, 417, 423, 428, 498
hepatitis 152, 153, 155, 162–3, 170
high blood pressure and treatments
480, 498, 605
on what is important 476, 477
influences 48, 81, 104, 232, 300–1,
334–5, 364, 387, 459, 460, 488, 507,
553–5, 559–60, 648
on his influence on others 325
on innocence 119, 131–3, 377
interviews 47, 182, 335–6, 356, 380,
465, 468, 470–1, 511, 528, 580, 611,
634–5, 649, 693
judging for awards 635
learning languages 127, 131, 393, 397
letter to be opened after his death 38–9
on letters 38, 131, 141, 372, 372, 408,
531–2, 675
letters of condolence 149, 228
on the literary scene 352, 375–6, 380,
392, 424, 514
on living alone/with others 74–5,
145–6
on living in/not in cities 91–2, 207
on loneliness 365
calls himself look-snob 436
on love 135–9, 614
on manuscripts 310–11
on marriage 678
on metaphors and symbolism 238,
364, 372, 376–8, 407, 447
on mimesis 504
on morality 131–2, 138
see also Values
National Service 9–11, 516
on notes to poems 89, 270, 508
on obscurity 270, 276, 383
and opera 394, 521, 568, 610
operatic project 66
on originality 595
on being out/closeted 67, 138, 336,
341, 387–8, 413, 449–50
on pacifism and militarism 12–13,
131–3, 188, 197, 200

on personal views in critical writing
372
PhD, work towards 67, 68, 103, 108,
109, 110
photographs of 356
on photographs of poets 99
on pity 132
see also on self-pity *in this entry*
on place names and identity 285
pleasure in shocking 584
on being a poet 40, 387
on poetry
definitions 438, 698
as explorations and adventures 471
interpretation 376–8, 492, 540–1
nature of 291, 698
punctuation 61, 237, 458
style and subject 504
theory of 168, 404, 434, 438, 526,
594
words and 434, 698
on poetry scene politics 352, 375–6,
380, 392, 424, 514
and politics 80, 184, 188, 197, 218,
221, 224, 234, 246, 253, 272, 299,
306–7, 376, 409, 457, 472, 495,
564–5, 582
abortion 502
cultural 563–4
see also gay rights campaigning
on politics and personal qualities 291
on politics in poetry 447–8, 454–5,
463, 484
and porn 21, 121, 138, 187, 295, 394,
626, 649, 658, 662, 665, 673
postcards 387; *see also* postcards
on posterity 585
on prizing clear structure 557–8
on pronouns 587, 608
prose writing projects 64, 81, 86, 122,
154, 170, 214, 340, 372; *see also*
under Bunting
on publishing letters 531–2
on racism 311, 381, 436, 457, 463
readings 78, 96, 226, 229, 230, 232,